C000263760

The Complete Record of

WEST INDIAN TEST CRICKETERS

By Bridgette Lawrence and Ray Goble

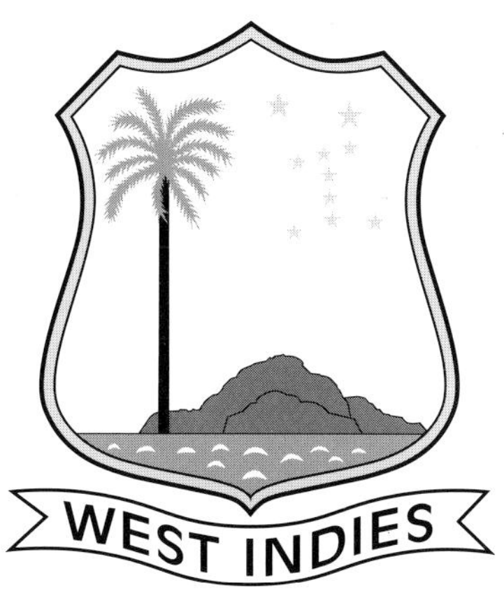

Published by
ACL & POLAR PUBLISHING (UK) LTD

Dedication

For my Mother, who introduced me to cricket and some of the other good things in life.

B.L.

First published in Great Britain by
ACL Colour Print & Polar Publishing (UK) Ltd
2, Uxbridge Road, Leicester LE4 7ST
England.

Copyright ACL & Polar 1991

ISBN 0 9514862 2 5

All rights reserved. No part of this publication may be reproduced, stored in a retrieval system, or transmitted, in any form or by any means without the prior written permission of the publisher and the authors.

Edited by
Julian Baskcomb

Printed by
ACL Colour Print & Polar Publishing (UK) Ltd
2, Uxbridge Road, Leicester, England.
Telephone: (0533) 610800

Photographs are courtesy of:
Allsport, Colorsport, Patrick Eagar, The Roger Mann Collection and David Munden.

Cover Photographs:
Front: (Clockwise); Clive Lloyd *(Colorsport)*, Viv Richards *(David Munden)*,
Gary Sobers *(Colorsport)*.
Back: Norbert Phillip *(Colorsport)*, George Headley *(Roger Mann Collection)*,
Learie Constantine *(Roger Mann Collection)*.

FOREWORD

by Sir Garfield Sobers

THIS book looks at the players who have contributed to the West Indian success story in Test cricket. I was quite fortunate to come on to the scene at a young age and have the opportunity of playing with some of the great names, people like the Three "W"s, Kanhai, Nurse, Butcher, Hall and Griffith, and Gibbs.

Those players took our game to new heights, and I put our unprecedented success of recent times down to our fast bowlers who have been supported by outstanding fielders. Although we have produced some great batsmen, it is our bowlers who have taken us to the top of world cricket and who have kept us there. Never before in the history of Test cricket have opposing batsmen had to cope with such a sustained pace attack, backed by top-class fielding.

I think the West Indies team will be a force to be reckoned with for a long time. Although we don't appear to have any young fast bowlers coming on stream at the moment, like young batsmen, they often appear from nowhere. I am sure there are one or two just waiting for an opportunity to emulate the likes of Ambrose and Bishop, who have already established themselves in the Test side. It also worries me that we have not been able to produce many top-class batsmen of late, although cricket is a funny game, and again one could appear out of the blue as a lot of school cricket is being played. Jamaica has produced some good players, Robert Haynes for example and, by all accounts, Brian Lara of Trinidad has a great future.

I believe batsmen must be nurtured at grass-roots level and it concerns me that Barbados, who have traditionally made such a strong contribution to the West Indies team, have not been able to produce the players recently. I put this down to our uncovered wickets that have allowed bowlers, who are not always that good, to dominate at the expense of batsmen. This situation needs to be rectified if our batsmen are going to have an opportunity to develop their skills; while bowlers need to get used to operating in conditions where the wickets are covered, which is the norm in Test cricket.

In 1989 we sent a West Indian team to Zimbabwe without a player from Barbados for the first time. I think that is a worrying trend, not because I am Barbadian but because Barbados, like Yorkshire and New South Wales, have historically always made substantial contributions to their respective Test sides. When for example Yorkshire has been weak so has England. At the moment we have some well known stalwarts in the batting department, but I am anxious to see some new faces appearing.

Having said that I believe the West Indies will continue to be a major force on the cricketing landscape and I think that many of our future players will come from the Leeward and Windward Islands, who have made such phenomenal progress in the last 10 years. But, wherever the new generation of Test players come from, I am confident they will carry the West Indies to more success over the next decade and certainly enhance any future update of this fascinating book.

CONTENTS

INTRODUCTION

THE Complete Record of West Indian Test Cricketers is probably the most comprehensive analysis of the careers of West Indian Test Cricketers ever to appear. A combination of my own research together with the detailed statistics provided by Ray Goble and some vintage photographs supplied by collector Roger Mann means that West Indian cricket lovers can now have in-depth coverage of all their favourite players - together with less well-known ones - at their fingertips.

It is perhaps surprising, given their remarkable success in world cricket in recent years, that only 195 players have appeared in the Test colours of the West Indies; and to complete the story we have added an appendix of the eight West Indian-born players who have played Test cricket for England.

This Complete Record which charts the great moments in the history of West Indian Test cricket through the eyes of the players themselves is a tribute to a side which began as the underdogs of world cricket and rose to dominate the game with a spirit and poise not previously seen in the international cricket arena. The West Indian Hall of Fame bulges with names whose feats on the field of play have become part of cricketing folklore: Headley's two centuries at Lord's in 1939, Sobers' 365 not out against Pakistan in 1958, Hall's last over against Australia at Brisbane in 1960 and Holding's 14 for 149 on a flat track at The Oval in 1976 provide just a taste. With moments like this to recall, illustrated with a wealth of photographs and statistics, this book should help to quench the thirst for knowledge of the West Indies' highly acclaimed and unsung heroes. We have made every effort to ensure that the factual details in this book are correct but, occasionally, especially with some of the older players, it has been impossible to get definitive information so we have used what appears to be the common fact, figure or spelling.

It has been a great joy to write this book and I hope that it will be equally pleasurable to read.

Bridgette Lawrence,
London 1991

Acknowledgements

I would like to thank the following for their support:

Julian Baskcomb for his faith, Julia Byrne for her inspiration, Ray Goble for his sense of humour (and statistics), Roger Mann and David Munden for their photographs and Sir Garfield Sobers for his foreword, together with his 202 fellow West Indian cricketers who have made this book possible.

The following also provided useful points of reference:

The Wisden Cricketers' Almanack, The Complete Who's Who of Test Cricketers by Christopher Martin-Jenkins, *West Indians at the Wicket* by Clayton Goodwin and *The Benson & Hedges West Indies Cricket Annuals.*

Bridgette Lawrence

To the people who have helped me in collecting the facts over the years I would like to say a big thank you.

The first two who started me off with my West Indies scorecards were Robert Brooke and Brian Cloudy; without them I don't think I would have ever made the start!

Michael Ronayne was also a great help, but the one person on whom I have had to call so many times, with all types of queries, is David Gallagher. He has been a tremendous help and has given me the encouragement to keep going. Thanks also to Julian Baskcomb for his belief and encouragement and Julia Byrne for her cheerful attention to detail. Finally I should like to thank my wife Joyce for all her help and support.

I am most grateful to you all and, if I have missed anyone, I thank you too!

Ray Goble

ACHONG, Ellis "Puss" Edgar

Born: 16 February 1904, Belmont, Port-of-Spain, Trinidad
Died: 29 August 1986
Role: Left-arm off-spin bowler

"PUSS" ACHONG won a place in cricketing folklore for inspiring the phrase 'Chinaman' in cricket's vocabulary. Many years later, Achong recalled how it came about after he had stumped England's Walter Robins during the Old Trafford Test of the West Indies tour in 1933: "It pitched perfectly and turned back nicely and when Robins saw it coming back at him, he opened his legs and the ball went through. On his way from the wicket, Robins turned to Learie [Constantine] and said: 'Fancy being out to a bloody Chinaman!' because it had been reported in the Press that I was the first person of Chinese origin to play Test cricket."

A slow left-armer, Achong made his Test debut against England at Port-of-Spain in 1930, after bowling Trinidad to victory against the visitors. However, Achong found the gap between domestic competition and Test cricket difficult to bridge, although he did account for England's match-winning batsman, Patsy Hendren, in that game.

A nasty injury sustained in that match hampered his cause and he did not play for the West Indies again until 1933 when, once more, a superb performance for Trinidad earned him selection for the tour of England: he took 10 for 147 against British Guiana in the final of the 1932 inter-colonial tournament. In England he took five Test wickets to put him second behind the superb Manny Martindale, who claimed 14 victims.

"Puss" Achong

Achong's Test figures fail to reflect his notable success at regional level in the West Indies and in the North of England leagues where he took over 1,000 wickets, including 10 in an innings for Burnley against Todmorden in 1945. The 'Chinaman' returned to the Caribbean in 1952 where he became a Test umpire and heavily involved in the development of the game in Trinidad & Tobago, coaching and selecting the island side.

Teams: *Trinidad, Combined XI, West Indies*
First-class debut: *22/1/30 Trinidad v M.C.C.*
First-class record: *110 wickets (30.23) and 503 runs (14.37)*
Tests: *6*
Test debut: *1/2/30 West Indies v England*
Test record: *8 wickets (47.25) and 81 runs (8.10)*

ALEXANDER, Franz Copeland "Gerry" Murray

Born: 2 November 1928, Kingston, Jamaica
Role: Wicket-keeper, right-hand batsman

"GERRY" ALEXANDER'S selection for the 1957 tour of England was met by consternation in many parts of the West Indies, especially as Kanhai, who could also keep wicket, was in the party. The selectors would doubtless have justified their decision by pointing to his familiarity with English conditions, as he had been a Cambridge blue in 1952 and 1953, while a century partnership with the young Wes Hall in a trial match probably clinched his place.

A poor series in England seemed to confirm the sceptics' view that 'establishment' connections rather than cricketing ability had won Alexander a place in the team. They must have been dismayed, therefore, when he was appointed captain for the subsequent home series against Pakistan, after Worrell had declined the job. But his elevation to the captaincy seemed to enhance his game and, after a successful series against the tourists, he led the West Indies to India and Pakistan in 1958-59. During their one moment of weakness in India - on the first day of the second Test at Kanpur, when Subhash Gupte reduced them to 88 for six - Alexander rallied his side with a stubborn 70, paving the way for victory, and inspiring his side to their huge totals in the other Tests. He also had another good series behind the stumps.

The loss of Gilchrist, who was sent home after a contretemps with his captain, and indifferent umpiring saw

"Gerry" Alexander

Inshan Ali

the West Indies lose the Test series in Pakistan. The defeat by England in the Caribbean in 1959-60, precipitated Alexander's demise as captain, even though he had just equalled the then world record of 23 dismissals in a series. By that time Worrell was back on the scene and in formidable form, so Alexander must have known his days as captain were numbered. Even so, he could take comfort from the fact that his style of captaincy had allowed the people who would set the 1960's ablaze - Hall, Sobers, Kanhai, Gibbs, Hunte and Butcher - to develop unhindered.

Ironically, after he was relieved of the captaincy, Alexander blossomed as a batsman and headed the averages with 60.50 in Australia in 1960-61. After the controversy that greeted his initial selection at Test level, Alexander matured into a cricketer of genuine international calibre and kept wicket in 25 consecutive Tests, with only Walcott of previous 'keepers playing in more than 10.

But, perhaps, Alexander's greatest contribution to West Indian cricket was the unobtrusive way in which he welded the Test side together after their triumph in India, nurturing the nucleus of the team that would go on to unprecedented success under Worrell.

Teams: *Jamaica, Cambridge University, West Indies, New Zealand Governor General's XI*
First-class debut: *30/4/52 Cambridge University v Leicestershire*
First-class record: *217 catches & 39 stumpings and 3,238 runs (29.17)*
Tests: *25*
Test debut: *25/7/57 West Indies v England*
Test record: *85 catches & 5 stumpings, and 961 runs (30.03)*

ALI, Imtiaz

Born: 18 July 1954, Trinidad
Role: Right-arm spin bowler

IMTIAZ ALI, a right-arm leg-spin and googly bowler, promised much with Trinidad & Tobago in the early 1970's, but was given scant opportunity to prove himself at international level. He played just one Test, against India in front of his home crowd at Port-of-Spain in 1976, when he took two for 89 and scored one not out.

Teams: *Trinidad, East Trinidad, North East Trinidad, West Indies*
First-class debut: *1/4/72 East Trinidad v Central Trinidad*
First-class record: *157 wickets (26.29) and 558 runs (11.16)*
Tests: *1*
Test debut: *7/4/76 West Indies v India*
Test record: *2 wickets (44.50) and 1 run*

ALI, Inshan

Born: 25 September 1949, Preyel Village, Trinidad
Role: Left-arm spin bowler

INSHAN ALI was a gifted spin bowler who never quite realised his potential at Test level. The Trinidadian was notoriously difficult to read, but his lack of consistency meant when he wasn't outwitting his opponents they were dispatching his bowling over the ropes.

Nonetheless, on his day, Ali was a real handful as the New Zealanders found out when he took five for 59 against them in the fifth Test at Port-of-Spain in 1972. Then, in England in 1973, he took 38 wickets from 11 matches and maintained his momentum in Australia in 1975-76 to finish second in the tour averages with 22 wickets at 25.54, although he only played one Test on each tour.

Teams: *Trinidad, South Trinidad, North Trinidad, Central Trinidad, S/C Trinidad, West Indies, Rest of the World XI*
First-class debut: *15/4/66 South Trinidad v North Trinidad*
First-class record: *328 wickets (28.93) and 1,341 runs (13.82)*
Tests: *12*
Test debut: *1/4/71 West Indies v India*
Test record: *34 wickets (47.67) and 172 runs (10.75)*

ALLAN, David Walter

Born: 5 November 1937, Hastings, Barbados
Role: Wicket-keeper

DAVID ALLAN had an auspicious start to his Test career: in his two games against India at Bridgetown and Kingston in 1962, he took eight catches and made two stumpings to make him first choice wicket-keeper for the 1963 tour of England. There, however, Allan was ousted by the prodigious Deryck Murray for the Tests. Even so the fair-haired Bajan performed admirably, making 46 catches and nine stumpings on the tour. He played two Tests on his second visit to England three years later, sharing the wicket-keeping duties with Hendriks. His last home Test appearance had come in the final match against the touring Australians at Port-of-Spain in 1965, when he took over from the injured Hendriks. Besides his wicket-keeping prowess, Allan was also a capable batsman.

Teams: *Barbados, West Indies*
First-class debut: *21/3/56 Barbados v E.W.Swanton's XI*
First-class record: *117 catches & 24 stumpings, and 764 runs (14.69)*
Tests: *5*
Test debut: *23/3/62 West Indies v India*
Test record: *15 catches & 3 stumpings, and 75 runs (12.50)*

AMBROSE, Curtly Elconn Lynwall

Born: 21 September 1963, Swetes, Antigua, Leeward Islands
Role: Right-arm fast bowler, left-hand batsman

CURTLY AMBROSE has given new meaning to the phrase 'meteoric rise': before the start of the 1988 Red Stripe Cup Ambrose had played in just one first class match, by the end of the competition he had taken a record-breaking 35 wickets and, at 6ft 7in, was being hailed as the new "Big Bird".

Despite his own preference for basketball and umpiring in cricket matches, the gangling youngster was persuaded to take playing cricket seriously and in his first match for Antigua, against arch-rivals St Kitts in the annual Leeward Islands tournament, snapped up seven for 67 in the first innings. As a result of his efforts, Ambrose played for the Leewards in their Shell Shield fixture against Guyana in 1986, and then won a Vivian Richards' Scholarship which earned him a season of league cricket in England later that year. In 1987 he enjoyed another successful summer in England, taking over 100 wickets in the Central Lancashire League, but the competition at home remained formidable: Baptiste, Benjamin, Ferris and Merrick were all vying for a place in the Leewards team, never mind the calibre of the opposition at Test level. However, it was the success of Baptiste and Benjamin that gave him his chance. With those two on tour in India with the West Indies for the start of the domestic season, Ambrose established himself in the Leewards team. He was at his most devastating later in the season, against Guyana at St John's, when he took 12 wickets in the match, including nine clean-bowled, and finished the Red Stripe season with a record 35 wickets to his credit.

By now Garner had retired from Test cricket, but Ambrose's high action, steep bounce and devastating yorker confirmed that Big Bird's match-winning weapons were in safe hands. With Holding also off the scene and Marshall injured, Ambrose was an automatic choice for the one-day series against Pakistan early in 1988. He bowled magnificently, taking 10 wickets in three matches; but was somewhat disappointing in the subsequent Test series, collecting seven wickets at over 50 apiece.

Nonetheless, his undoubted talent secured his ticket to England, where he justified the selectors' faith taking 22 Test wickets (20.22); in the subsequent series against Australia, he bowled even better to top the Test averages with 26 wickets at 21.46. Although he was less successful against India later in 1989, his magnificent performance against England in 1989-90, when he took 20 wickets (15.35) including best bowling figures of eight for 45 in the fourth Test at Bridgetown to level the series for West Indies, confirmed that he seems destined to become a leading figure on the contemporary Test scene.

Teams: *Leeward Islands, West Indies, Northamptonshire*
First-class debut: *12/2/86 Leeward Islands v Guyana*
First-class record: *251 wickets (22.77) and 1,116 runs (16.41)*
Tests: *20*
Test debut: *2/4/88 West Indies v Pakistan*
Test record: *80 wickets (24.35) and 332 runs (14.43)*

Curtly Ambrose (and on facing page)

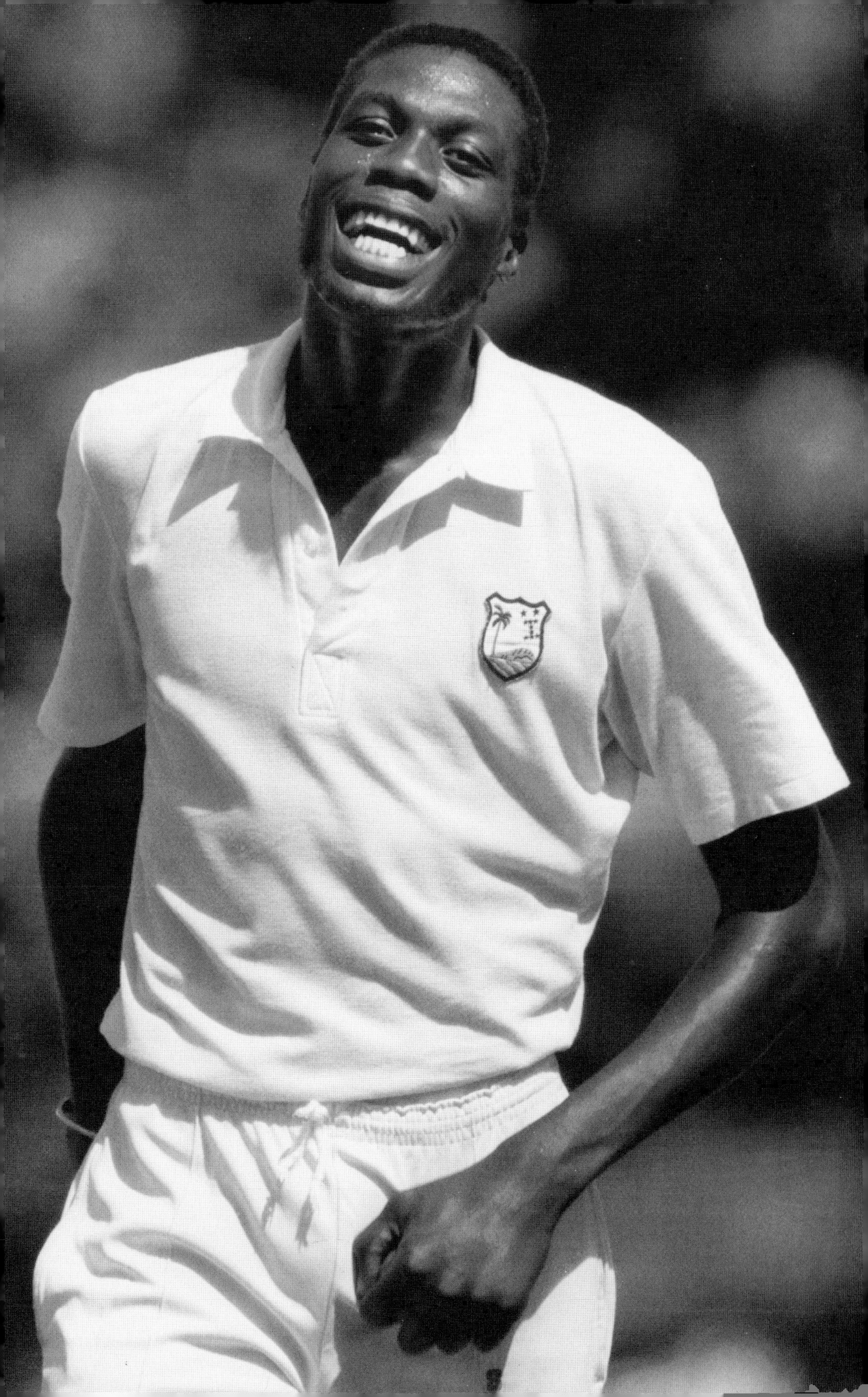

ARTHURTON, Keith Lloyd Thomas

Born: 21 February 1965, Nevis, Leeward Islands
Role: Left-hand batsman

KEITH ARTHURTON, who averaged over 50 in his first two full seasons of cricket in the West Indies, booked his passage to England in 1988 after scoring two centuries in representative matches - for the West Indies Board XI and the Under-23 XI - against the touring Pakistanis earlier that year.

He became the third West Indian player from the tiny Leeward island of Nevis, whose population is just 15,000, to play Test cricket (after Elquemedo Willett and Derick Parry) when he made his debut against England at Headingley, scoring 27 in his only innings. He toured Australia in 1988-89, but didn't make the Test side; and after a disappointing home series against the Indians was not picked when England visited the Caribbean early in 1990.

Despite these set-backs Arthurton is an exceptionally fit and strong batsman whose left-handed batting, with a little more luck and a lot more consistency, could bring variety to the West Indies middle order, now that Lloyd and Gomes have retired. His outstanding fielding, especially in the covers, is another factor in his favour.

Teams: *Leeward Islands, West Indies*
First-class debut: *24/1/86 Leeward Islands v Barbados*
First-class record: *2,483 runs (42.81) and 12 wickets (29.00)*
Tests: *5*
Test debut: *21/7/88 West Indies v England*
Test record: *105 runs (17.50)*

ASGARALI, Nyron Sultan

Born: 28 December 1920, St. James, Port-of-Spain, Trinidad
Role: Right-hand batsman

NYRON ASGARALI was a a sound opening batsman who first caught the public eye in the 1951-52 season - more than 10 years after his first- class debut - when he scored 103, 128 and

Keith Arthurton

83 in successive matches for Trinidad against British Guiana. He was one of three specialist openers selected for the 1957 tour of England - the other two being Andy Ganteaume and Bruce Pairaudeau - but disappointed in his two Test appearances. His best Test score was 29, although he scored over 1,000 first-class runs on that trip. Asgarali subsequently became a professional in the Lancashire League.

Nyron Asgarali

Teams: *Trinidad, South Trinidad, West Indies, Commonwealth XI*
First-class debut: *1/2/41 Trinidad v Barbados*
First-class record: *2,761 runs (32.86) and 23 wickets (42.00)*
Tests: *2*
Test debut: *20/6/57 West Indies v England*
Test record: *62 runs (15.50)*

ATKINSON, Denis St Eval

Born: 9 August 1926, Christ Church, Barbados
Role: Right-hand batsman, off-spin bowler

DENIS ATKINSON would doubtless have shone more brightly at Test level if he had come to cricketing maturity in an era when the West Indies were less inundated with batting stars. As it was he played in the shadow of the three "W"s, Stollmeyer and Rae and, when he occasionally got his chance to shine, lack of practice usually found him out.

Apart from 45 on his Test debut against India in 1948, his showing in Test cricket was modest until the series against the touring MCC side in 1953-54. He made 53 in the second Test at Bridgetown and another two half centuries in the fourth match at Port-of-Spain, although a stubborn 40 in the last encounter at Kingston could not prevent England from levelling the series. These performances did not go unnoticed and he was appointed vice-captain to Jeff Stollmeyer for the visit by Australia in 1954-55. However, the Barbadian unwittingly found himself caught up in a political storm when Stollmeyer was injured and Atkinson, a white insurance salesman with a mediocre Test record, found himself at the helm for three of the four Tests. Amidst a volatile political climate, prompted by the prospect of decolonisation and the upheaval that would bring, there was much pressure to have Atkinson removed from the captaincy.

Eventually the storm passed and Atkinson quelled most of his remaining critics with one of the most memorable rearguard actions in the history of Test cricket, in front of his home crowd in the fourth match at Bridgetown. He and fellow Barbadian, Clairmonte Depeiza, added a world record 347 for the seventh wicket, after Australia had scored 668 and then reduced West Indies to 146 for six. Atkinson, who made his highest Test score of 219 (and only century in Test cricket), then took five Australian wickets in the tourists' second innings, and thereby became the first West Indian captain to score a century and take five wickets in a Test innings.

Atkinson led the West Indies to victory in New Zealand in 1955-56, but was dismissed from the captaincy after losing the last Test in Auckland, even though his medium pace had accounted for seven home batsmen in the second innings. His removal from the captaincy seemed particularly harsh given that Stollmeyer had retired and, although Atkinson made the tour to England in 1957, a shoulder injury sustained early on hampered him greatly.

Denis Atkinson

In another time, Atkinson's all-round cricketing skills might have made a greater impact on West Indian cricket. Yet for a man whose main interest was fishing until he left school, Atkinson left behind a considerable

cricketing legacy: besides his historic partnership with Depeiza, he shared in a record ninth-wicket stand of 106 with Robert Christiani on his first trip to India and put on a record-breaking 143 for the seventh wicket with John Goddard in New Zealand in 1956.

Teams: *Barbados, Trinidad, West Indies*
First-class debut: *28/9/46*
Barbados v British Guiana
First-class record: *2,812 runs (28.40) and 200 wickets (26.45)*
Tests: *22*
Test debut: *10/11/48 West Indies v India*
Test record: *922 runs (31.79) and 47 wickets (35.04)*

ATKINSON, Eric St Eval

Born: 6 November 1927, Christ Church, Barbados
Role: Right-hand batsman, fast-medium bowler

ERIC ATKINSON was a useful all-round cricketer, and younger brother of Denis. He played in the home series against Pakistan in 1957-58: in the third Test in Kingston his fast-medium bowling brought him match figures of eight for 78, in a game dominated by batsmen (including Sobers' 365 not out). He went on tour to India and Pakistan in 1958-59, and took nine wickets (13.22) in two Tests in Pakistan.

Teams: *Barbados, West Indies*
First-class debut: *9/2/50*
Barbados v British Guiana
First-class record: *61 wickets (26.72) and 696 runs (21.75)*
Tests: *8*
Test debut: *17/1/58 West Indies v Pakistan*
Test record: *25 wickets (23.56) and 126 runs (15.75)*

AUSTIN, Richard Arkwright

Born: 3 September 1954 , Kingston, Jamaica
Role: Right-hand batsman, right-arm bowler

RICHARD AUSTIN was a gifted all-rounder: an accomplished batsman, he could also bowl medium pace or off-spin. Indeed, his talents had just won him a place in the West Indies Test side, when he signed to play world series cricket for Kerry Packer in 1978. He was one of the Packer players then dropped from the team for the third Test against Australia at Georgetown - having apparently told the West Indies Board that he would be available for the imminent trip to India - which prompted the remaining Packer players to withdraw from the contest on the eve of the match.

Despite the controversy off the field, Austin enjoyed a vintage season in domestic cricket that year and finished as Jamaica's leading batsman in the Shell Shield with an average of over 60. For good measure, he also took 18 Shield wickets, including match figures of 12 for 116, against Trinidad & Tobago.

However, after the Packer crisis was resolved, Austin did not get another chance at international level. Deducing his Test days were over, he accepted an invitation to tour South Africa with the first unofficial West Indies team to visit the Republic in 1982-83.

Teams: *Jamaica, West Indies, West Indies 'Rebels XI'*
First-class debut: *21/3/75*
Jamaica v Trinidad
First-class record: *2,097 runs (33.82) and 73 wickets (31.21)*
Tests: *2*
Test debut: *3/3/78 West Indies v Australia*
Test record: *22 runs (11.00) and 0-5*

Richard Austin

BACCHUS, Sheik Faoud Ahumul Fasiel

Born: 31 January 1954, Georgetown, British Guiana
Role: Right-hand batsman

FAOUD BACCHUS was one of several players elevated to Test status after the rift between the cricketing establishment and the world series players became public. After making a name for himself as a gifted young batsman in Guyana, Bacchus' first taste of Test cricket came in the last two matches against the Australians in 1978, where he was disappointing.

He returned to his best form on the subsequent tour of India, crashing 96 in the second Test at Bangalore and 61, as the tourists followed on, in the fifth match in Delhi. But he kept his most spectacular batting for the last Test at Kanpur where he scored a match-winning double hundred, in the face of three centuries from the opposition. Bacchus crashed 250 in 512 minutes to help the tourists save face and himself to the highest individual Test score ever recorded on the ground.

Bacchus was included in West Indies World Cup squad of 1979, but then fell out of favour before returning for the tours to England, Pakistan and Australia between 1980-82. Significantly he was also invited to captain the West Indies Under-26 side to Zimbabwe during that period. However, patience was not one of Bacchus' most noted qualities and, when he was overlooked for the home series against India in 1983 (having played in the one-day internationals) and Haynes had won his spurs as Greenidge's new opening partner, Bacchus seemed to give up hope of commanding a regular Test place and defected to South Africa.

He performed well out there - scoring 664 runs from just 12 matches - which suggests if he had been a little more patient, he could have become a regular member of the full West Indies side.

Teams: *Guyana, Demerara, West Indies, West Indies U-26 XI, West Indies 'Rebels' XI, Border, Western Province*
First-class debut: *30/10/71 Demerara v Berbice*
First-class record: *5,944 runs (35.17) and 8 wickets (24.62)*
Tests: *19*
Test debut: *15/4/78 West Indies v Australia*
Test record: *782 runs (26.06) and 0-3*

BAICHAN, Leonard

Born: 12 May 1946, Berbice, British Guiana
Role: Left-hand batsman

LEONARD BAICHAN'S most enviable asset was his intense powers of concentration. The left-handed opener was selected for the tour of India and Pakistan in 1974-75 and scored centuries in his first two innings in India. He seemed destined for a memorable trip, before a car accident ruled him out of the Indian Test series. He recovered in time for the first Test against Pakistan in Lahore to join the distinguished band of cricketers who have made a hundred on their Test debut but, after an indifferent tour of Australia in 1975-76, he faded from the scene.

Teams: *Guyana, Berbice, West Indies*
First-class debut: *27/2/69 Guyana v Barbados*
First-class record: *4,504 runs (51.77) and 0-34*
Tests: *3*
Test debut: *15/2/75 West Indies v Pakistan*
Test record: *184 runs (46.00)*

Faoud Bacchus

Eldine Baptiste

BAPTISTE, Eldine Ashworth Elderfield

Born: 12 March 1960, Liberta, Antigua, Leeward Islands
Role: Right-hand batsman, right-arm medium-fast bowler

ELDINE BAPTISTE is a gifted all-rounder, who made his English county debut - for Kent against Oxford University in 1981 - a year before he donned the Leeward colours. Groomed by knowledgeable Kentish hands, he enjoyed an excellent season with his adopted club in 1983 - which included a career-best score of 136 not out against Yorkshire - and was selected for the West Indies side to tour India at the end of that year.

The tall Antiguan got few opportunities on that trip, but his familiarity with English conditions stood him in good stead when the West Indies toured England in 1984. He took eight valuable wickets in the series in his role as a stock bowler and, in the first Test at Edgbaston, raced to an unbeaten 87 in a record ninth wicket partnership of 150 with Holding. An impressive performance for the Leeward Islands against the visiting Australians earlier in 1984, secured his place in the side for the subsequent trip 'Down Under', although he only played four matches on the tour.

A versatile all-rounder Baptiste, like many West Indians before, has suffered from a surfeit of talent around him. But, on several occasions, he has steered them through a difficult session, and lack of opportunity - he played two matches on West Indies' visit to India in 1987-88 and just one Test in the home series against England in 1989-90 - has often been a bigger enemy than lack of talent. He confirmed this by being one of the key figures in the Leeward Islands' historic victory in the Red Stripe Cup, finishing as their leading wicket-taker in the competition with 26 at an average of 17.50.

Teams: *Leeward Islands, West Indies, Kent*
First-class debut: *17/6/81*
Kent v Oxford University
First-class record: *5,196 runs (28.08) and 426 wickets (25.24)*
Tests: *10*
Test debut: *21/10/83 West Indies v India*
Test record: *233 runs (23.30) and 16 wickets (35.18)*

BARRETT, Arthur George

Born: 4 April 1942, Kingston, Jamaica
Role: Right-arm leg-spin bowler

ARTHUR BARRETT was an accurate leg-break bowler who played in three Test series: at home against India in 1970-71 and England in 1973-74, and away against India and Pakistan in 1974-75. However, he could only muster 13 expensive wickets in an era when fast bowling submerged even talented leg-spinners.

Teams: *Jamaica, West Indies*
First-class debut: *8/2/67*
Jamaica v Trinidad
First-class record: *169 wickets (31.21) and 1,086 runs (17.51)*
Tests: *6*
Test debut: *18/2/71 West Indies v India*
Test record: *13 wickets (46.38) and 40 runs (6.66)*

BARROW, Ivan

Born: 6 January 1911, Kingston, Jamaica
Died: 2 April 1979
Role: Wicket-keeper, right-hand batsman

IVAN BARROW'S greatest achievement was to become the first West Indian to score a Test century in England, beating Headley by a few minutes, as the pair put on 200 in almost even time in the Old Trafford Test of 1933. It proved to be the high point of his series, as the wicket-keeper-batsman registered 28 dismissals and scored over 1,000 runs on that trip. Barrow had set a precedent for sharing large partnerships with Headley, when they put on 248 for the third wicket for Jamaica against Lord Tennyson's side at Kingston in 1932. Then, Barrow hit his highest first-class score of 169.

He made his Test debut against England at Sabina Park in 1930. In a high-scoring match, Barrow failed with the bat, but stumped 50-year-old George Gunn off the bowling of Frank Martin. But, Barrow made a sufficiently good impression to be selected for the first tour to Australia in 1930-31. He was retained for the series against England in 1933 and was promoted to open the innings with Clifford Roach, a practice maintained with subsequent wicket-keepers, as the West Indies searched in vain for a dependable opening pair.

By the time of England's visit to the Caribbean in 1934-35, Barrow had been superceded as wicket-keeper by Cyril Christiani. The latter had been his deputy in England, but Barrow returned to open the innings in the final Test at Kingston - a match which saw Barrow, Christiani and the Barbadian wicket-keeper, Derek Sealy, filling three of the top four batting places. After Christiani's untimely death from malaria in 1938, Barrow was recalled for the trip to England in 1939. However, the Jamaican had been living in the United States and was out of top-class match practice. He struggled early on in the tour and, after the first Test, Sealy took over the gloves.

Barrow played for Jamaica again in 1946 and later became his country's first cricket broadcaster.

Ivan Barrow

Teams: *Jamaica, West Indies*
First-class debut: *21/2/29 Jamaica v Julien Cahn's XI*
First-class record: *71 catches & 27 stumpings, and 2,551 runs (23.84)*
Tests: *11*
Test debut: *3/4/30 West Indies v England*
Test record: *17 catches & 5 stumpings, and 276 runs (16.23)*

Edward Bartlett

BARTLETT, Edward Lawson

Born: 18 March 1906, Barbados
Died: 21 December 1976
Role: Right-hand batsman

EDWARD BARTLETT was another of West Indies' pioneering batsmen, who played in the inaugural Test series in England in 1928 and Australia in 1930-31.

Unlike some of his illustrious colleagues, at just 22 "Barto" was not past his best by the time Test status arrived, but he did not excel on those tours as he would have liked. His best Test innings was 84 against Australia in the first match at Adelaide, which would have disappointed the hard-hitting right-hander, whose cause was hampered further by a nasty hand injury he incurred during the second Test. He played with more characteristic panache against British Guiana in 1926-27, when he added 216 for the eighth wicket with "Snuffy" Browne, to help Barbados to 715 for nine. Unhappily for Bartlett, he was never this fluent at the highest level.

Teams: *Barbados, West Indies, Combined XI*
First-class debut: *19/2/24 Barbados v Trinidad*
First-class record: *1,581 runs (23.25)*
Tests: *5*
Test debut: *11/8/28 West Indies v England*
Test record: *131 runs (18.71)*

Winston Benjamin

BENJAMIN, Winston Keithroy Matthew

Born: 31 December 1964, All Saints, Antigua, Leeward Islands
Role: Right-arm fast bowler, right-hand batsman

WINSTON BENJAMIN made his Test debut in India at the end of 1987, but was given his first real chance when Pakistan toured the Caribbean the following year. In the three-match series the Antiguan paceman took 12 wickets at 24.41 and, for good measure, scored 31 and 40 not out in the third Test at Bridgetown. Then, in England in 1988, he topped the averages with 12 wickets at 12.58 - including four for 52 in the final Test at The Oval - bowling in the company of Marshall, Ambrose, Patterson and Walsh.

Although he was chosen for the subsequent trip to Australia he did not play in a Test match and, although he had one Test against India early in 1989, he was overlooked again when England visited the Caribbean in 1989-90. With the recent progress of Ambrose and newcomer, Ian Bishop, Benjamin knows he must fire on all cylinders if he is to forge a regular place in the West Indies pace attack.

Teams: *Leewards Islands, West Indies, Leicestershire, Rest of World XI*
First-class debut: *8/9/85 Rest of World XI v D.B. Close's XI*
First-class record: *285 wickets (24.91) and 2,094 runs (23.52)*
Tests: *8*
Test debut: *25/11/87 West Indies v India*
Test record: *26 wickets (21.69) and 124 runs (13.77)*

BEST, Carlisle Alonza

Born: 14 May 1959, Barbados
Role: Right-hand batsman

CARLISLE BEST'S Test career got underway with characteristic gusto when he hooked Ian Botham for six to get off the mark in his first Test, at Kingston in 1986. After three prolific seasons for Barbados in the Shell Shield, Best now seemed set to make his mark in the Test arena. But, after this flamboyant start, he became more introverted and lost his confidence, and his place, after three games.

An orthodox right-hander, Best first caught the public eye in 1976 when, as a schoolboy, he scored over 800 runs in the Barbados Association's Division II. Those efforts won him a place in the Barbados team for the West Indies youth championships, and a sparkling hundred against Guyana in that competition secured his passage with the West Indies youth team to England in 1978.

Best established himself in the full Barbados team when several of his compatriots went to South Africa, and he assumed the captaincy of the side in 1984 while the top Bajans were on Test duty in India and Australia. Leading from the front - he averaged over 40 with the bat, which included his maiden first-class hundred, against the Windward Islands - Best chaperoned his side to success in the Shield.

Although Barbados could not maintain their momentum the following year, Best's purple patch continued unabated. He thrashed 437 runs, including centuries off Guyana and Jamaica, which earned him a trip with the West Indies to Sharjah and Pakistan, although he didn't get a game on that tour.

He excelled in the Shield again in 1986 - topping the averages for the second successive year with over 500 runs - this time in the company of the regular Test players. However, the success of those players, notably Greenidge and Haynes, means that Best has to bat at number three for Barbados and even lower down in the Test line-up. Despite the competition, this likeable character has the will and the talent to be a regular member of both sides for several years to come.

After a four year break from Test cricket, Best enjoyed great success against England in the West Indies early in 1990. He averaged almost 50 from three Tests, which included a

Carlisle Best

Ian Bishop

majestic maiden Test hundred in front of his adoring home crowd in the fourth match at Bridgetown. If he can maintain that kind of form Best seems assured of an international future, but he knows if things don't work out he has plenty of other options: he has a degree in economics from the University of the West Indies and has built up a formidable reputation as a commentator, albeit on his own batting when he is out in the middle! He is also a member of the Barbados Labour Party, and even a career in politics has been mooted after his playing days are over.

Teams: *Barbados, West Indies, Rest of World XI*
First-class debut: *28/3/80 Barbados v Trinidad*
First-class record: *4,289 runs (44.21) and 11 wickets (34.72)*
Tests: *6*
Test debut: *21/2/86 West Indies v England*
Test record: *320 runs (40.00)*

BETANCOURT, Nelson

Born: 4 June 1887, Trinidad
Died: 12 October 1947
Role: Wicket-keeper, right-hand batsman

NELSON BETANCOURT had a very brief and relatively distinguished Test career. In keeping with the policy of choosing an indigenous captain, Betancourt skippered the West Indies in his sole Test appearance, on his home ground at Port-of-Spain against England in 1930. A capable wicket-keeper for Trinidad, he did not keep in that match, but batted admirably for 39 and 13 in a losing cause.

Teams: *Trinidad, West Indies*
First-class debut: *14/8/05 Trinidad v Jamaica*
First-class record: *442 runs (18.41) and 1 wicket (98.00)*
Tests: *1*
Test debut: *1/2/30 West Indies v England*
Test record: *52 runs (26.00)*

Nelson Betancourt

BINNS, Alfred Phillip

Born: 24 July 1929, Kingston, Jamaica
Role: Wicket-keeper, right-hand batsman

Alfie Binns

ALFIE BINNS was one of several wicket-keepers tried at Test level by the selectors during the mid-1950's, but the capable Binns only rarely played at his best in Tests. He went on the 'blooding' tour to New Zealand in 1955-56 and had played at home against India and Australia in two preceding series, but was never able to make the wicket-keeping position his own.

Teams: *Jamaica, West Indies*
First-class debut: *25/1/50 Jamaica v Trinidad*
First-class record: *48 catches & 17 stumpings, and 1,446 runs (37.07)*
Tests: *5*
Test debut: *21/1/53 West Indies v India*
Test record: *14 catches & 3 stumpings, and 64 runs (9.14)*

BIRKETT, Lionel Sidney

Born: 14 April 1905, Barbados
Role: Right-hand batsman, right-arm medium-pace bowler

LIONEL BIRKETT first hit the headlines when he scored a majestic double century against British Guiana at Georgetown in 1929-30. A fluent right-handed batsman, he was also a useful change bowler, although he only took one wicket in a Test match when he bowled Alan Kippax at Brisbane in 1931. After his showing in the 1929-30 domestic season he was made vice-captain for West Indies' first visit to Australia in 1930-31. He began promisingly, scoring 64 in the first Test at Adelaide, but was disappointing in the remainder of the series.

Teams: *Barbados, Trinidad, British Guiana, Combined XI, R.S.Grant's XI, West Indies*
First-class debut: *21/1/25 Barbados v Jamaica*
First-class record: *1,295 runs (33.20) and 9 wickets (56.00)*
Tests: *4*
Test debut: *1/1/31 West Indies v Australia*
Test record: *136 runs (17.00) and 1 wicket (71.00)*

BISHOP, Ian Raphael

Born: 24 October 1967, Port-of-Spain, Trinidad
Role: Right-arm fast bowler, right-hand batsman

IAN BISHOP didn't play in a Test match on his first tour of England in 1988, but made such an impression in the county fixtures that, by the end of the season, several wanted to sign him.

It was only a quirk of fate that ensured he was selected: by playing league cricket in England in 1987, he could not take part in the annual West Indies youth championships and was, therefore, not considered for the inaugural youth World Cup in Australia. If he had played in that competition he would have missed most of the Red Stripe Cup matches, where he enhanced his reputation as he out-bowled his new ball partner for Trinidad & Tobago, Tony Gray.

His 19 wickets at less than 14 runs apiece meant that he headed the Red Stripe averages and prompted the selectors to pick him for the three representative matches against Pakistan and the tour to England in 1988. Although the youngster's international appearances were restricted to the one-day games, by the end of the summer a cluster of counties were lining up for his signature: in the end, he opted, sensibly, to join Derbyshire where he enjoyed a season of expert tuition under the experienced eye of Michael Holding in 1989.

Bishop played five first-class matches on the tour of Australia in 1988-89 and finally made his Test debut against India when they visited the Caribbean early in 1989. He enjoyed a magnificent first series, taking 16 wickets (23.12) including a wicket with his first ball in the second Test at Bridgetown and six for 87 in the second innings. The Trinidadian continued his splendid run against England in the Caribbean, early in 1990, to finish as the leading wicket-taker, with 21 victims, at under 20 apiece.

Like several distinguished pace bowlers before him, Bishop began his cricketing career as a batsman - he used to open the innings for his club side when he could fit it in around his other sporting interests including football, basketball and table tennis - but was invited to bowl in an under-16 schools' competition 'just to help out'. It was the first step towards a promising career at the highest level and one suspects, if he can maintain his momentum, there will be many batsmen in the future who will wish he stuck to opening the innings.

Teams: *Trinidad, West Indies, Derbyshire*
First-class debut: *3/4/87 Trinidad v Guyana*

Lionel Birkett

Keith Boyce

First-class record: *237 wickets (21.28) and 909 runs (15.94)*
Tests: *8*
Test debut: *25/3/89 West Indies v India*
Test record: *37 wickets (21.32) and 124 runs (20.66)*

BOYCE, Keith David

Born: 11 October 1943, St. Peter, Barbados
Role: Right-hand batsman, right-arm fast-medium bowler

KEITH BOYCE struggled to live up to his early reputation after turning in some memorable performances as a young all-rounder in Barbados - a task made even more difficult after premature comparisons with Constantine. After showing touches of brilliance for Barbados and then Essex, the Test match public were only rarely treated to such performances from Boyce: as when he crashed 72 runs off the English bowlers in the first Test at The Oval in 1973 then, sharing the new ball with Bernard Julien, returned match figures of 11 for 147 to sweep West Indies to their first Test victory for four years.

"Snuffy" Browne

He had a modest return series against England in the Caribbean, but was back to his something near his best against India in the second Test in Delhi at the end of 1974. There, he scored 68 glorious runs, sharing in a century partnership with the up-and-coming Viv Richards; while, in the bowling department, he had the young Andy Roberts to keep up with. But there was still plenty of life in Boyce: he produced a match-winning bowling performance in the 1975 World Cup final, taking four of the five Australian wickets to fall; and performed reasonably with the bat on the subsequent miserable tour of Australia. His best moment came in the fifth Test at Adelaide: his unbeaten 95 saved the follow-on almost single-handedly, although an equally resolute 69 in the second innings could not stave off another defeat, as Jeff Thomson and Dennis Lillee reigned supreme.

Boyce's failure to deliver at Melbourne signalled the end of his Test career but his overall contribution had been important, not least by filling the huge gap left by Hall and Griffith until the emergence of Roberts & Co.

This swashbuckling all-rounder was one of the first and best-loved players to appear regularly in English county cricket and during a distinguished career with Essex, he became the first player to reach 1,000 runs and 100 wickets in limited-overs cricket.

Teams: *Barbados, West Indies, Essex, Commonwealth XI, Rest of World XI, T.N.Pearce's XI, M.C.C.*
First-class debut: *25/2/65 Barbados v Cavaliers XI*
First-class record: *8,800 runs (22.39) and 852 wickets (25.02)*
Tests: *21*
Test debut: *19/3/71 West Indies v India*
Test record: *657 runs (24.33) and 60 wickets (30.01)*

BROWNE, Cyril Rutherford "Snuffy"

Born: 8 October 1890, Bridgetown, Barbados
Died: 12 January 1964
Role: Right-hand batsman, spin bowler

"SNUFFY" BROWNE really made his mark in cricket before West Indies' elevation to Test status, although he played in the inaugural series in England in 1928 and in Australia in 1930-31. However, Browne's cricketing prowess was at its height in the 1920's: on the 1923 tour to England he bowled well to capture 75 wickets, including six for 66 against Somerset. He played well against Freddie Calthorpe's touring MCC side in 1925-26, scoring an unbeaten century in the third representative match at Georgetown - despite having been hit on the head earlier on - to help the home side to hold their own in the three match series.

Almost 40 by the time West Indies played their first Test, Browne's cause was hampered further by the inclusion of Constantine and Griffith in the squad, while Joe Small's batting abilities reduced his chances still further. Nonetheless "Snuffy" was far from a spent force: he scored 44 as West Indies were overwhelmed in the first Test at Lord's and, in the county matches, he took eight for 81 against Derbyshire and plundered a match-winning century in an hour against Kent.

When West Indies registered their first Test win, against England at Georgetown in 1930, due in the main to big innings from Headley and Roach, Browne finished the job by batting quickly, but sensibly, for 70 priceless runs. As late as the 1937-38 season, Browne was making an impact on the field, when he took seven for 13 against Barbados. When he finally retired, Browne became the first black West Indian to be elected to honorary life membership of MCC.

Teams: *Barbados, British Guiana, West Indies*
First-class debut: *13/1/09 Barbados v British Guiana*
First-class record: *2,077 runs (19.97) and 278 wickets (22.40)*
Tests: *4*
Test debut: *23/6/28 West Indies v England*
Test record: *176 runs (25.14) and 6 wickets (48.00)*

Basil Butcher

BUTCHER, Basil Fitzherbert

Born: 3 September 1933, Port Mourant, Berbice, British Guiana
Role: Right-hand batsman, right-arm leg-spin bowler

BASIL BUTCHER was one of the rising stars to emerge from British Guiana in the mid-1950's, after Walcott went there as coach. Although he quickly established himself at home, when his Test opportunity arrived in 1958, Butcher found himself struggling to hold his own in the illustrious company of Hunte, Sobers, Kanhai and Worrell.

More of an accumulator of runs than a lavish stroke-maker, Butcher was given the chance to prove himself in India and Pakistan in 1958-59. He hit his maiden Test hundred in the third game at Calcutta, sharing in a double century stand with Kanhai; and went on to make 142 out of 500 in the first innings of the fourth Test at Madras. He finished the series with an average of almost 70. Butcher then lost favour with the selectors after some puzzlingly poor home performances against England in 1959-60, but he returned to the fold for the West Indies tour of England in 1963. There, he enjoyed a vintage season scoring almost 1,300 runs, including a match-saving century in the Lord's Test - a marvellously determined rearguard action that included two sixes and 17 fours. Further good performances at Headingley and The Oval meant that, this time, he kept his place. His 71 against Australia in the first Test at Kingston in 1965, as he shared in a century partnership with Sobers, was instrumental in securing West Indies' victory over the tourists, and he followed that up with 117 in the second Test at Port-of-Spain.

Butcher was always at his most resilient against England: on the 1966 tour he played an heroic innings to set up victory for the tourists in the third match at Trent Bridge. West Indies' cause looked lost when Butcher arrived at the crease, with the visitors two wickets down and still behind on the first innings. But, in a gallant rearguard action, Butcher scored an unbeaten double century in seven and three-quarter hours, before Hall, Griffith and Gibbs capitalised on his good work.

Butcher made the headlines again, this time when England visited the Caribbean in 1967-

68: after hitting timely fifties in the first and third Tests, he took five English wickets for 34 with his leg-spin in the fourth match at Port-of-Spain, inducing Sobers to make an ill-judged second innings declaration. Set 215 to win in 164 minutes, the tourists romped to victory, as Butcher failed to repeat the magical form of his first innings.

The Guyanese's fine form in Australia and New Zealand in 1968-69, won him a place in the tour party to England later that year. There, he found himself the centre of high drama in the final Test at Headingley. West Indies were chasing 303 to win and, with Butcher playing at his most fluent and the score on 219 for three, the tourists seemed poised for victory. But Butcher was given out on 91 in a hotly disputed catch behind by Alan Knott off Derek Underwood, and the subsequent speedy removal of Sobers meant the loss of the match - by 30 runs - and the series.

When he finally got going Butcher made a considerable contribution to West Indian Test cricket: when the more flamboyant players had failed, he could invariably be relied on to hold the middle order together, as he saved his best performances for West Indies' most critical moments.

Teams: *British Guiana, Guyana, Berbice, West Indies, Commonwealth XI, Rest of World XI, F.Worrell's XI, Indian President's XI*
First-class debut: *29/1/55 British Guiana v Barbados*
First-class record: *11,628 runs (49.90) and 40 wickets (30.42)*
Tests: *44*
Test debut: *28/11/58 West Indies v India*
Test record: *3,104 runs (43.11) and 5 wickets (18.00)*

BUTLER, Lennox Stephen "Bunny"

Born: 9 February 1929, Port-of-Spain, Trinidad
Role: Right-arm fast-medium bowler

"BUNNY" BUTLER was a fast-medium bowler who impressed the selectors when he took five for 93 for Trinidad against the touring Australians at Port-of-Spain in 1955. Indeed, the locals were so taken with his performance, comparisons were made with Ray Lindwall, but they proved to be unduly optimistic. Butler took two for 151 in the second Test in front of his home crowd, as the visitors galloped to 600 for nine declared, and was not selected again.

Teams: *Trinidad, West Indies*
First-class debut: *23/2/49 Trinidad v Barbados*

Clyde Butts

First-class record: *29 wickets (33.48) and 161 runs (14.63)*
Tests: *1*
Test debut: *11/4/55 West Indies v Australia*
Test record: *2 wickets (75.50) and 16 runs (16.00)*

BUTTS, Clyde George

Born: 8 July 1957, Perseverance, Georgetown, British Guiana
Role: Off-spin bowler

CLYDE BUTTS comes from a village called Perseverance, about 30 miles outside Georgetown, and that was just the quality required of the tall, lean off-spinner when he won his first Test cap, against New Zealand on a beautiful batting wicket at Bourda in 1985. He had been the leading first-class wicket-taker that season, with 32 at 19.21 apiece but, against New Zealand he bowled 47 overs for figures of nought for 113. Promoted to number three in the batting order, the Guyanese scored just nine and, clearly in need of a lift, got married on the rest day of that Test.

Prior to his elevation to the Test team, Butts had been making huge waves in domestic cricket in Guyana: when they won the Shield in 1983 he took 25 wickets for less than 19 runs each and is now the leading wicket-taker for Guyana in the Shell Shield/Red Stripe Cup with 179 victims. His achievement is all the more worthy when one considers that he came from a relatively poor family - he was the last of 10 children - and cricket invariably had to take second place. Even after Lance Gibbs had invited him to play a few games for Demerara at intermediate level, the cost of commuting proved too much and he returned home to join the police force.

However, he never completely abandoned his cricket and, after a few Case Cup matches, he made his Shield debut against Trinidad & Tobago at Bourda in 1981. Roger Harper was away playing for the President's XI against England and Butts was not about to squander his big chance. After making solid progress, culminating in his outstanding Shield performance in 1983, he was selected for the West Indies "B" team to tour Zimbabwe in October. He bowled well on that tour, and took six wickets in the first 'Test' to enhance his reputation further; but could not remove the steel grip of the pacemen on the subsequent tours of England and Australia.

In 1985 he enjoyed another vintage year in Shield cricket: this time he took 32 inexpensive wickets and finally achieved recognition at the highest level when he was selected to play in the second Test against New Zealand in front of his home crowd in 1985.

He had a successful tour of Pakistan in 1986-87, taking six wickets in the two Tests he played, including four for 73 in the third match at Karachi. Indeed, he appeared to be edging ahead of Roger Harper for the title of best off-spinner in the West Indies, when he was selected for the tour of New Zealand in 1987 and played in three Tests compared to Harper's one on the subsequent trip to India, after Harper injured himself. However, cricket is a funny game - as Butts knows only too well - and neither he nor Harper have been able to establish themselves in a West Indies side that continues to keep faith with its match-winning pacemen.

Teams: *Guyana, Demerara, West Indies*
First-class debut: *23/1/81*
Guyana v Trinidad
First-class record: *253 wickets (25.32)*
and 1,029 runs (15.13)
Tests: *7*
Test debut: *2/4/85*
West Indies v New Zealand
Test record: *10 wickets (59.50)*
and 108 runs (15.42)

BYNOE, Michael Robin

Born: 23 February 1941, Christ Church, Barbados
Role: Right-hand batsman, left-arm medium-pace bowler

ROBIN BYNOE made his Test match debut as an 18-year-old schoolboy against Pakistan in 1959. An elegant opening batsman he enjoyed considerable success on his first tour, scoring over 500 runs for an average of 34 in India and Pakistan in 1958-59. But then Bynoe, who was a useful change bowler with his left-arm medium pace, disappeared from the scene until his services were called upon for the tour to India in 1966-67. He was disappointing in the Tests on that trip, seemingly unable to cope with the spinners - although it must have been of some consolation to him that Erapally Prasanna, one of his tormentors, became his only victim in Test cricket, when he bowled him in the third match at Chepauk - and thereafter lost his place altogether. Like many before him, and doubtless many to come, Bynoe was never able to reproduce his regional form at Test level.

Teams: *Barbados, West Indies*
First-class debut: *11/1/58*
Barbados v Pakistan
First-class record: *3,572 runs (41.05)*
and 9 wickets (27.33)
Tests: *4*
Test debut: *26/3/59 West Indies v Pakistan*
Test record: *111 runs (18.50)*
and 1 wicket (5.00)

Steve Camacho

CAMACHO, George Stephen

Born: 15 October 1945, Georgetown, British Guiana
Role: Right-hand batsman

STEVE CAMACHO made an impressive start to his Test career: when he hit 57 against England in the Bridgetown Test of 1968 and 87 in the subsequent match at Port-of-Spain, it seemed that Camacho would take over Conrad Hunte's opening mantle. However, it was a premature conclusion. Despite topping the Test averages in England in 1969 - aided by 67 and 45 in the second match at Lord's against some fearsome pace bowling from John Snow - he subsequently failed to maintain his consistency, as the West Indies searched in vain for successors to Rae and Stollmeyer. Having played well in the two series against England, Camacho was eventually obliged to make way for Lawrence Rowe.

After his retirement Camacho became a highly respected cricket administrator in the Caribbean and Secretary of the West Indies Board of Control.

Teams: *British Guiana, Guyana, Demerara, West Indies*
First-class debut: *7/4/65 British Guiana v Australia*
First-class record: *4,079 runs (34.86)*
Tests: *11*
Test debut: *19/1/68 West Indies v England*
Test record: *640 runs (29.09) and 0-12*

C

CAMERON, Francis James

Born: 22 June 1923, Kingston, Jamaica
Role: Right-hand batsman, off-spin bowler

JIMMY CAMERON was a useful batsman and capable off-break bowler, who played club cricket in England for many years. He was studying in North America when the West Indies selectors called him up for the tour of India and Pakistan in 1948-49, where he enjoyed only moderate success: he scored 330 runs (25.38) and took 18 expensive wickets. His best performance in the Tests came in the second match at Bombay, where he scored a hard-hit 75 not out. He is the younger brother of John Cameron.

Teams: *Jamaica, West Indies, Canada*
First-class debut: *3/7/46 Jamaica v Trinidad*
First-class record: *551 runs (25.04) and 29 wickets (48.65)*
Tests: *5*
Test debut: *10/11/48 West Indies v India*
Test record: *151 runs (25.16) and 3 wickets (92.66)*

CAMERON, John Hensley

Born: 8 April 1914, Kingston, Jamaica
Role: Right-hand batsman, off-spin bowler

JOHN CAMERON was regarded as something of a cricketing prodigy at Taunton School and went on to play successfully for Cambridge University in the mid-1930's. His all-round cricketing skills - including a cleverly disguised googly - also brought him success at Somerset. His knowledge of English conditions helped secure his appointment as vice-captain for West Indies' tour of England in 1939 but, by that time, his googly had deserted him and he had an undistinguished summer. His father, incidentally, had toured England with Harold Austin's side in 1906, while younger brother, Jimmy, was selected for West Indies' trip to India after the War.

Teams: *Jamaica, West Indies, Somerset, Cambridge University, Combined Universities, Gentlemen's XI*
First-class debut: *27/8/32 Somerset v Warwickshire*
First-class record: *2,772 runs (18.23) and 184 wickets (30.77)*
Tests: *2*
Test debut: *24/6/39 West Indies v England*
Test record: *6 runs (2.00) and 3 wickets (29.33)*

John Cameron

CAREW, George McDonald

Born: 4 June 1910, Bridgetown, Barbados
Died: 9 December 1974, Barbados
Role: Right-hand batsman

GEORGE CAREW was a dependable batsman who had an erratic Test career. He first came to the fore in 1934-35, scoring 46, 43 and 68 off the touring MCC side, which won him a place in the Test side for the first match at Bridgetown. Opening the innings with Roach, he was dismissed for a duck and didn't play another Test until England visited the Caribbean after the War. Then, in the second match at Port-of-Spain in 1948, he enjoyed his finest hour. Batting in nonchalant fashion, complete with dark brown felt hat and an endless supply of chewing gum, he thrashed the English bowlers for 107, adding 173 for the first wicket with Andy Ganteaume. He played in one more Test in that series and was selected for the tour to India in 1948-49, but failed to impress.

Teams: *Barbados, West Indies*
First-class debut: *21/9/34 Barbados v British Guiana*
First-class record: *2,131 runs (34.37) and 13 wickets (46.15)*
Tests: *4*
Test debut: *8/1/35 West Indies v England*
Test record: *170 runs (28.33) and 0-2*

CAREW, Michael "Joey" Conrad

Born: 15 September 1937, Woodbrook, Port-of-Spain, Trinidad
Role: Left-hand batsman, right-arm spin bowler

"JOEY" CAREW personified the late developer. As a promising youngster for Trinidad, he scored a century against Jamaica in 1959 and the following year hit 102 not out and 70 in two matches against the MCC. But it was not until the 1968-69 tour of Australia and New Zealand that Carew established himself at the highest level. In the first Test at Brisbane, he shared in century stands with Kanhai in the first innings and Lloyd in the second, playing a decisive role in West Indies' only win of the series; while a swashbuckling 90 later in the rubber, at Adelaide, helped West Indies to a morale-boosting 616 and the safety of a draw. He completed a successful series by scoring 64 in a losing cause in the fifth match at Sydney. So Carew, the surprise choice for the trip, turned out to be the surprise success, scoring over 1,200 runs for an average of 45.

The Trinidadian reached the high point of his career in New Zealand, scoring his only Test hundred in the first match at Auckland, as he added 172 with Nurse. The rest of the side collapsed in the wake of their partnership and it needed a brilliant century in the second innings from Nurse to turn the tide in West Indies' favour. The pair were dominant again in the

"Joey" Carew

CHALLENOR, George

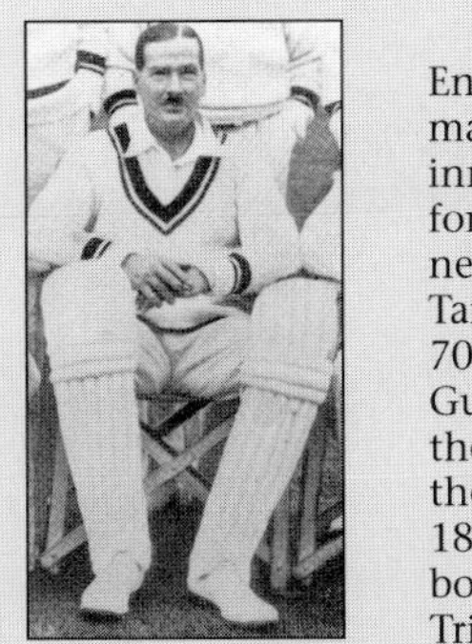

Born: 28 June 1888, Waterloo, Barbados
Died: 20 July 1947, Barbados
Role: Right-hand batsman

GEORGE CHALLENOR is universally acknowledged as the father of West Indian batting. Indeed, that title reveals why he failed to make the impact he surely would have in Test cricket if he had been born 20 years later. When Test status finally arrived, on 23 June 1928, Challenor was within five days of his 40th birthday: the accolade had come too late for the man who had done so much to bring it about.

As early as 1906 - on his first tour of England - Challenor was making the news, hitting a hundred against Nottinghamshire, one of the strongest sides in the country, then 90 off Scotland. Batting for Barbados, he took two centuries off the touring MCC side in successive matches in 1912-13, before the First World War interrupted his flow of runs.

Even so, his performance on the 1923 tour of England, when he scored almost 1,600 first class runs, with eight centuries - including 155 not out against Surrey as he carried his bat and his side to victory by 10 wickets - confirmed the widely-held view that he was the best batsman to visit England between Victor Trumper and Don Bradman. His efforts that summer led to him being specially elected to the MCC. A scintillating 124 for Barbados against the next touring MCC side made the English realise they could no longer legitimately block West Indies' path to Test status.

Despite his success in England, Challenor played many of his most outstanding innings in the Caribbean and formed a famous opening partnership for Barbados with Tim Tarilton. Barbados scored over 700 runs against British Guiana and then Trinidad in the 1927 domestic series: in the first match the pair put on 183 for the first wicket, as they both hit centuries; against Trinidad, they shared in a spectacular 292-run partnership, in which Challenor made 220 and Tarilton 123.

Challenor's Test record - which included an impressive 46 against the fearsome pace of Harold Larwood in the final match of the 1928 series - fails completely to reflect his true ability. However, even if Challenor had been born a generation too soon, it must have been of some consolation to followers of West Indian cricket that, as one of West Indies' earliest master batsmen and a teacher in Barbados, he was able to encourage the likes of Worrell and Walcott to develop their batting and take the game seriously.

Teams: *Barbados, West Indies, M.C.C., H. Leveson-Gower's XI, Gentlemen's XI, Combined XI*
First-class debut: *8/1/06*
Barbados v British Guiana
First-class record: *5,822 runs (38.55) and 54 wickets (23.88)*
Tests: *3*
Test debut: *23/6/28*
West Indies v England
Test record: *101 runs (16.83)*

third match at Christchurch, this time sharing in a stand of 231, with Carew playing a more restrained innings as he took over five hours for his 91. However, once more West Indies failed to capitalise on their efforts and were dismissed relatively cheaply.

Ironically, having played so well on that tour, the gifted left-hander's success seemed to ring the death-knell of his Test career. Although he was selected for the trip to England in 1969, after failing in the first innings of the first Test at Old Trafford, he was unceremoniously dropped despite making amends in the second innings, as he added 92 with Fredericks. Nonetheless he continued to play well on the tour, making 677 runs in his 12 matches, including three centuries, in spite of a hand injury. He was given a short-lived international reprieve when India toured the Caribbean in 1970-71 and then against New Zealand in 1971-72 but, thereafter, faded from the scene.

Teams: *Trinidad, North Trinidad, West Indies, The Rest XI, F.Worrell's XI*
First-class debut: *31/3/56*
Trinidad v E.W. Swanton's XI
First-class record: *7,810 runs (38.47) and 108 wickets (29.76)*
Tests: *19*
Test debut: *6/6/63 West Indies v England*
Test record: *1,127 runs (34.15) and 8 wickets (54.62)*

CHANG, Herbert Samuel

Born: 22 July 1952, Jamaica
Role: Left-hand batsman

HERBERT CHANG was a small left-handed stroke-maker, known for his powers of concentration. Several years of consistent batting for Jamaica in the Shell Shield were finally rewarded when he was selected for West Indies' visit to the Indian subcontinent in 1978-79. However, he was only given one chance to play in a Test - the fourth at Madras - and couldn't produce the goods, being dismissed for six and two.

Chang was not given another opportunity to prove himself in official international cricket and, after a vintage Shield season in 1981-82 when he scored 426 runs from nine innings, an offer to join the first team of West Indians to tour South Africa proved too tempting.

Teams: *Jamaica, West Indies*
First-class debut: *19/1/73 Jamaica v Barbados*
First-class record: *3,273 runs (35.19)*
Tests: *1*
Test debut: *10/1/79 West Indies v India*
Test record: *8 runs (4.00)*

CHRISTIANI, Cyril Marcel

Born: 28 October 1913, Georgetown, British Guiana
Died: 4 April 1938
Role: Wicket-keeper

CYRIL CHRISTIANI toured England in 1933 as deputy wicket-keeper to Ivan Barrow, and quickly revealed himself to have the makings of a top-class wicket-keeper-batsman. Indeed, by the time of the return series in the Caribbean in 1935, Christiani was first choice 'keeper. He kept superbly throughout the series, with his seven dismissals helping West Indies to clinch their first Test rubber.

Christiani was also a capable batsman, as he showed when batting with one of his brothers, E. S. Christiani. Opening for British Guiana, the pair added a record 196 for the first wicket against East India CC, and it seemed, at last, that West Indies might have found a specialist wicket-keeper who could bat as well. Yet, it was not to be, for in April 1938 Cyril died of malaria. He was the older brother of Robert Christiani.

Cyril Christiani

Teams: *British Guiana, West Indies, G.C.Grant's XI*
First-class debut: *22/1/32 British Guiana v Trinidad*
First-class record: *44 catches & 20 stumpings, and 658 runs (16.45)*
Tests: *4*
Test debut: *8/1/35 West Indies v England*
Test record: *6 catches & 1 stumping, and 98 runs (19.60)*

CHRISTIANI, Robert Julian

Born: 19 July 1920, Georgetown, British Guiana
Role: Right-hand batsman, wicket-keeper, off-spin bowler

ROBERT CHRISTIANI was one of several players who had the misfortune to reach cricketing maturity at a time when the West Indies had a wealth of batting talent at their disposal. In Christiani's case, he had to compete with the likes of the three "W"s, Stollmeyer and Gomez. Nonetheless he began his international career promisingly enough with 99 against England in the second innings of the first Test at Bridgetown in 1948 - even though his untimely departure caused him and his supporters to shed a few tears. He carried his momentum into the third Test, hitting a stylish half century in front of his home crowd. The Georgetown supporters were used to seeing Christiani in full flow: at his peak, the right-hander held most of Guiana's batting records.

His performances against England won him a place on the trip to India in 1948-49. He opened his account with a maiden Test century in the first match in Delhi, before snapping up three Indian wickets for good measure; and hit 74 lower down the order in the second match at Bombay. Like his older brother, Cyril, Robert was a capable wicket-keeper and distinguished himself with a catch and two stumpings in the third Test at Calcutta, standing in for Walcott.

The Guyanese followed his success on the subcontinent with over 1,000 first-class runs in England the following summer, but the plethora of gifted batsmen available to the tourists meant that he didn't come in until number seven and therefore had little opportunity to show his true class.

Even so, he went on the trip to Australia and New Zealand in 1951-52 and made some useful contributions with the bat: notably when he top-scored with 76 in the second Test at

Sydney and hit the winning run at Adelaide to secure West Indies' only victory of the series. After that his Test appearances were few, but a first-class average of over 40 confirms that he was a gifted batsman.

Teams: *British Guiana, West Indies*
First-class debut: *25/8/38*
British Guiana v R.S.Grant's XI
First-class record: *5,103 runs (40.50), 98 catches & 12 stumpings, and 18 wickets (60.44)*
Tests: *22*
Test debut: *21/1/48 West Indies v England*
Test record: *896 runs (26.35), 19 catches & 2 stumpings, and 3 wickets (36.00)*

CLARKE, Dr. Carlos Bertram

Born: 7 April 1918, Bridgetown, Barbados
Role: Right-arm leg-spin bowler

BERTIE CLARKE comes into the category of 'surprise choice' for a tour. He was included for the trip to England in 1939 on the recommendation of Headley and - as so often with surprise choices - Clarke came off, capturing 87 wickets at just over 20 apiece. If the pundits were taken aback, so was Clarke himself, who recalls: "I'd read all about the English stars, the Huttons and the Comptons and came here on tour with a great feeling of deference. To my amazement, I found myself getting these stars out!" Unusually Clarke had started life as a pace bowler, but quickly picked up the art of spin bowling from a school library book and equally quickly developed his famous googly.

Although the Second World War interrupted his Test career, Clarke was a familiar face on the English club scene, as he maintained his cricket while studying medicine at Guy's hospital in London. Besides playing, the tall leg-spinner also made cricketing contributions on the BBC's World Service. Clarke played for Northamptonshire between 1946-49 (during which time he took 156 wickets) and for the BBC on Sundays; he appeared for Essex in 1959 and 1960 and maintained his club cricket links well into his sixties.

Clarke might have had a more distinguished Test career, but for his decision to pursue his medical career in England. With the emergence of the National Health Service, he put his faith in medicine rather than the precarious life of an international sportsman,

Robert Christiani

despite being invited to join the West Indies squad to play England in the first Test series after the War.

> ***Teams:*** *Barbados, West Indies, Northamptonshire, Essex, M.C.C.*
> ***First-class debut:*** *27/9/37 Barbados v British Guiana*
> ***First-class record:*** *333 wickets (26.37) and 1,292 runs (12.30)*
> ***Tests:*** *3*
> ***Test debut:*** *24/6/39 West Indies v England*
> ***Test record:*** *6 wickets (43.50) and 3 runs (1.00)*

Sylvester Clarke

CLARKE, Sylvester Theophilus

Born: 11 December 1954, Lead Vale, Christ Church, Barbados
Role: Right-arm fast bowler

SYLVESTER CLARKE could be described as a laid-back cricketer, just so long as you never had the misfortune to be facing him as he hurtled towards the wicket. The man who terrorised batsmen the world over during much of the 1980's, was nurtured in school and club cricket in Barbados. Then, he burst on to the first-class scene in 1978, taking a hat-trick against Trinidad in his first season.

The wrangling at Test level at that time provided him with an unexpected chance once the Packer schism was out in the open, and he took six wickets on his debut - despite several dropped catches - against Australia at Georgetown in 1978. Only injury - which plagued him throughout his career - curtailed his involvement in the series.

Clarke topped the bowling averages with 21 wickets (34.33) in the subsequent rubber in India and, after an interval when the Packer players were back in favour, he played in the series against Pakistan and Australia between 1980-82. In Pakistan, after Holding had been injured, Clarke took 14 wickets (17.28) in four Tests. For good measure he crashed 35 runs in 30 balls - including three successive sixes - in the second Test at Faisalabad. He blotted his copy-book in the fourth match at Multan when, after being provoked by spectators, he threw a brick being used as a boundary marker into the crowd. A student was quite badly injured in the incident, but recovered and Clarke escaped with a suspension from the West Indies Board.

The Barbadian enjoyed a distinguished career in English county cricket, spearheading Surrey's attack for ten seasons until his dismissal early in 1989. He enjoyed particular success with them in 1986, as his 48 victims cost just 16.79 each, and returned career-best bowling

Bertie Clarke

figures of seven for 31 against Essex at The Oval the following year.

Yet Clarke's Test appearances were never as regular as he would have liked, which was a factor that influenced his decision to join Transvaal and then the unofficial West Indies team that toured South Africa in 1983. He continued to play in his own unassuming way and equalled the Currie Cup record in 1984-85, when he took 58 wickets at 13 runs apiece. Clarke believes he was treated unfairly by the West Indies selectors, so switched his allegiance elsewhere. With a cooler head on his shoulders he may have had a more expansive Test career but, then, he may have been a less effective bowler.

Teams: *Barbados, West Indies, West Indies 'Rebels XI', Surrey, Transvaal, Northern Transvaal, Orange Free State.*
First-class debut: *19/1/78 Barbados v Combined Islands*
First-class record: *942 wickets (19.52) and 3,269 runs (14.79)*
Tests: *11*
Test debut: *31/3/78 West Indies v Australia*
Test record: *42 wickets (27.85) and 172 runs (15.63)*

CONSTANTINE, Sir Learie Nicholas

Born: 21 September 1901, Petit Valley, Trinidad
Died: 1 July 1971
Role: Fast bowler, medium-pace bowler, right-hand batsman

LEARIE CONSTANTINE came to symbolise all that is best in West Indian cricket: during the 1930's his outstanding natural talent and unquenchable enthusiasm made him one of the biggest crowd-pullers of his day.

Constantine's grandfather had been a slave, while his father had toured England as a cricketer in 1900 and enjoyed the distinction of being the first West Indian to score a century in England. Learie revealed how deep the family's cricketing roots were when he wrote in *Wisden*: "My mother could keep wicket almost as well as a Test 'keeper; my sister had as much aptitude for batting as I had; one of my uncles was an international player and another was just as skilled."

The younger Constantine was selected for the 1923 tour to England and impressed with his brilliant bowling and fielding, while his batting, if a little erratic, was often just as effective, as when he hit 60 out of a West Indies total of 97 against Derbyshire in a game ruined by the weather. But it was his bowling that provided the real talking point. Jack Hobbs, who had faced the lethal Australian combination of Ted McDonald and Jack Gregory at their peak, thought Constantine's first few overs against him in the 1928 Test series were as quick as anything he had faced. As he got older, Constantine modified his style so he remained an effective force throughout his career.

In 1928 he performed brilliantly in the county matches: against Middlesex, after the home side had made 352 for six and then reduced West Indies to 79 for five, Constantine scored 50 runs in less than 20 minutes, and went on to a top score of 86 in their total of 230; he then snapped up seven Middlesex wickets for 57, including a spell of six for 11 off 39 balls. As if that were not enough, the tourists collapsed to 121 for five in their second innings, leaving Constantine to bring off a remarkable victory as he hit 103 out of 133, with two sixes and 12 fours.

Later in the tour, he repeated his one-man show against Northamptonshire as his pace broke through their batting to give him figures of seven for 45. He then turned on them with his bat, racing to 107 in 90 minutes, before a second innings hat-trick gave him 13 wickets in the match and victory for West Indies. He finished the tour as the leading wicket-taker with 107, including West Indies' first Test victim, Charles Hallows, dismissed in the first session at Lord's, the leading batsman with 1,381 runs and the leading fielder with 33 catches. But, as was to be the case on subsequent occasions, he failed to carry this form into the Test arena, where he took just five wickets and scored a mere 89 runs from six Test innings.

He seemed more at ease when England visited the Caribbean in 1929-30. Opening the bowling with Herman Griffith in the first Test at Bridgetown, he dismissed three good batsmen without the help of any fielder and held three catches. He was the top-scorer with 58 in the second Test in Trinidad; and was instrumental in achieving the long-awaited victory at Georgetown, as he broke through England's batting on the first day to collect four wickets for 35, before completing the rout in the second innings by taking five for 87.

The Trinidadian was generally disappointing on the inaugural visit to Australia but, by the time of the series in England in 1933, he was making such a mark in Lancashire League cricket that he was only released for the second Test at Old Trafford. There, he was top-scorer in the tourists' second innings with 64 and, along with Martindale, subjected the English to a spell of 'bodyline', after the home side had tried to tame the tourists with the same. His performance enabled West Indies to secure a draw, while in the other two matches in which he did not play they were heavily defeated.

Constantine was at his best for England's second visit to the Caribbean, in 1934-35. After missing the first Test, he played a decisive role in the second at Port-of-Spain. He hit 90 in West Indies' first innings, before removing two English batsmen as the tourists slumped to 28 for five. Even though England eventually rallied to 258, they failed to stave off defeat as, with the penultimate ball of the game, Constantine trapped Maurice Leyland leg before wicket to level the series, and give himself bowling figures of three wickets for 11 runs.

He played a leading role in West Indies' historic victory at Kingston, to ensure that the home side won their first-ever Test rubber: after being instrumental with Martindale in enforcing the follow-on, and taking an astonishing catch to end Les Ames' rearguard innings of 126, Constantine had the satisfaction of leading West Indies to victory, after Jackie Grant was forced to retire with an ankle injury. In an inspired piece of captaincy, Constantine brought on Derek Sealy to allow himself and Martindale to change ends. Thoughtfully, Sealy took a wicket, whereupon Constantine returned to take three others to finish the job, before the rains swept in from the Blue Mountains.

Despite advancing years, Constantine continued to turn in superb performances: in England in 1939 he bowled more overs (493.4) and took more wickets (103 at 17.77) than anyone else. It was, perhaps, fitting that he shone so brightly in his last Test appearance, at The Oval. There, he snapped up five for 75 and hit a majestic 79 out of 103 added in an hour, as he stroked the ball to all parts of the ground. The Second World War meant that he wasn't given an opportunity to maintain this kind of form in Test cricket, that he produced so readily in league cricket. Nonetheless, he played for the Dominions during the War and led them to victory over England at Lord's in 1945.

If his services were no longer required on the field of play, his talents were put to even better use off it as he threw his weight against racial discrimination. By his very deeds and demeanour, Constantine was already challenging many racial stereotypes and, at the start of the War, joined the Ministry of Labour's Welfare Office, helping to look after the interests of fellow West Indians. He also studied law and was called to the Bar in 1954. When Trinidad & Tobago became independent in 1962, he was elected an MP and later became Minister of Works in the Trinidadian government. He was High Commissioner for Trinidad & Tobago in London between 1962-64. He was knighted in 1962 and created a life peer in 1969 and, among the various posts he held, he was a member of the Race Relations Board and the Sports Council, and became a Governor of the BBC. Constantine wrote and broadcast on cricket, and when he died in 1971 his country awarded him its highest honour, the Trinity Cross.

For all his achievements in the political and social arena, it is perhaps indicative of his worth as a cricketer that it is for his exploits on the field of play that Constantine is most remembered and most loved.

Teams: *Trinidad, Barbados, West Indies, Freelooters (India), Dominions XI, Combined XI.*
First-class debut: *19/9/21 Trinidad v Barbados*
First-class record: *439 wickets (20.48) and 4,475 runs (24.05)*
Lancashire League record: *790 wickets (9.90) and 6,673 runs (38.35)*
Tests: *18*
Test debut: *23/6/28 West Indies v England*
Test record: *58 wickets (30.10) and 635 runs (19.24)*

CROFT, Colin Everton Hunte

Born: 15 March 1953, Demerara, British Guiana
Role: Right-arm fast bowler

COLIN CROFT was a big, mean-looking pace bowler who took full advantage of the opportunity to establish himself in the West Indies Test side when injury ruled Holding and Daniel out of the home series against Pakistan in 1977.

Already a force to be reckoned with in his native Guyana, Croft collected seven wickets on his debut, in the first Test at Bridgetown, and was in even better form for the second match in Trinidad. His lift and movement off the pitch made him unplayable, as he returned the sensational figures of eight for 29 to smash Holding's record of six for 57 set against England the previous year. In a devastating opening spell, Croft forced Sadiq Mohammad to retire, and then removed three more of Pakistan's top-order batsmen before Majid Khan and Wasim Raja steadied the innings briefly. In one of the most spectacular bursts of fast bowling ever seen, five of Croft's victims were removed in just 10.5 overs at a cost of nine runs. This effort proved to be the shape of things to come and he finished the series with 33 wickets, equalling Alf Valentine's record for a West Indian bowler.

Colin Croft

His performance brought him rich rewards: a regular place in the Test team and a county contract with Lancashire.

Ironically, having made such an impact in official Test circles, and having bowled splendidly in the first two Tests against the touring Australians in 1978, Croft then signed for Kerry Packer. When the rift was finally patched up, Croft's return to the official fold was delayed until after the 1979 World Cup. His return to favour seemed to inspire him and on the tour of Australia in 1979-80 he was the leading wicket-taker with 16 scalps, as the West Indies won their first rubber in Australia. His 24 wickets at 18.95 apiece against England in the Caribbean in 1981 confirmed his calibre, but a subsequent lean spell saw him fall victim to the lure of the South African rand. It must have been a decision taken in a fit of pique as, even in the esteemed company of Roberts and Holding, Croft invariably finished on top. After his sojourn to South Africa, he moved to the United States.

Teams: *Guyana, Demerara, West Indies, Lancashire, West Indies 'Rebels XI'*
First-class debut: *27/1/72 Guyana v Jamaica*
First-class record: *428 wickets (24.60) and 865 runs (10.54)*
Tests: *27*
Test debut: *18/2/77 West Indies v Pakistan*
Test record: *125 wickets (23.30) and 158 runs (10.53)*

DA COSTA, Oscar Constantine

Born: 11 September 1907, Jamaica
Died: 1 October 1936
Role: Right-hand batsman, medium-pace bowler

OSCAR DA COSTA was a gifted all-round cricketer, being a capable batsman, useful medium-pacer and agile fielder. He demonstrated these skills on his Test debut, against England, in the fourth Test at Kingston in 1930. He scored 39 in his only innings, took a wicket in each of the English innings and held three catches in the match. He was selected for West Indies' tour of England in 1933 and scored over 1,000 first-class runs (26.82), including his maiden century, 105 against Essex at Leyton, and took 31 wickets (34.03), but he was unimpressive in the Tests.

Da Costa was, however, the joker in the pack: he carried a rubber stamp with his signature to save him from writers' cramp lest he be bombarded by autograph-hunters! In his last international appearance, in the second Test against England at Port-of-Spain in 1935, he scored 25 and 19 not out, before his untimely death the following year.

Teams: *Jamaica, West Indies, G.C. Grant's XI.*
First-class debut: *21/2/29 Jamaica v Julien Cahn's XI*
First-class record: *1,563 runs (29.49) and 44 wickets (40.13)*
Tests: *5*
Test debut: *3/4/30 West Indies v England*
Test record: *153 runs (19.12) and 3 wickets (58.33)*

Oscar Da Costa

Wayne Daniel

DANIEL, Wayne Wendell

Born: 16 January 1956, St Philip, Barbados
Role: Right-arm fast bowler

WAYNE DANIEL was the backbone of Middlesex's pace attack for well over a decade, although he would have preferred to have been donning the maroon colours of his native West Indies more often. But he never found regular favour with the selectors.

Daniel first made an impression at Middlesex when he visited England in 1974 with the Young West Indies side; two years later he had graduated to representative honours with Barbados, Middlesex and the West Indies. He made his Test debut against India early in 1976 and on the subsequent tour of England, took 52 wickets bowling in the company of Holding, Roberts, Holder and Julien. Tony Cozier noted: "[Daniel] was the least experienced of the lot [and] accordingly the wildest but, on occasion, the fastest."

Thereafter, the man who worshipped two of his island's greatest fast bowlers, Hall and Griffith, and who enjoyed the benefit of Seymour Nurse's advice, enjoyed only fleeting international recognition (he was selected for West Indies' World Cup squad in 1983 and toured India with them later that year). So he channelled his energies into a career with Middlesex where, on his day, he bowled as fast as anyone on the English county circuit. Daniel helped Middlesex to five county championships and in his benefit year with the club in 1985 finished as their leading wicket-taker.

Teams: *Barbados, West Indies, Middlesex, Western Australia*
First-class debut: *16/1/76 Barbados v Trinidad*
First-class record: *867 wickets (22.47) and 1,551 runs (11.48)*
Tests: *10*
Test debut: *21/4/76 West Indies v India*
Test record: *36 wickets (25.27) and 46 runs (6.57)*

DAVIS, Bryan Alan

Born: 2 May 1940, Belmont, Port-of-Spain, Trinidad
Role: Right-hand batsman, leg-spin bowler

BRYAN DAVIS was a gifted batsman, who often opened the innings. He distinguished himself in domestic cricket in 1966-67 when he carried his bat for 188 for North against South of Trinidad at

Port-of-Spain. The same year, Davis toured the Indian subcontinent with the West Indies, but was not selected for any of the Tests. However, he had played in four matches against the visiting Australians in 1965, opening in three of them as the selectors searched in vain for a regular partner for Conrad Hunte. Davis enjoyed most success in the second Test at Port-of-Spain: in front of his home crowd, the elegant right-hander hit two half-centuries, adding 116 and 91 for the first wicket with Hunte. He had two successful seasons with Glamorgan, scoring over 1,000 runs in 1969 and 1970. He is the older brother of Charlie Davis.

> ***Teams:*** *Trinidad, North Trinidad, West Indies, Glamorgan*
> ***First-class debut:*** *2/10/59 Trinidad v Jamaica*
> ***First-class record:*** *6,231 runs (34.81) and 9 wickets (48.22)*
> ***Tests:*** *4*
> ***Test debut:*** *26/3/65 West Indies v Australia*
> ***Test record:*** *245 runs (30.62)*

Left: Bryan Davis

Below: Charlie Davis

DAVIS, Charles Alan

Born: 1 January 1944, Belmont, Port-of-Spain, Trinidad
Role: Right-hand batsman, medium-pace bowler

CHARLIE DAVIS, like many before him, initially found the gap between territorial and Test cricket difficult to bridge. As early as 1960 he was scoring centuries in domestic cricket in Trinidad and eight years later thrashed 158 for the President's X1 against the touring MCC side. He was rewarded with a trip to Australia and New Zealand in 1968-69, but had a dismal time with the bat although, ironically, he headed the bowling averages with 24 wickets, including career-best bowling figures of seven for 106 against South Australia.

However, he proved himself as a batsman in England in 1969, averaging over 40, which included a six-and-a-half-hour century in the second Test at Lord's after he had been involved in a run-out mix-up with his mentor, Sobers. Davis was prolific against India in 1970-71, averaging 132.25 in four Tests - a figure boosted by centuries in the third game at Georgetown and one in front of his home crowd in the final Test in Trinidad. He continued his fine run by averaging almost 60 in the series against New Zealand in 1971-72. During that rubber, he scored 183 in the third Test at Bridgetown, sharing in an infinitely more fruitful partnership with Sobers, as the pair added 254 for the sixth wicket. It was another marathon effort by the right-hander: this time his innings lasted for 10 hours, after he had been dropped in the slips on 18.

Davis seemed to be riding high but, suddenly, as had happened to so many before him, he was dropped from the Test side without warning and left to cherish a remarkably high Test average of 54.20.

Teams: *Trinidad, North Trinidad, West Indies*
First-class debut: *7/4/61 Trinidad v E.W. Swanton's XI*
First-class record: *5,538 runs (41.32) and 63 wickets (39.36)*
Tests: *15*
Test debut: *26/12/68 West Indies v Australia*
Test record: *1,301 runs (54.20) and 2 wickets (165.00)*

DAVIS, Winston Walter

Born: 18 September 1958, Kingstown, St Vincent, Windward Islands
Role: Right-arm fast bowler

WINSTON DAVIS might not be the first name that springs to mind when thinking of a West Indian bowler who set two distinguished records in 1983. But it was the wiry Vincentian who set the record for the most wickets in a Shell Shield season, when he took 33 at 18.78 apiece, and went on to return the best bowling analysis in the World Cup later that year, when he snapped up seven for 51 in West Indies' clash with Australia at Headingley - indeed, his first five overs went for 33 runs before he skittled out seven Australians for 18 runs in five amazing overs.

Coming from one of the smaller Caribbean islands, Davis is also one of fast bowling's smaller figures, but he is tremendously strong. He received his first formal coaching when he and his compatriot, Linton Lewis, won official sponsorship to attend Alf Gover's cricket school in London. Davis had already made his mark in youth cricket and in 1978 had been in England with West Indies' Young Cricketers. Two years later he made his Shield debut, appearing for the Combined Islands. After a quiet start - although he impressed sufficiently to be included in West Indies Under-26 tour party to Zimbabwe in 1981 - he signalled the shape of things to come by collecting 22 Shield wickets at 22.77 each in 1982. Later that year, Davis joined Glamorgan after Ezra Moseley had been put out of action with a back injury; ironically it was Moseley's back problem which had made space for Davis on the tour to Zimbabwe.

After making his Test debut against India in 1983, Davis made his first appearance against England, in the fourth match at Old Trafford in 1984, this time as a replacement for the injured Malcolm Marshall. Surprisingly, he made his biggest impact with the bat, hitting 77 as nightwatchman, as he shared in a stand of 170 with Greenidge. He toured Australia with West Indies in 1984-85 and returned his best Test figures when New Zealand visited the Caribbean later that year, taking four for 19 in the fourth game at Kingston.

After being somewhat hampered by injury while playing for Tasmania in the Sheffield Shield in 1985-86, Davis was rejuvenated by a summer of Lancashire League cricket with Rishton in 1986, and then signed a county contract with Northamptonshire. He toured India in 1987-88, bowling more overs than anyone part from Clyde Butts, and captured 13 wickets in the Tests.

Teams: *Windward Islands, Combined Islands, West Indies, Glamorgan, Tasmania, Northamptonshire*
First-class debut: *11/3/80 Windward Islands v Leeward Islands*
First-class record: *582 wickets (28.54) and 2,211 runs (14.08)*
Tests: *15*
Test debut: *28/4/83 West Indies v India*
Test record: *45 wickets (32.71) and 202 runs (15.53)*

Winston Davis

De CAIRES, Francis Ignatius

Born: 12 May 1909, British Guiana
Died: 2 February 1959
Role: Right-hand batsman

Frank De Caires

FRANK De CAIRES distinguished himself with two masterful innings in the first-ever Test in the West Indies, against England at Bridgetown in 1930. Only a century from Roach in the first innings and one from Headley in the second overshadowed de Caires' 80 and 70, which helped the West Indies to a worthy draw. He was selected for the first trip to Australia later that year, but didn't make the Test side.

Teams: *British Guiana, West Indies*
First-class debut: *31/1/29 British Guiana v Trinidad*
First-class record: *945 runs (28.63) and 1 wicket (48.00)*
Tests: *3*
Test debut: *11/1/30 West Indies v England*
Test record: *232 runs (38.66) and 0-9*

DEPEIZA, Clairmonte Cyril

Born: 10 October 1927, St James, Barbados
Role: Wicket-keeper, right-hand batsman

CLAIRMONTE DEPEIZA'S capable wicket-keeping feats seemed to pale by comparison after his world record seventh wicket partnership of 347 with Denis Atkinson against Australia in the Bridgetown Test of 1955. Prior to that innings Depeiza had never scored a first-class 50. After the tourists had scored 668 in their first innings, West Indies were reduced to a dubious 146 for six before Depeiza joined his captain at the wicket. Amazingly, they batted on and on for over a day in front of their disbelieving compatriots, as they both went on to career-best scores of 122 for Depeiza and 219 for Atkinson. Although they failed to prevent the follow-on, they tired the opposing bowlers, spearheaded by Ray Lindwall and Keith Miller, to such an extent that the visitors could not risk another session in the field immediately. Lack of time meant that Australia were not in a position to make a realistic second innings declaration and, fittingly, Atkinson and Depeiza played out the last half hour for a draw. Indeed, Depeiza's studious pushes forward - a technique he carried into the second innings - prompted a local wag to nickname him 'the Leaning Tower Depeiza'!

Depeiza's elevation to Test status forms part of West Indies' on-going saga to find a reliable wicket-keeper in the mid-1950's. The Barbadian met with more success than his immediate predecessors, Alfie Binns and Clifford McWatt, who had been restricted to one home Test each. Once Depeiza was selected - for the third Test at Georgetown - he achieved the rare accolade for a 'keeper in those days of being retained for the whole series. Depeiza and Binns were the two selected for the 1955-56 tour to New Zealand; both were given a chance behind the stumps: Depeiza played in two Tests 'keeping in one and bowling in the other, with Binns behind the stumps. Depeiza's skilful 'keeping to the spinners, Ramadhin and Valentine, in the second Test at Christchurch helped the West Indies to a decisive victory.

Depeiza's creditable performances in New Zealand and the fact that Binns and McWatt were rated as better 'keepers, made the decision to take Gerry Alexander to England in 1957 seem somewhat bizarre; while the omission of the gifted Jackie Hendriks made it even more difficult to understand. It has been suggested that some of the selectors thought that Depeiza had been chosen but, in the end, did not make the tour because his whereabouts were unknown. This seems strange given that both he and Conrad Hunte, the other surprise omission, were both available for English sides.

However, when given a chance, Depeiza put his all-round talents to good use. He could look back on a career that, besides the acclaim he won for his wicket-keeping, had brought him fleeting fame as an international batsman and more sustained appreciation as a bowler in league cricket in the UK.

Teams: *Barbados, West Indies*
First-class debut: *24/1/52 Barbados v Jamaica*
First-class record: *31 catches & 9 stumpings, and 623 runs (32.78)*
Tests: *5*
Test debut: *26/4/55 West Indies v Australia*
Test record: *7 catches & 4 stumpings, and 187 runs (31.16) and 0-15*

DEWDNEY, David Thomas

Born: 23 October 1933, Kingston, Jamaica
Role: Right-arm fast bowler

TOM DEWDNEY was a tall, strong fast bowler from Jamaica, who rarely sacrificed accuracy for pace. He was on the edge of international selection for most of the 1950's and finally made his Test debut against Australia in the fourth match at Bridgetown in 1955. Although it was only his third first-class match, the youngster was far from over-awed returning the creditable figures of four for 125 off 33 overs, as the tourists poured on the agony with a first innings total of 668. This performance won him a place on the 'blooding' tour to New Zealand in 1955-56 where he was used sparingly, although he performed admirably in the fourth Test at Auckland capturing five wickets for 21 in just 19.5 overs. These spurts of brilliance must have made the selectors think they had found a genuine paceman to subdue the opposition, but he disappointed on the tour of England in 1957 and had little success when Pakistan visited the Caribbean the following year. His career was not helped by being involved in a car accident in England in September 1959, in which Gary Sobers was also travelling and "Collie" Smith was killed.

Dewdney was perhaps unlucky with his Test career in that his best chances always seemed to come against strong English and Australian batting sides: in a different setting he might have lasted longer.

Teams: *Jamaica, West Indies, Commonwealth XI*
First-class debut: *12/2/55 Jamaica v Trinidad*
First-class record: *92 wickets (30.73) and 171 runs (5.70)*
Tests: *9*
Test debut: *14/5/55 West Indies v Australia*
Test record: *21 wickets (38.42) and 17 runs (2.42)*

Tom Dewdney

DOWE, Uton George

Born: 29 March 1949, St Mary, Jamaica
Role: Right-arm fast-medium bowler

UTON DOWE was a sturdy figure who bowled fast-medium. He played four Test matches, all at home, against India, New Zealand and Australia between 1971 and 1973. However, he failed to establish himself - after a promising debut when he took four for 69 against India at Kensington Oval - and was often erratic, so much so that in the first Test against Australia at Sabina Park, his home supporters began chanting 'Dowe shall not bowl!'

Teams: *Jamaica, West Indies*
First-class debut: *7/2/70 Jamaica v Cavaliers XI*
First-class record: *97 wickets (27.86) and 128 runs (7.11)*
Tests: *4*
Test debut: *1/4/71 West Indies v India*
Test record: *12 wickets (44.50) and 8 runs (8.00)*

DUJON, Peter Jeffrey Leroy

Born: 28 May 1956, Kingston, Jamaica
Role: Wicket-keeper, right-hand batsman

JEFF DUJON is rightly acknowledged as one of the finest wicket-keeper-batsmen of all time. His athletic prowess behind the stumps, as he swoops and dives to gather seemingly unpluckable balls from the air have become his trademark.

Dujon has a formidable cricketing pedigree: his father played first-class cricket and his brother, Dean, was similarly gifted until he decided to pursue a career in medicine. But it was Jeffrey - who, as a toddler, was a familiar sight at Kingston Cricket Club - who has made the most indelible mark. His rise was truly meteoric: he appeared for Kingston at the age of 13, for Jamaica at 18 and two years later hit his maiden century, having already impressed on West Indies Young Cricketers' tour to England in 1974.

Solid performances in Zimbabwe in 1981, when he toured with West Indies' Under-26 side, earned him a place on the short trip to Australia in 1981-82. There, he enhanced his reputation with his efficient 'keeping and stylish batting and headed the Test averages with 45.50. Dujon's cause was aided further with the defection to South Africa of some of his leading wicket-keeping rivals before the next series against India, where he was determined to secure the long-term succession to Deryck Murray. He crowned a splendid series against India by becoming the first West Indian wicket-keeper for over 20 years to score a century in a Test, as he put on 207 for the sixth wicket with Lloyd in the final Test in Antigua. Earlier, in the first match of the series in Kingston, Dujon equalled the record for the most catches in an innings by a West Indian 'keeper by snapping up five - a feat he repeated against England at Bridgetown in 1986 - and then won the game for West Indies by hitting a six over square-leg in the last over, to the delight of his home crowd.

The Jamaican kept up this record-breaking form in the home series against Australia at the start of 1984, crashing 130 in the second Test at Port-of-Spain and then set a record for a West Indian 'keeper by making 20 dismissals in the series.

His boundless energy allowed him to motor on against England later that year: his impeccable wicket-keeping and more fine batting - including a century in the Old Trafford Test - confirmed him as the best in his field. He was on the attack against Australia again, this time in Australia at the end of 1984, when he hit 139 in the first Test at Perth, having retired hurt after being hit on the head with a bouncer before he had scored. He struck 77 and 32 in the third game at Adelaide and wrapped up a successful series with 49 at Melbourne.

Jeff Dujon

Inevitably, his purple patch had to come to an end and it happened in Pakistan in 1986. However, he wasn't off song for long and returned to almost his best form in the subsequent series in New Zealand. Although he had a below par tour to India in 1987-88, he lifted himself when Pakistan visited the Caribbean in 1988. He scored 106 not out in the drawn second Test in Trinidad, and shared in a vital unbroken ninth wicket partnership of 61 with Benjamin to level the series in the third match in Barbados. He was also in fine form in England in 1988, taking 20 catches in the Test series and again finished high in the batting averages with 305 runs at 50.83.

In West Indies' most recent series he has performed more modestly by his own high standards. But, with an overall batting average approaching 40 and 223 dismissals from 68 Tests, "Dooj", as he is known to his team mates, remains the outstanding contemporary wicket-keeper-batsman, which was reflected in his invitation to keep wicket for the Rest of the World XI in MCC's bi-centenary Test in 1987.

Teams: *Jamaica, West Indies, Rest of World XI*
First-class debut: *21/3/75 Jamaica v Trinidad*
First-class record: *8,163 runs (39.62) and 361 catches & 17 stumpings and 1 wicket (45.00)*
Tests: *68*
Test debut: *26/12/81 West Indies v Australia*
Test record: *2,994 runs (35.22) and 218 catches & 5 stumpings*

EDWARDS, Richard Martin "Prof"

Born: 3 June 1940, Worthing, Barbados
Role: Right-arm fast bowler

"PROF" EDWARDS is an amiable soul, who served his apprenticeship as a pace bowler under Hall and Griffith on the 1968-69 tour of Australia. However, the self-effacing Bajan - who normally let his bowling do the talking - struggled on the Australian wickets and his 14 scalps were expensive. His figures would have been better if he hadn't been the victim of some poor fielding by his team mates in the second Test at Melbourne: Ian Chappell was dropped off his bowling on 10 and went on to 165, and then Bill Lawry enjoyed the same good fortune when he was missed off the unlucky Edwards on 132, and went on to a double century.

Despite his difficulties in Australia, Edwards kept his spirits up and recovered in New Zealand where he took six for 129 in the first Test at Auckland and seven for 126 in the second at Wellington, including five for 84 in the first innings. These performances helped him to finish as the leading wicket-taker with 15 at 23.46 apiece but, by that time, the selectors were already making plans for a new-look pace attack, in which Edwards did not figure. So the genial Edwards faded from the Test scene, although he continued to be heavily involved in cricket in Barbados. He is an enthusiastic supporter of youth cricket and his son is a leading light at his old club, Wanderers.

"Prof" Edwards

Teams: *Barbados, West Indies, New Zealand Governor's XI*
First-class debut: *21/10/61 Barbados v British Guiana*
First-class record: *78 wickets (36.29) and 389 runs (11.78)*
Tests: *5*
Test debut: *26/12/68 West Indies v Australia*
Test record: *18 wickets (34.77) and 65 runs (9.28)*

FERGUSON, Wilfred F

Born: 14 December 1917, Longdenville, Trinidad
Died: 23 February 1961
Role: Right-arm leg-spin bowler, right-hand batsman

WILF FERGUSON was a short, stocky player whose specialism was well-pitched leg-breaks and hard-hit runs late in the order. He enjoyed a splendid series against England immediately after the War, taking 23 wickets at an average of 24.65. He was seen at his best in the second Test at Port-of-Spain when, on a docile wicket, he returned the fine figures of 11 for 229 in 73.2 overs. Just as people thought he might not come off with the bat, he hit a memorable 75 in one and three-quarter hours in the fourth Test at Kingston. He made the 1948-49 tour to India and played once against England in 1954. Selected for the fourth Test at Queen's Park Oval, his chief contribution in a drawn match was 44 in the second innings when he was promoted to opener.

A jovial character, besides his brisk innings, Ferguson's other trademark was his bald head which, when he took his cap off, invariably caused much amusement among spectators.

Teams: *Trinidad, West Indies*
First-class debut: *20/2/43 Trinidad v Barbados*
First-class record: *165 wickets (31.55) and 1,225 runs (23.55)*
Tests: *8*
Test debut: *21/1/48 West Indies v England*
Test record: *34 wickets (34.26) and 200 runs (28.58)*

Wilf Ferguson

FERNANDES, Maurius Pacheco "Maurice"

Born: 12 August 1897, British Guiana
Died: 8 May 1981
Role: Right-hand batsman

"MAURICE" FERNANDES' chief contribution to the history of West Indian cricket came when he led his side to their first Test match victory, against England at Georgetown in 1930. Fernandes had played representative cricket against England seven years earlier and, despite a bout of malaria, scored over 500 runs (34.86) on the 1923 tour. And, in 1925-26, he made 120 for British Guiana against Freddie Calthorpe's touring team, to secure a draw for the home side.

But, as with so many top players, by the time the West Indies were admitted to Test cricket, Fernandes was past his best. He struggled in England in 1928, but achieved his real moment of glory before his home crowd at Georgetown in 1930. After Constantine and Francis had bowled the tourists out for 145, Fernandes wisely rested his bowlers in preference to enforcing the follow-on. His decision reaped rich rewards as Constantine took five for 87 in the second innings to sweep West Indies to a decisive first win.

Despite overseeing that historic victory, the West Indies selectors continued with their practice of rarely picking players outside of their home territory - due, in the main, to economic considerations - and Fernandes' Test career came to an abrupt end. Fernandes took out any disappointment he may have felt on Barbados by scoring a splendid century against them in the domestic championship of that year.

"Maurice" Fernandes

Teams: *British Guiana, West Indies*
First-class debut: *23/9/22 British Guiana v Trinidad*
First-class record: *2,087 runs (28.20) and 5 wickets (36.60)*
Tests: *2*
Test debut: *23/6/28 West Indies v England*
Test record: *49 runs (12.25)*

FINDLAY, Thaddeus Michael

Born: 19 October 1943, Troumaca, St Vincent, Windward Islands
Role: Wicket-keeper

MIKE FINDLAY was a first-rate wicket-keeper - and sometime goal-keeper for St Vincent - whose admirable technique made him only the second player from his island to play international cricket since Charles Ollivierre two generations earlier.

Findlay had an impressive first-class debut against the visiting Australians in 1965 but, nonetheless, was considered lucky to be included on the trip there in 1968-69 as deputy to Hendriks, in preference to the prodigious Deryck Murray. But the Vincentian played well and, on the subsequent tour of England, was chosen to keep wicket in two of the three Tests in front of Hendriks. But, as so often in the past, it seemed that the wicket-keeper's position was in a state of flux and Findlay's modest batting meant that Desmond Lewis, who was a specialist opener and 'keeper, took over the gloves later in the home series against India in 1970-71. However, Lewis failed to make a real impression and Findlay was recalled for the trip to New Zealand in 1971-72. He retained the position for the first Test against Australia in Jamaica the following year but, with Murray now available having completed his studies, Findlay must have known his indifferent performance in that game made his position vulnerable. And so it was: Murray took over for the second Test at Bridgetown and, although Findlay was selected for and played well during the 1976 tour of England, the tenacious Trinidadian proved impossible to dislodge from the Test team.

Mike Findlay

Teams: *Windward Islands, Combined Islands, West Indies*
First-class debut: *22/5/65 Windward Islands v Australia*
First-class record: *209 catches & 43 stumpings, and 2,927 runs (20.18)*
Tests: *10*
Test debut: *26/6/69 West Indies v England*
Test record: *19 catches & 2 stumpings, and 212 runs (16.30)*

FOSTER, Maurice Linton Churchill

Born: 9 May 1943, Retreat, St Mary, Jamaica
Role: Right-hand batsman, off-spin bowler

MAURICE FOSTER was a capable all-rounder, who could be relied on to bolster the middle order and frequently work the oracle with his off-break bowling. He captained Jamaica for several years, and became one of the most prolific and consistent run-scorers in Shell Shield cricket. He was selected for the tour to England in 1969, but enjoyed most success when Australia visited the Caribbean in 1972-73. He averaged over 40 with the bat, helped by the only Test hundred of his career - which came in front of his home crowd in the first match at Kingston - as he added 210 for the fifth wicket with Kanhai in even time. It was only fitting that the amiable Foster should have reached this landmark as, two years earlier, he had come within one run of a century in the fifth Test against India in Trinidad.

Thereafter Foster's Test career was patchy, hampered by his unavailability for the tour of India in 1974-75 and he was eventually squeezed out by the wealth of batting talent that blossomed under the aegis of Clive Lloyd. Besides his cricketing prowess, Foster was also a top-class table tennis player and became champion of the West Indies.

Teams: *Jamaica, West Indies*
First-class debut: *9/1/64 Jamaica v Cavaliers XI*
First-class record: *6,731 runs (45.17) and 132 wickets (30.72)*
Tests: *14*
Test debut: *12/6/69 West Indies*
Test record: *580 runs (30.52) and 9 wickets (66.66)*

Maurice Foster

FRANCIS, George Nathaniel

Born: 7 December 1897,
Bridgetown, Barbados
Died: 12 January 1942
Role: Right-arm fast bowler

GEORGE FRANCIS bowled fast and straight. The penetrative nature of his bowling - which included a wicked yorker - meant that as often as not he took the new ball as a matter of course.

The Barbadian was at his peak on West Indies' tour of England in 1923, after Harold Austin, the captain of that side, had demanded his inclusion. He lived up to his promise and was soon running through the county sides: he took 10 wickets against Sussex, six for 34 in an innings against Middlesex and a match-winning 10 for 76 against Surrey at The Oval. To confirm his remarkable talent Francis then ripped through the best of England's batting in the end-of-tour match against Henry Leveson-Gower's XI at Scarborough. An England line-up that included Jack Hobbs, Ernest Tyldesley, Percy Chapman, Wilfred Rhodes and Percy Fender predictably secured a substantial first innings lead and, needing just 28 runs for victory in the fourth, it seemed the contest would be a one-sided walk-over. But Francis had other ideas and removed Hobbs after just three runs had been scored. He and his more experienced partner, George John, then proceeded to push West Indies to the edge of a remarkable victory, reducing the home side to 19 for six. In the end, the hosts scraped home by four wickets, with Francis returning figures of four for 12, and acknowledgement from the English that Test status could not be put off much longer.

Francis finished that tour with 82 wickets (15.58) and maintained his momentum against Freddie Calthorpe's MCC tourists in 1925-26. This time he was partnered by his compatriot, Herman Griffith, who caused the English more anguish. The pair took nine wickets each in MCC's opening match against Barbados, as the visitors collapsed to their only defeat of the tour. Francis nearly inspired another victory when he took seven English wickets in the first innings of the tourists' second game against Barbados.

Predictably, by the time of West Indies' first Test series, Francis had lost much of his accuracy as he strove to maintain his speed. Even so, it was fitting that the man who had done so much to hasten the granting of Test status should bowl their first ball in Test cricket. He returned figures of 25-4-72-2 in that first innings, his two wickets being the illustrious Herbert Sutcliffe and later Tyldesley, who became the first player to score a Test hundred against the West Indies. In the last match at The Oval, Hobbs and Sutcliffe combined to put on 155 for the first wicket, before Francis accounted for them both, allowing Griffith to mop up the middle order. Although he had passed his 30th birthday, Francis still had enough energy to capture 56 wickets on that tour at just over 30 apiece.

Francis was delighted to have been included in the West Indies team that secured their first Test victory, against England at Georgetown in 1930, and would have counted his blessings that that was the match his employers had allowed him leave for. He performed admirably taking six wickets altogether, including four for 40 in the first innings. That haul, together with his relative wealth of international experience, ensured he was selected for the inaugural tour of Australia. It was a punishing trip, made worthwhile by their exhilarating win in the final Test in Sydney. Against a strong Australian attack, the West Indies reached 350 for six, to give their bowlers a reasonable target to defend. For the first time in the series Francis and Griffith came off together, with Francis capturing four for 48, to increase his Test tally by more than a third to 11, as Australia were left trailing on the first innings by 126. Jackie Grant was sufficiently impressed by his pace duo to set Australia a target of 250; the pair rewarded his faith by sweeping the visitors to a morale-boosting win: Francis' accuracy pinned them down, while Griffith snapped up four crucial wickets.

Francis' only appearance of the 1933 series in England came at Lord's because of his commitments in the Central Lancashire League. The

George Francis

Bajan was a popular figure in league cricket and enjoyed a considerable reputation; indeed, it was West Indies' loss that Test recognition arrived rather too late for him. However, they and he could take heart from the fact that he was able to pass on his expertise and experience of English conditions to the up-and-coming players who would trouble the 'old country' in the not too distant future.

Teams: *Barbados, West Indies, Combined XI, C.A. Merry's XI*
First-class debut: *23/5/23 West Indies v Sussex*
First-class record: *223 wickets (23.13) and 874 runs (12.85)*
Tests: *10*
Test debut: *23/6/28 West Indies v England*
Test record: *23 wickets (33.17) and 81 runs (5.78)*

FREDERICK, Michael Campbell

Born: 6 May 1927, St Peter, Barbados
Role: Opening batsman

MICHAEL FREDERICK was a reliable opening batsman whose sole Test appearance came in the first match against England at Kingston in 1954. He made nought and 30. Earlier, in 1949, he had had a similarly fleeting career as an amateur for Derbyshire when, this time, he appeared twice. He also appeared briefly for Barbados and Jamaica.

Teams: *Barbados, Jamaica, West Indies, Derbyshire*
First-class debut: *2/10/44 Barbados v British Guiana*
First-class record: *294 runs (29.40)*
Tests: *1*
Test debut: *15/1/54 West Indies v England*
Test record: *30 runs (15.00)*

Michael Frederick

FREDERICKS, Roy Clifton

Born: 11 November 1942, Blairmont, Berbice, British Guiana
Role: Left-hand batsman

ROY FREDERICKS was one of West Indies' finest opening batsmen. When he first graduated to the position, perhaps conscious of the short-lived careers of his immediate predecessors, he was relatively guarded in his approach. This was personified by his innings against England at Edgbaston in 1973, when he took eight-and-a-half hours over 150. The Guyanese was lambasted by many for his slow scoring, but his efforts helped win the series for the West Indies. Although he was picked for the 1968-69 tour to Australia - prompted by two splendid hundreds against Barbados in the 1967 Shell Shield - it was in England in 1969 that he established himself, underlining his ability with 63 and 60 in the Lord's Test.

Apart from a solid 80 in the second Test of the home series against India in 1970-71, Fredericks played indifferently, but elevated himself to his former level when New Zealand visited the Caribbean in 1971-72. He played superbly to score his maiden Test century in the first match at Kingston - a performance eclipsed only by a double hundred from Rowe - as the pair put on 269. He played two good innings against Australia when they toured the West Indies in 1972-73, in preparation for his metamorphosis which would turn him into a formidable opponent. He was determined to become more consistent and, after his marathon innings at Edgbaston, passed 50 in six of his next seven Tests.

Fredericks was in prolific form when England visited the Caribbean in 1973-74. He scored 94 in a record-breaking stand of 206 with Rowe in the second Test at Kingston and was out again in the nineties at Georgetown. He maintained his momentum in India in 1974-75, hitting centuries at Calcutta and in the deciding match at Bombay. However, of more significance for the future of West Indian cricket, he formed a partnership with the young Gordon Greenidge, which was to become the most lasting since that of Rae and Stollmeyer.

However, in Australia in 1975-76, Fredericks must have thought the

Barbadian would be another passing companion as Greenidge's loss of form meant he had to open the innings with Julien, Kallicharran and finally Richards, as the West Indies only once passed 50 for the first wicket. Fredericks enjoyed his finest hour in the second Test at Perth, when he played what is regarded as one of the great innings of Test cricket: in a savage display of batting he crashed 169 runs in 217 minutes, with one six and 27 fours, off the mighty duo of Lillee and Thomson to help sweep the tourists to their only success of the series.

When the Indians visited the Caribbean in 1975-76, Fredericks paired up with Rowe in the fourth Test at Kingston, and put on 105 to help West Indies win the series. And, his attacking play against England at Lord's in 1976 could have conjured an unlikely win for the tourists but, in the end, a combination of inclement weather and Fredericks being caught out playing his favourite hook shot for 138, condemned the match to a draw.

It was in that series that Fredericks cemented his partnership with Greenidge: they added 116 in the second innings of the Old Trafford Test, and both scored centuries in the fourth match at Headingley, rattling up 192 off the English attack before the first wicket fell. Fredericks ended the series with a partnership of 159 with Richards in the first innings at The Oval, and an unbeaten stand of 182 with Greenidge in just over two hours in the second, as both openers passed 500 runs for the series.

The West Indies seemed more vulnerable when Pakistan visited the Caribbean in 1977, but the openers kept them going with some useful scores. The hosts went into the fifth match with the series level and Fredericks on the eve of his retirement. It was only fitting therefore that the Guyanese should share in a match-winning stand with Greenidge. He score 83 fluent runs, adding 182 with the Barbadian, before they were dismissed in successive overs in a poignant end to one of the great opening partnerships in Test cricket.

Teams: *British Guiana, Guyana, Berbice, Demerara, West Indies, Glamorgan, Cavaliers XI, New Zealand Governor's XI*
First-class debut: *5/3/64 British Guiana v Jamaica*
First-class record: *16,384 runs (45.89) and 75 wickets (37.94)*
Tests: *59*
Test debut: *26/12/68 West Indies v Australia*
Test record: *4,334 runs (42.49) and 7 wickets (78.28)*

FULLER, Richard Livingston

Born: 30 January 1913, St Ann, Jamaica
Died: 3 May 1987
Role: Right-hand batsman, fast-medium bowler

DICKIE FULLER was an outstanding club cricketer for Melbourne in Jamaican senior cup cricket in the 1930's. But it was a distinguished performance for Jamaica against England in 1935, when he took four for 69 in the visitors' first innings and then clattered an unbeaten century - including four successive fours off Jim Smith - that earned him a place in the Test side for the fourth match at Sabina Park. However, his services were hardly required, and he scored just one run in West Indies' declared total of 535 for seven and bowled eight overs for 12 runs in the the match, as England lost by an innings. After this frustrating start to his international career, Fuller was discarded without ever being given a proper chance to prove himself.

Teams: *Jamaica, West Indies*
First-class debut: *5/3/35 Jamaica v M.C.C.*
First-class record: *280 runs (28.00) and 12 wickets (43.66)*
Tests: *1*
Test debut: *14/3/35 West Indies v England*
Test record: *1 run and 0-12*

FURLONGE, Hammond Alan

Born: 19 June 1934, Apex Oilfields, Trinidad
Role: Right-hand batsman

HAMMOND FURLONGE was an opening batsman who enjoyed fleeting glory for Trinidad when he staved off defeat almost single-handedly against the touring Australians at Port-of-Spain in 1955. Showing great maturity for his years, the youngster scored 57 and 150 not out - his maiden first-class century - in a display of batting that would doubtless have impressed Wally Hammond, whom he had been named after. This performance earned him a place in the Test side against the Australians and a tour to New Zealand in 1955-56 but, apart from a stubborn 64 out of a total of 145 in the fourth Test at Auckland, Furlonge was simply never able to capitalise on his chances at the highest level and soon drifted out of the international picture.

Teams: *Trinidad, West Indies, North Trinidad*
First-class debut: *5/2/55 Trinidad v Jamaica*
First-class record: *808 runs (32.33)*
Tests: *3*
Test debut: *11/6/55 West Indies v Australia*
Test record: *99 runs (19.80)*

Dickie Fuller

GANTEAUME, Andrew Gordon

Born: 22 January 1921, Port-of-Spain, Trinidad
Role: Right-hand batsman, wicket-keeper

ANDY GANTEAUME enjoys the dubious distinction of being the only player ever to have scored a century in his sole Test appearance. The slightly-built right-hander, who also kept wicket, was selected for the second match against England at Port-of-Spain in 1948, as replacement for his injured compatriot, Jeff Stollmeyer. Ganteaume batted resiliently for 112, putting on 173 for the first wicket with George Carew in his only innings. Then, in one of the more remarkable acts of selectorial impetuosity, he was discarded for the rest of the series.

Although he toured England in 1957 as one of three specialist openers - and was dropped down the batting order in the match against Kent, because he arrived late after visiting Canterbury Cathedral - he never made the Test side, so this strange cricketing statistic remained intact.

Andy Ganteaume

Teams: *Trinidad, West Indies*
First-class debut: *8/2/41 Trinidad v Barbados*
First-class record: *2,785 runs (34.81)*
Tests: *1*
Test debut: *11/2/48 West Indies v England*
Test record: *112 runs (112.00)*

GARNER, Joel

Born: 16 December 1952, Christ Church, Barbados
Role: Right-arm fast bowler

JOEL GARNER was one of the most familiar figures in Test cricket standing 6ft 8in tall and weighing 17 stone. This remarkable frame allowed him to get extra bounce off a short run, making him the most effective bowler of his type for many years.

His talent was nurtured by Seymour Nurse and Wes Hall in his early years, although it was some advice from Charlie Griffith to change his action that turned him into a world-class bowler. Yet as there was such a plethora of talent at the time, Garner did not make his first-class debut until he was 23 - and that was prompted by the absence of Boyce and Holder. Similarly, it needed injuries to Daniel and Holding before he could get into the Test side. Having waited so long, though, he did not waste his chance and - having bowled well for the President's XI against Pakistan in 1977 - took 25 wickets (27.52) in the Test series, including eight for 148 at Georgetown. This performance kept his place for the subsequent series against Australia, but then he opted out of the official fold to play world series cricket where, again, he shone.

Garner's class was quickly recognised in England where he and Viv Richards helped Somerset to unprecedented success. The "Big Bird"s' familiarity with English conditions produced match-winning results in the 1979 World Cup final when he took five Australian wickets for 38, including bowling four batsmen for four runs in 11 balls. After this the Barbadian became an established figure in the West Indies side, helping them to win their first Test series in Australia in 1979-80, and performed similarly well in New Zealand. Indeed, he played a leading role in all their successes in the early 1980's until a shoulder injury - which hampered him against India in the Caribbean in 1983 - prompted him to opt out of the return series on the subcontinent. He returned prematurely for the world series one-day tournament in Australia, although recovered to take 10 wickets in the three finals. He was back to his best by the

time Australia toured in 1984 - again West Indies were without key bowlers, this time Holding and Marshall due to injury - and Garner finished the series with 31 wickets (16.87), a new record for a series against Australia.

The Barbadian finished as the leading wicket-taker, with 29, in the five Test series against England in 1984 and 19 from five matches against Australia in 1984-85, making him one of the key players during the record 11 successive Test wins the West Indies enjoyed during this period.

Besides the remarkable success he enjoyed at Test level, Garner was an inspiration for Barbados. He enjoyed a vintage year as captain in 1986, taking 28 wickets at 13.5 each - the most by a Barbadian in a Shield season - and carried this form into the Test series against England in the Caribbean early in 1986. Then, he took 27 wickets to equal the record for a West Indian in a home rubber against England. For good measure, he also led Barbados to victory over the tourists.

After topping the bowling averages in New Zealand in 1987, Garner announced his retirement from Test cricket. A jovial character, whose personality matches his massive frame, it was fitting that "the Bird" should go out on top, even if it did leave the West Indies with a huge gap to fill - in more ways than one!

Teams: *Barbados, West Indies, Somerset, South Australia*
First-class debut: *30/1/76 Barbados v Combined Islands*
First-class record: *881 wickets (18.53) and 2,964 runs (16.74)*
Tests: *58*
Test debut: *18/2/77 West Indies v Pakistan*
Test record: *259 wickets (20.97) and 672 runs (12.44)*

GASKIN, Berkeley Bertram McGarrell

Born: 21 March 1908, Georgetown, British Guiana
Died: 2 May 1979
Role: Right-arm medium pace bowler

BERKELEY GASKIN could, perhaps, best be described as a late developer, making his Test debut in his 40th year. However, he was certainly very fit, opening the attack with his medium pace in the first post-War Tests against England at Bridgetown and Port-of-Spain. He met with meagre success, and made a more lasting impression as manager of the victorious West Indies team that visited England in 1963.

Joel Garner

Berkeley Gaskin

Teams: *British Guiana, West Indies*
First-class debut: *31/1/29*
British Guiana v Trinidad
First-class record: *138 wickets (31.84) and 782 runs (14.21)*
Tests: *2*
Test debut: *28/1/48 West Indies v England*
Test record: *2 wickets (79.00) and 17 runs (5.66)*

GIBBS, Glendon Lionel

Born: 27 December 1925, Georgetown, British Guiana
Died: 21 February 1979
Role: Left-hand batsman, left-arm spin bowler

GLENDON GIBBS made his mark in West Indian cricketing circles when he scored 216 for British Guiana against Barbados at Georgetown in 1951-52, adding a record 390 for the first wicket with Leslie Wight. Although this performance did not win him immediate recognition at Test level, his consistency for Guiana won him a place in the West Indies side for the first Test against Australia at Kingston in 1955. His performance was disappointing: he made 12 and nought, spun the ball for a few overs without taking a wicket and made one catch. He was not give a second chance.

Teams: *British Guiana, West Indies*
First-class debut: *9/2/50*
British Guiana v Barbados
First-class record: *1,730 runs (36.80) and 23 wickets (53.47)*
Tests: *1*
Test debut: *26/3/55 West Indies v Australia*
Test record: *12 runs (6.00) and 0-7*

GIBBS, Lancelot Richard

Born: 29 September 1934, Georgetown, British Guiana
Role: Right-arm off-spinner

LANCE GIBBS was, perhaps, the finest player ever to spin a ball in Test cricket. Indeed, his skill was such that he achieved the unlikely distinction of overshadowing the quick bowlers on many occasions.

A product of the powerful Demerara cricket club, Gibbs began life as a leg-spinner but, after getting on the wrong side of Robert Christiani's bat, he became an off-spinner. He had an unorthodox chest-on action, while his great height allowed him to get extra bounce and spin from most pitches. This, and his variation of pace and flight combined with pin-point accuracy, made him a formidable opponent.

Gibbs had a dream start to his Test career, heading the bowling averages with 17 wickets (23.05) in the home series against Pakistan in 1958; but was somewhat sidelined by the success of Hall and Gilchrist on the subsequent trip to India and Pakistan. But, he bounced back in the third Test of the memorable tour to Australia in 1960-61. Finding his best form, Gibbs came close to a hat-trick as he collected three wickets in four balls to propel the visitors to a most comprehensive victory. He made no mistake however in the next game at Adelaide, snapping up the wickets of Ken MacKay, Wally Grout - who succumbed to Gibbs' guile for his third successive duck - and Frank Mission to complete the first

Lance Gibbs

Lance Gibbs

Test hat-trick in Australia since 1903-04. That was one of the highlights of a remarkable series and, after playing in three Tests, Gibbs once again found himself at the top of the averages with 19 wickets at 20.78 each.

Although the Indian tourists were intimidated by the pace of Hall in 1962, the most comprehensive collapse was inspired by Gibbs in the third Test at Bridgetown. West Indies had secured a lead of 217 and, by lunch on the final day, the tourists were 158 for two and seemed content to settle for a draw, but Gibbs had other plans. In 15.3 overs after the interval, he entranced the batsmen and the crowd, as he bowled 14 maidens and collected eight wickets for six runs to bring off an incredible victory. Thereafter, Gibbs was acknowledged as the finest bowler of his type for over a decade.

He bowled well in England in 1963, including returning the match-winning figures of nine for 157 in the Test at Old Trafford, and then turned his match-winning style on the Australians again, this time at home in 1965. As so often, he was at his best in front of his home crowd, taking three for 51 and six for 29 in the third Test at Georgetown, with the second innings dismissal of Bill Lawry taking Gibbs past the coveted 100 Test wicket landmark.

As West Indies' leading wicket-taker - he took nine others in the rubber - Gibbs was instrumental in securing their first ever series victory over Australia.

As the pace duo of Hall and Griffith began to lose some of their bite, Gibbs was used increasingly as a stock bowler. He bowled almost 100 overs more than Hall against England in 1966, topping the averages again. Once more he bowled splendidly at Old Trafford, taking 10 wickets in the match and was instrumental in England's defeat in the fourth game at Headingley, where he took six second innings wickets for 39.

A solid series in India in 1966-67, was followed by another good performance against England in 1968. He was the leading actor in the fifth Test at Georgetown, which West Indies had to win to level the series. Gibbs brought them within a whisper of victory taking six for 60 but, in the end, he was thwarted by the fast bowler, Jeff Jones, who defended stoutly in Gibbs' last over to ensure that England clinched the rubber. On West Indies' disappointing trip to Australia in 1968-69, Gibbs - along with Sobers - was the best of a poor bowling bunch and, after a modest showing in England later in 1969, the Guyanese was rested until Australia visited the Caribbean four years later. It was a distinguished return for Gibbs, who finished the series with 26 wickets.

Back in the groove, Gibbs spun England to defeat in the first Test at Port-of-Spain in 1974 and continued his match-winning ways in India, when he ran through the home side's batting in the second Test in Delhi to finish with figures of six for 76. He completed a magnificent series by taking seven for 98 in the first innings of the fifth match at Bombay. On the 1975-76 trip to Australia, the years of toil began to show, but he kept his place in the team in the hope that he would surpass Fred Trueman's world record haul of Test wickets. This he did when he had Ian Redpath caught on the first day of the final match at Melbourne and, for a while, remained the leading wicket-taker with 309 victims.

Gibbs' contribution to West Indian cricket is perhaps best summed up by his cousin and long-time colleague, Clive Lloyd. He said: "There was never a more whole-hearted cricketer for the West Indies, nor an off-spinner in anything like his class. He was by no means a mechanical spinner, instead always thinking about the game, working an opponent out, assessing his strengths and weaknesses and laying the trap for him. A fierce competitor, he would be giving total effort, no matter if the pitch was flat and docile, no matter if the total was 300 for two and the sun scorching, no matter if his finger had been rubbed raw."

Teams: *British Guiana, Guyana, Demerara, West Indies, Warwickshire, Rest of World XI, Commonwealth XI, South Australia, C. Hunte's XI*
First-class debut: *17/2/54 British Guiana v M.C.C.*
First-class record: *1,024 wickets (27.22) and 1,729 runs (8.55)*
Tests: *79*
Test debut: *5/2/58 West Indies v Pakistan*
Test record: *309 wickets (29.09) and 488 runs (6.97)*

GILCHRIST, Roy

Born: 28 June 1934, Seaforth, Jamaica
Role: Right-arm fast bowler

ROY GILCHRIST was brought up on a sugar plantation in Jamaica. He was a short, stocky man with long arms and powerful shoulders, who developed his bowling technique without any formal coaching.

"Gilly" was selected for the tour to England in 1957 - along with Wes Hall - after an excellent season in Jamaica. Even so, most people thought Ramadhin and Valentine would work their trickery again, and Gilchrist was not used to his best effect. Nonetheless his talent could not be overlooked and he was selected to play against Pakistan at home in 1958, where his fearful pace brought him 21 wickets and a place on the tour to India and Pakistan in 1958-59.

But the seeds of his downfall had already been sown: Gilchrist had begun his international career under Worrell, but was now being skippered by Alexander. Although they were both from Jamaica, that was about all they had in common and their personality clash came to a head in India. Gilchrist had begun auspiciously enough as, in partnership with Hall, the pair overwhelmed their hosts. "Gilly" was at his most lethal in the third Test at Calcutta where he took six for 55: he clean-bowled five of his victims, three with the total on 131, to propel the tourists to a comprehensive victory. In the fifth Test in Delhi, Gilchrist's burst was decisive as he finished India's second innings by inducing Chandrakant Borde to hit his wicket on 96, and then bowled the two tail-enders as three wickets fell for one run.

It turned out to be Gilchrist's last appearance for West Indies as the dispute between him and Alexander made his position untenable after an episode involving an overdose of beamers. Gilchrist was sent home and West Indies lost their most talented bowler since Martindale.

The decision to remove Gilchrist from Test match consideration had far-reaching consequences for West Indian cricket: there can be little doubt that if he had been able to partner Hall in the series against England and Australia at the turn of the decade, the narrow defeats would almost certainly have been pulled round in their favour. As it was the West Indies were obliged to wait for the emergence of Charlie Griffith as a world-class bowler in 1963.

Roy Gilchrist

Teams: *Jamaica, West Indies, Hyderabad, South Zone, Chidambaram's XI, Chief Minister's XI*
First-class debut: *11/10/56 Jamaica v British Guiana*
First-class record: *167 wickets (26.00) and 258 runs (7.81)*
Tests: *13*
Test debut: *30/5/57 West Indies v England*
Test record: *57 wickets (26.68) and 60 runs (5.45)*

GLADSTONE, George

Born: 14 January 1901, Jamaica
Died: 19 May 1978
Role: Left-arm spin bowler

GEORGE GLADSTONE was a useful slow bowler and reasonable bat who enjoyed one season in first-class cricket in 1929-30. It was certainly a full year: after snapping up four frontline batsmen for Jamaica Colts Fifteen in their match against the touring MCC side at Kingston, he maintained his momentum for the full Jamaica side against the same opponents a few days later, returning figures of nine for 252 in 75.3 overs. That convinced the selectors he should be given a chance in the Test match at Sabina Park: he made 12 not out and returned the unflattering match analysis of 50-5-189-1, figures that marred his brief first-class career.

Teams: *Jamaica, West Indies*
First-class debut: *28/3/30 Jamaica v M.C.C.*
First-class record: *10 wickets (44.10) and 26 runs*
Tests: *1*
Test debut: *3/4/30 West Indies v England*
Test record: *1 wicket (189.00) and 12**

GODDARD, John Douglas Claude

Born: 21 April 1919, Bridgetown, Barbados
Died: 20 August 1987, London
Role: Left-hand batsman, Right-arm off-spinner

JOHN GODDARD made his mark in West Indian cricket as a selector, even though he was still playing when, as captain of the tour party to England in 1950, he insisted on the inclusion of Ramadhin and Valentine, two unknown spinners.

Goddard was no mean cricketer himself: he was one of the most prolific batsmen in the War Goodwill Inter-Colonial series between 1941-46, scoring nearly 1,400 runs at an average of over 70. In the 1943-44 series, Goddard shared in an unbroken fourth wicket stand of 502 with Worrell for Barbados against Trinidad at Bridgetown, registering his career-best score of 218 not out.

John Goddard

He made his Test debut against England at

Bridgetown in 1948 and was promoted to the captaincy after two Tests. He put his all-round talents to good use: in his first match as captain he swept West Indies to victory by taking five for 31 on a drying Georgetown pitch; and then led them to a 10-wicket win in the final Test at Kingston, chipping in with 46 in the second innings, as he and Stollmeyer knocked off the arrears without incident.

The Barbadian retained the captaincy for the series in India in 1948-49, where he averaged 47 with the bat. But it was a deadlocked contest, broken only by the tourists' handsome innings victory in the fourth match at Madras. But this was enough to ensure that Goddard led them on their triumphant tour of England in 1950; however, although the team enjoyed almost unbroken success, Goddard's personal contribution was slight.

His captaincy was criticised in Australia when, in the fourth Test at Melbourne in 1952, he was accused of losing control at crucial stages of the match, in particular when lack of discipline allowed Australia's last pair to score the 38 runs needed for victory. Stollmeyer skippered the side in the last game at Sydney, with the official reason for Goddard's absence being that he was unfit. Whatever the truth, his Test career appeared to be over. But, he enjoyed a successful come-back four years later, when he went as player-manager with the team of up-and-coming youngsters to New Zealand, and was recalled to the captaincy for the tour of England in 1957.

Chosen more for his white, upper-class background than his now waning cricketing talents, Goddard struggled - apart from hitting 61 in a match-saving stand of 174 with Collie Smith at Trent Bridge - as his side slid to a 3-0 defeat.

In 1987 he was invited to attend the MCC's bi-centenary match at Lord's, where he must have preferred to cast his mind back to the glories of the 1950 tour and his 'two little pals', Ramadhin and Valentine, who had won him such early acclaim. Clearly enjoying the nostalgia of the occasion, Goddard seemed relaxed as he met up with old friends but, two days after the game, he died suddenly.

Teams: *Barbados, West Indies, R.S. Grant's XI, M.C.C.*
First-class debut: *16/1/37 Barbados v Trinidad*
First-class record: *3,769 runs (33.35) and 146 wickets (26.33)*
Tests: *27*
Test debut: *21/1/48 West Indies v England*
Test record: *33 wickets (31.81) and 859 runs (30.67)*

Larry Gomes

GOMES, Hilary Angelo

Born: 13 July 1953, Arima, Trinidad
Role: Left-hand batsman, right-arm medium-pace bowler, off-spinner

LARRY GOMES was a gifted batsman who took a long time to establish himself in the Test team, often being overshadowed by the more gregarious characters in the side.

He made his first-class debut against New Zealand in 1972 three years after another gregarious personality, his elder brother, Sheldon, had made the news with some fine innings. But it was the more consistent, less spectacular, Larry who was to become the backbone of a weak Trinidadian batting side in the 1970's. During this time, Larry played briefly for Middlesex and it was his familiarity with English conditions that won him a place on the trip to England in 1976. He made his debut at Lord's, but struggled to command a regular Test place in the face of fierce batting competition. Even so, he was prolific against the counties, scoring nearly 1,400 runs, with five centuries.

The self-effacing Gomes then enjoyed two splendid summers with Nelson in the Lancashire League: he scored over 1,000 runs both times and in his first year with the club passed Constantine's record seasonal aggregate. But by that time, Gomes had lost his place in the Test side to Collis King and it wasn't until the Packer episode that he got a second chance. He certainly seemed determined to make no mistake then: with a century for Trinidad & Tobago against the touring Australians already behind him, he hammered them for another hundred in the third Test at Georgetown and hit a resolute 115 out of a total of 280 in the final match at Kingston.

Gomes had a successful tour of India in 1978-79 and was surprisingly dropped for the trip to England in 1980; but he returned to the fold for the tour to Pakistan. There, he finished second in the averages with just under 50 and seemed at last to have established himself. He played consistently in the home series against England in 1981, including making a polished 90 in the Test at Kingston, and confirmed his arrival by topping the averages in the subsequent three match rubber against Australia, which included an important innings in Adelaide to square the series for the visitors.

He proved his worth again, this time against India early in 1983, when he scored 123, sharing in a double century partnership with Lloyd in the second Test at Port-of-Spain after the first three wickets had fallen for one run. Some punters were surprised when Gomes was preferred to the more attacking Richardson for the first Test against England at Edgbaston in 1984. But it proved to be a sound decision as the thoughtful Gomes scored 143, adding 206 for the third wicket with Richards. The quiet left-hander shared in an unbroken match-winning stand with Greenidge in the Lord's Test and completed a hat-trick of success when he fought a magnificent rearguard action in the third match at Headingley. The tourists had collapsed from 201 for four to 206 for seven, before a timely century from Gomes - helped by sensible batting from Holding - turned a potential deficit into a match-winning lead.

Gomes was similarly successful in Australia - where he scored six Test hundreds altogether - in 1984-85; again he headed the batting averages, aided by two memorable centuries in the Tests at Perth and Adelaide. Although he was less prolific on the subsequent tours to Pakistan and New Zealand, he still finished his career with an admirable Test average, confirming him as a top-class batsman, who had that priceless quality of saving some of his best innings for when West Indies were in trouble.

Teams: *Trinidad, East Trinidad, North East Trinidad, West Indies, Middlesex*
First-class debut: *3/3/72 Trinidad v New Zealand*
First-class record: *12,982 runs (40.56) and 107 wickets (39.32)*
Tests: *60*
Test debut: *3/6/76 West Indies v England*
Test record: *3,171 runs (39.63) and 15 wickets (62.00)*

GOMEZ, Gerald Ethridge

Born: 10 October 1919, Woodbrook, Port-of-Spain, Trinidad
Role: Right-hand batsman, right-arm medium pace bowler

GERRY GOMEZ scored his first runs in Test cricket in 1939, but had to wait until after the Second World War to take his first Test wicket. The Trinidadian made his Test debut against England along with his compatriot and school friend, Jeff Stollmeyer, and the pair were keen to get back into international competition once hostilities had ceased, as they showed in the 1946-47 season. Batting together for Trinidad against British Guiana they put on 434 runs, falling just 11 short of the world record for a third wicket partnership.

Gomez top-scored with 86 in West Indies' first post-War innings, in 1948 against England at Bridgetown, and was made captain for the second game at Port-of-Spain, when Stollmeyer was injured. After batting well in the first innings and taking the wicket of Billy Griffith, he could have led his side to victory if rain hadn't intervened. John Goddard took over the captaincy for the Georgetown Test and Gomez kept a low profile for the rest of the series.

Gomez had flourished in domestic cricket during and immediately after the War, indeed, 1948-49 was the only season when he failed to make a hundred at Port-of-Spain. As soon as international cricket was back on its feet again, Gomez was determined to make an impact. He enjoyed all-round success in India in 1948-49: his best batting came when he hit a century in the first Test in Delhi and, as the tour progressed, his bowling came to the fore. In the end, he was asked to open the Test attack with Prior Jones, having taken a record nine wickets for 24 against the strong South Zone side at Madras. He finished the series with commendable figures: 16 wickets at just under 30 apiece and 256 runs for an average of 36.57.

In England in 1950 he occasionally took the new ball with Worrell, but is best remembered for his stubborn 70 scored during the famous 'calypso' Test at Lord's, when he shared in a match-winning double century partnership with Walcott. He revealed the stubborn trait in his character under more trying circumstances in Australia the following year when he stood almost alone against the 'barrage of bumpers' that emanated from Ray Lindwall and Keith Miller to head the batting averages and, just to keep the opposition on their toes, took seven wickets for 55 in their first innings in the fifth Test at Sydney. Although he played in the home series against India and England in the mid-1950's, his performance in Australia was the high point in his career.

Gerry Gomez

The quiet Trinidadian could not have anticipated being on a Test field with the Australians some 14 years later, but it happened when he was invited to umpire during the third Test between West Indies and Australia at Georgetown in 1965. He stood in briefly, after some disquiet with an earlier choice and transport difficulties with his replacement. When the latter finally arrived, Gomez was seen making a quick dash to the commentary box, where he was supposed to be summarising the day's events for a local radio station!

Teams: *Trinidad, West Indies, R.S.Grant's XI, M.C.C.*
First-class debut: *4/10/37 Trinidad v British Guiana*
First-class record: *6,764 runs (43.63) and 200 wickets (25.26)*
Tests: *29*
Test debut: *22/7/39 West Indies v England*
Test record: *1,243 runs (30.31) and 58 wickets (27.41)*

GRANT, George Copeland "Jackie"

Born: 9 May 1907, Port-of-Spain, Trinidad
Died: 26 October 1978
Role: Right-hand batsman

"JACKIE" GRANT, at the tender age of 23, became the youngest man ever to lead the West Indies, when he was made captain for their first tour to Australia in 1930-31. Although he had played cricket at Cambridge University, Grant seemed an unwise choice being out of match practice and having no experience of captaincy. But, after meeting his team mates for the first time when he joined them on the ship going to Australia at the Panama Canal, he was one of the few players to enjoy a successful trip.

Two unbeaten innings in the first Test at Adelaide helped him to head the batting averages with 42.50. Although West Indies lost the first four Tests, inspired captaincy from Grant meant they finished on a winning note beating Sheffield Shield champions, New South Wales, and Australia in an historic Test victory in the fifth match at Sydney. Martin and Headley laid the foundations with centuries to take the visitors to 350 for six, before Grant declared after overnight rain had affected the wicket. Griffith and Francis then bowled Australia out for 224 and, by the end of the third day, the tourists had a lead of 250. Rain washed out the fourth day's play, prompting Grant to make his second adventurous declaration of the match in bright sunshine on the fifth morning. That put the onus on the revitalised pace duo of Griffith and Francis, who responded accordingly and swept West Indies to victory by 30 runs.

After this success, it was inevitable that Grant would retain the captaincy for the tour of England in 1933. But, apart from a top-score of 26 out of a first innings total of 97 at Lord's, he had little success with the bat in the Test series, although he scored almost 1,200 first-class runs on the trip.

But it was his astute handling of the side that was Grant's main contribution to their success and the selectors wisely made him captain for the entire series against England in the Caribbean in 1935. On an almost unplayable wicket at Bridgetown, Grant nearly conjured another amazing win: the hosts had managed only 102 in their first innings before England stumbled to 81 for seven. Bob Wyatt, the England captain, decided to declare the innings closed at that point to try and avoid the worst of the pitch. In an imaginative response, Grant reversed his batting order to similarly shield his best players, but another downpour spoiled his plan and the English bowlers were able to take advantage in virtually unplayable conditions. The situation deteriorated to such an extent that Grant decided to declare on 51 for six, with a miserly lead of 72, even though top-order batsmen remained in the pavilion. Like West Indies, England sent in their fast bowlers to open the batting. When Martindale accounted for five of them, it seemed West Indies might come out on top but lack of support for Martindale and 29 priceless runs from Wally Hammond allowed England to scrape home.

"Jackie" Grant

Even so the West Indies continued to play well, and their win at Kingston - which gave them their first ever series victory - made the excitement at Bridgetown seem a distant memory. Sadly Grant, who had done so much to allow them to taste the fruits of success, was not on the field when victory was finally posted, after injuring his ankle earlier in the day.

The irony of Grant's own success was that his initial selection had been a gamble, but it succeeded in proportion to the success of his own risk-taking on the field. But like the best gamblers, Grant decided to quit while he was ahead, and retired at the end of that season to take up missionary work in Africa, and thus kept his remarkable cricketing legacy intact.

Teams: *Trinidad, West Indies, G.C.Grant's XI, Cambridge University, Rhodesia*
First-class debut: *13/6/28*
Cambridge University v Northamptonshire
First-class record: *3,831 runs (32.19) and 19 wickets (51.00)*
Tests: *12*
Test debut: *12/12/30*
West Indies v Australia
Test record: *413 runs (25.81) and 0-18*

GRANT, Rolph Stewart

Born: 15 December 1909, Port-of-Spain, Trinidad
Died: 18 October 1977
Role: Right-hand batsman, off-spinner

ROLPH GRANT succeeded his elder brother, Jackie, as captain of West Indies after the latter decided to retire at his peak. The younger Grant was a remarkable all-round athlete, winning blues at Cambridge for cricket and football and a half-blue for boxing. If that were not enough, he also became amateur goal-keeper for England and heavyweight boxing champion of Trinidad.

On the cricket field, besides being a capable batsman and off-spinner, he was a top-class fielder and, together with Constantine, set new standards for the West Indies. Grant's athleticism helped his side to level the series against England in the second Test at Port-of-Spain in 1935, as he returned match figures of 40-11-86-4 and held three catches to dismiss top-order batsmen in the tourists' first innings. Then, in the fourth match at Kingston, he shone with the bat hitting 77 elegant runs, as he and Headley put on a record 147 for the seventh wicket, to clinch West Indies' first series victory.

Grant captained West Indies in England in 1939 and enjoyed most success in the second Test at Old Trafford, scoring 47 out of a total of

Rolph Grant (right) is introduced to King George VI.

133, after England had declared on a deteriorating wicket. It was a marvellous knock, lasting just 38 minutes and included three sixes, as 56 runs were added while he was at the crease. That performance helped the visitors to the safety of a draw and kept the series alive.

Having shown such promise that summer, it was unfortunate that the gathering clouds of war prevented him from having a chance to emulate the feats of his brother as captain for, at the end of that season, Rolph decided to hang up his cricketing boots for good.

Teams: *Trinidad, West Indies, R.S. Grant's XI, Cambridge University*
First-class debut: *4/5/32 Cambridge University v Kent*
First-class record: *1,883 runs (28.53) and 79 wickets (25.17)*
Tests: *7*
Test debut: *8/1/35 West Indies v England*
Test record: *220 runs (22.00) and 11 wickets (32.09)*

GRAY, Anthony Hollis

Born: 23 May 1963, Belmont, Trinidad
Role: Right-arm fast bowler

TONY GRAY is a big man: at 6ft 6in tall and weighing 15 stone, he seemed tailor-made to take over from Joel Garner in the West Indies side, after an excellent Shell Shield season in 1985. Then his 23 wickets helped Trinidad & Tobago to win the Shield and Gray to a county contract with Surrey, after Sylvester Clarke had been injured. There, he topped the bowling averages with 79 wickets (22.98), before being catapulted into the West Indies team for their trip to Sharjah and Pakistan. However, since those heady days Gray has been somewhat overshadowed by the emergence of his compatriot, Ian Bishop, who has staked a place in the Test team.

But Gray has been building his reputation over a long period: he won a scholarship to the Alf Gover Cricket School at the age of 18 and made his first-class debut for North against South in Trinidad in 1984 and, later the same season, made his Shield debut against Barbados. The pace man took seven wickets that year, as a prelude to his vintage season in 1985, which included his best Shield figures of six for 78 against Jamaica in Kingston. His arrival at The Oval in May of that year saw his hunger for wickets continue unabated. He took more than five wickets in an innings six times, including eight for 40 against Yorkshire at Sheffield, which featured the only hat-trick of his career. Indeed, it was largely due to the efforts of their new arrival that Surrey were able to finish sixth in the county championship, in a season where they were plagued by injuries.

Gray was rewarded the following year when he was included in the West Indies tour party to Pakistan, after Garner and Holding had decided to opt out. It was a successful sojourn for the youngster, who took 14 wickets (16.21) including his best Test figures of four for 39 in the first match at Faisalabad, to help him to second in the bowling averages behind Marshall. He maintained this sparkling form in the three match series against New Zealand in 1987, collecting eight wickets at 18.75 each, and again finished second in the averages, this time to Garner.

However, Gray now seems to have reached an impasse in his international career and will need to draw on all his qualities of courage and maturity besides his undoubted bowling talents if he is to establish himself as a regular member of the Test side. He took an important step in that direction by performing splendidly on West Indies' "B" tour of Zimbabwe in 1989, when he took 18 wickets at under 10 apiece.

Tony Gray

Teams: *Trinidad, North Trinidad, West Indies, Surrey, North-East Trinidad*
First-class debut: *5/1/84*
North Trinidad v South Trinidad
First-class record: *359 wickets (21.97) and 909 runs (11.50)*
Tests: *5*
Test debut: *24/10/86*
West Indies v Pakistan
Test record: *22 wickets (17.13) and 48 runs (8.00)*

GREENIDGE, Alvin Ethelbert

Born: 20 August 1956, Barbados
Role: Right-hand batsman

ALVIN GREENIDGE is no relation to his illustrious namesake, Gordon, or his somewhat less illustrious namesake, Geoffrey. Although they are all Bajan and all right-handed openers, the comparisons really stop there. Alvin came to the fore as a batsman in 1977-78, when he enjoyed a productive season in the Shell Shield and hit 96 for Barbados against the touring Australians. He was given his opportunity at Test level after the Packer players defected mid-way through the rubber. Despite his lack of experience, he performed admirably scoring 56 in his first Test innings, in the third game at Georgetown, and 69 in the second innings of the fourth match at Port-of-Spain.

Those performances secured his passage to India the following year, but he could only muster 80 runs from four Tests and, once the Packer split had healed, the amiable Greenidge was out of the reckoning. He continued to play well for Barbados and was their top-scorer in the 1982 Shield, with 172 against Jamaica. He also played professional cricket in Holland and, indeed, was summoned from his Dutch club to field for the injury-hit Test side against England at The Oval in 1980.

Teams: *Barbados, West Indies, West Indies 'Rebels XI'*
First-class debut: *14/3/75 Barbados v Trinidad*
First-class record: *2,319 runs (30.51) and 5 wickets (29.40)*
Tests: *6*
Test debut: *1/4/78 West Indies v Australia*
Test record: *222 runs (22.20)*

Alvin Greenidge

GREENIDGE, Cuthbert Gordon

Born: 1 May 1951, Black Bess, St Peter, Barbados
Role: Right-hand batsman

GORDON GREENIDGE is the most prolific West Indian opening batsman to have played Test cricket: With over 7,000 Test runs to his credit, he has been a remarkable run-scoring machine for his country since the mid-1970's.

Despite spending his formative cricketing years in England, Greenidge still bats with the bravado of a West Indian: indeed his flamboyant stroke-making - notably an insatiable desire to smatter his innings with huge sixes - has become his hallmark. Born in St Peter in Barbados, he joined his mother in England at the age of 14 and quickly made an impact in youth cricket in the south. He impressed the Hampshire coach, Arthur Holt, who decided to snap him up before anyone else had a chance to sign him. The young Greenidge joined Hampshire in 1967, but impetuous batting and even more erratic fielding meant that his contract nearly wasn't renewed. In the winter of 1969-70, he resolved to become more professional in his attitude and trained very hard. The first fruits of his efforts were born the following August when he shared in his first opening partnership with the South African, Barry Richards. The pair were to become one of the greatest post-War opening combinations and certainly the best confined to domestic cricket.

Four years later Greenidge began another illustrious partnership, when he made his Test debut against India at Bangalore, opening the innings with Roy Fredericks. But although the Barbadian began promisingly, scoring 93 and 107, a disastrous trip to Australia the following year - including a pair in the first Test at Brisbane - suggested their partnership would be short-lived. The selectors seemed to confirm this when his most significant role in the home series against India in 1976 was appearing as 12th man at Bridgetown.

However, Greenidge was chosen to tour England later that year, where he established himself as one of the finest batsmen in contemporary cricket. He peaked in the third Test at Old Trafford, scoring 134 runs out of 211 in difficult batting conditions, and followed that with 111 in the second innings, thus becoming only the second West Indian after Headley to score a century in each innings of a Test in England. Altogether, his match aggregate was 38 more than the whole England team. In the next game at Headingley, Greenidge and Fredericks put on 192 for the first wicket, with 147 runs coming off 27 overs before lunch; and confirmed their class with an unbeaten partnership of 182 off 32 overs in the final Test at The Oval. Greenidge topped 500 runs for the series and repeated this feat in the subsequent series against Pakistan, sharing in a large match-winning partnership with Fredericks, who was making his final Test appearance, in the fifth game at Kingston.

Before he signed for Kerry Packer, Greenidge had time to cement a new partnership, this time with his compatriot Desmond Haynes, as the pair shared in a three figure stand in front of their home crowd in the second Test against Australia at Bridgetown in 1978.

The Packer players returned to the official fold for the short series in Australia in 1979-80 where, once more, Greenidge was disappointing, although he lifted his game in New Zealand and was back to his impressive best against England at home early in 1981. By that time Greenidge and Haynes were recognised as the premier opening pair in Test cricket and confirmed it against India in the fifth Test in Antigua in 1983, when they shared in a record stand of 296 for the first wicket. It was a brilliant performance, sadly marred when Greenidge had to curtail his innings on 154 to join his young daughter who was fatally ill. Greenidge scored centuries in the opening Tests of the next two series, against India and Australia. On the latter occasion, he added 250 with Haynes for the first wicket at Georgetown and shared in further century stands at Bridgetown and Kingston, scoring the only hundred of the match at Sabina Park.

In spite of his outstanding success, as soon as he falters, Greenidge, along with virtually every other member of recent West Indian Test teams, comes under scrutiny. He found himself in such a position after an indifferent start to the tour of England in 1984. Having made just 19 and one in his first two Test innings, he knew he needed a large score to maintain his standing. With West Indies set 342 to win on the final day of the second Test at Lord's, he had a perfect opportunity. Greenidge did not waste it - despite losing Haynes early on - and stroked his way to a marvellous double century supported by the phlegmatic Gomes, who gave the Barbadian as much of the strike as possible. The pair shared in an unbroken match-winning stand of 287, as Greenidge scored at almost a run a ball, with two sixes and 29 fours, to overhaul the target. He maintained his dominant form in the next match at Old Trafford, scoring 223 in 10 hours and in dismal weather to help him to an average that far exceeded any of his team-mates.

Having learnt his cricket in England, it is not surprising that Greenidge has always thrived in English conditions. He enjoyed a marvellous career with Hampshire and at one time held the record for the highest individual score in each of the three English limited-overs tournaments: 173 not out in 55 overs in a Benson & Hedges Cup match against the Minor Counties South in 1973, 177 in a 60-over Gillette Cup match against Glamorgan in 1975 and 163 not out in 40 overs in a Sunday League match in 1979. He was also a prolific scorer in the county championship: in 1975 he scored 259 runs, with a record 13 sixes, against Sussex and headed the national batting averages in 1986 with over 2,000 runs, including four successive centuries.

Greenidge has enjoyed similar success with Barbados - first appearing for them in 1972 -

and was appointed captain in 1982-83, after many of their leading players had gone to South Africa. He celebrated in predictable style, scoring a quite majestic double hundred against the touring Indians.

The Barbadian enjoyed a prolific home series against Australia in 1983-84, scoring two centuries, but struggled again in Australia in 1984-85, although he came within five runs of his first Test century 'Down Under' in the third match in Adelaide; and was back to his usual prolific ways when New Zealand visited the Caribbean in 1985. A relatively modest series in Pakistan preceded a vintage one against the unfortunate New Zealanders, as he scored more than twice as many runs as any other visiting batsman on the 1987 tour. He hit another Test double hundred at Auckland, in a match-winning performance that included seven sixes, 20 fours and three dropped catches; and returned home to hit 202 for Barbados against Trinidad & Tobago in his mandatory Shell Shield appearance.

Gordon Greenidge displays the Wisden Trophy in August 1988.

Greenidge scored 260 runs (43.33) against India in 1987-88, and would have had a better aggregate but for some dubious umpiring decisions that went against him in the first two Tests and a dislocated thumb which ruled him out of the last Test and the one-day series, just as he ran into form with 141 and 69 in the third Test in Calcutta. The Barbadian was more sedate against Pakistan, but lifted his game in England, scoring 282 runs (47.00) from four Tests, including the only century for the tourists in the second match at Lord's.

Then, in Australia in 1988-89, 14 years and four tours after his ignominious start, he finally made his mark - even if he did leave it until the last minute! After a series in which he and Haynes shared in their first century opening stand in Australia - in the first Test at Brisbane - Greenidge reached his own personal landmark when he scored his first Test hundred in Australia on the last day of the series in Adelaide, where he had come so close four years earlier.

The Barbadian enjoyed more success in the subsequent series against India and England, and confirmed himself as one of the finest batsmen of his generation when he crowned his 100th Test match appearance, in the fifth game against England at St John's in 1990, with his 18th Test hundred and completed 7,000 runs in Test cricket; he also joined Javed Miandad as the only batsmen to have scored centuries in both their first and 100th Tests. It was fitting that the man who has forged more world-class opening partnerships than any other should have added a record 298 for the first wicket in that game - the highest for the West Indies against all countries - with his friend, compatriot and greatest partner, Desmond Haynes. These partnerships have immortalised Greenidge's name in the annals of West Indian cricket, but it is a tribute to his remarkable talent that his own batting would have done that anyway.

Teams: *Barbados, West Indies, Hampshire, D.H. Robins' XI, M.C.C., Rest of World XI*
First-class debut: *5/8/70 Hampshire v Sussex*
First-class record: *36,434 runs (46.23) and 17 wickets (27.76)*
Tests: *100*
Test debut: *22/11/74 West Indies v India*
Test record: *7,134 runs (46.02) and 0-4*

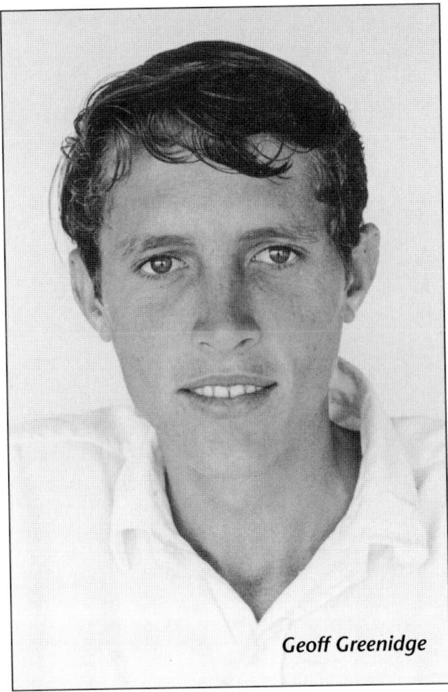

Geoff Greenidge

GREENIDGE, Geoffrey Alan

Born: 26 May 1948, Bridgetown, Barbados
Role: Right-hand batsman, leg-spin bowler

GEOFF GREENIDGE had a dream debut to his first-class career when he scored 205 for Barbados against the Leeward Islands and took seven first innings wickets for 124 in 1967. He did not make his Test debut until five years later, against New Zealand at Georgetown in 1972, where he gave two polished performances and scored 85 runs for once out. However, despite other opportunities, he could not maintain his momentum and was soon off the selectors' short-list.

He played with success for Barbados, although in 1976 he was the centre of controversy when the Guyanese government called off their side's Shell Shield fixture against Barbados at Georgetown because Greenidge had accompanied an International Wanderers side to Rhodesia just before the start of the domestic season. Barbados refused to field a team without Greenidge and the side was called home; in the end, in a season badly hit by the weather, the Board of Control declared the first tie in the history of the Shield, with Trinidad & Tobago and Barbados sharing the title. Prior to all this excitement, Greenidge appeared in county cricket for Sussex between 1968-75 with some success.

Teams: *Barbados, West Indies, Sussex, D.H.Robins' XI, International XI*
First-class debut: *9/2/67 Barbados v Leeward Islands*
First-class record: *9,112 runs (29.39) and 13 wickets (72.92)*
Tests: *5*
Test debut: *6/4/72 West Indies v New Zealand*
Test record: *209 runs (29.85) and 0-75*

GRELL, Mervyn George

Born: 18 December 1899, Trinidad
Died: 11 January 1976
Role: Right-hand batsman, medium-pace bowler

MERVYN GRELL was another West Indian who only played in one Test. Grell, who was a reliable batsman and useful medium-pacer, enjoyed his moment of glory when he was selected for the second Test against England at Port-of-Spain in 1930. As so often in those days, he owed his selection more to being one of the better players on the island rather than having genuine Test credentials, as the West Indies sought to keep travelling expenses to a minimum. In those early years, Grell was not alone in winning Test honours as much for his proximity to the ground as for his cricketing ability. He didn't let himself down, though, scoring 21 and 13, took nought for 17 and held one catch.

Teams: *Trinidad, West Indies*
First-class debut: *22/1/30 Trinidad v M.C.C.*
First-class record: *489 runs (28.76) and 5 wickets (34.40)*
Tests: *1*
Test debut: *1/2/30 West Indies v England*
Test record: *34 runs (17.00) and 0-17*

GRIFFITH, Charles Christopher

Born: 14 December 1938, St Lucy, Barbados
Role: Right-arm fast bowler

CHARLIE GRIFFITH was the most feared fast bowler of his day. However, like his partner and friend, Wes Hall, Griffith began life as a spin bowler before taking the new ball - and seven wickets - for his local club one Saturday afternoon in a move that transformed his career.

Charlie Griffith

Barbados' new fast bowling find made an impressive debut for the island against the touring England side in 1959, accounting for some of their frontline batsmen. But after a modest showing in the final Test of that year, he was overlooked for the trip to Australia.

He was back in the reckoning to face the Indians in 1962, but it was not a good year for Griffith. He almost fatally injured the visiting captain, Nariman Contractor, when the latter ducked into a bouncer from Griffith in India's match against Barbados, and later in that game he was accused of 'throwing'. Although Griffith was exonerated by hours of film of his action and many distinguished figures jumping to his defence, it was a label he was never able to shake off and which caused him much personal anguish.

However, Griffith enjoyed stunning success in England in 1963, taking 32 Test wickets (16.21) which helped him to a tally of 119 (12.83) for the trip, as he and his illustrious partner, Hall, became the toast of the tour. By the time of the fourth Test at Headingley, Griffith already had 14 scalps to his credit and had been studying the action of Fred Trueman during their match against Yorkshire: "what especially struck me about Freddie", Griffith remarked, "was the way in which he used the crease and how he controlled his speed. He used to come in close to the stumps to bowl the out-swinger and he had these subtle variations of pace that troubled us all." Those observations brought Griffith rich rewards in the Test as he took six for 36 in England's first innings to set up victory and an unassailable lead in the series. However, his efforts were marred by further questions over his action, after he had been 'called' in several county matches; and he was plagued by similar accusations during the home series against Australia in 1965 which, despite being cleared once more, seemed to affect his performance adversely. After he was called for throwing during the Old Trafford Test of 1966, it seemed that Griffith was to be condemned as the 'big, bad boy of cricket'; but he enjoyed a new lease of life in India in 1966-67. In the first Test at Bombay, Hall and Griffith began by reducing the hosts to 14 for three on a docile wicket, before Gibbs eventually spun the tourists to victory. In the third game at Madras, Griffith snapped up four for 61 in India's second innings and then, enjoying unusual success with the bat, hit 40 not out to help West Indies to the safety of a draw, after the top-order had faltered.

After that trip though, it was clear that one of the great bowling partnerships in Test cricket was nearing its end. Even though their reputation carried them through another three series, it was evident that Hall and Griffith had run out of steam: against England in 1968 they could only muster 19 wickets between them compared to 48 in 1963, and they finally exhausted themselves in Australia and New Zealand the following year, when they were rarely fit together.

Teams: *Barbados, West Indies, F. Worrell's XI, Commonwealth XI, Indian President's XI, Rest of World XI*
First-class debut: *30/12/59 Barbados v M.C.C.*
First-class record: *332 wickets (21.60) and 1,502 runs (17.26)*
Tests: *28*
Test debut: *25/3/60 West Indies v England*
Test record: *94 wickets (28.54) and 530 runs (16.56)*

GRIFFITH, Herman Clarence

Born: 1 December 1893, Port-of-Spain, Trinidad
Died: 18 March 1980
Role: Right-arm fast bowler

HERMAN GRIFFITH was one of the first in a long line of distinguished fast bowlers to emerge from Barbados. After his top-class performance in the 1921-22 domestic series, exemplified by his seven for 38 against Trinidad, it seemed he would be an automatic choice for the tour to England in 1923. But he failed to make the trip and there was some talk that his explosive fast bowling was sometimes reflected in his behaviour, as he barracked people on the field and acquired a reputation of being difficult to handle.

His bowling did the talking against Freddie Calthorpe's MCC tourists in 1925-26 when, partnered by George Francis, the pair helped Barbados to a stunning victory, as they took nine wickets each. By the time of the 1928 series, it would have been difficult to leave Griffith at home and he was selected as first change bowler. He performed splendidly and finished second in the averages to Constantine, aided by a splendid performance in the third Test at The Oval where he took six for 103. In an hour of

Herman Griffith

fast and furious bowling with the second new ball, he accounted for four batsmen as England added just 44. Unfortunately for the visitors, when Griffith tired, no one else seemed able to maintain his momentum and West Indies' advantage disappeared.

The Barbadian was similarly frustrated against England in the second Test in Trinidad in 1930 when, after taking five wickets in the first innings and dismissing two top-order batsmen in the second, no one capitalised on his efforts and West Indies slid to defeat. Ironically, Griffith did not play in the third match at Georgetown, where the elusive first Test victory finally came.

By the time of West Indies' inaugural visit to Australia, Griffith was almost 40. Even so, he still managed to dismiss Don Bradman for his first duck in Test cricket in the fifth match at Sydney - which prompted the cocky Griffith to nickname the great man 'his rabbit' - and in the second innings took four for 50 to help West Indies to their first win over Australia. That was sweet revenge for the Barbadian who had suffered at the hands of Bradman during his double century in Brisbane.

Griffith made the trip to England in 1933 but, with age creeping up on him, was obliged to make way for the prodigious Martindale. As with so many of his pioneering colleagues, Griffith's Test record does not reflect his true calibre, although the sight of an opposing batsmen always seemed to erase some of his years.

Teams: *Barbados, West Indies, Combined B/J XI*
First-class debut: *21/9/21 Barbados v Trinidad*
First-class record: *258 wickets (28.27) and 1,204 runs (15.05)*
Tests: *13*
Test debut: *23/6/28 West Indies v England*
Test record: *44 wickets (28.25) and 91 runs (5.05)*

GUILLEN, Simpson "Sammy" Clairmonte

Born: 24 September 1924, Port-of-Spain, Trinidad
Role: Wicket-keeper, right-hand batsman

"SAMMY" GUILLEN was a talented wicket-keeper-batsman who enjoyed a successful tour of Australia and New Zealand in 1951-52. He played in five Tests - after Walcott had been injured - and ended the trip with 34 dismissals (24 caught, 10 stumped) from 11 matches. Indeed, Guillen was so taken with New Zealand that he decided to stay there. He took out residency and kept wicket for Canterbury before achieving the unusual distinction of playing

"Sammy" Guillen

Test cricket for a second country - when he was selected by New Zealand for the series against West Indies in 1956. He also played in three unofficial Tests against Australia the following year. Guillen certainly blossomed in New Zealand and made his highest first-class score there, 197 for Canterbury against Fiji in 1953-54.

Teams: *Trinidad, West Indies, Canterbury, New Zealand*
First-class debut: *4/2/48 Trinidad v M.C.C.*
First-class record: *111 catches & 34 stumpings, and 2,672 runs (26.97)*
Tests: *8 [5 for West Indies, 3 for New Zealand]*
Test debut: *22/12/51 West Indies v Australia*
Test record: *for West Indies - 9 catches & 2 stumpings, and 104 runs (26.00); for New Zealand - 4 catches & 1 stumping, and 98 runs (16.33)*

HALL, Wesley Winfield

Born: 12 September 1937, Christ Church, Barbados
Role: Right-arm fast bowler

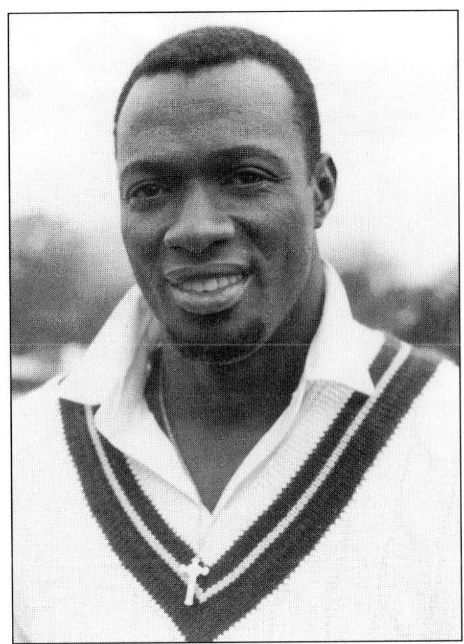

Wes Hall

WES HALL is a remarkable exception to the idea that cricketers should begin their careers at a young age: at 18, Hall had not bowled a ball in competition and, after leaving school, played as opening batsman and wicket-keeper for his office side, Cable & Wireless. His conversion to fast bowling has a fairy-tale ring to it: one Saturday afternoon he was invited to open Cable's attack against Wanderers, after the regular opener had failed to appear. Obligingly Hall took the new ball and six wickets, to herald the start of a spectacular career.

With just one first-class match to his name, he was taken to England in 1957. It was not a particularly profitable gamble on the part of the selectors, as Hall struggled with his run-up, line and length and failed to make his Test debut, even when several of the side were sidelined through injury. After being overlooked for the next home series, it needed a stroke of luck to rescue his international career. It came when Worrell withdrew from the squad to tour India and Pakistan in 1958-59, and Hall was selected as late replacement and deputy to Jaswick Taylor.

It was to be the turning point of Hall's career, as his fearsome pace against Baroda, the domestic champions, brought him a haul of wickets and a place in front of Taylor in the Test side. Bowling in tandem with Gilchrist, Hall surpassed everyone's expectations (including probably his own) and took a fifth of all his Test wickets in that series, bagging 46 (17.76) from eight matches. He was dominant in the second Test at Kanpur, returning figures of 11 for 126 to sweep West Indies to victory. By the Pakistan leg of the tour, he was almost unplayable: in the second Test at Dacca, his movement through the air reduced the home side to 22 for five, as he finished with four for 49 in the first innings, and wrapped up Pakistan's tail in the second, taking the last four wickets in the course of 14 runs - albeit in a losing cause. He took a match-winning five for 87 in the final Test at Lahore, including the only hat-trick of his Test career.

Hall had a classical fast bowling action, and it served him well against England in the third Test at Kingston in 1960, when he took seven for 69, as only a century from Colin Cowdrey kept the tourists in the game.

But he needed more than just his bowling know-how in Australia in 1960-61, when he found himself the leading actor in one of cricket's most famous dramas. It occurred in the first Test at Brisbane as Australia were chasing 233 to win, a target boosted by Hall's first Test 50. Six runs were required off the last (eight-ball) over of the match, to be bowled by Hall. Richie Benaud, who had shared in what appeared to be a match-winning stand of 134 with Alan Davidson, was caught behind off the second ball of the over; a dropped catch off his fifth saved Wally Grout and brought Australia two more precious singles. Ian Meckiff played the sixth ball to backward square-leg and, attempting a third run, Grout was run out by Conrad Hunte, as the scores drew level. Having been warned by Worrell of his likely fate when he got back home if he transgressed the popping-crease, Hall bowled the last ball of the match: Lindsay Kline, Australia's last man, managed to get a touch and raced towards the bowler's end. Joe Solomon, who had run out Davidson a few minutes earlier, threw down the stumps to run out Meckiff and secure the first tie in the history of Test cricket.

Having reached such a pitch of excitement, it seemed it would be difficult to emulate those efforts in the remainder of the series, but both teams came close to it. In the next match at Melbourne, Hall took four for 51 in the first innings including clean-bowling the famed duo of Benaud and Davidson but, thereafter, the pitches were more conducive to spin and Hall was able to share the workload with Gibbs and Valentine. Nonetheless Hall had made his mark: he was invited to play Sheffield Shield cricket for Queensland and, later, had a major influence on the development of Australia's great fast bowling phenomenon, Dennis Lillee.

The Barbadian was lethal against India in 1962, snapping up 27 wickets at 15.74 apiece, including the magnificent return of five for 20 in the high-scoring fourth Test in Trinidad; and, along with Charlie Griffith, received unprecedented acclaim when he arrived in England the following year. He lived up to his reputation as an outstanding athlete when he bowled unchanged for three hours and 20 minutes in the Test at Lord's. A fine 70 from Brian Close almost brought England victory, but more top-class bowling from Hall, who finished with four for 93, secured a draw, even though the result could have gone either way in the last tense over. Hall and Griffith dominated that series - no Englishman scored over 85 - in a way that was not emulated until the arrival of Roberts and Holding in 1976.

Hall took 16 wickets in the series against Australia in 1965, including best bowling figures of five for 60 in the first Test in Jamaica, playing an instrumental role in securing West Indies' first series victory over Australia. By the time of West Indies' next rubber, in England in 1966, Hall and Griffith had lost some of their energy and on the subsequent tour of India, nearly a decade after he had brought the subcontinent's batsmen to their knees, Hall was unable to find his best form on some unhelpful pitches. He retired from Test cricket, along with Griffith, after touring Australia and New Zealand in 1968-69.

But his name was already secure in cricketing history as one of the most gifted fast bowlers of all-time, and Hall himself summed up the nature of his contribution in the title of his autobiography: "Pace like Fire".

After he retired, Hall became an MP in Barbados' House of Assembly and, fittingly, as one of their greatest sportsmen and, indeed, something of a tourist attraction, was later appointed Minister of Tourism and Sport.

Teams: *Barbados, Trinidad, West Indies, Jamaican XI, Queensland, Commonwealth XI, F. Worrell's XI, Rest of World XI, Indian President's XI*
First-class debut: *21/3/56 Barbados v E.W. Swanton's XI*
First-class record: *546 wickets (26.14) and 2,673 runs (15.10)*
Tests: *48*
Test debut: *28/11/58 West Indies v India*
Test record: *192 wickets (26.38) and 818 runs (15.73)*

HARPER, Roger Andrew

Born: 17 March 1963, Georgetown, British Guiana
Role: Right-arm off-spin bowler, right-hand batsman

ROGER HARPER has been mooted as a possible West Indies captain of the future. But, currently, he seems to be failing the test put by Clayton Goodwin, when he asked "can any slow bowler, however good, be sure of selection on merit for every Test match the captain is required to play"? Harper has vied with Clyde Butts for several seasons to carve a niche in the West Indies side as their resident spinner but, as yet, neither of them has made the place - when it is available at all - their own.

But his talent has never been in doubt: even as a young boy, Harper was given special dispensation to play for the prestigious Demerara club in preference to his school, where he

Roger Harper

appeared as an off-spinner, batting at number eight. By the age of 16 he was playing national youth cricket and appeared for the West Indies youth team immediately after his 17th birthday. He made his debut for Guyana in 1980, under the captaincy of his boyhood hero, Roy Fredericks, and collected 17 wickets in the last four games of the Shell Shield.

In 1982 Harper led the Young West Indies to a 2-0 victory over England in their 'Test' series and, after taking 24 wickets in the Shield in 1983, graduated to the full side for West Indies' tour of India at the end of that year, making his Test debut in the fifth match in Calcutta. He maintained his momentum in England in 1984, taking 13 Test wickets at just over 20 apiece, including six for 57 in the fourth match at Old Trafford. Harper finished the tour with 37 wickets and enhanced his reputation as a fielder of remarkable agility, all of which prompted Northamptonshire to offer him a contract before anyone else had a chance. He accepted and, when given the opportunity, met with considerable success, notably in 1986 when he topped their bowling averages. The same year he scored a career-best 234 against Gloucestershire, to set a new record for a number seven batsman in England, the day he arrived back from the Caribbean.

He also bowled well for Guyana, taking 22 wickets and scoring 262 runs in their Shield season in 1986, having performed well in Australia in 1984-85 and again in his two Test appearances against England in 1986. But he went off the boil in Pakistan and poor form in the extended series of one-day internationals in Australia in 1986-87 lost him his place for the following tour to New Zealand. So he returned home and shepherded Guyana to victory in the Shell Shield. Leading from the front Harper scored 277 runs (138.50) and took seven wickets (33.28), as his team gelled to take the trophy.

As a result of these performances, the Guyanese was appointed vice-captain for West Indies' World Cup campaign in 1987 and their subsequent tour of India. However, he had the misfortune to twist his knee so badly in the first one-day international of the Indian trip that he only played in one more match before returning to England for an operation. Harper missed the series against Pakistan, but bounced back against England in 1988, to lie third in the batting averages with 49, including his highest Test score of 74 at Old Trafford, although he only bowled two overs of spin in the match. Indeed, he only bowled 29 overs in the entire series as, once again, the pace men dominated.

In Australia in 1988-89 his opportunities were limited: he scored 267 runs and took 11 expensive wickets on the tour, playing just one Test. Harper did not appear in the subsequent home series against India and England although, as a positive and philosophical character, he knows if he can return to his best form, he will never be far from the selectors' short-list.

Teams: *Guyana, Demerara, West Indies, D.B.Close's XI, Northamptonshire, Rest of World XI*
First-class debut: *20/10/79 Demerara v Berbice*
First-class record: *5,523 runs (31.38) and 458 wickets (27.37)*
Tests: *24*
Test debut: *10/12/83 West Indies v India*
Test record: *532 runs (19.00) and 45 wickets (27.82)*

HAYNES, Desmond Leo

Born: 15 February 1956, Holder's Hill, St James, Barbados
Role: Right-hand batsman

DESMOND HAYNES forms one half of the most enduring opening partnerships in the history of Test cricket. Up to the end of the series against England in the Caribbean in 1990, he had opened the innings 127 times with Gordon Greenidge in a Test match. Altogether, they have shared in 11 century opening stands which speaks volumes for the contribution the pair have made to the success of the West Indies for more than a decade now.

A prolific scorer of runs wherever he goes, the happy-go-lucky Haynes took the first tentative steps towards Test acclaim when he hit 136 for Barbados against the touring Pakistanis in 1977. After a disappointing start to his domestic career, he only won this reprieve after injury had obliged Greenidge to withdraw from the match. Haynes secured the vacant opener's place in the Test side when he hit a brilliant 148 off the touring Australians in the first one-day international in 1978, and made a promising start to his Test career by scoring 61 in the first match at Port-of-Spain and 66 in the first innings of the second at Bridgetown. There were enthusiastic celebrations in Barbados, when he and Greenidge put on a match-winning 131 in the second innings as the locals celebrated the birth of a new Bajan partnership. But, almost before these celebrations had died down, the pair had opted out of official cricket to join Packer's world series. On his return to official circles, for the 1979-80 tour to Australia and New Zealand, Haynes had an indifferent series averaging under 30.00 with the bat; but he recaptured his best form on the second leg of the tour, scoring 105 in the first Test at Dunedin and 122 in the second at Christchurch, as he shared in a double century stand with Greenidge for the first wicket. He maintained his good form against England in 1980, and was seen at his best during the Lord's Test when he cracked 184 runs off the English attack in just over eight hours. Even so, his run thirst remained unquenched and in the return series in the Caribbean, he scored 96 in the first Test in Trinidad and 84 in the fifth in Jamaica.

The spinners had foiled him in Pakistan in 1980-81 and he had difficulties against the Indians when they visited the Caribbean in 1983. He did, however, put them to one side in the fifth Test on a docile Antiguan wicket, as he scored 136 and shared in a record-breaking stand of 296 with Greenidge.

Many of Haynes' most memorable innings have come in limited-overs cricket. He has a record number of one-day centuries to his credit and scored three of them in succession for once out in Australia in 1984, and followed that with almost 500 runs in the subsequent Test series for an average of 93.60, including 145 at Bridgetown - his first Test century on his home ground. Although he struggled against England in the early part of the 1984 series, it seemed as if he couldn't get through a series without reaching three figures and duly hoisted his hundred in the final match at The Oval.

He was in majestic form when England visited the Caribbean in 1986, hammering 131 in the fifth Test in St John's, as he scored 117 out of 228 for four on a testing first day to set up victory for West Indies, and help himself to an average of almost 80 for the series. He topped the batting in Pakistan in 1986, but against New Zealand the following year had a leaner time in the Tests, apart from a century in the first match at Wellington, in a prelude to poor series against India and Pakistan. But he hauled himself back up the averages, scoring 235 runs (47.00) against England in 1988, including an unbeaten 77 in the fifth Test at The Oval.

Even so, Haynes arrived in Australia later that year without a century for 13 Tests. Keen to re-establish himself, he topped the batting with a record 537 runs (59.66), including 143 out of 256 on a turning pitch in the fourth Test at Sydney - quelling the notion that he was vulnerable against spin - as he became the sixth West Indian to pass 5,000 Test runs. This, together with 500 runs in the one-day internationals, won him the title of International Cricketer of the Year. He was similarly prolific in the home series against India scoring 280 runs at 46.66 and eased himself into the new decade with 371 runs at 53.00 against England in the Caribbean.

A friendly, affable man Haynes fitted in well at Middlesex after the untimely death of Wilf Slack and hit a career-best 255 not out for his adopted county against Sussex at Lord's in 1990. Still only 35, but with the energy and enthusiasm of a 17-year-old, he seems determined to continue in his role as one of West Indies' greatest batting assets, if not quite into the next century, then at least for several more years to come.

Desmond Haynes

Teams: *Barbados, West Indies, D.B. Close's XI, Rest of World XI, Middlesex*
First-class debut: *7/1/77 Barbados v Jamaica*
First-class record: *17,126 runs (45.66) and 6 wickets (32.66)*
Tests: *89*
Test debut: *3/2/78 West Indies v Australia*
Test record: *5,711 runs (41.99) and 1 wicket (8.00)*

HEADLEY, George Alphonso

Born: 30 May 1909, Panama, U.S.A.
Died: 30 November 1983
Role: Right-hand batsman

GEORGE HEADLEY, for many people, is the greatest West Indian batsman of them all: some get close, but no one touches him. That feeling was summed up by Berkeley Gaskin, who played under him when Headley became the first black man to captain the West Indies in a Test, in the first match against England at Bridgetown in 1948. When asked some years later, how he would compare Headley with the then outstanding players, headed by the three "W"s and Sobers, Gaskin replied: "They could sit in the same cathedral as George, but not in the same pew."

Headley's messianic following was brought about by his remarkable deeds on the cricket field and nonchalant attitude to them off it. He was born in Panama, after his father had gone there to help build the Panama canal, and grew up in a sporting environment. The youngster was taken to Jamaica in 1919 and appeared for the renowned St Catherine cricket club in 1927. He gave the first signs of his genius the following season when, still in his teens, he hit 71, 211 and 71 for Jamaica in matches against Lionel Tennyson's touring team.

George Headley

Headley seemed a certainty for West Indies' first official tour of England in 1928 and there was widespread surprise when he was omitted from the side. As if to underline the error of the selectors' ways, he scored a century when his debut finally arrived, against England at Bridgetown in 1930, in his maiden first-class match outside Jamaica. Indeed, his gifts were such that the selectors soon realised he was worth his weight in gold and, exceptionally, he played in all four Tests in that first series in the Caribbean. He was instrumental in West Indies' first Test victory, at Georgetown in 1930, when he savaged the English attack for 114 runs in the first innings and 112 in the second, to become the first West Indian to score two centuries in the same Test.

As was his habit, "King George" saved his best innings for his home crowd and scored a suitably majestic double century, with 28 boundaries, in the final drawn Test at Sabina Park. This effort took him to a record aggregate of 703 runs for his first series, and an average of almost 90.

His reputation went ahead of him to Australia in 1930-31 and he was soon subduing strong state sides with his masterful strokeplay. Then, to everyone's surprise, he ran into difficulties. Having arrived in Australia as a strong off-side player, he had to modify his technique in the face of some testing leg-break bowling from Clarrie Grimmett. Alterations to his stance and grip improved his game and, by the time of the third Test in Brisbane, his mastery of the bowlers had returned as he scored 102 not out, albeit in a losing cause, and thereby became the first West Indian to score a Test hundred in Australia.

In a bleak series for West Indies, Headley was a lone beacon of hope: invariably he held the innings together almost single-handedly, so it must have been especially satisfying when he at last found support in the shape of his compatriot, Frank Martin, in the final Test at Sydney. Headley scored his second century of the series, adding 152 for the second wicket with Martin, who carried his bat for 123.

After his return from Australia, Headley maintained his brilliant form against Lord Tennyson's side who, perhaps unwisely, were visiting the Caribbean again. In a series of matches spread over a month Headley scored 344 not out, sharing in a world record undefeated partnership of 487 for the sixth wicket with his school friend, Clarence Passailaigue, 84, 155 not out and 140. The disbelieving Lord reported: "I cannot recollect such perfection of timing nor variety of shots, and the delight of it all was that he himself was, I am sure, unconscious that he was doing anything out of the ordinary..."

Headley was irrepressible when he finally toured England in 1933, scoring 2,320 first-class runs including a splendid hundred in the Old Trafford Test. The fact that he would head the averages was a foregone conclusion but it was the gulf between him and the next man, as he scored nearly twice as many runs as anyone else, that marked him out as a player of rare quality.

Nicknamed the "Black Bradman" - although West Indians preferred to call Bradman the "White Headley" - the Jamaican was largely responsible for England's defeat in the Caribbean in 1935. His remarkable ability and the disastrous nature of the pitch in the first Test at Bridgetown were revealed as he top-scored with 44 in the home side's first innings and made a duck in their second, as England secured a fortuitous victory. He played well at Port-of-Spain and Georgetown, but was at his most fluent before his home supporters when he scored West Indies' only century of the series, thrashing 270 runs, with 30 fours, in 500 minutes. That scintillating performance was decisive in giving West Indies a sufficiently large total for their bowlers, headed by Martindale, to sweep aside the opposition and register their first victory in a Test series.

The finest jewel in Headley's crown came during West Indies' tour of England in 1939. It was put in place when he became the first player to score two centuries in a Test at Lord's. He made 106 and 107 in another losing cause, but kept the statisticians busy as he became only the second man in the history of Test cricket to score two centuries in the same Test on two different occasions. The Second World War deprived the world of some of Headley's best cricketing years but, with the resumption of Test cricket in the Caribbean in 1948, he became the first black man to lead the West Indies when he was appointed captain for the first Test at Bridgetown. The fact that he was only appointed for the first Test and the fourth, in Jamaica, merely revealed the blatant nature of colonial prejudice at the time; his cause was hampered further when he pulled a muscle in Bridgetown that ruled him out of the rest of the series.

Even though he didn't captain the West Indies as often as his ability warranted, the senior players, including less gifted ones whose background nonetheless made them more acceptable captains, invariably deferred to his encyclopedic knowledge of the game. Headley's appreciation of cricketing strategy and tactics were second to none, and most people drew on his expertise whenever the opportunity arose.

Headley became the oldest man ever to represent the West Indies when he was brought over from England, where he was playing league cricket, for one final Test appearance at his beloved Sabina Park. At the age of almost 45, his adoring Jamaican public raised over £1,000 to pay for his passage home and his fans virtually obliged the selectors to include him in the side for the first Test against England in 1954. History has judged the decision harshly, as the great man could muster only 16 and one in a sad end to a brilliant career.

In a sense, though, it hardly mattered: Headley has become immortalised in the annals of West Indian cricket. His standards of batsmanship set the tone for the new generation of players. He carried West Indies' pre-War batting, like Martindale did the bowling, but even his genius could not always bridge the gap: in 15 out of 35 Test innings he was the top scorer, in 11 of those he made at least a third of the runs and in three it was over half. At his peak, in the 1930's, he scored a century in every other Test, while the remaining West Indian batsmen could only manufacture five between them. But, the statistics are only half the story, his cool composure on and off the field, often in trying circumstances, as he grappled with the injustices of his day, make his story all the more remarkable.

Teams: *Jamaica, West Indies, Combined Jam/BG XI, Commonwealth XI, L. Parkinson's XI*
First-class debut: *9/2/28 Jamaica v L.H. Tennyson's XI*
First-class record: *9,921 runs (69.86) and 51 wickets (36.11)*
Tests: *22*
Test debut: *11/1/30 West Indies v England*
Test record: *2,190 runs (60.83) and 0-230*

Ron Headley

HEADLEY, Ronald George Alphonso

Born: 29 June 1939, Rollington Town, Kingston, Jamaica
Role: Left-hand batsman

RON HEADLEY played most of his cricket in England, predictably under the shadow of his illustrious father, George. An almost impossible act to follow, Ron nonetheless enjoyed a distinguished first-class career opening for Worcestershire between 1958-74 and, more fleetingly for Jamaica in 1965-66 and 1973-74, and played some one-day games for Derbyshire. It was while he was contracted to Worcestershire that his chance at Test level came, when he got the call from an injury-hit West Indian side in 1973. He scored eight and 42 in the first Test at The Oval and one and 11 in the second at Edgbaston, but was never given a proper chance to establish himself and returned to county cricket, where his swashbuckling style brought him considerable success.

Teams: *Jamaica, West Indies, Worcestershire, Commonwealth XI, Cavaliers XI*
First-class debut: *28/6/58 Worcestershire v Cambridge University*
First-class record: *21,695 runs (31.12) and 12 wickets (49.00)*
Tests: *2*
Test debut: *26/7/73 West Indies v England*
Test record: *62 runs (15.50)*

HENDRIKS, John "Jackie" Leslie

Born: 21 December 1933, Kingston, Jamaica
Role: Wicket-keeper, right-hand batsman

"JACKIE" HENDRIKS is regarded as one of the finest wicket-keepers ever produced by the Caribbean. Ironically, therefore, his Test appearances were limited by a susceptibility to injury and playing in the shadow of Gerry Alexander.

Although he was widely recognised as the best wicket-keeper in the West Indies, it was not until the 1962 series against the Indians that Hendriks made his Test debut, after the retirement of Alexander.

Tragically, after his long apprenticeship, Hendriks broke his finger during the first innings of the opening game in Trinidad and, despite bravely top-scoring with 64 in the home side's reply, he took no further part in the series. It was more than two long years before he regained his place after the prodigious Deryck Murray made his mark in England in 1963, as Hendriks missed out on selection for that trip because of business commitments in America.

When Murray stayed in the UK to study, Hendriks was recalled and, for almost a decade, the identity of West Indies' wicket-keeper was largely determined by Murray's academic timetable and the fitness of the injury-prone Hendriks. Indeed, the serious injury he sustained on his return to the side stretched the boundaries of ill fortune. He was hit on the side of the head by a ball from Graham McKenzie in the fourth Test against Australia at Bridgetown in 1965,

"Jackie" Hendriks

and only narrowly avoided brain damage. Earlier in the series, Hendriks had distinguished himself when he made two fine stumpings and took two catches in Australia's second innings at Georgetown to wrap up the match in favour of West Indies.

After recovering from his accident at Bridgetown, Hendriks was selected for the trips to England, India, and Australia and New Zealand in the second half of the decade although, predictably, injury and his job meant he missed the series against England in the Caribbean in 1968.

Yet, through all his ups and downs, Hendriks played in the knowledge that his peers rated him as the finest and most consistent 'keeper of his day, as he stood up to the might of Hall and Griffith with the same ease as he coped with the variety of Sobers and the guile of Gibbs. Indeed, he is the only West Indian to have kept wicket in three innings which have passed 500 runs without conceding a bye: when Barbados made 521 for seven declared at Bridgetown in 1967, and when Australia made 510 at Melbourne and 619 at Sydney in 1968-69.

After his playing days were were over, Hendriks became an influential administrator in West Indian cricket. His jovial, but tactful character was perhaps put to its best use when he managed the triumphant Test sides in England in 1984 and 1988.

Teams: *Jamaica, West Indies, New Zealand Governor's XI*
First-class debut: *8/2/54 Jamaica v M.C.C.*
First-class record: *140 catches & 50 stumpings, and 1,568 runs (17.42)*
Tests: *20*
Test debut: *16/2/62 West Indies v India*
Test record: *42 catches & 5 stumpings, and 447 runs (18.62)*

HOAD, Edward Lisle Goldsworthy

Born: 29 January 1896, Richmond, Bridgetown, Barbados
Died: 5 March 1986
Role: Right-hand batsman, leg-spin bowler

TEDDY HOAD was a solid batsman and leg-break change bowler, who scored heavily in the West Indies during the inter-War years. He enjoyed particular success in the inter-colonial tournament of 1926-27, scoring 115 for Barbados against British Guiana and an unbeaten 174 against Trinidad in Bridgetown.

When he arrived in England in 1928, with the first official West Indies side he struggled to acclimatise and only appeared in the second Test at Old Trafford, although he picked up in the second half of the tour and finished as the leading batsman with 765 runs (36.42) including three hundreds.

Teddy Hoad

Hoad had the honour of captaining the West Indies in the first ever Test in the Caribbean, against England at Bridgetown in 1930, although he never seemed able to carry his sparkling domestic form into the Test arena. (Even so, Hoad knew a Test-class batsman when he saw one and spotted the potential of the young Everton Weekes early in his career). Hoad toured England again in 1933 as vice-captain and scored over 1,000 first-class runs, including sharing in a record-breaking last wicket partnership of 138 with Herman Griffith against Sussex at Hove.

Teams: *Barbados, West Indies, Combined T/BG XI*
First-class debut: *21/9/22 Barbados v Trinidad*
First-class record: *3,502 runs (38.48) and 53 wickets (36.28)*
Tests: *4*
Test debut: *21/7/28 West Indies v England*
Test record: *98 runs (12.25)*

A royal handshake for Vanburn Holder (right)

HOLDER, Vanburn Alonza

Born: 8 October 1945, Bridgetown, Barbados
Role: Right-arm fast-medium bowler, right-hand batsman

VANBURN HOLDER played an invaluable role in West Indian cricket as a stop-gap bowler between the retirement of Hall and Griffith and the emergence of Roberts and Holding.

Although he was never as fast as any of them, Holder made an important contribution. He met with moderate success in England in 1969, returning his best figures of four for 48 in the third Test at Headingley. He bowled consistently, although without much luck, against India in 1971 and topped the averages against New Zealand in 1972, in a deadlocked series where unusually the West Indies lacked the firepower to bowl out the visitors twice.

Holder went to England in 1973 as part of a three-pronged pace attack, along with Keith Boyce and Bernard Julien, and took four for 56 in England's first innings of the Lord's Test to help West Indies to a decisive win.

Whether playing for the West Indies, Barbados or Worcestershire, Holder could always be relied on to give his best. He enjoyed a vintage year in domestic cricket in 1974: his bowling helped Worcestershire to the county championship - including returning his best championship figures of seven for 40 against Glamorgan - having hit a career-best 122 for Barbados against Trinidad & Tobago in the Shell Shield earlier in the year.

Holder toured India and Pakistan in 1974-75, and was seen at his most potent in the fifth and deciding Test at Bombay. Extracting bounce and movement from a wearing pitch, the Barbadian finished with six for 39 to clinch the series for West Indies.

But with the arrival of Roberts and Holding in the mid-seventies, Holder's role became that of a change bowler in the subsequent series in Australia and England. It seemed that the amiable Barbadian would be put out to grass, but he made a surprise return to the international arena as vice-captain to Kallicharran in the wake of the Packer crisis.

This out-of-the-blue opportunity seemed to inspire Holder, who returned the best performance of his Test career, when he took six for 28 with the new ball against Australia in the fourth match in Trinidad, to help clinch another series for West Indies.

Although he was selected for the following tour to India, Holder was too old to enjoy a second career at the highest level and, when the Packer players returned to the fold, the hardworking Bajan was sidelined for good.

Teams: *Barbados, West Indies, Worcestershire, Rest of World XI, Orange Free State*
First-class debut: *22/2/67 Barbados v Trinidad*
First-class record: *950 wickets (24.52) and 3,593 runs (12.97)*
Tests: *40*
Test debut: *12/6/69 West Indies v England*
Test record: *109 wickets (33.27) and 682 runs (14.20)*

HOLDING, Michael Anthony

Born: 16 February 1954, Half-Way Tree, Kingston, Jamaica
Role: Right-arm fast bowler

MICHAEL HOLDING lifted himself into the category of great fast bowlers with a record-breaking performance on a dead track at The Oval in 1976. There, his sustained pace accounted for 14 England players at a cost of just 149 runs. His feat is put into its true perspective by the other six fast or medium-fast men who could only muster six wickets between them. Altogether 28 wickets fell in the match at a cost of 53.80 runs apiece, while Holding's were less than a fifth of that at 10.90 each.

And to think at the start of the decade, as a gifted 400-metre runner and university graduate, Holding might have been lost to cricket. But he stayed and quickly made his mark: in 1972 he played in the West Indies youth tournament and the following year made his maiden first-class appearance for Jamaica. Then, with just a few first-class games to his name, he was picked to partner Andy Roberts on West Indies' tour of Australia in 1975-76. He began impressively, albeit with the bat, when he made two fifties in the opening state games, before taking six for 60 against New South Wales at Sydney to secure his place for the first Test at Brisbane. He had an inauspicious beginning, returning match figures of nought for 127, but lifted himself in the next game at Perth, where he took four wickets for 88, including three in his second over on the second day. But later in that game, he sustained a muscle injury which hampered him for the rest of the series and he finished with 10 expensive wickets, although Holding thought it should have been 11 after Ian Chappell refused to walk in a controversial incident in the fourth Test at Sydney.

After the rigours of his first tour, the young Jamaican bounced back for the home series against India to head the bowling averages with 19 wickets at under 20 apiece, including his best figures of six for 65 in the third Test in Trinidad. He was lethal on his home ground in the fourth match in Kingston, where he exploited a ridge at the northern end of the Sabina Park ground, and his venomous deliveries accounted for four Indian batsmen as only 82 runs were added. Indeed, after two touring batsmen were injured by rising balls, India declared. Facing a deficit of 85, India went in again, but when three men were dismissed on 97, five others withdrew from the contest 'absent hurt' after complaints about intimidatory bowling which would have worried the English who were preparing to entertain Holding et al at home later that summer.

Holding and Roberts dominated that series - as Griffith and Hall had the 1963 contest - taking 56 wickets between them. After mesmerising the cream of England's batting in an early game on the tour against MCC at Lord's, Holding missed the first Test after a case of mild glandular fever and was struggling for fitness in the second. But in the third at Old Trafford, the Jamaican sent England crashing to defeat as he took five wickets for nine runs in 7.5 overs, before his magnificent display at The Oval, which included a record eight for 92 in England's second innings, then the best Test figures by a West Indian.

A combination of injury and involvement

Michael Holding

in world series cricket then removed him from the official scene for a while but, unhappily for England, Holding was back to his best by the time West Indies toured in 1980. He took six for 67 in the Lord's Test and, in an inspired spell at the start of England's second innings in the fourth match at The Oval, unceremoniously removed both openers, to leave England swaying on 10 for two.

Geoff Boycott is another opener who will readily vouch for the blistering pace of Holding, particularly after facing a terrifying first over from him in the third Test at Bridgetown in 1981. Even a batsman of Boycott's skill failed to survive that; and comparable pace from Holding claimed 24 Australian wickets (14.33), including five or more in four innings out of six, in the subsequent short series in Australia.

Like all great bowlers, even when he cut down his run, Holding remained effective as the Indians discovered at the end of 1983 when they suffered at his hands, as he collected 30 wickets at 22.10 during the Test series on the subcontinent.

By the time of the 1984 series against Australia, Holding had passed his 30th birthday and was regarded as the elder statesman of the pace attack. Yet Holding did not take kindly to that title and, in the first Test at Perth, bowled out Australia for their lowest total of 76 against West Indies, taking six for 21 in just 35 balls.

Given that the West Indies batsmen were usually as complete in their assaults with the willow as Holding was with the ball, the Jamaican rarely had an opportunity to shine with the bat. But, against England in the first Test at Edgbaston in 1984, he demonstrated a sound technique, scoring 69 runs in a record ninth wicket stand of 150 with Baptiste. In the third match at Headingley, he was at it again, this time in more trying circumstances: West Indies were 64 runs adrift, before Holding slammed 59 runs - including five sixes off Bob Willis - sharing in a stand of 82 with Gomes, which helped the tourists to a first innings lead and eventual victory in the match, as Holding finished the series with a batting average of over 30.

When he returned to The Oval - the scene of his record performance eight years earlier - for the final Test of that series, Holding also returned to his full run-up and, in a few overs of breathtaking pace, removed Chris Broad, David Gower and the in-form Allan Lamb. Another two wickets gave him figures of five for 43, as he ushered West Indies to another conclusive victory. When England visited the Caribbean early in 1986, Holding was waiting for them again. This time, West Indies' newly appointed vice-captain took 16 wickets in the series (24.06) and ran riot with the bat in the third Test in Antigua, as his 73 included four sixes and six fours.

Holding toured New Zealand in 1987 and then announced his retirement from Test cricket. He had been one of the vital components in the West Indies' pace machine that helped them dominate world cricket for most of Holding's career. But opposing batsmen should not sleep too easily in their beds for the 'Rolls-Royce of fast bowling' is now tutoring one of West Indies' newest models, in the shape of the young Ian Bishop.

Teams: *Jamaica, West Indies, Lancashire, International XI, Tasmania, Derbyshire, Canterbury*
First-class debut: *19/1/73 Jamaica v Barbados*
First-class record: *778 wickets (23.43) and 3,600 runs (15.00)*
Tests: *60*
Test debut: *28/11/75 West Indies v Australia*
Test record: *249 wickets (23.68) and 910 runs (13.78)*

HOLFORD, David Anthony Jerome

Born: 16 April 1940, Bridgetown, Barbados
Role: Right-hand batsman, right-arm leg-spin bowler

DAVID HOLFORD won a reputation as a cricketer of exceptional talent, after some splendid performances as a young man in his native Barbados. Indeed, he seemed to have the world at his feet and, as a cousin of Sobers, had an impeccable pedigree.

Holford was a top-class leg-break bowler and more than useful middle-order batsman. After Joe Solomon left the Test scene, it seemed that Holford would slip easily into his shoes. He began promisingly when, in his first Test against England at Old Trafford in 1966, he shared in a century partnership with Sobers, and then bowled well in tandem with Sobers and Gibbs. Holford made his finest performance

David Holford

in Test cricket a family affair when he scored 105 not out, in a record unbroken sixth wicket partnership of 274 with Sobers, as the pair almost snatched victory from the jaws of defeat, in the drawn second Test at Lord's. When Holford arrived at the wicket, at 95 for five, West Indies had only just edged into the lead; but, despite his lack of experience and known unsteadiness early in his innings, Holford was more than a match for the occasion as he registered the only Test hundred of his career.

Those performances seemed to confirm the prediction that he had a glowing future ahead of him and he was included in the tour party to India in 1966-67. He scored 80 in his only innings and took five wickets in the opening Test at Bombay, and appeared to be going from strength to strength. But then he was struck down by a severe attack of pleurisy, which sidelined him for the rest of the tour and, sadly, seemed to take some of the zest out of his cricket.

He toured England, Australia and New Zealand in the late 1960's, but only met with limited success. Although, thereafter, he faded from the Test scene, he was never entirely out of the reckoning until he joined Kerry Packer's ranks: indeed he bowled so well when New Zealand were in the Caribbean in 1972, there was talk that he might captain West Indies in England the following year but, in the event, he was not selected for the trip at all; then, against India in 1976, he took a match-winning five for 23 in the first Test at Bridgetown.

Three years later Holford retired from a game that had not brought him as much success as it had promised early on, and channelled his considerable energies into a career as an agronomist.

Teams: *Barbados, Trinidad, North Trinidad, West Indies*
First-class debut: *26/1/61 Barbados v Trinidad*
First-class record: *3,821 runs (31.31) and 253 wickets (32.00)*
Tests: *24*
Test debut: *2/6/66 West Indies v England*
Test record: *768 runs (22.58) and 51 wickets (39.39)*

HOLT (Jnr.), John Kenneth

Born: 12 August 1923, Kingston, Jamaica
Role: Right-hand batsman

JOHN HOLT Junior caused a lot of excitement in his brief Test career. He waited a long time for international recognition and when it finally came, in the first Test against England at Kingston in 1954, he was determined to do well. Everything seemed to be going according to the script until Brian Statham made a successful leg before wicket appeal against him when he was on 94; his home supporters were not imp-ressed and voiced their opinions noisily.

John Holt (Jnr.)

But Holt made sure of his century in the next match at Bridgetown, where he scored a scintillating 166 - 110 of them in boundaries - sharing in a second wicket partnership of 222 with Worrell.

Holt remained in the spotlight in the next encounter at Georgetown. This time crowd trouble flared after Clifford McWatt, the home batsman, was run out attempting a second run, after a partnership of 99 with the Jamaican, who was batting with a runner. Despite his muscle injury, Holt top-scored in the second innings with 64 and hit 40 in a losing cause in the fourth game in Trinidad.

His excellent batting against England in 1954 meant he kept his place in the team when Australia toured the following year. He began well, making 60 in the first Test at Kingston but, like most of the other batsmen, fell away in the wake of Ray Lindwall's and Keith Miller's pace later in the series.

Holt was omitted from the tours to New Zealand and England in the mid-1950's, but enjoyed a revival in India in 1958-59 when he scored over 900 first-class runs, including 63 and 81 not out in the fourth Test at Madras and a splendid 123 in the fifth in Delhi, before he and his partner, Conrad Hunte, were dropped after poor performances in the opening games in Pakistan. Hunte's demise turned out to be temporary, but Holt was not selected again and was probably especially disappointed that he never came to England, where his father had toured with Harold Austin's team in 1923.

Teams: *Jamaica, West Indies, Commonwealth XI*
First-class debut: *26/6/46 Jamaica v Trinidad*
First-class record: *4,258 runs (41.33) and 5 wickets (35.40)*
Tests: *17*
Test debut: *15/1/54 West Indies v England*
Test record: *1,066 runs (36.75) and 1 wicket (20.00)*

HOOPER, Carl Llewellyn

Born: 15 December 1966, Georgetown, Guyana
Role: Right-hand batsman

Carl Hooper

CARL HOOPER burst on to the cricket scene, when he topped the batting in West Indies' youth championships in 1984. A tall right-hander, with powerful arms and shoulders, Guyana hauled him out of the Young West Indies side that were playing England in 1985, as he was considered too important to their domestic campaign. They were proved right, as he scored a century in his first innings, against Barbados, and then toured Zimbabwe with the West Indies "B" team before, predictably, moving into the full side. In 1986 he had made his mark in the Central Lancashire League when, appearing for Werneth, he overhauled Frank Worrell's record league aggregate set in 1951, by scoring 1,715 runs.

Hooper was chosen for the 1987 tour of New Zealand, but was obliged to sit out the Tests, although he had an auspicious debut in the first one-day international at Dunedin, where he hit a polished 48. When his opportunity at Test level finally came, he fulfilled all expectations by slamming an unbeaten century against India in his second Test innings in the third match at Calcutta at the end of 1987, as he finished second in the averages with 49 behind Richards.

The Guyanese was less prolific in 1988 as the touring Pakistanis halved his average from India, which was only boosted when he made 54 in the final Test at Bridgetown. Against England later that year, he slipped further down the batting making just 166 runs (23.71) from five Tests, after starting impressively with a top score of 84 in the first Test at Trent Bridge; and was even more disappointing in the following series in Australia. In fact, on that tour he impressed more in the bowling department, as his off-spin accounted for 16 wickets. He missed the series against India through injury and, when he had recovered and been recalled, was less than prolific against England in the Caribbean early in 1990.

After his explosive start in first-class cricket, Hooper seems to have lost some of his dynamism, but it is difficult to believe that a player with such gifts will not be able to rekindle the magic that continues to make him one of the most exciting batting prospects around.

Teams: *Guyana, Demerara, West Indies*
First-class debut: *8/10/83*
Demerara v Berbice
First-class record: *2,805 runs (32.24) and 96 wickets (29.31)*
Tests: *19*
Test debut: *11/12/87 West Indies v India*
Test record: *710 runs (23.66) and 7 wickets (81.14)*

HOWARD, Anthony Bourne

Born: 27 August 1946, Barbados
Role: Right-arm off-spin bowler

TONY HOWARD got his chance at Test level, after bowling well in Barbados' match against the touring New Zealanders in 1972. He played in the fourth match against the Kiwis at Georgetown, taking two for 140 off 62 overs in one innings. He didn't get a chance to bat and was given no further opportunities in Test cricket.

Teams: *Barbados, West Indies*
First-class debut: *18/2/66*
Barbados v Guyana
First-class record: *85 wickets (27.30) and 310 runs (10.00)*
Tests: *1*
Test debut: *6/4/72*
West Indies v New Zealand
Test record: *2 wickets (70.00)*

HUNTE, Conrad Cleophas

Born: 9 May 1932, St Andrew, Barbados
Role: Right-hand batsman

CONRAD HUNTE began his cricketing career as a carefree stroke-maker in Barbados and ended it as one of West Indies' most reliable, albeit more defensive, openers.

It was the West Indies' misfortune that they were unable to find as consistent a batsman to open with him; as it was Hunte had to get used to 12 different partners in his 44 Tests.

He made his first-class debut in 1951 and, having scored prolifically in Barbados, seemed a certainty for the tour to England in 1957. But, he was left out of the party, apparently, because the selectors could not contact him.

As if to make up for lost time, he scored a century on his debut, in front of his home crowd in the first Test against Pakistan in 1958, and hammered 260 in the third at Kingston, sharing in a record second wicket partnership of 446 with Sobers, who went on to his record-breaking 365 not out.

Hunte lost some of his momentum in India later that year and was dropped from the side early on the Pakistan leg of the tour. But he maintained his place for the home series against England, where a courageous 72 not out, after being hit by a bumper from Fred Trueman, in the fifth Test in Trinidad, earned him a place in the team to Australia in 1960-61.

He showed his calibre with an outstanding 110, made in difficult conditions in the second Test at Melbourne, as the visitors followed on 167 behind. Although he had become more defensive in his approach, he hit 79 in the fourth Test at Adelaide, sharing in a century partnership with Kanhai before the latter ran him out after Hunte had suggested some tight singles because of poor fielding by the Australians.

Hunte had a more restrained series against India in 1962, seeming to save his best for more testing circumstances. He was appointed vice-captain to Worrell for the 1963 tour of England and celebrated by topping the batting averages with almost 60. This was helped by a splendid century at Old Trafford and it seemed he had returned to his attacking ways when he hit Trueman's first three balls to the boundary in the next Test at Lord's. But, thereafter, he reverted to his more circumspect ways and his solid batting in the final match at The Oval, where he made 80 and 108, was decisive in setting up victory for West Indies.

Besides his sound batting, Hunte had been a competent vice-captain and it must have been a bitter blow when the leadership passed to Sobers after Worrell's retirement but, in keeping with his generous nature, he knuckled down and threw his weight behind the new skipper.

Back in the Caribbean, Hunte headed the averages against Australia in 1965. He was the

Conrad Hunte

model of consistency, scoring six fifties in the rubber, including an unbeaten 60 out of a total of 131 in the final Test at Port-of-Spain, to become the first West Indian to carry his bat in a Test in the Caribbean.

After a promising start in England in 1966, when he scored 135 on the first day of the Test series, it seemed he might enjoy another vintage summer, but he lost his momentum quickly. He picked up in India later that year and was the only touring batsman to score a Test century. It seemed that Hunte would simply go on and on but, after seeing the film 'The Crowning Experience' in Australia, he abandoned cricket to devote his life to the Moral Re-armament Movement.

Teams: *Barbados, West Indies, Jamaican XI, Commonwealth XI, C. Hunte's XI, Indian Prime Minister's XI, Rest of World XI*
First-class debut: *21/2/51 Barbados v Trinidad*
First-class record: *8,916 runs (43.92) and 17 wickets (37.88)*
Tests: *44*
Test debut: *17/1/58 West Indies v Pakistan*
Test record: *3,245 runs (45.06) and 2 wickets (55.00)*

HUNTE, Errol Ashton Clairmore

Born: 3 October 1905, Port-of-Spain, Trinidad
Died: 26 June 1967
Role: Opening batsman, wicket-keeper

ERROL HUNTE was a sound opening batsman and competent wicket-keeper. He was selected for three Tests against England in the Caribbean in 1930. His best performance came in the second on his home ground at Port-of-Spain, where he kept wicket and scored 58 and 30 then, in the third game at Georgetown, he shared in an opening stand of 144 with Clifford Roach in West Indies' first innings. Although he went on the inaugural trip to Australia in 1930-31, he did not play in a Test match.

Teams: *Trinidad, West Indies*
First-class debut: *31/1/29 Trinidad v British Guiana*
First-class record: *472 runs (20.52) and 28 catches & 8 stumpings*
Tests: *3*
Test debut: *11/1/30 West Indies v England*
Test record: *166 runs (33.20) and 5 catches*

Errol Hunte

HYLTON, Leslie George

Born: 29 March 1905, Kingston, Jamaica
Died: 17 May 1955
Role: Right-arm fast bowler

LESLIE HYLTON, at the height of his bowling powers, ranked only slightly behind Constantine and Martindale. Indeed, it was England's misfortune to run into this trio when they visited the Caribbean in 1934-35: they shared 47 Test wickets in a victorious series, with Hylton's haul being 13. A thickly-set man, the Jamaican had excellent control over his length and swing, and was in no way overshadowed by his illustrious bowling colleagues. Hylton was at his best in the third Test at Georgetown when he took four for 27 in England's first innings to foil the visitors' attempts to edge ahead in the series. However, despite his success at home, he had a disappointing tour to England in 1939. Hylton didn't make the news again until 1955 when he was hanged for the murder of his wife.

Leslie Hylton

Teams: *Jamaica, West Indies, G.C. Grant's XI, Combined J/B XI*
First-class debut: *19/2/27 Jamaica v L.H. Tennyson's XI*
First-class record: *120 wickets (25.62) and 843 runs (18.73)*
Tests: *6*
Test debut: *8/1/35 West Indies v England*
Test record: *16 wickets (26.12) and 70 runs (11.66)*

JOHNSON, Hophnie Horace Hines

Born: 13 July 1910, Kingston, Jamaica
Died: 24 June 1987
Role: Right-arm fast bowler

HINES JOHNSON had a reputation as a formidably fast bowler in Jamaica from the time he made his debut for the island in 1934-35. But, in spite of bowling well in the trial matches in Port-of-Spain, he missed the 1939 tour to England and had to wait until after the War to make his first international appearance, against England at Kingston in 1948. Although he was 37 years old, spurred on by his home crowd, he finished with the remarkable figures of 10 for 96, including removing both openers in England's first innings.

It seemed that West Indies' fast bowling prayers had been answered, but Johnson, perhaps thinking he was never going to find favour with the Test selectors, was in the process of setting up an electrical business and therefore unavailable for the subsequent tour of India. When he came to England in 1950, he was hampered by a muscle injury and disappointing in his two Test appearances: his best performance came in the third match at Trent Bridge, when he took three for 59 in England's first innings and amused the crowd by sheltering under the covers protecting the wicket, rather than retiring to the pavilion, during a storm.

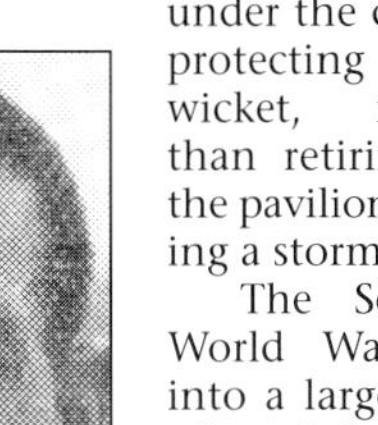

Hines Johnson

The Second World War ate into a large part of Johnson's career and when he was finally given a chance at Test level, apart from his remarkable debut, he was too old to establish himself. However, it would have been of some consolation to him that he featured in two of West Indies' earliest series wins over England.

Teams: *Jamaica, West Indies*
First-class debut: *9/3/35 Jamaica v M.C.C.*
First-class record: *68 wickets (23.36) and 316 runs (17.55)*
Tests: *3*
Test debut: *27/3/48 West Indies v England*
Test record: *13 wickets (18.30) and 38 runs (9.50)*

JOHNSON, Tyrell Francis

Born: 10 January 1917, Tunapuna, Trinidad
Died: 5 April 1985
Role: Left-arm fast bowler

TYRELL JOHNSON was a towering pace bowler, who was selected to tour England in 1939. He had an impressive action that belied his miserly figures: in his sole Test, the third at The Oval, he scored nine not out, took three for 129 and held one catch. He was, however, a good starter: he took a wicket with his first ball of the tour and also with his first ball in Test cricket.

Teams: *Trinidad, West Indies*
First-class debut: *29/1/36 Trinidad v Barbados*
First-class record: *50 wickets (21.50) and 90 runs (9.00)*
Tests: *1*
Test debut: *19/8/39 West Indies v England*
Test record: *3 wickets (43.00) and 9**

Tyrell Johnson

JONES, Charles Ernest Llewellyn

Born: 3 November 1902, British Guiana
Died: 10 December 1959
Role: Left-hand batsman, left-arm bowler

CHARLES JONES was a capable batsman and useful slow bowler who played against England in 1930 and 1935. His first Test appearance came in the victorious setting of Georgetown, when West Indies beat England in the third Test, although his own contribution was marginal as he made six and two batting low in the order. He made three appearances in the subsequent home series: predictably he struggled with the rest of the team in the quagmire at Bridgetown and, opening the innings with Cyril Christiani in the next match at Port-of-Spain, scored 19 on each occasion. His last appearance, like his first, came on his home ground at Georgetown where again he was disappointing with the bat and failed to take a wicket.

Teams:
British Guiana,
West Indies,
Combined T/BG XI,
Barbados XI,
R.S. Grant's XI
First-class debut:
1/10/25
British Guiana v Barbados
First-class record:
917 runs (21.83)
and 24 wickets (44.12)
Tests: *4*
Test debut: *21/2/30*
West Indies v England
Test record: *63 runs*
(9.00) and 0-11

Charles Jones

JONES, Prior Erskine

Born: 6 June 1917, Princes Town, Trinidad
Role: Right-arm medium-fast bowler

PRIOR JONES was a talented medium-fast bowler who had the unusual misfortune to play in the shadow of an illustrious spin bowling partnership, namely that of Ramadhin and Valentine. Selected for the 1950 tour to England, along with his Trinidadian compatriot, Lance Pierre, and the Jamaican, Hines Johnson, the trio found themselves reduced to admiring spectators in the wake of the spinners' success.

Jones had played just one Test against England before that series, when he took four for 54 at Bridgetown in 1948. He was selected for the subsequent trip to India and, despite having to bowl on slower pitches, finished with 37 wickets (22.56) including 17 Test victims. His most impressive performance came in the fourth game at Madras, where he took a match-winning four for 30, which clinched the series for the tourists. He maintained his momentum into the final Test at Bombay: India were set 361 runs to win in 395 minutes, Jones took five for 85 in the innings, including centurion Vijay Hazare, and seemed on the verge of engineering an unlikely win, before a bizarre end to the game ensued. Jones prepared to bowl the last delivery of the match, with India needing six runs to win, with eight wickets down and the wicket-keeper unable to bat because of injury. Then, just as the bowler was about to start his run-up, the umpire removed the bails and called time, realising he had miscounted the over amidst the excitement.

Prior Jones

The big Trinidadian toured Australia in 1951-52 and, although he played in most of the state games, he only appeared in one Test, the second at Sydney. Indeed the tourists might have been able to reverse the result if Lindsay Hassett hadn't been dropped off the bowling of Jones, when he was on nine. But, thereafter, the diminutive Australian made no further mistakes and steered his side to victory with a splendid century.

So Jones' career came to an end and, as future West Indian pace men subdued opposing batsmen the world over, he must have rued coming to cricketing maturity when the spinners were enjoying fleeting pre-eminence and the overseas wickets on which he bowled were not always conducive to his style.

Teams: *Trinidad, West Indies*
First-class debut: *8/2/41*
Trinidad v Barbados
First-class record: *169 wickets (26.81)*
and 775 runs (14.09)
Tests: *9*
Test debut: *21/2/48 West Indies v England*
Test record: *25 wickets (30.04)*
and 47 runs (5.22)

JULIEN, Bernard Denis

Born: 13 March 1950, Carnage Village, Trinidad
Role: Right-hand batsman, left-arm fast-medium bowler, orthodox left-arm spinner, left-arm chinaman and googly bowler

BERNARD JULIEN was a top-class all-rounder whose career suffered from premature comparisons with Sobers.

Julien had an illustrious start as a schoolboy cricketer and by the age of 16 had scored a double century for St Mary's College. Soon after he was making his mark for North against South in Trinidad: in one game he took a hat-trick, and eventually finished with eight for 58, opening with the new ball and later switching to left-arm spin. He was also an unorthodox chinaman and googly bowler, as well as being a fine close-in fielder. Indeed, that was part of Julien's problem, he was jack of all trades and failed to take time out to master one or two. Yet, for all that, he remained a very talented cricketer, and impressed Colin Cowdrey sufficiently during a visit to Trinidad, for the former England captain to invite him to join Kent. Julien joined the club in 1970 and, as with his Test career, his performances for them were either outstanding or decidedly ordinary.

As a result of his association with Kent, Julien was a familiar face to English cricket lovers by the time of his Test debut against England in 1973. He began promisingly - scoring 54 in the second Test at Edgbaston - before exploding with a brilliant innings of 121 off 127 balls in the third match at Lord's. He shared in a record seventh wicket partnership of 155 in less than two hours with Sobers, which earned him an extended run in the side.

Julien was in fine form with the bat again for the return series in the Caribbean, scoring 86 not out in a lone show of support for Kallicharran, as the pair engineered a seven-wicket win in the first Test in Trinidad. He followed that with 66 in the next game in Jamaica, and returned his best Test bowling figures of five for 57 in the third match in Barbados. But, after that, Julien ran out of steam and did not shine again until the final match against Pakistan in 1975, when he hit the second hundred of his Test career in Karachi. However, his occasional bursts of brilliance - which could be decisive in one-day cricket - meant he held on to his place for the first World Cup later in 1975. It turned out to be a sound decision: he got West Indies off to a good start by taking four for 20 against

Bernard Julien

Sri Lanka in their opening fixture and took four important wickets for 27 against New Zealand to ease his side into the final.

Julien struggled along with the rest of the side in Australia in 1975-76, but scored 25 crucial runs, adding 91 with Fredericks, in the second Test in Perth, as the pair laid the platform for West Indies' sole win of the series. Although hardly anyone enhanced their reputation on that tour, Julien must have known his days were numbered with the emergence of Richards in the batting department, and the fledgling partnership of Roberts and Holding in the bowling.

Disappointing performances with bat and ball in 1976 sealed his fate at Test level and, after a spell in world series cricket, he joined Lawrence Rowe's team for their tour of South Africa in 1983. Julien later renounced the system of apartheid and had his name removed from the UN blacklist. He returned to play for Trinidad & Tobago, but did not end his career with the same aplomb as he had begun it almost 20 years earlier.

Teams: *Trinidad, North Trinidad, West Indies, Kent, West Indies 'Rebels XI', North-East Trinidad*
First-class debut: *19/4/68 North Trinidad v South Trinidad*
First-class record: *5,793 runs (24.44) and 483 wickets (28.72)*
Tests: *24*
Test debut: *26/7/73 West Indies v England*
Test record: *866 runs (30.92) and 50 wickets (37.36)*

JUMADEEN, Raphick Rasif

Born: 12 April 1948, Harmony Hall, Gasparillo, Trinidad
Role: Left-arm spin bowler

RAPHICK JUMADEEN invariably got a lot of turn out of helpful wickets with his slow left-arm spin; although he was known more for his consistency than the penetrative nature of his bowling. He had a modest Test debut against New Zealand in April 1972, but went on to take nine wickets (30.88) from four Tests in the home series against India in 1976. He was selected to tour England later that year, but received few opportunities, as the pace men ran through England's batting. As a result, he played in just one Test, but took 58 wickets (30.00) in all first-class matches.

After that trip Jumadeen fell from favour, but was recalled to face Australia in 1978 after the defection of the Packer players. He took 11 wickets in two Tests, including three for 34 in the fourth innings of the fourth Test in Trinidad, as he and Derick Parry spun West Indies to victory; and four for 72 in the first innings in Kingston, as Australia made some amends by amassing a total of 343.

Jumadeen played two more Tests, against India in 1978-79, but only increased his wicket-haul by three, although he bowled long, tight spells.

Teams: *Trinidad, South Trinidad, S/C Trinidad, West Indies*
First-class debut: *14/4/67 South Trinidad v North Trinidad*
First-class record: *347 wickets (27.91) and 604 runs (8.50)*
Tests: *12* ***Test debut:*** *20/4/72 West Indies v New Zealand*
Test record: *29 wickets (39.34) and 84 runs (21.00)*

Alvin Kallicharran

KALLICHARRAN, Alvin Isaac

Born: 21 March 1949, Paidama, Berbice, British Guiana
Role: Left-hand batsman

ALVIN KALLICHARRAN almost achieved the impossible by allowing his controversial behaviour to frequently overshadow his world-class batsmanship.

However, there was no debate over his prodigious cricketing ability. After making a significant mark in the Guyana schools team in the West Indies championships in 1966, he became one of the youngest players to appear for Guyana in the Shell Shield the following year.

Like his mentor Kanhai, the diminutive Kallicharran was a touch player and derived his power from his impeccable timing. He was a top-class player of spin bowling, as Clive Lloyd remarked: "[He] is one of the best players of spin bowling I have seen, and one only needs to glance at his scores at Queen's Park Oval - a traditional spinners' paradise - to be convinced of this. This is not to say that he was inadequate against pace and, at his best, is the complete player."

Kallicharran gave notice of the success he was to enjoy in international cricket when he scored a century on his Test debut, against New Zealand in 1972, before his home Georgetown crowd. His last 41 runs were made in just 60 minutes after his innings had been interrupted by a bottle-throwing incident; and he confirmed his class with another hundred in his second Test innings in the final match in Trinidad, making him an automatic choice to meet the touring Australians the following year. He played solidly in that series, almost conjuring a surprise win for West Indies by scoring 53 and 91 on a treacherous Port-of-Spain wicket in the third Test.

He averaged over 40 on the tour of England in 1973, aided by 80 in each innings of the first Test at The Oval; and maintained his momentum in the return series, cracking 158 in the first Test at Port-of-Spain (after being notoriously 'run out' by Tony Greig on 142. Julien had played the last ball of the day to Greig at short-leg, who then ran out Kallicharran, as he began walking back to the pavilion without first grounding his bat. The umpire was obliged to answer Greig's appeal positively, which sparked a huge row and, eventually, resulted in Kallicharran being reinstated after the appeal had been withdrawn), 93 in the second at Kingston and 119 in the third at Bridgetown, adding a record 249 runs for the second wicket with Rowe.

He was majestic in India and Pakistan in 1974-75, scoring 124, 29, 44, 0, 57, 17, 51, 98, 34*, 92, 44, and 115 from seven Tests; and maintained his momentum against the searing pace of Dennis Lillee in an early round of the inaugural World Cup. His breath-taking innings inspired West Indies' victory, as he raced to 78, including crashing one six and seven fours in 10 balls, and then top-scored to help beat New Zealand in the semi-finals. Having cut his teeth against them in the World Cup, Kallicharran stood up well to Lillee and Jeff Thomson - including sustaining a broken nose - on the subsequent dismal visit to Australia. He had another consistent series against the touring Indians in 1976, finishing second in the averages to Richards. The pair shared in a double century third wicket stand in the opening Test in Barbados, before Kallicharran predictably hit an unbeaten 103 in the third Test on his favourite Port-of-Spain ground.

Soon afterwards, the Guyanese was afflicted with fibrositis in his shoulder, which hampered him in England later that year. He grafted for 97, adding 303 for the third wicket with Richards, in the first Test at Trent Bridge, but a pair at Lord's and further discomfort at Old Trafford ruled him out of the rest of the tour. He was clearly below par for the visiting Pakistanis, with his only innings of note being 72 in the third Test at Georgetown.

The left-hander then made headline news as he became one of the first players to sign for Packer's world series cricket - only to back out when he realised it contravened an earlier contract he had signed with a radio station in Queensland. After extricating himself from this delicate situation, Kallicharran returned to lead the official West Indies side who, by this time, were severely depleted by the loss of the other Packer players. Therefore, for the second half of the Test series against Australia in 1978, West Indies fielded what was effectively a second X1 team and won the fourth Test at Port-of-Spain due more to Kallicharran's splendid batting than his captaincy.

There has never been any question over Kallicharran's batting ability, and the runs continued to flow when he skippered West Indies in India in 1978-79, but his captaincy left something to be desired and after becoming the first West Indian to lose a series on the subcontinent, he would not have been surprised to lose it when Lloyd and his fellow Packer players returned to the official fold.

Ironically, however, the loss of the captaincy seemed to have a detrimental effect on his batting and, apart from a century at Adelaide early in 1980, he had a modest tour of Australia and New Zealand and struggled on the subsequent visits to England and Pakistan. Perhaps disenchanted with the way things were going, Kallicharran made the remarkable decision to join the South African side, Transvaal, and thereby had the decidedly dubious distinction of becoming the first West Indian to play Currie Cup cricket in the republic. Not surprisingly, his decision caused uproar in the West Indies, particularly in his native Guyana, who have been one of the most hardline opponents of the government in Pretoria.

But Kallicharran carried on, seemingly unaffected by the controversy, and was one of the most prolific run-scorers in first-class cricket in the early 1980's. Indeed, he came to look on county cricket as his Test cricket and in 1982 scored over 2,000 runs for Warwickshire, with three championship double hundreds - including 230 not out as he shared in a record fourth wicket stand of 470 with Geoff Humpage against Lancashire at Southport - and five single hundreds. Indeed in five of his first seven seasons with Warwickshire, he passed 1,000 first-class runs and has 52 championship centuries to his credit - including a record nine in 1984 - and six double hundreds.

However, mid-way through the 1990 season Kallicharran was forced to announce his retirement after a recurring hand injury hampered his scoring. The Guyanese, who made his home in Birmingham, had convinced the TCCB that he could play for Warwickshire - and even England - as a qualified English man. But, in the end, time ran out on Kallicharran and he was forced to hang up his boots on a glittering career, sometimes marred by controversy.

> ***Teams:*** *Guyana, Berbice, West Indies, Warwickshire, Rest of World XI, Queensland, West Indies 'Rebels XI', Transvaal, Orange Free State*
> ***First-class debut:*** *15/3/67 Guyana v Windward Islands*
> ***First-class record:*** *32,650 runs (43.64) and 84 wickets (47.97)*
> ***Tests:*** *66*
> ***Test debut:*** *6/4/72 West Indies v New Zealand*
> ***Test record:*** *4,399 runs (44.43) and 4 wickets (39.00)*

KANHAI, Rohan Babulal

Born: 26 December 1935, Port Mourant, Berbice, British Guiana
Role: Right-hand batsman, wicket-keeper

ROHAN KANHAI was one of the finest batsmen of his generation. His talent came to the fore when Clyde Walcott went to British Guiana in the 1950's as national coach. They had plenty in common as, apart from their batting talent, both players began their careers as capable wicket-keepers. Indeed, on his first overseas tour, to England in 1957, Kanhai kept in three Tests. He performed admirably, coping with the pace of Gilchrist and Hall behind the stumps and, as makeshift opener in the Tests, that of Fred Trueman and Brian Statham in front of them.

A sparkling 96 runs in the second Test in Trinidad and 62 in front of his home Georgetown crowd against the touring Pakistanis the following year, earned him a place on the trip to India and Pakistan in 1958-59. Forced to open the innings again, he top-scored with 66 in the first Test in Bombay, but was seen at his most glorious when, batting at number three in the third match in Calcutta, he scored 256 out of 614 for five declared, sharing in a double century partnership with Butcher. That innings proved to be a watershed in Kanhai's career, as his extravagant stroke-play marked him out as a player of the highest quality. He was the leading batsman on the tour, and would have increased his aggregate if some careless running had not cost him his wicket when he was on 99 in the fourth Test at Madras.

When West Indies' openers struggled in Pakistan, Kanhai was once again drafted into that role, but he was never comfortable there and confirmed this in the final Test at Lahore when, restored to the number three slot, he scored a match-winning 217, which was more

Rohan Kanhai

than the combined total of any other player on that leg of the tour. He might have changed the outcome of the following home series against England when, having scored 110 in a losing cause in the second Test in Trinidad, he was refused a runner in the next game in Jamaica. West Indies were chasing 230 to win in just over four hours and were hoping Kanhai might lift them to victory. But the Guyanese was hampered by a muscle injury and when, in a mistaken decision, he was not allowed a runner the game drifted into a dull draw.

Kanhai was at his best in Australia in 1960-61. He began ominously well, scoring a hundred against an Australian X1 and a double hundred against Victoria. He made 54 in the first Test at Brisbane and 84 out of a total of 181 in the next match at Melbourne, but saved his best form for the fourth match in Adelaide, where he scored a century in each innings; and made another two Test hundreds against the touring Indians in 1962.

Although he did not reach three figures in the series against England in 1963, his contributions were invariably decisive. He hit 90 in the opening Test at Old Trafford before a moment of rashness cost him his wicket, when he was run out. He top-scored with 73 in the next match at Lord's and missed out on his century again, this time at Headingley, where he scored 92. He was at his most menacing in the final match at The Oval, as England strove to win the game so they could level the series. But Kanhai would have none of this and scored 77 glorious runs in less than even time to scupper their chances.

The Guyanese confirmed his liking for the Australian attack when they toured the Caribbean in 1964-65. He scored a match-winning 89 in difficult conditions in the third Test at Georgetown and 129 on a friendlier Bridgetown pitch, sharing in a double century stand with Nurse. He showed a refreshing consistency by then scoring 121 out of 224 in the final Test at Port-of-Spain to complete an excellent series.

Kanhai's batting set up victory against England at Trent Bridge in 1966, as his uncharacteristically dull 63 helped erase the first innings deficit, before a double century from Butcher gave West Indies an invincible lead in the series. Kanhai then ended a pleasing summer by scoring his first Test hundred in England, in the fifth match at The Oval.

The Guyanese was always at home in England and for many years a prolific run-scorer for Warwickshire: he hit 31 first-class centuries for the club, including 213 in a world record undefeated second wicket stand of 465 with John Jameson against Gloucestershire at Edgbaston in 1974.

In India in 1966-67, Kanhai top-scored with 90 in the second Test at Calcutta which, once again, secured the rubber for the tourists and, after scoring 77 in the final match at Madras, took a well-earned rest from international cricket before returning refreshed to tackle England when they visited the Caribbean in 1967-68. He was in quite sparkling form in the last two matches of that series: he scored 153 in the fourth Test in Trinidad - his fourth century in as many series on the Port-of-Spain ground, adding 273 with Nurse; and followed that with 150 at Georgetown, as this time he shared in a double century stand with Sobers.

He then endured a lean spell in Australia in 1968-69 - apart from 94 in the opening Test at Brisbane - and opted out of the subsequent tour to England. He enjoyed a brief revival against India in 1971 when he prevented the tourists from gaining an early lead in the series by top-scoring with 56 in the first innings of the first Test in Kingston and, following on, helped himself to another 158 runs off the Indian bowlers. However, after that - apart from 85 in the Barbados Test - he went into another temporary decline before surprisingly being elevated to the captaincy for the series against the visiting Australians in 1973. Although West Indies lost the series, consistent batting from Kanhai ensured he retained the captaincy for the short tour of England later that year. A majestic century in the final Test at Lord's from the visiting captain helped clinch the rubber, as West Indies completed their first series win since 1967. However, the jubilation was short-lived as Kanhai had a modest time with the bat in the return rubber and, after England squared the series in the final Test in Trinidad, he was relieved of the captaincy.

Kanhai has gone down in cricketing history as one of West Indies' greatest batsmen - although his obsession with scoring runs quickly occasionally hampered the West Indies as much as his more careful innings helped them. Walcott provided an insight into Kanhai's thinking when he explained that his fetish for keeping the scoreboard moving reflected his desire not to disappoint the people who had such high expectations of him. Nonetheless, this tendency meant that although he was a heavy scorer for the West Indies, Kanhai was never as reliable as someone like Sobers.

Besides his batting, Kanhai's role as interim captain also served West Indian cricket well. He was the first Guyanese to lead the West Indies for an extended period and, in his 13 Tests as captain, he instilled the killer instinct into the side that Lloyd would use to such great effect over the next decade.

Teams: *British Guiana, Guyana, Berbice, West Indies, Trinidad, Commonwealth XI, A.E.R. Gilligan's XI, C. Hunte's XI, Western Australia, Rest of World XI, Indian President's XI, Warwickshire, Tasmania, International XI*
First-class debut: *5/2/55 British Guiana v Barbados*
First-class record: *28,774 runs (49.01), 318 catches & 7 stumpings, and 18 wickets (56.05)*
Tests: *79*
Test debut: *30/5/57 West Indies v England*
Test record: *6,227 runs (47.53), 50 catches, and 0-85*

KENTISH, Esmond Seymour Maurice

Born: 21 November 1916, Cambridge, Jamaica
Role: Right-arm fast bowler

ESMOND KENTISH was a pace bowler, known for his staying power. He made two Test appearances in 1948 and 1954, both against England and both on his home ground at Kingston, and became the oldest man to appear in a varsity match when he played for Oxford against Cambridge at Lord's in 1956, at the age of 39.

In his first Test, he opened the bowling with Hines Johnson and returned match figures of three for 106, but distinguished himself six years later when, bowling at the leg-stump to an on-side field of seven men, he took a match-winning five for 49, as seven wickets crashed for six runs, to give West Indies an early series lead.

Esmond Kentish

After his retirement, Kentish became an administrator in West Indian cricket, serving on the Board of Control and managing several overseas tours. He was later appointed as Governor of the Bank of Jamaica.

Teams: *Jamaica, West Indies, Oxford University*
First-class debut: *6/10/47 Jamaica v British Guiana*
First-class record: *78 wickets (26.71) and 109 runs (13.62)*
Tests: *2*
Test debut: *27/3/48 West Indies v England*
Test record: *8 wickets (22.25) and 1 run (1.00)*

KING, Collis Llewellyn

Born: 11 June 1951, Christ Church, Barbados
Role: Right-hand batsman, medium-pace bowler

COLLIS KING will be remembered above all for his firecracker innings in the 1979 World Cup final. After England had made a remarkably good start by reducing West Indies to 99 for four, King arrived at the wicket to thrash 86 runs off 66 balls. In 21 unbelievable overs of power hitting, the flamboyant Barbadian and, for once, more subdued Richards, added 139 runs and effectively put the game out of England's reach.

King's batting panache was never far from the surface: even during West Indies' vintage summer for batsmen in 1976, he held his own scoring 1,320 first-class runs (55.00), including six glorious hundreds, and took 27 wickets. In the Tests, too, he gave fair warning of what he could do, crashing fifty off 39 balls at Headingley and a sizzling 63 in the run riot at The Oval. His other spectacular innings came in New Zealand in 1980 when he entertained the

Christchurch crowd with an unbeaten century.

Indeed, these type of innings sometimes handicapped him, as when he was banned from playing in the North Wales league for being too good in 1979 - the Welsh had obviously taken their cue from his World Cup performance and the 283 he scored in an afternoon match the year before! Luckily for King, the Lancashire League felt able to cope with his batting excesses.

However, King was lost to official world cricket after he opted to tour South Africa in 1982-84, but even a delicate political situation failed to stem his flow of runs as he topped the batting averages on both trips.

Teams: *Barbados, West Indies, Glamorgan, Worcestershire, West Indies 'Rebels XI', International XI, D.B. Close's XI, Natal*
First-class debut: *6/1/73 Barbados v Combined Islands*
First-class record: *6,770 runs (38.24) and 128 wickets (34.21)*
Tests: *9*
Test debut: *8/7/76 West Indies v England*
Test record: *418 runs (32.15) and 3 wickets (94.00)*

KING, Frank McDonald

Born: 14 December 1926, Bridgetown, Barbados
Role: Right-arm fast bowler

FRANK KING's scathing pace against India in 1953 provided West Indies with the false hope that they had found a new fast bowler to spearhead their attack. He took 17 wickets at under 30 apiece in that series, including his best Test figures of five for 74 in the visitors' first innings in the third match at Port-of-Spain. However, as the only genuine pace man around, he was probably over-bowled in the home series against England and Australia in the mid-1950's. This exacerbated his fitness problems and his Test career ended when his slender frame folded under the pressure in New Zealand in 1956.

Teams: *Barbados, Trinidad, West Indies*
First-class debut: *9/1/48 Barbados v M.C.C.*
First-class record: *90 wickets (28.75) and 237 runs (9.11)*
Tests: *14*
Test debut: *21/1/53 West Indies v India*
Test record: *29 wickets (39.96) and 116 runs (8.28)*

Collis King

KING, Lester Anthony

Born: 27 February 1939, St Catherine Parish, Jamaica
Role: Right-arm fast-medium bowler

Lester King

LESTER KING had a short, but relatively sweet, Test career. A busy fast-medium bowler, he played in two Tests. His most dramatic appearance came on his debut, against India in the final Test at Kingston in 1962, where he dismissed five touring batsmen in an hour to finish with figures of five for 46, and set up victory for the hosts, who completed a whitewash in the series.

King was selected for the 1963 tour of England, but played in the shadow of Hall and Griffith, although he did take 47 wickets (27.31) against the counties. He also toured India in 1966-67 and Australia and New Zealand in 1968-69 but, again, did not appear in the Tests. His final Test appearance had been in the interim series, against England in the final match at Georgetown, but he was not as spectacular as he had been on his debut. Besides, his native Jamaica, King also played for various Indian sides.

Teams: *Jamaica, West Indies, Bengal, The Rest XI, C. Hunte's XI, East Zone, Chidambaram's XI, Chief Minister's XI, Bombay Governor's XI, New Zealand Governor's XI*
First-class debut: *13/10/61 Jamaica v Barbados*
First-class record: *142 wickets (31.42) and 1,404 runs (20.64)*
Tests: *2*
Test debut: *13/4/62 West Indies v India*
Test record: *9 wickets (17.11) and 41 runs (10.25)*

LASHLEY, Patrick "Peter" Douglas

Born: 11 February 1937, Christ Church, Barbados
Role: Left-hand batsman

"PETER" LASHLEY won a place on West Indies' tour of Australia in 1960-61 after a superb double hundred for Barbados against British Guiana at Bridgetown the year before. However, the left-hander failed to live up to his promise, averaging just 19.40. His best performance came in the fifth Test at Melbourne when he scored 41, bolstering the middle order with Joe Solomon. But despite their sensible batting, the tourists trailed on the first innings and eventually lost the game and, with it, the series. Lashley was given a second chance to prove himself, when he was selected for the trip to England in 1966 but, again, was unimpressive in the Tests - apart from a watchful 49 at Trent Bridge, when he opened the innings with Conrad Hunte. Indeed, Lashley never did himself justice at Test level as his remarkable all-round record for Barbados reveals: he is their leading run scorer in the Shell Shield with 2,736 at an average of 55.83 and only Carlisle Best has passed his record of six centuries for the island.

Teams: *Barbados, West Indies*
First-class debut: *11/2/58 Barbados v Pakistan*
First-class record: *4,932 runs (41.44) and 27 wickets (35.48)*
Tests: *4*
Test debut: *9/12/60 West Indies v Australia*
Test record: *159 runs (22.71) and 1 wicket (1.00)*

"Peter" Lashley

LEGALL, Ralph Archibald

Born: 25 February 1926, Bridgetown, Barbados
Died: Deceased - date unknown
Role: Wicket-keeper, right-hand batsman

RALPH LEGALL was one of several distinguished wicket-keepers who briefly held the position in the Test side in the mid-1950's, as West Indies struggled to find a replacement for Walcott, whose back injury had ended his career behind the stumps.

Legall was initiated into Test cricket for the home series against India in 1953. After Alfie Binns had kept in the first Test, Legall took over for the four remaining matches of the series - the only ones of his Test career.

Born in Barbados, Legall moved to Trinidad after being stationed there with the armed forces just after the War. He soon revealed his remarkable all-round sporting talent: besides playing cricket for Trinidad, he also represented them at basketball, soccer and table tennis. Legall also played Davis Cup tennis for the West Indies, which almost certainly makes him the most gifted sportsman ever to emerge from the Caribbean.

Teams: *Trinidad, West Indies*
First-class debut: *15/3/47 Trinidad v British Guiana*
First-class record: *32 catches & 10 stumpings, and 485 runs (22.04)*
Tests: *4*
Test debut: *7/2/53 West Indies v India*
Test record: *8 catches & 1 stumping, and 50 runs (10.00)*

LEWIS, Desmond Michael

Born: 21 February 1946, Kingston, Jamaica
Role: Right-hand batsman, wicket-keeper

DESMOND LEWIS was a highly talented batsman, who also kept wicket. He had his first taste of Test cricket when India visited the Caribbean in 1970-71. In the three matches in which he played he kept tidily and showed great promise with the bat, scoring 81 not out in his first Test at Georgetown, 88 in his second at Bridgetown, where he opened the innings with Fredericks, and 72 in his third at Port-of-Spain, where again he opened the innings. But, by the time of the next series he had been discarded in favour of the specialist 'keeper, Mike Findlay, and was left to cherish a Test average of almost Bradmanesque proportions.

Teams: *Jamaica, West Indies*
First-class debut: *25/7/70 Jamaica v Glamorgan*
First-class record: *67 catches & 11 stumpings, and 1,623 runs (31.82)*
Tests: *3*
Test debut: *19/3/71 West Indies v India*
Test record: *8 catches, and 259 runs (86.33)*

LLOYD, Clive Hubert

Born: 31 August 1944, Queenstown, Georgetown, British Guiana
Role: Left-hand batsman

CLIVE LLOYD is the most successful Test captain of all time. He led the West Indies in a record 74 matches, including 26 successive games without defeat, and to a record 36 victories. Besides his remarkable leadership qualities, Lloyd is also one of West Indies' greatest batsmen - only Sobers and Richards have a higher Test aggregate - and a world class fielder. He has held more catches for the West Indies than anyone apart from Sobers, Richards, Greenidge and wicket-keepers, Deryck Murray and Jeff Dujon. Lloyd rose quickly through the ranks of youth cricket in his native Guiana, appearing regularly for the powerful Demerara team, who had previously enjoyed the services of his illustrious cousin, Lance Gibbs. He played for the national side in 1964 but was dropped after an indifferent game against Jamaica and failed to distinguish himself against the touring Australians the following year.

It seemed Lloyd might struggle to establish himself in top-class cricket when he was dismissed by Sobers for a duck in his first Shell Shield innings, against Barbados in 1966. But a second innings century against the bowling of Sobers and Charlie Griffith allayed any doubts, while 194 against Jamaica in the next match at Kingston, confirmed his potential. He was selected to tour India in 1966-67, and immediately proved his worth with 82 and 78 not out in his first Test at Bombay, sharing in a match-winning century stand with Sobers in the second innings; and followed that up with hundreds against the Prime Minister's XI in Delhi and Ceylon at Colombo.

Lloyd was one of the star batsmen when England visited the Caribbean in 1967-68, hitting timely centuries in the Tests at Port-of-Spain and Bridgetown in what turned out to be a trying series for the hosts. He began well in Australia in 1968-69, scoring a hundred in the opening Test at Brisbane before his form dipped with the rest of the side. He lifted himself in the short series in England in 1969 - the first year he appeared for Lancashire - scoring a rapid 70 in the Lord's Test and an exhilarating double century against Glamorgan at Swansea.

The retirement of Butcher and Nurse put the batting spotlight on Lloyd, something he did not appear to relish as he struggled to repeat his overseas successes in three consecutive home series. Indeed, his undistinguished showing against the New Zealanders in 1972 meant that his inclusion to meet the touring Australians the following year was widely criticised. But Lloyd answered his critics when he slammed 178 - with one six and 24 fours - on his home ground in the fourth Test at Georgetown, adding a record 187 for the fourth wicket with his compatriot, Kanhai.

Lloyd confirmed his revival with a vintage summer in England in 1973, averaging over 60 in the three-match Test series. Indeed, he has always thrived in England and was a central figure in Lancashire's renaissance in the early 1970's, including helping them to win the Gillette Cup four times in the first half of the decade, as he collected a record eight Man of the Match awards. He was appointed captain of the county in 1981.

Despite his usual success against England, fate did not smile on him when they visited the Caribbean in 1973-74 but, nonetheless, he was appointed captain for the trip to India and Pakistan later that year. The responsibility seemed to bring added consistency to his batting, as he made 14 of his 19 Test hundreds as skipper. His first came in the first Test at Bangalore, as he crashed 163 runs, sharing in a double century stand with Greenidge for the fourth wicket. He completed a superb series with a career-best 242 not out in the final match at Bombay, sharing in another double century stand, this time with Deryck Murray. Altogether, Lloyd scored 636 runs (79.50) in the series, which was decisive in helping West Indies to win the rubber as, in the two Tests they lost, Lloyd failed with the bat.

He was in match-winning form in the first World Cup final in 1975, as his century secured the trophy for the West Indies; but he faced a far stiffer test against the same opponents, Australia, over an extended period 'Down Under' in 1975-76. Despite enduring a drubbing at the hands of their hosts, Lloyd excelled with the bat, hammering 149 in the second Test at Perth and 102 and 91 not out in the two matches played in Melbourne, to make him the most successful touring batsman.

And, despite the intense disappointment felt at the time, Lloyd had learnt a vital lesson in Australia: catches win matches, but so do fast bowlers. By the time India toured the Caribbean in 1975-76, Roberts and Holding, supported by Julien, provided Lloyd with a penetrating pace attack

Left: Clive Lloyd

and this together with fine batting - including Lloyd's 10th Test hundred in his 50th Test, in the opening match at Bridgetown - overwhelmed the tourists, despite an unexpected win in the third Test in Trinidad, after Lloyd had misjudged the declaration.

Lloyd's pace bowlers - now joined by Daniel and Holder - enjoyed unprecedented success in England later that year and, on the only occasion that the batting faltered, in the first innings of the Lord's Test, Lloyd lifted them with 50, and then crashed another half century off the demoralised English attack in the final match at The Oval. Altogether, he scored over 1,000 first-class runs on that tour, including another unbeaten double century off Glamorgan, this time in just two hours, to equal the record for the fastest double hundred in first-class cricket.

Lloyd scored an impressive century against the touring Pakistanis in the first Test at Bridgetown in 1977; and continued in this rich vein against the Australians the following year, before pulling out of the rubber to join Kerry Packer's world series cricket. It was a significant step for this was the first time that an incumbent West Indian captain had resigned and there was no guarantee he would ever play Test cricket again, far less be re-appointed to the captaincy. However, his gifts as a batsman and captain were such that when the rift had healed, he was the natural choice to take over again. He confirmed the wisdom of his re-appointment, leading West Indies to success in the 1979 World Cup and then secured their first series win in Australia immediately afterwards.

The success of the West Indies continued unabated: they predictably overwhelmed England in 1980, as the Guyanese lifted his team with 101 in front of his adopted 'home' crowd in the third Test at Old Trafford. Lloyd never scored less than 50 in the return rubber in the Caribbean, even if his series average of 76 was almost 100 short of his Shield average of 172.50 for that year; and then hit a match-winning 77 not out in the third Test against Australia in the short series of 1981-82, to level the series and end premature talk of West Indies' tumble from the top of world cricket.

During these years, however, Lloyd's success was not all at international level and in 1983 he led Guyana to a unique double success in the Shell Shield and the Geddes Grant-Harrison Line Trophy, before returning to the international arena to hit two hundreds against the touring Indians, and ease West Indies to a 2-0 victory in the series.

Known as 'supercat' for his feline prowess in the covers, Lloyd and his team then exacted a savage revenge over the Indians in India after they had been defeated by them in the World Cup in mid-summer, an event Lloyd rates as his biggest disappointment. Like injured lions, the West Indies stalked their prey, winning the one-day series 5-0 and the Test series 3-0, as Lloyd topped the batting averages in the Tests with 82.66, helped by another two centuries.

The West Indies machine seemed unstoppable: they defeated Australia decisively in the Caribbean at the beginning of 1984 and romped to their third successive victory in England, as they defeated the home country five matches to nil later that year. Then came Lloyd's opportunity to set the record straight in Australia after his team's mauling almost a decade earlier. The Guyanese left nothing to chance, thrashing 114 runs in the second Test at Brisbane to give his side a two-nil lead in the five match series; he scored 78 at Adelaide and wrapped up a gratifying campaign with a masterful 72 on a difficult wicket at Sydney. In recognition of his services to cricket, Lloyd was awarded the Order of Australia at the end of that tour, and also received the second highest honour in his native Guyana, the Order of Roirama.

Now, at last, having completed a record-breaking 11 consecutive Test victories with the win in the third match at Adelaide, Lloyd could retire a satisfied man. So, what was the secret of his success? Joel Garner, one of Lloyd's regular match-winners, argued that "Worrell inspired his men, Sobers led mainly by example and Lloyd combined the best features of both". That is probably an accurate assessment of his approach, but Lloyd himself revealed perhaps the most crucial ingredient when he wrote, just before his retirement, "The most important requirement for a successful captain is respect. I have been fortunate that my players have respected me as a man and a cricketer and consequently as a skipper."

Teams: *British Guiana, Guyana, West Indies, Lancashire, Rest of World XI, New Zealand Governor's XI*
First-class debut: *5/3/64 British Guiana v Jamaica*
First-class record: *31,232 runs (49.26) and 114 wickets (36.00)*
Tests: *110*
Test debut: *13/12/66 West Indies v India*
Test record: *7,515 runs (46.67) and 10 wickets (62.20)*

LOGIE, Augustine Lawrence

Born: 28 September 1960, La Brea, Sobo, Trinidad
Role: Right-hand batsman

GUS LOGIE certainly makes up in ability what he lacks in stature. The 5ft 4in right-hander made his Test debut against India early in 1983 after a succession of good scores for Trinidad & Tobago in the Shell Shield and impressing with 163 for Young West Indies against Young England in St Lucia in 1980.

However, he did not have an auspicious start to his Test career: in his first three matches, his scores were 13, 10, 13 and 0 before he put his nerves behind him and scored a splendid 130 in the fourth match at Bridgetown, after being given a 'life' early in his innings. That innings won him a place on the tour to the subcontinent for the return series but, again, he seemed ill at ease and a pair in the third Test at Ahmedabad brought his international career to a temporary halt. Indeed, Logie might have anticipated a long wait before getting a second chance given the emergence of Richardson and the renaissance of Gomes.

But more domestic success speeded his recall and he appeared against the visiting Australians in 1984. He shone in front of his home crowd in the second Test at Port-of-Spain, scoring 97, as he shared in partnerships of 100 for the fifth wicket with Richards and 158 for the sixth with Dujon. Although he was still not an automatic choice for the Test side, he made the tour to England in 1984 and the subsequent trip to Australia. He was particularly impressive in England where his fluent batting - which brought him 585 first-class runs (73.12) - and brilliant fielding won him many fans.

Logie didn't make a Test appearance against Pakistan in 1986 and was disappointing in New Zealand in 1987, but finally found the consistency that his batting had always promised on the subsequent tour of India: his 46 in the first Test at Delhi provided crucial support to Richards' match-winning effort, before he scored a chanceless century at Calcutta, and wrapped up a pleasing series with a skilful 67 in a losing cause on a vicious Madras pitch. For good measure, he was a constant and quick scorer in the one-day games.

He averaged over 40 in that series and - apart from a leaner time in Pakistan in 1988 and against Australia in 1988-89 - has kept up that momentum, finally rewarding the faith the selectors have shown in him. Indeed, he had a vintage summer in England in 1988, topping the averages with 72.80, including 81 and 95 not out at Lord's - a performance that won him the Man of the Match award - and a cameo innings of 47, as he added 69 with Dujon in the only substantial partnership of the innings, in the final Test at The Oval.

He maintained his momentum when India visited the Caribbean in 1989 and his 212 runs (42.40) in the following series against England suggests that he has at last reached maturity as a Test batsman. Indeed, it is critical for his game that he continues to get international exposure, as he adamantly refuses to play for anyone other than his third division club side, Texaco-Brighton, at home, arguing: "When you're a nobody no one wants to know you, but when you make it all the bigger clubs want to grab you. I've always had this policy that if I start here, I finish here. I've made the Trinidad team and now the West Indies team and I have no reason to change." The moral of the tale, as West Indies' selectors have found out with Logie, is surely that loyalty often pays.

Teams: *Trinidad, South Trinidad, S/C Trinidad, West Indies*
First-class debut: *6/1/78 South Trinidad v Central Trinidad*
First-class record: *6,241 runs (35.26) and 3 wickets (42.66)*
Tests: *40*
Test debut: *23/2/83 West Indies v India*
Test record: *1,919 runs (34.89) and 0-4*

Gus Logie

McMORRIS, Easton Dudley Ashton St John

Born: 4 April 1935, Kingston, Jamaica
Role: Right-hand batsman

EASTON McMORRIS made an undistinguished Test debut against Pakistan at Port-of-Spain in 1958; and then appeared against England at Bridgetown in 1960 and suffered the ultimate nightmare: without having faced a delivery, he was run out off a no-ball backing up at the non-strikers end. He seemed fated when he was injured in the third Test at Kingston, but nonetheless scored a brave 73 in front of his home supporters. But it was all to no avail as he was left out of the tour to Australia in 1960-61, and had to wait until the Indians visited the Caribbean in 1961-62 for a recall. He was in fine form against them scoring 125 in the second Test at Kingston - as he shared in a record double hundred partnership with Kanhai - and 50 and 56 in the fourth game at Port-of-Spain, which produced an average of almost 60 for the series. McMorris toured England in 1963 and 1966, but disappointed in his four Test appearances. He seemed far happier on hard, true Caribbean pitches and for a while was the leading run-scorer for Jamaica in the Shell Shield, whom he captained successfully for several years.

Easton McMorris

Teams: *Jamaica, West Indies, The Rest XI, F. Worrell's XI*
First-class debut: *11/10/56 Jamaica v British Guiana*
First-class record: *5,906 runs (42.18)*
Tests: *13*
Test debut: *5/2/58 West Indies v Pakistan*
Test record: *564 runs (26.85)*

McWATT, Clifford Aubrey

Born: 1 February 1923, British Guiana
Role: Wicket-keeper, left-hand batsman

CLIFFORD McWATT was one of the merry and distinguished band of wicket-keepers tried out at Test level in the mid-1950's. As with the others, his appearances were somewhat irregular. He toured India as deputy to Walcott in 1948-49, but didn't make his Test debut until the first match against England at Kingston in 1954. He kept tidily and scored 54 and 36 not out, which secured his place for the remainder of the series. He maintained his batting momentum in the third Test at Georgetown: again he scored 54, adding 99 for the eighth wicket with John Holt, after the first seven home wickets had fallen for 139. A tight single as he strove for the century partnership resulted in McWatt being run out, and his home fans showing their anger by showering the out-field with bottles and other debris. After that series McWatt made only one other Test appearance, in the second match against Australia at Port-of-Spain in 1955, as the selectors reverted to their more erratic ways.

Clifford McWatt

McWatt was a lucky batsman which earned him the nickname of 'McCatt' (nine lives) and he had a particular liking for the Trinidadian attack as he showed when he made 123 not out against them at Port-of-Spain in 1946-47 and 128 at Georgetown in 1953.

Teams: *British Guiana, West Indies*
First-class debut: *11/3/44 British Guiana v Trinidad*
First-class record: *1,673 runs (28.84), 45 catches & 6 stumpings, and 2 wickets (47.50)*
Tests: *6*
Test debut: *15/1/54 West Indies v England*
Test record: *202 runs (28.85), 9 catches and 1 stumping, and 1 wicket (16.00)*

MADRAY, Ivan Samuel

Born: 2 July 1934, Berbice, British Guiana
Role: Right-hand batsman, leg-spin bowler

IVAN MADRAY was a useful middle-order batsman and gifted leg-break bowler, who played in the second Test at Port-of-Spain and the fourth at Georgetown against Pakistan in 1958. However, he failed to distinguish at this level, scoring just three runs and did not take a wicket.

Teams: *British Guiana, West Indies*
First-class debut: *20/4/55 British Guiana v Australia*
First-class record: *73 runs (9.12) and 16 wickets (38.81)*
Tests: *2*
Test debut: *5/2/58 West Indies v Pakistan*
Test record: *3 runs (1.00) and 0-108*

M

MARSHALL, Malcolm Denzil

Born: 18 April 1958, Pine, Bridgetown, Barbados
Role: Right-arm fast bowler, right-hand batsman

MALCOLM MARSHALL secured the title of the fastest bowler in the world when he ran through India's batting in the two series played by the West Indies in 1983. In the second series, hosted on the subcontinent at the end of that year, he equalled the record number of wickets taken by a West Indian in India by dismissing 33 batsmen.

It was all a long way from his early cricketing days: the Barbadian started out as a promising batsman, who bowled gentle medium-pacers, before stepping up several gears in the bowling department under the auspices of Charlie Griffith and Seymour Nurse.

After making his mark in school and club cricket in Barbados, Marshall made his first-class debut against Jamaica in the final match of the 1977-78 Shell Shield season. With the announcement of the West Indies tour party to India and Sri Lanka later that year imminent, Marshall bowled his heart out to take six for 77, which won him a place in the squad. Despite finishing as the leading wicket-taker in the first-class matches with 42, his im-pact in the Tests was marginal, as he struggled on the sluggish Indian pitches. But 25 scalps in the subsequent Shield series kept his place in the West Indies World Cup squad even though, by this time, the Packer players had returned to the fold.

Malcolm Marshall

In the event he had to sit out the World Cup, but was compensated by the success he enjoyed that year in his first season with Hampshire, including taking nine wickets on his debut against Glamorgan.

He matured as a Test bowler in Pakistan in 1980-81 taking 13 wickets in the four match series at 24 apiece, including four for 25 in the second Test in Faisalabad. Yet after five tours, Marshall still had only 11 Tests to his name. But the clearing up of a nagging back injury after the trip to Australia in 1981-82 brought rich rewards for his adopted county. Fully fit for the 1982 English season he took a record 134 victims - 49 more than the next bowler - for a 22-match season, including 39 from just four games.

By 1983 Marshall was an automatic choice for the West Indies team and acknowledged as the fastest bowler in the world. He took 21 wickets (23.57) against India in the Caribbean in 1982-83, including five for 37 bowling round the wicket on a rain-affected pitch in the second Test in Trinidad. He peaked in India at the end of 1983, as his 33 wickets included four in each innings of the first Test at Kanpur and a remarkable six for 37 in the fifth in Calcutta. He finished a memorable series by taking five for 72 in India's only innings in the sixth Test at Madras, including dismissing both openers without a run on the board. For good measure, the Barbadian had also scored 92 hard-hit runs at Kanpur to ease the visitors to a decisive victory.

He collected another 21 wickets (22.85) against the touring Australians in 1984, including five for 42 at Bridgetown as the visitors collapsed to a record-low 97 all out in their second innings and wrapped up the series with five for 51 in the fifth Test in Kingston.

Always keen to do well against England, Marshall enjoyed a remarkable match against them at Headingley in 1984. Despite a broken thumb he joined Gomes at the wicket and stayed around long enough for the Trinidadian to reach his century, and even managed to hit a boundary himself. Then, in a remarkable bowling performance in England's second innings, Marshall returned his best Test figures of seven for 53 off a shortened run. Incredibly he was able to take a sharp return catch off his own bowling to dismiss Graeme Fowler, the top scorer in the innings, and took another wicket with his next ball.

By this time he seemed almost invincible and humbled the Australians in 1984-85. He took five wickets in an innings on four successive occasions, and accounted for 10 batsmen in the third Test at Adelaide. When he failed to take a wicket, in the fifth match at Sydney, West Indies lost their first Test for three years. Marshall finished the campaign with 28 wickets (19.78) which won him the Man of the Series award, a title he collected in the subsequent series against New Zealand and England, as he took 27 economical Test wickets against each country. He saved his best performance for his home crowd against the New Zealanders in the third Test at Bridgetown: he removed two batsmen before they had scored so, at one stage, the tourists' first innings stood at one run for three wickets. After scoring 63 himself, he returned to capture seven more New Zealand wickets coming round the wicket.

Marshall took his 200th Test wicket against England in the second Test at Port-of-Spain in 1986 in a shorter time than any other West Indian bowler. He celebrated by thrashing an unbeaten 62 off the English attack and followed this assault with a quick-fire 76 in the fifth match in Antigua.

Appointed vice-captain for the tour to Pakistan in 1986, Marshall predictably finished as the leading wicket-taker, although he was less impressive in New Zealand as his nine wickets were uncharacteristically costly at over 32 apiece - costly that is by his own remarkable standards. Not surprisingly jaded by the huge amount of top-class cricket he has packed into his career, Marshall opted out of the subsequent tour of India. Against Pakistan in 1988, a knee injury meant he missed four of the one-day internationals and the first Test. Although he bowled at top pace at the start of Pakistan's first innings in Trinidad and on the third evening of the Barbados Test, he relied more on control and movement for his 15 wickets.

Invariably at his best against England, he was in record-breaking form against them later in 1988, as he took a remarkable 35 Test wickets (12.65) including seven for 22 at Old Trafford, shaking off the challenge of any young pretenders who had thoughts of wresting the title of world's premier fast bowler from him. He had a more modest series in Australia but confirmed his pre-eminence when he became West Indies' leading wicket-taker, with 310, when he dismissed Mohammed Azharuddin in the second Test against India at Bridgetown to the delight of his home supporters. Indeed, Lance Gibbs, the previous record holder, was among the Bajan crowd as his record fell and Marshall went on to yet another five-wicket haul in a Test innings. The pace man demonstrated his commitment by taking 11 wickets in the third Test in Trinidad despite an injury to his right hand, that was diagnosed as a fractured wrist a few weeks later.

At the age of 33, and with a crop of hungry fast bowlers hard on his heels, Marshall has now relinquished his role as West Indies' main strike bowler. But, he has already been successful in modifying his action to accommodate his advancing years and could certainly pass 400 Test wickets. It is indicative of his remarkable talent that, of those players who have reached 300 Test wickets, Marshall has the best strike rate.

Teams: *Barbados, West Indies, Hampshire, M.C.C.*
First-class debut: *17/2/78 Barbados v Jamaica*
First-class record: *1,396 wickets (18.22) and 8,757 runs (24.46)*
Tests: *68*
Test debut: *15/12/78 West Indies v India*
Test record: *329 wickets (20.76) and 1,457 runs (18.44)*

MARSHALL, Norman Edgar

Born: 27 February 1924, St Thomas, Barbados
Role: Right-hand batsman, off-spin bowler

NORMAN MARSHALL was a capable all-rounder, whose sole Test appearance came against Australia in the third match at Georgetown in 1955. He made nought and eight and took two for 62, and was not given another chance to establish his credentials at Test level. He is the older brother of Roy Marshall.

Teams: *Barbados, Trinidad, North Trinidad, West Indies*
First-class debut: *8/2/41 Barbados v Trinidad*
First-class record: *1,337 runs (30.38) and 90 wickets (31.72)*
Tests: *1*
Test debut: *26/4/55 West Indies v Australia*
Test record: *8 runs (4.00) and 2 wickets (31.00)*

MARSHALL, Roy Edwin

Born: 25 April 1930, St Thomas, Barbados
Role: Right-hand batsman, off-spinner

ROY MARSHALL was a top-class opening batsman who would surely have enjoyed a prolific Test career had he not opted to play for Hampshire in the days before such county allegiances were allowed.

Roy Marshall

Always a heavy run-scorer, after making his debut for Barbados at the age of 15, Marshall hit 191 against British Guiana at Bridgetown in 1949 before he was 20. This secured him a place in the West Indies' tour party to England where, as the youngest member, he enjoyed great success: he scored over 1,000 first-class runs (39.89) including centuries against Leicestershire, Surrey and, significantly, his future employers, Hampshire.

Yet the opening partnership of Rae and Stollmeyer remained intact for the Tests and it wasn't until the subsequent trip to Australia and New Zealand that Marshall finally got his chance in Test cricket. He made his debut in the first match at Brisbane, where he hit his best score of the series - a disappointing 30 - as injury to other players forced him down the order to bolster the middle batting. However, he was seen at his best against New South Wales in Sydney and Otago at Dunedin, where he cracked sparkling hundreds.

However, Marshall ruled himself out of further contention for a Test place when he signed for Hampshire in 1953. He enjoyed 20 glorious seasons with the county and by the end of his career had amassed more first-class runs than any other West Indian player. Altogether Marshall scored 60 centuries for Hampshire including 212 to clinch a famous victory over Somerset at Bournemouth in 1961, a year in which his batting played a decisive role in his adopted county winning their first championship, as he scored over 2,600 first-class runs.

Although he would have been the perfect foil for Conrad Hunte during these years for the West Indies Test side, Marshall could take heart from the fact that his style of batting set the tone for the West Indian batsmen of the future who would entrance the cricket-loving public in England with their bravado.

Teams: *Barbados, West Indies, Hampshire, Commonwealth XI, M.C.C., The South XI, Duke of Norfolk's XI, The Players XI, T.N. Pearce's XI, Rest of League XI, International XI, Cavaliers XI, Rest of World XI*
First-class debut: *26/1/46 Barbados v Trinidad*
First-class record: *35,725 runs (35.94) and 176 wickets (28.93)*
Tests: *4*
Test debut: *9/11/51 West Indies v Australia*
Test record: *143 runs (20.42) and 0-15*

MARTIN, Frank Reginald

Born: 12 October 1893, Jamaica
Died: 23 November 1967
Role: Left-hand batsman, off-spinner

FRANK MARTIN was one of the key figures in West Indies' first victory over Australia, at Sydney in 1931, when he carried his bat for 123 runs.

Martin invariably saved his best innings for auspicious occasions: on his first-class debut he hit 195 for Jamaica against Barbados at Bridgetown in 1925 and scored well against Freddie Calthorpe's MCC side the following season. Then he scored 270 runs from three matches against Lionel Tennyson's England touring teams in 1926-27 and again in 1928-29.

The Jamaican was not overawed batting in a Test setting either, scoring 44 in West Indies' first-ever Test at Lord's in 1928 and 41 in the third game at The Oval, to help top the Test averages with almost 30. Indeed, he was the leading scorer on the tour, hitting almost 1,400 runs and, for good measure, took 19 wickets with his slow off-spin.

When England toured the Caribbean in 1929-30 Martin, like some of his colleagues, could not get time off from work to play in all of the Tests and only appeared in the fourth on his home ground at Sabina Park. However, it would have pleased him that he was selected for the first tour to Australia the following year and was instrumental in securing their first Test victory after a difficult series. Having been completely out-played in their first four matches, Martin was one of two West Indian centurions to lift the visitors to a morale-boosting win, as he added 70 for the first wicket with Roach and 152 with the other century-maker, Headley.

Martin's contributions were not limited to the batting department, as the docile Australian pitches meant that he was called upon to bowl extensively, once the pace men started to struggle.

He was selected for the trip to England in 1933 and, after performing well in the early county matches, seemed set for a good Test series before he stood on the ball and wrenched his ankle in the game against Middlesex, which put him out of contention.

Martin had an enigmatic temperament: although he was usually a calm and composed figure, he sometimes suffered from rushes of blood to the head which resulted in him sacrificing his wicket in a seemingly careless manner while, on other occasions, he would play sensibly for long periods. This was particularly useful when he was promoted to open the innings with Roach - as had happened in Sydney - who was a flamboyant player, who benefited from batting with a calm partner.

Teams: *Jamaica, West Indies*
First-class debut: *21/1/25 Jamaica v Barbados*
First-class record: *3,589 runs (37.78) and 74 wickets (42.55)*
Tests: *9*
Test debut: *23/6/28 West Indies v England*
Test record: *486 runs (28.58) and 8 wickets (77.37)*

Frank Martin

MARTINDALE, Emmanuel Alfred

Born: 25 November 1909, Barbados
Died: 17 March 1972
Role: Right-arm fast bowler

MANNY MARTINDALE carried West Indies' pace attack in their early years of Test match status with the same skill and panache as Headley did their batting.

A relatively short, but powerful, man Martindale quickly won recognition as West Indies' first great Test fast bowler. He bowled 'bodyline' at England in 1933 - splitting Wally Hammond's chin in the second Test at Old Trafford - as he and Constantine gave the hosts a taste of their own medicine. Altogether Martindale collected 14 wickets (17.92) from three Test innings, including four for 85 at Lord's and five for 73 at Old Trafford. The next most successful bowler was "Puss" Achong, who took five wickets.

On a difficult tour Martindale finished with 103 wickets and doubtless wished he could have shared the new ball with Constantine for more than one Test, as the latter had commitments in the Lancashire League. Indeed, the potential difference was revealed when the pair joined forces for the home series in the Caribbean in 1935. Ironically, Martindale enjoyed his finest hour on the marshy wicket served up at Bridgetown in the only Test in which Constantine did not play. In impossible batting conditions, Martindale became the local hero as he took five English wickets for 22, even though the tourists juggled their batting to try and keep their best batsmen away from the Bajan magician until the pitch improved. In an altogether curious match Martindale finished with figures of eight for 61, but West Indies lacked the firepower to complete the job and Hammond ushered England home with a chancy 29 not out, including a winning six over extra-cover off Martindale.

In the deciding Test in Kingston, Martindale once again damaged a batsman's features as, this time, he fractured the England captain, Bob Wyatt's jaw. He finished the match with seven wickets for 84 and Constantine with six for 68, as the pair lifted West Indies to their first series victory over England.

Another four years elapsed before the two sides met again and, although Martindale had been playing league cricket during this time, he was past his best. It is a telling feature of early West Indian Test cricket that, in his six year career, Martindale played just 10 matches. But if his figures are analysed pro-rata, it quickly becomes apparent that Martindale compares with the finest fast bowlers of today.

Like many West Indian quick bowlers, Martindale enjoyed batting and made 134 in an

Manny Martindale

inter-territorial match against Trinidad, sharing in a partnership of 255 for the eighth wicket with "Foffie" Williams in 1935-36, which remains a West Indian record.

Teams: *Barbados, West Indies, C.A. Merry's XI*
First-class debut: *24/9/29 Barbados v British Guiana*
First-class record: *203 wickets (25.64) and 972 runs (15.18)*
Tests: *10*
Test debut: *24/6/33 West Indies v England*
Test record: *37 wickets (21.72) and 58 runs (5.27)*

MATTIS, Everton Hugh

Born: 11 April 1957, Jamaica
Role: Right-hand batsman

EVERTON MATTIS enjoyed fleeting recognition at Test level when he appeared in the home series against England in 1981. A succession of good scores for Jamaica, culminating in a superb 132 against Guyana, catapulted him into the Test side but, once there, he did not do as well as expected. He made a duck on his debut in the first match in Trinidad and 16 and 24 in the third in Barbados. Although he lifted himself with 71 and 34 in the final two Tests of the series, he was not selected for the subsequent tour to Australia.

Instead he went with West Indies' Under-26 side to Zimbabwe, where he improved his form. His success on that trip and more heavy scoring for Jamaica in 1981-82 made a Test recall seem highly likely, but he squandered his chances when he agreed to tour South Africa in 1982-83. He justified his decision by claiming he was in severe financial difficulties. It was an unfortunate end to a promising Test career. Perhaps if he had been taken to Australia in 1981-82 he would have realised his early potential, but Mattis was not prepared to risk being permanently on the edge of Test selection when there was a lucrative alternative on offer.

Teams: *Jamaica, West Indies, West Indies 'Rebels XI'*
First-class debut: *28/1/77 Jamaica v Combined Islands*
First-class record: *2,064 runs (33.29) and 9 wickets (9.88)*
Tests: *4*
Test debut: *13/2/81 West Indies v England*
Test record: *145 runs (29.00) and 0-14*

MENDONCA, Ivor Leon

Born: 13 July 1934, British Guiana
Role: Wicket-keeper, right-hand batsman

IVOR MENDONCA was a fine wicket-keeper-batsman who had the misfortune to reach cricketing maturity at a time when several other such players had already laid claim to the position in the Test side.

His only chances at Test level came when he stood in for Hendriks after the latter had been injured, in the second and fourth Tests against India in 1962. Mendonca met with considerable success, especially on his debut at Kingston. In a pleasing all-round performance he scored 78 runs, adding 127 for the seventh wicket with Sobers, and took four catches and made one stumping in the match; he duplicated that wicket-keeping effort by making a further five dismissals in the game in Trinidad. Despite this commendable effort he was replaced by Deryck Murray for the 1963 series against England and did not represent the West Indies again.

Teams: *British Guiana, West Indies*
First-class debut: *24/1/59 British Guiana v Barbados*
First-class record: *25 catches & 5 stumpings, and 407 runs (31.30)*
Tests: *2*
Test debut: *7/3/62 West Indies v India*
Test record: *8 catches & 2 stumpings, and 81 runs (40.50)*

MILLER, Roy

Born: 24 December 1924, Jamaica
Died : Deceased - date unknown
Role: Right-hand batsman, right-arm fast-medium bowler

ROY MILLER was a capable all-rounder who played just one Test, the fourth match of the series against India at Georgetown in 1953. Coming in at number eight he scored 23 and took nought for 28 in the tourists' first innings. He was not given another opportunity to prove himself at the highest level.

Teams: *Jamaica, West Indies*
First-class debut: *10/3/51 Jamaica v British Guiana*
First-class record: *231 runs (25.66) and 14 wickets (45.35)*
Tests: *1*
Test debut: *11/3/53 West Indies v India*
Test record: *23 runs (23.00) and 0-28*

Everton Mattis

Cyril Merry

MERRY, Cyril Arthur

Born: 20 January 1911, Scarborough, Tobago
Died: 19 April 1964
Role: Right-hand batsman

CYRIL MERRY was the first player from Tobago to play Test cricket. On his day, he was a breath-taking batsman with all the strokes at his command. He toured England in 1933 and made 856 first-class runs (28.53), including 146 against Warwickshire. He and Headley entertained the Edgbaston crowd with some majestic batting, adding 228 for the fifth wicket in just 120 minutes. However, he was unable to reproduce that kind of form in the Test matches.

Many years later Jeff Stollmeyer argued that Merry was not, perhaps, Test match material at that time, but felt he was very unlucky to miss out on the 1939 tour to England. By then Stollmeyer believed Merry was the best batsman in Trinidad & Tobago and wrote: "Experienced, mature and with a resounding cover drive I can conclude that if he had been selected I would have been omitted".

Teams: *Trinidad, West Indies, C.A. Merry's XI*
First-class debut: *22/1/30 Trinidad v M.C.C.*
First-class record: *1,547 runs (27.14) and 33 wickets (22.60)*
Tests: *2* ***Test debut:*** *24/6/33 West Indies v England*
Test record: *34 runs (8.50)*

MOSELEY, Ezra Alphonsa

Born: 5 January 1958, Christ Church, Barbados
Role: Right-arm fast-medium bowler, right-hand batsman

EZRA MOSELEY made his Test debut at the age of 32 against England in Trinidad in 1990, becoming the first West Indian player to benefit from the ICC resolution that provided an amnesty for cricketers who had been to South Africa prior to 1 April 1989.

Moseley's decision to tour the republic with Lawrence Rowe's rebel side in the early 1980's sidelined him from first-class competition, but commendable all-round performances on the highly competitive club circuit in Barbados and equally pleasing efforts in the north of England leagues enabled him to maintain his form and fitness. An outstanding Red Stripe Cup season in 1990, when he finished as Barbados' leading wicket-taker with 22 (24.63), catapulted him into the Test side. In his first match, Moseley took three wickets, scored 26 runs, held one catch and broke Graham Gooch's left little finger, which put the England captain out of the series. Moseley took another three wickets in the next game at Bridgetown, before being replaced by Baptiste for the final Test. Moseley has played county cricket for Glamorgan.

Ezra Moseley

Teams: *Barbados, West Indies, West Indies 'Rebels XI', Glamorgan, Eastern Province, Rest of World XI*
First-class debut: *30/4/80 Glamorgan v Essex*
First-class record: *223 wickets (24.39) and 1,259 runs (18.51)*
Tests: *2*
Test debut: *23/3/90 West Indies v England*
Test record: *6 wickets (43.50) and 35 runs (8.75)*

MUDIE, George H.

George Mudie

Born: 25 November 1915, Jamaica
Role: Left-hand batsman, off-spin bowler

GEORGE MUDIE made an impact against England when they visited the Caribbean in 1934-35. Batting confidently in Jamaica's two matches against the tourists, he scored 94 and 60 not out. These performances won him a place in the Test side for the match at Kingston where, in the event, he was more effective with the ball. In his only Test appearance he scored five runs and took three wickets for 40. Mudie made a more telling contribution to West Indian fortunes at Test level by coaching the young Alf Valentine for a while.

Teams: *Jamaica, West Indies, G.C. Grant's XI*
First-class debut: *27/2/32 Jamaica v L.H. Tennyson's XI*
First-class record: *578 runs (22.23) and 42 wickets (35.45)*
Tests: *1*
Test debut: *14/3/35 West Indies v England*
Test record: *5 runs (5.00) and 3 wickets (13.33)*

MURRAY, David Anthony

Born: 29 September 1951, Carrington, Bridgetown, Barbados
Role: Wicket-keeper, right-hand batsman

DAVID MURRAY might have enjoyed a distinguished Test career had his Trinidadian namesake, Deryck, not been available at the same time. For many years, David was the top wicket-keeper in Barbados. He performed well on Young West Indies' visit to England in 1970 and, touring with the full side as deputy to

Deryck three years later, enhanced his reputation by taking 28 catches and making eight stumpings from 10 matches. For good measure, he also averaged 35.62 with the bat, including an unbeaten century against Kent.

However, he could not dislodge the incumbent 'keeper for the Tests and had to wait five years and the Packer crisis to make his debut. He grabbed his opportunity eagerly making nine dismissals in the last three Tests against Australia in 1978 and a further 18 on the subsequent tour of India, including five catches in India's only innings in the fifth Test in Delhi. He was also in fine form with the bat again, hitting a sparkling 84 in the first Test at Bombay and top-scored with 66 in the third at Calcutta, but was seen at his best against Central Zone when he crashed a career-best 206 not out.

By the time of the 1980-81 tour to Pakistan, Murray had at last secured the succession as West Indies' first choice wicket-keeper. Again, he performed soundly behind and in front of the stumps and maintained his momentum against England in the Caribbean, despite being heckled during the first Test in Trinidad, as the locals would have preferred to see Deryck keeping wicket. But by this time David was safely installed and confirmed his expertise when he set a new record during the first Test of the tour to Australia in 1981-82, by taking nine catches in the match at Melbourne.

David Murray

Given this train of events, it came as something of a surprise when it transpired that the Barbadian had opted to join the rebel tours to South Africa. After his long apprenticeship, Murray could have looked forward to a distinguished career at the highest level, but the South African offer proved more enticing.

Teams: *Barbados, West Indies, West Indies 'Rebels XI'*
First-class debut: *22/1/71 Barbados v Combined Islands*
First-class record: *292 catches & 31 stumpings and 4,503 runs (30.84)*
Tests: *19*
Test debut: *31/3/78 West Indies v Australia*
Test record: *57 catches & 5 stumpings and 601 runs (21.46)*

MURRAY, Deryck Lance

Born: 20 May 1943, Port-of-Spain, Trinidad
Role: Wicket-keeper, left-hand batsman

DERYCK MURRAY monopolised the wicket-keeping position in the West Indies Test side for over a decade, despite several self-imposed breaks. His Test career began when he was selected for the tour of England in 1963, as deputy to David Allan. After the latter fell ill early on in the tour, the 20-year-old took over the gloves and never relinquished the position finishing the Test series with a record 24 dismissals.

But Murray was as much an academic as a cricketer - he went to Cambridge and Nottingham Universities - and after his first tour to England preferred to study for a degree than play Test cricket. (He played for Cambridge University in 1965 and 1966, and later on for Nottinghamshire and Warwickshire). As a result, he did not return to the Test fold until five years later when England were touring the Caribbean. He took over from the outstanding Hendriks after the latter had been injured but, out of top-class match practice, Murray had an undistinguished come-back and Hendriks was chosen to tour Australia, as Murray returned to England to pursue his studies.

A further five years elapsed before Murray reappeared in Test cricket, this time for the home series against Australia in 1973. After the incumbent, Mike Findlay, had struggled in the opening match, Murray took over the reins for the second Test; competent batting from the Trinidadian - including 90 in his first match at Bridgetown - secured his place once and for all. He played in the subsequent series against England and, on the next tour of India, besides his now expected efficiency behind the stumps, he made his highest Test score of 91 in the last match in Bombay, sharing in a record stand of 250 with Lloyd.

As well as his acknowledged prowess in the five day game, Murray's all-round skills were often put to good use in one-day cricket. He was seen at his best in an early round of the inaugural World Cup in 1975. West Indies needed 64 runs to win their match against Australia when Murray was joined by the last man, Andy Roberts. It seemed an impossible task, but the Trinidadian played superbly for an unbeaten 61 and coaxed Roberts to stay with him as the pair brought off a spectacular victory with two balls to spare.

Murray's batting talents were revealed again, as West Indies struggled in Australia in 1975-76. In the first Test in Brisbane, he top-scored with 66 in the first innings and made 55 in the second. He followed that up with 63 in the next match at Perth, before scoring 50 out of 128 in the fourth Test at Sydney.

After the upward turn in West Indies' batting fortunes in 1976, Murray was not called upon to hold the fort so often but he nonetheless continued to plug the gap with timely innings as, for example, when he helped West Indies to a lead by scoring 60 in the second Test against Australia at Bridgetown in 1978, and also took five catches in the match.

But Murray's talents were never confined to the cricket field alone and he was a key figure in the West Indies Test Players' Association. As part of his campaign to improve players' wages he played a crucial role in negotiations on behalf of the West Indians who signed for Packer. When he and two others were dropped for the third Test against Australia in 1978 as a result of their activities, the remaining Packer players withdrew from the game. Once the rift was healed, Murray's career was resurrected for the series against Australia and New Zealand in 1979-80 and England in 1980.

In spite of the various interruptions to his career, Murray was the first West Indian wicket-keeper to claim over 100 Test victims. A man of the highest skill, he kept to two generations of fast bowlers at their peak: Hall and Griffith, and Roberts and Holding.

Nonetheless, it was his skills off the field that were often as crucial as those on it: his vibrant personality helped maintain morale during the difficult years of the early 1970's, and he became vice-captain to Lloyd for the tour to India in 1974-75. Murray captained West Indies when Lloyd was hurt in the first Test against Australia at Brisbane in 1979, and was only injured himself once in a Test when he was hit on the head by a ball deflected by Dennis Amiss at Port-of-Spain in 1974.

Having played a decisive role in discussions with Kerry Packer, it was perhaps inevitable that his negotiating skills would come to the fore when he retired. Murray served as Trinidad & Tobago's representative on the West Indies Board with his father, who also played for Trinidad, and has represented his country on a diplomatic level at the United Nations.

Teams: *Trinidad, North Trinidad, West Indies, F. Worrell's XI, M.C.C., Cambridge University, Nottinghamshire, N/E Trinidad, Rest of World XI, Warwickshire, A.E.R. Gilligan's XI*
First-class debut: *7/4/61 Trinidad v E.W. Swanton's XI*
First-class record:
741 catches & 108 stumpings and 13,291 runs (28.33)
Tests: *62*
Test debut: *6/6/63 West Indies v England*
Test record: *181 catches & 8 stumpings and 1,993 runs (22.90)*

Deryck Murray

NANAN, Ranjie

Born: 29 May 1953, Trinidad
Role: Off-spin bowler, right-hand batsman

Ranjie Nanan

RANJIE NANAN was a talented all-round cricketer as he showed in his one Test appearance, against Pakistan at Faisalabad in 1980. Although he only scored 16 runs in the match, his two for 54 in Pakistan's first innings and two for 37 in their second, along with two catches were vital in helping the tourists to win the game.

Nanan has an enviable record in domestic cricket for Trinidad & Tobago - he is their leading wicket-taker in Shell Shield/Red Stripe matches and in 1981-82 took a record 32 wickets from five Shield games all, incidentally, away from the relaid pitch at Queen's Park Oval, once a spinners' paradise. Indeed, had it not been for the glut of fast bowlers produced by West Indies while he was at his peak, Nanan would surely have won more Test caps.

Away from the cricket field, Nanan is a police officer.

Teams: *Trinidad, Central Trinidad, S/C Trinidad, West Indies*
First-class debut: *19/1/73 Central Trinidad v East Trinidad*
First-class record: *351 wickets (22.81) and 2,533 runs (21.46)*
Tests: *1*
Test debut: *8/12/80 West Indies v Pakistan*
Test record: *4 wickets (22.75) and 16 runs (8.00)*

NEBLETT, James M

Born: 13 November 1901, Barbados
Died: 28 March 1959
Role: Left-hand batsman, medium-pace bowler

JAMES NEBLETT was a useful batsman and accurate bowler, and a member of the first official touring team to England in 1928. However, he failed to impress on that visit and his sole Test appearance came against England seven years later in the third match at Georgetown. In that game he scored 11 not out and five, and took one for 75. Besides his native Barbados, Neblett also played first-class cricket for Guiana.

Teams: *British Guiana, Barbados XI, Combined Jam/Bar XI, West Indies*
First-class debut: *9/2/26 British Guiana v M.C.C.*
First-class record: *526 runs (18.78) and 29 wickets (41.55)*
Tests: *1*
Test debut: *14/2/35 West Indies v England*
Test record: *16 runs (16.00) and 1 wicket (75.00)*

NOREIGA, Jack Mollison

Born: 15 April 1936, St Joseph, Trinidad
Role: Right-arm off-spin bowler

JACK NOREIGA made his Test debut at the age of almost 35 against India in 1971, after Lance Gibbs had temporarily lost form. Having been kept in the background so long by the prolific Guyanese, Noreiga seemed determined to make his own mark. In the second Test in Trinidad - dominated by spinners - he took nine for 95 in 49.4 overs in the first innings total of 352 and, in the fifth also in Trinidad, returned figures of five for 129 in 53.4 overs on a turning wicket to complete two remarkable home performances. His nine for 95 was the best innings analysis ever returned for the West Indies. Although he did not shine so brightly at the other Test venues, he certainly distinguished himself in the brief time allowed by Gibbs' absence.

Teams: *Trinidad, North Trinidad, East Trinidad, West Indies*
First-class debut: *9/2/62 Trinidad v India*
First-class record: *68 wickets (29.67) and 181 runs (9.05)*
Tests: *4*
Test debut: *18/2/71 West Indies v India*
Test record: *17 wickets (29.00) and 11 runs (3.66)*

James Neblett

NUNES, Robert Karl

Born: 7 June 1894, Kingston, Jamaica
Died: 22 July 1958
Role: Left-hand batsman, wicket-keeper

KARL NUNES was West Indies' first Test captain. A product of Wolmer's Boys' School in Kingston and Dulwich College in England, Nunes' curriculum vitae met the social requirements for chaperoning the West Indies through their first official Test series, against England in 1928.

Nunes was a gifted opening batsman who also kept wicket. As the tourists did not have a specialist 'keeper in the party, Nunes took over the gloves and dropped himself down the batting order. The ploy failed, as a deflection from Herbert Sutcliffe's bat was the only one that stuck in Nunes' gloves, and he himself scored just 87 runs from six Test innings. *The Cricketer* took a sympathetic view, commenting: "He has a horrid job. He does not consider himself or his hands. As captain, he could give himself a rest from acting all day long as a target for fast bowling."

Nunes was one of six players in the 1928 side to have toured England five years earlier under the captaincy of Harold Austin. Nunes had enjoyed greater batting success then when he did not have to worry about keeping wicket and the captaincy. Even so, as vice-captain, he often took over from the 47-year-old Austin, who had originally been named as captain for the 1928 series until the selectors decided he was too old for the job. However, it is interesting to muse on how much closer that first series might have been if the composed Nunes had been allowed to open the innings with the more flamboyant Roach, free from the constraints of captaincy.

Nunes had revealed his batting prowess against Freddie Calthorpe's MCC side in 1925-26 when, opening the innings for Jamaica, he hit 83 and 140 not out and the following season crashed an unbeaten double century and 108 for the island against Lionel Tennyson's team.

Nunes captained West Indies again in the fourth Test against England at Kingston in 1930 and, opening the innings once more, top-scored with 66, as the home side struggled in the face of a massive England total. In the end, West Indies were set 836 to win this celebrated 'timeless Test'. Nunes scored 92, sharing in a double century stand with Headley, before the rains swept down from the Blue Mountains to spoil the fun.

As President of the West Indies Board of Control between 1945-52, Nunes was a key

Karl Nunes

figure in consolidating West Indies' Test status in the important years immediately after the War, while the R. K. Nunes Trophy, which is awarded to the West Indian who makes the most impact in each Test series, ensures his memory lives on.

Teams: *Jamaica, West Indies*
First-class debut: *19/5/23 West Indies v Cambridge University*
First-class record: *2,695 runs (31.33), 31 catches & 8 stumpings and 3 wickets (27.66)*
Tests: *4*
Test debut: *23/6/28 West Indies v England*
Test record: *245 runs (30.62) and 2 catches*

NURSE, Seymour MacDonald

Born: 10 November 1933, Bayville, Bridgetown, Barbados
Role: Right-hand batsman

SEYMOUR NURSE typified all that is best in West Indian batting: flamboyant stroke-play combined with powerful hitting and an insatiable appetite for runs. After scoring heavily in first division cricket in Barbados, Nurse made his first-class debut in 1958 and, in his second match, hit a majestic 128 against Jamaica. He liked to score his runs quickly, an approach that frequently cost him his wicket and, for a while, kept him on the edge of Test selection.

International recognition finally came when he was selected for the third Test against England at Kingston in 1960, after he had scored a double hundred off the tourists for Barbados. Nurse hit 70 on his debut and must have been aggrieved when he was dropped to make room for Walcott. However he was back in favour for the trip to Australia in 1960-61, and got another 70 in the second Test at Melbourne as he and Kanhai put on 123 out of 181 runs scored. After scoring two forties in the third and fourth Tests, he missed out on the final match because of a leg injury, which left him on crutches for a while. He played one Test against India in 1962 and toured England in 1963, but another injury prevented him from making an impact in the Tests. In all, Nurse had played five Tests over three series and had yet to make a hundred. But, with the retirement of Worrell and a return to full fitness, Nurse was given an extended run in the side.

Opening the batting in the first Test against Australia in 1965 he failed to reach 20 in either innings, but a return to the middle order for the third Test in Bridgetown revived his form. Encouraged by enthusiastic home supporters, he thrashed his way to a majestic double century, which could have brought off a surprise win for West Indies. Fittingly, before the match was over, Nurse's wife produced her own double when she gave birth to twin girls.

By the time of the 1966 series against England, Nurse still had a mere nine Tests to his credit. As if to make up for lost time, he got stuck into the English bowlers and scored over 500 Test runs to finish second in the averages to Sobers with 62.62. His best performance, in a pleasing series, came in the fourth Test at Headingley where he helped himself to 137, adding 265 for the fifth wicket with Sobers, to lift the tourists to victory by an innings.

Nurse was less prolific in India in 1966-67 and, with Hunte's departure, he was tried in the opener's position again when England toured West Indies in 1967-68. But he was never happy there, even though he helped Sobers save the second Test in Kingston with a stubborn 73. The West Indies always got the best out of Nurse when he was allowed to bat lower down the order. He proved this in the fourth Test in Trinidad when, coming in at number three, he scored a brilliant 136, sharing in a double century stand with Kanhai.

Almost a decade after he made his Test debut, Nurse enjoyed his finest series in New Zealand in 1969. He scored heavily on the Australian leg of the trip - including making 137 in the final Test in Sydney - and announced his arrival in New Zealand by scoring 95 in the first Test in Auckland, adding 172 for the second wicket with Carew. After the tourists had conceded an unlikely lead, Nurse hit a match-winning 168 in just over three-and-a-half hours of glorious stroke-play.

In the final Test at Christchurch, he powered his way to a career-best 258 - the highest score recorded on the ground - out of a West Indies total of 417 as, this time, he shared in a double century stand with Carew. Altogether on that tour, he scored 1,520 runs (52.41), and then announced his retirement from Test cricket.

That was a severe blow to the West Indies, who were deprived of a world class batsman who could have eased them through the difficult years of the early 1970's. But Nurse was not lost to West Indian cricket, as he became a government coach in Barbados. His influence as a coach, together with his own often dazzling performances at the highest level, have been an inspiration to several members of the current West Indies team.

Teams: *Barbados, West Indies, Rest of World XI, The Rest XI, C. Hunte's XI, Commonwealth XI, Indian Prime Minister's XI, E.W. Swanton's XI*
First-class debut: *19/7/58 Barbados v Jamaica*
First-class record: *9,489 runs (43.93) and 12 wickets (32.41)*
Tests: *29*
Test debut: *17/2/60 West Indies v England*
Test record: *2,523 runs (47.60) and 0-7*

Seymour Nurse

PADMORE, Albert Leroy

P

Born: 17 December 1946, St James, Barbados
Role: Off-spin bowler

ALBERT PADMORE modelled his action on that of Lance Gibbs, and by the mid-1970's was probably the finest off-spinner in the Caribbean. But his slow bowling skills could not penetrate the pace attack that by this time had begun to monopolise the bowling places in the Test side. He made his Test debut against India early in 1976 but, by the time of the tour to England later that year, the fast men had strengthened their grip on the side: in his only Test appearance of that long, hot summer - which provided ideal conditions for spinners - he bowled just three overs. Having taken 59 wickets (23.38) on the tour, Padmore obviously felt his opportunities at Test level were going to be limited and he signed up to play world series cricket. He blotted his copybook once and for all when he began managing tours to South Africa in 1983.

Albert Padmore

Teams: *Barbados, West Indies, West Indies 'Rebels XI'*
First-class debut: *19/1/73 Barbados v Jamaica*
First-class record: *193 wickets (29.94) and 562 runs (13.06)*
Tests: *2*
Test debut: *7/4/76 West Indies v India*
Test record: *1 wicket (135.00) and 8 runs (8.00)*

PAIRAUDEAU, Bruce Hamilton

Born: 14 April 1931, Georgetown, British Guiana
Role: Right-hand batsman

BRUCE PAIRAUDEAU looked like he might open the innings for West Indies for several seasons after he scored a century on his Test debut, against India in the first match at Port-of-Spain in 1953. One of three successive hundreds, the Guyanese shared in a double century partnership with Weekes, which made the selectors think he could blossom in

Bruce Pairaudeau

the opener's position. However, although he scored 58 in the final game at Kingston, he could not maintain his momentum and often seemed unhappy against fast bowling.

Pairaudeau lifted himself with 71 against England at Bridgetown in 1954, sharing in a century stand with Walcott, that helped West Indies to win the game. He lost his place against the touring Australians, but continued to score prolifically for Guiana - he had scored his maiden first-class century for them against Jamaica in 1947, aged 16 years and five months, having made his debut when he was still 15 - which earned him a place in the young team that toured New Zealand in 1955-56.

There, he seemed more comfortable with his batting, scoring 68 in the third Test at Wellington and was the only visiting batsman other than Weekes to score a century on the tour.

The right-hander's performances secured his place on the trip to England in 1957 where he opened the innings in the first Test at Edgbaston. However he made just eight runs in that match, although he spent a disproportionate amount of time in the middle as runner for Walcott and Worrell, and was at the wicket as 387 runs were added. On his other Test match appearance of the tour at Headingley, he was similarly disappointing.

Pairaudeau had felt most at home in New Zealand and emigrated there the following year. Between 1958-67 he enjoyed a successful career with Northern Districts and like his Test colleague, Sammy Guillen before him, was one of the first overseas players to captain a provincial side.

Teams: *British Guiana, West Indies, Commonwealth XI, Northern Districts*
First-class debut: *15/3/47*
British Guiana v Trinidad
First-class record: *4,930 runs (32.01)*
Tests: *13*
Test debut: *21/1/53 West Indies v India*
Test record: *454 runs (21.61) and 0-3*

PARRY, Derick Ricaldo

Born: 22 December 1954, Charlestown, Nevis, Leeward Islands
Role: Right-arm off-spin bowler, right-hand batsman

DERICK PARRY was a highly talented off-spinner and gifted batsman, who became the second man from the Leeward Island of Nevis to play Test cricket, when he made his debut against Australia at Georgetown in 1978.

Having enjoyed a vintage season for the Combined Leeward and Windward Islands, the Packer crisis gave him an unexpected opening to prove himself at the highest level. However, his debut was memorable for the wrong reasons: he got a 'golden' duck and then bowled a wide with his first ball in Test cricket. By the time of the second innings, though, he was more relaxed and, as night-watchman, scored 51 runs, albeit in a losing cause.

Parry was properly into his stride for the fourth Test in Trinidad: he scored 65 in West Indies' second innings, to help set the visitors a target of 293 to square the rubber. Australia were quickly reduced to 72 for five, before Parry spun West Indies to victory in the series by collecting five wickets for six runs in 28 balls. He bowled four of his five victims, as the tourists were dismissed for 94.

The off-spinner was disappointing in India in 1978-79, making just 170 runs in six Tests - including 55 in the opening game in Bombay

Derick Parry

- and taking nine expensive wickets. But the selectors kept faith with him and he toured Australia and New Zealand, and England and Pakistan at the turn of the decade.

But like specialist slow bowlers before and after him, Parry found it virtually impossible to make an impression on the Test side in the face of an all-conquering pace attack. That was presumably a crucial factor in his decision to tour South Africa with the rebel West Indian teams in 1983 and 1984.

Teams: *Leeward Islands, Combined Islands. West Indies, West Indies 'Rebels XI'*
First-class debut: *5/1/76 Leeward Islands v Windward Islands*
First-class record: *251 wickets (28.95) and 2,522 runs (26.86)*
Tests: *12*
Test debut: *3/3/78 West Indies v Australia*
Test record: *23 wickets (40.69) and 381 runs (22.41)*

PASSAILAIGUE, Clarence Charles

Born: 4 August 1902, Jamaica
Died: 7 January 1972
Role: Right-hand batsman

CLARENCE PASSAILAIGUE was a childhood friend of George Headley, with whom he shared in several high-scoring partnerships, most notably their world record unbroken stand of 487 for the sixth wicket for All Jamaica against Lionel Tennyson's touring team at Kingston in 1931-32. On that occasion Passailaigue scored 261 not out and had been in similarly prolific, if not quite such devastating, form against England in 1929-30. He hit 183 for Jamaica against the tourists and had a pleasing start to his Test career when he was selected for the fourth and final match against them at Kingston. He scored 46 runs in the match - for once out - held three catches and took nought for 15. The Jamaican must have been disappointed, therefore, not to be included in the first tour party to Australia in 1930-31. In spite of his world record performance, Passailaigue never found favour with the Test selectors again.

Teams: *Jamaica, West Indies, G.C. Grant's XI*
First-class debut: *28/3/30 Jamaica v M.C.C.*
First-class record: *788 runs (52.53) and 1 wicket (1-56)*
Tests: *1*
Test debut: *3/1/30 West Indies v England*
Test record: *46 runs (46.00) and 0-15*

PATTERSON, Balfour Patrick

Born: 15 September 1961, Portland, Jamaica
Role: Right-arm fast bowler

PATRICK PATTERSON announced his arrival in Test cricket by taking four English wickets for 29 on the first day of the first Test at Kingston in 1986. He finished the game with seven for 73 - which earned him the Man of the Match award - and the observation from *The Times* that some of his deliveries were "just about as fast as a man can bowl". He finished the series with 19 wickets at 22.42 each.

Patterson had served notice of his intentions on the tourists when, in the first one-day international, also in Kingston, he took two for 17 in seven overs of scorching pace.

Yet things were not always so effortless for

Patrick Patterson

the 6ft 2in Jamaican. He had made his first-class debut in 1983 and, prior to 1986, had been struggling to hold his own in the Jamaican team. But, of one thing there was no doubt: his desire to bowl as fast as humanly possible. Indeed a brief session on the receiving end of his thunderbolts in the nets in 1984, as he warmed up to face the visiting Australians, was enough to persuade Clive Lloyd that his services would be appreciated by Lancashire and Tasmania. As Patterson put it: "It was the break I needed." Yet, as with Jamacia, he didn't make an immediate impact with either club; indeed, his most newsworthy performance in Australia came when he was dropped from the side for bouncing the captain in the nets!

By 1985-86 Patterson realised he would need accuracy and stamina as well as pace if he wanted to make it at the highest level. He began working on his game with a new resolve and on the first day of the Shell Shield took seven for 24 from 7.1 overs against Guyana at Kingston and a further seven wickets in the next home match against the Leeward Islands. He removed Richie Richardson in both innings and also accounted for the great Richards himself. Although Patterson was not such a potent force in Jamaica's three away games, his 22 wickets were enough to win him Test recognition.

After his splendid showing against England, he was selected to tour Pakistan at the end of that year but only managed three fairly expensive wickets in the three match series, and played just one match on the subsequent tour to New Zealand.

He made his come-back when West Indies visited India in 1987-88 and what a come-back it was: bowling with genuine speed and hostility he bowled an incisive spell between lunch and tea on the final day of the second Test at Bombay, finishing the innings with five for 68, which nearly secured an improbable victory for the tourists and demolished the early Indian batting in two of the one-day internationals. He finished second in the averages to Walsh with 17 wickets at 26.82, including five for 24 in the first Test at Delhi. A knee injury restricted him to one Test against the touring Pakistanis and he was disappointing in England later in 1988, mustering only four very expensive wickets. He improved slightly against Australia but not sufficiently to keep his place for the home series

PAYNE, Thelston Rodney O'Neal

Born: 13 February 1957, St Philip, Barbados
Role: Left-hand batsman, wicket-keeper

THELSTON PAYNE became the first Barbadian to score three hundreds in a Shell Shield season in 1983. He had made his first-class debut four years earlier, but only became a regular member of the first team line-up when three players went to South Africa. Having waited so long, the left-hander was not about to waste his opportunity and scored 517 runs at an average of 78.85. This together with his wicket-keeping ability won him a place on the tour of England in 1984 but, with Dujon in top form, his opportunities were limited, although in the seven games he played he kept well and averaged almost 40 with the bat.

Payne was selected to tour Australia and Pakistan as Dujon's reserve, but didn't make his Test debut until the second match against England at Port-of-Spain in 1986, after the Jamaican had broken a finger. He performed admirably behind the stumps, holding five catches, although he only scored five runs. Like several illustrious wicket-keepers before him, though, it seems that Payne might have a long wait for another Test appearance assuming that Dujon maintains his form and fitness.

Teams: *Barbados, West Indies*
First-class debut: *16/3/79 Barbados v Jamaica*
First-class record: *3,391 runs (36.85), 103 catches & 8 stumpings*
Tests: *1*
Test debut: *7/3/86 West Indies v England*
Test record: *5 runs (5.00) and 5 catches*

against India, and took just one wicket in his sole Test appearance against England in the Caribbean early in 1990.

As a man who briefly laid claim to the title of fastest bowler in the world, Patterson knows he will have to perform much more consistently to become a permanent member of West Indies' pace attack.

Teams: *Jamaica, West Indies, Lancashire, Tasmania*
First-class debut: *11/2/83 Jamaica v Leeward Islands*
First-class record: *403 wickets (27.39) and 505 runs (6.08)*
Tests: *18*
Test debut: *21/2/86 West Indies v England*
Test record: *60 wickets (30.73) and 90 runs (7.50)*

PHILLIP, Norbert

Born: 12 June 1948, Bioche, Dominica, Windward Islands
Role: Right-hand batsman, right-arm medium-fast bowler

Norbert Phillip

NORBERT PHILLIP was a highly talented all-rounder who batted and bowled his heart out for whoever he played.

Phillip came from a family who played club cricket to a high standard, while Norbert played for the Combined Islands in the only schools championship ever to be held in the West Indies in 1966.

He made his debut for the full Combined Islands side in 1971 and a superb all-round performance in the Shell Shield in 1978, when he averaged 76 with the bat and took 21 wickets at 17.71 each - including 10 wickets and 160 runs for once out against Guyana - made a Test call seem highly likely. It became inevitable after the Packer schism and he took the new ball with Sylvester Clarke for the third Test against Australia at Georgetown in 1978. He began promisingly collecting six wickets in the match, and hit a crucial 46 in the next game in Trinidad to help West Indies to victory. The Dominican maintained his fine form with a splendid first summer at Essex in 1978: he took 71 wickets for the county and scored 645 runs, including a century against Gloucestershire.

He performed reasonably in India in 1978-79 taking 19 wickets (34.21), including seven for 85 in the fourth Test at Madras and, if several more catches had been held off his bowling, his tally would have been higher. He was no slouch with the bat either, averaging over 35.

In 1979 Phillip was instrumental in helping Essex to win the Benson & Hedges Cup and the county championship; and two years later hit a match-winning 83 against Surrey at The Oval to clinch the Sunday league trophy. He enjoyed similar all-round success at home and seemed to find extra inspiration when the Windward Islands competed on their own in the Shell Shield for the first time in 1982. He took 21 wickets (16.28), including seven for 33 in the second innings of the match against the Leewards - including three wickets in four balls - while a brilliant 62 against Barbados helped the Windwards to an historic win in Bridgetown. In the end, the Windwards were runners-up to Barbados in the Shield, as Phillip finished second only to Garner in the overall bowling averages.

Phillip was appointed captain of the Windwards in 1983 and celebrated by taking six wickets against the touring Indians. However, with the emergence of Marshall as West Indies' latest fast bowling weapon, the more sedate Phillip was out of Test match consideration.

Teams: *Windward Islands, Combined Islands, West Indies, Essex*
First-class debut: *7/4/70 Windward Islands v Glamorgan*
First-class record: *7,013 runs (23.61) and 688 wickets (24.75)*
Tests: *9*
Test debut: *1/4/78 West Indies v Australia*
Test record: *297 runs (29.70) and 28 wickets (37.17)*

PIERRE, Lancelot Richard

Born: 5 June 1921, Woodbrook, Port-of-Spain, Trinidad
Died: 15 April 1989, Port-of-Spain, Trinidad
Role: Right-arm seam bowler

LANCE PIERRE, along with Prior Jones, made up the best new-ball pairing ever produced by Trinidad & Tobago. Besides his pace and control, Pierre was known for his sharp outswingers. But, like Jones, he had very little opportunity to bowl at all when he toured England in 1950, given the success of the spin twins, Ramadhin and Valentine. Pierre's cause was not helped when he was injured and he played in 12 first-class matches, taking 24 wickets (23.20), including his best first-class figures of eight for 51 against Lancashire at Liverpool. His poor eyesight hampered his batting and he did not score his first run on the tour until the beginning of August and managed just two from seven innings.

Pierre had had equally few chances in his sole Test appearance, in the rain-affected match against England at Georgetown in 1948, where he took nought for 28 from seven overs and did not get a bat. It was unfortunate that the Trinidadian was at his peak during the War years - he took 69 wickets from 19 inter-territorial matches for Trinidad between 1941-46 - but he was a popular team man wherever he went, with his penchant for the piano and fine baritone voice.

Teams: *Trinidad, West Indies*
First-class debut: *1/2/41 Trinidad v Barbados*
First-class record: *102 wickets (24.72) and 131 runs (6.23)*
Tests: *1*
Test debut: *3/3/48 West Indies v England*
Test record: *0-28*

Allan Rae

R

RAE, Allan Fitzroy

Born: 30 September 1922, Kingston, Jamaica
Role: Left-hand batsman

ALLAN RAE provided West Indies with one half of their first reliable opening partnership in Test cricket. He combined with Jeff Stollmeyer to bring a stability to the position previously unknown.

Rae had a solid defence and preferred to accumulate his runs quietly rather than going in for spectacular batting displays. His father, Ernest, had been a member of the first official tour party to England and a generation later the younger Rae was chosen for the tour to India in 1948-49. He had only two first-class matches behind him, although he had scored a century in each innings of Jamaica's game against Barbados at Kingston in 1946-47.

He collected his first Test hundred in the second match against India at Bombay - as he and Stollmeyer shared in a century opening partnership - and reached three figures again in the fourth match at Madras. This time the visiting openers put on a record partnership of 239 which stood until 1983; while 97 in the final Test at Bombay from the accomplished Jamaican helped him to an average of 53.42 for the series.

This ensured him a place in the side for the tour party to England in 1950, which had been a happy hunting ground for Rae as a law student and sometime club cricketer for Winchmore Hill and the BBC. The success of the openers on that trip was a vital ingredient in West Indies' triumph: Rae's finest hour came on the first day of the Lord's Test when he scored 106 against some testing early bowling, and went on to share in partnerships of 91 with Worrell and 105 with Weekes. Rae scored another determined century at The Oval to help him to a Test average of 62.83 and over 1,000 first-class runs for the tour, including 179 against Sussex at Hove as he shared in a record first wicket stand of 355 with Stollmeyer.

However it was a different story in Australia, where he struggled against the extreme pace of Ray Lindwall and Keith Miller. His dismissal for a duck by Lindwall with the third ball of the series set the tone and he averaged a miserly 14.50 from three Tests. Rae recovered his composure somewhat in New Zealand, falling one short of his century in the second Test at Auckland, as he and Stollmeyer shared in an opening stand of 197.

Rae played his first home Test match against India at Port-of-Spain in 1953. Seemingly recovered from the shell-shock of Australia he made 63 not out and hoisted yet another century partnership with Stollmeyer. But the selectors were looking to the future and decided to promote the 21-year-old Bruce Pairaudeau to the opener's role. This seemed rather harsh on Rae, whose style had brought unprecedented consistency to West Indies' top order batting.

Rae became captain of Jamaica and continued to play first-class cricket until 1960, the year in which he shared in a record partnership of 258 with Easton McMorris for the island against Trinidad & Tobago.

On his retirement Rae devoted his energies to his legal career and was President of the West Indies Board of Control between 1981 and 1988, where his legal brain was stretched to the full as he handled negotiations with Kerry Packer and coped with the aftermath of the rebel tours to South Africa, as well as the financial difficulties besetting domestic cricket in the Caribbean, which led to the 1987 Shell Shield programme being cut by half.

Teams: *Jamaica, West Indies*
First-class debut: *22/3/47*
Jamaica v Barbados
First-class career: *4,798 runs (39.65)*
Tests: *15*
Test debut: *10/11/48*
West Indies v India
Test record: *1,016 runs (46.18)*

RAMADHIN, Sonny

Born: 1 May 1929, Esperance Village, Trinidad
Role: Right-arm spinner

SONNY RAMADHIN appeared from nowhere to take the cricket world by storm. Prior to the 1950 tour of England, Ramadhin, along with his partner Valentine, were little-known spinners in the Caribbean. But after he had taken 12 wickets in two trial matches, John Goddard, the West Indies captain, insisted that the slightly-built Trinidadian was included in the tour party, in what proved to be one of the most successful gambles in the history of Test cricket.

Ramadhin, who was the first East Indian to appear for West Indies in a Test match, played senior cricket for the Trinidad Leaseholds Oil Company. He baffled the most observant batsmen with his unorthodox grip, which meant they could not tell his leg-break from his off-break, that is, if they hadn't already been totally bemused by his insistence upon bowling in a cap with sleeves buttoned down to the wrist!

Just 21 years old by the time the Test series began, Ramadhin took 135 wickets on the tour, including 26 (23.33) from four Tests. In the second game at Lord's, Ramadhin returned match-winning figures of 11 for 152, including six for

Sonny Ramadhin

86 off 72 overs in the second innings, as the tourists secured their first victory on English soil. *Wisden* commented: "No blame could be attached to the pitch...Ramadhin bowled with the guile of a veteran. He pitched a tantalising length, bowling straight at the wicket and spun enough to beat the bat. No English batsman showed evidence of having mastered the problems of deciding which way Ramadhin would spin."

His bowling technique ensured another famous victory in the next Test at Trent Bridge, where this time he took five for 135. His success was celebrated enthusiastically at home and booked his place in the Test side for over a decade.

Even so, he was less successful in Australia in 1951-52 - apart from a five wicket haul in the opening Test at Brisbane - but foiled the New Zealanders, taking nine wickets in the first Test at Christchurch.

Again, he seemed to have lost a little of his magic when India visited the Caribbean in 1953, even though he and Valentine were cheered on by record crowds. But his efforts were decisive in the second Test at Bridgetown, when he returned match-winning figures of five for 26 in the visitors' second innings, to hand the home side the initiative in the series.

Ramadhin was the most successful bowler on either side in the rubber against England in 1954 and finished with 23 wickets (24.30), including six for 113 in the third Test at Georgetown.

However, it was an uphill struggle for Ramadhin who shouldered much of the bowling on his own during those years against powerful English and Australian batting sides. In particular, he struggled against the Australians in 1955, but the New Zealanders still hadn't worked him out by 1956. He mesmerised them in the first Test at Dunedin, taking six for 23 off 21.2 overs, including four batsmen before they had scored. He took a further six wickets in the Test at Christchurch, to help him to a tally of 20 at 15.80 apiece for the series. On that trip he also showed what he could do with the willow, scoring 44 at Dunedin and 33 at Christchurch. Ramadhin seemed to have lost none of his flair on his second visit to England, in 1957, as by the first Test he had taken a remarkable 38 wickets. He maintained his momentum in that first match collecting seven for 49 in unhelpful conditions. After dismissing Peter Richardson and Doug Insole in the second innings, he seemed set to run through the English batting once more. But Colin Cowdrey and Peter May thwarted him by making exaggerated use of their front pad and added a record 411 runs for the fourth wicket. But their tactics were widely frowned upon and eventually led to a change in the LBW law.

Altogether Ramadhin bowled 129 overs in that match, including a record 98 in the second innings, in the absence of the injured Worrell and Gilchrist. That performance took its toll on Ramadhin and he played a less prominent role in the remainder of the series, although he shared in a match-saving last wicket stand of 55 with Worrell at Trent Bridge and took four wickets in the final game at The Oval. Even so, he confirmed his outstanding calibre by topping the tour bowling averages with 119 wickets (13.98).

After that series Ramadhin was a less potent force, although he took four for 25 to help West Indies to victory over Pakistan at Lahore in 1959 and four for 73 against England in the final Test on his home ground in 1960.

But the Trinidadian had been instrumental in putting West Indian spin bowling on the international cricketing map and, for one glorious summer in 1950, the name of Ramadhin and that of his partner, Valentine, were on everyone's lips.

Teams: *Trinidad, West Indies, Commonwealth XI, Lancashire, International XI, E.W. Swanton's XI, M.C.C.*
First-class debut: *25/1/50 Trinidad v Jamaica*
First-class career: *758 wickets (20.24) and 1,092 runs (8.66)*
Tests: *43*
Test debut: *8/6/50 West Indies v England*
Test record: *158 wickets (28.98) and 361 runs (8.20)*

RICHARDS, Isaac Vivian Alexander

Born: 7 March 1952, St John's, Antigua, Leeward Islands
Role: Right-hand batsman, off-spinner

VIV RICHARDS was undoubtedly the finest batsman of his generation. He combined eagle-eyesight, perfect balance and timing with an unqualified self-confidence - some say arrogance - to lift himself into a class above all others. In his heyday, like Headley before him, Richards seemingly had the ability to deliver a big innings whenever the fancy took him.

Richards comes from a cricketing family: his father, Malcolm, spear-headed Antigua's fast bowling attack for many years and his two brothers have appeared for the island. But it is Vivian's charismatic batting which has always attracted intense public interest. As early as 1969 he was hitting the headlines when his followers forced an official to overrule an umpire and reinstate Richards after he had been given out in a Leeward Islands tournament. They did him no favours, though, as he was suspended for two years and did not make his first-class debut until 1972.

But of his talent there was no doubt and he was sponsored, along with Andy Roberts, to attend Alf Gover's Cricket School in England in 1973. His remarkable talent was soon noticed by many influential figures, including Len Creed, a Somerset committee member, who invited the youngster to join the county.

At Somerset Richards came under the watchful eye of Brian Close, who inspired the youngster to tighten his game - to the detriment of bowlers the world over, not least English ones! For over 10 years Richards could be relied on to score 1,000 first-class runs for his adopted county until his controversial dismissal in 1986. With his Test colleague, Joel Garner, he lifted Somerset cricket from the doldrums of never having won a trophy to unprecedented success in the early 1980's. The nature of his contribution to the club was epitomised when he scored 322 in a day against Warwickshire at Taunton on 1 June 1985. It was the Antiguan's highest first-class score and included eight sixes and 42 fours; he hit eight other championship centuries that summer to help him to an average of 76.50.

Even so, Richards could be considered a surprise choice when he was selected for his first full overseas tour, to India and Pakistan in 1974-75. He soon proved his worth, scoring a match-winning 192 not out in the second Test in Delhi, as he dominated partnerships with Lloyd and Boyce. However, apart from 50 in the Test at Madras, undisciplined batting in the other matches meant his aggregate was lower than it should have been.

In common with the rest of the side, Richards struggled for most of the subsequent tour of Australia. He began auspiciously enough with 175 against Western Australia, but a duck in the first Test at Brisbane saw him fall into a trough that he did not emerge from until he was promoted to open the innings later on the tour against Tasmania. In Hobart he made 100 in each innings and, maintaining the opener's position for the fifth Test at Adelaide, began one of the most remarkable sequences of scores ever seen in Test cricket. In eight incredible months he

Viv Richards

scored 1,710 Test runs as Australian, Indian and English bowlers all felt the weight of his mighty bat. He scored a century at Adelaide, a further three in the home series against India where, incidentally, in both Tests in Trinidad his score was more than the combined total of the rest of the side, and three more against England in 1976, including 232 in the first Test at Trent Bridge and 291 in the last at The Oval. *Wisden* wrote of his run-scoring that season: "If he fails to make another run in Test cricket his performance in this single year will always be a source of conversation for the enthusiasts and inspiration to young batsmen."

His performances against England in 1976, when he scored 829 runs from four Tests for an average of 118.42 to give him the highest aggregate ever by a West Indian - indeed, only three other batsmen have hit more runs in a series, but they all needed five Tests - caused *Wisden* particular excitement: "Mere figures cannot convey his perfect style and stroke-play. His cover driving was superb and with his feet always in the right position the way he flicked the ball on his leg-stump to square-leg had to be seen to be believed."

After his success in England there was a sense of inevitability about his match-winning 138 in the 1979 World Cup final; and he played a similarly decisive innings for Somerset later that year in the Gillette Cup final, to become the first man to score two centuries in two cup finals at Lord's in the same year.

It seemed that nothing could dull his appetite for runs: his batting had an enormous influence on the outcome of the short series in Australia in 1979-80 as, by scoring almost 100 runs every time he went to the wicket, he helped secure West Indies' first series victory on Australian soil.

He was majestic in England in 1980, shining with his usual brightness at Lord's, as he stroked the ball to all parts of the ground for 145 glorious runs; and enjoyed more success on the subsequent tour to Pakistan. Then, after making nought and 182 against England in the third Test at Bridgetown in 1981, the tourists might have anticipated that he was saving something extra special for the fourth Test, which was to be staged for the first time at the Recreation Ground in Antigua. Indeed, it was largely in tribute to his remarkable contribution to West Indian cricket that the ground was elevated to Test status. *Pelham Cricket Year* captured the mood perfectly: "That the man would hit a Test century on his own ground to mark its use as an international arena for the first time was one of cricket's more predictable happenings. He began in dominant mood, rested for a while, then flourished again before easing off to his hundred. It was his first week of married life, his home ground and his fourteenth Test hundred."

Ironically, after this performance his more restrained showing in Australia in 1981-82 confirmed he was a man and not a machine; but a lull in the international fixture list revitalised him and he was back to his best against the touring Indians, crashing 109 in the Georgetown Test of 1983, in an innings spread over four days due to a bank holiday and inclement weather.

When Australia visited the Caribbean in 1984, Richards and his young protege, Richardson, made it a local affair in the fourth Test in Antigua as they scored 178 and 154 respectively, sharing in a triple century stand, prompting the local papers to enthuse: "Richards and Son, specialists in batting."

Richards had an uncharacteristically modest tour of England in 1984 limiting himself to one Test 100, in the first match at Edgbaston. On that tour the Antiguan will be remembered most for his chanceless 189 off 170 balls in the first one-day game at Old Trafford. It was the highest innings in the history of limited-overs cricket and included five huge sixes and 21 fours. Richards made his runs out of a total of 272, after West Indies' ninth wicket had fallen on 161. On the subsequent tour of Australia, Richards had another quiet series, but the sleeping giant finally awoke for the fourth Test in Melbourne as he stroked his way to 208 - the highest Test score by a West Indian in Australia.

In 1985 Richards became the first player from the Leeward Islands to captain the West Indies, when he succeeded Lloyd for the series against New Zealand. By leading the West Indies to victory, he began by achieving one of the few feats to elude his predecessor and went on to emulate him by defeating England 5-0 in the subsequent series in the Caribbean. Richards scored 331 runs (66.20) against the visitors, including his seemingly compulsory century in the Test in Antigua which in terms of balls was the fastest in Test cricket coming off only 56 deliveries - including 15 where he failed to score.

After all that hectic activity, the years finally seemed to be catching up with him as he had more modest series against Pakistan and New Zealand. It seemed that perhaps Richards and his world-beating team were coming to the end of their run. But such talk only inspired them to lift their game once more. After a summer of Lancashire League cricket, the West Indies captain returned to the international fold for the World Cup in 1987. In a preliminary round match against Sri Lanka, he powered his way to the highest score ever recorded in the competition: 181 off just 125 balls, including six sixes and 16 fours in a brilliant display of batting from a man hungry for more success. He later became the first player to score 1,000 runs in

In eight incredible months Viv Richards scored 1,710 Test runs as Australian, Indian and English bowlers all felt the weight of his mighty bat.

the World Cup, but that achievement was submerged in the disappointment felt by Richards when West Indies failed to reach the semi-final stage of the competition for the first time.

Indeed, Richards' position as captain was questioned after their performance in the World Cup, but he re-asserted himself on the subsequent tour of India. Leading from the front he fashioned several crucial innings of the highest quality, notably an unbeaten 109 that turned the close first Test in Delhi into a comfortable West Indian victory and an equally invaluable 68 in the first innings of the final Test at Madras, which helped him to top the batting averages with 295 runs (59.00).

Richards was troubled by haemorrhoids when Pakistan visited the Caribbean in 1988 causing him to miss most of the one-day series and the first Test (which West Indies lost). His return was decisive as he top-scored in each innings of the drawn Trinidad Test, including an imperative century in the second, took two wickets and a vital catch in the tense closing stages, to prevent Pakistan from clinching the series. Despite playing one match less than the other batsmen, Richards still finished as the leading run-scorer with 278 (69.50).

In England in 1988 he confirmed his standing as a Test match captain by repeating the now familiar drubbing of the hosts, although he had a less productive series with bat, with his best score of 80 coming in the drawn opening Test at Trent Bridge. Richards created history in Australia in November of that year when a century against New South Wales made him the first West Indian to score 100 first-class centuries - completed in 658 innings, fewer than many of the cricketing greats who belong to the exclusive 100 Test Centuries Club - while the first Test at Brisbane was his 100th and he held his 100th catch during that game. He went on to enjoy his usual success in an Australian rubber scoring 446 runs (55.75), including 146 off 150 balls in the second match at Perth and a resolute innings of 68 not out in the final game at Adelaide which guaranteed the safety of his side.

The series against India in the Caribbean was not one of Richards' happier ones: he had a modest time with the bat scoring just 135 runs including 110 of them in the final Test at Sabina Park, although his innings was marred when he was involved in a dispute with the Indian fielders over his controversial dismissal, which incited the crowd to more disturbances and eventually resulted in a fine for the West Indies captain. Neither was he seen at his best in the home series against England in 1990 as, once again, a short temper and poor health hampered his cause; and, more unusually, England played exceptionally well.

Richards is now in the twilight of his cricketing career, but his remarkable feats on the field of play have made him a legend in his own lifetime: 24 centuries and 116 catches in Test cricket and over 6,500 runs in one-day internationals, including his world record innings of 189.

Although over the years he has been sharply criticised in many quarters for his alleged arrogance, insensitivity to the needs of his team mates and general temperamental disposition, there can be no doubt that what will live on long after Richards has left the playing scene is the killer instinct in his batting and the joy he brought to hundreds of thousands of cricket lovers who were fortunate enough to see him in full flow.

Teams: *Leeward Islands, Combined Islands, West Indies, Somerset, Glamorgan, Queensland, International XI*
First-class debut: *15/1/72 Leeward Islands v Windward Islands*
First-class career: *33,033 runs (50.20) and 210 wickets (44.52)*
Tests: *111*
Test debut: *22/11/74 West Indies v India*
Test record: *7,990 runs (51.21) and 32 wickets (58.03)*

RICHARDSON, Richard Benjamin

Born: 12 January 1962, Five Islands, Antigua, Leeward Islands
Role: Right-hand batsman

RICHIE RICHARDSON won Test recognition after performing well against his fast bowling colleagues in domestic competition. Hundreds off the likes of Holding, Walsh, Patterson, Marshall and Daniel batting against Jamaica and Barbados in the Shell Shield in 1983 earned him a place in the tour party to India at the end of that year.

However, he had an inauspicious beginning, being dismissed for a duck - albeit the victim of an unfortunate LBW decision - on his Test debut, having made nought in his first game of the tour as, indeed, he had in his first first-class match. More untimely noughts hampered his cause further, but he finally revealed his form in the finals of the one-day series in Australia in 1984 and later in the Test series against Australia in the Caribbean.

But, again, his start was unpromising: in the first two Tests he made 19 and 23 and was dropped; but Logie's withdrawal through illness earned him a reprieve and he finally came into his own in the third match at Bridgetown. There, he hit 131 not out, sharing in a century partnership with Haynes, and followed that up with 154 sparkling runs in the next game in Antigua as he and his mentor, Richards,

Richie Richardson

produced a record partnership of 308 for the home fans. Just to prove his impetuosity hadn't left him completely Richardson made his customary duck at Kingston but still finished the series with an average of over 80.

Richardson lost his momentum again in England in 1984, but perked up in Australia, scoring a majestic century in the second Test at Brisbane, having made a duck in the opening encounter at Perth. He was the most successful batsman in the home series against New Zealand scoring 378 runs for an average of 63, including 185 in the second Test at Georgetown, as he added 181 for the second wicket with Haynes.

Richardson maintained his form against England in the Caribbean early in 1986, scoring hundreds in the second Test in Trinidad and the third in Barbados; and in the Leewards' game against the visitors collected the only wickets of his first-class career, five for 40, bowling medium pace after George Ferris had been sidelined through injury.

The Antiguan confirmed his promise in the subsequent series against Pakistan, New Zealand and India. He then played consistently well in the home Test series against Pakistan in 1988 and topped the batting in the one-day internationals with an average of 80.25; in a vintage season he also scored 176 for the Leewards against Barbados at Bridgetown.

But in England later that year he scored just 71 runs from three Tests, struggling against the moving ball and was further hampered by injury. Indeed, by the end of that trip he had gone 17 Tests without a century and, after an impoverished start to the subsequent tour of Australia, seemed destined to continue on his downward spiral. But the Antiguan rallied in time for the first Test and topped 500 runs for the series at an average of almost 60, treating the Melbourne and Adelaide crowds to his overdue centuries.

Richardson enjoyed remarkable success in the subsequent home series against India scoring 619 runs (88.42) - an incredible 339 more runs than the next man - boosted by a marvellous 194 in the first Test in Georgetown and 156 in the last at Sabina Park; in the intervening two he missed his century by seven and one runs respectively. In less than six months he had scored 1,147 runs from nine Tests with four hundreds and five fifties for an average of 67.47, aided by his decision to stop chasing full length balls wide of the off-stump!

He scored more modestly against England in the Caribbean early in 1990 but, given the cyclical nature of his run-scoring and the faith the selectors have in him, Richardson seems destined to continue riding his luck for the West Indies for several years to come.

Teams: *Leeward Islands, West Indies, Rest of World XI*
First-class debut: *20/3/82*
Leeward Islands v Barbados
First-class career: *7,312 runs (40.62) and 5 wickets (32.00)*
Tests: *49*
Test debut: *24/11/83*
West Indies v India
Test record: *3,515 runs (46.25) and 0-12*

RICKARDS, Kenneth Roy

Born: 23 August 1923, Rollington Town, Kingston, Jamaica
Role: Right-hand batsman

Ken Rickards

KEN RICKARDS began his Test career promisingly when he scored 67 against England at Kingston in 1948, having scored a century against the tourists for Jamaica. He toured Australia and New Zealand in 1951-52 but failed to distinguish himself, making 15 and 22 opening the batting in his sole Test appearance in the fourth match at Melbourne. He enjoyed a distinguished first-class career in the Caribbean and played one game for Essex in 1953. He also played league cricket in the UK.

Teams: *Jamaica, West Indies, Commonwealth XI, Essex*
First-class debut: *28/6/46 Jamaica v Trinidad*
First-class career: *2,065 runs (38.96) and 1 wicket (128.00)*
Tests: *2*
Test debut: *27/3/48 West Indies v England*
Test record: *104 runs (34.66)*

ROACH, Clifford Archibald

Born: 13 March 1904, Port-of-Spain, Trinidad
Died: 18 April 1988, Trinidad
Role: Right-hand batsman

CLIFFORD ROACH enjoyed the unusual distinction of playing in West Indies' early Test series with considerable success as a batsman.

A gregarious cricketer, whose style took him to the heights and depths of batting, he provided an important link between Challenor, the acknowledged 'father' of West Indian batting, and the emergence of Headley.

Despite the erratic nature of his play, Roach still scored 1,000 first-class runs in England in 1928, including two fifties and two ducks in the three-match Test series. One of the highlights of the rubber for West Indies was a partnership of 91 between himself and Challenor in less than even time against the pace of Harold Larwood in the last match at The Oval.

When England played their first official Test series in the Caribbean in 1930, Roach became the first West Indian to score a Test century - he scored 80 of his 122 runs in boundaries, including successive fours off Wilfred Rhodes to reach his century - in the opening game at Bridgetown, and hit a similarly entertaining 77 in the second innings. Then he entered a downward spiral and could only muster 24 runs from his next six first-class innings, including a pair in the second Test at Port-of-Spain. Roach was so despondent over his poor form that he planned to miss the third Test in Georgetown. However, the selectors did not agree with that form of therapy and he was drafted into the side, whereupon the Trinidadian rewarded their faith by becoming the first West Indian to score a double century in a Test match. He hit a career-best 209, scoring 122 of his runs in 98 minutes after tea on the first day, to help lift West Indies to their first-ever Test victory, aided by substantial partnerships with Errol Hunte and Headley.

Roach was less successful in Australia in 1930-31, scoring just one fifty in the Test series and, in England in 1933, bagged another pair, this time at Lord's. But he lifted his game with a bright 64 in the second match at Old Trafford and thumped 56 in a hopeless cause in the third and final match at The Oval. Indeed, he seemed to enjoy batting at The Oval, having scored 180 at more than a run-a-minute in the tourists' match against Surrey.

Clifford Roach

The hallmark of Roach's batting was its entertainment value: however long or brief his innings, the crowd was always kept on the edge of their seats. Besides his own seemingly inherent inconsistency, Roach was hampered, like many of his successors, by not having a regular opening partner. In 12 consecutive Tests between 1928-35, he opened with nine different partners, four of them in 1930.

A solicitor by profession, Roach developed diabetes in later life which caused him to have both legs amputated. It was especially sad for a man like Roach who had always been quick-footed on the field and like lightning between the wickets, but he had artificial legs fitted in England and continued to work and follow cricket with the same energy that had been characteristic of his play.

Teams: *Trinidad, West Indies, Combined Trin/B.G.XI, C.A. Merry's XI*
First-class debut: *14/2/24 Trinidad v British Guiana*
First-class career: *4,851 runs (28.04) and 5 wickets (105.20)*
Tests: *16*
Test debut: *23/6/28 West Indies v England*
Test record: *952 runs (30.70) and 2 wickets (51.50)*

ROBERTS, Alphonso Theodore

Born: 18 September 1937, Kingstown, St Vincent, Windward Islands
Role: Right-hand batsman

ALFIE ROBERTS was the first player from the 'smaller' islands to play Test cricket. The slightly-built Vincentian was selected as a member of the predominantly youthful team that toured New Zealand in 1955-56. He made his debut in the fourth Test at Auckland at the age of 19 and made 28 - the joint second highest score of the innings - and nought. Immediately afterwards he collected a fluent 45 against the New Zealand Colts, to give him a tour aggregate of 137 runs (19.55).

In another era Roberts might have had a second chance at Test level, but with the three "W"s back in contention for the tour of England he was brushed aside. Besides the Windward Islands, Roberts also played for Trinidad & Tobago.

Teams: *Trinidad, Windward Islands, West Indies*
First-class debut: *20/1/56 West Indies v Auckland*
First-class career: *153 runs (13.90)*
Tests: *1*
Test debut: *9/3/56 West Indies v New Zealand*
Test record: *28 runs (14.00)*

ROBERTS, Anderson Montgomery Everton

Born: 29 January 1951, Urlings Village, Antigua, Leeward Islands
Role: Right-arm fast bowler

ANDY ROBERTS was the first of the famous quartet of fast bowlers to gain a stranglehold on the world's best batsmen, which enabled West Indies to dominate international cricket for over 10 years from the late 1970's.

He did not play cricket seriously until the age of 16, but developed his skills at the Rising Sun Club of St John's, with Antigua's other cricketing protege, Viv Richards. The pair made such an impression that they were sent to the Alf Gover School in England for some formal coaching, before being unleashed into the Test arena in the mid-1970's.

Andy Roberts

Although Roberts bowled well against England in their match with the Leeward Islands in 1974, he struggled on his Test debut on a placid Bridgetown wicket. Even so, he established his credentials with Hampshire later that year, topping the national first-class averages with 119 wicket (13.62) from 21 games. Soon his phenomenal pace, which brought him 100 Test match wickets in the record time of two years and 142 days, would be terrorising batsmen in international competition.

In 1974-75 he took a record 32 wickets in the Test series against India, including 12 for 121 in the fourth game at Madras ironically in a losing cause, and another 12 from two matches in Pakistan. In 1975 John Arlott wrote of him: "Andy Roberts is the rare combination of fire, settled physique and mature mind in a young fast bowler - and he is not yet at his peak."

After winning acclaim as a batsman in the inaugural World Cup, when he shared in a nail-biting last wicket partnership of 64 with Deryck Murray to bring off a famous victory for West Indies against Pakistan early in the competition, Roberts was the dominant bowler in the subsequent Test series in Australia. He collected 22 wickets (26.36), including a match-winning seven for 54 in the second Test at Perth, in a series which also saw the birth of his partnership with Holding.

Injury to Roberts prevented the touring Indians suffering too much at his hands early in 1976, but later that year he caused havoc in England as, aided and abetted by Holding, he took 28 wickets at 19.17 apiece. In the second match he became the first West Indian to take 10 wickets in a Test at Lord's and at Old Trafford found himself on a hat-trick twice in the second innings. Drinks were taken before Roberts returned to see his second hat-trick ball dropped in the slips; the disappointment was met by a glum look to the heavens by the laconic Antiguan. He still finished with six for 37 in the innings as the triumphant West Indies machine gathered pace.

Roberts was less impressive against the visiting Pakistanis in 1977, but lifted his side to victory in the first Test against Australia at Port-of-Spain in 1978 with five for 56 in the visitors' second innings. By this time however the burden of continuous cricket had started to take its toll and, as one of Kerry Packer's recruits, he left Hampshire halfway through the English season to concentrate on his world series commitments. Roberts subsequently returned to the official Test fray suitably rejuvenated to become the third West Indian to take 200 Test wickets.

Having lost some of his momentum in the Test series at the turn of the decade, he warmed up for England's visit in 1981 by taking 25 wickets from four Shield games for the Combined Islands. However, he performed modestly in the Test series and when he lost his place for the final game and was dropped in the second match of the subsequent tour of Australia, his international prospects seemed bleak. But the Antiguan lifted himself for the final Test in Adelaide to set up victory for West Indies with four first innings wickets, and returned to the Caribbean to take 24 wickets in four Shield games.

He was in devastating form against the visiting Indians in 1983, finishing as the leading wicket-taker with 24 victims (22.70) and took a further 28 wickets at under 20 apiece for the Leewards, whom he captained, in the Shell Shield. During this purple patch, Roberts took a hat-trick against Barbados and 11 for 114 against the Windward Islands, having taken nine wickets in the first Test against India the week before, including five for 39 in the second innings as the last four touring batsmen fell in the space of 20 balls.

Roberts toured India later in 1983 and in

Willie Rodriguez

the fifth match at Calcutta took his 200th Test wicket when he dismissed Roger Binny; he celebrated by making his highest first-class score of 68, sharing in a ninth wicket stand of 161 with Lloyd as West Indies romped to a decisive victory.

Like all great fast bowlers, towards the end of his career, Roberts remained effective when he cut down his pace and was used in shorter spells. Until late in his playing days, he inspired fear in the hearts of batsmen as he ran into bowl and, after his retirement, returned to his native Antigua to nurture the game on the island that, along with Richards, he had put on the cricketing map.

> ***Teams:*** *Leeward Islands, Combined Islands, West Indies, Hampshire, Leicestershire, New South Wales*
> ***First-class debut:*** *16/1/70 Leeward Islands v Windward Islands*
> ***First-class career:*** *856 wickets (20.92) and 3,328 runs (15.47)*
> ***Tests:*** *47*
> ***Test debut:*** *6/3/74 West Indies v England*
> ***Test record:*** *202 wickets (25.61) and 762 runs (14.94)*

RODRIGUEZ, William Vincente

Born: 25 June 1934, Woodbrook, Port-of-Spain, Trinidad
Role: Right-hand batsman, medium-pace bowler

WILLIE RODRIGUEZ was a useful all-round cricketer who would often play a timely innings or take a crucial wicket, but these performances rarely came in a Test match.

He had a pleasing debut, when he hit 50 against India in front of his home crowd in the fourth Test at Port-of-Spain in 1962. He was expected to perform well in England and included in the 1963 tour party, but injury marred most of his visit. He recovered sufficiently to play in the fifth Test at The Oval, where he opened the innings with Conrad Hunte. The Trinidadian made 28 in the second innings as the pair hoisted 78 for the first wicket, before Kanhai arrived to take up the challenge.

Thereafter, Rodriguez's Test appearances were few and far between, but he managed the West Indies side in Australia and New Zealand in 1979-80. Rodriguez was also a top-class footballer and represented West Indies in international competition.

> ***Teams:*** *Trinidad, North Trinidad, West Indies, C. Hunte's XI*
> ***First-class debut:*** *16/10/53 Trinidad v British Guiana*
> ***First-class career:*** *2,061 runs (24.83) and 119 wickets (28.08)*
> ***Tests:*** *5*
> ***Test debut:*** *7/3/62 West Indies v India*
> ***Test record:*** *96 runs (13.71) and 7 wickets (53.42)*

Lawrence Rowe

ROWE, Lawrence George

Born: 8 January 1949, Whitfield Town, Kingston, Jamaica
Role: Right-hand batsman

LAWRENCE ROWE confirmed his cricketing genius on his Test debut when he scored a remarkable 314 runs for once out against New Zealand at Kingston in 1972. His performance was without precedent in Test cricket, as he stroked his way to 214 in the first innings sharing in a double century partnership for the second wicket with Fredericks, and an unbeaten 100 in the second innings.

It seemed another batting giant had come of age to compare with the likes of Headley and the three "W"s, but his future career was beset by injury and health problems, including an allergy to grass! The first sign of his uphill struggle for fitness came when he wrenched his ankle in the third Test against Australia at Trinidad in 1973 - having scored 76 in the opening match at Sabina Park - which ruled him out of the series; while further injury problems severely hampered him in England later that year.

Indeed, after his spectacular start in Test cricket, Rowe struggled in his subsequent intermittent appearances and, but for the lack of other candidates, probably would not have been selected for the home series against England in 1974. However, he was promoted to open the innings with Fredericks and enjoyed something of a renaissance as the pair shared in four century partnerships in the five match series. Indeed, the Jamaican seemed to be back to his very best as he thrilled his home fans with a majestic century in the second Test; and lifted his game into another gear for the next encounter at Bridgetown as this time he became only the second West Indian to score a triple century in a Test match, stroking 302, with a six and 34 fours. Just to confirm his world class ability, Rowe played a superb defensive innings of 123 in seven-and-a-quarter hours on a turning wicket in a losing cause in the final match at Port-of-Spain.

It had been a vintage series for Rowe, but he was not to enjoy the same success again, as once more he was plagued by injury and his grass allergy came to the fore. His cause was hampered further by the emergence of Greenidge as an opener of world class potential. But he showed touches of his former self, as when he scored 107, batting at three in the first Test against Australia at Brisbane in 1975, adding 198 for the fourth wicket with Kallicharran in what could have been a match-winning stand had the subsequent batsmen been able to capitalise on their efforts.

When India visited the Caribbean in 1975-76 he was promoted to open the innings again, but failed to make the impact he had against England in that position, and his best score of the series was 47. Rowe lost his place to Greenidge for the Test series in England in 1976, but was included in the tour party and played in the last two Tests when Kallicharran was injured. Once more the crowds were treated to a taste of his magic as he scored 50 in the fourth match at Headingley and 70 in the fifth at The Oval.

But after a reasonable showing in Australia and New Zealand in 1979-80 his career was blighted by injury again and, doubtless frustrated by the traumas of his sporting life, he accepted an invitation to captain a West Indies team in South Africa in 1983.

For many, Rowe was the most natural stroke-maker of his generation - more gifted than either Richards or Greenidge - but, in the end, a number of outside factors combined to sabotage his international prospects.

Teams: *Jamaica, West Indies, Cavaliers XI, Derbyshire, West Indies 'Rebels XI'*
First-class debut: *25/1/69*
Jamaica v Windward Islands
First-class career: *8,755 runs (37.58) and 2 wickets (112.00)*
Tests: *30*
Test debut: *16/2/72*
West Indies v New Zealand
Test record: *2,047 runs (43.55) and 0-44*

Edwin St Hill

ST HILL, Edwin Lloyd

Born: 9 March 1904, Port-of-Spain, Trinidad
Died: 21 May 1957
Role: Right-arm bowler, right-hand batsman

EDWIN ST HILL was a capable all-rounder who played in two Tests against England in 1930. Although he performed modestly in that series he was still taken on the inaugural trip to Australia in 1930-31. He played in four matches against state sides, taking 16 wickets (29.81), but was not selected for any of the Tests.

Teams: *Trinidad, West Indies*
First-class debut: *14/2/24 Trinidad v British Guiana*
First-class career: *64 wickets (28.62) and 274 runs (11.91)*
Tests: *2*
Test debut: *11/1/30 West Indies v England*
Test career: *3 wickets (73.66) and 18 runs (4.50)*

ST HILL, Wilton H

Born: 6 July 1893, Port-of-Spain, Trinidad
Died: 1957
Role: Right-hand batsman

WILTON ST HILL was one of the first successful black batsmen. He was especially strong on the off-side and put the full weight of his athletic 6ft frame into his batting. A master of the late cut and a splendid leg-glancer, St Hill demonstrated all his skills when he scored 105 in 150 minutes for Trinidad against MCC in 1925-26, prompting Lord Harris to remark that he thought St Hill was the best batsman in the West Indies. But he failed to live up to that title on the first tour to England in 1928, scoring a mere 54 runs from four Test innings, including a top score of 38 at Old Trafford. Indeed, it was a thoroughly disappointing tour for him as he scored just 262 runs at an average of 10.91.

Although less flamboyant than he had been against Lord Harris' side, St Hill still scored a century for Trinidad against the MCC side that toured the West Indies in 1929-30. But, having prospered so much against touring teams at Queen's Park Oval in a non-Test setting, when his chance to play a big Test innings on his home ground came, against England in 1930, his best score was 33.

Teams: *Trinidad, West Indies, Combined T/BG XI*
First-class debut: *12/1/12 Trinidad v British Guiana*
First-class career: *1,928 runs (27.15) and 5 wickets (41.80)*
Tests: *3*
Test debut: *23/6/28 West Indies v England*
Test career: *117 runs (19.50) and 0-9*

Wilton St Hill

SCARLETT, Reginald Osmond

Born: 15 August 1934, Kingston, Jamaica
Role: Off-spinner, right-hand batsman

REG SCARLETT was a capable all-rounder whose testing off-spin was complemented by some hard-hit innings.

Having been on the verge of Test selection for several years, he made his debut in the first Test against England at Bridgetown in 1960. He made seven in his only innings and took one for 58 in the match. That performance was not enough to keep his place in the side, but an outstanding performance for Jamaica against the tourists - when he scored 139 for once out and dismissed three leading batsmen - won him a reprieve and he appeared in the third and fourth Tests of that series.

Reg Scarlett

Later in 1960 Scarlett came to live in England and became a top coach. He spent 15 years playing league cricket in the UK and is a familiar figure at charity games. He returned to Jamaica for four years in 1975 where he served on the Jamaican Board of Control and was given special responsibility for the development of youth cricket. His work at home stood him in good stead when he returned to England and became a leading figure in the development of grass-roots cricket in London, most notably with Haringey Cricket College in Tottenham.

Teams: *Jamaica, West Indies*
First-class debut: *17/1/52*
Jamaica v Barbados
First-class career: *48 wickets (34.12) and 477 runs (23.85)*
Tests: *3*
Test debut: *6/1/60 West Indies v England*
Test career: *2 wickets (104.50) and 54 runs (18.00)*

SCOTT, Alfred P H

Born: 29 July 1934, Jamaica
Role: Right-arm leg-spin bowler

ALF SCOTT was a useful leg-break bowler who tied the touring Indians up in knots in their match against Jamaica in 1953. He took seven wickets which won him a place in the Test side to face the visitors at Kingston. However, he was less successful in the Test match arena and finished with figures of nought for 140. He is the son of Tommy Scott, one of West Indies' pioneer Test cricketers.

Teams: *Jamaica, West Indies*
First-class debut: *9/10/52*
Jamaica v British Guiana
First-class career: *18 wickets (33.00) and 38 runs (12.66)*
Tests: *1*
Test debut: *28/3/53 West Indies v India*
Test career: *0-140 and 5 runs (5.00)*

SCOTT, Oscar "Tommy" Charles

Born: 25 August 1893, Jamaica
Died: 16 June 1961
Role: Right-hand batsman, leg-spin bowler

"TOMMY" SCOTT was a first-rate all-rounder who appeared in the first three Test series played by the West Indies. He performed moderately overall in England scoring 322 runs (20.12) and taking 25 wickets (36.24) although, in the Tests, he finished second in the batting averages with 74 runs (24.66) including a top-score of 35 at The Oval.

He bowled a marathon spell in England's first innings at Kingston in 1930 to return the figures of 80.2-13-266-5, as the visitors scored 849. His leg-spin was especially effective in

"Tommy" Scott

Australia, where he took 40 wickets (33.22) including 11 Test victims. In the first Test at Adelaide he mopped up the last four wickets in nine deliveries without addition to the score.

> ***Teams:*** *Jamaica, West Indies*
> ***First-class debut:*** *3/4/11 Jamaica v M.C.C.*
> ***First-class career:*** *1,317 runs (24.38) and 182 wickets (30.52)*
> ***Tests:*** *8*
> ***Test debut:*** *21/7/28 West Indies v England*
> ***Test career:*** *171 runs (17.10) and 22 wickets (42.04)*

SEALEY, Benjamin James

Born: 12 August 1899, St Joseph, Trinidad
Died: 12 September 1963
Role: Right-hand batsman, leg-spin bowler

BEN SEALEY had a sound pair of hands, whether he was using them for batting, bowling or taking catches. An entertaining cricketer to watch with his attacking batting and athletic fielding, he toured England in 1933. It was a successful trip for the Trinidadian, who scored 1,072 runs (39.70) including three centuries and took 19 wickets at just under 40 apiece. In his sole Test appearance, in the last match at The Oval, he top-scored with 29 out of a first innings total of 100, made 12 in the second innings and took one for 10.

> ***Teams:*** *Trinidad, West Indies, C.A. Merry's XI, Combined T/BG XI, R.S. Grant's XI, Barbados XI*
> ***First-class debut:*** *14/2/24 Trinidad v British Guiana*
> ***First-class career:*** *2,115 runs (29.37) and 78 wickets (25.97)*
> ***Tests:*** *1*
> ***Test debut:*** *12/8/33 West Indies v England*
> ***Test career:*** *41 runs (20.50) and 1 wicket (10.00)*

Ben Sealey

SEALY, James Edward Derek

Born: 11 September 1912, Barbados
Died: 3 January 1982
Role: Right-hand batsman, wicket-keeper, medium-pace bowler

DEREK SEALY was still a school-boy when he made history by becoming the youngest man to play Test cricket when he appeared against England at Bridgetown in 1930, at the age of 17 years and 122 days.

Although younger players have since appeared, Sealy remains the youngest West Indian. He was encouraged to play straight by Joe Hardstaff, the former England player who was umpiring in the game, and scored 58 and 15.

The youngster struggled with the rest of the side in Australia in 1930-31, and missed a Test century by nine runs against England at Kingston in 1935 as he shared in a record double century stand with Headley, having been dismissed in the nineties earlier in the series. He played an unexpected role as a bowler in winning the game at Kingston, when he was introduced into the attack to allow Constantine and Martindale to change ends. During his over, Sealy dismissed Errol Holmes, before Constantine returned to mop up the innings and usher West Indies to their first victory in a Test rubber. The series was a personal triumph for Sealy, who averaged 45 with the bat.

Incidentally, seven years later, Sealy proved his bowling ability more emphatically when he returned the best first-class figures ever recorded in the Caribbean with eight for eight for Barbados against Trinidad on a wet Bridgetown wicket, as the visitors were bowled out for 16.

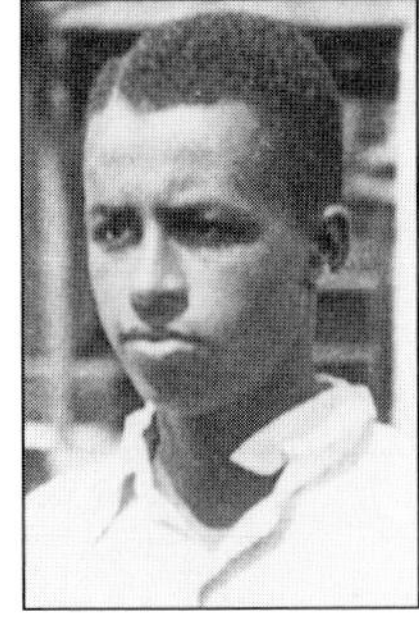
Derek Sealy

Surprisingly omitted from the tour to England in 1933, Sealy was included six years later, but disappointed in the Tests. Indeed, his most important contribution came when he kept wicket in the final two Tests when Ivan Barrow's return proved not as successful as hoped following the untimely death of Cyril Christiani. The Barbadian fared much better against the counties scoring almost 900 runs, including a career-best 181 in three-and-a-half hours against Middlesex.

After the War Sealy moved to Trinidad, where he kept wicket, and scored his last first-class century for his adopted island against his native Barbados at Kensington Oval in 1948.

After he retired Sealy became heavily involved in the administration of cricket in Trinidad & Tobago, but his biggest contribution was the influence he had on the young Frank Worrell, who was one of his sporting proteges at his old school, Combermere, in Barbados, where he taught. Clyde Walcott also came under his wing, as Sealy deservedly took the credit for nurturing the talents of two of West Indies' greatest players.

Teams: *Barbados, Trinidad, West Indies, C.A. Merry's XI, R.S. Grant's XI*
First-class debut: *5/2/29 Barbados v Trinidad*
First-class career: *3,831 runs (30.40), 67 catches & 13 stumpings, and 63 wickets (28.60)*
Tests: *11*
Test debut: *11/1/30 West Indies v England*
Test career: *478 runs (28.11), 6 catches & 1 stumping, and 3 wickets (31.33)*

SHEPHERD, John Neil

Born: 9 November 1943, Belleplaine, Barbados
Role: Right-hand batsman, right-arm medium-pace bowler

JOHN SHEPHERD enjoyed a first-class career spanning almost two decades. His reliable swing bowling and gutsy batting brought him rich rewards at Kent and, to a lesser extent, with West Indies. He made his Test debut against England in 1969 and, despite a heavy workload, finished the three match series with 12 wickets at 22.16 apiece. He played two Tests against India in the Caribbean in 1971, but struggled on less helpful wickets than those he had been used to in England.

John Shepherd

Shepherd became the first black cricketer, along with Younis Ahmed, to tour South Africa when he went there with a Derrick Robins team in 1973. Disgruntled by the lack of opportunities to coach at home, he claimed he could secure a job more easily in the republic, although he subsequently declined to return.

But it is his rumbustious performances on the field for which the Barbadian is best remembered. He hit 170 against Northamptonshire at Folkestone in 1968 and returned bowling figures of eight for 83 against Lancashire at Tunbridge Wells in 1977. In a match against Sussex in 1975 he bowled unchanged in both innings and finished with the remarkable figures of eight for 93 in the first innings off 32.5 overs and seven for 54 off 39 overs in the second.

Towards the end of his career, Gloucestershire enjoyed the benefit of his know-how when Shepherd moved there to coach their second team and made occasional appearances in the first XI.

Teams: *Barbados, West Indies, Kent, Gloucestershire, D.H. Robins' XI, International XI, Rhodesia*

First-class debut: *25/2/65*
Barbados v Cavaliers XI
First-class career: *13,359 runs (26.34) and 1,157 wickets (27.71)*
Tests: *5*
Test debut: *12/6/69 West Indies v England*
Test career: *77 runs (9.62) and 19 wickets (25.21)*

SHILLINGFORD, Grayson Cleophas

Born: 25 September 1944, Dunblanc, Dominica, Windward Islands
Role: Right-arm fast-medium bowler, left-hand batsman

GRAYSON SHILLINGFORD was a useful fast-medium bowler who toured England in 1969 as one of the new generation of fast bowlers to replace Hall and Griffith, and returned there for the visit in 1973. Early on his first trip he tore a muscle which sidelined him for the first month, but he bounced back to take 36 wickets at 18.58 apiece, including four in the second Test at Lord's. He played in the home series against India in 1971 and New Zealand the following year, but failed to establish himself, lacking the penetration and consistency to hold off the later challenge of Boyce and Julien to take the new ball. He is the first cousin of Irvine Shillingford.

Grayson Shillingford

Teams: *Windward Islands, Combined Islands, West Indies*
First-class debut: *8/3/68*
Windward Islands v M.C.C.
First-class career: *217 wickets (26.54) and 791 runs (10.14)*
Tests: *7*
Test debut: *26/6/69 West Indies v England*
Test career: *15 wickets (35.80) and 57 runs (8.14)*

SHILLINGFORD, Irvine Theodore

Born: 18 April 1944, Dominica, Windward Islands
Role: Right-hand batsman

IRVINE SHILLINGFORD was a gifted batsman, who scored prolifically for the Windward Islands after making his debut against the touring Australians in 1965. But he had to wait for over a decade to make his first Test appearance, against Pakistan in 1977. He played three Tests in that series, the highlight being his 120 in the second match at Georgetown, when he was particularly severe on Imran Khan.

In 1978 he scored a double century against the Leeward Islands at Castries and must have thought he had a good chance of revitalising his Test career when the Packer players disappeared from the official scene. Indeed, he was picked for the third Test against Australia at Georgetown but, after making just three and 16, was dropped and not given another chance to prove his undoubted talent at the highest level.

Teams: *Windward Islands, Combined Islands, West Indies*
First-class debut: *6/10/61*
Combined Islands v British Guiana
First-class career: *5,449 runs (36.57) and 1 wicket (85.00)*
Tests: *4*
Test debut: *4/3/77 West Indies v Pakistan*
Test career: *218 runs (31.14)*

SHIVNARINE, Sewdatt

Born: 13 May 1952, Berbice, British Guiana
Role: Left-arm spinner, right-hand batsman

SEW SHIVNARINE grabbed his chance to play Test cricket eagerly when the Packer crisis produced unexpected opportunities for those on the verge of selection. A useful all-round cricketer, who bowled slow left-arm orthodox and batted right-handed, he made an immediate

Irvine Shillingford

impact on his debut, against Australia at Georgetown in 1978, after performing well for Guyana against the tourists. On his Test debut, he hit 53 and 63 and scored another pleasing half century in the Test at Kingston. His performances won him a place in the tour party to India in 1978-79 but, apart from a match-saving innings at Calcutta, he struggled in unfamiliar conditions and thereafter faded from the scene. However, in August 1989 Shivnarine did pop up again as captain of a USA Select XI during two one-day matches in New York against West Indies.

Teams: *Guyana, Berbice, West Indies*
First-class debut: *27/2/71 Guyana v Jamaica*
First-class career: *2,182 runs (32.56) and 67 wickets (36.52)*
Tests: *8*
Test debut: *1/4/78 West Indies v Australia*
Test career: *379 runs (29.15) and 1 wicket (167.00)*

Phil Simmons

SIMMONS, Philip Verant

Born: 18 April 1963, Arima, Trinidad
Role: Right-hand batsman, medium-pace bowler

PHIL SIMMONS had an early set-back to his international career when he received a blow on the side of the head from David Lawrence in West Indies' tour match against Gloucestershire at the end of May 1988. Batting in poor light and without a helmet, Simmons had finished the first day unbeaten on 41 out of 91 for two. Early on the second morning he was felled by Lawrence, but walked from the ground unaided. He was taken to a nearby hospital for a precautionary check-up, but collapsed at the door and needed a life-saving operation to remove a blood-clot from his brain. He spent over a week in hospital, making a complete recovery, but took no further part in the tour.

Simmons, a tall upright player, had toured England with the Young West Indies team in 1983 and subsequently enjoyed several seasons in club cricket. A good showing in the 1987 World Cup, when he played in place of Greenidge, secured his place on the trip to India later that year.

He made his debut in the fourth Test at Madras early in 1988 after an injury to Greenidge, scoring 22 runs in the match in the wake of the success of India's debutant, Narendra Hirwani, who took 16 wickets in the match; and had a further chance against the touring Pakistanis in the first Test at Georgetown in 1988, after performing well in the one-day series. Opening with Haynes, he made 16 and 11, with Greenidge captaining the side and batting down the order. But when Richards returned, Greenidge resumed as opener and there was no room for the young Trinidadian.

Then came his injury in England. After that Simmons did not play in another first-class match until the start of the Red Stripe Cup tournament early in 1989, when he was appointed captain of Trinidad & Tobago. He gave everyone a fright in the second match, against Barbados, when he was hit in the face attempting to hook fast bowler, Emmerson Jordan. Fortunately the damage was limited to a cut under his eye and he played for the rest of the season.

With retirement beckoning for Greenidge, Simmons will hope that he has had his share of misfortune and will be able to concentrate on developing his undoubted talent to forge a regular place for himself in the Test side.

Teams: *Trinidad, N/E Trinidad, West Indies*
First-class debut: *7/1/83 North/East Trinidad v South/Central Trinidad*
First-class career: *2,880 runs (30.00) and 11 wickets (59.72)*

Tests: *2*
Test debut: *11/1/88 West Indies v India*
Test career: *49 runs (12.25)*

SINGH, Charran Kamkaran

Born: 24 November 1935, San Juan, Trinidad
Role: Left-arm slow bowler

CHARRAN SINGH had a controversial Test debut: playing in front of his home crowd, against England at Port-of-Spain in 1960, he was run out for nought to leave West Indies swaying on 98 for eight in the face of England's total of 382. The crowd were unimpressed with the decision and showed their dismay by showering the out-field with missiles before pouring onto the field themselves.

A few weeks earlier, Singh had taken five for 57 in 34 overs in England's first innings against Trinidad in considerably quieter conditions. He appeared in the fourth Test at Georgetown, but failed to make a significant impression and was not chosen again.

Teams: *Trinidad, North Trinidad, West Indies*
First-class debut: *2/10/59 Trinidad v Jamaica*
First-class career: *48 wickets (23.93) and 102 runs (8.50)*
Tests: *2*
Test debut: *28/1/60 West Indies v England*
Test career: *5 wickets (33.20) and 11 runs (3.66)*

SMALL, Joseph A

Born: 3 November 1892, Princes Town, Trinidad
Died: 26 April 1958
Role: Right-hand batsman, off-spin bowler

JOE SMALL was one of West Indies' pioneering all-rounders in Test cricket. He was a gifted batsman with all the strokes at his command, a medium-pace off-break bowler and competent slip fielder. He shone on the 1923 tour of England, scoring 776 runs (31.04), including a brilliant 94 against Lancashire at Old Trafford, and took 19 wickets (33.47). In 1928 he was less successful with the bat scoring 595 runs at 18.59, but excelled in his bowling finishing with 50 wickets at under 30 apiece. He showed his fighting spirit by top-scoring with 52 in a hopeless cause in the first Test at Lord's and played two other Tests, the third match of that series at The Oval and the second against England in the West Indies, at Port-of-Spain in 1930.

Joe Small

Teams: *Trinidad, Combined T/BG XI, West Indies*
First-class debut: *11/11/09 Trinidad v W.C.Shepherd's XI*
First-class career: *3,063 runs (26.17) and 165 wickets (27.81)*
Tests: *3*
Test debut: *23/6/28 West Indies v England*
Test career: *79 runs (13.16) and 3 wickets (61.33)*

SMALL, Milton Aster

Born: 12 February 1964, St Philip, Barbados
Role: Right-arm fast bowler

MILTON SMALL's pace accounted for eight batsmen for 110 when he made his debut for Barbados against Trinidad & Tobago in the Shell Shield in 1984. Although it was a pleasing start, it came as something of a surprise when he was picked for the second Test against Australia later that season, and an even bigger one when he was selected to tour England in 1984, given that his Test figures then stood at one for 75.

Small bowls accurate in-swingers that test most batsmen, although he does not rank with the quickest of West Indian bowlers. Nonetheless he was a worthy replacement for the injured Holding for the second Test at Lord's, as his three for 40 in the second innings helped secure victory for the tourists. A knee injury forced him to return home early and he only played in one Shield match the following season.

Small then spent three years in the wilderness before returning to be Barbados' leading wicket-taker in the 1989 Red Stripe Cup with 20 wickets at 22.05.

Teams: *Barbados, West Indies*
First-class debut: *20/1/84 Barbados v Trinidad*
First-class career: *56 wickets (25.96) and 50 runs (4.54)*
Tests: *2*
Test debut: *16/3/84 West Indies v Australia*
Test career: *4 wickets (38.25) and 3 runs*

Milton Small

SMITH, Cameron Wilberforce

Born: 29 July 1933, Christ Church, Barbados
Role: Right-hand batsman, wicket-keeper

CAMMIE SMITH was an attacking batsman who feared no bowler. He delighted in taking on the quicker men on West Indies' tour of Australia in 1960-61 but, apart from a hard-hit 55 in the third Test at Sydney, he failed to impress and wavered against the spinners.

Besides his exuberant batting, Smith was a competent wicket-keeper and stood in for Hendriks after the latter was injured on the first day of the first Test against India in Trinidad in 1962.

As with most impetuous batsmen, Smith's innings oscillated between the memorable and the menial. He showed his brilliance against England during Barbados' match against the tourists in 1959-60. The island scored over 500 runs before the visitors began to struggle against the unknown Charlie Griffith. Just as England thought they were safe, Smith lit up a gloomy Kensington Oval with a dazzling innings that lifted his side to victory by 10 wickets, as the last 58 runs were scored in 25 minutes.

Cammie Smith

Smith subsequently managed several West Indian teams abroad and is a leading figure in the development of cricket in Barbados.

Teams: *Barbados, West Indies, Commonwealth XI, New Zealand Governor General's XI*
First-class debut: *29/9/51 Barbados v British Guiana*
First-class career: *2,277 runs (37.32), 32 catches & 3 stumpings, and 3 wickets (32.33)*
Tests: *5*
Test debut: *9/12/60 West Indies v Australia*
Test career: *222 runs (24.66) and 4 catches & 1 stumping*

SMITH, "Collie" O'Neil Gordon

Born: 5 May 1933, Kingston, Jamaica
Died: 9 September 1959
Role: Right-hand batsman, right-arm off-spin bowler

"COLLIE" SMITH brought the Boys' Town spirit of club cricket into the Test match arena, as his infectious enthusiasm touched everyone who played with him.

Brought up in one of Kingston's poorest districts, he made his debut for Jamaica in 1955. In his third match for the island he thrashed 169 against the touring Australians, sharing in a double century stand with Alfie Binns, which won him his first Test cap. Smith had a dream debut, scoring 44 and 104 in the front of his home crowd in the first Test at Kingston against the pace of Keith Miller and Ray Lindwall. But the Jamaican discovered what a great leveller the game is when he made a pair in the second Test at Port-of-Spain and was unceremoniously dropped. He returned for the last two Tests of the series, but was unimpressive. Nonetheless, as one of West Indies' up-and-coming batsmen, it was appropriate that he was included in the young team that toured New Zealand in 1955-56, along with Sobers who became his great friend. Although the series was dominated by Weekes, Smith emerged as one of the successes of the tour. He scored 64 in the first Test at Dunedin, sharing in a century partnership with Weekes; while his four for 75 - including New Zealand's best batsman, John Reid - in the host's second innings was decisive in securing victory for the tourists in the second Test at Christchurch.

"Collie" Smith

Smith was one of the few players to enhance his reputation in England in 1957: he scored 161 glorious runs in the first Test at Edgbaston to secure a draw for the tourists and earn himself the nickname of "Mighty Mouse". He was instrumental in staving off defeat at Trent Bridge when, this time, he hit 168 in seven hours, sharing in century partnerships with Denis Atkinson and John Goddard, against the pace of Fred Trueman and Brian Statham.

The Jamaican maintained his form against the touring Pakistanis in 1958, taking four for 74 including three frontline batsmen, to ease West Indies to victory in the second Test in Trinidad; and was successful with the bat in the other Test at Port-of-Spain, top-scoring with 86 in a losing cause.

He was less successful in India and Pakistan in 1958-59, although he played well in the first and last Tests in India. He scored 63 and 58 at Bombay and exactly 100 in Delhi and took eight wickets in the match, including five for 90 in the second innings as only Chandrakant Borde - who he dismissed in the first innings - stood between West Indies and victory. Apart from these two matches, Smith had not been on top form and knew that competition for batting and bowling places was becoming more intense and he would have to perform at his very best to be sure of regular selection.

Smith came to England again in 1959 to play Lancashire League cricket. In the last week of the season he was travelling to a charity match in a car with Gary Sobers and Tom Dewdney when they were involved in an accident which resulted in Smith receiving fatal injuries.

His death was a tragic loss to the world of cricket and the Jamaican public in particular who had found a hero who never lost touch with his roots. They turned out in their tens of thousands for his funeral in Kingston and would have echoed the words of J. F. Dare, the President of the West Indies Board of Control, who observed: "He was one of a diminishing band who play a game for the game's sake and he had a great future before him."

Teams: *Jamaica, West Indies, Commonwealth XI*
First-class debut: *5/2/55 Jamaica v Trinidad*
First-class career: *4,031 runs (40.31) and 121 wickets (31.02)*
Tests: *26*
Test debut: *26/3/55 West Indies v Australia*
Test career: *1,331 runs (31.69) and 48 wickets (33.85)*

SOBERS, Sir Garfield St Aubrun

Born: 28 July 1936, Bridgetown, Barbados
Role: Left-hand batsman, left-arm fast-medium bowler, orthodox left-arm spinner, left-arm chinaman and googly bowler

GARY SOBERS is, without doubt, the finest all-rounder ever to have played Test cricket. A world-class batsman, he also bowled everything in the book: fast-medium, orthodox left-arm spin, and slow chinamen and googlies; he was also a top-class fielder in any position.

As a small boy, Sobers revealed his class in soft-ball cricket and rose rapidly through the ranks of domestic competition in Barbados, making his international debut for Barbados against India in 1953, at the age of just 16. He took seven wickets in the match to signal the start of a brilliant career in which he would confound opposing batsmen and bowlers the world over.

Sobers made his Test debut in the last match against England at Kingston in 1954 and took four for 75 in the tourists' first innings. He batted well in the subsequent series against Australia, including hitting a brilliant 43 in the fourth Test at Bridgetown as he crashed 10 boundaries in his innings, four of them off Keith Miller's first over. He performed modestly on the 'blooding' tour to New Zealand in 1955-56, but was one of the few successes in England in 1957, as he scored over 1,600 runs - passing 40 in four of the five Tests - and took 37 wickets. Yet, despite his unquestioned ability, by that time Sobers had played in four Test series without reaching three figures. As if conscious of this blot on his record when it came, he made it a big one: 365 not out, against Pakistan at Kingston in 1958. It was a dazzling innings that overhauled Len Hutton's record by one run and, aided by 34 boundaries, was three hours shorter than Hutton's; indeed, his record partnership of 446 for the second wicket with Hunte almost paled by comparison.

It was a golden season for Sobers which established him as the best batsman of his generation. He stroked 183 for Barbados in the first match of Pakistan's tour, while his scores for the Test series were 52, 52, 80, 365*, 125, 109, 14 and 27. That was the first time he scored over 500 runs in a Test series and he was to do it on no less than five other occasions. In India in 1958-59 he scored centuries in the first three games: 142 not out at Bombay, 198 at Kanpur and 106 not out at Calcutta. He also bowled splendidly throughout the tour finishing third in the averages behind Gilchrist and Hall.

He passed 140 three times in the series against England in 1960, including 226 in front of his home crowd in the first Test at Bridgetown, sharing in a record stand of 399 for the fourth wicket with Worrell. In Australia in 1960-61, his bowling confirmed him as the best all-rounder in the world, as his batsmanship was already without equal. He began by showing off his batting skills with a superb 132 to set up the thrilling tie at Brisbane and played what many consider to be his best Test innings in the third match at Sydney, when he scored 168 in four-and-a-half hours (106 of his runs coming in boundaries) to level the series for the visitors. In the fifth and deciding game at Melbourne, Sobers top-scored with 64 in West Indies' first innings and then took five for 120 in Australia's reply. In the end, a dubious umpiring decision and a lucky extra clinched the series for Australia but nothing could detract from Sobers' contribution and he returned to play for South Australia in the Sheffield Shield.

He was in all-conquering form against India in 1962, taking 23 wickets and scoring two centuries in the rubber. Inevitably fatigued by continuous competition, he restricted himself to one century against England in 1963. He was appointed captain for the home series against Australia in 1965 and confirmed his tactical know-how by leading West Indies to their first series victory over Australia. He was seen at his best in the third Test at Georgetown, where he hit 45 and 42, took four wickets in each of his bowling styles and held four catches.

Gary Sobers

The Barbadian had a majestic series in England in 1966. Leading by example, he scored 722 Test runs, including centuries at three of the five Test venues and fell a mere six short of his 100 at Trent Bridge and 19 short at The Oval. He also took 20 wickets at under 28 apiece - often opening the attack despite the presence of Hall and Griffith - and held 10 catches, not to mention winning five tosses. He was particularly spectacular in the fourth match at Headingley thrashing 174, as he collected a century between lunch and tea on the first day, and went on to add 265 for the fifth wicket with Nurse. He then wreaked havoc among the England batsmen as his pace and spin brought him eight wickets for 80 in the match and his side victory by an innings.

Sobers had another pleasing series against India in 1966-67 and was in similarly good form when England visited the Caribbean the following year. After a closely-fought series, the hosts finally lost out as England seized the initiative after Sobers set them 215 to win in 164 minutes in the fourth Test in Trinidad. With Griffith sidelined through injury, England won with seven wickets and eight balls to spare. These risque tactics did not go down well with the home supporters, who hung an effigy of Sobers in Independence Square in Port-of-Spain. The Barbadian hit back in the final match at Georgetown, as he tried to salvage the rubber almost single-handedly. He scored 247 runs for once out and took six wickets in the match, but England were determined to maintain their grip on the series.

Sobers returned his best Test bowling figures of six for 73 in the first match against Australia at Brisbane in 1968 and scored two centuries later in the rubber. But West Indies lost the series 3-1 and Sobers' leadership came in for severe criticism in some quarters. Doubtless affected by the adverse Press, Sobers did not reach his own remarkable standards in the short series against England in 1969, although his five for 42 in England's second innings of the third and deciding match briefly gave the tourists an opportunity to level the rubber. But when they lost their captain for a duck in the subsequent run-chase, England pushed home their advantage to secure the series.

Despite being more conservative in his approach to the captaincy - nine of the 10 Tests in the subsequent series against India and New Zealand were drawn - Sobers' personal performances continued to entrance the cricketing public. He scored centuries against India in the last three Tests of the 1971 home series and 142 in front of his adoring Bridgetown crowd in the subsequent rubber against New Zealand, but could not conjure a win from any of those situations.

Sobers was involved in a controversy off the field when Australia visited the Caribbean in 1972-73. He still felt delicate after a cartilage operation in England the previous summer and had asked to be left out of the team for the first Test. But when the selectors asked him to prove his fitness before returning to the side, the Barbadian preferred to miss the series, saying he had always kept the Board informed of any injury problems in the past. Australia won the series, but Ian Chappell, their competitive captain, was quick to point out that victory would have been sweeter if Sobers had been in the side.

But he returned to the fold for one more tour, appropriately enough to England in 1973, where he had played so much of his cricket and had such a tremendous following. Relieved of the pressures of captaincy, he signed off at Lord's with a superb 150 not out and took a record six catches close to the wicket in a fitting overseas swansong; and had one more go at the old enemy in the return rubber in the Caribbean, where he continued to taunt the Englishmen with bat and ball, albeit with more modest results.

Sobers made a remarkable contribution to cricket at all levels of the game: besides his feats at Test level, he enjoyed success in domestic cricket in England with Nottinghamshire, scoring over 7,000 championship runs and taking 281 wickets, besides providing cricket lovers with an unforgettable television clip when he slammed six sixes off Glamorgan's Malcolm Nash at Swansea; and enjoyed similar success in Australia becoming the only man to score 1,000 runs and take 50 wickets in an Australian season, a feat he achieved twice. He also played what is regarded as one of the great innings of all time in Australia when he scored 254 for the Rest of the World against Australia at Melbourne in 1971-72.

In recognition of his unique contribution to the game Sobers became the third West Indian cricketer to receive a knighthood, an honour bestowed upon him by the Queen in 1975 on the Garrison Savannah in Barbados, less than a mile from where he grew up.

Teams: *Barbados, West Indies, Commonwealth XI, Jamaican XI, A.E.R. Gilligan's XI, M.C.C., South Australia, C. Hunte's XI, E.W. Swanton's XI, Rest of World XI, Nottinghamshire, Cavaliers XI*
First-class debut: *31/1/53 Barbados v India*
First-class career: *28,315 runs (54.87) and 1,043 wickets (27.74)*
Tests: *93*
Test debut: *30/3/54 West Indies v England*
Test career: *8,032 runs (57.78) and 235 wickets (34.03)*

SOLOMON, Joseph Stanislaus

Born: 26 August 1930, Corentijn, Berbice, British Guiana
Role: Right-hand batsman, right-arm leg-spin bowler

JOE SOLOMON ensured that his batting and bowling contributions to West Indian cricket would be marginalised when he secured the first tie in the history of Test cricket by running out Ian Meckiff in the first Test against Australia at Brisbane in 1960.

Nonetheless, he was a gifted all-rounder who was selected for the 1958-59 tour to India and Pakistan and could be relied on to buttress the middle-order batting when the better-known names had failed. He made 45 and 86 on his debut in the second Test at Kanpur and an unbeaten 69 in the next game at Calcutta, sharing in a century stand with Sobers in even time. His 100 not out in the fifth match at Delhi, together with several other unbeaten innings, helped the Guyanese to head the batting averages in India; and he maintained his momentum in Pakistan, scoring 66 in the defeat at Karachi and 56 in the win at Lahore.

Joe Solomon

After an experiment at opening the innings against England in 1960 had failed, Solomon returned to the middle order with more success for the subsequent series in Australia. He made 67 and 45 at Brisbane, before his fielding transformed the game. A century partnership between Alan Davidson and Richie Benaud suggested that Australia would coast to victory, but two throws of pinpoint accuracy from Solomon changed the course of the match. On the first occasion he ran out Davidson, with just one stump to aim at; and with the scores level threw out last man Meckiff in almost identical fashion from the dramatic final ball of the match.

Solomon rarely showed that sort of flair as a batsman in a Test match, feeling obliged to play a more defensive role, which often proved invaluable for the West Indies; while his bowling was precise more than penetrative. He was more fluent as a batsman for his strong Berbice club, and made his highest first-class score of 201 not out for them against England in 1959-60.

The Guyanese toured England in 1963 and scored 56 at Lord's and 62 at Headingley, while his 76 against Australia in the first Test at Kingston in 1965 helped the home side to a decisive victory. Although his cricket was never as gregarious as many of his contemporaries, Solomon could invariably be relied upon to plug any gaps in the batting or bowling departments when the more extravagant players disappointed. Indeed, the value of his contributions were most keenly felt after he left the Test scene and, for a couple of years, there was no obvious candidate for the West Indies to turn to when stars failed to shine.

Teams: *British Guiana, Guyana, Berbice, West Indies, C. Hunte's XI*
First-class debut: *11/10/56 British Guiana v Jamaica*
First-class career: *5,318 runs (41.54) and 51 wickets (38.23)*
Tests: *27*
Test debut: *12/12/58 West Indies v India*
Test career: *1,326 runs (34.00) and 4 wickets (67.00)*

STAYERS, Sven Conrad "Charlie"

Born: 9 June 1937, British Guiana
Role: Right-hand batsman, right-arm fast-medium bowler

"CHARLIE" STAYERS was a tall all-rounder, whose gangling bowling action brought him moderate success as West Indies overwhelmed India in the Test series in the Caribbean in 1962. He appeared in four matches, returning his best bowling figures of three for 65 in the first innings of the first Test in Trinidad, while his best batting came in the second match in Kingston, when he finished unbeaten on 35 in a West Indies total of 631 for eight declared.

Teams: *British Guiana, West Indies, Bombay, West Zone, Chief Minister's XI*
First-class debut: *6/3/58 British Guiana v Pakistan*
First-class career: *485 runs (28.52) and 68 wickets (26.10)*
Tests: *4*
Test debut: *16/2/62 West Indies v India*
Test career: *58 runs (19.33) and 9 wickets (40.44)*

STOLLMEYER, Jeffrey Baxter

Born: 11 April 1921, Santa Cruz, Trinidad
Died: 10 September 1989, Miami, Florida
Role: Right-hand batsman

JEFF STOLLMEYER was a central figure in West Indian cricket for 50 years. He made his international debut against England in the first Test at Lord's in 1939 at the age of just 18 and, with Allan Rae, went on to provide West Indies with their first reliable opening partnership in Test cricket.

Stollmeyer had already won a reputation as a gifted batsman in Trinidad when he was selected as deputy to his brother, Victor, for the trip to England. But when the latter fell ill, Jeff took his place and performed admirably. He scored 59 at Lord's sharing in a century partnership with Headley, before the pair repeated their double act at The Oval.

The tall Trinidadian flourished in domestic competition during World War Two: he hit 210, 106 and 107 against Barbados and shared in several double century partnerships with Gomez, and one with his brother, during these years. In 1947 he made his career-best score of 324 against British Guiana - the highest score in inter-colonial matches - adding a record 434 for the third wicket with Gomez.

These performances made him an automatic choice for the first post-War series against England, and he began promisingly with 78 and 31 at Bridgetown. But a back injury ruled him out of the next two Tests, including the second at Port-of-Spain, where he had been nominated captain; indeed, injury and poor health interrupted Stollmeyer's Test career on more than one occasion.

The opener was appointed vice-captain to John Goddard for the tour of India in 1948-49, which was where he established his partnership with Rae. The pair shared in a century opening stand in the second Test at Bombay and a record 239 for the first wicket in the fourth at Madras, as Stollmeyer scored his maiden Test century which helped him to an average of almost 70 for the series.

The trip was a resounding success for Stollmeyer and he maintained his momentum in England in 1950, scoring over 1,000 first-class runs, including 198 against Sussex at Hove, as he and Rae put on a record 355 in just over four-and-a-half hours. In the Tests his best performance came at Old Trafford, where he top-scored with 78 out of a total of 183 in difficult conditions. One of the vital ingredients for the triumphant outcome of that tour - along with the success of Ramadhin and Valentine, whose selection Stollmeyer had supported - was the consistency of the openers.

Stollmeyer needed to draw on all his qualities of courage and resilience in Australia in

Jeff Stollmeyer

1951-52 and, despite being bombarded with bumpers from Keith Miller and Ray Lindwall in the fifth Test at Sydney, became the first West Indian skipper to score a century in a Test, as he stood in for Goddard. More success in New Zealand earned him the captaincy for the subsequent home series against the Indians. There his resolute approach ensured victory for West Indies, even though he had his partnership with Rae disrupted despite their notable success. The pair had averaged a remarkable 71 runs per innings (the highest of all West Indian first wicket pairs, Greenidge and Haynes included) but, after sharing in an unbroken century stand in the first Test in Trinidad, the selectors decided to blood Bruce Pairaudeau in place of Rae.

Stollmeyer did not score so freely against England in 1954 and his captaincy came in for criticism when the visitors levelled the series, after trailing by two matches. His decision not to enforce the follow-on in the first Test at Kingston had also caused considerable controversy but, in the end, rapid scoring from Weekes extricated his captain as the home side won comfortably.

His susceptibility to injury in the subsequent series against Australia restricted him to two Test appearances and finally forced him to retire from the game altogether. However, after his playing days were over, Stollmeyer became heavily involved in the administration of the game and, having represented the West Indies on the International Cricket Conference committee, became President of the West Indies Board of Control in 1974 - a post that stretched his considerable powers of diplomacy to the full, especially in the wake of the Packer crisis.

After such a worthy life, Stollmeyer met a tragic end when he was attacked during a burglary at his home in Port-of-Spain in 1989. He was shot during the incident and died of his injuries in a Florida hospital. Just before the attack he was named Australia's first honorary consul in Trinidad & Tobago; and early in 1990 a stand at Queen's Park Oval was dedicated to his memory.

Teams: *Trinidad, West Indies, R.S. Grant's XI*
First-class debut: *13/8/38 R.S. Grant's XI v British Guiana*
First-class career: *7,942 runs (44.61) and 55 wickets (45.12)*
Tests: *32*
Test debut: *24/6/39 West Indies v England*
Test career: *2,159 runs (42.33) and 13 wickets (39.00)*

STOLLMEYER, Victor Humphrey

Born: 24 January 1916, Santa Cruz, Trinidad
Role: Right-hand batsman

VIC STOLLMEYER was a stylish batsman, who liked to score his runs quickly. He toured England in 1939 and despite being hampered by illness made over 500 first-class runs at 30.11. He saved his best innings of the tour for the sole Test match appearance of his career, in the third game at The Oval. There he hit a brilliant 96 in two-and-a-half hours before he was stumped, after running out George Headley. A heavy scorer in inter-colonial cricket, Stollmeyer captained Trinidad & Tobago in the early 1940's. He is the older brother of Jeff Stollmeyer.

Teams: *Trinidad, West Indies*
First-class debut: *5/2/36 Trinidad v British Guiana*
First-class career: *2,096 runs (42.77) and 15 wickets (40.80)*
Tests: *1*
Test debut: *19/8/39 West Indies v England*
Test career: *96 runs (96.00)*

Vic Stollmeyer

TAYLOR, Jaswick Ossie

Born: 3 January 1932, Trinidad
Role: Right-arm fast-medium bowler

JASWICK TAYLOR toured India and Pakistan in 1958-59 and took 35 wickets, including five in his two Test appearances, which were limited due to the success of the young Wes Hall. He had performed admirably on his Test debut, in the fifth match against Pakistan at Port-of-Spain in 1958, taking five for 109 in a total of almost 500, which secured his selection for the tour of the subcontinent as partner for Roy Gilchrist. However, at that stage, no-one could have anticipated the success of Hall, who only made the trip as a late replacement and proceeded to oust Taylor from the limelight.

Teams: *Trinidad, West Indies*
First-class debut: *9/10/53 Trinidad v British Guiana*
First-class career: *50 wickets (26.22) and 62 runs (5.63)*
Tests: *3*
Test debut: *26/3/58 West Indies v Pakistan*
Test career: *10 wickets (27.30) and 4 runs (2.00)*

John Trim

TRIM, John

Born: 24 January 1915, Berbice, British Guiana
Died: 12 November 1960
Role: Right-arm fast-medium bowler

JOHN TRIM played four Test matches over three series. He made his first appearance against England in 1948 after taking nine for 104 in British Guiana's match against the tourists. He took two for six in the first innings of the third Test in Georgetown and one wicket in the second; these performances won him a place on the tour to India in 1948-49, where he bowled splendidly. Altogether he took 37 wickets (22.10) on the subcontinent, including seven for 76 in the fourth Test at Madras, as his speed found the home batsmen wanting.

The pace man was selected for the tour to Australia in 1951-52, and enjoyed success in the fourth Test at Melbourne where incisive bowling with the new ball helped him to first innings figures of five for 34. Indeed, whenever he donned the maroon colours of the West Indies, Trim could be relied on to perform well and he could be regarded as very unlucky not to have had more opportunities at the highest level.

Teams: *British Guiana, West Indies*
First-class debut: *11/3/44 British Guiana v Trinidad*
First-class career: *96 wickets (30.01) and 386 runs (11.69)*
Tests: *4*
Test debut: *3/3/48 West Indies v England*
Test career: *18 wickets (16.16) and 21 runs (5.25)*

VALENTINE, Alfred Lewis

Born: 29 April 1930, Kingston, Jamaica
Role: Left-arm off-spinner

ALF VALENTINE gave notice of his exceptional talent when he took eight wickets for 104 on his first day in Test cricket - including five before lunch - against England at Old Trafford in 1950.

The Jamaican had not been as impressive in the trial matches as his partner-to-be, Ramadhin, but Jack Mercer, an English cricketer who coached Valentine, recalled: "I saw him in a trial match bowling an eight ball over to an established Test batsman who played at the lot and connected once to mid-off, and that on a billiard table wicket. It was the best piece of bowling I ever saw in a very long association with the game."

Valentine's performance against Lancashire at Old Trafford when he took 13 for 67 won him selection for the first Test on that ground. After his remarkable debut, he went on to a record-breaking performance in the third Test at Trent Bridge as he sent down 92 overs in an innings and, in the final match at The Oval, took 10 for 160, including six for 39 in the second innings, to sweep West Indies to a hat-trick of wins.

The Jamaican took a record number of wickets for his first Test series: 33 at 20.42 each from 422.3 overs, including Len Hutton's three times. Altogether he claimed 123 first-class scalps (17.94) including five wickets for six runs against Kent, as his bowling partnership with Ramadhin won world acclaim.

He was one of the few successes on West Indies' difficult tour of Australia in 1951-52, finishing as the leading wicket taker on either side in the Test series with 24 wickets (28.79), including five for 99 at Brisbane, six for 102 in the victory at Adelaide and five for 88 at Melbourne.

The prodigious off-spinner performed admirably in front of the record crowds who attended the home series against India in 1953, taking 28 wickets; and collected his 100th Test victim in the unusually quick time for a spin bowler of three years and 263 days when he dismissed Jim Laker in the third Test against England at Georgetown in 1954. Valentine enjoyed more success in New Zealand in 1955-56, but illness and injury restricted his appearances on the subsequent tour of England to a mere 26 overs in the Test series.

His career seemed to have reached a terminal impasse before he was picked as surprise choice for the tour to Australia in 1960-61 and, once again, lived up to everyone's expectations. He finished second in the bowling averages to

Alf Valentine

Hall, collecting eight wickets in West Indies' sole win at Sydney, and found himself at the centre of the excitement in the deciding game at Melbourne. With Australia poised for victory, Valentine bowled Peter Burge and Richie Benaud and then seemed to dislodge Wally Grout's bail. But the unsighted umpire ruled him not out and, although Grout got himself out immediately afterwards, the ensuing runs were allowed to stand and Australia won by two wickets.

Although Valentine toured England in 1963 with a formidable cricketing pedigree behind him, he didn't make the Test side, and he and his many followers would doubtless have preferred to reminisce on that magical summer of 1950 and all the success associated with it.

Teams: *Jamaica, West Indies, Commonwealth XI, The Rest XI, F. Worrell's XI*
First-class debut: *25/1/50 Jamaica v Trinidad*
First-class record: *475 wickets (26.21) and 470 runs (5.00)*
Tests: *36*
Test debut: *8/6/50 West Indies v England*
Test record: *139 wickets (30.32) and 141 runs (4.70)*

VALENTINE, Vincent A

Born: 4 April 1908, Port Antonio, Jamaica
Died: 6 July 1972
Role: Right-arm fast-medium bowler

VIN VALENTINE was an affable pace bowler, known for his swinging deliveries. He bowled with pinpoint accuracy and was a useful batsman and capable in the field. He toured England in 1933 as a substitute for Constantine (who was contracted to play Lancashire League cricket for most of the series) and took 36 wickets (42.80) and made 391 runs (17.00). He played in the second and third Tests of the series, but failed to make a real impression in the company of the likes of Manny Martindale and Herman Griffith.

Teams: *Jamaica, West Indies, G.C. Grant's XI*
First-class debut: *20/2/32 Jamaica v L.H. Tennyson's XI*
First-class record: *49 wickets (40.40) and 500 runs (17.85)*
Tests: *2*
Test debut: *22/7/33 West Indies v England*
Test record: *1 wicket (104.00) and 35 runs (11.66)*

Vin Valentine

WALCOTT, Clyde Leopold

Born: 17 January 1926, Bridgetown, Barbados
Role: Right-hand batsman, wicket-keeper, medium-pace bowler

CLYDE WALCOTT was a superb all-round sportsman. Besides his renowned cricketing skills, he was an able footballer and represented Combermere School and Harrison College at athletics.

But it was at cricket that he made his name. He established himself as one of Barbados' top players during the War years, and was just 19 years old when he hit his career-best score of 314 not out against Trinidad at Port-of-Spain in an unbroken stand of 574 with his friend, Worrell - which remains the record for any West Indian wicket.

Walcott made his Test debut against England in 1948, alongside the other two "W"s, Worrell and Weekes, but disappointed after being invited to open the batting. However, Walcott was also a gifted wicket-keeper and this talent kept him his place in the side. He recovered his best batting form on the subsequent trip to India, top-scoring with 152 in the first Test in Delhi, as he added 267 with Gomez. Another Test hundred in Calcutta helped him to top 1,000 runs for the tour at the splendid average of 75.88. Walcott was equally enthusiastic in his fielding, chasing a ball from his wicket-keeping position to just inside the boundary as India failed by six runs to square the series in the final match at Bombay.

Clyde Walcott

The Barbadian kept superbly in England in 1950 making a vital contribution to the success of Ramadhin and Valentine and made 168 not out in the second Test at Lord's, sharing in a record match-winning double century stand for the sixth wicket with Gomez.

His success dried up in Australia the following year, as he scored just 87 runs from six Test innings - including 60 in the second Test at Sydney - against the unrelenting pace of Ray Lindwall and Keith Miller. It also marked a watershed in his career as, after slipping a disc in his back, he gave up wicket-keeping on the advice of an Australian doctor. On that tour the unfortunate Walcott also had his nose broken. He lifted himself in New Zealand, scoring a century in the Auckland Test, and returned to his best for the home series against India in 1953. He handed his side the initiative with 98 hard-hit runs in the second Test at Bridgetown, before being given out LBW by his uncle, who was umpiring; and went on to score his first century in the Caribbean in the fourth Test at Georgetown, when he hit 125, and rounded off a memorable series with 118 at Kingston.

England must have approached the 1954 series in the Caribbean with trepidation as they contemplated the prospect of all three "W"s succeeding together. Walcott enjoyed a splendid series, peaking with a double hundred which he served up for his home supporters in the second match at Bridgetown. His 220 made out of 383 transformed the situation, as West Indies were able to drive home their advantage and secure a decisive victory. In the fourth game in Trinidad, the Barbadian raced to 124 - the second time all three "W"s made centuries in a Test - and finished a memorable series with 50 and 116 in a losing cause at Kingston. Altogether he scored 698 runs for an average of 87.25.

Walcott lived up to his reputation as the best batsman in the world when Australia visited the Caribbean in 1954-55. Determined to erase the memories of his first encounter with the Australians he scored five centuries in three Tests against a bowling attack that included his old adversaries, Lindwall and Miller, who nonetheless continued to torment the other West Indian batsmen in a dismal series for the hosts. Walcott scored a record 827 runs (82.70) in the series, including a century in each innings of the Tests at Port-of-Spain and Kingston, and thereby became the first player to achieve this feat twice in the same series. Incidentally, his Test scores at Kingston since his debut read: 45, 118, 5*, 65, 25, 50,116, 155 and 110.

He looked like he would maintain that tremendous form in England in 1957 after his showing in the early county matches and a thunderous 90 in the first Test, albeit with the aid of a runner because of a thigh injury. However after that innings his next best score of the series was 38, even though he scored almost 1,500 runs on the tour. But the slow-down was only temporary and he found his best form again when Pakistan visited the Caribbean. He scored almost 400 runs from four matches at the remarkable average of 96.25, including 88 not out in the third Test at Kingston and 145 in the fourth at Georgetown. It therefore came as a great relief to Test bowlers the world over when he announced his retirement at the end of that series. Even so, he was persuaded to make a brief return for the rubber against England in 1960 and showed his old sparkle by scoring 53 in the final game in Trinidad.

After his retirement Walcott moved to Guiana and became cricket organiser and coach on the estates of the Sugar Producers' Association, where he uncovered a wealth of batting talent. Just as he had re-written many batting records during the 1950's so he nurtured the likes of Kanhai, Butcher, Gibbs and Lloyd who were to lift West Indies to unprecedented success in the 1960's and beyond.

Having been involved in the administration of cricket in the Caribbean, including managing several successful West Indian teams abroad, Walcott was elected President of the West Indies Board of Control in 1988.

Courtney Walsh

Teams: *Barbados, British Guiana, West Indies, Commonwealth XI, F. Worrell's XI, The Rest XI*
First-class debut: *17/1/42 Barbados v Trinidad*
First-class record: *11,820 runs (56.55), 174 catches & 33 stumpings, and 35 wickets (36.25)*
Tests: *44*
Test debut: *21/1/48 West Indies v England*
Test record: *3,798 runs (56.68), 53 catches & 11 stumpings, and 11 wickets (37.09)*

WALCOTT, Leslie Arthur

Born: 18 January 1894, Barbados
Died: 28 February 1984
Role: Right-hand batsman, off-spin bowler

LESLIE WALCOTT was a competent all-rounder whose sole Test appearance came in the first match ever played in the Caribbean, against England at Bridgetown in 1930. In a drawn game he scored 24 and 16 not out and bowled tidily, taking one for 17 in the second innings with his nippy off-spin.

Teams: *Barbados, West Indies*
First-class debut: *1/10/25 Barbados v British Guiana*
First-class record: *16 wickets (29.50) and 555 runs (30.83)*
Tests: *1*
Test debut: *11/1/30 West Indies v England*
Test record: *1 wicket (32.00) and 40 runs (40.00)*

WALSH, Courtney Andrew

Born: 30 October 1962, Kingston, Jamaica
Role: Right-arm fast bowler

COURTNEY WALSH quickly established himself as one of West Indies' top fast bowlers after rising rapidly through the ranks of school and youth cricket in Jamaica.

He had his first taste of international competition at the age of 17 when he appeared for the Jamaica youth team against the England youth team, and went on to play in West Indies youth championships. He joined the illustrious Melbourne cricket club and made his first-class debut for Jamaica in 1982, and finished the season as his island's leading wicket-taker with 15. An impressive trip to England later that year with the Young West Indies side secured his selection for the "B" tour to Zimbabwe in 1983. More success in Africa and a record 30 wickets for Jamaica in the subsequent Shell Shield in 1984 made his selection for the tour to England later that year almost inevitable. But he struggled in England, especially with his run-up, and could only muster 14 expensive wickets which, predictably, failed to earn him a Test cap.

Walsh had ironed out these difficulties by the time of the tour to Australia and a morale-boosting five for 60 against Western Australia ensured he made his debut in the first Test at Perth. Altogether he took 13 wickets (33.23) in the series and finished as leading wicket-taker overall, with 37.

Courtney Walsh

The amiable Jamaican made an immediate impact at Gloucestershire, pushing them 14 places up the county championship table in his first full season with them in 1985, as he finished with 85 wickets (20.07). He continued to worry the England batsmen when they toured the Caribbean early in 1986, taking five wickets in their game against Jamaica and a match-winning four for 74 in the second innings of the second Test in Trinidad, his only appearance of the series. He enjoyed another excellent Shield season, taking 29 wickets (15.89).

His adrenalin continued to flow in England in 1986 as he became the first bowler to take 100 championship wickets on 9 August, earlier than anyone since Lance Gibbs in 1971 and went on to head the national averages with 118 wickets (18.17).

Walsh was prolific against Pakistan later that year and in the one-day series in Sharjah returned the remarkable bowling figures of five wickets for one run off 4.3 overs against Sri Lanka; and was West Indies' best bowler as they struggled in the one-day tournaments held in Australia early in 1987. He was the leading bowler in New Zealand later that year - including returning his best Test figures of five for 73 in the second match at Auckland.

Besides his competence in the five-day game, Walsh's temperament has been severely tested in one-day cricket. He was involved in two nail-biting finishes in 1987: in the Geddes Grant-Harrison Line Trophy he won the match for Jamaica against the Leeward Islands even though only two runs were needed off his last over. Ironically he was less successful against England and Pakistan in the World Cup of that year when 18 and 14 were needed off his final over; indeed, in the match against Pakistan, Walsh warned a batsman for backing up too far rather than removing the bails which would have won the game for West Indies.

But, with the traumas of his last overs in the World Cup behind him, he enjoyed an outstanding tour of India in 1987-88, where he finished far and away the best bowler with 26 Test wickets (16.80) followed by Patterson with 17. However, by the time Pakistan visited the Caribbean, the Jamaican was clearly exhausted and could only muster four expensive wickets; and still appeared jaded in England in 1988 where he took 12 relatively costly wickets in the five match series.

Walsh recovered his form for the subsequent rubber in Australia to take 17 wickets at just under 30 apiece, which included one of the highlights of the series when he became the third West Indian, after Hall and Gibbs, to take a hat-trick in a Test. Walsh's was especially exciting, as it was spread over two innings: having dismissed Tony Dodemaide with the last ball of Australia's first innings, he then accounted for Mike Valetta and Graeme Wood when he was introduced as first-change bowler in the second innings. The affable Walsh appeared unaware of his feat until the public address announcement after Allan Border had played down his next delivery.

He maintained his good form for the home series against India, topping the bowling averages with 18 wickets (14.88), including 10 in the Test at Sabina Park, with India's lone century-maker Navjot Sidhu being among his victims.

Now a fully-fledged member of West Indies' pace attack, Walsh continued to be a thorn in England's flesh in the series in the Caribbean early in 1990. It is a role he clearly relishes and he seems determined to prey upon the world's best batsmen for some time to come.

Teams: *Jamaica, West Indies, Gloucestershire, Rest of World XI*
First-class debut: *12/2/82 Jamaica v Leeward Islands*
First-class record: *776 wickets (23.23) and 2,343 runs (13.38)*
Tests: *37*
Test debut: *9/11/85 West Indies v Australia*
Test record: *134 wickets (23.88) and 302 runs (9.74)*

WATSON, Chester Donald

Born: 1 July 1938, Westmoreland, Jamaica
Role: Right- arm fast bowler

CHESTER WATSON had a wristy action that disguised the speed of his deliveries, a characteristic which many batsmen failed to pick out. In fact 16 England players failed to read him during the Test series in the Caribbean in 1960, as they fell victim to the Jamaican. However, he was relatively expensive with his wickets costing just under 40 apiece, although he bowled splendidly in the second innings of the third Test at Kingston when he took four for 62.

Chester Watson

He toured Australia in 1960-61 and made one Test appearance, at Melbourne, but was eventually eclipsed by the development of Gary Sobers as a fast bowler. Watson was a successful participant in Lancashire League cricket for many years, and also a leading figure on the Jamaican Board of Control.

Teams: *Jamaica, West Indies, Commonwealth XI, New Delhi, West Zone, Indian Governor's XI, Cavaliers XI*
First-class debut: *5/7/58*
Jamaica v Leeward Islands
First-class record: *85 wickets (32.07) and 197 runs (7.57)*
Tests: *7*
Test debut: *6/1/60*
West Indies v England
Test record: *19 wickets (38.10) and 12 runs (2.40)*

WEEKES, Everton de Courcey

Born: 26 February 1925, Bridgetown, Barbados
Role: Right-hand batsman

EVERTON WEEKES, like Walcott, won his batting spurs after performing well in inter-island cricket in the mid-1940's.

However, after all the excitement his batting had caused in Barbados he disappointed in his first taste of Test cricket, against England in 1948, and was dropped to make way for Headley for the final Test at Kingston. But fate intervened in his favour when Headley was obliged to withdraw through injury and Weekes won a reprieve. However, the partisan Jamaican crowd would have preferred to have seen John Holt play and they booed Weekes every time he fielded the ball after he had arrived late from Barbados. However, they soon changed their minds as he went after the English bowling and scored 141 majestic runs.

That performance won him a place on the tour of India, where he set about establishing himself as the best batsman in the world. He scored a record 779 runs on that trip for a remarkable average of 111.28 as he set a world record by scoring five successive Test hundreds, including two in the third Test at Calcutta, and it would surely have been six, but for a controversial decision that resulted in him being run out for 90 at Madras.

Soon after the Lancashire League crowds were treated to a taste of his prolific run-scoring as he took every opportunity to fine-tune his game. Indeed by the time of the 1950 tour of England, virtually no one seemed able to check his run-scoring and he scored 2,310 runs - including a triple hundred against Cambridge University - for an average of almost 80 although, ironically, by his own remarkable standards he was somewhat restrained in the Tests with 338 runs (56.33). Weekes was also a top-class fielder and snapped up many close-in catches off the bowling of Ramadhin and Valentine, including five to help West Indies to victory in the final Test at The Oval.

Everton Weekes

When West Indies toured Australia in 1950-51, the Barbadian showed remarkable courage in the face of venomous bowling from Ray Lindwall and Keith Miller in the first Test, carving his way to 70 stylish runs and top-scored again with 56 in the next match at Sydney. But he found it impossible to sustain that form, especially after he was injured, and struggled along with the rest of the side in the second half of the series.

He recovered his form against the touring Indians in 1953: in the first Test at Port-of-Spain he powered his way to 207, sharing in a double century stand with Bruce Pairaudeau and, in case anyone had missed him in the first match in Trinidad, scored 161 and 55 not out in the third Test there. He scored another hundred at Kingston, to help himself to a three figure average for the series and, for good measure, had made 253 for Barbados against the tourists.

He played a match-winning innings with a quick-fire 90 not out in the first Test against England in 1954 and, having fallen six short of his century in the third at Georgetown, made the visitors pay with a superb 206 in the fourth game at Port-of-Spain, as he shared in stand of 338 for the third wicket with Worrell.

Like Walcott, Weekes was anxious to put the record straight against Australia and the pair took the opportunity to demonstrate their batting skills against the tourists in 1955. Weekes scored 139 and 87 not out in the second Test at Port-of-Spain, sharing in two huge third wicket partnerships with Walcott and in the second innings was just 13 short of scoring five centuries in seven Test innings at Queen's Park Oval. In New Zealand in 1955-56, he achieved the unlikely feat of exceeding his own remarkable scoring record. As one of the senior members of a predominantly youthful team, he scored 940 runs (104.44) including six hundreds - four of them in succession - from eight first-class matches. In the first three Tests he scored centuries in his only innings to lift his side to decisive victories and when he missed out at Auckland, even though he top-scored in the visitors' second innings with 31, his side collapsed to defeat.

Those performances suggested he would dominate the series in England in 1957 but, apart from a brave 90 on a lively Lord's wicket scored after he had been hit on the finger, his tour was blighted by poor health. But a return to full fitness in time for the series against Pakistan in the Caribbean the following year, also saw him return to his best cricketing form. His finest innings came when he crashed 197 in the first Test in Barbados, an innings which was followed by more sedate fifties in the two games in Trinidad.

Even though the runs had started to flow again, Weekes was still troubled by a thigh injury which hampered his movement and an unsuccessful operation prompted his retire-

WEEKES, Kenneth "Bam Bam" Hunnell

Born: 24 June 1912, USA
Role: Left-hand batsman, wicket-keeper

KEN WEEKES was a fast-scoring, albeit unorthodox, batsman equally strong on either side of the wicket. Besides his stylish stroke-play he was also a capable reserve wicket-keeper. He toured England in 1939, scoring 803 first-class runs (29.74) including his career-best score of 146 against Surrey at The Oval and confirmed his liking for the south London ground when he scored a cavalier 137 in two-and-a-quarter hours against England at the same venue in the third Test. His promising international career was then cut short by the outbreak of war.

Teams: *Jamaica, West Indies*
First-class debut: *10/8/38*
Jamaica v Combined Universities
First-class record: *1,731 runs (40.25), 21 catches & 1 stumping and 12 wickets (38.66)*
Tests: *2*
Test debut: *24/6/39 West Indies v England*
Test record: *173 runs (57.66)*

Ken Weekes meets King George VI

ment. It was most unfortunate that his glittering Test career was brought to a premature end but it was understandable that a man, known for his merciless attacks on top-class bowling, would have wanted an even contest, even if many of those bowlers would probably have still felt vulnerable against a less-than-fit Weekes.

Teams: *Barbados, West Indies, Commonwealth XI, E.W. Swanton's XI, International XI, F. Worrell's XI, The Rest XI*
First-class debut: *24/2/45 Barbados v Trinidad*
First-class record: *12,010 runs (55.34) and 17 wickets (43.00)*
Tests: *48*
Test debut: *21/1/48 West Indies v England*
Test record: *4,455 runs (58.61) and 1 wicket (77.00)*

WHITE, Anthony Wilbur

Born: 20 November 1938, Bridgetown, Barbados
Role: Right-hand batsman, medium-pace bowler, off-spin bowler

TONY WHITE was a competent all-rounder, who could frequently be relied upon to hit a timely innings or stem the flow of runs with his medium-pace or off-spin bowling. These qualities earned him a call-up from the West Indies team in England in 1963 when Willie Rodriguez was ruled out through injury. Even though he made 228 runs and took 28 wickets from nine matches, he did not make the Test side.

International recognition came during the home series against Australia in 1965 when he was selected for the first two Tests. He had a promising debut, top-scoring with 57 not out coming in low in the order and took three wickets at Kingston, but a less impressive showing in the next match in Trinidad brought his Test career to an abrupt end.

Tony White

Teams: *Barbados, West Indies, F. Worrell's XI, The Rest XI*
First-class debut: *19/7/58 Barbados v Jamaica*
First-class record: *996 runs (25.53) and 95 wickets (28.05)*
Tests: *2*
Test debut: *3/3/65 West Indies v Australia*
Test record: *71 runs (23.66) and 3 wickets (50.66)*

Vibart Wight

WIGHT, Claude Vibart

Born: 28 July 1902, Georgetown, British Guiana
Died: 4 October 1969
Role: Right-hand batsman

VIBART WIGHT was appointed vice-captain to Karl Nunes for West Indies' first Test series, against England in 1928, even though he had no captaincy experience at first-class level. He had a disappointing time in England scoring just 343 runs (20.17) including 23 and 12 not out in his one Test appearance of the series, in the third match at The Oval. He won his only other Test cap when he played against England on his home Bourda ground in 1930, where he scored 10 and 22.

Teams: *British Guiana, West Indies, Combined T/BG XI*
First-class debut: *1/10/25 British Guiana v Barbados*
First-class record: *1,547 runs (30.94) and 3 wickets (69.66)*
Tests: *2* ***Test debut:*** *11/8/28 West Indies v England*
Test record: *67 runs (22.33) and 0-6*

WIGHT, George Leslie

Born: 28 May 1929, Georgetown, British Guiana
Role: Right-hand batsman

LESLIE WIGHT was a dour batsman, known for his defensive approach. In his only Test appearance, against India at Georgetown in 1953, he lingered over 21 runs in his one innings. He had been more prolific against Barbados at Georgetown in 1951-52 when he scored 262 not out for British Guiana, sharing in a record opening stand of 390 with Glendon Gibbs. That innings helped him to an unusually high first-class average.

Teams: *British Guiana, West Indies*
First-class debut: *9/2/50*
British Guiana v Barbados
First-class record: *1,260 runs (66.31)*
Tests: *1*
Test debut: *11/3/53 West Indies v India*
Test record: *21 runs (21.00)*

WILES, Charles Archibald

Born: 11 August 1892, Bridgetown, Barbados
Died: 4 November 1957
Role: Right-hand batsman

ARCHIE WILES was a reliable batsman who performed well against the touring MCC side in 1925-26. His dashing batting helped Trinidad to win the inter-colonial tournament in 1931-32, and won him a place in the tour party to England in 1933. However he was just three weeks from his 41st birthday when he made his Test debut, in the second match at Old Trafford, and could not lift his game to meet the occasion.

Teams: *Trinidad, West Indies, Barbados XI, C.A. Merry's XI, Combined T/BG XI*
First-class debut: *6/2/20*
Trinidad v Barbados
First-class record: *1,766 runs (27.59)*
Tests: *1*
Test debut: *22/7/33 West Indies v England*
Test record: *2 runs (1.00)*

WILLETT, Elquemedo Tonito

Born: 1 May 1953, Charlestown, Nevis, Leeward Islands
Role: Left-arm spin bowler

ELQUEMEDO WILLETT was the first man from the Leeward Islands to play Test cricket. A slow left-arm orthodox spinner, he made his Test debut at the age of just 19

Archie Wiles

Elquemedo Willett

against Australia in the second match at Bridgetown in 1973. He bowled steadily, taking two wickets, while a similar approach brought him 30 economical wickets on the 1973 tour of England although, this time, he could not break into the Test side.

His selection for the tour of India and Pakistan in 1974-75 lifted the morale of the other smaller West Indian islands, some of whom were to make a considerable impact over the next decade. Even so, he was unfortunate to bowl at a time when there was little consistency in the choice of spinners and, after two Test appearances on the subcontinent, faded from the picture.

Teams: *Leeward Islands, Combined Islands, West Indies*
First-class debut: *14/11/71*
Leeward Islands v Windward Islands
First-class record: *286 wickets (28.43) and 1,100 runs (12.94)*
Tests: *5*
Test debut: *9/3/73 West Indies v Australia*
Test record: *11 wickets (43.81) and 74 runs (14.80)*

WILLIAMS, Alvadon Basil

Born: 21 November 1949, Kingston, Jamaica
Role: Right-hand batsman

BASIL WILLIAMS established his credentials as a top-class batsman when he fell one short of 400 runs in the 1977-78 Shell Shield, for an average of 79.80. These timely efforts won the Jamaican opener a Test cap once the Packer players had disappeared from the scene. He quickly confirmed his calibre as a gifted strokemaker, by scoring a century on his debut against Australia at Georgetown in 1978, and hit 257 runs (42.83) altogether in the last three matches of the series. This secured his place in the tour party to India, where he scored 212 runs (35.33) including another Test hundred at Calcutta. But when the world series cricketers returned to the fold, Williams was discarded.

Teams: *Jamaica, West Indies*
First-class debut: *19/2/70*
Jamaica v Guyana
First-class record: *2,603 runs (34.70)*
Tests: *7*
Test debut: *1/4/78 West Indies v Australia*
Test record: *469 runs (39.08)*

WILLIAMS, Ernest Albert Vivian "Foffie"

Born: 10 April 1914, Bridgetown, Barbados
Role: Right-hand batsman, fast-medium bowler

"FOFFIE" WILLIAMS was a high class all-rounder whose immense stamina meant that he could bowl fast for long spells and this, combined with his powerful batting and athletic fielding, made him a formidable opponent.

His career might have been even more distinguished but for the Second World War. He scored 131 not out against Trinidad at Bridgetown in 1935-36, sharing in a record stand of 255 for the eighth wicket with Martindale. He toured England in 1939 and played in the second Test at Old Trafford, but failed in his only innings.

However, Williams showed he had lost none of his vivacity when, in the first Test after the War against England at Bridgetown in 1948, he opened his account by blasting two sixes and two fours off the first four balls from Jim Laker and hit two

"Foffie" Williams

more fours off the next two deliveries from Jack Ikin in an unprecedented start to a Test innings; he made another 44 runs at a more sedate pace. His first spell of bowling in the match was equally impressive as his figures read 11-8-3-1, and finished with a final analysis of three for 51 from 33 overs. And all this from a man who had only been selected because Worrell had been struck down with food poisoning!

Teams: *Barbados, West Indies*
First-class debut: *21/9/34*
Barbados v British Guiana
First-class record: *1,479 runs (28.69) and 116 wickets (29.19)*
Tests: *4*
Test debut: *22/7/39 West Indies v England*
Test record: *113 runs (18.83) and 9 wickets (26.77)*

WISHART, Kenneth Leslie

Born: 28 November 1908, British Guiana
Died: 18 October 1972
Role: Left-hand batsman

KEN WISHART scored 88 and 77 in successive games - and in trying circumstances - for British Guiana against England at Georgetown in 1929-30, but had to wait until England toured the Caribbean in 1934-35 for Test recognition. He made 52 and nought in his only Test appearance, in the drawn match on his home ground, and thereafter was given no more opportunities at Test level.

He served as British Guiana's (later Guyana's) representative on the West Indies Board of Control from 1949 until shortly before his death.

Teams: *British Guiana, West Indies*
First-class debut: *31/1/29*
British Guiana v Trinidad
First-class record: *706 runs (23.53)*
Tests: *1*
Test debut: *14/2/35 West Indies v England*
Test record: *52 runs (26.00)*

WORRELL, Sir Frank Mortimore Maglinne

Born: 1 August 1924, Bank Hall, Bridgetown, Barbados
Died: 13 March 1967
Role: Right-hand batsman, left-arm medium-pace bowler

FRANK WORRELL was the first black man to be appointed captain of the West Indies for more than one match. Aware of the political significance of the move, Worrell was determined to succeed and did so in such a way that his influence can still be seen today.

Worrell began his cricketing life as a left-arm spinner who could bat a little and developed his game in the first-class environment in which his school, Combermere, operated, where he was greatly influenced by his teacher, the former Test player Derek Sealy.

He made his debut for Barbados at the age of 17 and was still looked on primarily as a bowler. But a splendid transformation was about to take place: the following year he was sent in as night-watchman in Barbados' game against Trinidad. He carried his bat for 64 and made 188 in the next match to make the opener's position his own. Against Trinidad in 1943-44 at Bridgetown, Worrell made his career-best score of 308 not out, sharing in an unbroken stand of 502 with John Goddard. Two years later he went after the Trinidadian bowling again as, this time, he scored 255 not out in another unbroken record fourth wicket stand with his school and Empire colleague, Walcott.

By the time of the first Test series after the War, Worrell, like the other two "W"s, was keen to show what he could do at the highest level. He had an early set-back when illness ruled him out of the first Test, but he made up for lost time in the second in Trinidad by scoring 97 against the English tourists and confirmed his calibre with 131 not out in the third match at Georgetown - more than twice as many as anyone else on either side - which helped him to a record average of 147 for his first series.

He missed the subsequent series in India because the West Indies Board refused to meet his pay demands, although he visited the subcontinent with various Commonwealth teams in the early 1950's.

Worrell returned to the Test fold for the tour to England in 1950. He was relatively subdued in the run feast at Lord's, before showing his class with a majestic 261 in the third match at Trent Bridge. It was his highest Test score and lasted just over five-and-a-half hours, as he shared in seven records, including 283 runs for the fourth wicket with Weekes. Earlier in the match, he had taken three for 40 in England's first innings. Another century in more testing circumstances at The Oval made him the highest scoring batsman of the series with 539 runs for an average of almost 90. In all Worrell scored 1,775 runs (68.26) with six hundreds and a record stand of 350 with Weekes against Cambridge University; he also took 39 wickets.

In common with the rest of his team mates, he had a more restrained series in Australia and it was his success with the ball that earned the tourists victory in the third match in Adelaide as, bowling throughout the first innings, he took six for 38. His brilliance as a batsman came to the fore in the fourth match at Melbourne as he hit 108 in just under four hours, with the next highest score being 37. Despite the difficult circumstances, Worrell once again finished as the leading visiting batsman with 337 runs (33.70) and took 17 wickets (17.35); and maintained his fine form on the New Zealand leg of the tour.

However the trip had taken its toll of Worrell and he had a quieter time against the visiting Indians in 1953 until the final match of the rubber at Kingston. There he lifted his game in front of his adopted home crowd - by then he had moved to Jamaica after becoming disgruntled over accusations of his alleged arrogance in his native Barbados - scoring a superb

Frank Worrell

237, as he shared in huge partnerships with Weekes and Walcott, as the three "W"s all scored centuries for the first time in the same Test innings.

He was appointed vice-captain for the home series against England in 1954 but, apart from an unbeaten half century at Bridgetown, Worrell was disappointing until the fourth match in Trinidad when he scored 167 and 56 in a masterful display of batting. But the loss of the vice-captaincy and more patchy form against the visiting Australians the following year could not have foretold the success he was to enjoy in England in 1957. Although he was hampered by academic commitments and injury problems he still scored 1,470 runs on the tour (58.80), including carrying his bat for 191 in a marathon performance at Trent Bridge, and took 39 wickets (24.33), seven of which he collected for just 70 runs in England's only innings at Headingley, prompting the *West Indies Challenge* to comment: "What the West Indian side would have done without Frank Worrell as a batsman and bowler it is hard to conjecture."

Given his standing in the cricket world and the changing social and political environment, Worrell seemed an obvious candidate to take over the captaincy of the West Indies and he was earmarked to lead the side against Pakistan in 1958 but, in the event, missed the next two series because of his studies.

He resumed his Test career against England at Bridgetown in 1960 and re-established himself with a painstaking 197 not out, lasting 11 hours and 29 minutes, as he added 399 in a record fourth wicket partnership with Sobers. Further solid, if not quite so protracted, performances in the remaining matches convinced the selectors that Worrell was the man to lead West Indies in Australia later that year.

The trip was a bigger triumph than anyone could have anticipated: on and off the field Worrell's team won respect and admiration for the way they played their cricket and they only lost the series by the narrowest of margins due, in no small part, to some dubious umpiring decisions. In the tied Test at Brisbane, Worrell scored 65 in both innings batting lower down the order to allow the younger talent to develop. It was appropriate, therefore, that he shared in a partnership of 174 for the fourth wicket with Sobers in the first innings. Then, in the dying moments of the match, he implored Hall not to overstep the popping-crease and the fielders to stay on their toes, as they contrived to tie the game.

Although, in the end, West Indies lost the rubber, they had helped to revive the popularity of cricket in Australia, a fact reflected in the presentation of the Frank Worrell Trophy to the Australian side, a prize that was competed for in subsequent series between the two countries.

In preparation for his final triumph, over England in 1963, he led West Indies to a crushing 5-0 series victory over India when they visited the Caribbean in 1961-62. For good measure, Worrell also headed the batting averages with 83.00, boosted by an unbeaten innings of 98 in the last match at Kingston.

Then, in England, although he was often unfit himself, he never failed to inspire his men. He hit 74 not out in the victory at Old Trafford and in the drawn match at Lord's, once more found himself urging Hall to maintain his accuracy as England began the last over needing eight runs for victory. After England won at Edgbaston, West Indies won the last two Tests to clinch the rubber in another exhilarating series which, on the initiative of Worrell, prompted a move to organise more frequent visits by West Indies. At the end of that tour, the visiting captain announced his retirement, saying: "My aim was always to see West Indies moulded from a rabble of brilliant island individualists into a real team - and I've done it."

Worrell was a fine ambassador for West Indian cricket and having won nine of his 15 Tests as skipper is considered one of the best Test captains ever. In 1964 he became the second West Indian cricketer to receive a knighthood. After his retirement from cricket, he continued to be involved in the game as an administrator and also became a senator in the Jamaican Parliament. The huge respect and esteem in which he was held was revealed when, after his untimely death from leukaemia in March 1967, a memorial service was held for him in Westminster Abbey, the first occasion that a sportsman had been honoured in such a way.

Teams: *Barbados, Jamaica, West Indies, Commonwealth XI, A.E.R. Gilligan's XI, M.C.C., F. Worrell's XI, Free Foresters XI*
First-class debut: *17/1/42*
Barbados v Trinidad
First-class record: *15,025 runs (54.24) and 349 wickets (28.98)*
Tests: *51*
Test debut: *11/2/48 West Indies v England*
Test record: *3,860 runs (49.48) and 69 wickets (38.72)*

APPENDIX A

West Indian-born cricketers who have played Test cricket for England

BUTCHER, Roland Orlando

Born: 14 October 1953, East Point, St Philip, Barbados
Role: Right-hand batsman

ROLAND BUTCHER enjoyed the distinction of being the first West Indian-born cricketer to play Test cricket for England during their 1980-81 tour of the Caribbean. Born in Barbados, he came to England at the age of 13 and was quickly snapped up by Middlesex who recognised his outstanding talent. Two brilliant match-winning hundreds in the English county championship and another two high class innings in limited-overs games for England and Middlesex in 1980 earned him a place in the tour party. The scene was set for a dream debut when he was selected for the third Test at Kensington Oval, but he disappointed himself, and the crowd, by scoring just 19 runs in the match. His best performance of the series came in the final game at Kingston when he hit 32. However, his inconsistency, which became his hallmark, prevented him from being given another opportunity at the highest level. He played for Barbados in the Shell Shield in 1974-75.

Teams: *Middlesex, Barbados, T.N. Pearce's XI, England, International XI, Tasmania, M.C.C.*
First class debut: *22/6/74 Middlesex v Yorkshire*
First-class career: *12,021 runs (31.22) and 4 wickets (45.50)*
Tests: *3*
Test debut: *13/3/81 England v West Indies*
Test record: *71 runs (14.20)*

Roland Butcher

Norman Cowans

COWANS, Norman George

Born: 17 January 1961, Enfield, St Mary, Jamaica
Role: Right-arm fast bowler

NORMAN COWANS must be considered very unlucky to have played so few Test matches; despite performing consistently well in domestic cricket in England, he has not been chosen that often for Tests. He burst onto the international scene when he was selected as the 'surprise choice' to Australia in 1982-83 - he had just 43 first-class wickets to his credit - and took a match-winning six for 77 in the fourth Test at Melbourne, suggesting that England had found a replacement for Bob Willis. Thereafter, he began to struggle, taking just 12 wickets (37.25) from four Tests against New Zealand in 1983; and was unimpressive on the subsequent tours of New Zealand and Pakistan.

Thereafter his Test appearances were spasmodic, although he toured India in 1984-85 with limited success. He then enjoyed a sustained revival in his game but, despite bowling splendidly in domestic cricket in England since the mid-1980's, it is surprising that he now either makes the "B" teams or is not selected at all.

Teams: *Middlesex, England, M.C.C., D.B. Close's XI*
First-class debut: *21/6/80 Middlesex v Oxford University*
First-class career: *576 wickets (23.84) and 1,345 runs (9.02)*
Tests: *19*
Test debut: *12/11/82 England v Australia*
Test record: *51 wickets (39.27) and 175 runs (7.95)*

DeFREITAS, Phillip Anthony Jason

Born: 18 February 1966, Scotts Head, Dominica, Windward Islands
Role: Right-arm fast-medium bowler, right-hand batsman

PHIL DeFREITAS was selected to tour Australia in 1986-87, having attracted attention with his all-round performances at Leicestershire. He enjoyed moderate success there and again in Pakistan the following year, when he took five for 86 in the third Test at Karachi. He had a bleak series against the West Indies in 1988; and was disappointing in his one match against the touring Australians the following year.

He was below par in his two Test appearances of the series in the Caribbean early in 1990; but improved in the subsequent short rubber against New Zealand - returning his best Test figures of five for 53 in the opening encounter at Trent Bridge - although he did not play in the Tests against India later that summer due to injury. However, a return to fitness saw him back in contention and his all-round capabilities suggest he will develop into a considerable force to be reckoned with for some time to come.

Teams: *Leicestershire, T.C.C.B.XI, England, M.C.C., Lancashire*
First-class debut: *1/5/85 Leicestershire v Oxford University*
First-class career: *3,321 runs (21.70) and 413 wickets (27.24)*
Tests: *17*
Test debut: *14/11/86 England v Australia*
Test record: *505 runs (21.04) and 38 wickets (45.07)*

Phil DeFreitas

Chris Lewis

LEWIS, Christopher Clairmonte

Born: 14 February 1968, Georgetown, Guyana
Role: Right-arm medium-fast bowler, right-hand batsman

CHRIS LEWIS won selection for England's "A" tour of Zimbabwe in early 1990 after some promising performances for Leicestershire; and then found himself on a 'plane to join the England Test team in the Caribbean after the West Indian-born Ricky Ellcock was sidelined by a recurrent back injury. Even so, Lewis had to wait until the third Test against New Zealand in England later that year to make his debut where, in a promising start, he took four for 127 and hit 32 in his first Test innings. He was less impressive in the two matches he played against India, but his all-round potential suggests that he is likely to remain at the forefront of the selectors' mind, as was reflected in his selection for the winter tour to Australia.

Teams: *Leicestershire, England*
First-class debut: *13/6/87 Leicestershire v Worcestershire*
First-class career: *150 wickets (27.92) and 1,460 runs (22.46)*
Tests: *3*
Test debut: *5/7/90 England v New Zealand*
Test record: *9 wickets (45.33) and 36 runs (12.00)*

Devon Malcolm

MALCOLM, Devon Eugene

Born: 22 February 1963, Kingston, Jamaica
Role: Right-arm fast bowler

DEVON MALCOLM had an unspectacular Test debut against Australia at Trent Bridge in 1989, but quickly rose through the ranks to become one of England's most potent fast bowling weapons. He came of age on England's tour of the West Indies early in 1990, finishing as the leading wicket-taker in the Tests with 19 scalps at 30.36. Malcolm played a key role in their surprise victory in the first Test in Jamaica, dismissing Viv Richards in both innings and, in the second, finished with four for 77. His best bowling of the series came in the third match at Port-of-Spain, when he returned figures of 10 for 137 which deservedly won him the Man of the Match award.

Malcolm consolidated his position with a splendid series against New Zealand in England, topping the bowling averages with 15 wickets at 17.93, as his eight wicket haul in the final Test at Edgbaston helped England to win the series. He performed modestly against the Indians in the second half of the summer, but his genuine pace suggests that he will have a crucial role to play in England's fortunes for the foreseeable future.

Teams: *Derbyshire, England*
First-class debut: *14/7/84 Derbyshire v Surrey*
First-class career: *260 wickets (30.20) and 530 runs (8.54)*
Tests: *11*
Test debut: *10/8/89 England v Australia*
Test record: *42 wickets (34.47) and 63 runs (7.87)*

SLACK, Wilfred Norris

Born: 12 December 1954, Troumaca, St Vincent, Windward Islands
Died: 15 January 1989
Role: Left-hand batsman, right-arm medium-pace bowler

WILF SLACK was obliged to make his Test debut in trying circumstances. Having scored almost 2,000 first-class runs in 1985, including a double century against the Australian tourists, he was considered unlucky to have missed out on selection for the main tour to the Caribbean the following year. Instead he went with the "B" team to Sri Lanka and was the side's leading batsman until an injury to Mike Gatting saw him heading to the West Indies as the replacement. On his arrival he played well for 34 in the one-day game in Port-of-Spain, which secured his place in the Test side. But he had a disappointing start, scoring two in his first innings and was run out for nought in his second. He lifted his game for the final Test in Antigua, scoring 52, as he shared in an opening stand of 127 with Graham Gooch, which was one of the highlights of a dismal tour.

That performance earned him selection for the first Test against the visiting Indians in 1986, but a disappointing showing saw him slip out of contention. He returned to the Middlesex fold where a string of good scores won him a place on the tour to Australia in 1986-87. It was during that tour that Slack experienced the first of his mystery black-outs, which culminated in his tragic death while on a private tour of The

Wilf Slack

Gambia in 1989. A man who lived for cricket, he was buried in his England blazer, bat at his side.

In the early 1980's Slack had been invited back home to play for the Windward Islands who, by this time, were competing on their own in the Shell Shield. There, his experience proved invaluable and he headed the batting averages with 41.42 in 1982 when the Windwards finished second in the championship, as his unbeaten 68 steered them to an historic victory over Barbados at Kensington Oval.

Teams: *Middlesex, Windward Islands, England, International XI*
First-class debut: *15/6/77 Middlesex v Cambridge University*
First-class career: *13,950 runs (38.96) and 21 wickets (32.76)*
Tests: *3*
Test debut: *7/3/86 England v West Indies*
Test record: *81 runs (13.50)*

SMALL, Gladstone Cleophas

Born: 18 October 1961, St George, Barbados
Role: Right-arm fast-medium bowler, right-hand batsman

GLADSTONE SMALL is the cousin of Milton Small. Born in Barbados, but educated in Birmingham, Gladstone went on to bowl, with considerable success, for Warwickshire in the early 1980's. He then went off the boil for a while, suffering from a plethora of no-balls, but returned to form in 1985 after shortening his run. A successful season with Warwickshire and more good results in domestic cricket in Australia won him selection for the last two Tests against New Zealand in 1986. He performed well, taking four for 98 on an unhelpful wicket at Trent Bridge, and was selected for the subsequent tour of Australia. There he bowled splendidly heading the tour averages with 33 wickets (18.96), including five for 48 in the fourth Test at Melbourne to help England retain the Ashes.

Despite these worthy performances, his services were not called upon again until West Indies visited England in 1988 and in his sole Test appearance, at Lord's, took four for 64 in the first innings; and was restricted to one appearance against Australia the following year. Although his four wickets in that match were expensive, he scored a determined 59 in the first innings which prevented England from having to follow-on.

He was a lynchpin of England's attack in the Caribbean early in 1990, taking five wickets in the victory at Kingston and eight for 183 before his 'home' crowd in the fourth Test at Bridgetown. All in all he performed admirably to finish with 17 wickets at under 30 apiece.

Gladstone Small

Small was disappointing with the ball in the subsequent series against New Zealand and missed out on the rubber against India later in 1990; but the selectors confirmed their faith in his undoubted ability by selecting him for the winter tour to Australia.

Teams: *Warwickshire, England, D.H.Robins' XI, International XI, South Australia, M.C.C.*
First-class debut: *22/3/80 D.H.Robins' XI v Northern Districts*
First-class career: *656 wickets (28.00) and 3,335 runs (14.82)*
Tests: *13*
Test debut: *7/8/86 England v New Zealand*
Test record: *46 wickets (31.45) and 221 runs (18.41)*

WILLIAMS, Neil Fitzgerald

Born: 2 July 1962, Hopewell, St Vincent, Windward Islands
Role: Right-arm fast-medium bowler, right-hand batsman

NEIL WILLIAMS forged a place in the Middlesex side as a pace bowler despite considerable competition and a susceptibility to back problems. Having been on the verge of Test recognition for some time, he made his debut in the final match against India at The Oval in 1990, taking two for 148 and scoring 38 impressive runs batting at number three as night-watchman. However, his performance was not spectacular enough to earn him selection for the tour of Australia. Williams has also appeared for the Windward Islands.

Teams: *Middlesex, Windward Islands, M.C.C., Tasmania, English Counties XI*
First-class debut: *28/4/82 Middlesex v Cambridge University*
First-class career: *394 wickets (29.13) and 2,777 runs (21.19)*
Tests: *1*
Test debut: *23/8/90 England v India*
Test record: *2 wickets (74.00) and 38 runs (38.00)*

Neil Williams

APPENDIX B

Career Statistics for West Indian Test Cricketers

Key and Denotes

B.C. - Beaumont Cup	This cup was donated in 1926 for a game between North and South Trinidad. Was given first-class status in 1959.
T.C. - Texaco Cup	Was introduced in 1971/72 and for a time replaced the Beaumont Cup.
N/E - North and East Trinidad **S/C** - South and Central Trinidad	These two sides contested for the Beaumont Cup from 1975/76 until its first-class status was removed in 1985.
J.C. - Jones Cup	Donated in 1954 and given first class status from 1971/72.
G.T. - Guystac Trophy	Took over from the Jones Cup in 1984 and was replaced by the K.S.M. Trophy in 1989.

N. Trinidad - North Trinidad
S. Trinidad - South Trinidad
C. Trinidad - Central Trinidad
E. Trinidad - East Trinidad

1. Players full totals under the heading 'West Indies' includes all types of matches representing the West Indies i.e. President's XI, Board XI, Awards XI, Under 23XI, Under 26XI, 'B'XI and W.I. XI.
2. When a player appears for an English County side the 'Opponents' column includes (where applicable) other matches such as the two Universities and touring sides etc.
3. When a player appears for an Australian State side this can also include other teams such as touring XI's etc.
4. Some of the figures given in the columns 'Overs' and 'Maidens' are inevitably open to debate regarding their complete accuracy, despite an extensive cross-check into a variety of statistical sources.

ACHONG, Ellis Edgar

				BATTING									BOWLING					
SEASON	TEAM	OPPONENTS	V	M	I	NO	RUNS	H.S.	AVGE	100	50	CT	OV	MD	RUNS	W	AVGE	B.B.
1929-30	Trinidad	M.C.C. Tourist	WI	2	4	1	17	*12	5.66			3	71	17	168	12	14.00	
1929-30	**WEST INDIES**	**ENGLAND TESTS**	**WI**	**1**	**2**	**1**	**5**	***4**	**5.00**			**2**	**24**	**3**	**76**	**2**	**38.00**	
1931-32	Trinidad	Barbados	IIs	1	1	1	7	*7					31.4	8	50	5	10.00	
1931-32	Trinidad	British Guiana	IIs	1	2		18	18	9.00			1	70	20	147	10	14.70	
1932-33	Combined T/B XI	Jam/BG XI	IIs	1	2	2	30	*23					24	7	53	1	53.00	
1933	West Indies	Tour of England	E	24	32	13	257	*25	13.52			8	865.3	174	2329	66	35.28	
1933	**WEST INDIES**	**ENGLAND TESTS**	**E**	**3**	**6**		**67**	**22**	**11.16**			**2**	**95**	**21**	**237**	**5**	**47.40**	
1933-34	Trinidad	Barbados	IIs	1	2	1	60	*45	60.00			1	41	14	65	4	16.25	
1934-35	**WEST INDIES**	**ENGLAND TESTS**	**WI**	**2**	**3**		**9**	**9**	**3.00**			**2**	**34**	**10**	**65**	**1**	**65.00**	
1934-35	Trinidad	M.C.C. Tourist	WI	2	1	1	33	*33				1	43.4	7	136	4	34.00	
		Trinidad		7	10	4	135	*45	22.50			6	257.2	66	566	35	16.17	
		Combined XI		1	2	2	30	*23					24	7	53	1	53.00	
		West Indies		30	43	14	338	*25	11.65			14	1018.3	208	2707	74	36.58	
		TEST RECORD		**6**	**11**	**1**	**81**	**22**	**8.10**	**0**	**0**	**6**	**153**	**34**	**378**	**8**	**47.25**	**2-64**
		CAREER		**38**	**55**	**20**	**503**	***45**	**14.37**	**0**	**0**	**20**	**1299.5**	**281**	**3326**	**110**	**30.23**	**7-73**

ALEXANDER, Franz Copeland Murray

				BATTING									BOWLING					
SEASON	TEAM	OPPONENTS	V	M	I	NO	RUNS	H.S.	AVGE	100	50	CT/St	OV	MD	RUNS	W	AVGE	B.B.
1952	Cambridge Univ.	Counties	E	12	16	7	291	54	32.33		1	19/12						
1953	Cambridge Univ.	Counties	E	15	25	1	720	99	30.00		5	20/5	2	0	7	0		
1956-57	Jamaica	Duke of Norfolk Tourist	WI	2	4	1	87	*41	29.00			9/1						
1957	West Indies	Tour of England	E	18	26	9	376	83	19.35		2	38/6						
1957	**WEST INDIES**	**ENGLAND TESTS**	**E**	**2**	**4**	**1**	**11**	**11**	**3.66**			**4/0**						
1957-58	**WEST INDIES**	**PAKISTAN TESTS**	**WI**	**5**	**6**		**133**	**57**	**21.66**		**1**	**16/3**						
1957-58	Jamaica	Pakistan Tourist	WI	1	2	1	7	*7	7.00			1/0						
1958-59	Jamaica	Barbados	IIs	2	4		152	70	38.00		2	3/2						
1958-59	West Indies	Tour of India	I	7	10	1	202	*72	22.44		1	19/3						
1958-59	**WEST INDIES**	**INDIA TESTS**	**I**	**5**	**5**	**1**	**156**	**70**	**39.00**		**1**	**18/0**						
1958-59	West Indies	Tour of Pakistan	P	2	2	1	119	*62	119.00		2	5/0						
1958-59	**WEST INDIES**	**PAKISTAN TESTS**	**P**	**3**	**5**		**69**	**21**	**13.80**			**9/1**						
1959-60	Jamaica	Trinidad	IIs	1	1		10	10	10.00			1/0						
1959-60	Jamaica	British Guiana	IIs	1	2		41	30	20.50			2/0						

SEASON	TEAM	OPPONENTS		V	M	I	NO	RUNS	H.S.	AVGE	100	50	CT	OV	MD	RUNS	W	AVGE	B.B.
1959-60	**WEST INDIES**	**ENGLAND TESTS**		**WI**	**5**	**8**	**2**	**108**	**33**	**18.00**			**22/1**						
1960-61	West Indies	Tour of Australia		A	5	9	2	250	58	35.71		1	15/1						
1960-61	**WEST INDIES**	**AUSTRALIA TESTS**		**A**	**5**	**10**	**2**	**484**	**108**	**60.50**	**1**	**5**	**16/0**						
1960-61	N.Z. Gov/Gen XI	M.C.C. Tourist		NZ	1	2	1	22	22	22.00			0/4						
		Jamaica			7	13	2	297	70	27.00		2	16/3						
		Cambridge Univ.			27	41	8	1011	99	30.63		6	39/17	2	0	7	0		
		West Indies			57	85	19	1908	108	28.90	1	13	162/15						
		N.Z. Gov/Gen XI			1	2	1	22	22	22.00			0/4						
		TEST RECORD			**25**	**38**	**6**	**961**	**108**	**30.03**	**1**	**7**	**85/5**						
		CAREER			**92**	**141**	**30**	**3238**	**108**	**29.17**	**1**	**21**	**217/39**	**2**	**0**	**7**	**0**		

ALI, Imtiaz

SEASON	TEAM	OPPONENTS		V	M	I	NO	RUNS	H.S.	AVGE	100	50	CT	OV	MD	RUNS	W	AVGE	B.B.
					BATTING									BOWLING					
1971-72	East Trinidad	S&C Trinidad	T.C.	T	2	3		23	16	7.66			2	71.4	24	150	13	11.53	
1972-73	Trinidad	Shell Shield		IIs	4	3	1	32	22	16.00			1	149	27	490	9	55.44	
1972-73	Trinidad	Australian Tourist		WI	1	1	1	21	*21					30	5	99	1	99.00	
1972-73	WI President's XI	Australian Tourist		WI	1	2		21	16	10.50				27	4	103	2	51.50	
1972-73	East Trinidad	S&C Trinidad	T.C.	T	2	4	1	28	*13	9.33			2	57	14	172	11	15.63	
1973-74	Trinidad	M.C.C. Tourists		WI	1	1	1	22	*22					53	11	166	5	33.20	
1973-74	Trinidad	Shell Shield		IIs	4	6		32	12	5.33			1	93	16	320	8	40.00	
1973-74	East Trinidad	Central Trinidad	T.C.	T	1	2		13	11	6.50			1	25	2	73	2	36.50	
1974-75	Trinidad	Shell Shield		IIs	4	7		30	17	4.28			2	121	25	400	16	21.05	
1974-75	East Trinidad	C&N Trinidad	T.C.	T	2	3	1	46	*28	23.00			1	60	14	169	11	15.36	
1975-76	Trinidad	Shell Shield		IIs	4	6		101	45	20.20			1	224.3	73	458	19	24.10	
1975-76	Trinidad	Indian Tourist		WI	1	1	1	9	*9				2	57	14	126	1	126.00	
1975-76	**WEST INDIES**	**INDIA TESTS**		**WI**	**1**	**1**	**1**	**1**	***1**					**34**	**10**	**89**	**2**	**44.50**	
1975-76	East Trinidad	North Trinidad	T.C.	T	1	1		24	24	24.00			1	28	8	60	2	30.00	
1976-77	Trinidad	Shell Shield		IIs	3	4	1	17	9	5.66			1	133	43	298	4	74.50	
1976-77	East Trinidad	S&C Trinidad	T.C.	T	2	2		24	17	12.00				63.1	16	144	16	9.00	
1976-77	N.E. Trinidad	S.C. Trinidad	B.C.	T	1	1	1	4	*4				2	9	1	38	1	38.00	
1977-78	East Trinidad	N.S. & C. Trinidad	T.C.	T	3	5		21	11	4.20			1	77.1	17	199	8	24.87	
1978-79	East Trinidad	N.S.C. Trinidad & Tob.	T.C.	T	4	4	1	10	10	3.33				80	13	239	9	26.55	
1979-80	Trinidad	Shell Shield		IIs	3	3	2	56	*48	56.00			2	72.2	16	234	9	26.00	
1979-80	N.E. Trinidad	S.C. Trinidad	BC	T	1	2		23	21	11.00			2	44.5	13	102	8	12.75	

SEASON	TEAM			BATTING M	I	NO	RUNS	H.S.	AVGE	100	50	CT	BOWLING OV	MD	RUNS	W	AVGE	B.B.
		Trinidad		25	32	7	320	*48	12.80			10	932.5	230	2591	72	35.98	
		East Trinidad		17	24	3	189	*28	9.00			8	462	108	1206	72	16.75	
		N.E. Trinidad		2	3	1	27	21	13.50			4	53.5	14	140	9	15.15	
		West Indies		2	3	1	22	16	11.00				61	14	192	4	48.00	
		TEST RECORD		**1**	**1**	**1**	**1**	***1**		**0**	**0**	**0**	**34**	**10**	**89**	**2**	**44.50**	**2-37**
		CAREER		**46**	**62**	**12**	**558**	***48**	**11.16**	**0**	**0**	**22**	**1509.4**	**366**	**4129**	**157**	**26.29**	**8-38**

ALI, Inshan

SEASON	TEAM	OPPONENTS	V	BATTING M	I	NO	RUNS	H.S.	AVGE	100	50	CT	BOWLING OV	MD	RUNS	W	AVGE	B.B.
1965-66	S. Trinidad	North Trinidad BC	T	1	2	1	2	*2	2.00				19.5	1	89	3	29.66	
1966-67	Trinidad	Shell Shield	IIs	2	3	1	15	10	7.50			1	40.4	13	131	9	14.55	
1966-67	N. Trinidad	South Trinidad BC	T	1	2	1	30	*30	30.00				28	3	97	2	48.50	
1967-68	Trinidad	M.C.C Tourist	WI	1	1		3	3	3.00				30	5	108	3	36.00	
1967-68	WI President's XI	M.C.C Tourist	WI	1	1		11	11	11.00				33	6	96	1	96.00	
1967-68	S. Trinidad	North Trinidad BC	T	1	1		0	0					14	4	42	2	21.00	
1968-69	Trinidad	Shell Shield	IIs	3	3	1	28	22	14.00			1	41	13	118	3	39.33	
1968-69	S. Trinidad	North Trinidad BC	T	1	2		21	19	10.50				23	1	76	2	38.00	
1969-70	Trinidad	Shell Shield	IIs	2	2	1	10	10	10.00			1	25	4	66	3	22.00	
1969-70	Trinidad	Duke of Norfolk Tourist	WI	1	1		12	12	12.00			1	59	13	153	12	12.75	
1969-70	Trinidad	Glamorgan Tourist	WI	1	1		55	55	55.00		1		28.1	10	53	7	7.57	
1969-70	S. Trinidad	North Trinidad BC	T	1	2		11	7	5.50				13	1	55	0		
1970-71	Trinidad	Shell Shield	IIs	3	2	1	34	*31	34.00			1	73.4	12	266	5	53.20	
1970-71	Trinidad	Indian Tourist	WI	1	1	1	9	*9					63	6	229	5	59.80	
1970-71	**WEST INDIES**	**INDIA TESTS**	**WI**	**1**	**D**							**1**	**38**	**5**	**125**	**1**	**125.00**	
1970-71	C. Trinidad	North Trinidad BC	T	1	2		37	37	18.50				32	4	107	1	107.00	
1971-72	Trinidad	Shell Shield	IIs	2	2	2	7	*7				1	54	4	177	8	22.12	
1971-72	Trinidad	New Zealand Tourist	WI	1	2	2	27	*20					40	12	88	6	14.66	
1971-72	**WEST INDIES**	**NEW ZEALAND TESTS**	**WI**	**3**	**5**	**1**	**56**	**25**	**14.00**				**192.3**	**53**	**391**	**11**	**35.54**	
1971-72	C. Trinidad	East Trinidad TC	T	1	2	1	31	*26	31.00				26.4	6	90	2	45.00	
1972-73	Trinidad	Shell Shield	IIs	3	3	1	59	*47	29.50			1	133.5	32	418	12	34.83	
1972-73	Trinidad	Australian Tourist	WI	1	2		73	57	36.50		1		47	3	202	2	101.00	
1972-73	**WEST INDIES**	**AUSTRALIA TESTS**	**WI**	**3**	**4**		**27**	**15**	**6.75**			**3**	**154.1**	**24**	**473**	**10**	**47.30**	
1972-73	C. Trinidad	East Trinidad TC	T	1	2		4	2	2.00			1	30	4	90	4	22.50	
1973	West Indies	Tour of England	E	10	6		103	63	17.16		1	5	318.2	78	919	37	24.83	

1973	**WEST INDIES**	**ENGLAND TESTS**		**E**	**1**	**2**	**1**	**20**	**15**	**20.00**				**34**	**9**	**101**	**1**	**101.00**	
1973-74	Rest of World XI	Tour of Pakistan		P	1	1		0	0				1	47	10	148	7	21.14	
1973-74	Trinidad	Shell Shield		IIs	4	5		33	24	6.60			5	158.4	38	434	27	16.07	
1973-74	**WEST INDIES**	**ENGLAND TESTS**		**WI**	**2**	**3**		**29**	**15**	**9.66**				**113**	**34**	**248**	**5**	**49.00**	
1973-74	C. Trinidad	East Trinidad	TC	T	1	1		38	38	38.00			2	35.2	8	67	10	6.70	
1974-75	Trinidad	Shell Shield		IIs	4	8	2	155	36	25.83				147	26	499	9	55.44	
1974-75	C. Trinidad	East Trinidad	TC	T	1	1		4	4	4.00				11	1	51	2	25.50	
1975-76	West Indies	Tour of Australia		A	5	6	1	85	29	17.00			6	123.7	20	438	21	20.85	
1975-76	**WEST INDIES**	**AUSTRALIA TESTS**		**A**	**1**	**2**		**36**	**24**	**18.00**				**27**	**1**	**124**	**1**	**124.00**	
1975-76	Trinidad	Indian Tourist		WI	1	1		16	16	16.00				60	6	182	6	30.33	
1975-76	C. Trinidad	East Trinidad	TC	T	1	1		14	14	14.00			1	21	6	56	7	8.00	
1976-77	Trinidad	Shell Shield		IIs	3	4		7	5	1.75			2	171.1	36	408	14	29.14	
1976-77	Trinidad	Pakistan Tourist		WI	1	2		13	9	6.50				40	8	121	4	30.25	
1976-77	**WEST INDIES**	**PAKISTAN TESTS**		**WI**	**1**	**2**		**4**	**4**	**2.00**			**3**	**52**	**11**	**159**	**5**	**31.80**	
1976-77	C. Trinidad	N&E Trinidad	TC	T	2	3		3	3	1.00			3	53.4	11	149	7	21.28	
1976-77	S/C Trinidad	N/E Trinidad	BC	T	1	2		34	22	17.00				35	7	90	2	45.00	
1977-78	Trinidad	Shell Shield		IIs	4	8		85	42	10.62			2	192.4	23	616	22	28.00	
1877-78	Trinidad	Australian Tourist		WI	1	2		22	22	11.00				38	11	129	2	64.50	
1977-78	C. Trinidad	N. S. & E. Trinidad	TC	T	3	3		49	25	16.33			1	81	22	280	9	31.11	
1978-79	Trinidad	Shell Shield		IIs	3	4	1	26	*12	8.66			1	78	7	342	6	57.00	
1979.80	Trinidad	Shell Shield		IIs	1	2	2	3	*2					28.1	5	110	4	27.50	
1979-80	S/C Trinidad	N/E Trinidad	BC	T	1	1		0	0					27	6	80	6	13.33	
		Trinidad			43	59	15	692	55	15.72		2	17	1549	287	4850	169	28.69	
		South Trinidad			4	7	1	34	19	5.66				69.5	7	262	7	37.42	
		North Trinidad			1	2	1	30	*30	30.00				28	3	97	2	48.50	
		Central Trinidad			11	15	1	180	38	12.85			8	290.4	62	890	42	21.19	
		S/C Trinidad			2	3		34	22	11.33				62	13	170	8	21.25	
		West Indies			28	31	3	371	63	13.25		1	18	1085.3	241	3074	93	33.05	
		Rest of World XI			1	1		0	0				1	47	10	148	7	21.14	
		TEST RECORD			**12**	**18**	**2**	**172**	**25**	**10.75**	**0**	**0**	**7**	**610.4**	**137**	**1621**	**34**	**47.67**	**5-59**
		CAREER			**90**	**118**	**21**	**1341**	**63**	**13.82**	**0**	**3**	**44**	**3132.2**	**623**	**9491**	**328**	**28.93**	**8-58**

ALLAN, David Walter

SEASON	TEAM	OPPONENTS	V	M	I	NO	RUNS	H.S.	AVGE	100	50	CT/St	OV	MD	RUNS	W	AVGE	B.B.
				BATTING									BOWLING					
1955-56	Barbados	E.W. Swanton's Tourist	WI	1	2	1	51	45	51.00			1/1						

SEASON	TEAM	OPPONENTS	V	BATTING M	I	NO	RUNS	H.S.	AVGE	100	50	CT/St	BOWLING OV	MD	RUNS	W	AVGE	B.B.
1957-58	Barbados	Pakistan Tourist	WI	1	1		0	0				2/0						
1958-59	Barbados	Jamaica	IIs	1	2		18	12	9.00			3/0						
1958-59	Barbados	British Guiana	IIs	1	1		0	0										
1959-60	Barbados	M.C.C Tourist	WI	1	D							1/0						
1960-61	Barbados	Trinidad	IIs	2	3	1	13	*7	6.50			3/2						
1961-62	Barbados	Indian Tourist	WI	1	1		8	8	8.00			2/1						
1961-62	**WEST INDIES**	**INDIA TESTS**	**WI**	**2**	**3**	**1**	**43**	***40**	**21.50**			**8/2**						
1962-63	Barbados	Trinidad	IIs	1	1		29	29	29.00			1/1						
1962-63	Barbados	British Guiana	IIs	1	2		43	33	21.50			1/0						
1963	West Indies	Tour of England	E	18	22	5	226	34	13.29			46/9						
1963-64	Barbados	British Guiana	IIs	1	1		0	0				2/0						
1963-64	Barbados	Jamaica	IIs	1	1		18	18	18.00			6/0						
1963-64	Barbados	Trinidad	IIs	1	2	1	22	*21	22.00			2/0						
1964-65	Barbados	Cavaliers Tourist XI	WI	1	D							2/0						
1964-65	Barbados	Australian Tourist	WI	1	1		8	8	8.00			1/0						
1964-65	**WEST INDIES**	**AUSTRALIA TESTS**	**WI**	**1**	**2**		**18**	**11**	**9.00**			**2/0**						
1965-66	Barbados	Shell Shield	IIs	4	4	1	58	*42	19.33			6/0						
1966	West Indies	Tour of England	E	12	13	2	195	56	17.72		2	22/7						
1966	**WEST INDIES**	**ENGLAND TESTS**	**E**	**2**	**2**		**14**	**13**	**7.00**			**5/1**						
		Barbados		19	22	4	268	45	14.88			34/5						
		West Indies		35	42	8	496	56	14.58		2	83/19						
		TEST RECORD		**5**	**7**	**1**	**75**	***40**	**12.50**	**0**	**0**	**15/3**						
		CAREER		**54**	**64**	**12**	**764**	**56**	**14.69**	**0**	**2**	**117/24**						

AMBROSE, Curtly Elconn Lynwall

SEASON	TEAM	OPPONENTS	V	BATTING M	I	NO	RUNS	H.S.	AVGE	100	50	CT	BOWLING OV	MD	RUNS	W	AVGE	B.B.
1985-86	Leeward Islands	Guyana (S/S)	IIs	1	1	1	0	*0					38	5	140	4	35.00	
1987-88	Leeward Islands	Red Stripe Cup	IIs	5	6	1	39	19	6.50			2	189.2	34	542	35	15.51	
1987-88	**WEST INDIES**	**PAKISTAN TESTS**	**WI**	**3**	**6**	**2**	**47**	***25**	**11.75**			-	**114.2**	**18**	**365**	**7**	**52.14**	
1988	West Indies	Tour of England	E	8	9	1	203	59	22.55		1	1	126	30	288	13	22.15	
1988	**WEST INDIES**	**ENGLAND TESTS**	**E**	**5**	**6**	**2**	**75**	**43**	**18.75**				**203.1**	**56**	**445**	**22**	**20.22**	
1988-89	West Indies	Tour of Australia	A	2	3		62	30	20.66			1	62.2	16	171	6	28.50	
1988-89	**WEST INDIES**	**AUSTRALIA TESTS**	**A**	**5**	**8**	**1**	**106**	**44**	**15.14**			**2**	**204.3**	**38**	**558**	**26**	**21.46**	

SEASON	TEAM	OPPONENTS	V	M	I	NO	RUNS	H.S.	AVGE	100	50	CT	OV	MD	RUNS	W	AVGE	B.B.
1988-89	Leeward Islands	Red Stripe Cup	IIs	1	2		51	34	25.50				20	3	44	2	22.00	
1988-89	**WEST INDIES**	**INDIA TESTS**	**WI**	**4**	**5**	**1**	**53**	**16**	**13.25**			**2**	**93.5**	**20**	**273**	**5**	**54.60**	
1989	Northamptonshire	Counties	E	9	14	5	127	*23	14.11			2	281	70	795	28	28.39	
1989-90	Leeward Islands	Red Stripe Cup	IIs	5	6	1	99	49	19.80			1	174.3	61	375	22	17.04	
1989-90	**WEST INDIES**	**ENGLAND TESTS**	**WI**	**3**	**5**	**1**	**51**	***20**	**12.75**			**1**	**132**	**32**	**307**	**20**	**15.35**	
1990	Northamptonshire	Counties	E	15	18	5	203	*55	15.61		1	1	503.4	122	1413	61	23.16	
		Leeward Islands		12	15	3	189	49	15.75			3	321.5	103	1101	63	17.47	
		West Indies		30	42	8	597	59	17.55		1	7	936.1	210	2407	99	24.31	
		Northamptonshire		24	32	10	330	*55	15.00		1	3	784.4	192	2208	89	24.80	
		TEST RECORD		**20**	**30**	**7**	**332**	**44**	**14.43**	**0**	**0**	**5**	**747.5**	**164**	**1948**	**80**	**24.35**	**8-45**
		CAREER		**66**	**89**	**21**	**1116**	**59**	**16.41**	**0**	**2**	**13**	**2142.4**	**505**	**5716**	**251**	**22.77**	**8-45**

ARTHURTON, Keith Lloyd Thomas

				BATTING									BOWLING					
SEASON	TEAM	OPPONENTS	V	M	I	NO	RUNS	H.S.	AVGE	100	50	CT	OV	MD	RUNS	W	AVGE	B.B.
1985-86	Leeward Islands	Shell Shield	IIs	1	1		9	9	9.00			1						
1985-86	Leeward Islands	English Tourist	WI	1	2		24	13	12.00									
1986-87	Leeward Islands	Shell Shield	IIs	3	5		281	132	56.20	1	1		8	1	33	1	33.00	
1987-88	Leeward Islands	Red Stripe Cup	IIs	5	8	2	380	122	63.33	1	2	4						
1987-88	WI President's XI	Pakistan Tourist	WI	1	1		41	41	41.00				2.3	0	6	1	6.00	
1987-88	WI Board XI	Pakistan Tourist	WI	1	2		136	132	68.00	1			2	0	7	0		
1987-88	WI Under 23 XI	Pakistan Tourist	WI	1	2		128	124	64.00	1		1	8	2	18	3	6.00	
1988	West Indies	Tour of England	E	9	12	3	472	121	52.44	2	2	8	27.1	8	80	3	26.66	
1988	**WEST INDIES**	**ENGLAND TESTS**	**E**	**1**	**1**		**27**	**27**	**27.00**									
1988-89	West Indies	Tour of Australia	A	5	8	1	182	72	26.00		2	3	26	2	71	0		
1988-89	Leeward Islands	Red Stripe Cup	IIs	2	4		311	154	77.75	1	2		4	0	17	0		
1988-89	WI President's XI	Indian Tourist	WI	1	2		52	38	26.00									
1988-89	**WEST INDIES**	**INDIA TESTS**	**WI**	**4**	**7**	**2**	**78**	**37**	**15.60**			**2**	**14**	**3**	**38**	**0**		
1989-90	Leeward Islands	Red Stripe Cup	IIs	5	9	2	230	*101	32.85	1	1	6	2.2	0	6	0		
1989-90	Leeward Islands	English Tourist	WI	1	2		93	86	46.50		1	1	27	9	54	3	18.00	
1989-90	WI President's XI	English Tourist	WI	1	2		39	37	19.50				5	0	18	1	18.00	
		Leeward Islands		18	31	4	1328	154	49.18	4	7	12	41.2	10	110	4	27.50	
		West Indies		24	37	6	1155	132	37.25	4	4	14	84.4	15	238	8	29.75	
		TEST RECORD		**5**	**8**	**2**	**105**	**37**	**17.50**	**0**	**0**	**2**	**14**	**3**	**38**	**0**		
		CAREER		**42**	**68**	**10**	**2483**	**154**	**42.81**	**8**	**11**	**26**	**126**	**25**	**348**	**12**	**29.00**	**3-14**

ASGARALI, Nyron Sultan

SEASON	TEAM	OPPONENTS		V	BATTING M	I	NO	RUNS	H.S.	AVGE	100	50	CT	BOWLING OV	MD	RUNS	W	AVGE	B.B.
1940-41	Trinidad	Barbados		IIs	1	2		33	33	16.50			1						
1941-42	Trinidad	Barbados		IIs	1	2		40	32	20.00									
1943-44	Trinidad	Barbados		IIs	1	2		4	4	2.00									
1945-46	Trinidad	Jamaica		IIs	1	2		25	19	12.50			2						
1946-47	Trinidad	British Guiana		IIs	1	2		42	42	21.00									
1948-49	Trinidad	Barbados		IIs	2	4		88	31	22.00			1	38	7	126	3	42.00	
1949-50	Trinidad	Jamaica		IIs	2	2	1	77	*77	77.00		1	1	8	4	12	0		
1950-51	Trinidad	Barbados		IIs	2	3		55	48	18.33			1	27.2	5	91	3	30.33	
1951-52	Trinidad	British Guiana		IIs	2	4		332	128	83.00	2	1	4	6	3	3	0		
1952-53	Trinidad	Indian Tourist		WI	1	1		47	47	47.00			1	8	2	19	0		
1953-54	Trinidad	British Guiana		IIs	2	4	1	217	*141	72.33	1		4						
1953-54	Trinidad	M.C.C Tourist		WI	1	2		98	65	49.00		1		29	9	90	2	45.00	
1954-55	Trinidad	Jamaica		IIs	1	2		144	124	72.00	1		1	8	2	23	0		
1955-56	Trinidad	E.W. Swanton's Tourist		WI	1	2		6	4	3.00			1	12	2	21	0		
1956	Comm. XI	England XI		E	1	1		38	38	38.00									
1956-57	Trinidad	Barbados		IIs	1	2		22	22	11.00				30	13	78	3	26.00	
1957	West Indies	Tour of England		E	19	33	3	949	*130	31.63	2	3	11	76	24	201	5	40.20	
1957	**WEST INDIES**	**ENGLAND TESTS**		**E**	**2**	**4**		**62**	**29**	**15.50**									
1957-58	Trinidad	Pakistan Tourist		WI	1	1		131	131	131.00	1			21	7	39	0		
1958-59	South Trinidad	North Trinidad	BC	T	1	2		117	98	58.50		1		28	4	70	1	70.00	
1959-60	Trinidad	Jamaica		IIs	1	2		16	14	8.00				28.1	12	55	3	18.33	
1959-60	Trinidad	M.C.C Tourist		WI	1	2		19	10	9.50				12	0	58	1	58.00	
1959-60	South Trinidad	North Trinidad	BC	T	1	2		50	39	25.00				14	3	20	2	10.00	
1960-61	South Trinidad	North Trinidad	BC	T	1	2		36	32	18.00				10	4	20	0		
1961-62	South Trinidad	North Trinidad	BC	T	1	2		100	55	50.00		1	1	12	2	24	0		
1962-63	South Trinidad	North Trinidad	BC	T	1	2		13	13	6.50				5	0	16	0		
		Trinidad			23	41	2	1396	*141	35.79	5	3	17	227.3	66	615	15	41.00	
		South Trinidad			5	10		316	98	31.60		2	1	69	13	150	3	50.00	
		West Indies			21	37	3	1011	*130	29.73	2	3	11	76	24	201	5	40.20	
		Comm. XI			1	1		38	38	38.00									
		TEST RECORD			**2**	**4**	**0**	**62**	**29**	**15.50**	**0**	**0**	**0**						
		CAREER			**50**	**89**	**5**	**2761**	***141**	**32.86**	**7**	**8**	**29**	**372.3**	**103**	**966**	**23**	**42.00**	**4-72**

ATKINSON, Denis St. Eval

SEASON	TEAM	OPPONENTS	V	BATTING M	I	NO	RUNS	H.S.	AVGE	100	50	CT	BOWLING OV	MD	RUNS	W	AVGE	B.B.
1946-47	Barbados	British Guiana	IIs	1	2		38	38	19.00				9	2	24	1	24.00	
1946-47	Barbados	Jamaica	IIs	1	2		70	68	35.00		1	1	34	7	98	1	98.00	
1947-48	Trinidad	M.C.C Tourist	WI	2	2	1	99	*83	99.00		1	1	50	10	131	3	43.66	
1948-49	West Indies	Tour of India	I	8	10	2	181	83	22.62		1	4	181	45	438	16	27.37	
1948-49	West Indies	Tour of Pakistan	P	1	1		8	8	8.00				15	5	43	2	21.50	
1948-49	**WEST INDIES**	**INDIA TESTS**	**I**	**4**	**6**	**2**	**79**	**45**	**19.75**			**5**	**94**	**17**	**224**	**5**	**44.80**	
1948-49	West Indies	Tour of Ceylon	C	1	1		74	74	74.00		1	1	54	10	133	5	26.60	
1949-50	Trinidad	Jamaica	IIs	2	2		8	8	4.00			2	25	5	74	2	37.00	
1950-51	Barbados	Trinidad	IIs	2	4		120	77	30.00		1	1	38	10	108	1	108.00	
1951-52	West Indies	Tour of Australia	A	5	9	2	76	23	10.85				92.4	19	310	17	18.23	
1951-52	**WEST INDIES**	**AUSTRALIA TESTS**	**A**	**2**	**3**		**23**	**15**	**7.66**			**1**	**14**	**2**	**43**	**0**		
1951-52	West Indies	Tour of New Zealand	NZ	1	1		26	26	26.00				33	10	66	2	33.00	
1951-52	**WEST INDIES**	**NEW ZEALAND TESTS**	**NZ**	**1**	**1**	**1**	**8**	***8**					**26**	**8**	**46**	**2**	**23.00**	
1952-53	Barbados	Indian Tourist	WI	1	1		81	81	81.00		1	1	58	30	76	1	76.00	
1953-54	Barbados	M.C.C Tourist	WI	1	2		152	151	76.00	1		2	71.1	32	127	4	31.75	
1953-54	**WEST INDIES**	**ENGLAND TESTS**	**WI**	**4**	**7**	**1**	**259**	**74**	**43.16**		**3**	**1**	**177**	**71**	**314**	**8**	**39.25**	
1954-55	Barbados	British Guiana	IIs	2	3		125	78	41.66		1	1	45	14	108	6	18.00	
1954-55	Barbados	Australian Tourist	WI	1	2		80	78	40.00		1		57.4	23	114	7	16.28	
1954-55	**WEST INDIES**	**AUSTRALIA TESTS**	**WI**	**4**	**8**	**1**	**311**	**219**	**44.42**	**1**		**2**	**215.1**	**77**	**459**	**13**	**35.30**	
1955-56	West Indies	Tour of New Zealand	NZ	3	4		48	28	12.00			2	69.2	32	124	8	15.50	
1955-56	**WEST INDIES**	**NEW ZEALAND TESTS**	**NZ**	**4**	**5**		**183**	**85**	**36.60**		**2**	**1**	**148.2**	**62**	**233**	**16**	**14.56**	
1956-57	Barbados	Trinidad	IIs	1	1		0	0				1	44	19	70	5	14.00	
1956-57	Barbados	British Guiana	IIs	1	2	1	28	*16	28.00				70	29	128	2	64.00	
1957	West Indies	Tour of England	E	14	19	3	269	*101	16.81	1		6	479.3	162	968	53	18.26	
1957	**WEST INDIES**	**ENGLAND TESTS**	**E**	**2**	**4**	**1**	**55**	**46**	**18.33**				**125.4**	**39**	**267**	**2**	**133.50**	
1957-58	Barbados	Pakistan Tourist	WI	1	2		38	37	19.00				52	23	99	3	33.00	
1957-58	**WEST INDIES**	**PAKISTAN TESTS**	**WI**	**1**	**1**		**4**	**4**	**4.00**			**1**	**62**	**35**	**61**	**1**	**61.00**	
1958-59	Barbados	Jamaica	IIs	2	4		132	100	33.00	1			44	19	81	1	81.00	
1958-59	Barbados	British Guiana	IIs	2	2		49	39	24.50			1	80.2	36	141	6	23.50	
1959-60	Barbados	M.C.C Tourist	WI	1	D							1	56.1	30	65	3	21.66	
1960-61	Barbados	Trinidad	IIs	2	4	1	188	*113	62.66	1	1	3	67	24	118	4	29.50	
		Barbados		19	31	2	1101	151	37.96	3	6	12	726.2	298	1357	45	30.15	
		Trinidad		4	4	1	107	*83	35.66		1	3	75	15	205	5	41.00	
		West Indies		55	80	13	1604	219	23.94	2	7	24	1786.4	594	3729	150	24.86	
		TEST RECORD		**22**	**35**	**6**	**922**	**219**	**31.79**	**1**	**5**	**11**	**862.1**	**276**	**1647**	**47**	**35.04**	**7-53**
		CAREER		**78**	**115**	**16**	**2812**	**219**	**28.40**	**5**	**14**	**39**	**2588**	**907**	**5291**	**200**	**26.45**	**8-58**

ATKINSON, Eric St. Eval

				BATTING									BOWLING					
SEASON	TEAM	OPPONENTS	V	M	I	NO	RUNS	H.S.	AVGE	100	50	CT	OV	MD	RUNS	W	AVGE	B.B.
1949-50	Barbados	British Guiana	IIs	2	3		81	50	27.00		1	1	49	12	127	3	42.33	
1950-51	Barbados	Trinidad	IIs	1	2		16	13	8.00			1	7	1	27	0		
1951-52	Barbados	British Guiana	IIs	2	3	1	99	47	49.50			1	47	5	137	0		
1951-52	Barbados	Jamaica	IIs	1	1		2	2	2.00			2	6	1	21	0		
1954-55	Barbados	British Guiana	IIs	1	1		31	31	31.00									
1954-55	Barbados	Australian Tourist	WI	1	2		24	23	12.00				10	0	40	0		
1955-56	Barbados	E.W. Swanton's Tourist	WI	1	1		77	77	77.00		1	1	18	3	57	0		
1956-57	Barbados	Trinidad	IIs	1	1		54	54	54.00		1		8	3	18	0		
1956-57	Barbados	British Guiana	IIs	1	2	1	27	17	27.00				14	1	53	2	26.50	
1957-58	Barbados	Pakistan Tourist	WI	1	2	1	42	27	42.00				31.5	8	84	4	21.00	
1957-58	**WEST INDIES**	**PAKISTAN TESTS**	**WI**	**3**	**3**		**19**	**19**	**6.33**				**127**	**21**	**307**	**12**	**25.58**	
1958-59	West Indies	Tour of India	I	7	8	2	72	*23	12.00			6	181.4	57	366	22	16.63	
1958-59	**WEST INDIES**	**INDIA TESTS**	**I**	**3**	**3**	**1**	**67**	**37**	**33.50**			**1**	**87**	**36**	**163**	**4**	**40.75**	
1958-59	West Indies	Tour of Pakistan	P	2	3		45	31	15.00				43	8	111	5	22.20	
1958-59	**WEST INDIES**	**PAKISTAN TESTS**	**P**	**2**	**3**		**40**	**20**	**13.33**			**1**	**58.2**	**20**	**119**	**9**	**13.22**	
		Barbados		12	18	3	453	77	30.20		3	6	190.5	34	564	9	62.66	
		West Indies		17	20	3	243	37	14.29			8	497	142	1066	52	20.50	
		TEST RECORD		**8**	**9**	**1**	**126**	**37**	**15.75**	**0**	**0**	**2**	**272.2**	**77**	**589**	**25**	**23.56**	**5-42**
		CAREER		**29**	**38**	**6**	**696**	**77**	**21.75**	**0**	**3**	**14**	**687.5**	**176**	**1630**	**61**	**26.72**	**4-70**

AUSTIN, Richard Arkwright

				BATTING									BOWLING					
SEASON	TEAM	OPPONENTS	V	M	I	NO	RUNS	H.S.	AVGE	100	50	CT	OV	MD	RUNS	W	AVGE	B.B.
1974-75	Jamaica	Shell Shield	IIs	4	7		181	74	25.85		2	2	65.3	9	184	6	30.66	
1975-76	Jamaica	Shell Shield	IIs	4	4		170	82	42.50		2	1	16	2	37	0		
1975-76	Jamaica	Indian Tourist	WI	1	2		149	141	74.50	1			4	1	16	0		
1976-77	Jamaica	Shell Shield	IIs	4	6		231	131	38.50	1	1	6	99.2	31	210	7	30.00	
1976-77	Jamaica	Pakistan Tourist	WI	1	2		28	27	14.00				37	11	103	9	11.44	
1976-77	WI President's XI	Pakistan Tourist	WI	1	1		1	1	1.00									
1977-78	Jamaica	Shell Shield	IIs	4	6		369	127	61.50	1	3	1	153.1	48	373	18	20.72	
1977-78	Jamaica	Australian Tourist	WI	1	2		96	58	48.00		1		28.3	1	86	3	28.66	
1977-78	**WEST INDIES**	**AUSTRALIA TESTS**	**WI**	**2**	**2**		**22**	**20**	**11.00**			**2**	**1**	**0**	**5**	**0**		
1979-80	Jamaica	Shell Shield	IIs	4	8		159	41	19.87			5	193.2	50	479	16	29.93	

				M	I	NO	RUNS	H.S.	AVGE	100	50	CT	OV	MD	RUNS	W	AVGE	B.B.
1980-81	Jamaica	Shell Shield	IIs	3	6	1	226	*87	45.20		2	3	60	14	183	6	30.50	
1980-81	Jamaica	English Tourist	WI	1	1		62	62	62.00		1	3	45	4	145	2	72.50	
1980-81	WI President's XI	English Tourist	WI	1	2		44	25	22.00				45	10	142	0		
1981-82	Jamaica	Shell Shield	IIs	5	10		225	118	22.50	1	1	2	85.1	15	280	6	46.66	
1982-83	WI Rebels XI	Tour of South Africa	SA	2	4		134	93	33.50		1	2	10	1	36	0		
		Jamaica		32	54	1	1896	141	35.77	4	13	23	787	186	2096	73	28.71	
		West Indies		4	5		67	25	13.40			2	46	10	147	0		
		WI Rebels XI		2	4		134	93	33.50		1	2	10	1	36	0		
		TEST RECORD		**2**	**2**	**0**	**22**	**20**	**11.00**	**0**	**0**	**2**	**1**	**0**	**5**	**0**		
		CAREER		**38**	**63**	**1**	**2097**	**141**	**33.82**	**4**	**14**	**27**	**843**	**197**	**2279**	**73**	**31.21**	**8-71**

BACCHUS, Sheik Faoud Ahumul Fasiel

				BATTING									BOWLING					
SEASON	**TEAM**	**OPPONENTS**	**V**	**M**	**I**	**NO**	**RUNS**	**H.S.**	**AVGE**	**100**	**50**	**CT**	**OV**	**MD**	**RUNS**	**W**	**AVGE**	**B.B.**
1971-72	Demerara	Berbice JC	G	1	2		17	9	8.50									
1972-73	Guyana	Australian Tourist	WI	1	2	1	67	*36	67.00									
1973-74	Guyana	Shell Shield	IIs	2	2		12	10	6.00			1	1	0	8	0		
1973-74	Guyana	M.C.C Tourist	WI	1	2		38	24	19.00									
1974-75	Guyana	Shell Shield	IIs	3	3	1	111	53	55.50		2	3						
1975-76	Demerara	Berbice JC	G	1	2		34	23	17.00									
1975-76	Guyana	Shell Shield	IIs	3	4		211	84	52.75		2							
1976-77	Guyana	Shell Shield	IIs	2	3		95	62	31.66		1		1	0	1	0		
1976-77	Guyana	Pakistan Tourist	WI	1	2		18	17	9.00			1						
1977-78	Guyana	Shell Shield	IIs	4	6		184	102	30.66	1		2						
1977-78	Guyana	Australian Tourist	WI	1	2		35	22	17.50									
1977-78	**WEST INDIES**	**AUSTRALIA TESTS**	**WI**	**2**	**4**		**42**	**21**	**10.50**			**3**						
1978-79	West Indies	Tour of India	I	6	12	1	450	*110	40.90	1	2	4						
1978-79	**WEST INDIES**	**INDIA TESTS**	**I**	**6**	**10**		**472**	**250**	**47.20**	**1**	**2**	**7**						
1978-79	West Indies	Tour of Sri Lanka	SL	2	3		108	56	36.00		1	4	4	2	4	0		
1978-79	Guyana	Shell Shield	IIs	4	5	1	196	*154	49.00	1			1	0	1	0		
1979-80	Demerara	Berbice JC	G	1	D													
1979-80	Guyana	Shell Shield	IIs	3	5		222	81	44.40		2	2						
1980	West Indies	Tour of England	E	10	17	2	589	*164	33.80	1	3	14	1	0	8	0		
1980	**WEST INDIES**	**ENGLAND TESTS**	**E**	**5**	**6**		**121**	**61**	**20.16**		**1**	**1**	**1**	**0**	**3**	**0**		
1980-81	West Indies	Tour of Pakistan	P	4	8	2	286	80	47.66		2	5	0.1	0	0	0		
1980-81	**WEST INDIES**	**PAKISTAN TESTS**	**P**	**4**	**6**		**119**	**45**	**19.83**			**4**						

				BATTING									BOWLING					
SEASON	TEAM	OPPONENTS	V	M	I	NO	RUNS	H.S.	AVGE	100	50	CT	OV	MD	RUNS	W	AVGE	B.B.
1980-81	Guyana	Shell Shield	IIs	4	7		204	86	29.14		1	3	3	1	2	0		
1981-82	WI Under 26 XI	Tour of Zimbabwe	Z	3	4	1	69	29	23.00			3						
1981-82	West Indies	Tour of Australia	A	4	6	2	291	85	72.75		4	2						
1981-82	**WEST INDIES**	**AUSTRALIA TESTS**	**A**	**2**	**4**		**28**	**27**	**7.00**			**2**						
1981-82	Guyana	Shell Shield	IIs	3	5	1	326	126	81.50	1	3	2	1	1	0	0		
1982-83	Guyana	Shell Shield	IIs	5	8		349	143	43.62	1	2	7						
1983-84	WI Rebels XI	Tour of South Africa	SA	7	13	1	432	88	36.00		4	3						
1984-85	Western Province	Currie Cup	SA	9	17		324	65	19.05		3	11	1	0	2	1	2.00	
1985-86	Border	Currie Cup	SA	7	12		494	134	41.16	1	2	4	64.2	10	168	7	24.00	
		Guyana		37	56	4	2068	154	39.76	4	13	21	7	2	12	0		
		Demerara		3	4		51	23	12.75									
		West Indies		48	80	8	2575	250	35.76	3	15	49	6.1	2	15	0		
		WI Rebels XI		7	13	1	432	88	36.00		4	3						
		Western Province		9	17		324	65	19.05		3	11	1	0	2	1	2.00	
		Border		7	12		494	134	41.16	1	2	4	64.2	10	168	7	24.00	
		TEST RECORD		**19**	**30**	**0**	**782**	**250**	**26.06**	**1**	**3**	**17**	**1**	**0**	**3**	**0**		
		CAREER		**111**	**182**	**13**	**5944**	**250**	**35.17**	**8**	**37**	**88**	**78.3**	**14**	**197**	**8**	**24.62**	**2-18**

BAICHAN, LEONARD

				BATTING									BOWLING					
SEASON	TEAM	OPPONENTS	V	M	I	NO	RUNS	H.S.	AVGE	100	50	CT	OV	MD	RUNS	W	AVGE	B.B.
1968-69	Guyana	Shell Shield	IIs	2	4		162	72	40.50		2							
1971-72	Guyana	Shell Shield	IIs	3	5	1	278	*114	69.50	1	1							
1971-72	WI President's XI	New Zealand Tourist	WI	1	1		96	96	96.00		1		1	0	4	0		
1971-72	Guyana	New Zealand Tourist	WI	1	2		20	10	10.00									
1972-73	Berbice	Demerara J.C.	G	1	2		87	82	43.50		1							
1972-73	Guyana	Shell Shield	IIs	2	3	1	167	134	83.50	1		1	3	0	16	0		
1972-73	Guyana	Australian Tourist	WI	1	2		35	32	17.50									
1973-74	Berbice	Demerara JC	G	1	2	1	318	*216	318.00	2								
1973-74	Guyana	Shell Shield	IIs	4	6		276	113	46.00	1	1	3	1	0	6	0		
1973-74	Guyana	M.C.C. Tourist	WI	1	2		72	71	36.00		1	1						
1973-74	WI President's XI	M.C.C. Tourist	WI	1	2	1	188	*139	188.00	1								
1974-75	West Indies	Tour of India	I	7	10	1	480	158	53.33	2	2		1	0	4	0		
1974-75	West Indies	Tour of Sri Lanka	SL	2	3		70	36	23.33			2						

1974-75	**WEST INDIES**	**PAKISTAN TESTS**	**P**	**2**	**4**	**2**	**161**	***105**	**80.50**	**1**		**2**						
1974-75	Guyana	Shell Shield	IIs	4	6	1	212	111	42.40	1	1	5						
1975-76	West Indies	Tour of Australia	A	6	9	1	305	72	38.12		2	4						
1975-76	**WEST INDIES**	**AUSTRALIA TESTS**	**A**	**1**	**2**		**23**	**20**	**11.50**									
1976-77	Berbice	Demerara J.C.	G	1	2	1	129	*83	129.00		1	3						
1976-77	Guyana	Shell Shield	IIs	4	7	1	246	63	41.00		2	4	1	0	4	0		
1976-77	Guyana	Pakistan Tourist	WI	1	2		137	115	68.50	1								
1976-77	WI President's XI	Pakistan Tourist	WI	1	1		62	62	62.00		1	1						
1977-78	Berbice	Demerara J.C.	G	1	2		157	81	78.50		2	2						
1977-78	Guyana	Shell Shield	IIs	4	6	1	169	85	33.80		1	2						
1977-78	Guyana	Australian Tourist	WI	1	2		60	40	30.00									
1978-79	Berbice	Demerara J.C.	G	1	1		4	4	4.00			1						
1978-79	Guyana	Shell Shield	IIs	4	5		238	85	47.60		3	2						
1979-80	Berbice	Demerara J.C.	G	1	D													
1979-80	Guyana	Shell Shield	IIs	2	4		64	40	16.00									
1981-82	Berbice	Demerara J.C.	G	1	1		55	55	55.00		1	2						
1982-83	Berbice	Demerara J.C.	G	1	2	1	233	132	233.00	2								
		Guyana		34	56	5	2136	134	41.88	5	12	17	5	0	26	0		
		Berbice		8	12	3	983	*216	109.22	4	5	8						
		West Indies		21	32	5	1385	158	51.29	4	6	10	2	0	8	0		
		TEST RECORD		**3**	**6**	**2**	**184**	***105**	**46.00**	**1**	**0**	**2**						
		CAREER		**63**	**100**	**13**	**4504**	***216**	**51.77**	**13**	**23**	**35**	**7**	**0**	**34**	**0**		

BAPTISTE, Eldine Ashworth Elderfield

				BATTING									BOWLING					
SEASON	TEAM	OPPONENTS	V	M	I	NO	RUNS	H.S.	AVGE	100	50	CT	OV	MD	RUNS	W	AVGE	B.B.
1981	Kent	Counties	E	15	22	4	359	*37	19.95			8	280.3	64	844	29	29.10	
1981-82	Leeward Islands	Shell Shield	IIs	4	7	1	126	46	21.00			3	90	12	349	9	38.77	
1982	Kent	Counties	E	9	12	3	319	*69	35.44		2	7	186.4	45	671	12	55.91	
1982-83	Leeward Islands	Shell Shield	IIs	5	9		171	44	19.00			2	154.4	31	508	26	19.53	
1982-83	Leeward Islands	Indian Tourist	WI	1	2		29	20	14.50			1	23	5	61	2	30.50	
1983	Kent	Counties	E	17	26	5	755	*136	35.95	2	3	10	376.3	88	1187	50	23.74	
1983-84	West Indies	Tour of India	I	4	6	3	175	*64	58.33		1	3	74.5	13	179	11	16.27	
1983-84	**WEST INDIES**	**INDIA TESTS**	**I**	**1**	**1**		**6**	**6**	**6.00**				**17**	**1**	**66**	**1**	**66.00**	
1983-84	Leeward Islands	Shell Shield	IIs	1	D							1	27	6	105	3	35.00	
1983-84	Leeward Islands	Australian Tourist	WI	1	2	1	60	*57			1		44	9	146	6	24.33	
1983-84	**WEST INDIES**	**AUSTRALIA TESTS**	**WI**	**3**	**3**		**44**	**27**	**14.66**			**1**	**62**	**15**	**155**	**6**	**25.83**	

				BATTING									BOWLING					
SEASON	TEAM	OPPONENTS	V	M	I	NO	RUNS	H.S.	AVGE	100	50	CT	OV	MD	RUNS	W	AVGE	B.B.
1984	West Indies	Tour of England	E	5	3		22	16	7.33				96.2	25	252	11	22.90	
1984	**WEST INDIES**	**ENGLAND TESTS**	**E**	**5**	**6**	**1**	**174**	***87**	**34.80**		**1**	**1**	**125**	**39**	**265**	**8**	**33.12**	
1984-85	West Indies	Tour of Australia	A	4	6		107	54	17.83		1	1	121.2	28	350	11	31.81	
1984-85	Leeward Islands	Shell Shield	IIs	2	3		62	38	20.66			3	56	17	138	11	12.54	
1985	Kent	Counties	E	23	36	5	972	82	31.35		6	12	562	116	1661	58	28.63	
1985-86	Leeward Islands	Shell Shield	IIs	1	2		71	58	35.50		1		13	4	24	1	24.00	
1986	Kent	Counties	E	7	8		273	113	34.12	1	1	1	146	40	351	13	27.00	
1986-87	West Indies 'B'	Tour of Zimbabwe	Z	5	6		137	55	22.83		1	2	156.5	41	408	29	14.06	
1986-87	Leeward Islands	Shell Shield	IIs	3	5	2	84	33	28.00			4	81	14	215	6	35.83	
1987	Kent	Counties	E	16	23	3	517	95	25.85		3	6	519.3	117	1495	56	26.69	
1987-88	West Indies	Tour of India	I	2	2	1	97	*75	97.00		1		60.3	13	172	12	14.33	
1987-88	Leeward Islands	Red Stripe Cup	IIs	3	4		189	99	47.25		2		51	5	125	3	41.66	
1988-89	Leeward Islands	Red Stripe Cup	IIs	5	9		231	95	25.66		1	4	99.4	22	272	21	12.95	
1989-90	Leeward Islands	Red Stripe Cup	II	5	7		118	46	16.85			2	191.1	60	455	26	17.50	
1989-90	Leeward Islands	English Tourist	WI	1	1		61	61	61.00		1		39	10	90	0		
1989-90	WI President's XI	English Tourist	WI	1	2		28	19	14.00				57.1	11	133	4	33.25	
1989-90	**WEST INDIES**	**ENGLAND TESTS**	**WI**	**1**	**1**		**9**	**9**	**9.00**				**23**	**5**	**77**	**1**	**77.00**	
		Leeward Islands		32	51	4	1202	99	25.57		6	20	869.3	195	2488	114	21.82	
		West Indies		31	36	5	799	*87	25.77		5	8	794	191	2057	94	21.88	
		Kent		87	127	20	3195	*136	29.85	3	15	44	2071.1	470	6209	218	28.48	
		TEST RECORD		**10**	**11**	**1**	**233**	***87**	**23.30**	**0**	**1**	**2**	**227**	**60**	**563**	**16**	**35.18**	**3-31**
		CAREER		**150**	**214**	**29**	**5196**	***136**	**28.08**	**3**	**26**	**72**	**3734.4**	**856**	**10754**	**426**	**25.24**	**8-76**

BARRETT, Arthur George

				BATTING									BOWLING					
SEASON	TEAM	OPPONENTS	V	M	I	NO	RUNS	H.S.	AVGE	100	50	CT	OV	MD	RUNS	W	AVGE	B.B.
1966-67	Jamaica	Shell Shield	IIs	2	2		0	0				1	86.3	17	253	7	36.14	
1968-69	Jamaica	Shell Shield	IIs	4	4	2	35	18	17.50			5	78	21	195	9	21.66	
1969-70	Jamaica	Shell Shield	IIs	4	7	2	196	*102	39.20	1		5	191.2	43	579	26	22.96	
1969-70	Jamaica	Canadian Tourist XI	WI	1	1		25	25	25.00			2	52	10	166	8	20.75	
1970	Jamaica	Tour of English Counties	E	4	4	1	87	*37	29.00			4	47.1	14	119	5	23.80	
1970-71	Jamaica	Shell Shield	IIs	4	6		68	42	11.33			9	165.1	40	521	17	30.64	
1970-71	Jamaica	Indian Tourist	WI	1	1		22	22	22.00			1	144.2	10	135	5	27.00	

1970-71	WI President's XI	Indian Tourist	WI	1	1		12	12	12.00			1	45	7	128	3	42.66	
1970-71	**WEST INDIES**	**INDIA TESTS**	**WI**	**2**	**4**		**33**	**19**	**8.25**				**80.4**	**19**	**194**	**4**	**48.50**	
1971-72	Jamaica	Shell Shield	IIs	2	4	1	58	*22	19.33				57	14	173	4	43.25	
1971-72	Jamaica	New Zealand Tourist	WI	1	1		10	10	10.00			1	61	23	113	4	28.25	
1972-73	Jamaica	Shell Shield	IIs	4	7		101	34	14.42			4	142	28	423	9	47.00	
1972-73	Jamaica	Australian Tourist	WI	1	2		3	3	1.50			2	28	2	113	1	113.00	
1973-74	Jamaica	Shell Shield	IIs	4	5		88	34	17.60			6	188.4	48	483	17	28.41	
1973-74	Jamaica	M.C.C. Tourist	WI	1	2	1	3	*3	3.00			1	35	8	81	2	40.50	
1973-74	WI President's XI	M.C.C. Tourist	WI	1	2		37	37	18.50			1	41	17	98	4	24.50	
1973-74	**WEST INDIES**	**ENGLAND TESTS**	**WI**	**2**	**1**		**0**	**0**					**124**	**46**	**260**	**7**	**37.14**	
1974-75	West Indies	Tour of India	I	6	6	1	117	*36	23.40			2	165	38	454	15	29.33	
1974-75	**WEST INDIES**	**INDIA TESTS**	**I**	**2**	**2**	**1**	**7**	***5**	**7.00**				**64**	**18**	**149**	**2**	**74.50**	
1974-75	West Indies	Tour of Pakistan	P	1	2	1	23	*12	23.00				25	3	81	0		
1974-75	Jamaica	Shell Shield	IIs	1	2		62	49	31.00			1	50	9	117	6	19.50	
1975-76	Jamaica	Shell Shield	IIs	4	4	1	34	21	11.33			5	93	23	216	6	36.00	
1980-81	Jamaica	Shell Shield	IIs	4	5	2	65	*23	21.66			3	72	10	225	8	28.12	
		Jamaica		41	57	10	857	*102	18.23	1		50	1491.1	320	3912	134	29.19	
		West Indies		15	18	3	229	37	15.26			4	544	148	1364	35	38.97	
		TEST RECORD		**6**	**7**	**1**	**40**	**19**	**6.66**	**0**	**0**	**0**	**268.4**	**83**	**603**	**13**	**46.38**	**3-43**
		CAREER		**57**	**75**	**13**	**1086**	***102**	**17.51**	**1**	**0**	**54**	**2035.5**	**468**	**5276**	**169**	**31.21**	**7-90**

BARROW, Ivan

				BATTING									BOWLING					
SEASON	**TEAM**	**OPPONENTS**	**V**	**M**	**I**	**NO**	**RUNS**	**H.S.**	**AVGE**	**100**	**50**	**CT/St**	**OV**	**MD**	**RUNS**	**W**	**AVGE**	**B.B.**
1928-29	Jamaica	Julien Cahn's XI	WI	2	4		83	61	20.75		1	4/2						
1928-29	West Indies XI	Julien Cahn's XI	WI	1	2		33	21	16.50									
1929-30	Jamaica	M.C.C. Tourist	WI	2	4	1	94	*42	31.33			1/0						
1929-30	**WEST INDIES**	**ENGLAND TESTS**	**WI**	**1**	**1**		**0**	**0**				**1/2**						
1930-31	West Indies	Tour of Australia	A	3	6		123	45	20.50			4/1						
1930-31	**WEST INDIES**	**AUSTRALIA TESTS**	**A**	**5**	**9**	**1**	**122**	**27**	**15.25**			**9/2**						
1931-32	Jamaica	L. Tennyson's Tourist	WI	3	4	1	249	169	83.00	1	1	4/3						
1933	West Indies	Tour of England	E	22	39	1	903	89	23.76		5	16/6	4	1	14	0		
1933	**WEST INDIES**	**ENGLAND TESTS**	**E**	**3**	**6**		**143**	**105**	**23.83**	**1**		**5/1**						
1934-35	Jamaica	M.C.C. Tourist	WI	2	3		207	108	69.00	1	1	2/1						

				BATTING									BOWLING					
SEASON	TEAM	OPPONENTS	V	M	I	NO	RUNS	H.S.	AVGE	100	50	CT/St	OV	MD	RUNS	W	AVGE	B.B.
1934-35	**WEST INDIES**	**ENGLAND TESTS**	**WI**	**1**	**1**		**3**	**3**	**3.00**			**1/0**						
1935-36	Jamaica	Yorkshire Tourist	WI	3	5		210	59	42.00		1	3/0	5	0	20	0		
1938-39	Jamaica	Combined University Tourist	WI	2	3		77	65	25.66		1	0/2						
1939	West Indies	Tour of England	E	15	23	1	296	41	13.45			19/6						
1939	**WEST INDIES**	**ENGLAND TESTS**	**E**	**1**	**2**	**1**	**8**	***6**	**8.00**			**1/0**						
1945-46	Jamaica	Trinidad	IIs	1	1		0	0				1/1						
		Jamaica		15	24	2	920	169	41.81	2	5	15/9	5	0	20	0		
		West Indies		52	89	4	1631	105	19.18	1	5	56/18	4	1	14	0		
		TEST RECORD		**11**	**19**	**2**	**276**	**105**	**16.23**	**1**	**0**	**17/5**						
		CAREER		**67**	**113**	**6**	**2551**	**169**	**23.84**	**3**	**10**	**71/27**	**9**	**1**	**34**	**0**		

BARTLETT, Edward Lawson

				BATTING									BOWLING					
SEASON	TEAM	OPPONENTS	V	M	I	NO	RUNS	H.S.	AVGE	100	50	CT	OV	MD	RUNS	W	AVGE	B.B.
1923-24	Barbados	Trinidad	IIs	1	2		1	1	0.50									
1924-25	Barbados	Jamaica	IIs	2	2		69	61	34.50		1	2						
1924-25	Barbados	Trinidad	IIs	1	2		13	7	6.50									
1925-26	Barbados	British Guiana	IIs	1	2		19	14	9.50									
1926-27	Barbados	British Guiana	IIs	1	1		88	88	88.00		1							
1926-27	Barbados	Trinidad	IIs	1	2		91	74	45.50		1							
1927-28	Combined B/J XI	Combined Trin/BG XI	IIs	1	2	1	19	*11	19.00									
1927-28	Barbados Born XI	West Indies XI	IIs	1	2	1	131	*93	131.00		1							
1928	West Indies	Tour of England	E	14	23	1	563	109	25.59	1	2	1						
1928	**WEST INDIES**	**ENGLAND TESTS**	**E**	**1**	**2**		**21**	**13**	**10.50**									
1929-30	Barbados	British Guiana	IIs	1	2		40	37	20.00			1						
1929-30	Barbados	M.C.C. Tourist	WI	2	3		109	67	36.33		1							
1930-31	West Indies	Tour of Australia	A	4	7		98	34	14.00									
1930-31	**WEST INDIES**	**AUSTRALIA TESTS**	**A**	**4**	**6**	**1**	**110**	**84**	**22.00**		**1**	**2**						
1931-32	Barbados	Trinidad	IIs	1	2		18	16	9.00			2						
1933-34	Barbados	British Guiana	IIs	1	2		26	19	13.00									
1933-34	Barbados	Trinidad	IIs	1	2		15	14	7.50									
1934-35	Barbados	British Guiana	IIs	1	2		15	10	7.50									
1935-36	Barbados	Trinidad	IIs	1	2		62	45	31.00									

SEASON	TEAM	OPPONENTS	V	M	I	NO	RUNS	H.S.	AVGE	100	50	CT	OV	MD	RUNS	W	AVGE	B.B.
1938-39	Barbados	Trinidad	IIs	1	2		68	44	34.00									
1938-39	Barbados	British Guiana	IIs	1	2		5	5	2.50									
		Barbados		18	32	1	770	*93	24.83		5	5						
		Combined XI		1	2	1	19	*11	19.00									
		West Indies		23	38	2	792	109	22.00	1	3	3						
		TEST RECORD		**5**	**8**	**1**	**131**	**84**	**18.71**	**0**	**1**	**2**						
		CAREER		**42**	**72**	**4**	**1581**	**109**	**23.25**	**1**	**8**	**8**						

BENJAMIN, Winston Keithroy Matthew

				BATTING									BOWLING					
SEASON	TEAM	OPPONENTS	V	M	I	NO	RUNS	H.S.	AVGE	100	50	CT	OV	MD	RUNS	W	AVGE	B.B.
1985	Rest of World XI	D.B. Close's XI	E	1	2	1	15	15	15.00				21	5	61	3	20.33	
1985-86	Leeward Islands	Shell Shield	IIs	4	5	1	61	21	15.25			1	111.2	24	303	16	18.93	
1985-86	Leeward Islands	English Tourist	WI	1	2		35	30	17.50			1	47.1	13	97	4	24.25	
1986	Leicestershire	Counties	E	20	20	10	404	*95	40.40		3	9	465.3	89	1541	46	33.50	
1986-87	West Indies	Tour of Pakistan	P	3	3		132	92	44.00		1		34.2	3	120	3	40.00	
1986-87	West Indies	Tour of Australia	A	1	2	1	5	*4	5.00				12	1	30	0		
1986-87	Leeward Islands	Shell Shield	IIs	3	5	1	60	44	15.00				111.1	25	294	15	19.60	
1987	Leicestershire	Counties	E	8	9	1	69	30	8.62			5	207.2	54	525	15	35.00	
1987-88	West Indies	Tour of India	I	2	2	2	44	*37				1	45	11	130	4	32.50	
1987-88	**WEST INDIES**	**INDIA TESTS**	**I**	**1**	**1**		**19**	**19**	**19.00**			**1**	**30**	**3**	**93**	**2**	**46.50**	
1987-88	Leeward Islands	Red Stripe Cup	IIs	3	3		7	4	2.33			1	83.4	21	239	14	17.07	
1987-88	WI President's XI	Pakistan Tourist	WI	1	1		18	18	18.00				34	11	98	4	24.50	
1987-88	**WEST INDIES**	**PAKISTAN TESTS**	**WI**	**3**	**6**	**1**	**89**	***40**	**17.80**			**1**	**100**	**16**	**293**	**12**	**24.41**	
1988	West Indies	Tour of England	E	7	8	4	93	*21	23.25			5	116.1	27	316	21	15.04	
1988	**WEST INDIES**	**ENGLAND TESTS**	**E**	**3**	**2**		**9**	**9**	**4.50**			**1**	**67**	**17**	**151**	**12**	**12.58**	
1988-89	West Indies	Tour of Australia	A	5	6	2	141	50	35.26		1	6	121	24	361	8	45.12	
1988-89	Leeward Islands	Red Stripe Cup	IIs	2	4		129	85	32.25		1		43	5	117	2	58.50	
1988-89	WI President's XI	Indian Tourist	WI	1	D								14	1	48	1	48.00	
1988-89	WI Board XI	Indian Tourist	WI	1	D								8	3	11	1	11.00	
1988-89	**WEST INDIES**	**INDIA TESTS**	**WI**	**1**	**1**		**7**	**7**	**7.00**				**11**	**2**	**27**	**0**		
1989	Leicestershire	Counties	E	15	19	2	273	41	16.05			7	484.1	145	1238	69	17.94	
1989-90	Leeward Islands	Red Stripe Cup	IIs	1	1		47	47	47.00			1	36	9	89	4	22.25	
1989-90	Leeward Islands	English Tourist	WI	1	1	1	0	*0					21	3	62	1	62.00	

SEASON	TEAM	OPPONENTS	V	M	I	NO	RUNS	H.S.	AVGE	100	50	CT	OV	MD	RUNS	W	AVGE	B.B.
				BATTING									BOWLING					
1990	Leicestershire	Counties	E	12	15	2	437	*101	33.61	1	4	3	284.3	63	858	28	30.64	
		Leeward Islands		15	21	3	339	85	18.83		1	4	453.2	100	1201	56	21.44	
		West Indies		29	32	10	557	92	25.31		2	15	592.3	119	1678	68	24.67	
		Leicestershire		55	63	15	1183	*101	24.64	1	7	24	1441.3	351	4162	158	26.34	
		Rest of World XI		1	2	1	15	15	15.00				21	5	61	3	20.33	
		TEST RECORD		**8**	**10**	**1**	**124**	***40**	**13.77**	**0**	**0**	**3**	**208**	**38**	**564**	**26**	**21.69**	**4-52**
		CAREER		**100**	**118**	**29**	**2094**	***101**	**23.52**	**1**	**10**	**43**	**2508.2**	**575**	**7102**	**285**	**24.91**	**7-54**

BEST, Carlisle Alonza

SEASON	TEAM	OPPONENTS	V	M	I	NO	RUNS	H.S.	AVGE	100	50	CT	OV	MD	RUNS	W	AVGE	B.B.
				BATTING									BOWLING					
1979-80	Barbados	Shell Shield	IIs	2	3		26	10	8.66			1						
1981-82	Barbados	Shell Shield	IIs	2	1		75	75	75.00		1	2						
1982-83	Barbados	Shell Shield	IIs	5	10	1	267	84	29.66		1	7						
1982-83	Barbados	Indian Tourist	WI	1	1		6	6	6.00			1						
1983-84	Barbados	Shell Shield	IIs	5	10		411	108	41.10	1	2	8	0.1	0	0	0		
1983-84	Barbados	Australian Tourist	WI	1	2		63	43	31.50			2	5	2	19	0		
1984-85	Barbados	Shell Shield	IIs	5	9	1	437	147	54.62	2	1	5	13	2	33	2	16.50	
1984-85	WI Awards XI	New Zealand Tourist	WI	1	2	1	37	28	37.00			2						
1984-85	WI President's XI	New Zealand Tourist	WI	1	2	1	69	*53	69.00		1							
1985-86	Barbados	Shell Shield	IIs	5	9		518	179	57.55	2	2	6	19	2	55	0		
1985-86	Barbados	English Tourist	WI	1	2		44	42	22.00			3	5.3	0	20	1	20.00	
1985-86	**WEST INDIES**	**ENGLAND TESTS**	**WI**	**3**	**4**	**1**	**78**	**35**	**26.00**			**4**						
1986-87	Barbados	Guyana	IIs	1	1		112	112	112.00	1		1						
1986-87	Barbados	Windward Islands	IIs	1	2		34	20	17.00			1	2	2	0	0		
1986-87	Barbados	Shell Shield	IIs	2	2		59	56	29.50		1	1						
1986-87	West Indies 'B'	Tour of Zimbabwe	Z	5	8	1	245	*58	35.00		2	13	4	1	9	0		
1987-88	Barbados	Red Stripe Cup	IIs	5	9		328	98	36.44		4	4	5	1	17	1	17.00	
1987-88	WI President's XI	Pakistan Tourist	WI	1	2	1	23	13	23.00			2	2	0	8	0		
1988-89	Barbados	Red Stripe Cup	IIs	5	7	1	422	*157	70.33	2	1	9	55.4	11	143	4	35.75	
1988-89	WI President's XI	Indian Tourist	WI	1	2	1	120	*104	120.00	1		1						
1988-89	WI Board XI	Indian Tourist	WI	1	1		58	58	58.00		1							
1989	Rest of World XI	M.C.C. XI	E	1	2		139	100	69.50	1								
1989-90	Barbados	Red Stripe Cup	IIs	5	8		310	175	38.75	1		5	17.5	3	44	3	14.66	

SEASON	TEAM	OPPONENTS	V	M	I	NO	RUNS	H.S.	AVGE	100	50	CT	OV	MD	RUNS	W	AVGE	B.B.
1989-90	Barbados	English Tourist	WI	1	2		166	95	83.00		2	3	6	0	15	0		
1989-90	**WEST INDIES**	**ENGLAND TESTS**	**WI**	**3**	**5**		**242**	**164**	**48.40**	**1**	**1**	**3**	**4**	**0**	**19**	**0**		
		Barbados		47	78	3	3278	179	43.70	9	15	59	129.1	23	346	11	31.45	
		West Indies		16	26	6	872	164	43.60	2	5	25	10	1	36	0		
		Rest of World XI		1	2		139	100	69.50	1								
		TEST RECORD		**6**	**9**	**1**	**320**	**164**	**40.00**	**1**	**1**	**7**	**4**	**0**	**19**	**0**		
		CAREER		**64**	**106**	**9**	**4289**	**179**	**44.21**	**12**	**20**	**84**	**139.1**	**24**	**382**	**11**	**34.72**	**2-17**

BETANCOURT, Nelson

				BATTING									BOWLING					
SEASON	TEAM	OPPONENTS	V	M	I	NO	RUNS	H.S.	AVGE	100	50	CT	OV	MD	RUNS	W	AVGE	B.B.
1905-06	Trinidad	Jamaica	IIs	1	2		12	11	6.00									
1907-08	Trinidad	British Guiana	IIs	1	2	1	37	25	37.00									
1907-08	Trinidad	Barbados	IIs	1	2	1	10	9	10.00			1	6	2	9	0		
1908-09	Trinidad	Barbados	IIs	1	2		9	6	4.50									
1911-12	Trinidad	British Guiana	IIs	1	1		3	3	3.00									
1911-12	Trinidad	Barbados	IIs	1	2		32	16	16.00									
1912-13	Trinidad	M.C.C. Tourist	WI	2	3		74	35	24.66			2	1	0	1	0		
1912-13	West Indies XI	M.C.C. Tourist	WI	1	1		31	31	31.00			1						
1922-23	Trinidad	British Guiana	IIs	1	2		28	19	14.00				5	0	23	0		
1922-23	Trinidad	Barbados	IIs	1	2		23	12	11.50				14	1	65	1	65.00	
1928-29	Trinidad	British Guiana	IIs	1	2	1	101	*71	101.00		1							
1928-29	Trinidad	Barbados	IIs	1	1		13	13	13.00			1						
1929-30	Trinidad	British Guiana	IIs	1	2	1	1	*1	1.00									
1929-30	Trinidad	M.C.C. Tourist	WI	1	2		16	11	8.00									
1929-30	**WEST INDIES**	**ENGLAND TESTS**	**WI**	**1**	**2**		**52**	**39**	**26.00**									
		Trinidad		14	25	4	359	71	17.09		1	5	26	3	98	1	98.00	
		West Indies		2	3		83	39				1						
		TEST RECORD		**1**	**2**	**0**	**52**	**39**	**26.00**	**0**	**0**	**0**						
		CAREER		**16**	**28**	**4**	**442**	***71**	**18.41**	**0**	**1**	**6**	**26**	**3**	**98**	**1**	**98.00**	**1-65**

BINNS, Alfred Phillip

SEASON	TEAM	OPPONENTS	V	BATTING M	I	NO	RUNS	H.S.	AVGE	100	50	CT/St	BOWLING OV	MD	RUNS	W	AVGE	B.B.
1949-50	Jamaica	Trinidad	IIs	2	4	1	77	*50	25.66		1	3/1						
1950-51	Jamaica	British Guiana	IIs	2	3		131	82	43.66		1	3/4						
1951-52	Jamaica	Barbados	IIs	2	4	1	197	*100	65.66	1	1	8/2						
1952-53	Jamaica	British Guiana	IIs	2	4	1	268	157	89.33	1	1	3/3						
1952-53	Jamaica	Indian Tourist	WI	1	2		9	7	4.50			5/0						
1952-53	**WEST INDIES**	**INDIA TESTS**	**WI**	**1**	**1**		**2**	**2**	**2.00**			**4/0**						
1953-54	Jamaica	M.C.C. Tourist	WI	1	2		60	43	30.00			1/0						
1954-55	Jamaica	Trinidad	IIs	2	3		86	47	28.66			2/2						
1954-55	Jamaica	Australian Tourist	WI	1	1		151	151	151.00	1		2/0						
1954-55	**WEST INDIES**	**AUSTRALIA TESTS**	**WI**	**1**	**2**		**0**	**0**				**0/1**						
1955-56	West Indies	Tour of New Zealand	NZ	3	5		117	34	23.40			5/2						
1955-56	**WEST INDIES**	**NEW ZEALAND TESTS**	**NZ**	**3**	**5**	**1**	**62**	**27**	**15.50**			**10/2**						
1956-57	Jamaica	British Guiana	IIs	1	1		151	151	151.00	1		0/0						
1956-57	Jamaica	Duke of Norfolk's Tourist	WI	3	6		135	47	22.50			2/0						
		Jamaica		17	30	3	1265	157	46.85	4	4	29/12						
		West Indies		8	13	1	181	34	15.08			19/5						
		TEST RECORD		**5**	**8**	**1**	**64**	**27**	**9.14**	**0**	**0**	**14/3**						
		CAREER		**25**	**43**	**4**	**1446**	**157**	**37.07**	**4**	**4**	**48/17**						

BIRKETT, Lionel Sidney

SEASON	TEAM	OPPONENTS	V	BATTING M	I	NO	RUNS	H.S.	AVGE	100	50	CT	BOWLING OV	MD	RUNS	W	AVGE	B.B.
1924-25	Barbados	Jamaica	IIs	2	1		10	10	10.00			3	35.3	12	56	4	14.00	
1924-25	Barbados	Trinidad	IIs	1	2		45	31	22.50			2	10	0	27	1	27.00	
1925-26	Barbados	M.C.C. Tourist	WI	2	2	1	77	*62	77.00		1	3	5	0	12	1	12.00	
1927-28	Combined B/J XI	Combined Trin/BG XI	IIs	2	4		14	14	3.50				7	1	26	0		
1928-29	Barbados	Trinidad	IIs	1	2		58	30	29.00				10	4	39	1	39.00	
1929-30	Trinidad	British Guiana	IIs	1	2		304	253	152.00	1	1	1	33	8	72	0		
1930-31	West Indies	Tour of Australia	A	7	12	1	363	*128	33.00	1		6	35	1	134	1	134.00	
1930-31	**WEST INDIES**	**AUSTRALIA TESTS**	**A**	**4**	**8**		**136**	**64**	**17.00**		**1**	**4**	**21**	**1**	**71**	**1**	**71.00**	
1937-38	Trinidad	British Guiana	IIs	1	2		164	121	82.00	1		1	15	2	47	0		
1938-39	R.S. Grant's XI	British Guiana	IIs	2	3	1	23	14	11.50				5	2	8	0		
1938-39	Trinidad	Barbados	IIs	1	1		40	40	40.00			1						

SEASON	TEAM	OPPONENTS	V	M	I	NO	RUNS	H.S.	AVGE	100	50	CT	OV	MD	RUNS	W	AVGE	B.B.
1938-39	Trinidad	British Guiana	IIs	1	1		9	9	9.00									
1944-45	British Guiana	Barbados	IIs	1	2		52	34	26.00			1	5	1	12	0		
		Barbados		6	7	1	190	*62	31.66		1	8	60.3	16	134	7	19.14	
		Trinidad		4	6		517	253	86.16	2	1	3	48	10	119	0		
		British Guiana		1	2		52	34	26.00			1	5	1	12	0		
		Combined XI		2	4		14	14	3.50				7	1	26	0		
		R.S. Grant's XI		2	3	1	23	14	11.50				5	2	8	0		
		West Indies		11	20	1	499	*128	26.26	1	1	10	56	2	205	2	102.50	
		TEST RECORD		**4**	**8**	**0**	**136**	**64**	**17.00**	**0**	**1**	**4**	**21**	**1**	**71**	**1**	**71.00**	**1-16**
		CAREER		**26**	**42**	**3**	**1295**	**253**	**33.20**	**3**	**3**	**22**	**181.3**	**32**	**504**	**9**	**56.00**	**2-6**

BISHOP, Ian Raphael

				BATTING									BOWLING					
SEASON	**TEAM**	**OPPONENTS**	**V**	**M**	**I**	**NO**	**RUNS**	**H.S.**	**AVGE**	**100**	**50**	**CT**	**OV**	**MD**	**RUNS**	**W**	**AVGE**	**B.B.**
1986-87	Trinidad	Shell Shield	IIs	2	4	3	22	*9	22.00				44	3	193	3	64.33	
1987-88	Trinidad	Red Stripe Cup	IIs	5	7	5	49	*19	24.50			1	96	13	260	19	13.68	
1987-88	WI President's XI	Pakistan Tourist	WI	1	1	1	0	*0				1	34	5	108	1	108.00	
1987-88	WI Under 23 XI	Pakistan Tourist	WI	1	2	1	0	*0				1	42.4	9	153	4	38.25	
1987-88	WI Board XI	Pakistan Tourist	WI	1	1	1	6	*6					35	2	140	3	46.66	
1988	West Indies	Tour of England	E	8	6	2	56	23	14.00			1	142	30	406	21	19.33	
1988-89	West Indies	Tour of Australia	A	5	7	2	64	20	12.80			1	120	17	408	10	40.80	
1988-89	Trinidad	Red Stripe Cup	IIs	2	2		10	8	5.00			1	75.4	12	213	16	13.31	
1988-89	**WEST INDIES**	**INDIA TESTS**	**WI**	**4**	**5**	**3**	**55**	***30**	**27.50**				**137**	**38**	**370**	**16**	**23.12**	
1989	Derbyshire	Counties	E	12	20	2	180	*28	10.00			2	337	66	920	41	22.43	
1989-90	Trinidad	Red Stripe Cup	IIs	4	8	2	65	21	10.83			2	130	23	330	23	14.34	
1989-90	**WEST INDIES**	**ENGLAND TESTS**	**WI**	**4**	**7**	**3**	**69**	**16**	**17.25**			**1**	**162.1**	**37**	**419**	**21**	**19.95**	
1990	Derbyshire	Counties	E	13	16	4	333	*103	27.75	1		2	407.3	92	1124	59	19.05	
		Trinidad		13	21	10	146	21	13.27			4	345.4	51	996	61	16.32	
		West Indies		24	29	13	250	*30	15.62			5	672.5	138	2004	76	26.36	
		Derbyshire		25	36	6	513	*103	17.10	1		4	744.3	158	2044	100	20.44	
		TEST RECORD		**8**	**12**	**6**	**124**	***30**	**20.66**	**0**	**0**	**1**	**299.1**	**75**	**789**	**37**	**21.32**	**6-87**
		CAREER		**62**	**86**	**29**	**909**	***103**	**15.94**	**1**	**0**	**13**	**1763**	**347**	**5044**	**237**	**21.28**	**6-39**

BOYCE, Keith David

SEASON	TEAM	OPPONENTS	V	BATTING									BOWLING					
				M	I	NO	RUNS	H.S.	AVGE	100	50	CT	OV	MD	RUNS	W	AVGE	B.B.
1964-65	Barbados	Touring Cavaliers XI	WI	1	1		55	55	55.00		1		25	5	65	2	32.50	
1966	Essex	Counties	E	2	3		6	6	2.00				55.5	7	172	14	12.38	
1967	Essex	Counties	E	30	51	6	910	78	20.22		6	33	810	160	2207	81	27.24	
1967-68	Comm. XI	Tour of Pakistan	P	7	9	1	90	23	11.25			2	128	26	487	13	37.46	
1968	Essex	Counties	E	28	46	2	908	90	20.63		2	17	749.4	147	2072	88	23.54	
1968-69	Barbados	Shell Shield	IIs	2	3		124	112	41.33	1		3	31	4	115	5	23.00	
1969	Essex	Counties	E	25	36	3	892	*147	27.03	2	4	28	585.4	100	1696	72	23.53	
1970	Essex	Counties	E	27	46	1	728	70	16.17		4	23	759.4	112	2303	87	26.47	
1970	M.C.C.	Yorkshire	E	1	2		22	18	11.00			1	15.3	3	48	1	48.00	
1970-71	Barbados	Shell Shield	IIs	3	5	1	121	45	30.25			2	58	10	182	7	26.00	
1970-71	Barbados	Indian Tourist	WI	1	1		74	74	74.00		1		23	3	69	1	69.00	
1970-71	WI President's XI	Indian Tourist	WI	1	1		41	41	41.00				34	11	71	2	35.50	
1970-71	**WEST INDIES**	**INDIA TESTS**	**WI**	**1**	**1**		**9**	**9**	**9.00**				**22.4**	**5**	**59**	**2**	**29.50**	
1971	Essex	Counties	E	25	38	1	690	67	18.64		2	20	599.3	113	1759	62	28.37	
1971	TN Pearce's XI	Indian Tourist	E	1	D								21.4	3	72	2	36.00	
1971-72	Barbados	Shell Shield	IIs	4	5		56	15	11.20			2	77	14	208	6	34.66	
1971-72	Barbados	New Zealand Tourist	WI	1	2		38	21	19.00			1	47	7	123	7	17.57	
1972	Essex	Counties	E	21	32		994	86	31.06		8	21	603.1	129	1608	81	19.85	
1972	T.N. Pearce's XI	Australian Tourist	E	1	2		29	25	14.50				13	2	49	1	49.00	
1972-73	Barbados	Shell Shield	IIs	3	6	2	109	36	27.25			2	53	7	165	3	55.00	
1972-73	Barbados	Australian Tourist	WI	1	2		46	44	23.00			2	33	4	117	3	39.00	
1972-73	**WEST INDIES**	**AUSTRALIA TESTS**	**WI**	**4**	**6**		**97**	**31**	**16.16**			**1**	**110.4**	**24**	**340**	**9**	**32.77**	
1973	West Indies	Tour of England	E	8	8	1	183	87	26.14		1	5	195.5	30	627	22	28.50	
1973	**WEST INDIES**	**ENGLAND TESTS**	**E**	**3**	**5**		**129**	**72**	**25.80**		**1**		**98.1**	**22**	**294**	**19**	**15.47**	
1973	Essex	Counties	E	6	7	1	291	83	48.50		3	5	145	34	380	18	21.11	
1973-74	Rest of World XI	Tour of Pakistan	P	2	4		54	40	13.50			1	53	5	198	4	49.50	
1973-74	Barbados	Shell Shield	IIs	2	3		67	60	22.33		1	2	45	8	146	10	14.60	
1973-74	**WEST INDIES**	**ENGLAND TESTS**	**WI**	**4**	**4**	**1**	**87**	***34**	**29.00**			**1**	**118.4**	**23**	**324**	**11**	**29.45**	
1974	Essex	Counties	E	12	16		335	75	20.93		1	7	313.4	55	868	35	24.80	
1974-75	West Indies	Tour of India	I	3	3		30	16	10.00				74	7	214	6	35.66	
1974-75	**WEST INDIES**	**INDIA TESTS**	**I**	**3**	**5**		**80**	**68**	**16.00**		**1**	**1**	**65**	**13**	**246**	**6**	**41.00**	
1974-75	West Indies	Tour of Sri Lanka	SL	2	3		27	22	9.00			1	46	8	144	7	20.57	
1974-75	**WEST INDIES**	**PAKISTAN TESTS**	**P**	**2**	**2**		**15**	**13**	**7.50**			**1**	**44**	**6**	**177**	**4**	**44.25**	
1974-75	Barbados	Shell Shield	IIs	4	6		105	51	17.50		1	3	110.3	23	316	14	22.57	
1975	Essex	Counties	E	15	22	2	555	113	27.75	1	3	15	471	92	1309	72	18.18	
1975-76	West Indies	Tour of Australia	A	5	5	1	24	14	6.00			2	91	14	403	14	28.75	

1975-76	**WEST INDIES**	**AUSTRALIA TESTS**	**A**	**4**	**7**	**2**	**240**	***95**	**48.00**		**2**	**1**	**82.2**	**6**	**361**	**9**	**40.11**	
1976	Essex	Counties	E	13	15	1	400	88	28.57		3	7	301.4	64	834	29	28.75	
1977	Essex	Counties	E	7	7	1	139	69	23.16		1	5	189.4	45	496	23	21.56	
		Barbados		22	34	3	795	112	25.64	1	3	17	502.3	85	1506	58	25.96	
		West Indies		40	50	5	962	*95	21.37		5	13	982.2	169	3260	111	29.36	
		Essex		211	319	18	6848	*147	22.75	3	37	181	5584.3	1058	15704	662	23.72	
		Comm. XI		7	9	1	90	23	11.25			2	128	26	487	13	37.46	
		Rest of World XI		2	4		54	40	13.50			1	53	5	198	4	49.50	
		T.N. Pearce's XI		2	2		29	25	14.50				34.4	5	121	3	40.33	
		M.C.C.		1	2		22	18	11.00			1	15.3	3	48	1	48.00	
		TEST RECORD		**21**	**30**	**3**	**657**	***95**	**24.33**	**0**	**4**	**5**	**540.3**	**99**	**1801**	**60**	**30.01**	**6-77**
		CAREER		**285**	**420**	**27**	**8800**	***147**	**22.39**	**4**	**45**	**215**	**7300.3**	**1351**	**21324**	**852**	**25.02**	**9-61**

BROWNE, Cyril Rutherford

							BATTING						BOWLING					
SEASON	**TEAM**	**OPPONENTS**	**V**	**M**	**I**	**NO**	**RUNS**	**H.S.**	**AVGE**	**100**	**50**	**CT**	**OV**	**MD**	**RUNS**	**W**	**AVGE**	**B.B.**
1908-09	Barbados	British Guiana	IIs	1	1		19	19	19.00			1	30.2	3	84	3	28.00	
1908-09	Barbados	Trinidad	IIs	1	1		4	4	4.00			1	22.3	8	41	4	10.25	
1909-10	Barbados	Trinidad	IIs	1	2		15	13	7.50			2	74	16	192	7	27.42	
1910-11	Barbados	British Guiana	IIs	1	2	1	19	13	19.00			2	26.5	14	37	8	4.62	
1910-11	Barbados	Trinidad	IIs	1	1		1	1	1.00			1	25	7	52	6	8.66	
1910-11	Barbados	M.C.C. Tourist	WI	2	2		15	14	7.50			3	68	11	178	16	11.12	
1910-11	West Indies XI	M.C.C. Tourist	WI	2	4	3	21	*11	21.00			5	100.3	19	288	11	26.18	
1921-22	British Guiana	Trinidad	IIs	1	2		19	19	9.50			2	27	9	45	3	15.00	
1922.23	British Guiana	Trinidad	IIs	1	2		5	5	2.50			1	36.4	4	107	11	9.72	
1923	West Indies	Tour of England	E	18	26	2	258	24	10.75			14	696	171	1672	75	22.29	
1923-24	British Guiana	Trinidad	IIs	1	2		7	7	3.50			2	48	9	111	10	11.10	
1925-26	British Guiana	Barbados	IIs	1	1		102	102	102.00	1		2	74	25	135	13	10.38	
1925-26	British Guiana	Trinidad	IIs	1	2		0	0				1	60.2	10	176	6	29.33	
1925-26	British Guiana	M.C.C. Tourist	WI	2	2		54	39	27.00				74	18	164	0		
1925-26	West Indies XI	M.C.C. Tourist	WI	3	4	1	189	*102	63.00	1	1	1	112.4	17	339	8	42.37	
1928	West Indies	Tour of England	E	19	29	2	469	103	17.37	1	2	9	380.3	77	986	30	32.86	
1928	**WEST INDIES**	**ENGLAND TESTS**	**E**	**2**	**4**		**84**	**44**	**21.00**			**1**	**47**	**7**	**125**	**2**	**62.50**	
1929-30	British Guiana	Barbados	IIs	1	2		150	95	75.00		2	2	94.3	38	137	7	19.57	
1929-30	British Guiana	Trinidad	IIs	1	2	1	107	83	107.00		1		67	7	190	11	17.27	
1929-30	British Guiana	M.C.C. Tourist	WI	2	4		135	61	33.75		1	2	63	14	146	1	146.00	

SEASON	TEAM	OPPONENTS	V	BATTING M	I	NO	RUNS	H.S.	AVGE	100	50	CT	BOWLING OV	MD	RUNS	W	AVGE	B.B.
1929-30	**WEST INDIES**	**ENGLAND TESTS**	**WI**	**2**	**4**	**1**	**92**	***70**	**30.66**		**1**		**93**	**31**	**163**	**4**	**40.75**	
1931-32	British Guiana	Trinidad	IIs	1	2		36	20	18.00			2	62	17	130	1	130.00	
1934-35	British Guiana	Barbados	IIs	1	2		18	14	9.00			1	71	17	143	10	14.30	
1934-35	British Guiana	Trinidad	IIs	1	1		2	2	2.00			2	33	7	74	6	12.33	
1934-35	British Guiana	M.C.C. Tourist	WI	2	3		37	37	12.33				49	5	131	2	65.50	
1935-36	British Guiana	Trinidad	IIs	1	1		12	12	12.00			1	36	10	62	7	8.85	
1936-37	British Guiana	Trinidad	IIs	1	2		28	26	14.00			1	55	14	101	4	25.25	
1937-38	British Guiana	Barbados	IIs	1	1		69	69	69.00		1		41	14	63	8	7.87	
1937-38	British Guiana	Trinidad	IIs	1	2		59	54	29.50		1		55	6	134	4	33.50	
1938-39	British Guiana	R.S. Grant's XI	IIs	1	2		51	34	25.50				9	2	22	0		
		Barbados		7	9	1	73	19	9.12			10	246.4	59	584	44	13.27	
		British Guiana		21	35	1	891	102	26.50	1	6	19	955.3	226	2071	104	19.91	
		West Indies		46	71	9	1113	103	17.95	2	4	30	1429.4	322	3573	130	27.48	
		TEST RECORD		**4**	**8**	**1**	**176**	***70**	**25.14**	**0**	**1**	**1**	**140**	**38**	**288**	**6**	**48.00**	**2-72**
		CAREER		**74**	**115**	**11**	**2077**	**103**	**19.97**	**3**	**10**	**59**	**2631.5**	**607**	**6228**	**278**	**22.40**	**8-58**

BUTCHER, Basil Fitzherbert

SEASON	TEAM	OPPONENTS	V	BATTING M	I	NO	RUNS	H.S.	AVGE	100	50	CT	BOWLING OV	MD	RUNS	W	AVGE	B.B.
1954-55	British Guiana	Barbados	IIs	2	4		105	62	26.25		1	2						
1954-55	British Guiana	Australian Tourist	WI	1	2		54	46	27.00				14	2	43	0		
1956-57	British Guiana	Jamaica	IIs	1	1	1	154	*154		1			3	0	7	0		
1956-57	British Guiana	Barbados	IIs	1	1		4	4	4.00									
1957-58	British Guiana	Pakistan Tourist	WI	1	1		122	122	122.00	1			4	0	11	0		
1958-59	West Indies	Tour of India	I	10	13	2	422	*95	38.36		3	5	1	0	5	0		
1958-59	**WEST INDIES**	**INDIA TESTS**	**I**	**5**	**8**	**1**	**486**	**142**	**69.42**	**2**	**3**	**1**	**6**	**1**	**17**	**0**		
1958-59	West Indies	Tour of Pakistan	P	2	3	1	92	90	46.00		1	1						
1958-59	**WEST INDIES**	**PAKISTAN TESTS**	**P**	**3**	**5**	**1**	**133**	**61**	**33.25**		**1**							
1959-60	British Guiana	Jamaica	IIs	1	1		27	27	27.00									
1959-60	British Guiana	M.C.C. Tourist	WI	1	2		123	123	61.50	1								
1959-60	Berbice	M.C.C. Tourist	WI	1	1	1	131	*131		1								
1959-60	**WEST INDIES**	**ENGLAND TESTS**	**WI**	**2**	**3**		**31**	**13**	**10.33**									
1960-61	Berbice	E.W. Swanton's Tourist	WI	1	2		73	73	36.50		1	1						
1960-61	British Guiana	E.W. Swanton's Tourist	WI	1	2		137	113	68.50	1								

1961-62	British Guiana	Combined Lee/Wind XI	IIs	1	1		38	38	38.00			1					
1961-62	British Guiana	Trinidad	IIs	1	2		79	56	39.50		1						
1961-62	British Guiana	Barbados	IIs	1	2		80	46	40.00			1					
1962-63	British Guiana	Barbados	IIs	1	2		89	73	44.50		1						
1963	West Indies	Tour of England	E	17	25	4	911	130	43.38	1	6	9	2.3	0	10	1	10.00
1963	**WEST INDIES**	**ENGLAND TESTS**	**E**	**5**	**9**	**1**	**383**	**133**	**47.87**	**1**	**2**						
1963-64	West Indies XI	The Rest XI	IIs	1	2		56	35	28.00				2	0	16	1	16.00
1963-64	F. Worrell's XI	C. Hunte's XI	IIs	1	2		157	108	78.50	1							
1963-64	Indian President's XI	Prime Minister's XI	I	1	2		49	37	24.50			1					
1963-64	British Guiana	Barbados	IIs	1	2		105	105	52.50	1		1	1	1	0	0	
1963-64	British Guiana	Jamaica	IIs	1	1		102	102	102.00	1		1					
1963-64	British Guiana	Trinidad	IIs	1	2		90	90	45.00		1	2	3	0	16	1	
1963-64	Comm. XI	Tour of Pakistan	P	6	8		269	95	33.62		3	2	24.4	5	108	2	54.00
1964	West Indies XI	Tour of England	E	3	4	1	103	74	34.33		1						
1964-65	Comm. XI	Tour of India	I	1	2	1	75	40	75.00			1					
1964-65	British Guiana	Australian Tourist	WI	1	2		196	157	98.00	1			5	1	16	0	
1964-65	**WEST INDIES**	**AUSTRALIA TESTS**	**WI**	**5**	**10**		**405**	**117**	**40.50**	**1**	**1**	**3**					
1965-66	British Guiana	Shell Shield	IIs	4	6		274	99	45.66		2	3					
1966	West Indies	Tour of England	E	14	17	1	685	137	42.81	2	2	3	2	0	7	0	
1966	**WEST INDIES**	**ENGLAND TESTS**	**E**	**5**	**8**	**1**	**420**	***209**	**60.00**	**1**	**1**	**5**					
1966-67	West Indies	Tour of India	I	5	8	2	469	84	78.16		6	5	27	2	125	3	41.66
1966-67	**WEST INDIES**	**INDIA TESTS**	**I**	**3**	**5**		**86**	**35**	**17.20**			**1**					
1966-67	West Indies	Tour of Ceylon	C	1	1		152	152	152.00	1		1	8	1	26	1	26.00
1966-67	Guyana	Shell Shield	IIs	4	6	2	505	*183	126.25	3			2	0	8	0	
1967-68	Guyana	M.C.C. Tourist	WI	1	2		37	19	18.50								
1967-68	**WEST INDIES**	**ENGLAND TESTS**	**WI**	**5**	**9**	**1**	**301**	**86**	**37.62**		**3**	**2**	**33.4**	**13**	**67**	**5**	**13.40**
1968	Rest of World XI	Tour of England	E	4	8	1	241	70	34.42		2	3	15	1	65	0	
1968-69	West Indies	Tour of Australia	A	7	13	1	786	172	65.50	3	2	5	35	1	200	6	33.33
1968-69	**WEST INDIES**	**AUSTRALIA TESTS**	**A**	**5**	**10**		**405**	**118**	**40.50**	**2**	**1**	**2**					
1968-69	West Indies	Tour of New Zealand	NZ	2	3		98	58	32.66		1	1	3	0	14	3	4.66
1968-69	**WEST INDIES**	**NEW ZEALAND TESTS**	**NZ**	**3**	**5**	**1**	**216**	***78**	**54.50**		**3**						
1969	West Indies	Tour of England	E	12	14	4	746	151	74.60	3	2	1	34	5	97	6	16.16
1969	**WEST INDIES**	**ENGLAND TESTS**	**E**	**3**	**6**		**238**	**91**	**39.66**		**1**	**1**	**3**	**1**	**6**	**0**	
1969-70	Guyana	Shell Shield	IIs	4	6	1	311	*203	62.20	1		1	61.1	14	167	6	27.83
1970-71	Guyana	Shell Shield	IIs	4	5		267	162	53.40	1	1	1	55	15	149	3	49.66
1970-71	Guyana	Indian Tourist	WI	1	2		80	44	40.00				4	0	7	0	
1971-72	Berbice	Demerara J.C.	G	1	1		30	30	30.00				14	3	30	2	15.00
		British Guiana/Guyana		35	55	4	2979	*203	58.41	12	7	13	152.1	33	424	10	42.40

SEASON	TEAM	OPPONENTS	V	BATTING M	I	NO	RUNS	H.S.	AVGE	100	50	CT	BOWLING OV	MD	RUNS	W	AVGE	B.B.
		Berbice		3	4	1	234	*131	78.00	1	1	1	14	3	30	2	15.00	
		West Indies		118	181	22	7624	*209	47.94	17	40	46	157.1	24	590	26	22.69	
		Comm. XI		7	10	1	344	95	38.22		3	3	24.4	5	108	2	54.00	
		Rest of World XI		4	8	1	241	70	34.42		2	3	15	1	65	0		
		F. Worrell's XI		1	2		157	108	78.50	1								
		Indian President's XI		1	2		49	37	24.50			1						
		TEST RECORD		**44**	**78**	**6**	**3104**	***209**	**43.11**	**7**	**16**	**15**	**42.4**	**15**	**90**	**5**	**18.00**	**5-34**
		CAREER		**169**	**262**	**29**	**11628**	***209**	**49.90**	**31**	**53**	**67**	**363**	**66**	**1217**	**40**	**30.42**	**5-34**

BUTLER, Lennox Stephen

SEASON	TEAM	OPPONENTS	V	BATTING M	I	NO	RUNS	H.S.	AVGE	100	50	CT	BOWLING OV	MD	RUNS	W	AVGE	B.B.
1948-49	Trinidad	Barbados	IIs	1	2	2	27	*18					32	0	142	2	71.00	
1950-51	Trinidad	Barbados	IIs	1	1		13	13	13.00				32	7	79	4	19.73	
1951-52	Trinidad	British Guiana	IIs	2	3	1	64	44	32.00				72.5	28	120	5	24.00	
1952-53	Trinidad	Indian Tourist	WI	1	1		17	17	17.00				37	21	62	1	62.00	
1953-54	Trinidad	British Guiana	IIs	2	2		11	11	5.50			1	59.3	18	153	5	30.60	
1954-55	Trinidad	Jamaica	IIs	1	2	1	2	*1	2.00				66	28	124	3	41.33	
1954-55	Trinidad	Australian Tourist	WI	1	1		0	0					26	5	93	5	18.60	
1954-55	**WEST INDIES**	**AUSTRALIA TESTS**	**WI**	**1**	**1**		**16**	**16**	**16.00**				**40**	**7**	**151**	**2**	**75.50**	
1955-56	Trinidad	E.W. Swanton's Tourist	WI	1	2		11	11	5.50				14	3	47	2	23.50	
		Trinidad		10	14	4	145	44	14.50			1	339.2	110	820	27	30.57	
		West Indies		1	1		16	16	16.00				40	7	151	2	75.50	
		TEST RECORD		**1**	**1**	**0**	**16**	**16**	**16.00**	**0**	**0**	**0**	**40**	**7**	**151**	**2**	**75.50**	**2-151**
		CAREER		**11**	**15**	**4**	**161**	**44**	**14.63**	**0**	**0**	**1**	**379.2**	**117**	**971**	**29**	**33.48**	**5-93**

BUTTS, Clyde George

SEASON	TEAM	OPPONENTS	V	BATTING M	I	NO	RUNS	H.S.	AVGE	100	50	CT	BOWLING OV	MD	RUNS	W	AVGE	B.B.
1980-81	Guyana	Shell Shield	IIs	2	3	1	15	*11	7.50			1	74.3	19	164	11	15.00	
1981-82	Demerara	Berbice JC	G	1	1		28	28	28.00			1	35	14	66	1	66.00	
1981-82	Guyana	Shell Shield	IIs	3	4	1	74	35	24.66			1	63	19	161	2	80.50	

SEASON	TEAM	OPPONENTS	V	M	I	NO	RUNS	H.S.	AVGE	100	50	CT	OV	MD	RUNS	W	AVGE	B.B.
1982-83	Demerara	Berbice JC	G	1	1		38	38	38.00				96	42	132	11	12.00	
1982-83	Guyana	Shell Shield	IIs	5	8	2	33	13	5.50			2	209.3	59	458	25	18.32	
1983-84	West Indies 'B'	Tour of Zimbabwe	Z	2	4		109	51	27.25		1	1	66	13	226	6	37.66	
1983-84	Guyana	Shell Shield	IIs	5	7		106	31	15.14			1	302.4	88	652	24	27.16	
1983-84	Guyana	Australian Tourist	WI	1	2	1	11	8	11.00				58	8	196	5	39.20	
1984-85	Demerara	Berbice JC	G	1	1		14	14	14.00			4	67.3	20	137	6	22.83	
1984-85	Guyana	Shell Shield	IIs	5	6	3	56	*30	18.66			1	300.2	81	615	32	19.21	
1984-85	WI Awards XI	New Zealand Tourist	WI	1	1		7	7	7.00				61.3	13	126	7	18.00	
1984-85	**WEST INDIES**	**NEW ZEALAND TESTS**	**WI**	**1**	**1**		**9**	**9**	**9.00**				**47**	**12**	**113**	**0**		
1985-86	Demerara	Berbice JC	G	1	1	1	12	*12				1	38.4	9	78	6	13.00	
1985-86	Guyana	Shell Shield	IIs	5	8	1	95	33	13.57			1	235.2	63	515	28	18.39	
1986-87	West Indies	Tour of Pakistan	P	3	3	1	57	*57	28.50		1	1	63.4	17	149	11	13.54	
1986-87	**WEST INDIES**	**PAKISTAN TESTS**	**P**	**2**	**3**		**35**	**17**	**11.66**				**60**	**24**	**95**	**6**	**15.83**	
1986-87	West Indies	Tour of New Zealand	NZ	2	1	1	3	*3				2	75	19	197	5	39.40	
1986-87	**WEST INDIES**	**NEW ZEALAND TESTS**	**NZ**	**1**	**1**	**1**	**8**	***8**					**38**	**10**	**82**	**2**	**41.00**	
1986-87	Guyana	Shell Shield	IIs	3	2		24	19	12.00			2	162.5	49	287	16	17.93	
1987-88	Demerara	Berbice GT	G	1	1		32	32	32.00			1	26	10	56	5	11.20	
1987-88	West Indies	Tour of India	I	3	3		65	47	21.66			1	60	3	223	2	111.50	
1987-88	**WEST INDIES**	**INDIA TESTS**	**I**	**3**	**3**		**56**	**38**	**18.66**			**2**	**114**	**24**	**305**	**2**	**152.50**	
1987-88	Guyana	Red Stripe Cup	IIs	4	5		45	16	9.00			2	128	27	308	7	44.00	
1987-88	WI Board XI	Pakistan Tourist	WI	1	1		48	48	48.00				67	13	173	3	57.66	
1988-89	Demerara	Berbice GT	G	1	D													
1988-89	Guyana	Red Stripe Cup	IIs	5	4		37	33	9.25			2	225.4	61	464	17	27.29	
1989-90	Demerara	Berbice KSMT	G	1	1		5	5	5.00			3	55	16	121	1	121.00	
1989-90	Guyana	Red Stripe Cup	IIs	3	5		7	4	1.40			1	131	34	307	12	25.28	
		Guyana		41	54	9	503	35	11.17			14	1890.5	508	4127	179	23.05	
		Demerara		7	6	1	129	*38	25.80			10	318.1	111	590	30	19.66	
		West Indies		19	21	3	397	*57	22.05		2	7	652.1	148	1689	44	38.38	
		TEST RECORD		**7**	**8**	**1**	**108**	**38**	**15.42**	**0**	**0**	**2**	**259**	**70**	**595**	**10**	**59.50**	**4-73**
		CAREER		**67**	**81**	**13**	**1029**	***57**	**15.13**	**0**	**2**	**31**	**2861.1**	**767**	**6406**	**253**	**25.32**	**7-56**

BYNOE, Michael Robin

				BATTING									BOWLING					
SEASON	TEAM	OPPONENTS	V	M	I	NO	RUNS	H.S.	AVGE	100	50	CT	OV	MD	RUNS	W	AVGE	B.B.
1957-58	Barbados	Pakistan Tourist	WI	1	2		76	47	38.00				5	0	19	0		
1958-59	Barbados	Jamaica	IIs	1	2		68	52	34.00		1							
1958-59	West Indies	Tour of India	I	7	12	2	259	76	25.90		2	4	3	1	9	0		

SEASON	TEAM	OPPONENTS	V	BATTING M	I	NO	RUNS	H.S.	AVGE	100	50	CT	BOWLING OV	MD	RUNS	W	AVGE	B.B.
1958-59	West Indies	Tour of Pakistan	P	3	6	2	255	70	63.75		1	2						
1958-59	**WEST INDIES**	**PAKISTAN TESTS**	**P**	**1**	**1**		**1**	**1**	**1.00**			**1**						
1959-60	Barbados	M.C.C. Tourist	WI	1	1		34	34	34.00				4	0	11	0		
1960-61	Barbados	Trinidad	IIs	2	4		44	18	11.00			1						
1962-63	Barbados	Trinidad	IIs	1	1		0	0				2	1	0	1	0		
1963-64	Barbados	British Guiana	IIs	1	2		146	81	73.00		2							
1963-64	Barbados	Jamaica	IIs	1	2		133	120	66.50	1								
1963-64	Barbados	Trinidad	IIs	1	2		21	18	10.50									
1964-65	Barbados	Cavaliers Touring XI	WI	1	2		149	110	74.50	1								
1964-65	Barbados	Australian Tourist	WI	1	1		24	24	24.00			2	4	2	11	0		
1965-66	Barbados	Shell Shield	IIs	4	5	1	251	104	62.75	1	2	5						
1966-67	West Indies	Tour of India	I	4	8	1	228	*94	32.57		2	9	5	0	21	2	10.50	
1966-67	**WEST INDIES**	**INDIA TESTS**	**I**	**3**	**5**		**110**	**48**	**22.00**			**3**	**5**	**4**	**5**	**1**	**5.00**	
1966-67	West Indies	Tour of Ceylon	C	1	1		43	43	43.00				28	7	94	4	23.00	
1966-67	Barbados	Shell Shield	IIs	3	5		63	26	12.60			3	10	1	29	0		
1966-67	Barbados	Rest of World XI	WI	1	2		45	37	22.50			1						
1967-68	Barbados	M.C.C. Tourist	WI	1	2	1	64	*64	64.00		1		2	0	14	0		
1968-69	Barbados	Shell Shield	IIs	4	7		421	114	60.14	1	3	6	6	0	21	0		
1969	Barbados	Tour of English Counties	E	2	4		174	75	43.50		1							
1969-70	Barbados	Shell Shield	IIs	3	6		265	124	44.16	1	1	3	1	1	0	0		
1970-71	Barbados	Shell Shield	IIs	3	6	1	275	72	55.00		3	2						
1970-71	Barbados	Indian Tourist	WI	1	2	1	73	48	73.00				2	1	5	0		
1971-72	Barbados	Shell Shield	IIs	4	6	1	350	190	70.00	1	1	1	5	1	6	3.00		
		Barbados		37	64	5	2676	190	45.35	6	15	26	40	6	117	2	58.50	
		West Indies		19	33	5	896	*96	32.00		5	19	41	12	129	7	18.42	
		TEST RECORD		**4**	**6**	**0**	**111**	**48**	**18.50**	**0**	**0**	**4**	**5**	**4**	**5**	**1**	**5.00**	**1-5**
		CAREER		**56**	**97**	**10**	**3572**	**190**	**41.05**	**6**	**20**	**45**	**81**	**18**	**246**	**9**	**27.33**	**2-7**

CAMACHO, George Stephen

SEASON	TEAM	OPPONENTS	V	BATTING M	I	NO	RUNS	H.S.	AVGE	100	50	CT	BOWLING OV	MD	RUNS	W	AVGE	B.B.
1964-65	British Guiana	Australian Tourist	WI	1	2		53	28	26.50			1	3	0	4	0		
1965-66	British Guiana	Shell Shield	IIs	3	4		156	106	39.00	1		1	9	3	23	1	23.00	
1966-67	Guyana	Shell Shield	IIs	1	2		80	66	40.00		1	1						

SEASON	TEAM	OPPONENTS	V	M	I	NO	RUNS	H.S.	AVGE	100	50	CT	OV	MD	RUNS	W	AVGE	B.B.
1967-68	WI President's XI	M.C.C. Tourist	WI	1	2		120	85	60.00		1		5	1	22	1	22.00	
1967-68	Guyana	M.C.C. Tourist	WI	1	2		22	11	11.00			1						
1967-68	**WEST INDIES**	**ENGLAND TESTS**	**WI**	**5**	**10**		**328**	**87**	**32.80**		**2**	**1**	**3**	**1**	**12**	**0**		
1968-69	West Indies	Tour of Australia	A	7	14	2	455	102	37.91	1	2	7	3	0	22	0		
1968-69	**WEST INDIES**	**AUSTRALIA TESTS**	**A**	**2**	**4**		**57**	**40**	**14.25**			**2**						
1968-69	West Indies	Tour of New Zealand	NZ	1	2		15	14	7.50			1						
1969	West Indies	Tour of England	E	14	21	1	559	101	27.95	1	3	9	13	2	31	1	31.00	
1969	**WEST INDIES**	**ENGLAND TESTS**	**E**	**2**	**4**		**187**	**71**	**29.66**		**2**	**1**						
1969-70	Guyana	Shell Shield	IIs	4	7	1	253	80	42.16		3	1	6	2	14	0		
1970-71	Guyana	Shell Shield	IIs	4	6	1	195	117	39.00	1	1	1	25	8	45	4	11.25	
1970-71	WI President's XI	Indian Tourist	WI	1	2		84	45	42.00			2						
1970-71	**WEST INDIES**	**INDIA TESTS**	**WI**	**2**	**4**		**68**	**35**	**17.00**			**1**						
1971-72	Demerara	Berbice JC	G	1	1		141	141	141.00	1		5	9	1	26	0		
1971-72	Guyana	Shell Shield	IIs	1	2		19	18	9.50									
1971-72	Guyana	New Zealand Tourist	WI	1	2		49	32	24.50				3	0	14	1	14.00	
1972-73	Guyana	Shell Shield	IIs	4	6		425	144	70.83	1	4	5						
1972-73	Guyana	Australian Tourist	WI	1	2		63	55	31.50		1							
1973	West Indies	Tour of England	E	2	4	1	97	63	32.33		1							
1974-75	Guyana	Shell Shield	IIs	3	4	1	42	13	14.00			1						
1975-76	Guyana	Shell Shield	IIs	3	4		147	60	36.75		2							
1975-76	Demerara	Berbice JC	G	1	1		166	166	166.00	1								
1977-78	Demerara	Berbice JC	G	1	2		25	22	12.50			1						
1977-78	Guyana	Shell Shield	IIs	4	6		111	50	18.50		1	3						
1978-79	Demerara	Berbice JC	G	1	1		19	19	19.00			1	4	1	3	0		
1978-79	Guyana	Shell Shield	IIs	4	4	1	143	63	47.66		1	1						
		Guyana/British Guiana		35	53	4	1758	144	35.87	3	14	16	46	13	100	6	16.66	
		Demerara		4	5		351	166	70.20	2		7	13	2	29	0		
		West Indies		37	67	4	1970	102	31.26	2	11	24	24	4	87	2	43.50	
		TEST RECORD		**11**	**22**	**0**	**640**	**87**	**29.09**	**0**	**4**	**4**	**3**	**1**	**12**	**0**		
		CAREER		**76**	**125**	**8**	**4079**	**166**	**34.86**	**7**	**25**	**47**	**83**	**19**	**216**	**8**	**27.00**	**3-10**

CAMERON, Francis James

				BATTING									BOWLING					
SEASON	**TEAM**	**OPPONENTS**	**V**	**M**	**I**	**NO**	**RUNS**	**H.S.**	**AVGE**	**100**	**50**	**CT**	**OV**	**MD**	**RUNS**	**W**	**AVGE**	**B.B.**
1945-46	Jamaica	Trinidad	IIs	2	3		87	50	29.00		1		72.2	11	222	9	24.66	
1948-49	West Indies	Tour of India	I	7	8	2	161	50	26.83		1	7	184.2	33	492	11	44.72	

SEASON	TEAM	OPPONENTS	V	M	I	NO	RUNS	H.S.	AVGE	100	50	CT	OV	MD	RUNS	W	AVGE	B.B.
				BATTING									BOWLING					
1948-49	**WEST INDIES**	**INDIA TESTS**	**I**	**5**	**7**	**1**	**151**	***75**	**25.16**		**1**		**131**	**34**	**278**	**3**	**92.66**	
1948-49	West Indies	Tour of Pakistan	P	1	1		9	9	9.00				44	16	101	4	25.25	
1948-49	West Indies	Tour of Ceylon	C	1	1	1	9	*9					18	2	61	0		
1954	Canada	Tour of England	E	4	6	1	127	39	25.40			2	66	7	257	2	128.50	
1959-60	Jamaica	Trinidad	IIs	1	1		7	7	7.00									
		Jamaica		3	4		94	50	23.50		1		72.2	11	222	9	24.66	
		West Indies		14	17	4	330	*75	25.38		2	7	377.2	85	932	18	51.77	
		Canada		4	6	1	127	39	25.40			2	66	7	257	2	128.50	
		TEST RECORD		**5**	**7**	**1**	**151**	***75**	**25.16**	**0**	**1**	**0**	**131**	**34**	**278**	**3**	**92.66**	**2-74**
		CAREER		**21**	**27**	**5**	**551**	***75**	**25.04**	**0**	**3**	**9**	**515.4**	**103**	**1411**	**29**	**48.65**	**4-52**

CAMERON, John Hensley

SEASON	TEAM	OPPONENTS	V	M	I	NO	RUNS	H.S.	AVGE	100	50	CT	OV	MD	RUNS	W	AVGE	B.B.
				BATTING									BOWLING					
1932	Somerset	Counties	E	2	3		13	9	4.33			3	34	3	149	2	74.50	
1934	Somerset	Counties	E	6	10		91	41	9.10			4	103.3	6	445	9	49.44	
1934	Cambridge Univ.	Counties	E	5	5		95	41	19.00			4	120	8	485	13	37.30	
1935	Somerset	Counties	E	13	19	2	326	111	19.17	1		11	214.4	43	648	16	40.50	
1935	Cambridge Univ.	Counties	E	11	19		195	40	10.26			11	298.1	46	883	44	20.06	
1935	Gentlemen's XI	Players XI	E	1	1		44	44	44.00			2	9	1	45	0		
1936	Somerset	Counties	E	11	20	1	274	43	14.42			5	15	0	62	0		
1936	Cambridge Univ.	Counties	E	12	17	2	213	46	14.20			8	250.1	21	972	25	38.88	
1937	Somerset	Counties	E	13	24	2	574	113	26.09	2	1	8	156.1	20	560	17	32.99	
1937	Cambridge Univ.	Counties	E	8	14	1	289	50	22.23		1	2	120.5	10	484	17	28.47	
1938-39	Combined UN XI	Tour of Jamaica	WI	2	4	1	116	62	38.66		1		36.3	1	120	5	24.00	
1939	West Indies	Tour of England	E	15	20	2	432	106	21.60	1	1	5	193.6	34	576	28	20.57	
1939	**WEST INDIES**	**ENGLAND TESTS**	**E**	**2**	**3**		**6**	**5**	**2.00**				**29**	**6**	**88**	**3**	**29.33**	
1945-46	Jamaica	Trinidad	IIs	1	1		9	9	9.00				19.1	3	44	4	11.00	
1947	Somerset	Counties	E	3	4	1	95	*38	31.66				32	7	101	1	101.00	
		Somerset		48	80	6	1373	113	18.37	3	1	31	555.2	79	1965	45	43.67	
		Cambridge Univ.		36	55	3	792	50	15.23		1	25	789.1	85	2824	99	25.53	
		Jamaica		1	1	0	9	9	9.00				19.1	3	44	4	11.00	
		West Indies		17	23	3	438	106	20.85	1	1	5	222.6	40	664	31	21.41	

		Combined University		2	4	1	116	62	38.66		1		36.3	1	120	5	24.00	
		Gentlemen's XI		1	1	0	44	44	44.00			2	9	1	45	0		
		TEST RECORD		**2**	**3**	**0**	**6**	**5**	**2.00**	**0**	**0**	**0**	**29**	**6**	**88**	**3**	**29.33**	**3-66**
		CAREER		**105**	**164**	**12**	**2772**	**113**	**18.23**	**4**	**4**	**63**	**1632.1**	**209**	**5662**	**184**	**30.77**	**7-73**

CAREW, George McDonald

				BATTING									BOWLING					
SEASON	TEAM	OPPONENTS	V	M	I	NO	RUNS	H.S.	AVGE	100	50	CT	OV	MD	RUNS	W	AVGE	B.B.
1934-35	Barbados	British Guiana	IIs	1	2		33	17	16.50									
1934-35	Barbados	M.C.C. Tourist	WI	2	4	1	157	68	52.33		1	1						
1934-35	**WEST INDIES**	**ENGLAND TESTS**	**WI**	**1**	**1**		**0**	**0**										
1935-36	Barbados	Trinidad	IIs	1	2		3	2	1.50			3	2	0	8	0		
1937-38	Barbados	British Guiana	IIs	1	2	1	101	67	101.00		1		15	1	47	0		
1938-39	Barbados	Trinidad	IIs	1	2		6	5	3.00									
1938-39	Barbados	British Guiana	IIs	1	2	1	31	*24	31.00			1						
1938-39	West Indies XI	Jamaica	WI	1	2		3	3	1.50				1	0	5	0		
1940-41	Barbados	Trinidad	IIs	2	4	1	191	100	63.66	1		1	19.2	1	92	3	30.66	
1941-42	Barbados	Trinidad	IIs	4	7		190	95	27.14		1	3	27	3	117	3	39.00	
1942-43	Barbados	Trinidad	IIs	2	4		116	55	29.00		1	1	16	3	72	1	72.00	
1943-44	Barbados	Trinidad	IIs	2	3		50	36	16.66				3	0	26	0		
1944-45	Barbados	British Guiana	IIs	2	3		132	97	44.00		1	1	2	0	22	0		
1945-46	Barbados	Trinidad	IIs	2	4		121	74	30.25		1	2	32	6	100	2	50.00	
1947-48	Barbados	M.C.C. Tourist	WI	2	3		157	81	52.33		1		3	2	1	0		
1947-48	**WEST INDIES**	**ENGLAND TESTS**	**WI**	**2**	**4**	**1**	**150**	**107**	**50.00**	**1**		**1**						
1948-49	West Indies	Tour of India	I	10	17	2	593	100	39.53	1	4	3	46	15	108	4	27.00	
1948-49	**WEST INDIES**	**INDIA TESTS**	**I**	**1**	**2**		**20**	**11**	**10.00**				**3**	**2**	**2**	**0**		
1948-49	West Indies	Tour of Ceylon	C	1	1		77	77	77.00		1							
		Barbados		23	42	4	1288	100	33.89	1	7	13	119.2	16	485	9	53.88	
		West Indies		16	27	3	843	107	35.12	2	5	4	50	17	115	4	28.75	
		TEST RECORD		**4**	**7**	**1**	**170**	**107**	**28.33**	**1**	**0**	**1**	**3**	**2**	**2**	**0**		
		CAREER		**39**	**69**	**7**	**2131**	**107**	**34.37**	**3**	**12**	**17**	**169.2**	**33**	**600**	**13**	**46.15**	**2-26**

CAREW, Michael Conrad

SEASON	TEAM	OPPONENTS		V	M	I	NO	RUNS	H.S.	AVGE	100	50	CT	OV	MD	RUNS	W	AVGE	B.B.
					BATTING									BOWLING					
1955-56	Trinidad	E.W. Swanton's Tourist		WI	1	2		25	17	12.50				7	0	31	0		
1958-59	N.Trinidad	S.Trinidad	BC	T	1	1		11	11	11.00			3						
1959-60	Trinidad	Jamaica		IIs	1	2		124	114	62.00	1		1	7	1	23	0		
1959-60	Trinidad	M.C.C. Tourist		WI	2	4	1	185	*102	61.66	1	1	2						
1959-60	N.Trinidad	S.Trinidad	BC	T	1	2		63	61	31.50		1	3						
1960-61	Trinidad	Barbados		IIs	2	4	1	101	*76	33.66		1		16	3	49	2	24.50	
1960-61	Trinidad	E.W. Swanton's Tourist		WI	1	2		60	53	30.00		1	1	3	0	9	0		
1960-61	N.Trinidad	S.Trinidad	BC	T	1	1		4	4	4.00									
1961-62	Trinidad	British Guiana		IIs	1	2		38	34	19.00			1						
1961-62	Trinidad	Indian Tourist		WI	1	2		66	55	33.00		1							
1961-62	N.Trinidad	S.Trinidad	BC	T	1	2		56	46	28.00			2						
1963	West Indies	Tour of England		E	19	35	3	1003	117	31.34	1	6	7	32	7	99	4	24.75	
1963	**WEST INDIES**	**ENGLAND TESTS**		**E**	**2**	**4**	**1**	**57**	**40**	**19.00**									
1963-64	The Rest XI	West Indies XI		WI	1	2		122	79	61.00		1		8	0	49	0		
1963-64	F.Worrell's XI	C.Hunte's XI		WI	1	2		84	47	42.00				11	0	48	1	48.00	
1963-64	Trinidad	Jamaica		IIs	1	2		14	8	7.00				2	0	4	0		
1963-64	Trinidad	Barbados		IIs	1	2		47	29	23.50			1	1	0	2	0		
1963-64	Trinidad	British Guiana		IIs	1	2		94	77	47.00		1							
1963-64	N.Trinidad	S.Trinidad	BC	T	1	2		152	88	76.00		2	2	9	3	18	0		
1964-65	Trinidad	Australian Tourist		WI	1	2		5	5	2.50			1						
1964-65	N.Trinidad	S.Trinidad	BC	T	1	2		76	64	38.00		1	2						
1965-66	Trinidad	Shell Shield		IIs	4	6		206	81	34.33		2		73.2	25	190	11	17.27	
1966	West Indies	Tour of England		E	17	27	1	718	132	27.61	1	2	9	230	78	520	16	32.50	
1966	**WEST INDIES**	**ENGLAND TESTS**		**E**	**1**	**2**		**2**	**2**	**1.00**				**3**	**0**	**11**	**1**	**11.00**	
1966-67	Trinidad	Shell Shield		IIs	4	7	1	165	*65	27.50		1	2	85.5	25	216	9	24.00	
1966-67	N.Trinidad	S.Trinidad	BC	T	1	1		30	30	30.00			1	33	11	64	2	32.00	
1967-68	Trinidad	M.C.C. Tourist		WI	1	2	1	118	*90	118.00		1		27	13	41	2	20.50	
1967-68	**WEST INDIES**	**ENGLAND TESTS**		**WI**	**1**	**2**	**1**	**76**	***40**	**76.00**				**32**	**20**	**42**	**1**	**42.00**	
1967-68	N.Trinidad	S.Trinidad	BC	T	1	1		18	18	18.00			2	11	3	28	0		
1968-69	West Indies	Tour of Australia		A	6	12	3	360	74	40.00		3	9	71.3	12	236	7	33.71	
1968-69	**WEST INDIES**	**AUSTRALIA TESTS**		**A**	**5**	**10**	**1**	**427**	**90**	**47.44**		**4**	**6**	**59**	**9**	**238**	**3**	**79.33**	
1968-69	West Indies	Tour of New Zealand		NZ	2	4		179	76	44.75		2	4	21	7	132	1	132.00	
1968-69	**WEST INDIES**	**NEW ZEALAND TESTS**		**NZ**	**3**	**5**		**256**	**109**	**51.20**	**1**	**1**	**1**	**27**	**9**	**54**	**3**	**18.00**	
1969	West Indies	Tour of England		E	11	16	3	632	*172	48.61	3	1	8	65.4	13	242	7	34.57	
1969	**WEST INDIES**	**ENGLAND TESTS**		**E**	**1**	**2**		**45**	**44**	**22.50**				**11**	**3**	**19**	**0**		
1969-70	Trinidad	Shell Shield		IIs	4	6		523	164	87.16	3	1		67.1	23	120	13	9.30	

SEASON	TEAM	OPPONENTS	V	M	I	NO	RUNS	H.S.	AVGE	100	50	CT	OV	MD	RUNS	W	AVGE	B.B.
1969-70	Trinidad	Duke of Norfolk's Tourist	WI	1	2		62	39	31.00				9	1	14	0		
1969-70	N.Trinidad	S.Trinidad BC	T	1	2		107	69	53.50		1		38	11	69	2	34.50	
1970-71	Trinidad	Shell Shield	IIs	4	7	1	347	91	57.83		3	3	56	16	144	4	36.00	
1970-71	**WEST INDIES**	**INDIA TESTS**	**WI**	**3**	**5**		**121**	**45**	**24.20**			**3**	**14**	**4**	**20**	**0**		
1970-71	N.Trinidad	C & E Trinidad BC	T	2	3		212	182	70.66	1			57.2	15	117	3	39.00	
1971-72	Trinidad	Shell Shield	IIs	4	6		227	78	37.83		2	1	50	18	101	5	20.20	
1971-72	Trinidad	New Zealand Tourist	WI	1	2		130	100	65.00	1			7	2	13	0		
1971-72	**WEST INDIES**	**NEW ZEALAND TESTS**	**WI**	**3**	**6**		**143**	**45**	**23.83**			**3**	**21**	**2**	**53**	**0**		
1972-73	Trinidad	Shell Shield	IIs	4	3		200	84	66.66		2	3	39	9	90	3	30.00	
1972-73	N.Trinidad	S.Trinidad TC	T	1	1		92	92	92.00		1	2	53	22	76	3	25.33	
1973-74	N.Trinidad	S.Trinidad TC	T	1	2		27	19	13.50				36.4	12	33	5	6.60	
		Trinidad		40	67	5	2737	164	44.14	6	17	16	450.2	136	1047	49	21.36	
		N.Trinidad		13	20		848	182	42.40	1	6	17	238	77	405	15	27.00	
		West Indies		74	130	13	4019	*172	34.35	6	19	50	587.1	163	1666	43	38.74	
		The Rest XI		1	2		122	79	61.00		1		8	0	49	0		
		F.Worrell's XI		1	2		84	47	42.00				11	0	48	1	48.00	
		TEST RECORD		**19**	**36**	**3**	**1127**	**109**	**34.15**	**1**	**5**	**13**	**167**	**46**	**437**	**8**	**54.62**	**1-11**
		CAREER		**129**	**221**	**18**	**7810**	**182**	**38.47**	**13**	**43**	**83**	**1294.3**	**376**	**3215**	**108**	**29.76**	**5-28**

CHALLENOR, George

				BATTING									BOWLING					
SEASON	**TEAM**	**OPPONENTS**	**V**	**M**	**I**	**NO**	**RUNS**	**H.S.**	**AVGE**	**100**	**50**	**CT**	**OV**	**MD**	**RUNS**	**W**	**AVGE**	**B.B.**
1905-06	Barbados	British Guiana	IIs	1	2		54	34	27.00									
1905-06	Barbados	Trinidad	IIs	1	2		40	36	20.00									
1906	West Indies	Tour of England	E	12	24		684	108	28.50	1	4	3						
1908-09	Barbados	Trinidad	IIs	1	2		37	32	18.50				2	0	13	1	13.00	
1909-10	Barbados	Trinidad	IIs	1	2		17	17	8.50				4.4	0	19	2	9.50	
1910-11	Barbados	British Guiana	IIs	1	2		51	43	25.50				7	1	15	0		
1910-11	Barbados	Trinidad	IIs	1	1		1	1	1.00				3	0	14	0		
1910-11	Barbados	M.C.C. Tourist	WI	2	2		27	16	13.50				20.1	3	43	7	6.14	
1910-11	West Indies XI	M.C.C. Tourist	WI	1	2		112	75	56.00		1		38	11	101	3	33.66	
1911-12	Barbados	Trinidad	IIs	1	2	1	7	*4	7.00			1	30.3	4	97	5	19.40	
1912-13	Barbados	M.C.C. Tourist	WI	2	2		227	118	113.50	2			72.5	19	249	10	24.90	
1912-13	West Indies XI	M.C.C. Tourist	WI	1	2		1	1	0.50				8	1	23	0		
1919-20	Barbados	Trinidad	IIs	2	2		123	104	61.50	1		1	45	8	125	7	17.85	
1921-22	Barbados	Trinidad	IIs	1	1		16	16	16.00			2	21	7	48	2	24.00	

SEASON	TEAM	OPPONENTS	V	M	I	NO	RUNS	H.S.	AVGE	100	50	CT	OV	MD	RUNS	W	AVGE	B.B.
				BATTING									BOWLING					
1922-23	Barbados	Trinidad	IIs	1	1		96	96	96.00		1		17	1	80	0		
1923	West Indies	Tour of England	E	20	35	5	1556	*155	51.86	6	8	4	17	3	54	2	27.00	
1923-24	Barbados	Trinidad	IIs	1	2		144	114	72.00	1			14	4	27	2	13.50	
1924-25	Barbados	Jamaica	IIs	2	2	1	279	*237	279.00	1		1	27	6	43	2	21.50	
1924-25	Barbados	Trinidad	IIs	1	2		66	56	33.00		1	1	13	3	39	2	19.50	
1925-26	Barbados	M.C.C. Tourist	WI	2	2		142	124	71.00	1			5	3	14	1	14.00	
1925-26	West Indies XI	M.C.C. Tourist	WI	3	5	1	161	82	40.25		2	1						
1926	M.C.C.	Universities & Yorkshire	E	3	6		129	47	21.50			1	13	4	40	1	40.00	
1926	H. Leveson-Gower's XI	Cambridge U & Glamorgan	E	2	4		154	65	38.50		1							
1926	Gentlemen's XI	Players' XI	E	2	3		104	56	34.66		1							
1926-27	Barbados	British Guiana	IIs	1	1		104	104	104.00	1		2	9	2	22	1	22.00	
1926-27	Barbados	Trinidad	IIs	1	2		231	220	115.50	1		2	32	6	75	3	25.00	
1927-28	Combined B/J XI	Combined Trin/BG XI	IIs	2	4		123	65	30.75		1							
1927-28	Barbados Born XI	West Indies XI	IIs	1	2		11	9	5.50				14	0	38	1	38.00	
1928	West Indies	Tour of England	E	21	34	1	973	97	29.48		8	6	17.2	4	80	2	40.00	
1928	**WEST INDIES**	**ENGLAND TESTS**	**E**	**3**	**6**		**101**	**46**	**16.83**									
1929-30	Barbados	M.C.C. Tourist	WI	1	1		51	51	51.00		1		6	1	31	0		
		Barbados		25	35	2	1724	*237	52.24	8	3	10	343.1	68	992	46	21.56	
		West Indies		61	108	7	3588	*155	35.52	7	23	14	80.2	19	258	7	36.85	
		M.C.C.		3	6		129	47	21.50			1	13	4	40	1	40.00	
		Gentlemens XI		2	3		104	56	34.66		1							
		H.Leveson-Gower's XI		2	4		154	65	38.50		1							
		Combined B/J XI		2	4		123	65	31.25		1							
		TEST RECORD		**3**	**6**	**0**	**101**	**46**	**16.83**	**0**	**0**	**0**						
		CAREER		**95**	**160**	**9**	**5822**	***237**	**38.55**	**15**	**29**	**26**	**436.3**	**91**	**1290**	**54**	**23.88**	**4-16**

CHANG, Herbert Samuel

SEASON	TEAM	OPPONENTS	V	M	I	NO	RUNS	H.S.	AVGE	100	50	CT	OV	MD	RUNS	W	AVGE	B.B.
				BATTING									BOWLING					
1972-73	Jamaica	Shell Shield	IIs	4	8	1	211	90	30.14		1	4						
1972-73	Jamaica	Australian Tourist	WI	1	2		103	64	51.50		1	1						
1973-74	Jamaica	Shell Shield	IIs	4	6	1	123	55	24.60		1	3	1	0	1	0		
1973-74	WI President's XI	M.C.C. Tourist	WI	1	2		68	64	34.00		1							
1973-74	Jamaica	M.C.C. Tourist	WI	1	2		41	22	20.50									

SEASON	TEAM	OPPONENTS	V	M	I	NO	RUNS	H.S.	AVGE	100	50	CT/St	OV	MD	RUNS	W	AVGE	B.B.
1974-75	Jamaica	Shell Shield	IIs	4	6	2	261	*108	65.25	1	1	3	3	0	15	0		
1975-76	Jamaica	Shell Shield	IIs	4	4		178	145	45.50	1		2						
1975-76	Jamaica	Indian Tourist	WI	1	2		25	24	12.50									
1976-77	Jamaica	Shell Shield	IIs	4	6		164	58	27.33		1	3						
1976-77	Jamaica	Pakistan Tourist	WI	1	2		100	50	50.00		2							
1977-78	Jamaica	Shell Shield	IIs	4	6		125	81	20.83		1	2	1	0	1	0		
1977-78	Jamaica	Australian Tourist	WI	1	2		75	64	37.50		1							
1978-79	West Indies	Tour of India	I	7	13		270	87	20.76		1	5	2	0	16	0		
1978-79	**WEST INDIES**	**INDIA TESTS**	**I**	**1**	**2**		**8**	**6**	**4.00**									
1978-79	West Indies	Tour of Sri Lanka	SL	1	2		80	67	40.00		1							
1978-79	Jamaica	Shell Shield	IIs	4	6		412	126	68.66	1	2							
1979-80	Jamaica	Shell Shield	IIs	4	8		358	132	44.75	1	2	3						
1980-81	Jamaica	Shell Shield	IIs	4	7	1	147	53	24.50		1	1						
1980-81	Jamaica	English Tourist	WI	1	1		12	12	12.00									
1981-82	Jamaica	Shell Shield	IIs	5	9		426	155	47.33	1	3	4						
1982-83	Jamaica	Shell Shield	IIs	1	2		86	64	43.00		1							
		Jamaica		48	79	5	2847	155	38.47	5	18	26	5	0	17	0		
		West Indies		10	19		426	87	22.42		3	5	2	0	16	0		
		TEST RECORD		**1**	**2**	**0**	**8**	**6**	**4.00**	**0**	**0**	**0**						
		CAREER		**58**	**98**	**5**	**3273**	**155**	**35.19**	**5**	**21**	**31**	**7**	**0**	**33**	**0**		

CHRISTIANI, Cyril Marcel

				BATTING									BOWLING					
SEASON	TEAM	OPPONENTS	V	M	I	NO	RUNS	H.S.	AVGE	100	50	CT/St	OV	MD	RUNS	W	AVGE	B.B.
1931-32	British Guiana	Trinidad	IIs	1	2		30	23	15.00									
1932-33	G.C. Grant's XI	C.A. Merry's XI	IIs	1	2	1	27	26	27.00			2/0						
1933	West Indies	Tour of England	E	13	19	1	179	40	9.94			27/4	1	0	6	0		
1933-34	British Guiana	Barbados	IIs	1	2		40	40	20.00			1/2						
1934-35	British Guiana	Barbados	IIs	1	2		49	32	24.50			3/0						
1934-35	British Guiana	Trinidad	IIs	1	1		25	25	25.00			1/2						
1934-35	British Guiana	M.C.C. Tourist	WI	2	3		19	10	6.33			1/3						
1934-35	**WEST INDIES**	**ENGLAND TESTS**	**WI**	**4**	**7**	**2**	**98**	***32**	**19.60**			**6/1**						
1935-36	British Guiana	Trinidad	IIs	1	1		28	28	28.00			1/4						
1936-37	British Guiana	Trinidad	IIs	1	2		113	79	56.50		1	1/0						
1937-38	British Guiana	Barbados	IIs	1	1		26	26	26.00			1/1						
1937-38	British Guiana	Trinidad	IIs	1	2		24	24	12.00			0/3						

SEASON	TEAM	M	I	NO	RUNS	H.S.	AVGE	100	50	CT/St	OV	MD	RUNS	W	AVGE	B.B.
		BATTING									BOWLING					
	British Guiana	10	16		354	79	22.15		1	9/15						
	West Indies	17	26	3	277	40	12.04			33/5	1	0	6	0		
	G.C. Grant's XI	1	2	1	27	26	27.00			2/0						
	TEST RECORD	**4**	**7**	**2**	**98**	***32**	**19.60**	**0**	**0**	**6/1**						
	CAREER	**28**	**44**	**4**	**658**	**79**	**16.45**	**0**	**1**	**44/20**	**1**	**0**	**6**	**0**		

CHRISTIANI, Robert Julian

SEASON	TEAM	OPPONENTS	V	M	I	NO	RUNS	H.S.	AVGE	100	50	CT/St	OV	MD	RUNS	W	AVGE	B.B.
				BATTING									BOWLING					
1938-39	British Guiana	R.S. Grant's XI	IIs	1	2	1	17	14	17.00									
1938-39	British Guiana	Trinidad	IIs	1	2		23	23	11.50			1/2						
1938-39	British Guiana	Barbados	IIs	1	2		31	30	15.50			3/0						
1938-39	West Indies XI	Jamaica	IIs	1	2		64	58	32.00		1							
1943-44	British Guiana	Trinidad	IIs	2	4		192	126	48.00	1	1	2	16	2	89	2	27.00	
1944-45	British Guiana	Barbados	IIs	2	4		168	128	42.00	1		3	10	0	59	2	39.50	
1945-46	British Guiana	Trinidad	IIs	2	4		98	75	24.50		1	4	8.3	1	36	1	36.00	
1946-47	British Guiana	Barbados	IIs	2	4		212	149	53.00	1		4	11	0	87	0		
1946-47	British Guiana	Trinidad	IIs	2	4		263	133	65.75	1	1	2	6	0	41	0		
1947-48	British Guiana	Jamaica	IIs	2	4		332	181	83.00	1	1	3	27	4	107	4	26.75	
1947-48	British Guiana	M.C.C. Tourist	WI	1	2	1	72	38	72.00			2	3	0	12	0		
1947-48	**WEST INDIES**	**ENGLAND TESTS**	**WI**	**4**	**6**		**175**	**99**	**29.16**		**2**	**6**						
1948-49	West Indies	Tour of India	I	8	10	1	337	85	37.44		3	9	11	1	45	0		
1948-49	**WEST INDIES**	**INDIA TESTS**	**I**	**5**	**7**		**294**	**107**	**42.00**	**1**	**1**	**5/2**	**38**	**1**	**106**	**3**	**35.33**	
1948-49	West Indies	Tour of Pakistan	P	2	2		58	34	29.00			1	29	2	104	1	104.00	
1948-49	West Indies	Tour of Ceylon	C	2	1		96	96	96.00		1	1	12	0	52	1	52.00	
1949-50	British Guiana	Barbados	IIs	2	4		199	121	49.75	1	1		19.4	1	117	3	39.00	
1950	West Indies	Tour of England	E	20	28	9	1012	*131	53.26	4	4	28/6						
1950	**WEST INDIES**	**ENGLAND TESTS**	**E**	**4**	**6**	**1**	**82**	**33**	**16.40**			**2/0**						
1950-51	British Guiana	Jamaica	IIs	2	4		148	61	37.00		2	5/1	6	0	42	0		
1951-52	West Indies	Tour of Australia	A	5	9	1	365	*107	45.62	1	2	1						
1951-52	**WEST INDIES**	**AUSTRALIA TESTS**	**A**	**5**	**10**	**1**	**261**	**76**	**29.00**		**1**	**2/0**						
1951-52	West Indies	Tour of New Zealand	NZ	2	3		97	66	32.33		1	0/1	3	1	12	0		
1951-52	**WEST INDIES**	**NEW ZEALAND TESTS**	**NZ**	**1**	**2**		**6**	**3**	**2.00**			**3/0**						
1952-53	British Guiana	Jamaica	IIs	2	3		115	43	38.33			1	17	4	69	0		
1952-53	British Guiana	Indian Tourist	WI	1	1		9	9	9.00			1						

SEASON	TEAM	OPPONENTS	V	M	I	NO	RUNS	H.S.	AVGE	100	50	CT	OV	MD	RUNS	W	AVGE	B.B.
1952-53	**WEST INDIES**	**INDIA TESTS**	**WI**	**2**	**4**	**1**	**42**	**33**	**14.00**			**1**						
1953-54	British Guiana	Trinidad	IIs	2	4		142	76	35.50		2	5	19	2	78	1	78.00	
1953-54	British Guiana	M.C.C. Tourist	WI	1	2		157	75	78.50		2	2	6	0	30	0		
1953-54	**WEST INDIES**	**ENGLAND TESTS**	**WI**	**1**	**2**		**36**	**25**	**18.00**				**1**	**0**	**2**	**0**		
		British Guiana		26	50	2	2178	181	45.37	6	12	39/3	149.1	14	767	13	59.00	
		West Indies		62	92	14	2925	*131	37.50	6	15	59/9	94	5	321	5	64.20	
		TEST RECORD		**22**	**37**	**3**	**896**	**107**	**26.35**	**1**	**4**	**19/2**	**39**	**1**	**108**	**3**	**36.00**	**3-52**
		CAREER		**88**	**142**	**16**	**5103**	**181**	**40.50**	**12**	**27**	**98/12**	**243.1**	**19**	**1088**	**18**	**60.44**	**3-11**

CLARKE, Dr. Carlos Bertram

				BATTING									BOWLING					
SEASON	TEAM	OPPONENTS	V	M	I	NO	RUNS	H.S.	AVGE	100	50	CT	OV	MD	RUNS	W	AVGE	B.B.
1937-38	Barbados	British Guiana	IIs	1	2		8	7	4.00				51	13	146	2	73.00	
1938-39	Barbados	Trinidad	IIs	1	2	2	21	*17					26	3	108	2	54.00	
1938-39	Barbados	British Guiana	IIs	1	1		14	14	14.00				24.1	3	108	8	13.50	
1938-39	West Indies XI	Jamaica	IIs	1	1	1	6	*6				1	32	3	123	1	123.00	
1939	West Indies	Tour of England	E	19	21	9	159	45	13.25			5	401.3	44	1637	81	20.20	
1939	**WEST INDIES**	**ENGLAND TESTS**	**E**	**3**	**4**	**1**	**3**	**2**	**1.00**				**57**	**2**	**261**	**6**	**43.50**	
1946	Northamptonshire	Counties	E	13	18	2	176	34	11.00			6	420.2	78	1413	44	32.11	
1947	Northamptonshire	Counties	E	24	44	6	477	86	12.55		1	17	688.5	92	2422	89	27.21	
1948	Northamptonshire	Counties	E	9	15	1	210	49	15.00			3	183.5	25	618	20	30.90	
1949	Northamptonshire	Counties	E	3	4	2	11	5	5.50			1	55	6	185	3	61.66	
1955	M.C.C.	Gloucestershire	E	1	1		6	6	6.00			2	43	3	122	4	30.50	
1956	M.C.C.	Cambridge University	E	1	2	1	17	*15	17.00				26.2	4	64	5	12.80	
1957	M.C.C.	Oxford University	E	1	2	1	7	7	7.00				45.3	14	134	8	16.75	
1959	Essex	Counties	E	9	15	8	95	39	13.57			4	243.2	42	796	36	22.11	
1960	Essex	Counties	E	9	12	6	82	28	13.66			2	194.2	46	557	22	25.31	
1961	M.C.C.	Gloucesteshire	E	1	1		0	0				1	20	2	88	2	44.00	
		Barbados		3	5	2	43	*17	14.33				101.1	19	362	12	30.16	
		West Cheshire		23	26	11	168	45	11.20			6	490.3	49	2021	88	22.96	
		Northamptonshire		49	81	11	874	86	12.48		1	27	1348	201	4638	156	29.73	
		Essex		18	27	14	177	39	13.61			6	437.4	88	1353	58	23.32	
		M.C.C.		4	6	2	30	*15	7.50			3	134.5	23	408	19	21.47	
		TEST RECORD		**3**	**4**	**1**	**3**	**2**	**1.00**	**0**	**0**	**0**	**57**	**2**	**261**	**6**	**43.50**	**3-59**
		CAREER		**97**	**145**	**40**	**1292**	**86**	**12.30**	**0**	**1**	**42**	**2512.1**	**380**	**8782**	**333**	**26.37**	**7-75**

CLARKE, Sylvester Theophilus

SEASON	TEAM	OPPONENTS	V	M	I	NO	RUNS	H.S.	AVGE	100	50	CT	OV	MD	RUNS	W	AVGE	B.B.
				BATTING									BOWLING					
1977-78	Barbados	Shell Shield	IIs	4	5	2	20	9	6.66				107.3	19	324	15	21.60	
1977-78	Barbados	Australian Tourist	WI	1	2	1	25	15	25.00				31	2	89	1	89.00	
1977-78	**WEST INDIES**	**AUSTRALIA TESTS**	**WI**	**1**	**2**	**1**	**11**	**6**	**11.00**				**49**	**8**	**140**	**6**	**23.33**	
1978-79	West Indies	Tour of India	I	3	4	1	49	22	16.33				73.1	25	165	12	13.75	
1978-79	**WEST INDIES**	**INDIA TESTS**	**I**	**5**	**7**	**2**	**39**	**15**	**7.80**			**1**	**233.5**	**39**	**712**	**21**	**34.33**	
1978-79	West Indies	Tour of Sri Lanka	SL	2	3		16	14	5.33			2	50.1	13	115	9	12.77	
1978-79	Barbados	Shell Shield	IIs	4	3	1	6	6	3.00			7	137.4	31	399	14	28.50	
1979	Surrey	Counties	E	11	11	3	90	25	11.25			6	320.1	106	757	43	17.60	
1979-80	Barbados	Shell Shield	IIs	4	4		89	36	22.25			2	121	22	420	14	30.00	
1980	Surrey	Counties	E	21	18	1	248	55	14.58		1	8	605.3	139	1700	79	21.51	
1980-81	West Indies	Tour of Pakistan	P	3	3	1	8	*5	4.00				78.4	16	225	14	16.07	
1980-81	**WEST INDIES**	**PAKISTAN TESTS**	**P**	**4**	**5**	**2**	**103**	***35**	**34.33**			**1**	**98**	**21**	**242**	**14**	**17.28**	
1980-81	Barbados	Shell Shield	IIs	3	4	1	26	*15	8.66			2	88.3	23	277	14	19.78	
1980-81	Barbados	English Tourist	WI	1	1		0	0				1	59	15	122	4	30.50	
1981	Surrey	Counties	E	10	14	1	342	*100	26.30	1	1	8	339.4	98	734	49	14.97	
1981-81	West Indies	Tour of Australia	A	3	1		0	0					57	5	185	8	23.12	
1981-82	**WEST INDIES**	**AUSTRALIA TESTS**	**A**	**1**	**2**		**19**	**14**	**9.50**				**32**	**13**	**76**	**1**	**76.00**	
1981-82	Barbados	Shell Shield	IIs	3	3	1	38	31	19.00			2	84	17	267	6	44.50	
1982	Surrey	Counties	E	22	25		408	52	16.32		1	11	659.3	159	1696	85	19.95	
1982-83	West Indies XI	International XI	WI	1	1		6	6	6.00				21	9	26	5	5.20	
1982-83	WI Rebels XI	Tour of South Africa	SA	2	4	2	30	25	15.00				93.5	27	210	14	15.00	
1983	Surrey	Counties	E	24	24	4	285	43	14.25			17	693.1	183	1773	79	22.44	
1983-84	WI Rebels XI	Tour of South Africa	SA	6	9	2	74	*23	10.57			3	220.1	61	573	31	18.48	
1983-84	Transvaal	Currie Cup	SA	4	6	1	136	*78	27.20		1	2	170.5	65	322	18	17.88	
1984	Surrey	Counties	E	28	25	3	329	35	14.95			23	651	165	1687	78	21.62	
1984-85	Transvaal	Currie Cup	SA	10	9	3	82	17	13.66			4	331	88	738	58	12.72	
1985-86	Transvaal	Currie Cup	SA	6	7	3	59	29	14.75			1	193	50	474	18	26.33	
1986	Surrey	Counties	E	14	13	4	156	*32	17.33			9	341.3	95	806	48	16.79	
1987	Surrey	Counties	E	15	15	1	131	44	9.35			8	456.4	124	1160	67	17.31	
1987-88	Orange Free State	Currie Cup	SA	7	14	1	201	60	15.46		1	9	240.4	58	504	32	15.75	
1988	Surrey	Counties	E	12	10	1	141	28	15.66			11	396.4	108	913	63	14.49	
1988-89	Northern Transvaal	Currie Cup	SA	2	4		36	25	9.00			4	34	8	95	2	47.50	
1989-90	Northern Transvaal	Currie Cup	SA	6	7	1	66	*42	11.00			4	200	53	471	20	23.55	
		Barbados		20	22	6	204	36	12.75			14	628.4	129	1898	68	27.91	
		West Indies		23	28	7	251	*35	11.95			4	692.5	149	1886	90	20.95	

SEASON	TEAM	OPPONENTS	V	M	I	NO	RUNS	H.S.	AVGE	100	50	CT	OV	MD	RUNS	W	AVGE	B.B.
		WI Rebels XI		8	13	4	104	25	11.55			3	314	88	783	45	17.40	
		Surrey		152	155	18	2130	*100	15.54	1	3	101	4463.5	1177	11226	591	18.99	
		Transvaal		20	22	7	277	*78	18.46		1	7	694.5	203	1534	94	16.94	
		Northern Transvaal		8	11	1	102	*42	10.20			9	234	61	566	22	25.72	
		Orange Free State		7	14	1	201	60	15.46		1	8	240.4	58	504	32	15.75	
		TEST RECORD		**11**	**16**	**5**	**172**	***35**	**15.63**	**0**	**0**	**2**	**412.5**	**81**	**1170**	**42**	**27.85**	**5-126**
		CAREER		**238**	**265**	**44**	**3269**	***100**	**14.79**	**1**	**5**	**146**	**7268.5**	**1865**	**18397**	**942**	**19.52**	**8-62**

CONSTANTINE, Learie Nicholas

				BATTING									BOWLING					
SEASON	TEAM	OPPONENTS	V	M	I	NO	RUNS	H.S.	AVGE	100	50	CT	OV	MD	RUNS	W	AVGE	B.B.
1921-22	Trinidad	Barbados	IIs	1	2		24	24	12.00			1	21	4	44	2	22.00	
1922-23	Trinidad	British Guiana	IIs	1	2		28	14	14.00			1	8	3	12	3	4.00	
1922-23	Trinidad	Barbados	IIs	1	2		30	17	15.00				45	10	97	1	97.00	
1923	West Indies	Tour of England	E	20	31	4	425	77	15.74		2	15	244.4	39	809	37	21.86	
1923-24	Trinidad	British Guiana	IIs	1	2		9	7	4.50				19	5	39	2	19.50	
1923-24	Trinidad	Barbados	IIs	1	2		29	25	14.50				29.2	10	70	10	7.00	
1924-25	Trinidad	British Guiana	IIs	1	2		1	1	0.50			4	11.1	2	39	0		
1924-25	Trinidad	Barbados	IIs	1	2		36	36	18.00				8	4	9	0		
1925-26	Trinidad	British Guiana	IIs	1	2	1	18	*16	18.00			1	23	4	55	3	18.33	
1925-26	Trinidad	M.C.C. Tourist	WI	2	3		43	29	14.33				32	7	100	2	50.00	
1925-26	West Indies	M.C.C. Tourist	WI	2	3		38	18	12.66			1	35	4	129	7	18.42	
1926-27	Trinidad	Barbados	IIs	1	2		24	13	12.00			2	58	5	211	3	70.33	
1927-28	Combined T/BG XI	Combined Bar/Jam XI	IIs	2	3		124	63	41.33		1	1	32.3	7	76	9	8.44	
1927-28	West Indies XI	Barbados Born XI	IIs	1	1		11	11	11.00				29	3	126	2	63.00	
1928	West Indies	Tour of England	E	23	37	3	1292	130	38.00	3	10	27	651.5	112	2194	102	21.50	
1928	**WEST INDIES**	**ENGLAND TESTS**	**E**	**3**	**6**		**89**	**37**	**14.83**			**6**	**71.4**	**19**	**262**	**5**	**52.40**	
1928-29	Trinidad	British Guiana	IIs	1	2		58	53	29.00		1	1	44.2	13	96	9	10.66	
1928-29	Trinidad	Barbados	IIs	1	1		133	133	133.00	1		3	20	5	71	7	10.14	
1928-29	West Indies XI	Julien Cahn's XI	WI	1	2		33	17	16.50			6	42	6	142	5	28.40	
1929-30	Trinidad	M.C.C. Tourist	WI	2	4		44	15	11.00			9	25.1	5	75	3	25.00	
1929-30	**WEST INDIES**	**ENGLAND TESTS**	**WI**	**3**	**6**		**100**	**52**	**17.66**		**1**	**7**	**163.4**	**42**	**497**	**18**	**27.61**	
1930-31	West Indies	Tour of Australia	A	8	13		636	100	48.92	1	5	12	172	10	543	39	13.92	
1930-31	**WEST INDIES**	**AUSTRALIA TESTS**	**A**	**5**	**10**		**72**	**14**	**7.20**			**9**	**127.3**	**15**	**407**	**8**	**50.87**	
1933	West Indies	Tour of England	E	4	7		86	51	12.28		1	3	91.3	21	255	13	19.61	
1933	**WEST INDIES**	**ENGLAND TESTS**	**E**	**1**	**2**		**95**	**64**	**47.50**		**1**	**2**	**25**	**5**	**55**	**1**	**55.00**	
1934-35	Freelooters	Indian Gold Cup	I	2	3		30	17	10.00				Unknown		254	15	16.93	

SEASON	TEAM	OPPONENTS	V	M	I	NO	RUNS	H.S.	AVGE	100	50	CT	OV	MD	RUNS	W	AVGE	B.B.
				BATTING									BOWLING					
1934-35	Trinidad	M.C.C. Tourist	WI	2	4		127	68	31.75		1	2	56.3	10	147	10	14.70	
1934-35	**WEST INDIES**	**ENGLAND TESTS**	**WI**	**3**	**5**		**169**	**90**	**33.80**		**1**	**3**	**114.1**	**36**	**197**	**15**	**13.13**	
1938-39	Barbados	British Guiana	IIs	1	2		12	11	6.00				19	6	69	4	17.25	
1939	West Indies	Tour of England	E	19	28	3	504	63	20.16		3	16	422.1	59	1503	92	16.33	
1939	**WEST INDIES**	**ENGLAND TESTS**	**E**	**3**	**4**		**110**	**79**	**27.50**		**1**	**1**	**71.3**	**8**	**328**	**11**	**29.81**	
1945	Dominions XI	England XI	E	1	2		45	40	22.50				21	2	80	1	80.00	
		Trinidad		17	32	1	604	133	19.48	1	2	24	400.3	87	1065	55	19.36	
		Barbados		1	2		12	11	6.00				19	6	69	4	17.25	
		West Indies		96	155	10	3660	130	25.24	4	25	108	2241.4	379	7447	355	20.97	
		Combined XI		2	3		124	63	41.33		1	1	32.3	7	76	9	8.44	
		Freelooters		2	3		30	17	10.00				Unknown		254	15	16.93	
		Dominions XI		1	2		45	40	23.50				21	2	80	1	80.00	
		TEST RECORD		**18**	**33**	**0**	**635**	**90**	**19.24**	**0**	**4**	**28**	**573.3**	**125**	**1746**	**58**	**30.10**	**5-75**
		CAREER		**119**	**197**	**11**	**4475**	**133**	**24.05**	**5**	**28**	**133**	**2714.5 +**	**481 +**	**8991**	**439**	**20.48**	**8-38**

CROFT, Colin Everton Hunte

SEASON	TEAM	OPPONENTS		V	M	I	NO	RUNS	H.S.	AVGE	100	50	CT	OV	MD	RUNS	W	AVGE	B.B.
					BATTING									BOWLING					
1971-72	Guyana	Shell Shield		IIs	1	2	1	1	1	1.00				15	2	75	0		
1975-76	Guyana	Shell Shield		IIs	1	D													
1975-76	Demerara	Berbice	JC	G	1	D							1	31	12	59	1	59.00	
1976-77	Demerara	Berbice	JC	G	1	2	1	21	*11	21.00			1	49	13	149	7	21.28	
1976-77	Guyana	Shell Shield		IIs	3	3	2	15	10	15.00			1	78.5	16	264	9	29.33	
1976-77	WI President's XI	Pakistan Tourist		WI	1	1	1	4	*4					32.2	10	109	10	10.90	
1976-77	**WEST INDIES**	**PAKISTAN TESTS**		**WI**	**5**	**8**	**7**	**53**	***23**	**53.00**			**6**	**217.5**	**45**	**676**	**33**	**20.48**	
1977	Lancashire	Counties		E	19	16	4	200	*46	16.66			2	476	120	1335	47	28.40	
1977-78	Demerara	Berbice	JC	G	1	2		12	12	6.00				39	6	134	2	67.00	
1977-78	Guyana	Shell Shield		IIs	4	5	1	26	*15	6.50			1	163.1	31	505	24	21.04	
1977-78	Guyana	Australian Tourist		WI	1	1		1	1	1.00			1	35	4	143	3	47.66	
1977-78	**WEST INDIES**	**AUSTRALIA TESTS**		**WI**	**2**	**2**	**1**	**7**	***4**	**7.00**			**1**	**55.1**	**13**	**170**	**9**	**18.88**	
1978	Lancashire	Counties		E	18	22	3	124	*19	6.52			1	431.3	101	1266	56	22.60	
1978-79	Demerara	Berbice	JC	G	1	1		4	4	4.00			1	32	8	84	2	42.00	
1978-79	Guyana	Shell Shield		IIs	1	2	2	8	*6					26	6	64	2	32.00	
1979-80	Demerara	Berbice	JC	G	1	D								6.5	1	28	3	9.33	
1979-80	West Indies	Tour of Australia		A	3	3	1	7	*7	3.50				96	16	310	13	23.84	

SEASON	TEAM	OPPONENTS	V	M	I	NO	RUNS	H.S.	AVGE	100	50	CT	OV	MD	RUNS	W	AVGE	B.B.
1979-80	**WEST INDIES**	**AUSTRALIA TESTS**	**A**	**3**	**4**	**2**	**15**	**12**	**7.50**				**121.3**	**20**	**378**	**16**	**23.62**	
1979-80	West Indies	Tour of New Zealand	NZ	1	D								23	4	61	1	61.00	
1979-80	**WEST INDIES**	**NEW ZEALAND TESTS**	**NZ**	**3**	**4**	**2**	**7**	**6**	**3.50**				**103**	**18**	**265**	**10**	**26.50**	
1979-80	Guyana	Shell Shield	IIs	3	6	3	20	12	6.66				95.4	17	357	16	22.31	
1980	West Indies	Tour of England	E	6	1	1	7	*7					126.3	29	384	16	24.00	
1980	**WEST INDIES**	**ENGLAND TESTS**	**E**	**3**	**3**	**2**	**1**	**1**	**1.00**				**104**	**25**	**306**	**9**	**34.00**	
1980-81	West Indies	Tour of Pakistan	P	2	3	3	3	*1					47	7	167	11	15.18	
1980-81	**WEST INDIES**	**PAKISTAN TESTS**	**P**	**4**	**6**	**2**	**17**	***7**	**4.25**				**130**	**32**	**302**	**17**	**17.76**	
1980-81	Guyana	Shell Shield	IIs	3	4		30	20	7.50				92	16	261	15	17.40	
1980-81	**WEST INDIES**	**ENGLAND TESTS**	**WI**	**4**	**5**	**3**	**54**	**33**	**27.00**			**1**	**157.5**	**34**	**455**	**24**	**18.95**	
1981-82	Demerara	Berbice JC	G	1	1		15	15	15.00				26	5	71	4	17.75	
1981-82	West Indies	Tour of Australia	A	3	3	1	44	34	22.00			3	113.5	18	312	11	28.36	
1981-82	**WEST INDIES**	**AUSTRALIA TESTS**	**A**	**3**	**5**	**3**	**4**	***4**	**2.00**				**138.1**	**25**	**361**	**7**	**51.37**	
1981-82	Guyana	Shell Shield	IIs	3	4	1	44	27	14.66				85.2	13	223	8	27.87	
1982	Lancashire	Counties	E	12	12	3	109	20	12.11			5	303	61	1003	33	30.39	
1983-84	WI Rebels XI	Tour of South Africa	SA	3	5	4	12	*5	12.00				66	12	253	9	28.11	
		Guyana		20	27	10	145	27	8.52			3	591	105	1892	77	24.57	
		Demerara		6	6	1	52	15	10.40			3	183.5	45	525	19	27.63	
		West Indies		43	48	29	223	34	11.73			11	1466.1	296	4256	187	22.75	
		WI Rebels XI		3	5	4	12	*5	12.00				66	12	253	9	28.11	
		Lancashire		49	50	10	433	*46	10.82			8	1210.3	282	3604	136	26.50	
		TEST RECORD		**27**	**37**	**22**	**158**	**33**	**10.53**	**0**	**0**	**8**	**1027.3**	**212**	**2913**	**125**	**23.30**	**8-29**
		CAREER		**121**	**136**	**54**	**865**	***46**	**10.54**	**0**	**0**	**25**	**3517.3**	**740**	**10530**	**428**	**24.60**	**8-29**

DA COSTA, Oscar Constantine

				BATTING									BOWLING					
SEASON	TEAM	OPPONENTS	V	M	I	NO	RUNS	H.S.	AVGE	100	50	CT	OV	MD	RUNS	W	AVGE	B.B.
1928-29	Jamaica	Julien Cahn's Tourist	WI	2	3	2	23	*10	11.50			1	36	5	120	1	120.00	
1929-30	Jamaica	M.C.C. Tourist	WI	2	4	1	121	*84	40.33		1	2	61	11	183	3	61.00	
1929-30	**WEST INDIES**	**ENGLAND TESTS**	**WI**	**1**	**1**		**39**	**39**	**39.00**			**3**	**27**	**2**	**95**	**2**	**47.50**	
1931-32	Jamaica	L Tennyson's Tourist	WI	3	5		165	66	33.00		1	5	53.5	9	171	4	42.75	
1932-33	G.C. Grant's XI	C.A. Merry's XI	WI	1	2		85	70	42.50		1		13	0	38	2	19.00	
1933	West Indies	Tour of England	E	24	39	6	976	*105	29.57	1	6	16	433.1	92	998	30	33.26	
1933	**WEST INDIES**	**ENGLAND TESTS**	**E**	**3**	**6**		**70**	**35**	**11.66**			**1**	**26**	**8**	**57**	**1**	**57.00**	
1934-35	Jamaica	M.C.C. Tourist	WI	2	2	1	40	*37	40.00			1	29	2	81	1	81.00	
1934-35	**WEST INDIES**	**ENGLAND TESTS**	**WI**	**1**	**2**	**1**	**44**	**25**	**44.00**			**1**	**9**	**3**	**23**	**0**		

SEASON	TEAM			BATTING M	I	NO	RUNS	H.S.	AVGE	100	50	CT	BOWLING OV	MD	RUNS	W	AVGE	B.B.
		Jamaica		9	14	4	349	*84	34.90		2	9	179.5	27	555	9	61.66	
		West Indies		29	48	7	1129	*105	27.53	1	6	21	495.1	105	1173	33	35.54	
		G.C. Grant's XI		1	2		85	70	42.50		1		13	0	38	2	19.00	
		TEST RECORD		**5**	**9**	**1**	**153**	**39**	**19.12**	**0**	**0**	**5**	**62**	**13**	**175**	**3**	**58.33**	**1-14**
		CAREER		**39**	**64**	**11**	**1563**	***105**	**29.49**	**1**	**9**	**30**	**688**	**132**	**1766**	**44**	**40.13**	**4-16**

DANIEL, Wayne Wendell

SEASON	TEAM	OPPONENTS	V	BATTING M	I	NO	RUNS	H.S.	AVGE	100	50	CT	BOWLING OV	MD	RUNS	W	AVGE	B.B.
1975-76	Barbados	Shell Shield	IIs	3	2		2	2	1.00				70.1	17	163	12	13.58	
1975-76	Barbados	Indian Tourist	WI	1	D								22.4	7	52	5	10.40	
1975-76	**WEST INDIES**	**INDIA TESTS**	**WI**	**1**	**1**		**11**	**11**	**11.00**				**23.2**	**7**	**64**	**2**	**32.50**	
1976	West Indies	Tour of England	E	11	6	1	44	30	8.80			3	263.3	60	789	39	20.23	
1976	**WEST INDIES**	**ENGLAND TESTS**	**E**	**4**	**4**	**2**	**18**	**10**	**9.00**			**2**	**108**	**28**	**317**	**13**	**24.38**	
1976-77	Barbados	Shell Shield	IIs	1	1		3	3	3.00				15	2	107	1	107.00	
1977	Middlesex	Counties	E	23	19	9	106	28	10.60			4	516.1	142	1233	75	16.44	
1977-78	Barbados	Australian Tourist	WI	1	2	1	19	*10	19.00				23	2	86	1	86.00	
1978	Middlesex	Counties	E	21	24	12	132	*30	11.00			3	453.3	113	1114	76	14.65	
1978-79	Barbados	Shell Shield	IIs	1	1		7	7	7.00				28	4	92	1	92.00	
1979	Middlesex	Counties	E	17	13	6	72	18	10.28			5	429.2	100	1170	52	22.50	
1979-80	Barbados	Shell Shield	IIs	3	3	3	65	*53			1		75.5	10	326	15	21.73	
1980	Middlesex	Counties	E	19	12	4	56	15	7.00			3	492.5	112	1454	67	21.70	
1980-81	Barbados	Shell Shield	IIs	1	1		9	9	9.00				21	4	86	5	17.20	
1980-81	Barbados	English Tourist	WI	1	1		21	21	21.00				49	9	133	1	133.00	
1981	Middlesex	Counties	E	21	22	11	195	*53	17.72		1	2	514.2	103	1494	67	22.29	
1981-82	WI Under 26 XI	Tour of Zimbabwe	Z	3	4	1	68	27	22.66				77.2	20	198	11	18.00	
1981-82	Western Australia	Sheffield Shield	A	2	2		23	21	11.50			1	63	13	180	1	180.00	
1981-82	Barbados	Shell Shield	IIs	2	3	2	6	5	6.00			1	73	11	270	7	38.57	
1982	Middlesex	Counties	E	19	15	9	88	21	14.66			13	468.5	107	1245	71	17.53	
1982-83	Barbados	Shell Shield	IIs	4	7	4	105	42	35.00			1	109.3	11	409	22	18.59	
1983	Middlesex	Counties	E	17	13	2	88	18	8.00			3	324.3	51	1106	48	23.04	
1983-84	West Indies	Tour of India	I	3	3	2	62	*28	62.00				47	7	142	3	47.33	
1983-84	**WEST INDIES**	**INDIA TESTS**	**I**	**3**	**4**	**1**	**7**	**5**	**2.33**			**1**	**98**	**12**	**332**	**14**	**23.71**	
1983-84	**WEST INDIES**	**AUSTRALIA TESTS**	**WI**	**2**	**2**	**1**	**10**	***6**	**10.00**			**1**	**63**	**13**	**197**	**7**	**28.14**	
1984	Middlesex	Counties	E	21	24	14	87	*16	8.70			4	462	86	1463	54	27.09	

SEASON	TEAM	OPPONENTS	V	M	I	NO	RUNS	H.S.	AVGE	100	50	CT	OV	MD	RUNS	W	AVGE	B.B.
1984-85	Barbados	Shell Shield	IIs	5	7	2	28	*7	5.60			1	151	26	458	22	20.81	
1985	Middlesex	Counties	E	22	15	5	48	*19	4.80			7	575.1	90	2111	79	26.72	
1986	Middlesex	Counties	E	16	16	6	140	33	14.00			3	402.1	52	1387	62	22.37	
1987	Middlesex	Counties	E	16	12	8	31	*9	7.75			5	348.1	47	1275	32	39.84	
1988	Middlesex	Counties	E	2	2		0	0					16	2	37	2	18.50	
		Barbados		23	28	12	265	*53	16.56		1	3	638.1	103	2182	92	23.71	
		West Indies		27	24	8	220	30	13.75			7	680.1	147	2039	89	22.91	
		Middlesex		214	187	86	1043	*53	10.32		1	52	5003	1005	15089	685	22.02	
		Western Australia		2	2		23	21	11.50			1	63	13	180	1	180.00	
		TEST RECORD		**10**	**11**	**4**	**46**	**11**	**6.57**	**0**	**0**	**4**	**292.2**	**60**	**910**	**36**	**25.27**	**5-39**
		CAREER		**266**	**241**	**106**	**1551**	***53**	**11.48**	**0**	**2**	**63**	**6384.2**	**1268**	**19490**	**867**	**22.47**	**9-61**

DAVIS, Bryan Alan

							BATTING								BOWLING			
SEASON	**TEAM**	**OPPONENTS**	**V**	**M**	**I**	**NO**	**RUNS**	**H.S.**	**AVGE**	**100**	**50**	**CT**	**OV**	**MD**	**RUNS**	**W**	**AVGE**	**B.B.**
1959-60	Trinidad	Jamaica	IIs	1	2		73	49	36.50									
1959-60	Trinidad	M.C.C. Tourist	WI	2	4		142	62	35.50		1							
1959-60	N.Trinidad	South Trinidad BC	T	1	2		48	37	24.00			1						
1960-61	Trinidad	Barbados	IIs	2	4		185	85	46.25		2	2						
1960-61	Trinidad	E.W. Swanton's Tourist	WI	1	2		142	74	71.00		2	1						
1960-61	N.Trinidad	South Trinidad BC	T	1	1		35	35	35.00			2						
1961-62	Trinidad	British Guiana	IIs	1	2		97	97	48.50		1							
1961-62	Trinidad	Indian Tourist	WI	1	2		95	57	47.50		1							
1961-62	N.Trinidad	South Trinidad BC	T	1	2		65	65	32.50		1	1						
1962-63	Trinidad	Barbados	IIs	1	2		94	72	47.00		1	1						
1962-63	N.Trinidad	South Trinidad BC	T	1	2	1	36	*36	36.00			1						
1963-64	Trinidad	Barbados	IIs	1	2		54	43	27.00									
1963-64	Trinidad	Jamaica	IIs	1	2		140	108	70.00	1		3						
1963-64	Trinidad	British Guiana	IIs	1	1		165	165	165.00	1								
1963-64	N.Trinidad	South Trinidad BC	T	1	2	1	53	*53	53.00		1							
1964-65	Trinidad	Australian Tourist	WI	1	2		56	30	28.00			5						
1964-65	**WEST INDIES**	**AUSTRALIA TESTS**	**WI**	**4**	**8**		**245**	**68**	**30.62**		**3**	**1**						
1965-66	Trinidad	Shell Shield	IIs	4	8	1	240	81	34.28		2	7						
1965-66	N.Trinidad	South Trinidad BC	T	1	2		62	42	31.00			1						
1966-67	West Indies	Tour of India	I	6	11		211	54	19.18		2	6	36	3	161	5	32.20	
1966-67	West Indies	Tour of Ceylon	C	1	1		7	7	7.00				11	4	34	0		

SEASON	TEAM	OPPONENTS	V	M	I	NO	RUNS	H.S.	AVGE	100	50	CT	OV	MD	RUNS	W	AVGE	B.B.
				BATTING									BOWLING					
1966-67	Trinidad	Shell Shield	IIs	4	7		338	176	48.28	1	1	7						
1966-67	N.Trinidad	South Trinidad BC	T	1	1	1	188	*188		1		2	2	0	6	0		
1967-68	Trinidad	M.C.C. Tourist	WI	1	2		31	30	15.50			4	1	0	2	0		
1968	Glamorgan	Counties	E	3	4		95	66	23.75		1	1	17	5	38	1	38.00	
1969	Glamorgan	Counties	E	28	43	5	1148	103	30.21	1	7	34	32.4	6	104	1	104.00	
1969-70	Trinidad	Shell Shield	IIs	4	5	1	282	90	70.50		3	6						
1969-70	Trinidad	Duke of Norfolk's Tourist	WI	1	1		12	12	12.00			4						
1969-70	Glamorgan	Tour of West Indies	WI	2	4		73	31	18.25			3	0.2	0	2	1	2.00	
1970	Glamorgan	Counties	E	27	52	3	1532	91	31.26		14	29	24	6	85	1	85.00	
1970-71	Trinidad	Shell Shield	IIs	4	7		139	72	19.85		1	4						
1970-71	Trinidad	Indian Tourist	WI	1	1		61	61	61.00		1	1	1	0	2	0		
1970-71	N. Trinidad	C & E Trinidad BC	T	2	2	1	87	87	87.00		1							
		Trinidad		32	56	2	2346	176	43.44	3	16	45	2	0	4	0		
		North Trinidad		9	14	4	574	*188	57.40	1	3	8	2	0	6	0		
		West Indies		11	20		463	68	23.15		5	7	47	7	195	5	39.00	
		Glamorgan		60	103	8	2848	103	29.97	1	22	67	74	17	229	4	57.25	
		TEST RECORD		**4**	**8**	**0**	**245**	**68**	**30.62**	**0**	**3**	**1**						
		CAREER		**112**	**193**	**14**	**6231**	***188**	**34.81**	**5**	**46**	**127**	**125**	**24**	**434**	**9**	**48.22**	**4-79**

DAVIS, Charles Alan

SEASON	TEAM	OPPONENTS	V	M	I	NO	RUNS	H.S.	AVGE	100	50	CT	OV	MD	RUNS	W	AVGE	B.B.
				BATTING									BOWLING					
1960-61	Trinidad	E.W. Swanton's Tourist	WI	1	2		69	58	34.50		1							
1960-61	N. Trinidad	South Trinidad BC	T	1	1		115	115	115.00	1								
1961-62	Trinidad	British Guiana	IIs	1	2		224	127	112.00	1	1		1	0	5	0		
1961-62	Trinidad	Indian Tourist	WI	1	2	1	34	28	34.00			2						
1961-62	N.Trinidad	South Trinidad BC	T	1	2		77	48	38.50				2	0	7	1	7.00	
1962-63	Trinidad	Barbados	IIs	1	2		5	4	2.50									
1962-63	N.Trinidad	South Trinidad BC	T	1	1		3	3	3.00			1	15	2	38	6	6.33	
1963-64	Trinidad	Barbados	IIs	1	2		36	32	18.00									
1963-64	Trinidad	Jamaica	IIs	1	2		61	42	30.50			1						
1963-64	Trinidad	British Guiana	IIs	1	2	1	12	*7	12.00			2						
1963-64	N.Trinidad	South Trinidad BC	T	1	1		45	45	45.00									
1964-65	Trinidad	Australian Tourist	WI	1	2		122	71	61.00		2							
1964-65	N.Trinidad	South Trinidad BC	T	1	2		48	32	24.00			1	2	2	0	0		

1965-66	Trinidad	Shell Shield		IIs	4	7	1	212	61	35.33		2	2	23	7	58	0		
1965-66	N.Trinidad	South Trinidad	BC	T	1	2		17	14	8.50			2	9	1	33	1	33.00	
1966-67	Trinidad	Shell Shield		IIs	4	7		254	154	26.28	1		2	14	3	40	1	40.00	
1966-67	N.Trinidad	South Trinidad	BC	T	1	1		12	12	12.00			3	4	1	10	0		
1967-68	WI President's XI	M.C.C. Tourist		WI	1	1	1	158	*158		1		2	7	0	17	0		
1967-68	Trinidad	M.C.C. Tourist		WI	1	2		130	68	65.00		2	1	8	3	9	0		
1967-68	N.Trinidad	South Trinidad	BC	T	1	1		19	19	19.00				4	1	12	0		
1968-69	West Indies	Tour of Australia		A	7	12		208	69	17.33		1	1	132.3	11	550	20	27.50	
1968-69	**WEST INDIES**	**AUSTRALIA TESTS**		**A**	**1**	**2**		**28**	**18**	**14.00**				**24**	**0**	**94**	**1**	**94.00**	
1968-69	West Indies	Tour of New Zealand		NZ	3	6		187	69	31.16		1	2	32	2	138	3	46.00	
1969	West Indies	Tour of England		E	13	19	5	640	*106	45.71	1	6	1	162.3	31	447	6	74.50	
1969	**WEST INDIES**	**ENGLAND TESTS**		**E**	**3**	**6**		**208**	**103**	**34.66**	**1**		**2**	**20**	**8**	**32**	**1**	**32.00**	
1969-70	Trinidad	Shell Shield		IIs	4	6	1	286	112	57.20	1	2	2	34	11	76	1	76.00	
1969-70	Trinidad	Duke of Norfolk's Tourist		WI	1	2	1	126	*96	126.00		1	2	5	2	8	0		
1969-70	Trinidad	Glamorgan Tourist		WI	1	2		7	5	3.50				15	1	36	2	18.00	
1969-70	N.Trinidad	South Trinidad	BC	T	1	2		17	9	8.50			1	28	8	55	4	13.75	
1970-71	Trinidad	Shell Shield		IIs	3	5		54	52	10.80		1		53	12	100	2	50.00	
1970-71	Trinidad	Indian Tourist		WI	1	1		100	100	100.00	1			24	2	69	0		
1970-71	**WEST INDIES**	**INDIA TESTS**		**WI**	**4**	**8**	**4**	**529**	***125**	**132.25**	**2**	**3**	**1**	**31**	**5**	**69**	**0**		
1970-71	N.Trinidad	East Trinidad	BC	T	1	2		14	8	7.00			1	16	4	46	1	46.00	
1971-72	Trinidad	Shell Shield		IIs	4	6	1	322	*180	64.40	1	2	1	14	3	45	2	22.50	
1971-72	Trinidad	New Zealand Tourist		WI	1	2		180	156	90.00	1		4	5	2	5	1	5.00	
1971-72	**WEST INDIES**	**NEW ZEALAND TESTS**		**WI**	**5**	**9**	**1**	**466**	**183**	**58.25**	**1**	**1**		**47**	**17**	**77**	**0**		
1972-73	N.Trinidad	South Trinidad	TC	T	1	1		12	12	12.00				22	9	31	2	15.50	
1972-73	Trinidad	Shell Shield		IIs	4	7	1	121	54	20.16		1	3	16	3	43	0		
1972-73	Trinidad	Australian Tourist		WI	1	2		77	63	38.50		1	1	8	3	27	0		
1972-73	**WEST INDIES**	**AUSTRALIA TESTS**		**WI**	**2**	**4**		**70**	**25**	**17.50**			**1**	**19**	**2**	**58**	**0**		
1974-75	N.Trinidad	East Trinidad	TC	T	1	2		162	162	81.00	1		1	51	16	128	5	25.60	
1975-76	N.Trinidad	S & C Trinidad	TC	T	2	2		71	40	35.50			1	42	14	117	3	39.00	
		Trinidad			37	65	7	2432	*180	41.93	6	16	23	220	52	521	9	57.88	
		North Trinidad			14	20		612	162	30.60	2		11	195	58	477	23	20.73	
		West Indies			39	67	11	2494	183	44.53	6	12	10	475	76	1482	31	47.80	
		TEST RECORD			**15**	**29**	**5**	**1301**	**183**	**54.20**	**4**	**4**	**4**	**141**	**32**	**330**	**2**	**165.00**	**1-27**
		CAREER			**90**	**152**	**18**	**5538**	**183**	**41.32**	**14**	**28**	**44**	**890**	**186**	**2480**	**63**	**39.36**	**7-106**

DAVIS, Winston Walter

				BATTING									BOWLING					
SEASON	TEAM	OPPONENTS	V	M	I	NO	RUNS	H.S.	AVGE	100	50	CT	OV	MD	RUNS	W	AVGE	B.B.
1979-80	Windward Is.	Leeward Islands	IIs	1	2	1	78	60	78.00		1		35	4	116	5	23.20	
1979-80	Combined Is.	Shell Shield	IIs	3	4	1	42	16	14.00			2	72	11	274	4	68.50	
1980-81	Windward Is.	Leeward Islands	IIs	1	2		19	10	9.50			1	18	5	60	1	60.00	
1980-81	Combined Is.	Shell Shield	IIs	4	5	2	43	*16	14.33				79	12	297	8	37.12	
1981-82	WI Under 26 XI	Tour of Zimbabwe	Z	1	1		5	5	5.00				22.2	5	51	4	12.75	
1981-82	Windward Is.	Shell Shield	IIs	4	6	1	23	10	4.60			1	173	34	501	22	22.77	
1982	Glamorgan	Counties	E	13	13	6	58	*20	8.25			3	391.5	70	1296	42	30.85	
1982-83	Windward Is.	Shell Shield	IIs	5	7	4	12	11	4.00			3	226.1	49	620	33	18.78	
1982-83	Windward Is.	Indian Tourist	WI	1	2	1	3	3	3.00				46.3	8	127	8	15.87	
1982-83	**WEST INDIES**	**INDIA TESTS**	**WI**	**1**	**1**		**14**	**14**	**14.00**			**1**	**52**	**5**	**175**	**4**	**43.75**	
1983	Glamorgan	Counties	E	15	18	9	135	*39	15.00			4	452.4	110	1389	52	26.71	
1983-84	West Indies	Tour of India	I	4	5	2	22	16	7.33				73	16	229	7	32.71	
1983-84	**WEST INDIES**	**INDIA TESTS**	**I**	**6**	**7**	**4**	**39**	**19**	**13.00**			**4**	**178.3**	**19**	**562**	**14**	**40.14**	
1983-84	Windward Is.	Australian Tourist	WI	1	1		12	12	12.00				35	4	135	5	27.00	
1983-84	**WEST INDIES**	**AUSTRALIA TESTS**	**WI**	**1**	**1**		**11**	**11**	**11.00**			**1**	**33**	**6**	**80**	**2**	**40.00**	
1984	West Indies	Tour of England	E	3	3	1	35	18	17.50			1	43	10	122	12	10.16	
1984	**WEST INDIES**	**ENGLAND TESTS**	**E**	**1**	**1**		**77**	**77**	**77.00**		**1**		**23**	**3**	**77**	**2**	**38.50**	
1984	Glamorgan	Counties	E	17	20	6	278	50	19.85		1	7	481.5	105	1526	48	31.79	
1984-85	West Indies	Tour of Australia	A	5	7	2	110	50	22.00		1	1	117.4	24	421	8	52.62	
1984-85	**WEST INDIES**	**NEW ZEALAND TESTS**	**WI**	**2**	**2**		**16**	**16**	**8.00**			**1**	**63.3**	**11**	**188**	**10**	**18.80**	
1985-86	Tasmania	Sheffield Shield	A	8	14	2	82	21	6.83			3	287.5	22	768	22	34.90	
1986-87	Windward Is.	Barbados	IIs	1	2		0	0				1	42	4	132	7	18.85	
1986-87	Windward Is.	Yorkshire Tourist	WI	1	1		9	9	9.00				33	4	119	3	39.66	
1986-87	Windward Is.	Shell Shield	IIs	2	4		36	18	9.00				91	14	259	11	23.54	
1987	Northamptonshire	Counties	E	19	18	5	186	*25	14.30			7	591.1	100	1906	70	27.22	
1987-88	West Indies	Tour of India	I	3	3	1	44	23	22.00			1	49	8	173	5	34.60	
1987-88	**WEST INDIES**	**INDIA TESTS**	**I**	**4**	**5**		**45**	**30**	**9.00**			**3**	**112.1**	**10**	**390**	**13**	**30.00**	
1987-88	Windward Is.	Red Stripe Cup	IIs	4	8	1	51	*16	7.28				130.2	16	395	9	43.88	
1988	Northamptonshire	Counties	E	15	18	3	306	43	20.40			5	538.2	91	1614	73	22.10	
1989	Northamptonshire	Counties	E	14	19	4	166	*40	11.06			4	440	68	1444	52	27.26	
1989-90	Windward Is.	Red Stripe Cup	IIs	4	8	1	153	35	21.85			1	107.3	14	355	13	27.30	
1990	Northamptonshire	Counties	E	9	7	1	101	47	16.83			2	237.5	27	812	13	62.46	
		Windward Islands		25	43	9	396	60	11.64		1	7	938.3	156	2819	117	24.09	
		Combined Islands		7	9	3	85	*16	14.16			2	151	23	571	12	47.58	
		West Indies		31	36	10	418	77	16.07		2	13	767.1	117	2468	81	30.46	

SEASON	TEAM	OPPONENTS	V	M	I	NO	RUNS	H.S.	AVGE	100	50	CT	OV	MD	RUNS	W	AVGE	B.B.
				BATTING									BOWLING					
		Glamorgan		45	51	21	471	50	15.70		1	14	1326.2	285	4211	142	29.65	
		Northamptonshire		57	62	13	759	47	15.48			18	1807.2	286	5776	208	27.76	
		Tasmania		8	14	2	82	21	6.83			3	287.5	22	768	22	34.90	
		TEST RECORD		**15**	**17**	**4**	**202**	**77**	**15.53**		**1**	**10**	**462.1**	**54**	**1472**	**45**	**32.71**	**4-19**
		CAREER		**173**	**215**	**58**	**2211**	**77**	**14.08**		**4**	**57**	**5278.1**	**889**	**16613**	**582**	**28.54**	**7-52**

DE CAIRES, Francis Ignatius

SEASON	TEAM	OPPONENTS	V	M	I	NO	RUNS	H.S.	AVGE	100	50	CT	OV	MD	RUNS	W	AVGE	B.B.
				BATTING									BOWLING					
1928-29	British Guiana	Trinidad	IIs	1	2		44	31	22.00			1						
1929-30	British Guiana	Barbados	IIs	1	2		59	59	29.50		1							
1929-30	British Guiana	Trinidad	IIs	1	2		145	133	72.50	1								
1929-30	British Guiana	M.C.C. Tourist	IIs	1	2		17	13	8.50									
1929-30	**WEST INDIES**	**ENGLAND TESTS**	**WI**	**3**	**6**		**232**	**80**	**38.66**		**2**	**1**	**2**	**0**	**9**	**0**		
1930-31	West Indies	Tour of Australia	A	4	7		165	76	23.57		2	2	6	0	20	1	20.00	
1931-32	British Guiana	Trinidad	IIs	1	2		43	29	21.50									
1933-34	British Guiana	Barbados	IIs	1	2		77	56	38.50		1	1						
1934-35	British Guiana	Barbados	IIs	1	2		39	28	19.50									
1934-35	British Guiana	M.C.C. Tourist	WI	2	4	1	100	*80	25.00		1		1	0	9	0		
1935-36	British Guiana	Trinidad	IIs	1	1		3	3	3.00			1						
1938-39	British Guiana	R.S. Grant's XI	IIs	1	2		21	21	10.50			1	2	0	10	0		
		British Guiana		11	21	1	548	133	27.40	1	3	4	3	0	19	0		
		West Indies		7	13		397	80	12.03		4	3	8	0	29	1	29.00	
		TEST RECORD		**3**	**6**	**0**	**232**	**80**	**38.66**	**0**	**2**	**1**	**2**	**0**	**9**	**0**		
		CAREER		**18**	**34**	**1**	**945**	**133**	**28.63**	**1**	**7**	**7**	**11**	**0**	**48**	**1**	**48.00**	**1-20**

DEPEIZA, Cyril Clairmonte

SEASON	TEAM	OPPONENTS	V	M	I	NO	RUNS	H.S.	AVGE	100	50	CT/St	OV	MD	RUNS	W	AVGE	B.B.
				BATTING									BOWLING					
1951-52	Barbados	Jamaica	IIs	1	2		20	16	10.00			2						
1952-53	Barbados	Indian Tourist	WI	1	1		26	26	26.00			1						
1953-54	Barbados	M.C.C. Tourist	WI	1	2	2	60	*44				2						

				BATTING									BOWLING					
SEASON	TEAM	OPPONENTS	V	M	I	NO	RUNS	H.S.	AVGE	100	50	CT/St	OV	MD	RUNS	W	AVGE	B.B.
1954-55	Barbados	British Guiana	IIs	2	3	1	116	64	58.00		2	5/1						
1954-55	Barbados	Australian Tourist	WI	1	2		27	27	13.50			3						
1954-55	**WEST INDIES**	**AUSTRALIA TESTS**	**WI**	**3**	**6**	**2**	**169**	**122**	**42.25**	**1**		**5/1**						
1955-56	West Indies	Tour of New Zealand	NZ	3	3		117	66	39.00		1	6/2						
1955-56	**WEST INDIES**	**NEW ZEALAND TESTS**	**NZ**	**2**	**2**		**18**	**14**	**9.00**			**2/3**	**5**	**0**	**15**	**0**		
1956-57	Barbados	Trinidad	IIs	1	1		65	65	65.00		1	3/2						
1956-57	Barbados	British Guiana	IIs	1	2		5	4	2.50			2						
		Barbados		8	13	3	319	65	31.90		3	18/3						
		West Indies		8	11	2	304	122	33.77	1	1	13/6	5	0	15	0		
		TEST RECORD		**5**	**8**	**2**	**187**	**122**	**31.16**	**1**	**0**	**7/4**	**5**	**0**	**15**	**0**		
		CAREER		**16**	**24**	**5**	**623**	**122**	**32.78**	**1**	**4**	**31/9**	**5**	**0**	**15**	**0**		

DEWDNEY, David Thomas

				BATTING									BOWLING					
SEASON	TEAM	OPPONENTS	V	M	I	NO	RUNS	H.S.	AVGE	100	50	CT	OV	MD	RUNS	W	AVGE	B.B.
1954-55	Jamaica	Trinidad	IIs	1	1		2	2	2.00			1	18	2	71	2	35.50	
1954-55	Jamaica	Australian Tourist	WI	1	1	1	13	*13				1	25	1	119	1	119.00	
1954-55	**WEST INDIES**	**AUSTRALIA TESTS**	**WI**	**2**	**3**		**2**	**2**	**0.66**				**67**	**13**	**263**	**5**	**52.60**	
1955-56	West Indies	Tour of New Zealand	NZ	3	3	2	4	*4	4.00				77.3	21	181	12	15.08	
1955-56	**WEST INDIES**	**NEW ZEALAND TESTS**	**NZ**	**3**	**4**	**2**	**9**	***4**	**4.50**				**83.5**	**29**	**174**	**8**	**21.75**	
1956-57	Jamaica	British Guiana	IIs	1	1		13	13	13.00			1	23	8	49	0		
1956-57	Jamaica	Duke of Norfolk's Tourist	WI	2	3		9	5	3.00				65.2	9	232	11	21.09	
1957	West Indies	Tour of England	E	15	16	7	48	*22	5.33			2	302.4	43	931	35	26.60	
1957	**WEST INDIES**	**ENGLAND TESTS**	**E**	**1**	**2**		**1**	**1**	**0.50**				**15**	**2**	**43**	**1**	**43.00**	
1957-58	Jamaica	Pakistan Tourist	WI	1	1		0	0				1	32	5	101	4	25.25	
1957-58	**WEST INDIES**	**PAKISTAN TESTS**	**WI**	**3**	**3**	**3**	**5**	***5**					**107.4**	**21**	**327**	**7**	**46.71**	
1960-61	West Indies	Tour of Australia	A	6	9	3	61	*37	10.16				71	9	296	5	29.20	
1961	Comm. XI	England XI	E	1	2	1	4	3	4.00				16	3	41	1	41.00	
		Jamaica		6	7	1	37	*13	6.16			4	163.2	25	572	18	31.77	
		West Indies		33	40	17	130	*37	5.65			2	724.4	138	2215	73	30.34	
		Comm. XI		1	2	1	4	3	4.00				16	3	41	1	41.00	
		TEST RECORD		**9**	**12**	**5**	**17**	***5**	**2.42**	**0**	**0**	**0**	**273.3**	**65**	**807**	**21**	**38.42**	**5-21**
		CAREER		**40**	**49**	**19**	**171**	***37**	**5.70**	**0**	**0**	**6**	**904**	**166**	**2828**	**92**	**30.73**	**7-55**

DOWE, Uton George

SEASON	TEAM	OPPONENTS	V	M	I	NO	RUNS	H.S.	AVGE	100	50	CT	OV	MD	RUNS	W	AVGE	B.B.
				BATTING									BOWLING					
1969-70	Jamaica	Cavaliers Tourist	WI	1	D								19.4	4	51	3	17.00	
1969-70	Jamaica	Shell Shield	IIs	1	1	1	1	*1					16.3	4	50	1	50.00	
1970-71	Jamaica	Shell Shield	IIs	4	5	2	47	18	15.66			1	130	36	378	24	15.75	
1970-71	Jamaica	Indian Tourist	WI	1	1	1	0	*0				1	44	3	150	2	75.00	
1970-71	**WEST INDIES**	**INDIA TESTS**	**WI**	**2**	**2**	**1**	**3**	**3**	**3.00**				**85**	**15**	**245**	**7**	**35.00**	
1971-72	Jamaica	Shell Shield	IIs	4	4	1	41	*25	13.66			1	129.5	19	495	13	38.07	
1971-72	Jamaica	New Zealand Tourist	WI	1	1		0	0				1	47	14	100	5	20.00	
1971-72	**WEST INDIES**	**NEW ZEALAND TESTS**	**WI**	**1**	**D**							**2**	**42**	**8**	**121**	**4**	**30.25**	
1972-73	Jamaica	Shell Shield	IIs	3	5		11	5	2.20			1	116	24	324	16	20.25	
1972-73	**WEST INDIES**	**AUSTRALIA TESTS**	**WI**	**1**	**1**	**1**	**5**	***5**				**1**	**42**	**7**	**168**	**1**	**168.00**	
1973-74	Jamaica	Shell Shield	IIs	4	4		11	8	2.75			1	114	24	329	14	23.50	
1973-74	Jamaica	M.C.C. Tourist	WI	1	1	1	9	*9					25.3	5	86	4	21.50	
1974-75	Jamaica	Shell Shield	IIs	1	1	1	0	*0					11	0	38	0		
1975-76	Jamaica	Indian Tourist	WI	1	1		0	0					29.4	5	98	3	32.66	
1976-77	Jamaica	Shell Shield	IIs	1	D								11	0	70	0		
		Jamaica		23	24	7	120	*25	7.05			6	694.1	138	2169	85	25.51	
		West Indies		4	3	2	8	*5	8.00			3	169	30	534	12	44.50	
		TEST RECORD		**4**	**3**	**2**	**8**	***5**	**8.00**	**0**	**0**	**3**	**169**	**30**	**534**	**12**	**44.50**	**4-69**
		CAREER		**27**	**27**	**9**	**128**	***25**	**7.11**	**0**	**0**	**9**	**863.1**	**168**	**2703**	**97**	**27.86**	**7-19**

DUJON, Peter Jeffrey Leroy

SEASON	TEAM	OPPONENTS	V	M	I	NO	RUNS	H.S.	AVGE	100	50	CT/St	OV	MD	RUNS	W	AVGE	B.B.
				BATTING									BOWLING					
1974-75	Jamaica	Shell Shield	IIs	4	6	1	278	110	55.60	1	1	5/1						
1975-76	Jamaica	Shell Shield	IIs	4	4		190	113	47.50	1	1	2	1	1	0	0		
1975-76	Jamaica	Indian Tourist	WI	1	2		21	14	10.50				1	0	1	0		
1976-77	Jamaica	Shell Shield	IIs	4	6		115	36	19.16			1						
1976-77	Jamaica	Pakistan Tourist	WI	1	2		76	69	38.00		1							
1977-78	Jamaica	Shell Shield	IIs	3	4		27	22	6.75			4						
1977-78	Jamaica	Australian Tourist	WI	1	2		68	50	34.00		1	2						
1978-79	Jamaica	Shell Shield	IIs	4	6		278	86	46.33		2							
1979-80	Jamaica	Shell Shield	IIs	3	6	2	166	*63	41.50		1							
1980-81	Jamaica	Shell Shield	IIs	3	4	2	168	*135	84.00	1	1	5/1						

SEASON	TEAM	OPPONENTS	V	BATTING M	I	NO	RUNS	H.S.	AVGE	100	50	CT/St	BOWLING OV	MD	RUNS	W	AVGE	B.B.
1980-81	Jamaica	English Tourist	WI	1	1		6	6	6.00			2/2						
1980-81	WI President's XI	English Tourist	WI	1	2	1	106	*105	106.00	1								
1981-82	WI Under 26 XI	Tour of Zimbabwe	Z	3	6		124	60	20.66		1	8/0						
1981-82	West Indies	Tour of Australia	A	2	2	1	105	104	105.00	1		6/0						
1981-82	**WEST INDIES**	**AUSTRALIA TESTS**	**A**	**3**	**6**	**1**	**227**	**51**	**45.50**		**1**	**9**						
1981-82	Jamaica	Shell Shield	IIs	5	9	2	270	81	38.57		2	9/1						
1982-83	West Indies XI	International XI	WI	1	1		19	19	19.00			3						
1982-83	Jamaica	Shell Shield	IIs	5	9	1	383	102	47.87	1	2	9/1						
1982-83	Jamaica	Indian Tourist	WI	1	2	1	110	104	110.00	1		1						
1982-83	**WEST INDIES**	**INDIA TESTS**	**WI**	**5**	**6**	**1**	**259**	**110**	**51.80**	**1**		**18/1**						
1983-84	West Indies	Tour of India	I	4	6	2	215	56	53.75		2	8/3						
1983-84	**WEST INDIES**	**INDIA TESTS**	**I**	**6**	**7**		**367**	**98**	**52.42**		**4**	**16/0**						
1983-84	**WEST INDIES**	**AUSTRALIA TESTS**	**WI**	**5**	**5**		**204**	**130**	**40.80**	**1**		**19/1**						
1984	West Indies	Tour of England	E	7	9	2	348	107	49.71	1	2	11/0						
1984	**WEST INDIES**	**ENGLAND TESTS**	**E**	**5**	**6**		**210**	**101**	**35.00**	**1**		**16/0**						
1984-85	West Indies	Tour of Australia	A	4	5	1	195	*151	48.75	1		8/0	9	3	43	1	43.00	
1984-85	**WEST INDIES**	**AUSTRALIA TESTS**	**A**	**5**	**8**	**1**	**341**	**139**	**48.71**	**1**	**1**	**19/0**						
1984-85	**WEST INDIES**	**NEW ZEALAND TESTS**	**WI**	**4**	**6**	**1**	**156**	**70**	**31.20**		**2**	**11/0**						
1985-86	Jamaica	Shell Shield	IIs	5	9	1	252	75	31.50		3	15/0						
1985-86	Jamaica	English Tourist	WI	1	2		70	39	35.00			2/0						
1985-86	**WEST INDIES**	**ENGLAND TESTS**	**WI**	**4**	**4**		**85**	**54**	**21.25**		**1**	**16/0**						
1986-87	West Indies	Tour of Pakistan	P	2	2	1	140	*126	140.00	1								
1986-87	**WEST INDIES**	**PAKISTAN TESTS**	**P**	**3**	**5**		**27**	**19**	**5.40**			**6/1**						
1986-87	West Indies	Tour of New Zealand	NZ	1	2	1	79	62	79.00		1	4/0						
1986-87	**WEST INDIES**	**NEW ZEALAND TESTS**	**NZ**	**3**	**4**		**144**	**77**	**36.00**		**1**	**9/0**						
1986-87	Jamaica	Shell Shield	IIs	2	3		45	27	15.00			7/2						
1987	Rest of World XI	M.C.C. & Gloucester	E	2	3	1	23	*14	11.50			3/0						
1987-88	West Indies	Tour of India	I	2	3	1	172	123	86.00	1		2/0						
1987-88	**WEST INDIES**	**INDIA TESTS**	**I**	**4**	**6**	**2**	**97**	***40**	**24.25**			**10/1**						
1987-88	Jamaica	Red Stripe Cup	IIs	3	4		241	108	60.25	1	1	7/0						
1987-88	**WEST INDIES**	**PAKISTAN TESTS**	**WI**	**3**	**6**	**2**	**185**	***106**	**46.25**	**1**		**5/1**						
1988	West Indies	Tour of England	E	7	9	3	296	141	49.33	1	1	11/0						
1988	**WEST INDIES**	**ENGLAND TESTS**	**E**	**5**	**7**	**1**	**305**	**67**	**50.83**		**4**	**20/0**						
1988-89	West Indies	Tour of Australia	A	5	8	1	195	*53	27.85		1	4/1	1	0	1	0		
1988-89	**WEST INDIES**	**AUSTRALIA TESTS**	**A**	**5**	**8**		**195**	**46**	**24.37**			**15/0**						
1988-89	Jamaica	Red Stripe Cup	IIs	1	2		69	64	34.50		1	3/0						
1988-89	**WEST INDIES**	**INDIA TESTS**	**WI**	**4**	**5**		**83**	**33**	**16.60**			**14/0**						

SEASON	TEAM	OPPONENTS	V	M	I	NO	RUNS	H.S.	AVGE	100	50	CT	OV	MD	RUNS	W	AVGE	B.B.
1989	Rest of World XI	M.C.C. XI	E	1	2	1	67	*42	67.00									
1989-90	Jamaica	Red Stripe Cup	IIs	3	5	1	252	92	63.00		2	1						
1989-90	**WEST INDIES**	**ENGLAND TESTS**	**WI**	**4**	**7**	**2**	**109**	**31**	**21.80**			**15/0**						
		Jamaica		55	88	11	3085	*135	40.06	6	19	75/8						
		West Indies		107	151	25	4988	*151	39.58	12	22	283/9	2	1	1	0		
		Rest of World XI		3	5	2	90	*42	30.00			3	10	3	44	1	44.00	
		TEST RECORD		**68**	**96**	**11**	**2994**	**139**	**35.22**	**5**	**14**	**218/5**						
		CAREER		**165**	**244**	**38**	**8163**	***151**	**39.62**	**18**	**41**	**361/17**	**12**	**4**	**45**	**1**	**45.00**	**1-43**

EDWARDS, Richard Martin

SEASON	TEAM	OPPONENTS	V	BATTING M	I	NO	RUNS	H.S.	AVGE	100	50	CT	BOWLING OV	MD	RUNS	W	AVGE	B.B.
1961-62	Barbados	British Guiana	IIs	1	2		22	15	11.00				17	1	57	1	57.00	
1962-63	Barbados	Trinidad	IIs	1	1	1	2	*2				1	24	5	71	2	35.50	
1962-63	Barbados	British Guiana	IIs	1	2		23	20	11.50				29.4	6	107	7	15.28	
1963-64	Barbados	Jamaica	IIs	1	1		7	7	7.00				42	8	115	3	38.33	
1963-64	Barbados	Trinidad	IIs	1	2	1	0	*0				1	24.2	2	69	5	13.80	
1964-65	Barbados	Cavaliers Tourist	WI	1	D							2	24	8	76	3	25.33	
1964-65	Barbados	Australian Tourist	WI	1	1		0	0				1	22	3	83	1	83.00	
1965-66	Barbados	Shell Shield	IIs	4	2	1	37	31	37.00			1	43.3	9	146	1	146.00	
1966-67	Barbados	Shell Shield	IIs	4	3	1	13	*13	6.50			3	79.2	17	283	10	28.30	
1967-68	WI President's XI	M.C.C. Tourist	WI	1	1		13	13	13.00			1	24	6	83	1	83.00	
1967-68	Barbados	M.C.C. Tourist	WI	1	1	1	9	*9				1	21	8	49	1	49.00	
1968-69	West Indies	Tour of Australia	A	6	7	2	61	*28	12.20			1	118.7	14	534	11	48.54	
1968-69	**WEST INDIES**	**AUSTRALIA TESTS**	**A**	**2**	**4**	**1**	**40**	**21**	**13.33**				**52**	**2**	**274**	**3**	**91.33**	
1968-69	West Indies	Tour of New Zealand	NZ	2	2		16	15	8.00				34	5	121	3	40.33	
1968-69	**WEST INDIES**	**NEW ZEALAND TESTS**	**NZ**	**3**	**4**		**25**	**22**	**6.25**				**111.7**	**23**	**352**	**15**	**23.46**	
1968-69	N.Z. Governor's XI	West Indies	NZ	1	2	1	35	34	35.00			2	16	1	72	3	24.00	
1969	Barbados	Tour of England	E	2	4		64	22	16.00				63	12	221	4	55.25	
1969-70	Barbados	Shell Shield	IIs	2	4	1	22	9	7.33			1	54	17	118	4	29.50	
		Barbados		20	23	6	199	31	11.70			11	443.5	96	1395	42	33.21	
		West Indies		14	18	3	155	*28	10.33			2	340.6	50	1364	33	41.33	
		N.Z. Governor's XI		1	2	1	35	34	35.00			2	16	1	72	3	24.00	
		TEST RECORD		**5**	**8**	**1**	**65**	**22**	**9.28**	**0**	**0**	**0**	**163.7**	**25**	**626**	**18**	**34.77**	**5-84**
		CAREER		**35**	**43**	**10**	**389**	**34**	**11.78**	**0**	**0**	**15**	**800.3**	**147**	**2831**	**78**	**36.29**	**6-45**

SEASON	TEAM	OPPONENTS	V	M	I	NO	RUNS	H.S.	AVGE	100	50	CT/St	OV	MD	RUNS	W	AVGE	B.B.
1924-25	British Guiana	Trinidad	IIs	1	2		35	19	17.50			1	11.3	0	25	0		
1925-26	British Guiana	Barbados	Iis	1	2		102	89	51.00		1							
1925-26	British Guiana	Trinidad	IIs	1	2		129	124	64.50	1			9	0	26	1	26.00	
1925-26	British Guiana	M.C.C. Tourist	WI	2	2		152	120	76.00	1		1	2	0	6	0		
1925-26	West Indies XI	M.C.C. Tourist	WI	1	1		3	3	3.00									
1926-27	British Guiana	Barbados	IIs	1	2		51	27	25.50			1	7	0	26	1	26.00	
1928	West Indies	Tour of England	E	19	31	1	573	73	19.10		3	19						
1928	**WEST INDIES**	**ENGLAND TESTS**	**E**	**1**	**2**		**8**	**8**	**4.00**									
1929-30	British Guiana	Barbados	IIs	1	2		142	141	71.00	1			3	0	6	0		
1929-30	British Guiana	Trinidad	IIs	1	2		142	88	71.00		2	1	4	0	17	0		
1929-30	British Guiana	M.C.C. Tourist	WI	2	4		56	34	14.00				5	0	37	0		
1929-30	**WEST INDIES**	**ENGLAND TESTS**	**WI**	**1**	**2**		**41**	**22**	**20.50**									
1931-32	British Guiana	Trinidad	IIs	1	2		85	78	42.50		1		8	0	29	2	14.50	
		British Guiana		13	24		939	141	39.12	3	4	5	53.3	0	183	5	36.30	
		West Indies		33	55	5	1148	110	22.96	1	5	25						
		TEST RECORD		**2**	**4**	**0**	**49**	**22**	**12.25**	**0**	**0**	**0**						
		CARFER		**46**	**79**	**5**	**2087**	**141**	**28.20**	**4**	**9**	**30**	**53.3**	**0**	**183**	**5**	**36.60**	**2-29**

FINDLAY, Thaddeus Michael

				BATTING									BOWLING					
SEASON	TEAM	OPPONENTS	V	M	I	NO	RUNS	H.S.	AVGE	100	50	CT/St	OV	MD	RUNS	W	AVGE	B.B.
1964-65	Windward Is.	Australian Tourist	WI	1	2	1	18	*10	18.00			2/1						
1965-66	Windward Is.	Leeward Islands	IIs	1	2	1	27	*20	27.00			1/0						
1966-67	Windward Is.	Shell Shield	IIs	3	6	1	143	*51	28.60		1	2/2						
1967-68	Windward Is.	M.C.C. Tourist	WI	1	1		15	15	15.00			5/0						
1968-69	West Indies	Tour of Australia	A	7	10	1	192	59	21.33		1	15/3						
1968-69	West Indies	Tour of New Zealand	NZ	3	6	2	73	35	18.25			4/3						
1969	West Indies	Tour of England	E	8	10		83	22	8.30			16/0						
1969	**WEST INDIES**	**ENGLAND TESTS**	**E**	**2**	**4**		**51**	**23**	**12.75**			**9/0**						
1969-70	Windward Is.	Leeward Islands	IIs	1	2		75	53	37.50		1	1/0						
1969-70	Combined Is.	Shell Shield	IIs	4	8		188	43	23.50			6/0						
1969-70	Windward Is.	Duke of Norfolk Tourist	WI	1	1		20	20	20.00			1/0						
1969-70	Windward Is.	Glamorgan Tourist	WI	1	2	1	59	51	59.00		1	3/0						
1970-71	Windward Is.	Leeward Islands	IIs	1	2		39	23	19.50			3/0						
1970-71	Combined Is.	Shell Shield	Iis	4	8		58	26	7.25			5/2						
1970-71	Windward Is.	Indian Tourist	WI	1	2		83	62	41.50		1	4/0						

FERGUSON, Wilfred F.

				BATTING									BOWLING					
SEASON	TEAM	OPPONENTS	V	M	I	NO	RUNS	H.S.	AVGE	100	50	CT	OV	MD	RUNS	W	AVGE	B.B.
1942-43	Trinidad	Barbados	IIs	1	1		37	37	37.00				13	0	61	0		
1943-44	Trinidad	British Guiana	IIs	1	1		60	60	60.00		1	3	23	1	83	9	9.22	
1944-45	Trinidad	Barbados	IIs	2	2		74	38	37.00			4	83.2	5	330	17	19.41	
1945-46	Trinidad	British Guiana	IIs	2	4		88	60	22.00		1	2	25	3	79	3	26.33	
1945-46	Trinidad	Barbados	IIs	2	3		55	35	18.33			2	58	3	248	3	82.66	
1945-46	Trinidad	Jamaica	IIs	3	6	1	73	34	14.60			3	62.3	3	260	3	86.66	
1946-47	Trinidad	British Guiana	IIs	2	3	1	39	25	19.50			3	112.2	15	411	15	27.40	
1947-48	Trinidad	M.C.C. Tourist	WI	1	1	1	14	*14					28.5	3	87	4	21.75	
1947-48	**WEST INDIES**	**ENGLAND TESTS**	**WI**	**4**	**5**	**1**	**138**	**75**	**34.50**		**2**	**5**	**216**	**43**	**567**	**23**	**24.65**	
1948-49	West Indies	Tour of India	I	6	5	2	49	*25	16.33			8	142.3	27	354	12	29.50	
1948-49	**WEST INDIES**	**INDIA TESTS**	**I**	**3**	**3**	**1**	**10**	**6**	**5.00**			**3**	**165**	**33**	**443**	**10**	**44.30**	
1948-49	West Indies	Tour of Ceylon	C	1	D								15	0	83	1	83.00	
1949-50	Trinidad	Jamaica	IIs	2	1		14	14	14.00				84	14	218	9	24.22	
1950-51	Trinidad	Barbados	IIs	2	4	1	122	90	40.66		1	2	64	6	304	4	76.00	
1951-52	West Indies	Tour of Australia	A	7	10	1	133	52	14.77		1	4	134.6	13	642	16	40.12	
1951-52	West Indies	Tour of New Zealand	NZ	2	3	2	74	45	74.00			3	72.4	11	228	12	19.00	
1953-54	Trinidad	British Guiana	IIs	2	2	1	70	*62	70.00		1		74.4	20	201	4	50.25	
1853-54	Trinidad	M.C.C. Tourist	WI	1	2		26	18	13.00			1	28	1	129	4	32.25	
1953-54	**WEST INDIES**	**ENGLAND TESTS**	**WI**	**1**	**2**	**1**	**52**	**44**	**52.00**			**3**	**47**	**7**	**155**	**1**	**155.00**	
1954-55	Trinidad	Jamaica	IIs	2	4		58	28	14.50			2	51.1	11	147	6	24.50	
1954-55	Trinidad	Australian Tourist	WI	1	1		18	18	18.00				23.5	4	73	4	18.25	
1955-56	Trinidad	E.W. Swanton's Tourist	WI	1	2		21	18	10.50				33	5	103	5	20.60	
		Trinidad		25	37	5	769	90	24.03		4	22	764.4	94	2734	90	30.27	
		West Indies		24	28	8	456	75	22.80		3	26	792.5	134	2472	75	32.96	
		TEST RECORD		**8**	**10**	**3**	**200**	**75**	**28.58**	**0**	**2**	**11**	**428**	**83**	**1165**	**34**	**34.26**	**6-92**
		CAREER		**49**	**65**	**13**	**1225**	**90**	**23.55**	**0**	**7**	**48**	**1557.3**	**228**	**5206**	**165**	**31.55**	**7-73**

FERNANDES, Maurius Pacheco

				BATTING									BOWLING					
SEASON	TEAM	OPPONENTS	V	M	I	NO	RUNS	H.S.	AVGE	100	50	CT	OV	MD	RUNS	W	AVGE	B.B.
1922-23	British Guiana	Trinidad	IIs	1	2		25	25	12.50			1	4	0	11	1	11.00	
1923	West Indies	Tour of England	E	11	19	4	523	110	34.86	1	2	6						
1923-24	British Guiana	Trinidad	IIs	1	2		20	17	10.00									

SEASON	TEAM	OPPONENTS	V	M	I	NO	BATTING RUNS	H.S.	AVGE	100	50	CT/St	BOWLING OV	MD	RUNS	W	AVGE	B.B.
1970-71	**WEST INDIES**	**INDIA TESTS**	**WI**	**2**	**4**	**1**	**37**	***30**	**12.33**			**3/1**						
1971-72	Windward Is.	Leeward Islands	IIs	1	2		79	57	39.50		1	4/3						
1971-72	Combined Is.	Shell Shield	IIs	4	8		115	38	14.37			3/0						
1971-72	W.I. President's XI	New Zealand Tourist	WI	1	1	1	3	*3										
1971-72	Windward Is.	New Zealand Tourist	WI	1	D							1/1						
1971-72	**WEST INDIES**	**NEW ZEALAND TESTS**	**WI**	**5**	**6**	**2**	**99**	***44**	**24.75**			**7/1**						
1972-73	Windward Is.	Leeward Islands	IIs	2	4		51	34	12.75			5/1						
1972-73	Combined Is.	Shell Shield	IIs	4	8	1	228	*68	32.57		2	6/6						
1972-73	Windward Is.	Australian Tourist	WI	1	2		25	15	12.50			1/1						
1972-73	**WEST INDIES**	**AUSTRALIAN TESTS**	**WI**	**1**	**2**		**25**	**13**	**12.50**									
1973-74	Windward Is.	Leeward Islands	IIs	1	2	1	93	*68	93.00		1	1/1						
1973-74	Combined Is.	Shell Shield	IIs	4	7	1	63	*33	10.50			15/2						
1974-75	Windward Is.	Leeward Islands	IIs	2	3		119	90	39.66		1	6/0						
1974-75	Combined Is.	Shell Shield	IIs	4	7	3	113	*46	28.25			9/1						
1975-76	Windward Is.	Leeward Islands	IIs	1	1		7	7	7.00			1/0						
1975-76	Combined Is.	Shell Shield	IIs	4	3		60	30	20.00			2/2						
1975-76	Windward Is.	Indian Tourist	WI	1	2		85	72	42.50		1							
1976	West Indies	Tour of England	E	18	21	7	276	*51	19.71		1	36/8						
1976-77	Windward Is.	Leeward Islands	IIs	1	2		62	36	31.00			2/0						
1976-77	Combined Is.	Shell Shield	IIs	4	6	1	22	11	4.40			13/2						
1976-77	W.I. President's XI	Pakistan Tourist	WI	1	1		19	19	19.00			2/0						
1976-77	Windward Is.	Pakistan Tourist	WI	1	2		4	2	2.00			2/0						
1977-78	Windward Is.	Leeward Islands	IIs	2	3		102	52	34.00		2	2/2						
1977-78	Combined Is.	Shell Shield	IIs	4	5		104	45	20.80			7/1						
1977-78	Windward Is.	Australian Tourist	WI	1	2		12	11	6.00			4/0						
		Windward Islands		26	45	5	1118	90	27.95		10	51/11						
		Combined Islands		36	60	6	951	*68	21.61		2	66/16						
		West Indies		48	65	14	858	59	16.82		2	92/16						
		TEST RECORD		**10**	**16**	**3**	**212**	***44**	**16.30**	**0**	**0**	**19/2**						
		CAREER		**110**	**170**	**25**	**2927**	**90**	**20.18**	**0**	**14**	**209/43**						

FOSTER, Maurice Linton Churchill

SEASON	TEAM	OPPONENTS	V	BATTING M	I	NO	RUNS	H.S.	AVGE	100	50	CT	BOWLING OV	MD	RUNS	W	AVGE	B.B.
1963-64	Jamaica	Cavaliers Tourist	WI	3	6	1	233	*136	46.60	1		2						
1963-64	Jamaica	Barbados	IIs	1	2		3	3	1.50									
1964-65	Jamaica	Cavaliers Tourist	WI	2	4		85	61	21.25		1	1						
1965-66	Jamaica	Shell Shield	IIs	4	8	1	215	71	30.71		1	1	84	13	221	5	44.20	
1965-66	Jamaica	Worcestershire Tourist	WI	1	2		82	73	41.00		1		37	10	101	3	33.66	
1966-67	Jamaica	Shell Shield	IIs	4	7		368	147	52.57	1	2	1	68	12	205	8	25.62	
1967-68	Jamaica	M.C.C. Tourist	WI	1	2		48	28	24.00				21	8	53	2	26.50	
1967-68	WI President's XI	M.C.C. Tourist	WI	1	2	1	34	20	34.00				31.5	13	67	5	13.40	
1968-69	Jamaica	Shell Shield	IIs	4	6		302	135	50.33	2		3	64	16	174	6	29.00	
1969	West Indies	Tour of England	E	13	17	4	389	*87	26.40		4	2	86.4	25	241	7	34.42	
1969	**WEST INDIES**	**ENGLAND TESTS**	**E**	**1**	**2**		**7**	**4**	**3.50**				**2**	**0**	**7**	**0**		
1969-70	Jamaica	Cavaliers Tourist	WI	1	2		21	11	10.50			2	5	0	20	0		
1969-70	Jamaica	Shell Shield	IIs	4	8		213	79	26.62		2	3	115.4	37	236	10	23.60	
1970	Jamaica	Tour of England	E	4	5	1	243	110	60.75	1	1	1	28	6	88	5	17.60	
1970-71	Jamaica	Shell Shield	IIs	4	6		334	146	55.66	1	2	1	89	35	163	5	32.60	
1970-71	Jamaica	Indian Tourist	WI	1	1		0	0					38	14	66	5	13.20	
1970-71	WI President's XI	Indian Tourist	WI	1	2		50	48	25.00				31.5	7	68	3	22.66	
1970-71	**WEST INDIES**	**INDIA TESTS**	**WI**	**2**	**4**	**2**	**177**	**99**	**88.50**		**1**	**1**	**39**	**14**	**52**	**1**	**52.00**	
1971-72	Jamaica	Shell Shield	IIs	4	7	1	511	160	85.16	3	1	1	105	43	220	11	20.00	
1971-72	Jamaica	New Zealand Tourist	WI	1	1		0	0				1	45	21	56	4	14.00	
1971-72	**WEST INDIES**	**NEW ZEALAND TESTS**	**WI**	**3**	**6**	**2**	**93**	***28**	**23.25**				**53**	**22**	**93**	**1**	**93.00**	
1972-73	Jamaica	Shell Shield	IIs	4	7	2	522	*145	104.40	3	1	1	105.4	49	159	4	39.75	
1972-73	Jamaica	Australian Tourist	WI	1	2		74	44	37.00				35	6	75	1	75.00	
1972-73	**WEST INDIES**	**AUSTRALIA TESTS**	**WI**	**4**	**7**	**1**	**262**	**125**	**43.66**	**1**		**1**	**111**	**39**	**249**	**3**	**83.00**	
1973	West Indies	Tour of England	E	14	19	7	819	127	68.25	1	7	4	83	28	189	7	27.00	
1973	**WEST INDIES**	**ENGLAND TESTS**	**E**	**1**	**1**		**9**	**9**	**9.00**				**1**	**0**	**2**	**0**		
1973-74	Jamaica	Shell Shield	IIs	4	5	1	400	186	100.00	2	1	2	107.3	43	148	6	24.66	
1973-74	Jamaica	M.C.C. Tourist	WI	1	2		11	10	5.50			1	19	10	20	0		
1973-74	WI President's XI	M.C.C. Tourist	WI	1	2		14	7	7.00			1	25	3	56	0		
1973-74	**WEST INDIES**	**ENGLAND TESTS**	**WI**	**1**	**D**								**16**	**5**	**32**	**0**		
1974-75	Jamaica	Shell Shield	Iis	4	6	1	273	78	54.60		4		133.4	67	200	7	28.57	
1975-76	Jamaica	Shell Shield	Iis	4	4		159	70	39.75		1	1	79.3	33	122	5	24.40	
1975-76	Jamaica	Indian Tourist	WI	1	1		62	62	62.00		1		19	6	33	0		
1976-77	Jamaica	Shell Shield	IIs	4	6		364	234	60.66	1	1		120.3	44	219	7	31.28	
1976-77	Jamaica	Pakistan Tourist	WI	1	2		33	23	31.50			1	9	2	29	0		
1976-77	**WEST INDIES**	**PAKISTAN TOURISTS**	**WI**	**1**	**2**		**19**	**15**	**9.50**				**35**	**15**	**75**	**3**	**25.00**	

SEASON	TEAM	OPPONENTS	V	M	I	NO	RUNS	H.S.	AVGE	100	50	CT	OV	MD	RUNS	W	AVGE	B.B.
				BATTING									BOWLING					
1977-78	Jamaica	Shell Shield	IIs	4	5	1	226	91	56.50		2	2	145	75	167	5	33.40	
1977-78	Jamaica	Australian Tourist	WI	1	2		63	63	31.50		1	2	39	11	60	2	30.00	
1977-78	**WEST INDIES**	**AUSTRALIA TESTS**	**WI**	**1**	**2**		**13**	**8**	**6.50**			**1**	**39**	**11**	**90**	**1**	**90.00**	
		Jamaica		68	109	9	4845	234	48.45	15	23	27	1512.3	561	2835	101	28.06	
		West Indies		44	66	17	1886	127	38.48	2	12	10	554.2	182	1221	31	39.38	
		TEST RECORD		**14**	**24**	**5**	**580**	**125**	**30.52**	**1**	**1**	**3**	**296**	**106**	**600**	**9**	**66.66**	**2-41**
		CAREER		**112**	**175**	**26**	**6731**	**234**	**45.17**	**17**	**35**	**37**	**2066.5**	**743**	**4056**	**132**	**30.72**	**5-65**

FRANCIS, George Nathaniel

SEASON	TEAM	OPPONENTS	V	M	I	NO	RUNS	H.S.	AVGE	100	50	CT	OV	MD	RUNS	W	AVGE	B.B.
				BATTING									BOWLING					
1923	West Indies	Tour of England	E	15	22	4	207	41	11.50			15	505.5	119	1278	82	15.58	
1924-25	Barbados	Jamaica	IIs	1	1		47	47	47.00				48	8	153	4	38.25	
1925-26	Barbados	M.C.C. Tourist	WI	2	D							1	65.1	13	147	18	8.16	
1925-26	West Indies XI	M.C.C. Tourist	WI	3	5	1	33	14	8.25			2	95.4	14	297	8	37.12	
1927-28	Combined B/J XI	Combined Trin/B.G. XI	IIs	2	4		83	37	20.75			1	46	9	194	6	32.33	
1927-28	Barbados Born XI	West Indies XI	IIs	1	1		12	12	12.00			1	28	1	92	4	23.00	
1928	West Indies	Tour of England	E	19	26	10	254	61	15.31		1	10	524.3	106	1538	50	30.76	
1928	**WEST INDIES**	**ENGLAND TESTS**	**E**	**3**	**6**	**1**	**28**	***19**	**5.60**			**2**	**75**	**12**	**252**	**6**	**42.00**	
1928-29	West Indies XI	Julien Cahn's Tourist	WI	1	2	1	36	22	36.00			1	28	8	92	2	46.00	
1929-30	Barbados	M.C.C. Tourist	WI	1	1		39	39	39.00				29	7	60	2	30.00	
1929-30	**WEST INDIES**	**ENGLAND TESTS**	**WI**	**1**	**2**	**1**	**7**	***5**	**7.00**			**2**	**47.5**	**16**	**109**	**6**	**18.16**	
1930-31	West Indies	Tour of Australia	A	6	9	3	61	*16	10.16			4	162.3	15	490	18	27.22	
1930-31	**WEST INDIES**	**AUSTRALIA TESTS**	**A**	**5**	**8**	**1**	**31**	**8**	**4.42**			**3**	**129**	**23**	**350**	**11**	**31.81**	
1932-33	C.A. Merry's XI	G.C. Grant's XI	IIs	1	2		21	18	10.50				17	3	55	6	9.16	
1932-33	**WEST INDIES**	**ENGLAND TESTS**	**E**	**1**	**2**	**1**	**15**	**11**	**15.00**				**18**	**3**	**52**	**0**		
		Barbados		5	3		98	47	32.66			2	170.1	29	452	28	16.14	
		West Indies		54	82	23	672	61	11.38		1	39	1586.2	316	4458	183	24.36	
		Combined XI		2	4		83	37	20.75			1	46	9	194	6	32.33	
		C.A. Merry's XI		1	2		21	18	10.50				17	3	55	6	9.16	
		TEST RECORD		**10**	**18**	**4**	**81**	***19**	**5.78**	**0**	**0**	**7**	**269.5**	**54**	**763**	**23**	**33.17**	**4-40**
		CAREER		**62**	**91**	**23**	**874**	**61**	**12.85**	**0**	**1**	**42**	**1819.3**	**357**	**5159**	**223**	**23.13**	**7-50**

FREDRICK, Michael Campbell

SEASON	TEAM	OPPONENTS	V	BATTING M	I	NO	RUNS	H.S.	AVGE	100	50	CT	BOWLING OV	MD	RUNS	W	AVGE	B.B.
1944-45	Barbados	British Guiana	IIs	1	1		8	8	8.00									
1949	Derbyshire	Counties	E	2	3		98	84	32.67		1	1						
1953-54	Jamaica	M.C.C. Tourist	WI	2	4		158	60	39.50		2	2						
1953-54	**WEST INDIES**	**ENGLAND TESTS**	**WI**	**1**	**2**		**30**	**30**	**15.00**									
		Barbados		1	1		8	8	8.00									
		Jamaica		2	4		158	60	39.50		2	2						
		West Indies		1	2		30	30	15.00									
		Derbyshire		2	3		98	84	32.67		1	1						
		TEST RECORD		**1**	**2**	**0**	**30**	**30**	**15.00**	**0**	**0**	**0**						
		CAREER		**6**	**10**	**0**	**294**	**84**	**29.40**	**0**	**3**	**3**						

FREDRICKS, Roy Clifton

SEASON	TEAM	OPPONENTS	V	BATTING M	I	NO	RUNS	H.S.	AVGE	100	50	CT	BOWLING OV	MD	RUNS	W	AVGE	B.B.
1963-64	British Guiana	Jamaica	IIs	1	1		25	25	25.00			1						
1963-64	British Guiana	Trinidad	IIs	1	2		47	25	23.50				1	1	0	0		
1964-65	British Guiana	Australian Tourist	WI	1	2		21	16	10.50			2						
1965-66	British Guiana	Shell Shield	IIs	3	5	1	95	31	23.75			1						
1966-67	Guyana	Shell Shield	IIs	4	7	1	499	*128	83.16	3		1	4	0	30	0		
1967-68	WI President's XI	M.C.C. Tourist	WI	1	2	1	86	*64	86.00		1	1	3	1	6	0		
1967-68	Guyana	M.C.C. Tourist	WI	1	2		65	57	32.50		1		3	0	18	0		
1968-69	West Indies	Tour of Australia	A	9	18	2	664	136	41.50	1	3	12						
1968-69	**WEST INDIES**	**AUSTRALIA TESTS**	**A**	**4**	**8**		**271**	**76**	**33.87**		**1**	**3**						
1968-69	West Indies	Tour of New Zealand	NZ	2	4		70	37	17.50			1	9	1	45	1	45.00	
1968-69	**WEST INDIES**	**NEW ZEALAND TESTS**	**NZ**	**3**	**5**		**50**	**23**	**10.00**			**4**						
1968-69	NZ Governor's XI	West Indies	NZ	1	2		76	62	38.00		1	2	1.7	0	8	2	4.00	
1969	West Indies	Tour of England	E	15	23	4	928	*168	48.84	3	4	9	4	0	16	0		
1969	**WEST INDIES**	**ENGLAND TESTS**	**E**	**3**	**6**		**204**	**64**	**34.00**		**3**	**3**						
1969	Cavaliers XI	Barbados Tourist	E	1	2		83	43	41.50			2						
1969-70	Guyana	Shell Shield	IIs	4	7		327	121	46.71	1	1		5	3	3	0		
1970-71	Guyana	Shell Shield	IIs	3	5	1	243	91	60.75		3	4	2	1	3	1	3.00	
1970-71	Guyana	Indian Tourist	WI	1	2		95	95	47.50		1		1	1	1	0		
1970-71	**WEST INDIES**	**INDIA TESTS**	**WI**	**4**	**8**		**242**	**80**	**30.25**		**1**	**3**	**5**	**0**	**10**	**0**		

SEASON	TEAM	OPPONENTS	V	M	I	NO	BATTING RUNS	H.S.	AVGE	100	50	CT	BOWLING OV	MD	RUNS	W	AVGE	B.B.
1971	Glamorgan	Counties	E	18	33	3	1377	*145	45.90	2	7	10	164.1	32	558	18	31.00	
1971-72	Guyana	Shell Shield	IIs	4	7		485	111	69.28	1	4	4	65	15	163	8	20.37	
1971-72	Guyana	New Zealand Tourist	WI	1	2	1	105	*100	105.00	1			1	0	4	0		
1971-72	**WEST INDIES**	**NEW ZEALAND TESTS**	**WI**	**5**	**10**	**1**	**487**	**163**	**54.11**	**1**	**2**	**3**	**21**	**7**	**37**	**0**		
1972	Glamorgan	Counties	E	21	35	5	1199	*228	39.96	4	3	8	25	8	64	2	32.00	
1972-73	Berbice	Demerara JC	G	1	2		80	62	40.00		1		28	4	108	7	15.42	
1972-73	Guyana	Shell Shield	IIs	3	4	1	339	118	113.00	1	3	1	30	4	114	2	57.00	
1972-73	Guyana	Australian Tourist	WI	1	2		276	158	138.00	2			4	0	20	0		
1972-73	**WEST INDIES**	**AUSTRALIA TESTS**	**WI**	**5**	**10**	**1**	**381**	**98**	**42.33**		**3**	**9**	**4**	**0**	**19**	**0**		
1973	West Indies	Tour of England	E	11	20	2	840	129	46.66	1	4	3	21	2	97	1	97.00	
1973	**WEST INDIES**	**ENGLAND TESTS**	**E**	**3**	**5**		**251**	**150**	**50.20**	**1**	**1**	**4**	**4**	**0**	**23**	**0**		
1973	Glamorgan	Counties	E	6	12		415	106	34.58	1	2	3	18	5	45	0		
1973-74	Guyana	Shell Shield	IIs	4	6		266	105	44.33	1	1	3	56.3	5	209	5	41.80	
1973-74	WI President's XI	M.C.C. Tourist	WI	1	2		8	8	4.00			2	5	0	22	0		
1973-74	Guyana	M.C.C. Tourist	WI	1	2	1	217	112	217.00	2			9	2	27	1	27.00	
1973-74	**WEST INDIES**	**ENGLAND TESTS**	**WI**	**5**	**7**	**1**	**397**	**98**	**66.16**		**4**	**10**	**34**	**7**	**93**	**1**	**93.00**	
1974-75	West Indies	Tour of India	I	5	6		457	202	76.16	2	1	6	50.2	14	129	6		
1974-75	**WEST INDIES**	**INDIA TESTS**	**I**	**5**	**8**		**323**	**104**	**40.37**	**2**		**4**	**26**	**6**	**74**	**1**	**74.00**	
1974-75	West Indies	Tour of Sri Lanka	SL	2	3		191	102	63.66	1	1	2	10	3	28	0		
1974-75	**WEST INDIES**	**PAKISTAN TESTS**	**P**	**2**	**4**	**1**	**135**	**77**	**45.00**		**1**	**3**	**13**	**3**	**49**	**1**	**49.00**	
1974-75	Guyana	Shell Shield	IIs	4	7	2	545	250	109.00	1	3	3	29	8	92	1	92.00	
1975-76	West Indies	Tour of Australia	A	6	11		311	108	28.27	1	2	4	16	0	97	1	97.00	
1975-76	**WEST INDIES**	**AUSTRALIA TESTS**	**A**	**6**	**11**		**417**	**169**	**37.90**	**1**	**1**	**4**	**13**	**1**	**62**	**1**	**62.00**	
1975-76	**WEST INDIES**	**INDIA TESTS**	**WI**	**4**	**7**	**1**	**202**	**82**	**33.66**		**2**	**2**	**6**	**2**	**10**	**0**		
1976	West Indies	Tour of England	E	16	28	2	733	114	28.19	1	2	16	81	15	282	11	25.63	
1976	**WEST INDIES**	**ENGLAND TESTS**	**E**	**5**	**10**	**1**	**517**	**138**	**57.44**	**2**	**3**	**3**	**43.4**	**11**	**119**	**1**	**119.00**	
1976-77	Guyana	Shell Shield	IIs	3	5		197	85	39.40		2	6	10.5	3	39	1	39.00	
1976-77	Guyana	Pakistan Tourist	WI	1	2		116	82	58.00		1	2	6	1	31	0		
1976-77	**WEST INDIES**	**PAKISTAN TESTS**	**WI**	**5**	**10**	**1**	**457**	**120**	**50.77**	**1**	**4**	**7**	**19.3**	**4**	**52**	**2**	**26.00**	
1979-80	Demerara	Berbice JC	G	1	D													
1979-80	Guyana	Shell Shield	IIs	4	7		249	90	35.57		2	5	7	1	39	0		
1982-83	Guyana	Shell Shield	IIs	2	2		320	217	160.00	2		1						
		Guyana		47	79	8	4532	250	63.83	15	22	34	234.2	45	793	19	41.73	
		Berbice		1	2		80	62	40.00		1		28	4	108	7	15.42	
		Demerara		1	D													
		West Indies		127	226	18	8622	202	41.45	18	44	118	388.3	77	1270	27	47.03	

Glamorgan		45	80	8	2991	*228	41.54	7	12	21	207.1	45	667	20	33.35	
Cavaliers XI		1	2		83	43	41.50			2						
N Z Governor's XI		1	2		76	62	38.00		1	2	1.7	0	8	2	4.00	
TEST RECORD		**59**	**109**	**7**	**4334**	**169**	**42.49**	**8**	**26**	**62**	**189.1**	**41**	**548**	**7**	**78.28**	**1-12**
CAREER		**223**	**391**	**34**	**16384**	**250**	**45.89**	**40**	**80**	**177**	**859.5**	**171**	**2846**	**75**	**37.94**	**4-36**

FULLER, Richard Livingston

SEASON	TEAM	OPPONENTS	V	M	I	NO	BATTING RUNS	H.S.	AVGE	100	50	CT	BOWLING OV	MD	RUNS	W	AVGE	B.B.
1934-35	Jamaica	M.C.C. Tourist	WI	2	2	1	127	*113	127.00	1		1	50	5	176	4	44.00	
1934-35	**WEST INDIES**	**ENGLAND TESTS**	**WI**	**1**	**1**		**1**	**1**	**1.00**				**8**	**2**	**12**	**0**		
1935-36	Jamaica	Yorkshire Tourist	WI	1	2		15	15	7.50			1	24	3	73	0		
1945-46	Jamaica	Trinidad	IIs	3	6	2	121	39	30.25			1	50	7	207	6	34.50	
1946-47	Jamaica	Barbados	IIs	1	2		16	9	8.00			2	18.2	2	56	2	28.00	
		Jamaica		7	12	3	279	*113	31.00	1		5	142.2	17	512	12	42.66	
		West Indies		1	1		1	1	1.00				8	2	12	0		
		TEST RECORD		**1**	**1**	**0**	**1**	**1**	**1.00**	**0**	**0**	**0**	**8**	**2**	**12**	**0**		
		CAREER		**8**	**13**	**3**	**280**	***113**	**28.00**	**1**	**0**	**5**	**150.2**	**19**	**524**	**12**	**43.66**	**4-69**

FURLONGE, Hammond Alan

SEASON	TEAM	OPPONENTS	V	M	I	NO	BATTING RUNS	H.S.	AVGE	100	50	CT	BOWLING OV	MD	RUNS	W	AVGE	B.B.
1954-55	Trinidad	Jamaica	IIs	2	4		79	27	19.75									
1954-55	Trinidad	Australian Tourist	WI	1	2	1	207	*150	207.00	1	1							
1954-55	**WEST INDIES**	**AUSTRALIA TESTS**	**WI**	**1**	**2**		**32**	**28**	**16.00**									
1955-56	West Indies	Tour of New Zealand	NZ	3	4	1	106	65	35.33		1	3						
1955-56	**WEST INDIES**	**NEW ZEALAND TESTS**	**NZ**	**2**	**3**		**67**	**64**	**22.33**		**1**							
1957-58	Trinidad	Pakistan Tourist	WI	1	1		4	4	4.00									
1959-60	N.Trinidad	South Trinidad BC	T	1	2		49	35	24.50									
1960-61	Trinidad	Barbados	IIs	2	4		177	106	44.25	1		2						
1960-61	Trinidad	E.W. Swanton's Tourist	WI	1	2		16	15	8.00			1						
1960-61	N.Trinidad	South Trinidad BC	T	1	1		38	38	38.00			1						
1961-62	Trinidad	British Guiana	IIs	1	2		33	31	16.50									

SEASON	TEAM		M	I	NO	RUNS	H.S.	AVGE	100	50	CT	OV	MD	RUNS	W	AVGE	B.B.
			BATTING									BOWLING					
		Trinidad	8	15	1	516	*150	36.85	2	1	3						
		North Trinidad	2	3		87	38	29.00			1						
		West Indies	6	9	1	205	65	25.62		2	3						
		TEST RECORD	**3**	**5**	**0**	**99**	**64**	**19.80**	**0**	**1**	**0**						
		CAREER	**16**	**27**	**2**	**808**	***150**	**32.33**	**2**	**3**	**7**						

GANTEAUME, Andrew Gordon

SEASON	TEAM	OPPONENTS	V	M	I	NO	RUNS	H.S.	AVGE	100	50	CT/St	OV	MD	RUNS	W	AVGE	B.B.
				BATTING									BOWLING					
1940-41	Trinidad	Barbados	IIs	1	1		87	87	87.00		1	1						
1941-42	Trinidad	Barbados	IIs	2	4		61	37	15.25			2						
1942-43	Trinidad	Barbados	IIs	2	3		16	9	5.33			0/1						
1943-44	Trinidad	Barbados	IIs	2	4		75	28	18.75			4						
1943-44	Trinidad	British Guiana	IIs	2	3		152	97	50.66		1	5						
1945-46	Trinidad	British Guiana	IIs	2	4		159	68	39.75		2	2						
1945-46	Trinidad	Barbados	IIs	2	3		224	112	74.66	1	1	1						
1945-46	Trinidad	Jamaica	IIs	3	6		202	159	33.66	1		3/1						
1946-47	Trinidad	British Guiana	IIs	2	3		87	50	29.00		1							
1947-48	Trinidad	M.C.C. Tourist	WI	2	4	1	243	101	81.00	1	1		3	0	21	0		
1947-48	**WEST INDIES**	**ENGLAND TESTS**	**WI**	**1**	**1**		**112**	**112**	**112.00**	**1**								
1948-49	Trinidad	Barbados	IIs	2	4		90	52	22.50		1	2						
1949-50	Trinidad	Jamaica	IIs	2	2		181	147	90.50	1		1						
1950-51	Trinidad	Barbados	IIs	2	4		183	68	45.75		2							
1953-54	Trinidad	British Guiana	IIs	1	2		41	34	20.50			1/1						
1956-57	Trinidad	Barbados	IIs	1	2		44	38	22.00									
1956-57	West Indies	Tour of England	E	19	32	3	800	92	27.58		7	11	3	0	20	0		
1957-58	Trinidad	Pakistan Tourist	WI	1	1		13	13	13.00				2	0	10	0		
1962-63	Trinidad	Barbados	IIs	1	2	1	15	11	15.00			1						
		Trinidad		30	52	2	1873	159	37.46	4	10	23/3	5	0	31	0		
		West Indies		20	33	3	912	112	30.40	1	7	11	3	0	20	0		
		TEST RECORD		**1**	**1**	**0**	**112**	**112**	**112.00**	**1**	**0**	**0**						
		CAREER		**50**	**85**	**5**	**2785**	**159**	**34.81**	**5**	**17**	**34/3**	**8**	**0**	**51**	**0**		

GARNER, Joel

				BATTING									BOWLING					
SEASON	TEAM	OPPONENTS	V	M	I	NO	RUNS	H.S.	AVGE	100	50	CT	OV	MD	RUNS	W	AVGE	B.B.
1975-76	Barbados	Shell Shield	IIs	2	1	1	14	*14				1	34	7	81	4	20.25	
1976-77	Barbados	Shell Shield	IIs	4	6	3	130	*44	43.33			2	122.1	22	388	23	16.86	
1976-77	WI President's XI	Pakistan Tourist	WI	1	1		10	10	10.00			1	31	10	86	7	12.28	
1976-77	Barbados	Pakistan Tourist	WI	1	D							2	39	5	132	3	44.00	
1976-77	**WEST INDIES**	**PAKISTAN TESTS**	**WI**	**5**	**8**		**92**	**43**	**11.50**			**6**	**219.3**	**41**	**688**	**25**	**27.52**	
1977	Somerset	Counties	E	5	6	1	91	37	18.20			5	215.1	60	539	27	19.96	
1977-78	**WEST INDIES**	**AUSTRALIA TESTS**	**WI**	**2**	**2**	**1**	**5**	***5**	**5.00**				**63.1**	**17**	**195**	**13**	**15.00**	
1978	Somerset	Counties	E	4	5	2	12	*6	4.00			2	170.1	61	351	22	15.95	
1978-79	Barbados	Shell Shield	IIs	2	2	1	62	51	62.00		1		64	20	147	6	24.50	
1979	Somerset	Counties	E	14	10	4	106	53	17.67		1	4	393.1	127	761	55	13.83	
1979-80	West Indies	Tour of Australia	A	4	4	2	81	39	40.50			5	92.3	14	340	18	18.88	
1979-80	**WEST INDIES**	**AUSTRALIA TESTS**	**A**	**3**	**4**	**1**	**106**	**60**	**35.33**		**1**	**3**	**127.4**	**34**	**301**	**14**	**21.50**	
1979-80	West Indies	Tour of New Zealand	NZ	1	2		5	3	2.50			2	25.1	7	53	5	10.60	
1979-80	**WEST INDIES**	**NEW ZEALAND TESTS**	**NZ**	**3**	**5**		**12**	**7**	**2.40**				**122.1**	**34**	**235**	**14**	**16.78**	
1979-80	Barbados	Shell Shield	IIs	2	2		79	67	39.50		1	3	65.5	19	219	13	16.84	
1980	West Indies	Tour of England	E	6	5		143	104	28.60	1		4	138.2	50	312	23	13.56	
1980	**WEST INDIES**	**ENGLAND TESTS**	**E**	**5**	**5**		**63**	**46**	**12.60**			**4**	**212.4**	**73**	**371**	**26**	**14.26**	
1980-81	West Indies	Tour of Pakistan	P	3	2	1	9	*8	9.00			2	52.4	11	159	8	19.87	
1980-81	**WEST INDIES**	**PAKISTAN TESTS**	**P**	**3**	**3**		**18**	**15**	**6.00**			**2**	**90.3**	**25**	**192**	**10**	**19.20**	
1980-81	Barbados	Shell Shield	IIs	1	2	1	11	*6	11.00				49	11	81	4	20.25	
1980-81	**WEST INDIES**	**ENGLAND TESTS**	**WI**	**4**	**4**		**84**	**46**	**21.00**			**4**	**151.2**	**48**	**303**	**10**	**30.30**	
1981	Somerset	Counties	E	18	18	2	324	90	20.25		2	10	605.4	182	1349	88	15.32	
1981-82	West Indies	Tour of Australia	A	2	2		30	18	15.00			1	43.3	14	97	11	8.81	
1981-82	**WEST INDIES**	**AUSTRALIA TESTS**	**A**	**3**	**5**		**20**	**12**	**4.00**			**3**	**122**	**37**	**275**	**12**	**22.91**	
1981-82	Barbados	Shell Shield	IIs	3	2		0	0				1	91.5	24	251	16	15.68	
1982	Somerset	Counties	E	10	11	5	98	*40	16.33			4	259.1	76	583	33	17.67	
1982-83	South Australia	Sheffield Shield	A	8	13	1	138	22	11.50			3	403.1	131	976	55	17.74	
1982-83	Barbados	Indian Tourist	WI	1	1		17	17	17.00			3	49.1	7	178	8	22.25	
1982-83	**WEST INDIES**	**INDIA TESTS**	**WI**	**4**	**4**	**4**	**24**	***21**				**4**	**113**	**36**	**301**	**7**	**43.00**	
1983	Somerset	Counties	E	10	16	6	265	44	26.50			10	277	74	708	35	20.22	
1983-84	**WEST INDIES**	**AUSTRALIA TESTS**	**WI**	**5**	**5**	**2**	**66**	***24**	**22.00**			**3**	**208.5**	**53**	**523**	**31**	**16.87**	
1984	West Indies	Tour of England	E	3	2		32	29	16.00			1	53	21	84	10	8.40	
1984	**WEST INDIES**	**ENGLAND TESTS**	**E**	**5**	**6**	**1**	**29**	***10**	**5.80**			**3**	**217.5**	**60**	**540**	**29**	**18.62**	
1984-85	West Indies	Tour of Australia	A	3	3	2	17	*9	17.00			1	60	21	102	6	17.00	
1984-85	**WEST INDIES**	**AUSTRALIA TESTS**	**A**	**5**	**6**	**2**	**41**	**17**	**10.25**			**2**	**177.4**	**33**	**566**	**19**	**29.78**	
1984-85	**WEST INDIES**	**NEW ZEALAND TESTS**	**WI**	**4**	**3**	**2**	**49**	***37**	**49.00**			**3**	**136.2**	**37**	**302**	**10**	**30.10**	

				BATTING									BOWLING					
SEASON	TEAM	OPPONENTS	V	M	I	NO	RUNS	H.S.	AVGE	100	50	CT	OV	MD	RUNS	W	AVGE	B.B.
1985	Somerset	Counties	E	15	11	3	92	22	11.50			4	295.4	75	739	31	23.83	
1985-86	Barbados	Shell Shield	IIs	5	8		166	56	20.75		1	4	141	31	378	28	13.50	
1985-86	Barbados	English Tourist	WI	1	2	1	27	*23	27.00				25	7	52	2	26.00	
1985-86	**WEST INDIES**	**ENGLAND TESTS**	**WI**	**5**	**5**	**1**	**52**	**24**	**13.00**			**2**	**156.1**	**30**	**436**	**27**	**16.14**	
1986	Somerset	Counties	E	18	15	4	182	47	16.54			8	419	95	1091	47	23.21	
1986-87	West Indies	Tour of Australia	A	1	1		1	1	1.00				10	1	19	0		
1986-87	West Indies	Tour of New Zealand	NZ	1	D								19.5	2	60	5	12.00	
1986-87	**WEST INDIES**	**NEW ZEALAND TESTS**	**NZ**	**2**	**3**		**11**	**11**	**3.66**			**3**	**77**	**16**	**205**	**12**	**17.08**	
1986-87	Barbados	Shell Shield	IIs	2	1		13	13	13.00			3	39	6	134	6	22.33	
1987-88	Barbados	Red Stripe Cup	IIs	5	9		137	61	15.22		1	1	148.5	26	450	23	19.56	
		Barbados		29	36	7	656	67	22.62		4	20	868.5	185	2491	136	18.31	
		West Indies		83	90	19	1000	104	14.08	1	1	59	2721.5	725	6745	352	19.16	
		Somerset		94	92	27	1170	90	18.00		3	47	635	750	6121	338	18.10	
		South Australia		8	13	1	138	22	11.50			3	403.1	131	976	55	17.74	
		TEST RECORD		**58**	**68**	**14**	**672**	**60**	**12.44**	**0**	**1**	**42**	**2195.5**	**574**	**5433**	**259**	**20.97**	**6-56**
		CAREER		**214**	**231**	**54**	**2964**	**104**	**16.74**	**1**	**8**	**129**	**6628.5**	**1791**	**16333**	**881**	**18.53**	**8-31**

GASKIN, Berkeley Bertram McGarrell

				BATTING									BOWLING					
SEASON	TEAM	OPPONENTS	V	M	I	NO	RUNS	H.S.	AVGE	100	50	CT	OV	MD	RUNS	W	AVGE	B.B.
1928-29	British Guiana	Trinidad	IIs	1	2		1	1	1.00				22	5	64	1	64.00	
1929-30	British Guiana	Barbados	IIs	1	2		11	7	5.50				24	4	66	1	66.00	
1933-34	British Guiana	Barbados	IIs	1	2	2	14	*8				1	52	11	92	2	46.00	
1934-35	British Guiana	Barbados	IIs	1	2	1	22	*16	22.00			2	32	9	70	3	23.33	
1934-35	British Guiana	Trinidad	IIs	1	1		17	17	17.00			1	24	7	54	3	18.00	
1934-35	British Guiana	M.C.C. Tourist	WI	1	1		0	0					14	3	37	0		
1935-36	British Guiana	Trinidad	IIs	1	1		39	39	39.00				14	2	40	2	20.00	
1936-37	British Guiana	Trinidad	IIs	1	2		21	14	10.50			1	21	6	43	3	14.33	
1937-38	British Guiana	Barbados	IIs	1	1		0	0					34.2	10	72	4	18.00	
1937-38	British Guiana	Trinidad	IIs	1	2	2	48	*43				1	24	2	85	1	85.00	
1938-39	British Guiana	Trinidad	IIs	1	2	1	6	*6	6.00				13	2	46	3	15.33	
1938-39	British Guiana	Barbados	IIs	1	2		4	4	2.00				24	1	96	2	48.00	
1938-39	West Indies XI	Jamaica	IIs	1	1		1	1	1.00			2	18	1	50	0		
1943-44	British Guiana	Trinidad	IIs	2	4	1	51	*30	17.00				74	9	234	8	29.25	

SEASON	TEAM	OPPONENTS	V	M	I	NO	RUNS	H.S.	AVGE	100	50	CT	OV	MD	RUNS	W	AVGE	B.B.
1944-45	British Guiana	Barbados	IIs	2	3		22	14	7.33				71.2	12	247	10	24.70	
1945-46	British Guiana	Trinidad	IIs	2	4	1	90	64	30.00		1		94.3	38	194	10	19.40	
1946-47	British Guiana	Barbados	IIs	2	3		113	60	37.66		1		104	15	316	8	39.50	
1946-47	British Guiana	Trinidad	IIs	2	4		70	48	17.50			3	100.5	10	402	9	44.66	
1947-48	British Guiana	Jamaica	IIs	2	4		62	40	15.50			1	86.1	18	237	9	26.33	
1947-48	British Guiana	M.C.C. Tourist	WI	1	1		15	15	15.00			1	67	21	152	3	50.66	
1947-48	**WEST INDIES**	**ENGLAND TESTS**	**WI**	**2**	**3**		**17**	**10**	**5.66**			**1**	**79**	**24**	**158**	**2**	**79.00**	
1949-50	British Guiana	Barbados	IIs	2	4		25	20	6.25			2	116	19	387	6	64.50	
1950-51	British Guiana	Jamaica	IIs	2	4	2	24	*10	12.00			1	88.2	17	275	13	21.15	
1951-52	British Guiana	Barbados	IIs	2	2	1	17	16	17.00				91.2	36	234	11	21.27	
1951-52	British Guiana	Trinidad	IIs	2	4	1	14	9	4.66				117.3	27	267	5	53.40	
1952-53	British Guiana	Jamaica	IIs	2	3	1	61	*35	30.50			1	100.4	39	192	8	24.00	
1952-53	British Guiana	Indian Tourist	WI	1	1		12	12	12.00			1	27	4	70	2	35.00	
1953-54	British Guiana	Trinidad	IIs	2	3		5	5	1.66			1	135.1	50	214	9	23.77	
		British Guiana		38	64	13	764	64	14.98		2	17	1572.1	377	4186	136	30.77	
		West Indies		3	4		18	10	4.50			3	97	25	208	2	104.00	
		TEST RECORD		**2**	**3**	**0**	**17**	**10**	**5.66**	**0**	**0**	**1**	**79**	**24**	**158**	**2**	**79.00**	**1-15**
		CAREER		**41**	**68**	**13**	**782**	**64**	**14.21**	**0**	**2**	**20**	**1669.1**	**402**	**4394**	**138**	**31.84**	**7-58**

GIBBS, Glendon Lionel

				BATTING									BOWLING					
SEASON	TEAM	OPPONENTS	V	M	I	NO	RUNS	H.S.	AVGE	100	50	CT	OV	MD	RUNS	W	AVGE	B.B.
1949-50	British Guiana	Barbados	IIs	2	4		39	14	9.75				35	2	168	2	84.00	
1951-52	British Guiana	Barbados	IIs	2	3	1	241	216	120.50	1		2	6	0	30	0		
1951-52	British Guiana	Trinidad	IIs	2	4		81	50	20.25		1		28	4	89	1	89.00	
1952-53	British Guiana	Jamaica	IIs	2	3		144	121	48.00	1		1	25	2	94	0		
1952-53	British Guiana	Indian Tourist	WI	1	2	1	46	*27	46.00				5	1	13	1	13.00	
1953-54	British Guiana	Trinidad	IIs	2	4		173	108	43.25	1		2	71	11	215	4	53.75	
1953-54	British Guiana	M.C.C. Tourist	WI	1	2		35	34	17.50			1	32.1	2	122	4	30.25	
1954-55	British Guiana	Barbados	IIs	2	4		139	93	34.75		1	2	79.4	15	221	9	24.55	
1954-55	British Guiana	Australian Tourist	WI	1	2		2	2	1.00				16	0	65	0		
1954-55	**WEST INDIES**	**AUSTRALIA TESTS**	**WI**	**1**	**2**		**12**	**12**	**6.00**			**1**	**4**	**1**	**7**	**0**		
1956-57	British Guiana	Jamaica	IIs	1	2	1	30	*18	30.00			1	25	2	85	0		
1956-57	British Guiana	Barbados	IIs	1	1		80	80	80.00		1							
1957-58	British Guiana	Pakistan Tourist	WI	1	1		28	28	28.00				8	0	33	0		
1958-59	British Guiana	Barbados	IIs	2	4		239	123	59.75	1	1	1	22	2	65	2	32.50	

SEASON	TEAM	OPPONENTS	V	M	I	NO	BATTING RUNS	H.S.	AVGE	100	50	CT	BOWLING OV	MD	RUNS	W	AVGE	B.B.
1959-60	British Guiana	Jamaica	IIs	1	1		92	92	92.00		1		3	0	19	0		
1959-60	British Guiana	M.C.C. Tourist	WI	1	2		82	78	41.00		1							
1960-61	British Guiana	E.W. Swanton's Tourist	WI	1	2		45	29	22.50			1						
1961-62	British Guiana	Combined Islands	IIs	1	1		36	36	36.00			1	2	0	4	0		
1961-62	British Guiana	Trinidad	IIs	1	2		173	129	86.50	1		1						
1961-62	British Guiana	Barbados	IIs	1	2		4	4	2.00									
1962-63	British Guiana	Barbados	IIs	1	2		9	5	4.50									
		British Guiana		27	48	3	1718	216	38.17	5	6	13	357.5	41	1223	23	53.17	
		West Indies		1	2		12	12	6.00			1	4	1	7	0		
		TEST RECORD		**1**	**2**	**0**	**12**	**12**	**6.00**	**0**	**0**	**1**	**4**	**1**	**7**	**0**		
		CAREER		**28**	**50**	**3**	**1730**	**216**	**36.80**	**5**	**6**	**14**	**361.5**	**42**	**1230**	**23**	**53.47**	**6-80**

GIBBS, Lancelot Richard

SEASON	TEAM	OPPONENTS	V	M	I	NO	BATTING RUNS	H.S.	AVGE	100	50	CT	BOWLING OV	MD	RUNS	W	AVGE	B.B.
1953-54	British Guiana	M.C.C. Tourist	WI	1	2	1	15	14	15.00				41	8	126	2	63.00	
1954-55	British Guiana	Barbados	IIs	2	4		7	6	1.75			2	44	10	131	1	131.00	
1956-57	British Guiana	Jamaica	IIs	1	D								80	35	113	4	28.25	
1956-57	British Guiana	Barbados	IIs	1	1		6	6	6.00			1	40	8	83	4	20.25	
1957-58	**WEST INDIES**	**PAKISTAN TESTS**	**WI**	**4**	**5**		**51**	**22**	**10.20**			**3**	**166.5**	**46**	**392**	**17**	**23.05**	
1958-59	West Indies	Tour of India	I	9	10	3	97	*25	13.85			5	189.5	61	418	18	23.22	
1958-59	**WEST INDIES**	**INDIA TESTS**	**I**	**1**	**1**		**16**	**16**	**16.00**				**30**	**12**	**61**	**0**		
1958-59	West Indies	Tour of Pakistan	P	2	2	1	23	21	23.00			1	57.3	20	109	9	12.11	
1958-59	**WEST INDIES**	**PAKISTAN TESTS**	**P**	**3**	**5**		**44**	**21**	**8.80**			**3**	**94.1**	**33**	**180**	**8**	**22.25**	
1959-60	British Guiana	Jamaica	IIs	1	1	1	11	*11					69	10	188	4	47.00	
1959-60	British Guiana	M.C.C. Tourist	WI	1	D							1	55	17	105	1	105.00	
1960-61	West Indies	Tour of Australia	A	6	9	1	101	43	12.62			5	181	23	527	15	35.13	
1960-61	**WEST INDIES**	**AUSTRALIA TESTS**	**A**	**3**	**5**		**55**	**18**	**11.00**			**1**	**192.2**	**65**	**395**	**19**	**20.78**	
1960-61	British Guiana	E.W. Swanton's Tourist	WI	1	1		6	6	6.00				40	7	111	6	18.50	
1961-62	British Guiana	Combined Islands	IIs	1	1	1	8	*8				1	26.1	6	62	4	15.50	
1961-62	British Guiana	Trinidad	IIs	1	1		21	21	21.00			1	58.1	13	151	3	50.33	
1961-62	British Guiana	Barbados	IIs	1	2		32	31	16.00				49	13	123	3	41.00	
1961-62	**WEST INDIES**	**INDIA TESTS**	**WI**	**5**	**5**		**25**	**15**	**5.00**			**4**	**264.5**	**93**	**490**	**24**	**20.41**	
1962-63	British Guiana	Barbados	IIs	1	2		5	5	2.50				42.2	12	86	10	8.60	

1963	West Indies	Tour of England	E	14	11	3	74	31	9.25	7	383.3	142	1010	52	19.42
1963	**WEST INDIES**	**ENGLAND TESTS**	**E**	**5**	**7**	**3**	**15**	**6**	**3.75**	**5**	**249.3**	**74**	**554**	**26**	**21.30**
1963-64	West Indies XI	The Rest XI	IIs	1	D					1	24.3	5	109	4	27.25
1963-64	C. Hunte's XI	F. Worrell's XI	IIs	1	2		20	12	10.00	1	28	2	116	3	38.66
1963-64	British Guiana	Barbados	IIs	1	1		0	0		2	87.3	27	178	6	29.66
1963-64	British Guiana	Jamaica	IIs	1	1	1	9	*9		1	17	6	25	2	12.50
1963-64	British Guiana	Trinidad	IIs	1	1		17	17	17.00		49	13	75	3	25.00
1964	West Indies XI	England XI	E	3	2	1	10	10	10.00	1	92.1	24	301	12	25.08
1964-65	Comm. XI	Tour of India	I	1	2		16	12	8.00	1	39	9	136	3	45.33
1964-65	**WEST INDIES**	**AUSTRALIA TESTS**	**WI**	**5**	**9**	**2**	**19**	**6**	**2.71**		**278.3**	**88**	**556**	**18**	**30.88**
1965	Rest of World XI	England XI	E	1	1	1	1	*1			11	3	41	0	
1965-66	British Guiana	Shell Shield	IIs	4	5	4	56	*23	56.00	1	288	77	402	12	33.50
1966	West Indies	Tour of England	E	12	12	5	76	19	10.85	6	335	104	670	26	25.76
1966	**WEST INDIES**	**ENGLAND TESTS**	**E**	**5**	**6**	**3**	**22**	**12**	**7.33**	**3**	**273.4**	**103**	**520**	**21**	**24.76**
1966-67	West Indies	Tour of India	I	3	3	2	13	*6	13.00		107.5	29	266	8	33.25
1966-67	**WEST INDIES**	**INDIA TESTS**	**I**	**3**	**4**	**2**	**8**	**5**	**4.00**	**3**	**204.5**	**59**	**397**	**18**	**22.05**
1966-67	West Indies	Tour of Ceylon	C	1	D						16	6	63	1	63.00
1966-67	Guyana	Shell Shield	IIs	4	3	1	13	6	6.50	2	121.5	39	232	9	25.77
1966-67	Rest of World XI	Barbados	WI	1	2	2	0	*0			40.2	14	72	6	12.00
1967	Warwickshire	Counties	E	3	D						108	29	265	9	29.44
1967	Rest of World XI	England XI & Sussex	E	2	D						82.5	18	234	12	19.50
1967-68	Guyana	M.C.C. Tourist	WI	1	2	1	0	*0			38	17	61	4	15.23
1967-68	**WEST INDIES**	**ENGLAND TESTS**	**WI**	**5**	**6**	**1**	**17**	**14**	**3.40**	**2**	**318.3**	**114**	**610**	**20**	**30.50**
1968	Warwickshire	Counties	E	27	25	15	66	*17	6.60	18	857	293	1808	72	25.11
1968-69	West Indies	Tour of Australia	A	5	4	3	4	3	4.00	5	128.1	26	389	12	32.41
1968-69	**WEST INDIES**	**AUSTRALIA TESTS**	**A**	**5**	**10**	**5**	**28**	**17**	**5.60**	**2**	**292.2**	**52**	**923**	**24**	**38.45**
1968-69	West Indies	Tour of New Zealand	NZ	2	3	1	8	5	4.00	1	17.3	2	93	6	15.50
1968-69	**WEST INDIES**	**NEW ZEALAND TESTS**	**NZ**	**3**	**4**	**3**	**3**	**2**	**3.00**	**6**	**132.4**	**28**	**362**	**8**	**42.25**
1969	West Indies	Tour of England	E	10	5	2	13	*10	4.33	5	183.3	52	403	13	31.00
1969	**WEST INDIES**	**ENGLAND TESTS**	**E**	**3**	**6**	**3**	**34**	***18**	**11.33**	**3**	**168.4**	**57**	**317**	**6**	**52.83**
1969	Warwickshire	Counties	E	9	9	6	33	19	11.00	2	216.1	76	443	19	23.31
1969-70	South Australia	Sheffield Shield	A	8	14	6	88	*21	11.00	6	254.4	74	632	18	35.11
1970	Rest of World XI	England (T)	E	4	5	3	7	*3	3.50	2	167	53	307	3	102.33
1970	Rest of World XI	T.N. Pearce's XI	E	1	1	1	4	*4		2	6	0	21	1	21.00
1970	Warwickshire	Counties	E	18	19	5	76	*20	5.42	14	698.3	229	1600	50	32.00
1970-71	Rest of World XI	Tour of Pakistan	P	1	2	2	2	*1		1	35	4	140	2	70.00
1970-71	Guyana	Shell Shield	IIs	3	4	1	10	6	3.33	3	129.3	45	255	11	23.18
1970-71	Guyana	Indian Tourist	WI	1	1	1	11	*11			48	17	80	1	80.00
1970-71	**WEST INDIES**	**INDIA TESTS**	**WI**	**1**	**1**		**25**	**25**	**25.00**		**40**	**17**	**65**	**0**	

SEASON	TEAM	OPPONENTS	V	M	I	NO	RUNS	H.S.	AVGE	100	50	CT	OV	MD	RUNS	W	AVGE	B.B.
				BATTING									BOWLING					
1971	Warwickshire	Counties	E	26	25	13	116	*23	9.66			24	1024.1	296	2475	131	18.89	
1971-72	Guyana	Shell Shield	IIs	2	4	3	21	*10	21.00			1	68.5	19	161	3	53.66	
1971-72	Guyana	New Zealand Tourist	WI	1	D								43	17	66	1	66.00	
1971-72	**WEST INDIES**	**NEW ZEALAND TESTS**	**WI**	**2**	**1**	**1**	**3**	***3**					**130**	**37**	**267**	**3**	**89.00**	
1972	Warwickshire	Counties	E	21	14	7	64	24	9.14			17	596.1	163	1428	52	27.46	
1972-73	Demerara	Berbice JC	G	1	2		7	6	3.50				69.3	30	129	10	12.90	
1972-73	Guyana	Shell Shield	IIs	4	4	2	14	6	7.00			1	182.3	48	355	22	16.13	
1972-73	**WEST INDIES**	**AUSTRALIA TESTS**	**WI**	**5**	**7**	**2**	**25**	**7**	**5.00**			**3**	**325**	**108**	**696**	**26**	**26.76**	
1973	West Indies	Tour of England	E	7	3	2	6	*4	6.00			2	197.3	59	449	15	29.93	
1973	**WEST INDIES**	**ENGLAND TESTS**	**E**	**3**	**4**	**3**	**8**	***3**	**8.00**			**4**	**135.1**	**46**	**227**	**9**	**25.22**	
1973	Warwickshire	Counties	E	5	4	2	15	12	7.50			5	110.5	37	262	5	52.40	
1973-74	Rest of World XI	Tour of Pakistan	P	1	2	1	5	5	5.00			1	19	5	64	0		
1973-74	Guyana	Shell Shield	IIs	2	3	1	1	1	0.50				102	37	200	5	40.00	
1973-74	**WEST INDIES**	**ENGLAND TESTS**	**WI**	**5**	**4**	**2**	**9**	***6**	**4.50**			**4**	**328.3**	**103**	**661**	**18**	**36.72**	
1974-75	West Indies	Tour of India	I	3	1	1	5	*5					73	21	154	0		
1974-75	**WEST INDIES**	**INDIA TESTS**	**I**	**5**	**6**	**2**	**34**	***14**	**8.50**				**259.5**	**103**	**454**	**21**	**21.61**	
1974-75	**WEST INDIES**	**PAKISTAN TESTS**	**P**	**2**	**2**	**1**	**4**	***4**	**4.00**			**2**	**89.5**	**27**	**210**	**7**	**30.00**	
1974-75	Guyana	Shell Shield	IIs	2	1	1	0	*0				1	109	37	220	6	36.66	
1975-76	West Indies	Tour of Australia	A	3	4	3	28	*15	28.00				59	9	166	1	166.00	
1975-76	**WEST INDIES**	**AUSTRALIA TESTS**	**A**	**6**	**11**	**6**	**43**	**13**	**8.60**			**4**	**232.5**	**48**	**652**	**16**	**40.75**	
		British Guiana/Guyana		39	45	19	263	31	10.11			18	1828.5	538	3589	127	28.25	
		Demerara		1	2		7	6	3.50				69.3	30	129	10	12.90	
		West Indies		160	178	67	946	43	8.52			91	6358.2	1895	14116	501	28.17	
		Warwickshire		109	96	48	370	24	7.70			80	3610.5	1123	8281	338	24.50	
		Rest of World XI		11	13	10	19	5	6.33			6	361.2	97	879	24	36.62	
		South Australia		8	14	6	88	*21	11.00			6	254.4	74	632	18	35.11	
		Comm. XI		1	2		16	12	8.00			1	39	9	136	3	45.33	
		C. Hunte's XI		1	2		20	12	10.00			1	28	2	116	3	38.66	
		TEST RECORD		**79**	**109**	**39**	**488**	**25**	**6.97**	**0**	**0**	**52**	**4208**	**1313**	**8989**	**309**	**29.09**	**8-38**
		CAREER		**330**	**352**	**150**	**1729**	**43**	**8.55**	**0**	**0**	**203**	**12550.1**	**3768**	**27878**	**1024**	**27.22**	**8-37**

GILCHRIST, Roy

				BATTING									BOWLING					
SEASON	TEAM	OPPONENTS	V	M	I	NO	RUNS	H.S.	AVGE	100	50	CT	OV	MD	RUNS	W	AVGE	B.B.
1956-57	Jamaica	British Guiana	IIs	1	1	1	8	*8				1	42	6	137	3	45.66	
1956-57	Jamaica	Duke of Norfolk's Tourist	WI	3	5		47	16	9.40				129.2	26	460	11	41.81	
1957	West Indies	Tour of England	E	11	9	3	45	20	7.50			2	241.5	35	710	27	26.29	
1957	**WEST INDIES**	**ENGLAND TESTS**	**E**	**4**	**7**	**2**	**22**	***11**	**4.40**			**1**	**152.3**	**19**	**466**	**10**	**46.00**	
1957-58	**WEST INDIES**	**PAKISTAN TESTS**	**WI**	**5**	**5**	**1**	**30**	**12**	**7.50**			**1**	**187.1**	**32**	**636**	**21**	**30.88**	
1958-59	West Indies	Tour of India	I	7	5	3	61	*43	30.50			2	188.4	44	545	45	12.11	
1958-59	**WEST INDIES**	**INDIA TESTS**	**I**	**4**	**2**		**8**	**7**	**4.00**			**2**	**198.1**	**73**	**419**	**26**	**16.11**	
1961-62	Jamaica	Barbados	IIs	1	2		5	5	2.50				40	5	177	2	88.50	
1962-63	Hyderabad	Bengal	I	1	1		0	0					84.3	9	235	9	26.11	
1962-63	South Zone	Central & West Zones	I	2	2		0	0					49	4	259	5	51.80	
1962-63	Chidambaram's XI	Ass. Cement Co.	I	1	1		7	7	7.00			1	22	2	69	3	23.00	
1962-63	Chief Minister's XI	Indian Starlets XI	I	2	3		25	16	8.33				41	4	229	5	45.80	
		Jamaica		5	8	1	60	16	8.57			1	211.2	37	774	16	48.37	
		West Indies		31	28	9	166	*43	8.73			8	968.2	203	2776	129	21.51	
		Indian XI's		6	7		32	16	4.57			1	196.3	19	792	22	36.00	
		TEST RECORD		**13**	**14**	**3**	**60**	**12**	**5.45**	**0**	**0**	**4**	**537.5**	**124**	**1521**	**57**	**26.68**	**6-55**
		CAREER		**42**	**43**	**10**	**258**	***43**	**7.81**	**0**	**0**	**10**	**1376.1**	**259**	**4342**	**167**	**26.00**	**6-16**

GLADSTONE, George

				BATTING									BOWLING					
SEASON	TEAM	OPPONENTS	V	M	I	NO	RUNS	H.S.	AVGE	100	50	CT	OV	MD	RUNS	W	AVGE	B.B.
1929-30	Jamaica	M.C.C. Tourist	WI	1	1	1	14	*14				1	75.3	12	252	9	28.00	
1929-30	**WEST INDIES**	**ENGLAND TESTS**	**WI**	**1**	**1**	**1**	**12**	***12**					**50**	**5**	**189**	**1**	**189.00**	
		Jamaica		1	1	1	14	*14				1	75.3	12	252	9	28.00	
		West Indies		1	1	1	12	*12					50	5	189	1	189.00	
		TEST RECORD		**1**	**1**	**1**	**12**	***12**		**0**	**0**	**0**	**50**	**5**	**189**	**1**	**189.00**	**1-139**
		CAREER		**2**	**2**	**2**	**26**	***14**		**0**	**0**	**1**	**125.3**	**17**	**441**	**10**	**44.10**	**6-142**

GODDARD, John Douglas Claude

SEASON	TEAM	OPPONENTS	V	BATTING M	I	NO	RUNS	H.S.	AVGE	100	50	CT	BOWLING OV	MD	RUNS	W	AVGE	B.B.
1936-37	Barbados	Trinidad	IIs	1	2		5	4	2.50				21	5	62	2	31.00	
1937-38	Barbados	British Guiana	IIs	1	2		16	14	8.00			1	14	1	51	0		
1938-39	R.S. Grant's XI	British Guiana	IIs	2	2		32	22	16.00			1	9	3	15	0		
1938-39	Barbados	British Guiana	IIs	1	2		49	30	24.50			1	5	0	15	0		
1941-42	Barbados	Trinidad	IIs	4	7	2	276	*98	55.20		3	3	16	1	61	1	61.00	
1942-43	Barbados	Trinidad	IIs	2	4	1	209	*101	69.66	1	1	1	32	6	98	4	24.50	
1943-44	Barbados	Trinidad	IIs	2	3	1	282	*218	141.00	1		1	19.7	2	72	1	72.00	
1944-45	Barbados	British Guiana	IIs	2	3		237	179	79.00	1	1		55	3	200	9	23.20	
1944-45	Barbados	Trinidad	IIs	2	4	1	217	*164	72.33	1			15.5	1	60	1	60.00	
1946-47	Barbados	British Guiana	IIs	2	3		141	114	47.00	1		3	42.5	7	116	6	19.33	
1946-47	Barbados	Jamaica	IIs	2	4		133	54	33.25		1	9	83	19	256	10	25.60	
1947-48	Barbados	M.C.C. Tourist	WI	2	3		75	52	25.00		1	1	33	8	74	3	24.66	
1947-48	**WEST INDIES**	**ENGLAND TESTS**	**WI**	**4**	**7**	**2**	**122**	***46**	**24.40**			**4**	**149.5**	**49**	**287**	**11**	**26.09**	
1948-49	West Indies	Tour of India	I	8	9	1	217	77			1	5	174.3	64	369	19	19.42	
1948-49	**WEST INDIES**	**INDIA TESTS**	**I**	**5**	**6**	**2**	**190**	**44**	**47.50**			**4**	**120.2**	**41**	**351**	**9**	**39.00**	
1948-49	West Indies	Tour of Pakistan	P	1	1		0	0				1	50	16	119	2	59.50	
1948-49	West Indies	Tour of Ceylon	C	2	1		4	4	4.00			3	33.1	3	144	5	28.80	
1949-50	Barbados	British Guiana	IIs	2	3	2	124	*56	124.00		2		37	12	79	1	79.00	
1950	West Indies	Tour of England	E	18	15	3	203	41	16.91			16	220.4	67	496	27	18.37	
1950	**WEST INDIES**	**ENGLAND TESTS**	**E**	**4**	**6**	**2**	**106**	***58**	**26.50**		**1**	**5**	**74.4**	**29**	**122**	**6**	**20.33**	
1950-51	Barbados	Trinidad	IIs	1	2	2	73	*66			1		1	0	1	0		
1951-52	West Indies	Tour of Australia	A	6	8	1	169	*48	24.14			5	78.4	20	216	3	72.00	
1951-52	**WEST INDIES**	**AUSTRALIA TESTS**	**A**	**4**	**7**	**1**	**156**	***57**	**26.00**		**1**	**1**	**41**	**7**	**126**	**4**	**31.50**	
1951-52	**WEST INDIES**	**NEW ZEALAND TESTS**	**NZ**	**2**	**1**		**26**	**26**	**26.00**			**1**	**14**	**4**	**36**	**1**	**36.00**	
1952-53	Barbados	Indian Tourist	WI	1	1	1	50	*50			1		7	2	14	0		
1953-54	Barbados	M.C.C. Tourist	WI	1	2		13	8	6.50				37	18	66	6	11.00	
1954-55	Barbados	British Guiana	IIs	2	3	1	40	17	20.00			3	24	11	38	3	12.66	
1954-55	Barbados	Australian Tourist	WI	1	2	2	88	*77			1	2	31.2	11	67	2	33.50	
1955-56	West Indies	Tour of New Zealand	NZ	2	2		43	34	21.50			2	3	3	0	0		
1955-56	**WEST INDIES**	**NEW ZEALAND TESTS**	**NZ**	**3**	**4**	**3**	**147**	***83**	**147.00**		**1**	**6**						
1956-57	Barbados	Trinidad	IIs	1	1		16	16	16.00			1	4	1	7	1	7.00	
1956-57	Barbados	British Guiana	IIs	1	1		11	11	11.00			1	15	6	20	1	20.00	
1957	West Indies	Tour of England	E	12	13	3	131	37	13.10			11	33	13	45	6	7.50	
1957	**WEST INDIES**	**ENGLAND TESTS**	**E**	**5**	**8**	**1**	**112**	**61**	**16.00**		**1**	**1**	**58**	**18**	**128**	**2**	**64.00**	
1957	M.C.C.	Yorkshire	E	1	2		9	5	4.50			1	5	1	15	0		
1957-58	Barbados	Pakistan Tourist	WI	1	1		47	47	47.00				10	4	18	0		

	M	I	NO	RUNS	H.S.	AVGE	100	50	CT	OV	MD	RUNS	W	AVGE	B.B.
Barbados	32	53	13	2102	*218	52.55	5	12	27	503.3	118	1376	51	26.98	
West Indies	75	88	19	1626	*83	23.56		5	65	1050.5	334	2439	95	25.67	
R.S. Grant's XI	2	2		32	30	16.00			1	9	3	15	0		
M.C.C.	1	2		9	5	4.50			1	5	1	15	0		
TEST RECORD	**27**	**39**	**11**	**859**	***83**	**30.67**	**0**	**4**	**22**	**457.5**	**148**	**1050**	**33**	**31.81**	**5-31**
CAREER	**111**	**145**	**32**	**3769**	***218**	**33.35**	**5**	**17**	**94**	**1568.2**	**456**	**3845**	**146**	**26.33**	**5-20**

GOMES, Hilary Angelo

					BATTING									BOWLING					
SEASON	TEAM	OPPONENTS		V	M	I	NO	RUNS	H.S.	AVGE	100	50	CT	OV	MD	RUNS	W	AVGE	B.B.
1971-72	Trinidad	New Zealand Tourist		WI	1	2		14	14	7.00				3	1	5	0		
1972-73	E. Trinidad	C. & S. Trinidad	TC	T	2	4		194	123	48.50	1	1	2	18	7	24	1	24.00	
1972-73	Trinidad	Australian Tourist		WI	1	2	1	29	*20	29.00			1	14	4	44	1	44.00	
1973	Middlesex	Counties		E	17	22	4	456	*65	25.33		2	8	63	21	145	4	36.25	
1973-74	Trinidad	Shell Shield		IIs	4	6	1	229	98	45.80		2	1						
1973-74	E. Trinidad	C. Trinidad	TC	T	1	2		57	39	28.50				4	1	6	0		
1974	Middlesex	Counties		E	12	19	1	222	85	12.33		1	2	105	24	308	6	51.33	
1974-75	Trinidad	Shell Shield		IIs	4	8	1	482	*171	68.85	1	4	1	1	0	13	0		
1974-75	E. Trinidad	C. & N. Trinidad	TC	T	2	3		75	52	25.00		1	2	19.5	4	60	2	30.00	
1975	Middlesex	Counties		E	12	20	3	479	*93	28.17		4	1	154.5	30	449	13	34.53	
1975-76	Trinidad	Shell Shield		IIs	4	7		213	82	30.28		2	4	42	11	111	3	37.00	
1975-76	E. Trinidad	N.Trinidad	TC	T	1	2		7	7	3.50			2	8	3	19	1	19.00	
1975-76	Trinidad	Indian Tourist		WI	1	1		110	110	110.00	1			2	0	18	0		
1976	West Indies	Tour of England		E	19	32	6	1382	190	53.15	5	5	4	144.3	39	408	14	29.14	
1976	**WEST INDIES**	**ENGLAND TESTS**		**E**	**2**	**3**		**11**	**11**	**3.66**			**1**	**13**	**2**	**26**	**0**		
1976	Middlesex	Counties		E	1	2	1	42	31	42.00				12	5	21	0		
1976-77	Trinidad	Shell Shield		IIs	4	8	1	398	100	56.85	1	3	2	15	7	41	1	41.00	
1976-77	E. Trinidad	S. & C. Trinidad	TC	T	2	4	1	76	*46	25.33			1	17	4	36	2	18.00	
1976-77	Trinidad	Pakistan Tourist		WI	1	2		59	41	29.50			1	5	4	5	1	5.00	
1976-77	WI President's XI	Pakistan Tourist		WI	1	1		4	4	4.00			2						
1977-78	Trinidad	Shell Shield		IIs	4	8		261	45	32.62			5	40	10	92	2	46.00	
1977-78	Trinidad	Australian Tourist		WI	1	2		135	120	67.50	1			8	3	27	1	27.00	
1977-78	**WEST INDIES**	**AUSTRALIA TESTS**		**WI**	**3**	**6**		**265**	**115**	**44.16**	**2**			**3**	**0**	**8**	**0**		
1977-78	E. Trinidad	N. S. & C. Trinidad	TC	T	3	6		328	126	54.66	1	2	1	11	4	33	1	33.00	
1978-79	West Indies	Tour of India		I	5	10	1	350	*121	38.88	1	2	1	26	8	56	2	28.00	
1978-79	**WEST INDIES**	**INDIA TESTS**		**I**	**6**	**10**		**405**	**91**	**40.50**		**4**	**1**	**16**	**3**	**65**	**1**	**65.00**	
1978-79	West Indies	Tour of Sri Lanka		SL	2	3	1	313	*173	156.50	2			8	1	20	2	10.00	

				BATTING									BOWLING					
SEASON	TEAM	OPPONENTS	V	M	I	NO	RUNS	H.S.	AVGE	100	50	CT	OV	MD	RUNS	W	AVGE	B.B.
1978-79	Trinidad	Shell Shield	IIs	4	6		367	131	61.16	2	1	4	22	4	70	1	70.00	
1979-80	West Indies	Tour of Australia	A	3	5	2	225	*137	75.00	1	1	1	2	0	15	0		
1979-80	West Indies	Tour of New Zealand	NZ	2	4	1	29	13	9.66				22	5	56	2	28.00	
1979-80	Trinidad	Shell Shield	IIs	3	6	1	344	*116	68.80	1	2		41	10	78	1	78.00	
1979-80	N/E Trinidad	S/C Trinidad BC	T	1	2		40	32	20.00			1	11	1	43	0		
1980-81	West Indies	Tour of Pakistan	P	3	4	1	240	86	80.00		2	1	3	0	14	0		
1980-81	**WEST INDIES**	**PAKISTAN TESTS**	**P**	**4**	**5**		**145**	**61**	**29.00**		**1**		**10**	**0**	**23**	**0**		
1980-81	Trinidad	Shell Shield	IIs	3	5	3	169	*68	84.50		1	1	43	13	92	4	23.00	
1980-81	Trinidad	English Tourist	WI	1	1		75	75	75.00		1		7	4	3	0		
1980-81	**WEST INDIES**	**ENGLAND TESTS**	**WI**	**4**	**5**	**1**	**199**	***90**	**49.75**		**2**	**1**	**37**	**13**	**57**	**1**	**57.00**	
1981-82	West Indies	Tour of Australia	A	4	4	1	319	*200	106.33	1	1		27	1	82	2	41.00	
1981-82	**WEST INDIES**	**AUSTRALIA TESTS**	**A**	**3**	**6**	**1**	**393**	**126**	**78.60**	**2**	**1**	**1**	**45**	**12**	**87**	**3**	**29.00**	
1981-82	Trinidad	Shell Shield	IIs	5	9		368	92	40.88		4	1	92.2	21	265	5	53.00	
1982-83	Trinidad	Shell Shield	IIs	1	2		74	67	37.00		1		2	0	8	0		
1982-83	Trinidad	Indian Tourist	WI	1	2		49	27	24.50				18	2	51	5	51.00	
1982-83	**WEST INDIES**	**INDIA TESTS**	**WI**	**5**	**5**		**178**	**123**	**35.60**	**1**		**3**	**84**	**20**	**203**	**3**	**67.66**	
1983-84	West Indies	Tour of India	I	6	11	3	218	65	27.25		1	1	68	18	190	10	19.00	
1983-84	**WEST INDIES**	**INDIA TESTS**	**I**	**6**	**10**	**3**	**223**	**38**	**31.85**			**3**	**65.1**	**5**	**178**	**2**	**77.00**	
1983-84	Trinidad	Shell Shield	IIs	1	2		4	3	2.00			2	14	2	56	2	28.00	
1983-84	Trinidad	Australian Tourist	WI	1	2		31	23	15.50			1	7	1	28	0		
1983-84	**WEST INDIES**	**AUSTRALIA TESTS**	**WI**	**2**	**2**		**13**	**10**	**6.50**			**1**	**63**	**8**	**146**	**1**	**146.00**	
1984	West Indies	Tour of England	E	7	9	2	441	143	63.00	2	2	1	44	15	81	2	40.50	
1984	**WEST INDIES**	**ENGLAND TESTS**	**E**	**5**	**8**	**3**	**400**	**143**	**80.00**	**2**	**1**	**1**						
1984-85	West Indies	Tour of Australia	A	5	6	1	170	85	34.00		1	1	53	13	107	1	107.00	
1984-85	**WEST INDIES**	**AUSTRALIA TESTS**	**A**	**5**	**9**	**2**	**451**	**127**	**64.42**	**2**	**2**	**1**	**15**	**4**	**30**	**2**	**15.00**	
1984-85	**WEST INDIES**	**NEW ZEALAND TESTS**	**WI**	**4**	**6**		**158**	**53**	**26.33**		**1**	**2**	**18**	**3**	**44**	**0**		
1985-86	Trinidad	Shell Shield	IIs	5	9	1	243	*168	30.37	1	1	2	7	1	25	0		
1985-86	**WEST INDIES**	**ENGLAND TESTS**	**WI**	**5**	**6**		**191**	**56**	**31.83**		**1**	**2**	**1**	**1**	**0**	**0**		
1986-87	West Indies	Tour of Pakistan	P	2	2		66	66	33.00		1							
1986-87	**WEST INDIES**	**PAKISTAN TESTS**	**P**	**3**	**5**		**67**	**33**	**13.40**									
1986-87	West Indies	Tour of Australia	A	1	2	1	184	*164	184.00	1			12	1	38	1	38.00	
1986-87	West Indies	Tour of New Zealand	NZ	2	3		75	73	25.00		1		14.2	2	33	3	11.00	
1986-87	**WEST INDIES**	**NEW ZEALAND TESTS**	**NZ**	**3**	**5**	**1**	**72**	**33**	**18.00**			**1**	**30**	**8**	**63**	**2**	**31.50**	
1987-88	Trinidad	Red Stripe Cup	IIs	5	7		165	66	23.57		1	1	2	1	2	0		
		Trinidad		55	97	9	3819	*171	43.39	8	23	27	385.2	99	1034	23	44.95	
		East Trinidad		11	21	1	737	123	36.85	2	4	8	77.5	23	178	7	25.42	

	M	I	NO	RUNS	H.S.	AVGE	100	50	CT	OV	MD	RUNS	W	AVGE	B.B.
North/East Trinidad	1	2		40	32	20.00			1	11	1	43	0		
West Indies	122	187	31	7187	*200	46.07	22	30	30	824	182	2030	54	37.59	
Middlesex	42	63	9	1199	*93	22.20		7	11	334.5	80	923	23	40.13	
TEST RECORD	**60**	**91**	**11**	**3171**	**143**	**39.63**	**9**	**13**	**18**	**400.1**	**77**	**930**	**15**	**62.00**	**2-20**
CAREER	**231**	**370**	**50**	**12982**	***200**	**40.56**	**32**	**64**	**77**	**1633**	**385**	**4208**	**107**	**39.32**	**4-22**

GOMEZ, Gerald Ethridge

				BATTING							BOWLING							
SEASON	TEAM	OPPONENTS	V	M	I	NO	RUNS	H.S.	AVGE	100	50	CT	OV	MD	RUNS	W	AVGE	B.B.
1937-38	Trinidad	British Guiana	IIs	1	2		54	39	27.00				3	0	15	0		
1938-39	R.S. Grant's XI	British Guiana	IIs	2	3	1	227	119	113.50	1	1	1	7	1	23	1	21.00	
1938-39	Trinidad	Barbados	IIs	1	1		0	0										
1938-39	Trinidad	British Guiana	IIs	1	1		1	1	1.00			1						
1938-39	Trinidad	Jamaica	IIs	1	2	1	163	*161	163.00	1								
1939	West Indies	Tour of England	E	17	27	2	697	90	27.88		5	9						
1939	**WEST INDIES**	**ENGLAND TESTS**	**E**	**2**	**3**		**22**	**11**	**7.33**			**2**						
1940-41	Trinidad	Barbados	IIs	2	3		72	51	24.00		1		3	0	10	0		
1941-42	Trinidad	Barbados	IIs	4	7	1	269	133	44.83	1		5	9	1	44	0		
1942-43	Trinidad	Barbados	IIs	2	2	1	333	*216	333.00	2		1	8	0	49	0		
1943-44	Trinidad	Barbados	IIs	2	3		147	94	49.00		1	2	2	0	16	0		
1943-44	Trinidad	British Guiana	IIs	1	1		12	12	12.00									
1944-45	Trinidad	Barbados	IIs	2	3	1	166	*108	83.00	1	1	2						
1945-46	Trinidad	British Guiana	IIs	2	4		142	60	35.50		1	1	12	4	24	0		
1945-46	Trinidad	Barbados	IIs	2	3	1	275	*213	137.50	1		3	15	0	78	1	78.00	
1945-46	Trinidad	Jamaica	IIs	3	6		161	62	26.83		1	3	50	3	166	2	83.00	
1946-47	Trinidad	British Guiana	IIs	2	3		232	190	77.33	1			39	7	90	2	45.00	
1947-48	Trinidad	M.C.C. Tourist	WI	2	3	1	235	*178	117.50	1		2	39	7	104	4	26.00	
1947-48	**WEST INDIES**	**ENGLAND TESTS**	**WI**	**4**	**6**	**1**	**232**	**86**	**46.40**		**2**	**4**	**9**	**2**	**31**	**1**	**31.00**	
1948-49	West Indies	Tour of India	I	9	13	4	384	58	42.66		2	4	323.3	98	606	44	13.77	
1948-49	**WEST INDIES**	**INDIA TESTS**	**I**	**5**	**7**		**256**	**101**	**36.57**	**1**	**1**	**1**	**257.3**	**84**	**454**	**16**	**28.37**	
1948-49	West Indies	Tour of Pakistan	P	2	2	1	18	*18	18.00			2	101.3	39	169	10	16.90	
1948-49	West Indies	Tour of Ceylon	C	1	D							4	47	17	99	1	99.00	
1949-50	Trinidad	Jamaica	IIs	2	1		99	99	99.00		1		43	13	84	0		
1950	West Indies	Tour of England	E	23	24	4	909	149	45.45	2	3	27	600.3	196	1244	53	23.47	
1950	**WEST INDIES**	**ENGLAND TESTS**	**E**	**4**	**6**	**1**	**207**	**74**	**41.40**		**2**	**5**	**80**	**25**	**163**	**2**	**81.50**	
1951-52	West Indies	Tour of Australia	A	5	9	1	211	*97	26.37		1	3	71.2	10	254	9	28.22	
1951-52	**WEST INDIES**	**AUSTRALIA TESTS**	**A**	**5**	**10**	**1**	**324**	**55**	**36.00**		**3**	**3**	**104.2**	**23**	**256**	**18**	**14.22**	

SEASON	TEAM	OPPONENTS	V	M	I	NO	RUNS	H.S.	AVGE	100	50	CT	OV	MD	RUNS	W	AVGE	B.B.
				BATTING									BOWLING					
1951-52	West Indies	Tour of New Zealand	NZ	1	1		20	20	20.00				9	4	11	0		
1951-52	**WEST INDIES**	**NEW ZEALAND TESTS**	**NZ**	**1**	**2**	**1**	**14**	***14**	**14.00**				**40**	**15**	**72**	**3**	**24.00**	
1952-53	Trinidad	Indian Tourist	WI	1	1		5	5	5.00				25.4	16	21	2	10.50	
1952-53	**WEST INDIES**	**INDIA TESTS**	**WI**	**4**	**5**		**62**	**35**	**12.40**			**1**	**219.1**	**91**	**351**	**11**	**31.90**	
1953-54	Trinidad	British Guiana	IIs	2	4	2	365	148	182.50	2	1	1	81	38	157	7	22.44	
1953-54	Trinidad	M.C.C. Tourist	WI	1	2	1	116	91	116.00		1	1	21	4	45	1	45.00	
1953-54	**WEST INDIES**	**ENGLAND TESTS**	**WI**	**4**	**7**	**1**	**126**	***47**	**21.00**			**2**	**128**	**38**	**263**	**7**	**37.57**	
1954-55	Trinidad	Australian Tourist	WI	1	1		45	45	45.00			1	24	9	57	1	57.00	
1955-56	Trinidad	E.W. Swanton's Tourist	WI	1	2		101	88	50.50		1	1	32	7	63	2	31.50	
1957	M.C.C.	Oxford University	E	1	2		62	31	31.00				15	5	33	2	16.50	
		Trinidad		36	55	9	2993	*216	65.06	10	9	24	406.4	109	1023	22	46.50	
		West Indies		87	122	17	3482	149	33.16	3	19	67	1990.5	642	3973	175	22.71	
		R.S. Grant's XI		2	3	1	227	119	113.50	1	1	1	7	1	23	1	23.00	
		M.C.C.		1	2		62	31	31.00				15	5	33	2	16.50	
		TEST RECORD		**29**	**46**	**5**	**1243**	**101**	**30.31**	**1**	**8**	**18**	**798**	**278**	**1590**	**58**	**27.41**	**7-55**
		CAREER		**126**	**182**	**27**	**6764**	***216**	**43.63**	**14**	**29**	**92**	**2419.3**	**757**	**5052**	**200**	**25.26**	**9-24**

GRANT, George Copeland

SEASON	TEAM	OPPONENTS	V	M	I	NO	RUNS	H.S.	AVGE	100	50	CT	OV	MD	RUNS	W	AVGE	B.B.
				BATTING									BOWLING					
1928	Cambridge Univ.	Counties	E	1	1	1	5	*5				1	8	1	24	0		
1929	Cambridge Univ.	Counties	E	14	23	1	691	98	31.40		5	7	121	16	419	5	83.80	
1930	Cambridge Univ.	Counties	E	11	18	2	716	100	44.75	1	1	9	51	5	191	2	95.50	
1930-31	West Indies	Tour of Australia	A	9	14		484	102	34.57	1	2	8						
1930-31	**WEST INDIES**	**AUSTRALIA TESTS**	**A**	**5**	**10**	**4**	**255**	***71**	**42.50**		**3**	**3**	**1**	**0**	**1**	**0**		
1931-32	Rhodesia	Currie Cup	SA	5	9		215	68	23.88		1	7	25	2	75	3	25.00	
1932-33	G.C. Grant's XI	C.A. Merry's XI	WI	1	2		6	6	3.00			1						
1933	West Indies	Tour of England	E	24	40	7	1093	115	33.12	2	4	21	43	1	234	9	26.00	
1933	**WEST INDIES**	**ENGLAND TESTS**	**E**	**3**	**6**		**102**	**28**	**17.00**			**2**	**2**	**0**	**12**	**0**		
1933-34	Trinidad	Barbados	IIs	1	2		85	80	42.50		1	1						
1934-35	Trinidad	British Guiana	IIs	1	2		42	23	21.00			1	2	0	6	0		
1934-35	Trinidad	M.C.C. Tourist	WI	2	4	1	81	35	27.00			5	2	0	2	0		
1934-35	**WEST INDIES**	**ENGLAND TESTS**	**WI**	**4**	**5**	**1**	**56**	**23**	**14.00**			**5**	**1**	**0**	**5**	**0**		

SEASON	TEAM	OPPONENTS	V	M	I	NO	RUNS	H.S.	AVGE	100	50	CT	OV	MD	RUNS	W	AVGE	B.B.
		Trinidad		4	8	1	208	80	29.71		1	7	4	0	8	0		
		West Indies		45	75	12	1990	115	31.58	3	9	39	47	1	252	9	28.00	
		Cambridge University		26	42	4	1412	100	37.15	1	6	17	180	22	634	7	90.57	
		Rhodesia		5	9		215	68	23.88		1	7	25	2	75	3	25.00	
		G.C. Grant's XI		1	2		6	6	3.00			1						
		TEST RECORD		**12**	**21**	**5**	**413**	***71**	**25.81**	**0**	**3**	**10**	**4**	**0**	**18**	**0**		
		CAREER		**81**	**136**	**17**	**3831**	**115**	**32.19**	**4**	**17**	**71**	**256**	**25**	**969**	**19**	**51.00**	**3-24**

GRANT, Rolph Stewart

				BATTING									BOWLING					
SEASON	TEAM	OPPONENTS	V	M	I	NO	RUNS	H.S.	AVGE	100	50	CT	OV	MD	RUNS	W	AVGE	B.B.
1932	Cambridge Univ.	Counties	E	3	6		72	22	12.00			6	31	4	105	2	52.50	
1933	Cambridge Univ.	Counties	E	7	11	2	158	29	17.55			12	158	49	378	15	25.20	
1933	West Indies	Cambridge University	E	1	2	1	16	10	16.00			3	7	2	11	3	3.66	
1933-34	Trinidad	Barbados	IIs	1	2		207	152	103.50	1	1	2	30	18	24	2	12.00	
1934-35	Trinidad	British Guiana	IIs	1	2		9	9	4.50			2	33	14	63	3	21.00	
1934-35	Trinidad	M.C.C. Tourist	WI	2	4		105	37	26.25			1	49	6	139	5	27.80	
1934-35	**WEST INDIES**	**ENGLAND TESTS**	**WI**	**4**	**6**	**1**	**122**	**77**	**24.40**		**1**	**9**	**120**	**27**	**245**	**9**	**27.22**	
1936-37	Trinidad	Barbados	IIs	1	1		3	3	3.00				59	26	81	6	13.50	
1936-37	Trinidad	British Guiana	IIs	1	1		28	28	28.00				18	8	31	0		
1938-39	R.S. Grant's XI	British Guiana	IIs	2	3		197	70	65.66		3	2	45	11	140	5	28.00	
1938-39	Trinidad	Barbados	IIs	1	1		93	93	93.00		1	2	6	1	21	0		
1938-39	Trinidad	British Guiana	IIs	1	1		5	5	5.00			2	8	3	19	1	19.00	
1938-39	Trinidad	Jamaica	IIs	1	1		0	0				1	15	3	43	3	14.33	
1938-39	West Indies XI	Jamaica	IIs	1	1		83	83	83.00		1	1	9	2	13	0		
1939	West Indies	Tour of England	E	18	27	4	687	95	29.86		3	19	178.3	28	568	23	24.69	
1939	**WEST INDIES**	**ENGLAND TESTS**	**E**	**3**	**5**		**98**	**47**	**19.60**			**4**	**33.2**	**5**	**108**	**2**	**54.00**	
		Trinidad		9	13		450	152	34.61	1	2	10	218	79	421	20	21.05	
		West Indies		27	41	6	1006	95	28.74		5	36	347.5	64	945	37	25.54	
		Cambridge University		10	17	2	230	29	15.33			18	189	53	483	17	28.41	
		R.S. Grant's XI		2	3		197	70	65.66		3	2	45	11	140	5	28.00	
		TEST RECORD		**7**	**11**	**1**	**220**	**77**	**22.00**	**0**	**1**	**13**	**153.2**	**32**	**353**	**11**	**32.09**	**3-68**
		CAREER		**48**	**74**	**8**	**1883**	**152**	**28.53**	**1**	**10**	**66**	**799.5**	**207**	**1989**	**79**	**25.17**	**4-41**

GRAY, Anthony Hollis

SEASON	TEAM	OPPONENTS		V	M	I	NO	RUNS	H.S.	AVGE	100	50	CT	OV	MD	RUNS	W	AVGE	B.B.
					BATTING									BOWLING					
1983-84	N Trinidad	South Trinidad	BC	T	1	2		28	21	14.00			1	20	0	94	1	94.00	
1983-84	Trinidad	Shell Shield		IIs	3	4	2	77	*31	38.50			1	51	5	221	7	31.57	
1983-84	Trinidad	Australian Tourist		WI	1	2	1	44	*41	44.00				25	5	91	2	45.50	
1984-85	N/E Trinidad	S/C Trinidad	BC	T	1	1		9	9	9.00			1	27	6	65	2	32.50	
1984-85	Trinidad	Shell Shield		IIs	5	7		69	26	9.85			1	125	15	458	23	19.91	
1984-85	WI Shell Awards XI	New Zealand Tourist		WI	1	1		9	9	9.00			2	33.2	6	88	6	14.66	
1984-85	WI Under 23 XI	New Zealand Tourist		WI	1	1		7	7	7.00				29	10	65	3	21.66	
1984-85	WI President's XI	New Zealand Tourist		WI	1	1		1	1	1.00			1	26	1	95	2	47.50	
1985	Surrey	Counties		E	19	10	1	48	20	5.33			3	524	99	1816	79	22.98	
1985-86	Trinidad	Shell Shield		IIs	5	8	2	84	*54	14.00		1	3	122.5	15	392	17	23.05	
1985-86	Trinidad	English Tourist		WI	1	1		2	2	2.00			1	35.3	11	89	7	12.71	
1986	Surrey	Counties		E	11	14	2	108	28	9.00			4	342.3	69	966	51	18.94	
1986-87	West Indies	Tour of Pakistan		P	1	1		1	1	1.00				11	2	39	5	7.80	
1986-87	**WEST INDIES**	**PAKISTAN TESTS**		**P**	**3**	**5**	**1**	**27**	***12**	**6.75**			**2**	**99**	**27**	**227**	**14**	**16.21**	
1986-87	West Indies	Tour of New Zealand		NZ	2	D								61	14	172	7	24.57	
1986-87	**WEST INDIES**	**NEW ZEALAND TESTS**		**NZ**	**2**	**3**	**1**	**21**	***10**	**10.50**			**4**	**49**	**10**	**150**	**8**	**18.75**	
1986-87	Trinidad	Shell Shield		IIs	1	2	1	15	*14	15.00				24	3	89	0		
1987	Surrey	Counties		E	10	8	3	67	35	13.40			4	291.1	59	748	48	15.58	
1987-88	Trinidad	Red Stripe Cup		IIs	5	7		130	47	18.57				108	15	349	14	24.92	
1987-88	WI President's XI	Pakistan Tourist		WI	1	1		20	20	20.00				34	3	85	1	85.00	
1987-88	WI Board XI	Pakistan Tourist		WI	1	1		15	15	15.00			1	39	8	123	2	61.50	
1988	Surrey	Counties		E	1	D								26	13	38	2	19.00	
1988-89	Trinidad	Red Stripe Cup		IIs	4	6	1	70	47	14.00			3	93.1	16	343	11	31.18	
1988-89	WI President's XI	Indian Tourist		WI	1	1		4	4	4.00			1	48	8	174	6	29.00	
1988-89	WI Board XI	Indian Tourist		WI	1	D								16.1	4	31	3	10.33	
1989-90	West Indies 'B'	Tour of Zimbabwe		Z	3	3		30	14	10.00			1	81.3	22	162	18	9.00	
1989-90	Trinidad	Red Stripe Cup		IIs	1	2		1	1	0.50				15	1	52	1	52.00	
1990	Surrey	Counties		E	7	2		22	11	11.00			7	239.5	43	666	19	35.05	
		Trinidad			26	39	7	492	*54	15.37		1	9	599.3	86	2084	82	25.41	
		North Trinidad			1	2		28	21	14.00			1	20	0	94	1	94.00	
		N/E Trinidad			1	1		9	9	9.00			1	27	6	65	2	32.50	
		West Indies			18	18	2	135	20	8.43			12	527	115	1411	75	18.81	
		Surrey			48	34	6	245	35	8.75			18	1423.3	283	4234	199	21.27	
		TEST RECORD			**5**	**8**	**2**	**48**	***12**	**8.00**			**6**	**148**	**37**	**377**	**22**	**17.13**	**4-39**
		CAREER			**94**	**94**	**15**	**909**	***54**	**11.50**		**1**	**41**	**2597**	**490**	**7888**	**359**	**21.97**	**8-40**

GREENIDGE, Alvin Ethelbert

				BATTING									BOWLING					
SEASON	TEAM	OPPONENTS	V	M	I	NO	RUNS	H.S.	AVGE	100	50	CT	OV	MD	RUNS	W	AVGE	B.B.
1974-75	Barbados	Shell Shield	IIs	3	6		156	72	26.00		1	3						
1976-77	Barbados	Pakistan Tourist	WI	1	2		52	51	26.00		1	1						
1977-78	Barbados	Shell Shield	IIs	4	7	1	293	164	49.16	1	1	4	4	0	17	0		
1977-78	Barbados	Australian Tourist	WI	1	2		107	96	53.50		1							
1977-78	**WEST INDIES**	**AUSTRALIA TESTS**	**WI**	**2**	**4**		**142**	**69**	**35.50**		**2**	**2**						
1978-79	West Indies	Tour of India	I	8	14		287	48	16.88			3	13	1	41	1	41.00	
1978-79	**WEST INDIES**	**INDIA TESTS**	**I**	**4**	**6**		**80**	**32**	**13.33**			**3**						
1978-79	West Indies	Tour of Sri Lanka	SL	2	3		30	26	8.66			2	4.4	2	6	1	6.00	
1978-79	Barbados	Shell Shield	IIs	4	6	1	260	109	52.00	1	1	4	24.4	2	82	3	27.33	2-52
1979-80	Barbados	Shell Shield	IIs	3	4		138	101	34.50	1		3						
1980-81	Barbados	Shell Shield	IIs	3	4	1	134	*74	44.60		1	1						
1981-82	Barbados	Shell Shield	IIs	5	7	1	315	172	52.50	1		2						
1982-83	WI Rebels XI	Tour of South Africa	SA	2	4	1	117	48	39.00									
1983-84	WI Rebels XI	Tour of South Africa	SA	6	12		208	43	17.33			4	1	0	1	0		
		Barbados		24	38	4	1455	172	42.79	4	6	18	28.4	2	99	3	33.00	
		West Indies		16	27		539	69	19.96		2	10	17.4	3	47	2	23.50	
		WI Rebels XI		8	16	1	325	48	21.66			4	1	0	1	0		
		TEST RECORD		**6**	**10**	**0**	**222**	**69**	**22.20**	**0**	**2**	**5**						
		CAREER		**48**	**81**	**5**	**2319**	**172**	**30.51**	**4**	**8**	**32**	**47.2**	**5**	**147**	**5**	**29.40**	**2-52**

GREENIDGE, Cuthbert Gordon

				BATTING									BOWLING					
SEASON	TEAM	OPPONENTS	V	M	I	NO	RUNS	H.S.	AVGE	100	50	CT	OV	MD	RUNS	W	AVGE	B.B.
1970	Hampshire	Counties	E	7	11	1	351	73	35.10		4	6	1	1	0	0		
1971	Hampshire	Counties	E	24	45	2	1164	102	27.02	1	6	13	25	7	57	5	11.40	
1972	Hampshire	Counties	E	22	38	1	1230	142	33.24	2	6	10	59	11	173	3	57.66	
1972-73	Barbados	Shell Shield	IIs	4	8		304	88	38.00		2	2	0.3	0	4	0		
1972-73	Barbados	Australian Tourist	WI	1	2		21	17	10.50				1.3	0	17	0		
1972-73	WI President's XI	Australian Tourist	WI	1	2		43	23	21.50			1	0.5	0	4	0		
1973	Hampshire	Counties	E	22	38	4	1656	*196	48.70	5	9	36	10.2	3	36	2	18.00	
1973-74	Barbados	Shell Shield	IIs	4	7	1	247	90	41.16		2	1						
1973-74	Barbados	M.C.C. Tourist	WI	1	2	1	41	36	41.00			3						
1973-74	WI President's XI	M.C.C. Tourist	WI	1	2		65	37	32.50				6	2	22	0		

				BATTING									BOWLING					
SEASON	TEAM	OPPONENTS	V	M	I	NO	RUNS	H.S.	AVGE	100	50	CT	OV	MD	RUNS	W	AVGE	B.B.
1974	Hampshire	Counties	E	21	31	1	804	120	26.80	1	6	22						
1974	D.H. Robins' XI	Pakistan Tourist	E	1	2	1	289	*273	289.00	1		1						
1974-75	West Indies	Tour of India	I	7	12	2	498	71	49.80		5	4	1	0	4	0		
1974-75	**WEST INDIES**	**INDIA TESTS**	**I**	**5**	**9**		**371**	**107**	**41.22**	**1**	**2**	**5**						
1974-75	West Indies	Tour of Pakistan	P	1	2	1	40	27	40.00									
1974-75	Barbados	Shell Shield	IIs	1	2		14	8	7.00									
1975	Hampshire	Counties	E	16	27		1120	259	41.48	2	4	26	19	4	92	5	18.40	
1975-76	West Indies	Tour of Australia	A	5	9		279	76	31.00		3	3						
1975-76	**WEST INDIES**	**AUSTRALIA TESTS**	**A**	**2**	**4**		**11**	**8**	**2.75**			**1**	**1**	**1**	**0**	**0**		
1975-76	Barbados	Shell Shield	IIs	1	1		106	106	106.00	1		1						
1975-76	Barbados	Indian Tourist	WI	1	1		21	21	21.00			2						
1976	West Indies	Tour of England	E	15	28	2	1360	130	52.30	5	6	21						
1976	**WEST INDIES**	**ENGLAND TESTS**	**E**	**5**	**10**	**1**	**592**	**134**	**65.77**	**3**	**2**	**7**						
1976-77	Barbados	Shell Shield	IIs	4	7		323	136	46.14	1	2							
1976-77	**WEST INDIES**	**PAKISTAN TESTS**	**WI**	**5**	**10**		**536**	**100**	**53.60**	**1**	**4**	**8**						
1977	Hampshire	Counties	E	19	32	3	1771	208	61.06	6	6	18	1	0	4	0		
1977-78	**WEST INDIES**	**AUSTRALIA TESTS**	**WI**	**2**	**3**	**1**	**131**	***80**	**15.50**		**1**	**1**						
1978	Hampshire	Counties	E	19	34	1	1771	211	53.66	5	9	34	4	2	8	1	8.00	
1978-79	Barbados	Shell Shield	IIs	1	1		31	31	31.00			1	4	0	10	0		
1979	Hampshire	Counties	E	17	30	2	1404	145	50.14	3	8	27						
1979-80	West Indies	Tour of Australia	A	3	5		135	45	27.00			10						
1979-80	**WEST INDIES**	**AUSTRALIA TESTS**	**A**	**3**	**6**	**1**	**173**	**76**	**34.60**		**1**	**3**						
1979-80	West Indies	Tour of New Zealand	NZ	2	4		136	116	34.00	1		1						
1979-80	**WEST INDIES**	**NEW ZEALAND TESTS**	**NZ**	**3**	**6**		**274**	**97**	**45.66**		**3**	**4**						
1980	West Indies	Tour of England	E	8	12	2	453	165	45.30	1	1	3	3	1	2	0		
1980	**WEST INDIES**	**ENGLAND TESTS**	**E**	**5**	**6**		**124**	**53**	**20.66**		**1**	**3**	**3**	**2**	**4**	**0**		
1980	Hampshire	Counties	E	3	6		167	65	27.83		1							
1980-81	West Indies	Tour of Pakistan	P	3	5		194	82	38.80		2							
1980-81	Barbados	Shell Shield	IIs	2	3		108	82	36.00		1	3						
1980-81	Barbados	English Tourist	WI	1	1		45	45	45.00			1						
1980-81	**WEST INDIES**	**ENGLAND TESTS**	**WI**	**4**	**5**		**223**	**84**	**44.60**		**3**	**6**						
1981	Hampshire	Counties	E	19	30	1	1442	140	49.72	4	9	24	0.4	0	1	0		
1981-82	West Indies	Tour of Australia	A	3	4		45	28	11.25			2						
1981-82	**WEST INDIES**	**AUSTRALIA TESTS**	**A**	**2**	**4**		**134**	**66**	**33.50**		**2**	**1**						
1981-82	Barbados	Shell Shield	IIs	3	4		216	101	54.00	1	1	2						
1982	Hampshire	Counties	E	21	41	8	1526	*183	46.24	3	4	23						
1982-83	West Indies XI	International XI	WI	1	1		43	43	43.00									

1982-83	Barbados	Shell Shield	IIs	5	10	1	155	38	17.22			6					
1982-83	Barbados	Indian Tourist	WI	1	1		237	237	237.00	1							
1982-83	**WEST INDIES**	**INDIA TESTS**	**WI**	**5**	**7**	**2**	**393**	***154**	**76.14**	**1**	**3**	**4**					
1983	Hampshire	Counties	E	15	27	5	1438	154	65.36	4	9	21					
1983-84	West Indies	Tour of India	I	4	7	2	304	*190	60.80	1	1	2					
1983-84	**WEST INDIES**	**INDIA TESTS**	**I**	**6**	**10**	**2**	**411**	**194**	**51.37**	**1**	**1**	**2**					
1983-84	Barbados	Shell Shield	IIs	1	2		60	45	30.00								
1983-84	**WEST INDIES**	**AUSTRALIA TESTS**	**WI**	**5**	**8**	**3**	**393**	**127**	**78.60**	**2**	**1**	**6**					
1984	West Indies	Tour of England	E	6	8	2	497	138	82.83	2	3	2	9	6	11	1	11.00
1984	**WEST INDIES**	**ENGLAND TESTS**	**E**	**5**	**8**	**1**	**572**	**223**	**81.71**	**2**		**3**					
1984-85	West Indies	Tour of Australia	A	4	7		255	79	36.42		2	4	3	0	7	0	
1984-85	**WEST INDIES**	**AUSTRALIA TESTS**	**A**	**5**	**8**		**214**	**95**	**26.75**		**1**	**5**					
1984-85	**WEST INDIES**	**NEW ZEALAND TESTS**	**WI**	**4**	**7**	**2**	**264**	**100**	**52.80**	**1**	**1**	**3**					
1985	Hampshire	Counties	E	19	32	2	1236	204	41.20	2	8	16	4	1	16	0	
1985-86	Barbados	Shell Shield	IIs	4	8	1	361	90	51.57		4	6					
1985-86	**WEST INDIES**	**ENGLAND TESTS**	**WI**	**5**	**6**		**217**	**58**	**36.16**		**1**	**3**					
1986	Hampshire	Counties	E	20	34	4	2035	222	67.83	8	6	18					
1986-87	West Indies	Tour of Pakistan	P	3	5	1	93	34	23.25			3					
1986-87	**WEST INDIES**	**PAKISTAN TESTS**	**P**	**3**	**5**		**132**	**75**	**26.40**		**1**	**3**					
1986-87	West Indies	Tour of Australia	A	1	1	1	16	*16									
1986-87	West Indies	Tour of New Zealand	NZ	1	1		39	39	39.00			2					
1986-87	**WEST INDIES**	**NEW ZEALAND TESTS**	**NZ**	**3**	**6**	**1**	**344**	**213**	**68.80**	**1**	**1**	**1**					
1986-87	Barbados	Shell Shield	IIs	1	1		202	202	202.00	1							
1987	Hampshire	Counties	E	11	16		725	163	45.31	2	5	21					
1987	M.C.C.	Rest of World XI	E	1	2		174	122	87.00	1	1						
1987-88	West Indies	Tour of India	I	2	3		269	174	89.66	1	1						
1987-88	**WEST INDIES**	**INDIA TESTS**	**I**	**3**	**6**		**260**	**141**	**43.33**	**1**	**1**	**4**					
1987-88	Barbados	Red Stripe Cup	IIs	3	6	1	215	70	43.00		1						
1987-88	**WEST INDIES**	**PAKISTAN TESTS**	**WI**	**3**	**6**		**135**	**43**	**22.50**			**6**					
1988	West Indies	Tour of England	E	7	10	1	480	111	53.33	2	3	2					
1988	**WEST INDIES**	**ENGLAND TESTS**	**E**	**4**	**6**		**282**	**103**	**47.00**	**1**	**1**	**4**					
1988-89	West Indies	Tour of Australia	A	4	6	1	403	213	80.60	1	2	1					
1988-89	**WEST INDIES**	**AUSTRALIA TESTS**	**A**	**5**	**10**	**1**	**397**	**104**	**44.11**	**1**	**2**	**4**					
1988-89	Barbados	Red Stripe Cup	IIs	1	1		0	0				1					
1988-89	**WEST INDIES**	**INDIA TESTS**	**WI**	**4**	**7**		**243**	**117**	**34.71**	**1**	**1**	**3**					
1989	Rest Of World XI	M.C.C. XI	E	1	2		30	25	15.00			1					
1989-90	Barbados	Red Stripe Cup	IIs	4	6	1	356	128	71.20	2	1	6					
1989-90	Barbados	English Tourist	WI	1	2		234	183	117.00	1	1	1					
1989-90	**WEST INDIES**	**ENGLAND TESTS**	**WI**	**4**	**7**		**308**	**149**	**44.00**	**1**		**3**					

SEASON	TEAM	OPPONENTS	V	M	I	NO	RUNS	H.S.	AVGE	100	50	CT	OV	MD	RUNS	W	AVGE	B.B.
				BATTING									BOWLING					
1990	Rest of World XI	Indian Tourist	E	1	2		23	23	11.50			1						
		Barbados		45	76	6	3297	237	47.10	8	15	36	6	0	31	0		
		West Indies		182	304	30	12781	223	46.64	32	63	154	26.5	12	54	1	54.00	
		Hampshire		275	472	35	19840	259	58.87	48	100	315	124	29	387	16	24.18	
		Rest of World XI		2	4		53	25	13.25			2						
		D. H. Robins' XI		1	2	1	289	*273	289.00	1		1						
		M.C.C.		1	2		174	122	87.00	1	1							
		TEST RECORD		**100**	**170**	**15**	**7134**	**223**	**46.02**	**18**	**34**	**93**	**4**	**3**	**4**	**0**		
		CAREER		**506**	**860**	**72**	**36434**	***273**	**46.23**	**90**	**179**	**508**	**156.5**	**41**	**472**	**17**	**27.76**	**5-49**

GREENIDGE, Geoffrey Alan

SEASON	TEAM	OPPONENTS	V	M	I	NO	RUNS	H.S.	AVGE	100	50	CT	OV	MD	RUNS	W	AVGE	B.B.
				BATTING									BOWLING					
1966-67	Barbados	Shell Shield	IIs	4	5		265	205	53.00	1		2	62.2	6	309	8	38.62	
1967-68	WI President's XI	M.C.C. Tourist	WI	1	1		28	28	28.00				9	1	31	0		
1968	Sussex	Counties	E	12	21	3	343	91	19.05		2	3	8	1	34	0		
1968-69	Barbados	Shell Shield	IIs	3	5		41	20	8.20				12	4	38	0		
1969	Sussex	Counties	E	12	19	1	426	141	23.66	1	3	8	6	2	20	1	20.00	
1970	Sussex	Counties	E	24	44		1305	172	29.65	5	3	10	53.3	6	220	4	55.00	
1971	Sussex	Counties	E	27	52	2	1334	*109	26.68	1	8	15	6	0	36	0		
1971-72	Barbados	Shell Shield	IIs	4	6	1	150	*58	30.00		1	2	7	2	24	0		
1971-72	Barbados	New Zealand Tourist	WI	1	2		132	126	66.00	1			3	0	12	0		
1971-72	**WEST INDIES**	**NEW ZEALAND TESTS**	**WI**	**2**	**4**	**1**	**144**	**50**	**48.00**		**1**	**2**	**15**	**4**	**36**	**0**		
1972	Sussex	Counties	E	22	40	3	1213	*142	32.78	2	7	10						
1972-73	Barbados	Shell Shield	IIs	3	6		308	99	51.33		4	1	4	1	15	0		
1972-73	Barbados	Australian Tourist	WI	1	2	1	169	*148	169.00	1		1						
1972-73	**WEST INDIES**	**AUSTRALIA TESTS**	**WI**	**3**	**5**	**1**	**65**	**24**	**16.25**			**1**	**11**	**0**	**39**	**0**		
1973	Sussex	Counties	E	21	41	4	1331	110	35.97	2	8	8	8	0	48	0		
1973-74	Barbados	Shell Shield	IIs	3	6	1	94	61	18.80		1	1						
1974	Sussex	Counties	E	21	42	3	1187	147	30.43	2	4	16	7	0	45	0		
1974-75	D.H. Robins' XI	Tour of South Africa	SA	1	D													
1975	Sussex	Counties	E	13	24		490	70	20.40		3	14	10	1	41	0		
1975-76	International XI	Tour of Rhodesia	R	1	2	1	9	*7	9.00									
1975-76	Barbados	Shell Shield	IIs	3	5		78	31	15.60			1						

SEASON	TEAM	OPPONENTS	V	M	I	NO	RUNS	H.S.	AVGE	100	50	CT	OV	MD	RUNS	W	AVGE	B.B.
		Barbados		22	37	3	1237	205	36.38	3	6	8	88.2	13	398	8	49.75	
		West Indies		6	10	2	237	50	29.62		1	3	35	5	106	0		
		Sussex		152	283	16	7629	172	28.57	13	38	84	98.3	10	444	5	88.80	
		D.H. Robins' XI		1	D													
		International XI		1	2	1	9	*7	9.00									
		TEST RECORD		**5**	**9**	**2**	**209**	**50**	**29.85**	**0**	**1**	**3**	**26**	**4**	**75**	**0**		
		CAREER		**182**	**332**	**22**	**9112**	**205**	**29.39**	**16**	**45**	**95**	**221.5**	**28**	**948**	**13**	**72.92**	**7-124**

GRELL, Mervyn George

				BATTING									BOWLING					
SEASON	TEAM	OPPONENTS	V	M	I	NO	RUNS	H.S.	AVGE	100	50	CT	OV	MD	RUNS	W	AVGE	B.B.
1929-30	Trinidad	M.C.C. Tourist	WI	2	4	1	128	54	42.66		1		23	2	62	4	15.50	
1929-30	**WEST INDIES**	**ENGLAND TESTS**	**WI**	**1**	**2**		**34**	**21**	**17.00**			**1**	**5**	**1**	**17**	**0**		
1933-34	Trinidad	Barbados	IIs	1	2		53	53	26.50		1		5	0	9	0		
1934-35	Trinidad	British Guiana	IIs	1	2		61	34	30.50				3	0	11	0		
1934-35	Trinidad	M.C.C. Tourist	WI	2	4		33	28	8.25									
1936-37	Trinidad	Barbados	IIs	1	2		83	53	41.50		1	1	16	2	41	1	41.00	
1936-37	Trinidad	British Guiana	IIs	1	1		20	20	20.00									
1937-38	Trinidad	British Guiana	IIs	1	2	1	77	*74	77.00		1		8	0	32	0		
		Trinidad		9	17	2	455	*74	30.33		4	1	55	4	155	5	31.00	
		West Indies		1	2		34	21	17.00			1	5	1	17	0		
		TEST RECORD		**1**	**2**	**0**	**34**	**21**	**17.00**	**0**	**0**	**1**	**5**	**1**	**17**	**0**		
		CAREER		**10**	**19**	**2**	**489**	***74**	**28.76**	**0**	**4**	**2**	**60**	**5**	**172**	**5**	**34.40**	**2-14**

GRIFFITH, Charles Christopher

				BATTING									BOWLING					
SEASON	TEAM	OPPONENTS	V	M	I	NO	RUNS	H.S.	AVGE	100	50	CT/St	OV	MD	RUNS	W	AVGE	B.B.
1959-60	Barbados	M.C.C. Tourist	WI	1	D							2	44	8	130	6	21.66	
1959-60	**WEST INDIES**	**ENGLAND TESTS**	**WI**	**1**	**1**	**1**	**5**	***5**					**24**	**3**	**102**	**1**	**102.00**	
1960-61	Barbados	Trinidad	IIs	1	1	1	0	*0					11	3	36	1	36.00	
1961-62	Barbados	Jamaica	IIs	1	1	1	13	*13					40	9	108	6	18.00	
1961-62	Barbados	British Guiana	IIs	1	2		35	35	17.50				40	10	88	5	17.60	
1961-62	Barbados	Indian Tourist	WI	1	1		19	19	19.00				19	7	50	5	10.00	
1962-63	Barbados	Trinidad	IIs	1	1		9	9	9.00			1	24.4	6	80	6	13.33	

				BATTING									BOWLING					
SEASON	TEAM	OPPONENTS	V	M	I	NO	RUNS	H.S.	AVGE	100	50	CT/St	OV	MD	RUNS	W	AVGE	B.B.
1962-63	Barbados	British Guiana	IIs	1	2		4	4	2.00			1	48	10	105	7	15.00	
1963	West Indies	Tour of England	E	15	16	5	132	*27	12.00			4	477.3	138	1008	87	11.58	
1963	**WEST INDIES**	**ENGLAND TESTS**	**E**	**5**	**7**	**2**	**32**	***13**	**6.40**			**3**	**223.5**	**54**	**519**	**32**	**16.21**	
1963-64	West Indies XI	The Rest XI	WI	1	1	1	6	*6					15	6	20	1	20.00	
1963-64	F. Worrell's XI	C. Hunte's XI	WI	1	1	1	23	*23				1	22	0	91	3	30.33	
1963-64	Comm. XI	Tour of Pakistan	P	5	6		180	98	30.00		1	2	159.4	37	434	15	28.93	
1963-64	Indian President's XI	Prime Minister's XI	I	1	2	1	13	*8	13.00			2	21	3	77	0		
1963-64	Barbados	British Guiana	IIs	1	1	1	1	*1					48.1	10	139	4	34.75	
1963-64	Barbados	Trinidad	IIs	1	2	1	12	12	12.00				32	8	75	0		
1963-64	Barbados	Jamaica	IIs	1	1	1	1	*1					44	11	124	4	31.00	
1964	West Indies XI	England XI	E	2	1		0	0				2	19	4	54	2	27.00	
1964-65	Barbados	Cavaliers Touring XI	WI	1	D								25	3	84	2	42.00	
1964-65	Barbados	Australian Tourist	WI	1	1		0	0					23	5	83	1	83.00	
1964-65	**WEST INDIES**	**AUSTRALIA TESTS**	**WI**	**5**	**9**	**2**	**134**	**54**	**19.14**		**1**	**1**	**154**	**22**	**480**	**15**	**32.00**	
1965	Rest of World XI	England XI	E	1	1		38	38	38.00				11.3	3	26	1	26.00	
1965-66	Barbados	Shell Shield	IIs	4	3		52	38	17.33			3	75.5	16	206	15	13.73	
1966	West Indies	Tour of England	E	11	14	5	215	*63	23.88		1	2	212.3	59	560	35	16.00	
1966	**WEST INDIES**	**ENGLAND TESTS**	**E**	**5**	**6**	**1**	**82**	**30**	**16.40**			**3**	**144.3**	**27**	**438**	**14**	**31.28**	
1966-67	West Indies	Tour of India	I	5	7	1	122	70	20.33		1	2	42.1	9	160	6	26.66	
1966-67	**WEST INDIES**	**INDIA TESTS**	**I**	**3**	**4**	**2**	**88**	***40**	**44.00**			**4**	**80**	**23**	**291**	**9**	**32.33**	
1966-67	Barbados	Shell Shield	IIs	1	D								13	3	34	0		
1966-67	Barbados	Rest of World XI	WI	1	2		15	15	7.50				44	5	167	7	23.85	
1967-68	**WEST INDIES**	**ENGLAND TESTS**	**WI**	**4**	**6**	**2**	**64**	**18**	**16.00**			**2**	**93.1**	**29**	**232**	**10**	**23.20**	
1968-69	West Indies	Tour of Australia	A	5	6	1	50	13	10.00			1	56.6	6	365	12	30.41	
1968-69	**WEST INDIES**	**AUSTRALIA TESTS**	**A**	**3**	**6**		**82**	**27**	**13.66**			**1**	**104**	**8**	**430**	**8**	**53.25**	
1968-69	West Indies	Tour of New Zealand	NZ	3	4	2	32	*22	16.00				40.5	6	185	7	26.42	
1968-69	**WEST INDIES**	**NEW ZEALAND TESTS**	**NZ**	**2**	**3**		**43**	**31**	**14.33**			**2**	**59.4**	**11**	**191**	**5**	**38.20**	
		Barbados		18	18	5	161	38	12.38			7	531.4	114	1509	69	21.86	
		West Indies		70	91	25	1087	70	16.46		3	27	1747.1	405	5035	244	20.63	
		Comm. XI		5	6		180	98	30.00		1	2	159.4	37	434	15	28.93	
		F. Worrell's XI		1	1	1	23	*23				1	22	0	91	3	30.33	
		Rest of World XI		1	1		38	38	38.00				11.3	3	26	1	16.00	
		Indian President's XI		1	2	1	13	*8	13.00			2	21	3	77	0		
		TEST RECORD		**28**	**42**	**10**	**530**	**54**	**16.56**	**0**	**1**	**16**	**883.1**	**177**	**2683**	**94**	**28.54**	**6-36**
		CAREER		**96**	**119**	**32**	**1502**	**98**	**17.26**	**0**	**4**	**39**	**2493**	**562**	**7172**	**332**	**21.60**	**8-23**

GRIFFITH, Herman Clarence

SEASON	TEAM	OPPONENTS	V	M	I	NO	RUNS	H.S.	AVGE	100	50	CT	OV	MD	RUNS	W	AVGE	B.B.
				BATTING									BOWLING					
1921-22	Barbados	Trinidad	IIs	1	1		34	34	34.00				46	13	91	8	11.32	
1922-23	Barbados	Trinidad	IIs	1	1		60	60	60.00		1		42	5	138	7	19.71	
1923-24	Barbados	Trinidad	IIs	1	2		1	1	0.50				30.1	6	78	10	7.80	
1924-25	Barbados	Jamaica	IIs	2	1		2	2	2.00				91	17	228	10	22.80	
1924-25	Barbados	Trinidad	IIs	1	2		18	13	9.00				39	7	124	9	13.77	
1925-26	Barbados	British Guiana	IIs	1	2	1	22	*21	22.00				34	6	112	2	56.00	
1925-26	Barbados	M.C.C. Tourist	WI	2	1	1	0	*0				4	63	11	161	13	12.38	
1926-27	Barbados	British Guiana	IIs	1	1		18	18	18.00			1	47	10	115	4	28.75	
1926-27	Barbados	Trinidad	IIs	1	1		28	28	28.00			1	64.1	9	205	9	22.77	
1927-28	Combined B/J XI	Combined Trin/BG XI	IIs	1	1	1	15	*15				1	25	3	95	4	23.75	
1928	West Indies	Tour of England	E	21	28	12	325	*61	20.31		1	6	560.2	104	1870	65	28.76	
1928	**WEST INDIES**	**ENGLAND TESTS**	**E**	**3**	**6**	**3**	**8**	**5**	**2.66**			**2**	**79.5**	**20**	**250**	**11**	**22.72**	
1928-29	Barbados	Trinidad	IIs	1	2		16	13	8.00			2	22	3	91	2	45.50	
1929-30	Barbados	M.C.C. Tourist	WI	1	1		38	38	38.00				36	6	95	2	47.50	
1929-30	**WEST INDIES**	**ENGLAND TESTS**	**WI**	**3**	**5**	**1**	**21**	**8**	**5.25**			**2**	**190.1**	**38**	**508**	**16**	**31.75**	
1930-31	West Indies	Tour of Australia	A	7	9	4	49	17	9.80			4	234.4	22	714	17	42.00	
1930-31	**WEST INDIES**	**AUSTRALIA TESTS**	**A**	**5**	**8**		**43**	**12**	**5.37**				**133.5**	**20**	**393**	**14**	**28.07**	
1931-32	Barbados	Trinidad	IIs	1	2		38	29	19.00				28	4	98	4	24.50	
1933	West Indies	Tour of England	E	19	24	3	396	84	18.85		2	10	556	132	1546	41	37.70	
1933	**WEST INDIES**	**ENGLAND TESTS**	**E**	**2**	**4**	**1**	**19**	**18**	**6.33**				**40**	**11**	**92**	**3**	**30.66**	
1934-35	Barbados	M.C.C. Tourist	WI	2	3		35	33	11.66			3	41	6	141	3	47.00	
1940-41	Barbados	Trinidad	IIs	2	3	1	18	16	9.00				30	2	149	4	37.25	
		Barbados		18	23	3	328	60	16.40		1	11	613.2	105	1826	87	20.98	
		West Indies		60	84	24	861	84	14.35		3	24	1794.5	347	5373	167	32.17	
		Combined B/J XI		1	1		15	*15				1	25	3	95	4	23.75	
		TEST RECORD		**13**	**23**	**5**	**91**	**18**	**5.05**	**0**	**0**	**4**	**443.5**	**89**	**1243**	**44**	**28.25**	**6-103**
		CAREER		**79**	**108**	**28**	**1204**	**84**	**15.05**	**0**	**4**	**36**	**2433.1**	**455**	**7294**	**258**	**28.27**	**7-38**

GUILLEN, Simpson Clairmonte

SEASON	TEAM	OPPONENTS	V	M	I	NO	RUNS	H.S.	AVGE	100	50	CT/St	OV	MD	RUNS	W	AVGE	B.B.
				BATTING									BOWLING					
1947-48	Trinidad	M.C.C. Tourist	WI	1	2		11	6	5.50			2/1						
1948-49	Trinidad	Barbados	IIs	2	4		63	29	15.75			4/1						

SEASON	TEAM	OPPONENTS	V	M	I	NO	RUNS	H.S.	AVGE	100	50	CT/St	OV	MD	RUNS	W	AVGE	B.B.
				BATTING									BOWLING					
1949-50	Trinidad	Jamaica	IIs	2	2		19	14	9.50			5/3						
1950-51	Trinidad	Barbados	IIs	1	2		12	12	6.00									
1951-52	West Indies	Tour of Australia	A	5	7	2	64	23	12.80			14/8						
1951-52	**WEST INDIES**	**AUSTRALIA TESTS**	**A**	**3**	**5**	**2**	**50**	***22**	**16.66**			**8/0**						
1951-52	West Indies	Tour of New Zealand	NZ	1	1		0	0				1/0						
1951-52	**WEST INDIES**	**NEW ZEALAND TESTS**	**NZ**	**2**	**1**		**54**	**54**	**54.00**		**1**	**1/2**						
1952-53	Canterbury	Plunket Shield	NZ	1	1	1	13	*13				2/1						
1953-54	Canterbury	Plunket Shield & Tourist	NZ	5	9	1	454	197	56.75	2	1	13/3						
1953-54	New Zealand XI	New Zealand	NZ	1	2	1	75	*54	75.00		1							
1954-55	Canterbury	Plunket Shield	NZ	5	10	1	110	*30	12.22			6/2						
1955-56	Canterbury	Plunket Shield	NZ	5	7	1	437	118	72.83	1	3	9/3						
1955-56	**NEW ZEALAND**	**WEST INDIES TESTS**	**NZ**	**3**	**6**		**98**	**41**	**16.33**			**4/1**						
1956-57	Canterbury	Plunket Shield & Tourist	NZ	6	10		314	96	31.40		2	12/4						
1956-57	New Zealand XI	Australia XI	NZ	3	4		40	23	10.00			3/0						
1957-58	Canterbury	Plunket Shield	NZ	5	8		232	62	29.00		2	8/3						
1958-59	Canterbury	Plunket Shield	NZ	4	8		221	76	27.62		2	8/2						
1959-60	Canterbury	Plunket Shield	NZ	5	10	1	244	57	27.11		2	9/0	20	9	49	1	49.00	
1960-61	Canterbury	Plunket Shield	NZ	6	10		161	41	16.10			2/0						
		Trinidad		6	10		105	29	10.50			11/5						
		West Indies		11	14	4	168	54	16.80		1	24/10						
		Canterbury		42	73	5	2186	197	32.14	3	12	69/18	20	9	49	1	49.00	
		New Zealand		7	12	1	213	*54	19.36		1	7/1						
		TEST RECORD	**WI**	**5**	**6**	**2**	**104**	**54**	**26.00**	**0**	**1**	**9/2**						
		TEST RECORD	**NZ**	**3**	**6**		**98**	**41**	**16.33**	**0**	**0**	**4/1**						
		CAREER		**66**	**109**	**10**	**2672**	**197**	**26.97**	**3**	**14**	**111/34**	**20**	**9**	**49**	**1**	**49.00**	**1-1**

HALL, Wesley Winfield

SEASON	TEAM	OPPONENTS	V	M	I	NO	RUNS	H.S.	AVGE	100	50	CT	OV	MD	RUNS	W	AVGE	B.B.
				BATTING									BOWLING					
1955-56	Barbados	E.W. Swanton's Tourist	WI	1	1	1	4	*4				2	24	1	112	0		
1957	West Indies	Tour of England	E	15	16	3	178	22	13.69			3	292	47	906	27	33.55	
1957-58	Barbados	Pakistan Tourist	WI	1	1		6	6	6.00				29	2	126	1	126.00	
1958-59	Barbados	Jamaica	IIs	2	3	1	4	3	2.00			1	83.4	16	240	11	21.81	
1958-59	West Indies	Tour of India	I	6	4	2	46	27	23.00			4	159.5	57	399	35	11.40	

1958-59	**WEST INDIES**	**INDIA TESTS**	**I**	**5**	**4**	**2**	**37**	**25**	**18.50**		**2**	**221.4**	**65**	**530**	**30**	**17.66**
1958-59	West Indies	Tour of Pakistan	P	2	2		17	16	8.50		1	37	27	96	6	16.00
1958-59	**WEST INDIES**	**PAKISTAN TESTS**	**P**	**3**	**5**		**17**	**7**	**3.40**		**1**	**100.5**	**18**	**287**	**16**	**17.93**
1959-60	**WEST INDIES**	**ENGLAND TESTS**	**WI**	**5**	**6**	**3**	**48**	**29**	**16.00**		**1**	**236.2**	**49**	**679**	**22**	**30.86**
1960-61	West Indies	Tour of Australia	A	7	9		60	12	6.66		1	115.6	8	493	19	25.94
1960-61	**WEST INDIES**	**AUSTRALIA TESTS**	**A**	**5**	**9**		**158**	**50**	**17.55**	**1**		**144.6**	**14**	**616**	**21**	**29.33**
1961	Comm. XI	England XI	E	1	2	1	6	*3	6.00			17	0	63	1	63.00
1961-62	Queensland	Sheffield Shield	A	8	12	3	166	43	18.44		6	204	30	871	43	20.25
1961-62	Barbados	Indian Tourist	WI	1	1		88	88	88.00	1	1	18	4	60	3	20.00
1961-62	**WEST INDIES**	**INDIA TESTS**	**WI**	**5**	**5**	**2**	**120**	***50**	**40.00**	**1**	**1**	**167.4**	**37**	**425**	**27**	**15.74**
1962-63	Queensland	Sheffield Shield & Tourist	A	9	14		243	50	17.35	1	3	217	28	1127	33	34.15
1962-63	Comm. XI	Tour of Rhodesia	R	1	2		10	6	5.00			15	1	48	1	48.00
1963	West Indies	Tour of England	E	15	14	1	185	*102	14.23	1	9	384.4	87	1072	58	18.48
1963	**WEST INDIES**	**ENGLAND TESTS**	**E**	**5**	**7**	**1**	**79**	**28**	**13.16**		**1**	**178**	**26**	**534**	**16**	**33.37**
1963-64	West Indies XI	The Rest XI	WI	1	1		5	5	5.00		1	14	2	44	2	22.00
1963-64	F. Worrell's XI	C. Hunte's XI	WI	1	1		27	27	27.00		1	14	1	62	1	62.00
1963-64	Indian President's XI	Prime Minister's XI	I	1	2		35	19	17.50		1	24	2	112	2	56.00
1963-64	Barbados	British Guiana	IIs	1	1		1	1	1.00			45	10	135	8	16.87
1963-64	Barbados	Trinidad	IIs	1	2		18	11	9.00			33.1	5	83	2	41.50
1963-64	Barbados	Jamaica	IIs	1	1		10	10	10.00			44.1	13	102	6	17.00
1964	West Indies XI	England XI	E	2	1		9	9	9.00		1	18	4	63	0	
1964-65	Jamaican XI	Cavaliers Touring XI	WI	1	2	1	26	16	26.00		1	23	2	87	5	17.40
1964-65	Barbados	Australian Tourist	WI	1	1		1	1	1.00			20	4	75	1	75.00
1964-65	**WEST INDIES**	**AUSTRALIA TESTS**	**WI**	**5**	**9**	**1**	**133**	**37**	**16.62**		**3**	**146**	**19**	**454**	**16**	**28.37**
1965	Rest of World XI	England XI	E	1	1		1	1	1.00			13	2	33	0	
1966	West Indies	Tour of England	E	14	15	3	177	*34	14.75		5	263.5	69	725	21	34.52
1966	**WEST INDIES**	**ENGLAND TESTS**	**E**	**5**	**6**	**2**	**69**	***30**	**17.25**		**1**	**175.3**	**35**	**555**	**18**	**30.83**
1966-67	West Indies	Tour of India	I	3	5	1	107	42	26.75		1	46	6	169	7	24.14
1966-67	**WEST INDIES**	**INDIA TESTS**	**I**	**3**	**3**		**67**	**35**	**22.33**			**73**	**10**	**266**	**8**	**33.25**
1966-67	West Indies	Tour of Ceylon	C	1	1		0	0				19	8	46	1	46.00
1966-67	Trinidad	Shell Shield	IIs	4	6		47	25	7.83		1	74	11	232	6	38.66
1966-67	Barbados	Rest of World XI	WI	1	2	1	5	4	5.00			35	6	137	5	27.40
1967-68	Trinidad	M.C.C. Tourist	WI	1	1	1	2	*2				19	3	54	2	27.00
1967-68	**WEST INDIES**	**ENGLAND TESTS**	**WI**	**4**	**7**	**3**	**50**	***26**	**12.50**			**122**	**29**	**353**	**9**	**39.22**
1968	Rest of World XI	Counties & Australia	E	3	4	2	26	10	13.00			64	3	253	5	50.60
1968-69	West Indies	Tour of Australia	A	7	10	2	140	78	17.50	1	1	132.7	18	641	22	29.13
1968-69	**WEST INDIES**	**AUSTRALIA TESTS**	**A**	**2**	**4**		**39**	**33**	**9.75**			**75.7**	**5**	**325**	**8**	**40.62**
1968-69	West Indies	Tour of New Zealand	NZ	1	2		56	29	28.00		1	10	1	36	1	36.00
1968-69	**WEST INDIES**	**NEW ZEALAND TESTS**	**NZ**	**1**	**1**		**1**	**1**	**1.00**		**1**	**16.2**	**5**	**42**	**1**	**42.00**

SEASON	TEAM	OPPONENTS	V	BATTING M	I	NO	RUNS	H.S.	AVGE	100	50	CT	BOWLING OV	MD	RUNS	W	AVGE	B.B.
1969	Barbados	Tour of England	E	2	4	1	111	55	37.00		1	2	32	6	106	2	53.00	
1969-70	Trinidad	Shell Shield	IIs	4	4		28	9	7.00				88	12	337	15	22.46	
1970-71	Barbados	Indian Tourist	WI	1	1		10	10	10.00				18	1	62	2	31.00	
		Barbados		13	18	4	258	88	18.42		2	6	382	68	1238	41	30.19	
		Trinidad		9	11	1	77	25	7.70			1	181	26	623	23	27.08	
		Jamaican XI		1	2	1	26	16	26.00			1	23	2	87	5	17.40	
		West Indies		122	146	26	1798	*102	14.98	1	3	39	3151.2	646	9756	391	24.95	
		Queensland		17	26	3	409	50	17.78		1	9	421	58	1998	76	26.28	
		Comm. XI		2	4	1	16	6	5.33				32	1	111	2	55.50	
		F. Worrell's XI		1	1		27	27	27.00			1	14	1	62	1	62.00	
		Rest of World XI		4	5	2	27	10	9.00				77	5	286	5	57.20	
		Indian President's XI		1	2		35	19	17.50			1	24	2	112	2	56.00	
		TEST RECORD		**48**	**66**	**14**	**818**	***50**	**15.73**	**0**	**2**	**11**	**1657.7**	**312**	**5066**	**192**	**26.38**	**7-69**
		CAREER		**170**	**215**	**38**	**2673**	***102**	**15.10**	**1**	**6**	**58**	**4305.2**	**809**	**14273**	**546**	**26.14**	**7-51**

HARPER, Roger Andrew

SEASON	TEAM	OPPONENTS		V	BATTING M	I	NO	RUNS	H.S.	AVGE	100	50	CT	BOWLING OV	MD	RUNS	W	AVGE	B.B.
1979-80	Demerara	Berbice	JC	G	1	D								1	0	1	0		
1979-80	Guyana	Shell Shield		IIs	4	7		82	38	11.71			6	207	52	462	17	27.17	
1980-81	Guyana	Shell Shield		IIs	3	5		49	26	9.80			4	148.5	23	415	7	59.28	
1980-81	WI President's XI	English Tourist		WI	1	2		0	0				1	66	11	200	6	33.33	
1981-82	Demerara	Berbice	JC	G	1	2	1	33	*18	33.00			1	30	5	69	1	69.00	
1981-82	Guyana	Shell Shield		IIs	3	4		87	37	21.75			5	84.2	22	184	9	20.44	
1982-83	Demerara	Berbice	JC	G	1	1		26	26	26.00			3	24	0	97	3	32.33	
1982-83	Guyana	Shell Shield		IIs	5	8		93	29	11.62			9	223	66	492	24	20.50	
1983	D.B. Close's XI	New Zealand Tourist		E	1	2		12	7	6.00				28	8	81	5	16.20	
1983-84	West Indies	Tour of India		I	6	8		204	70	25.50		1	5	190	45	447	24	18.62	
1983-84	**WEST INDIES**	**INDIA TESTS**		**I**	**2**	**2**		**0**	**0**				**3**	**50**	**9**	**124**	**1**	**124.00**	
1983-84	Guyana	Shell Shield		IIs	1	1		7	7	7.00			1	47.3	20	102	11	9.27	
1983-84	Guyana	Australian Tourist		WI	1	2		91	86	45.50		1		58	8	169	2	84.50	
1983-84	**WEST INDIES**	**AUSTRALIA TESTS**		**WI**	**4**	**4**		**56**	**27**	**14.00**			**5**	**138**	**35**	**303**	**10**	**30.30**	
1984	West Indies	Tour of England		E	8	6	1	232	73	46.40		2	6	173.3	59	356	24	14.83	
1984	**WEST INDIES**	**ENGLAND TESTS**		**E**	**5**	**6**	**1**	**96**	***39**	**19.20**			**8**	**128.4**	**47**	**276**	**13**	**21.73**	
1984	D.B. Close's XI	Sri Lanka Tourist		E	1	D								12	3	44	0		
1984-85	West Indies	Tour of Australia		A	4	6	1	64	*38	12.80			5	181.5	41	447	9	49.66	

1984-85	**WEST INDIES**	**AUSTRALIA TESTS**	**A**	**2**	**3**		**40**	**26**	**13.33**			**1**	**72**	**15**	**211**	**8**	**26.37**	
1984-85	WI Under 23 XI	New Zealand Tourist	WI	1	1		20	20	20.00				23	7	64	0		
1984-85	**WEST INDIES**	**NEW ZEALAND TESTS**	**WI**	**1**	**2**	**1**	**11**	***11**	**11.00**			**2**	**36**	**18**	**52**	**2**	**26.00**	
1985	Northamptonshire	Counties	E	23	26	7	734	127	38.63	1	3	20	748.4	188	2023	56	36.12	
1985	Rest of World XI	D.B. Close's XI	E	1	2		29	15	14.50			2	26.5	4	84	2	42.00	
1985-86	Demerara	Berbice JC	G	1	2	1	71	61	71.00		1	1	30	9	88	4	22.00	
1985-86	Guyana	Shell Shield	IIs	5	9	1	262	72	32.75		2	10	179.5	40	410	22	18.63	
1985-86	**WEST INDIES**	**ENGLAND TESTS**	**WI**	**2**	**3**	**1**	**100**	**60**	**50.00**		**1**	**2**	**38**	**15**	**55**	**4**	**13.75**	
1986	Northamptonshire	Counties	E	25	30	4	933	234	35.88	1	2	32	825.2	275	1700	62	27.41	
1986-87	West Indies	Tour of Pakistan	P	3	3		97	77	32.33		1	2	93	35	163	12	13.58	
1986-87	**WEST INDIES**	**PAKISTAN TESTS**	**P**	**3**	**5**		**49**	**28**	**9.80**			**3**	**36.5**	**9**	**69**	**2**	**34.50**	
1986-87	West Indies	Tour of Australia	A	1	2		138	118	69.00	1			19	5	65	2	32.50	
1986-87	Guyana	Barbados	IIs	1	2		142	120	71.00	1		4	62.5	16	122	10	12.20	
1986-87	Guyana	Shell Shield	IIs	3	3	1	277	128	138.50	2		3	94.3	22	233	7	33.28	
1987	Northamptonshire	Counties	E	6	7	3	167	*127	41.75	1		6	202	49	465	19	24.47	
1987	Rest of World XI	M.C.C. XI	E	1	2	2	26	*17				1	54	7	197	2	98.50	
1987-88	West Indies	Tour of India	I	2	3		108	82	36.00		1	3	35	9	113	4	28.25	
1987-88	**WEST INDIES**	**INDIA TESTS**	**I**	**1**	**1**		**4**	**4**	**4.00**			**5**	**12**	**3**	**13**	**0**		
1987-88	Guyana	Red Stripe Cup	IIs	1	1		29	29	29.00			2	23.3	3	60	3	20.00	
1987-88	WI President's XI	Pakistan Tourist	WI	1	1		30	30	30.00			3	52	11	121	5	24.20	
1987-88	WI Board XI	Pakistan Tourist	WI	1	2	1	10	*10	10.00				57	5	159	3	53.00	
1988	West Indies	Tour of England	E	9	10	5	475	*217	95.00	1	2	17	198.3	59	458	16	28.62	
1988	**WEST INDIES**	**ENGLAND TESTS**	**E**	**3**	**3**		**147**	**74**	**49.00**		**2**	**5**	**29**	**11**	**63**	**5**	**12.60**	
1988-89	West Indies	Tour of Australia	A	5	8	3	238	82	46.60		2	6	164.4	25	494	11	44.90	
1988-89	**WEST INDIES**	**AUSTRALIA TESTS**	**A**	**1**	**2**		**29**	**17**	**14.50**			**1**	**37**	**9**	**86**	**0**		
1988-89	Guyana	Red Stripe Cup	IIs	2	3		126	51	42.00		1	3	87	19	175	7	25.00	
1988-89	WI Board XI	Indian Tourist	WI	1	D							1	7	3	13	0		
1989	Rest of World XI	M.C.C. XI	E	1	1		27	27	27.00			2	39	14	97	4	24.25	
1989-90	Demerara	Berbice K.S.M.T	G	1	1		12	12	12.00			1	48	11	115	8	14.37	
1989-90	Guyana	Red Stripe Cup	IIs	3	5		43	21	8.60			5	83	13	199	7	28.42	
1990	Rest of World XI	Indian Tourist	E	1	1		17	17	17.00			1	33.4	8	104	5	20.80	
		Guyana		32	50	2	1288	128	26.83	3	4	52	1299.2	304	3023	126	23.99	
		Demerara		5	6	2	142	61	35.50	0	1	6	133	25	370	16	23.12	
		West Indies		67	83	14	2148	*217	31.13	2	12	84	1838	486	4352	161	27.03	
		Northamptonshire		54	63	14	1834	234	37.42	3	5	58	1776	512	4188	137	30.56	
		D.B. Close's XI		2	2		12	7	6.00				40	11	125	5	25.00	
		Rest of World XI		4	6	2	99	27	24.75			6	153.3	33	482	13	37.07	
		TEST RECORD		**24**	**31**	**3**	**532**	**74**	**19.00**	**0**	**3**	**35**	**577.3**	**171**	**1252**	**45**	**27.82**	**6-57**
		CAREER		**164**	**210**	**34**	**5523**	**234**	**31.38**	**8**	**22**	**206**	**5239.5**	**1371**	**12540**	**458**	**27.37**	**6-57**

HAYNES, Desmond Leo

SEASON	TEAM	OPPONENTS	V	BATTING M	I	NO	RUNS	H.S.	AVGE	100	50	CT/St	BOWLING OV	MD	RUNS	W	AVGE	B.B.
1976-77	Barbados	Shell Shield	IIs	3	5		75	37	15.00			1						
1976-77	Barbados	Pakistan Tourist	WI	1	2		161	136	80.50	1								
1977-78	Barbados	Shell Shield	IIs	4	7	1	310	79	51.66		4							
1977-78	Barbados	Australian Tourist	WI	1	2		64	40	32.00									
1977-78	**WEST INDIES**	**AUSTRALIA TESTS**	**WI**	**2**	**3**		**182**	**66**	**60.66**		**3**	**1**						
1978-79	Barbados	Shell Shield	IIs	2	3	1	150	107	75.00	1		1	1	1	0	0		
1979-80	West Indies	Tour of Australia	A	3	6	1	159	58	31.80		1	3						
1979-80	**WEST INDIES**	**AUSTRALIA TESTS**	**A**	**3**	**6**	**1**	**139**	**42**	**27.80**			**2**						
1979-80	West Indies	Tour of New Zealand	NZ	2	4		96	58	24.00		1	3						
1979-80	**WEST INDIES**	**NEW ZEALAND TESTS**	**NZ**	**3**	**6**		**339**	**122**	**56.50**	**2**	**1**	**2**						
1979-80	Barbados	Shell Shield	IIs	4	6	1	256	73	51.20		3	5						
1980	West Indies	Tour of England	E	9	16	3	566	82	43.53		5	2						
1980	**WEST INDIES**	**ENGLAND TESTS**	**E**	**5**	**6**		**308**	**184**	**51.33**	**1**	**1**		**1**	**0**	**2**	**0**		
1980-81	West Indies	Tour of Pakistan	P	5	9	1	381	98	47.62		3	3						
1980-81	**WEST INDIES**	**PAKISTAN TESTS**	**P**	**4**	**6**		**104**	**40**	**17.33**			**4**	**1**	**0**	**2**	**1**	**2.00**	
1980-81	Barbados	Shell Shield	IIs	4	6		304	160	50.66	1		2						
1980-81	Barbados	English Tourist	WI	1	1		44	44	44.00				1	0	2	0		
1980-81	**WEST INDIES**	**ENGLAND TESTS**	**WI**	**4**	**5**		**234**	**96**	**46.80**		**2**	**3**	**1**	**0**	**4**	**0**		
1981-82	WI Under 26 XI	Tour of Zimbabwe	Z	3	6	1	169	69	33.80		1	3	1	1	0	0		
1981-82	West Indies	Tour of Australia	A	3	5		258	139	51.60	1	1	2						
1981-82	**WEST INDIES**	**AUSTRALIA TESTS**	**A**	**3**	**6**		**125**	**51**	**20.83**		**1**	**1**						
1981-82	Barbados	Shell Shield	IIs	5	7		164	34	23.42									
1982	D.B. Close's XI	Pakistan Tourist	E	1	1		4	4	4.00			2						
1982-83	West Indies XI	International XI	WI	1	1		96	96	96.00		1							
1982-83	Barbados	Shell Shield	IIs	5	10		367	97	36.70		3	4						
1982-83	Barbados	Indian Tourist	WI	1	1		25	25	25.00			1	2	0	12	0		
1982-83	**WEST INDIES**	**INDIA TESTS**	**WI**	**5**	**7**	**1**	**333**	**136**	**55.55**	**1**	**1**	**4**						
1983-84	West Indies	Tour of India	I	5	9	1	384	*67	48.00		3	3	0.4	0	6	1	6.00	
1983-84	**WEST INDIES**	**INDIA TESTS**	**I**	**6**	**10**		**176**	**55**	**17.60**		**1**	**2**						
1983-84	Barbados	Australian Tourist	WI	1	2		85	70	42.50		1	1						
1983-84	**WEST INDIES**	**AUSTRALIA TESTS**	**WI**	**5**	**8**	**3**	**468**	**145**	**93.60**	**2**	**3**	**2**						
1984	West Indies	Tour of England	E	7	9	1	397	89	49.62		4	6						
1984	**WEST INDIES**	**ENGLAND TESTS**	**E**	**5**	**8**		**235**	**125**	**29.37**	**1**		**3**						
1984	D.B. Close's XI	Sri Lanka Tourist	E	1	1		111	111	111.00	1		1						
1984-85	West Indies	Tour of Australia	A	5	8	1	388	155	55.42	1	2	1	6	0	27	0		
1984-85	**WEST INDIES**	**AUSTRALIA TESTS**	**A**	**5**	**9**		**247**	**63**	**27.44**		**3**	**4**						

1984-85	**WEST INDIES**	**NEW ZEALAND TESTS**	**WI**	**4**	**8**	**2**	**344**	**90**	**57.33**		**4**	**5**						
1985-86	Barbados	Shell Shield	IIs	5	9		445	118	49.44	2	2	3						
1985-86	**WEST INDIES**	**ENGLAND TESTS**	**WI**	**5**	**9**	**3**	**469**	**131**	**78.16**	**1**	**3**	**3**						
1986-87	West Indies	Tour of Pakistan	P	2	3	1	110	*50	55.00		1	2						
1986-87	**WEST INDIES**	**PAKISTAN TESTS**	**P**	**3**	**5**	**1**	**149**	***88**	**37.25**		**1**	**3**						
1986-87	West Indies	Tour of Australia	A	1	2		82	67	41.00		1	1						
1986-87	West Indies	Tour of New Zealand	NZ	2	3	1	180	112	90.00	1	1	1						
1986-87	**WEST INDIES**	**NEW ZEALAND TESTS**	**NZ**	**3**	**6**	**1**	**160**	**121**	**32.00**	**1**	**1**							
1987	Rest of World XI	M.C.C. XI & Gloucester	E	2	4	1	156	130	52.00	1		4/1	1	0	4	1	4.00	
1987-88	West Indies	Tour of India	I	1	1		70	70	70.00		1							
1987-88	**WEST INDIES**	**INDIA TESTS**	**I**	**4**	**8**	**1**	**201**	**58**	**28.71**		**1**	**1**						
1987-88	Barbados	Red Stripe Cup	IIs	3	6	1	198	64	39.60		1							
1987-88	**WEST INDIES**	**PAKISTAN TESTS**	**WI**	**3**	**6**		**75**	**48**	**12.50**			**3**						
1988	West Indies	Tour of England	E	10	16	2	668	158	47.71	1	4	3						
1988	**WEST INDIES**	**ENGLAND TESTS**	**E**	**4**	**7**	**2**	**235**	***77**	**47.00**		**3**	**3**						
1988	Rest of World XI	M.C.C. XI	E	1	2		61	46	30.50									
1988-89	West Indies	Tour of Australia	A	4	7		250	102	35.71	1	2	3	1	0	3	0		
1988-89	**WEST INDIES**	**AUSTRALIA TESTS**	**A**	**5**	**10**	**1**	**537**	**143**	**59.66**	**2**	**2**	**5**						
1988-89	Barbados	Red Stripe Cup	IIs	1	1		82	82	82.00		1		6	4	2	1		
1988-89	**WEST INDIES**	**INDIA TESTS**	**WI**	**4**	**7**	**1**	**280**	***112**	**46.66**	**1**	**1**	**3**						
1989	Middlesex	Counties	E	20	37	5	1446	*206	45.18	3	8	12	6	3	13	0		
1989-90	Barbados	Red Stripe Cup	IIs	5	9	1	285	108	35.82	1	1	2						
1989-90	Barbados	English Tourist	WI	1	2		22	13	11.00				3	1	6	0		
1989-90	**WEST INDIES**	**ENGLAND TESTS**	**WI**	**4**	**7**		**371**	**167**	**53.00**	**2**		**1**						
1990	Middlesex	Counties	E	23	39	5	2346	*255	69.00	8	7	14	35	7	113	2	56.50	
		Barbados		47	79	5	3037	160	41.04	6	16	20	13	6	22	1	22.00	
		West Indies		152	258	30	9965	184	43.70	19	63	92	11.4	1	44	2	22.00	
		D.B. Close's XI		2	2		115	111	57.50	1		3						
		Rest of World XI		3	6	1	217	130	43.40	1		4/1	1	0	4	1	4.00	
		Middlesex		43	76	10	3792	*255	57.45	11	15	26	41	10	126	2	63.00	
		TEST RECORD		**89**	**153**	**17**	**5711**	**184**	**41.99**	**14**	**31**	**56**	**3**	**0**	**8**	**1**	**8.00**	**1-2**
		CAREER		**247**	**421**	**46**	**17126**	***255**	**45.66**	**38**	**94**	**145/1**	**66.4**	**17**	**196**	**6**	**32.66**	**1-2**

HEADLEY, George Alphonso

SEASON	TEAM	OPPONENTS	V	BATTING M	I	NO	RUNS	H.S.	AVGE	100	50	CT	BOWLING OV	MD	RUNS	W	AVGE	B.B.
1927-28	Jamaica	L.H. Tennyson's Tourist	WI	3	5		409	211	81.80	1	2	2	7	2	17	1	17.00	
1928-29	Jamaica	Julien Cahn's Tourist	WI	2	4		139	57	34.75		1	6	21	3	73	1	73.00	
1928-29	West Indies XI	Julien Cahn's Tourist	WI	1	2		187	143	93.50	1								
1929-30	Jamaica	M.C.C. Tourist	WI	2	3		188	72	62.66		3	5	10	1	31	0		
1929-30	**WEST INDIES**	**ENGLAND TESTS**	**WI**	**4**	**8**		**703**	**223**	**87.87**	**4**		**4**	**23**	**2**	**77**	**0**		
1930-31	West Indies	Tour of Australia	A	8	15		730	131	48.66	2	4	6	7	0	39	0		
1930-31	**WEST INDIES**	**AUSTRALIA TESTS**	**A**	**5**	**10**	**1**	**336**	**105**	**37.33**	**2**		**1**						
1931-32	Jamaica	L.H. Tennyson's Tourist	WI	3	4	2	723	*344	361.50	3	1	2	11	1	39	1	39.00	
1932-33	Combined J/BG XI	Combined Trin/Bar XI	IIs	1	2		51	30	25.50									
1933	West Indies	Tour of England	E	20	32	2	2043	*224	68.10	6	10	13	211.2	35	640	21	30.47	
1933	**WEST INDIES**	**ENGLAND TESTS**	**E**	**3**	**6**	**1**	**277**	***169**	**55.40**	**1**	**1**	**4**	**19**	**1**	**81**	**0**		
1934-35	Jamaica	M.C.C. Tourist	WI	2	3		152	127	50.66	1		1	3	0	20	0		
1934-35	**WEST INDIES**	**ENGLAND TESTS**	**WI**	**4**	**6**	**1**	**485**	***270**	**97.00**	**1**	**2**	**4**	**5**	**3**	**3**	**0**		
1935	L Parkinson's XI	Leicestershire	E	1	2		152	134	76.00	1			8	0	37	1	37.00	
1935-36	Jamaica	Yorkshire Touring XI	WI	3	5		266	118	53.20	1	2	3	44	9	91	1	91.00	
1938-39	Jamaica	Trinidad	IIs	1	1		160	160	160.00	1		3						
1938-39	Jamaica	West Indies XI	WI	1	1		103	103	103.00	1								
1939	West Indies	Tour of England	E	17	25	6	1411	*234	74.26	4	6	10	6	1	13	1	13.00	
1939	**WEST INDIES**	**ENGLAND TESTS**	**E**	**3**	**5**		**334**	**107**	**66.80**	**2**	**2**		**4**	**0**	**17**	**0**		
1945-46	Jamaica	Trinidad	IIs	3	4	1	170	99	56.66		2	3	43	8	137	8	17.12	
1946-47	Jamaica	Barbados	IIs	2	3	3	339	*203		1	2	2	43	12	102	5	20.40	
1947-48	Jamaica	British Guiana	IIs	2	2	1	40	36	40.00			2	75	10	227	5	45.40	
1947-48	Jamaica	M.C.C. Tourist	WI	2	2	1	101	65	101.00		1	1						
1947-48	**WEST INDIES**	**ENGLAND TESTS**	**WI**	**1**	**2**	**1**	**36**	**29**	**36.00**				**6**	**1**	**11**	**0**		
1948-49	West Indies	Tour of India	I	2	2		9	8	4.50			1	48	4	95	3	31.66	
1948-49	**WEST INDIES**	**INDIA TESTS**	**I**	**1**	**1**		**2**	**2**	**2.00**				**3**	**0**	**18**	**0**		
1948-49	West Indies	Tour of Pakistan	P	1	1	1	57	*57			1	1	20	11	21	2	10.50	
1951	Comm. XI	England XI	E	1	1		20	20	20.00			1						
1952	Comm. XI	England XI	E	1	2		159	98	79.50		2							
1953-54	Jamaica	M.C.C. Tourist	WI	1	2	1	58	*53	58.00		1		13.3	3	30	1	30.00	
1953-54	**WEST INDIES**	**ENGLAND TESTS**	**WI**	**1**	**2**		**17**	**16**	**8.50**			**1**	**5**	**0**	**23**	**0**		
1954	Comm. XI	England XI	E	1	1		64	64	64.00		1							
		Jamaica		27	39	9	2848	*344	94.93	9	15	30	270.3	49	767	23	33.34	
		West Indies		71	117	13	6627	270	63.72	23	26	45	357.2	58	1038	37	38.44	
		Comm. XI		3	4		243	98	60.75		3	1						

	M	I	NO	RUNS	H.S.	AVGE	100	50	CT	OV	MD	RUNS	W	AVGE	B.B.
Combined J/BG XI	1	2		51	30	25.50									
L. Parkinson's XI	1	2		152	134	76.00	1			8	0	37	1	37.00	
TEST RECORD	**22**	**40**	**4**	**2190**	***270**	**60.83**	**10**	**5**	**14**	**65**	**7**	**230**	**0**		
CAREER	**103**	**164**	**22**	**9921**	***344**	**69.86**	**33**	**44**	**76**	**635.5**	**107**	**1842**	**51**	**36.11**	**5-33**

HEADLEY, Ronald George Alphonso

				BATTING									BOWLING					
SEASON	TEAM	OPPONENTS	V	M	I	NO	RUNS	H.S.	AVGE	100	50	CT	OV	MD	RUNS	W	AVGE	B.B.
1958	Worcestershire	Counties	E	2	4	1	67	29	22.33			1						
1959	Worcestershire	Counties	E	14	26	2	522	93	21.75		2	6	58.2	8	218	2	109.00	
1960	Worcestershire	Counties	E	32	59	4	1241	108	22.56	2	6	24	14	6	26	0		
1961	Worcestershire	Counties	E	35	67	5	2026	*150	32.67	4	11	22						
1961	Comm. XI	M.C.C.	E	1	2		14	12	7.00			1						
1962	Worcestershire	Counties	E	17	31	3	710	90	25.35		5	8						
1963	Worcestershire	Counties	E	31	55	6	1432	108	29.22	1	10	29	65.4	22	159	7	22.71	
1964	Worcestershire	Counties	E	31	53	5	1697	*117	35.35	4	9	50	57.2	16	149	3	49.66	
1964-65	Worcestershire	Tour of Rhodesia	R	1	2		21	11	10.50				3	0	16	0		
1964-65	Cavaliers XI	Tour of Jamaica	WI	2	4	1	180	76	60.00		2		5	1	10	0		
1965	Worcestershire	Counties	E	30	54	7	1537	123	32.70	2	9	30						
1965-66	Jamaica	Shell Shield	IIs	4	7		286	86	40.85		2	3						
1965-66	Worcestershire	Jamaican XI	WI	1	2		20	20	10.00			3						
1966	Worcestershire	Counties	E	29	47	4	1028	137	23.90	1	4	38						
1967	Worcestershire	Counties	E	30	58	7	1500	104	29.41	2	8	36						
1968	Worcestershire	Counties	E	27	51	3	1415	82	29.47		9	22						
1969	Worcestershire	Counties	E	27	48	3	1241	106	27.57	1	7	20						
1970	Worcestershire	Counties	E	24	44	4	1670	*148	41.75	5	6	17						
1971	Worcestershire	Counties	E	23	42	2	1805	187	45.12	4	9	16						
1971	Comm. XI	Tour of Pakistan	P	1	1		8	8	8.00									
1972	Worcestershire	Counties	E	19	32	1	961	131	31.00	1	5	7						
1973	West Indies	Tour of England	E	5	9		230	62	25.55		2	3						
1973	**WEST INDIES**	**ENGLAND TESTS**	**E**	**2**	**4**		**62**	**42**	**15.50**			**2**						
1973	Worcestershire	Counties	E	11	19	1	755	113	41.94	2	4	5						
1973-74	Jamaica	Shell Shield	IIs	4	6		203	79	33.83		2	3	2	0	10	0		
1973-74	Jamaica	M.C.C. Tourist	WI	1	D							1						
1974	Worcestershire	Counties	E	19	31	2	1064	137	36.68	3	5	9						
		Jamaica		9	13	0	489	86	37.61	0	4	7	2	0	10	0		

SEASON	TEAM	M	I	NO	RUNS	H.S.	AVGE	100	50	CT	OV	MD	RUNS	W	AVGE	B.B.
					BATTING								BOWLING			
	West Indies	7	13	0	292	62	22.46	0	2	5						
	Worcestershire	403	725	60	20712	187	31.14	32	109	343	198.2	52	568	12	47.33	
	Comm. XI	2	3	0	22	12	7.33	0	0	1						
	Cavaliers XI	2	4	1	180	76	60.00	0	2		5	1	10	0		
	TEST RECORD	**2**	**4**	**0**	**62**	**42**	**15.50**	**0**	**0**	**2**						
	CAREER	**423**	**758**	**61**	**21695**	**187**	**31.12**	**32**	**117**	**356**	**205.2**	**53**	**588**	**12**	**49.00**	**4-40**

HENDRIKS, John Leslie

SEASON	TEAM	OPPONENTS	V	M	I	NO	RUNS	H.S.	AVGE	100	50	CT/St	OV	MD	RUNS	W	AVGE	B.B.
							BATTING								BOWLING			
1953-54	Jamaica	M.C.C. Tourist	WI	1	1		24	24	24.00			3						
1958-59	Jamaica	Leeward Islands	IIs	1	D							3/1						
1958-59	West Indies	Tour of India	I	7	7	1	137	73	22.83		1	18/5						
1958-59	West Indies	Tour of Pakistan	P	2	3	1	21	15	10.50			1						
1959-60	Jamaica	M.C.C. Tourist	WI	1	2		43	23	21.50									
1960-61	West Indies	Tour of Australia	A	4	7	1	191	82	31.83		3	5/5						
1961-62	Jamaica	Barbados	IIs	1	2		36	18	18.00			1						
1961-62	**WEST INDIES**	**INDIA TESTS**	**WI**	**1**	**1**		**64**	**64**	**64.00**		**1**	**1**						
1963-64	Jamaica	Cavaliers Touring XI	WI	3	6	2	86	44	21.50			4/3						
1963-64	Jamaica	Barbados	IIs	1	2	1	73	*73	73.00		1	1/1						
1963-64	Jamaica	Trinidad	IIs	1	2		16	15	8.00			2/2						
1963-64	Jamaica	British Guiana	IIs	1	2		10	7	5.00			1/1						
1964-65	Jamaica	Cavaliers Touring XI	WI	2	2		49	27	24.50			5						
1964-65	Jamaica	Australian Tourist	WI	1	2		25	15	12.50			1/1						
1964-65	**WEST INDIES**	**AUSTRALIA TESTS**	**WI**	**4**	**7**	**2**	**102**	***31**	**20.40**			**7/2**						
1965-66	Jamaica	Shell Shield	IIs	4	7	1	110	51	18.33		1	9/3						
1965-66	Jamaica	Worcestershire Tourist	WI	1	1		0	0				2/1						
1966	West Indies	Tour of England	E	11	12	4	133	28	16.62			18/10						
1966	**WEST INDIES**	**ENGLAND TESTS**	**E**	**3**	**4**	**1**	**11**	***9**	**3.66**			**7**						
1966-67	West Indies	Tour of India	I	3	3		17	17	5.66			3	6	0	49	0		
1966-67	**WEST INDIES**	**INDIA TESTS**	**I**	**3**	**4**		**62**	**48**	**15.50**			**9/1**						
1966-67	Jamaica	Shell Shield	IIs	4	6	1	20	*5	4.00			4/6						
1968-69	West Indies	Tour of Australia	A	3	4		24	19	6.00			5/3						
1968-69	**WEST INDIES**	**AUSTRALIA TESTS**	**A**	**5**	**10**	**3**	**118**	***37**	**16.85**			**9/2**						
1968-69	West Indies	Tour of New Zealand	NZ	1	2	1	5	*5	5.00			1	1	1	0	0		

1968-69	**WEST INDIES**	**NEW ZEALAND TESTS**	**NZ**	**3**	**4**	**1**	**84**	***54**	**28.00**		**1**	**8**						
1968-69	NZ Governor's XI	West Indies	NZ	1	2	1	1	*1	1.00			1	1	0	12	0		
1969	West Indies	Tour of England	E	9	6	1	100	*69	20.00		1	10/3						
1969	**WEST INDIES**	**ENGLAND TESTS**	**E**	**1**	**2**	**1**	**6**	***5**	**6.00**			**1**						
		Jamaica		22	35	5	492	*73	16.40		2	36/19						
		West Indies		60	76	17	1075	82	18.22		7	103/31	7	1	49	0		
		NZ Governor's XI		1	2	1	1	*1	1.00			1	1	0	12	0		
		TEST RECORD		**20**	**32**	**8**	**447**	**64**	**18.62**	**0**	**2**	**42/5**						
		CAREER		**83**	**113**	**23**	**1568**	**82**	**17.42**	**0**	**9**	**140/50**	**8**	**1**	**61**	**0**		

HOAD, Edward Lisle Goldsworthy

				BATTING									BOWLING					
SEASON	TEAM	OPPONENTS	V	M	I	NO	RUNS	H.S.	AVGE	100	50	CT	OV	MD	RUNS	W	AVGE	B.B.
1921-22	Barbados	Trinidad	IIs	1	1		0	0				1	4	0	16	0		
1922-23	Barbados	Trinidad	IIs	1	1		24	24	24.00			1	46	2	169	8	21.12	
1923-24	Barbados	Trinidad	IIs	1	2		19	13	9.50			1	11	2	31	1	31.00	
1924-25	Barbados	Jamaica	IIs	3	2	1	206	*150	206.00	1	1	1	93	14	246	5	49.20	
1924-25	Barbados	Trinidad	IIs	1	2		25	14	12.50			2	11	3	31	1	31.00	
1925-26	Barbados	British Guiana	IIs	1	2		95	79	47.50		1	1	31.3	2	90	5	18.00	
1925-26	Barbados	M.C.C. Tourist	WI	2	2		100	71	50.00		1	4	14	1	53	3	17.66	
1925-26	West Indies XI	M.C.C. Tourist	WI	1	2	1	0	*0				1	16	0	56	1	56.00	
1926-27	Barbados	British Guiana	IIs	1	1		115	115	115.00	1			39.4	5	90	3	30.00	
1926-27	Barbados	Trinidad	IIs	1	2	1	174	*174	174.00	1		2	35	3	122	4	30.50	
1927-28	Combined T/BG XI	Combined B/J XI	IIs	1	1		47	47	47.00				14	1	56	1	56.00	
1927-28	Barbados XI	The Rest XI	IIs	1	2		158	153	79.00	1			11	1	43	0		
1928	West Indies	Tour of England	E	14	22	3	748	*149	39.36	2	3	5	29	2	193	2	96.50	
1928	**WEST INDIES**	**ENGLAND TESTS**	**E**	**1**	**2**		**17**	**13**	**8.50**									
1929-30	Barbados	British Guiana	IIs	1	2		144	97	72.00		1		64	10	176	7	25.14	
1929-30	Barbados	M.C.C. Tourist	WI	2	3		157	147	52.33	1		1	27	0	95	0		
1929-30	**WEST INDIES**	**ENGLAND TESTS**	**WI**	**1**	**2**		**24**	**24**	**12.00**			**1**						
1931-32	Barbados	Trinidad	IIs	1	2		89	69	44.50		1		6	1	21	1	21.00	
1933	West Indies	Tour of England	E	22	39	4	1026	*149	29.31	1	3	3	28	1	150	3	50.00	
1933	**WEST INDIES**	**ENGLAND TESTS**	**E**	**2**	**4**		**57**	**36**	**14.25**									
1934-35	Barbados	British Guiana	IIs	1	2		98	71	49.00		1	2	52.3	8	140	7	20.00	
1934-35	Barbados	M.C.C. Tourist	WI	2	4	2	122	69	61.00		1		5	0	33	0		
1937-38	Barbados	British Guiana	IIs	1	2	1	57	*57	57.00		1		36	3	112	1	112.00	

SEASON	TEAM		M	I	NO	RUNS	H.S.	AVGE	100	50	CT	OV	MD	RUNS	W	AVGE	B.B.
						BATTING								BOWLING			
		Barbados	21	32	5	1583	*174	58.62	5	8	16	486.4	55	1468	46	31.91	
		West Indies	41	71	8	1872	*149	29.71	3	6	10	73	3	399	6	66.50	
		Combined T/BG XI	1	1		47	47	47.00				14	1	56	1	56.00	
		TEST RECORD	**4**	**8**	**0**	**98**	**36**	**12.25**	**0**	**0**	**1**						
		CAREER	**63**	**104**	**13**	**3502**	***174**	**38.48**	**8**	**14**	**26**	**573.4**	**59**	**1923**	**53**	**36.28**	**5-34**

HOLDER, Vanburn Alonza

SEASON	TEAM	OPPONENTS	V	M	I	NO	RUNS	H.S.	AVGE	100	50	CT	OV	MD	RUNS	W	AVGE	B.B.
							BATTING								BOWLING			
1966-67	Barbados	Shell Shield	IIs	1	2		10	6	5.00			1	12	2	44	1	44.00	
1967-68	Barbados	M.C.C. Tourist	WI	1	1		0	0					25	6	82	0		
1968	Worcestershire	Counties	E	20	24	3	164	*41	7.80			5	474.1	100	1299	59	22.01	
1968-69	Barbados	Shell Shield	IIs	4	6	3	15	11	5.00			2	135	39	300	19	15.78	
1969	West Indies	Tour of England	E	10	5	2	24	*15	8.00			1	219	60	572	21	27.23	
1969	**WEST INDIES**	**ENGLAND TESTS**	**E**	**3**	**6**		**80**	**35**	**13.33**			**1**	**148.5**	**52**	**335**	**9**	**37.22**	
1969	Worcestershire	Counties	E	9	10	3	51	14	7.28			3	234.1	49	631	21	30.04	
1969-70	Barbados	Shell Shield	IIs	4	5	1	40	16	10.00				151.2	34	380	16	23.75	
1969-70	Barbados	Duke of Norfolk's Tourist	WI	1	2		20	17	10.00			1	30	8	51	4	12.75	
1970	Worcestershire	Counties	E	23	20	5	158	52	10.53		1	10	707.3	141	1773	84	21.10	
1970-71	Barbados	Shell Shield	IIs	3	4	2	42	*20	21.00				67.5	8	188	6	31.33	
1970-71	Barbados	Indian Tourist	WI	1	1	1	5	*5				1	32	9	74	4	18.50	
1970-71	**WEST INDIES**	**INDIA TESTS**	**WI**	**3**	**3**		**35**	**14**	**11.66**			**2**	**82.2**	**28**	**192**	**6**	**32.00**	
1971	Worcestershire	Counties	E	26	31	13	287	*36	15.94			15	788.1	192	2064	76	27.15	
1971-72	Barbados	Shell Shield	IIs	4	4		36	12	9.00				137.5	44	273	20	13.65	
1971-72	**WEST INDIES**	**NEW ZEALAND TESTS**	**WI**	**4**	**5**	**1**	**103**	**42**	**25.75**			**3**	**153**	**52**	**285**	**12**	**23.75**	
1972	Worcestershire	Counties	E	21	18	6	139	*23	11.58			4	636.2	131	1647	79	20.84	
1972-73	Barbados	Shell Shield	IIs	4	5		2	2	0.40			1	106.3	29	240	5	48.00	
1972-73	**WEST INDIES**	**AUSTRALIA TESTS**	**WI**	**3**	**4**	**1**	**25**	**12**	**8.33**				**129**	**28**	**275**	**4**	**68.75**	
1973	West Indies	Tour of England	E	9	8		72	17	9.00			3	238	63	550	21	26.19	
1973	**WEST INDIES**	**ENGLAND TESTS**	**E**	**2**	**3**	**1**	**39**	***23**	**19.50**			**2**	**80**	**24**	**174**	**7**	**24.85**	
1973	Worcestershire	Counties	E	5	6	2	58	22	14.50				178.5	50	386	23	16.78	
1973-74	Rest of World XI	Tour of Pakistan	P	2	4	1	78	30	26.00			2	42.1	12	111	3	37.00	
1973-74	Barbados	Shell Shield	IIs	4	6		163	122	27.16	1		2	111.4	28	286	11	26.00	
1973-74	Barbados	M.C.C. Tourist	WI	1	1		4	4	4.00			1	50.2	12	94	7	13.85	
1973-74	**WEST INDIES**	**ENGLAND TESTS**	**WI**	**1**	**1**		**8**	**8**	**8.00**				**42**	**12**	**105**	**2**	**52.50**	

1974	Worcestershire	Counties	E	21	23	4	204	29	10.73			7	659	146	1493	94	15.88	
1974-75	West Indies	Tour of India	I	4	1	1	25	*25				1	94	30	202	11	18.36	
1974-75	**WEST INDIES**	**INDIA TESTS**	**I**	**4**	**7**	**1**	**37**	***26**	**6.16**			**1**	**150.2**	**41**	**315**	**17**	**18.52**	
1974-75	West Indies	Tour of Sri Lanka	SL	2	3	1	28	19	14.00				50	10	118	6	19.66	
1974-75	West Indies	Tour of Pakistan	P	1	D							1	35	7	115	1	115.00	
1974-75	**WEST INDIES**	**PAKISTAN TESTS**	**P**	**2**	**2**		**33**	**29**	**16.50**			**2**	**58**	**14**	**187**	**5**	**37.40**	
1974-75	Barbados	Shell Shield	IIs	4	6		117	37	19.50			1	126	42	276	15	18.40	
1975	Worcestershire	Counties	E	10	11	4	59	18	8.42			1	253.3	54	636	19	33.47	
1975-76	West Indies	Tour of Australia	A	4	5		30	9	6.00				84	8	389	13	29.92	
1975-76	**WEST INDIES**	**AUSTRALIA TESTS**	**A**	**3**	**6**	**1**	**82**	**24**	**16.40**			**1**	**109**	**7**	**513**	**13**	**39.46**	
1975-76	Barbados	Indian Tourist	WI	1	1	1	23	*23					17	2	54	4	13.50	
1975-76	**WEST INDIES**	**INDIA TESTS**	**WI**	**1**	**1**	**1**	**36**	***36**					**33**	**6**	**70**	**0**		
1976	West Indies	Tour of England	E	9	8	3	123	*42					229.1	61	637	37	17.21	
1976	**WEST INDIES**	**ENGLAND TESTS**	**E**	**4**	**6**	**3**	**50**	***19**	**16.66**			**2**	**158**	**48**	**367**	**15**	**24.46**	
1976-77	Barbados	Shell Shield	IIs	4	5		107	35	21.40			4	112	25	383	8	47.87	
1976-77	Barbados	Pakistan Tourist	WI	1	1	1	1	*1				1	35	5	113	3	37.66	
1976-77	**WEST INDIES**	**PAKISTAN TESTS**	**WI**	**1**	**1**		**6**	**6**					**4**	**0**	**13**	**0**		
1977	Worcestershire	Counties	E	21	28	4	206	27	8.58			2	639.5	151	1653	69	23.95	
1977-78	Barbados	Shell Shield	IIs	4	5	2	108	56	36.00		1	2	104	32	201	10	20.10	
1977-78	Barbados	Australian Tourist	WI	1	2		49	40	24.50				29	3	101	1	101.00	
1977-78	**WEST INDIES**	**AUSTRALIA TESTS**	**WI**	**3**	**6**		**69**	**31**	**11.50**			**1**	**110**	**21**	**248**	**11**	**22.54**	
1978	Worcestershire	Counties	E	5	5		30	23	6.00			1	179	31	468	15	31.20	
1978-79	West Indies	Tour of India	I	5	6		169	89	28.16		2	1	85	25	184	5	36.80	
1978-79	**WEST INDIES**	**INDIA TESTS**	**I**	**6**	**8**	**2**	**79**	**27**	**13.16**			**1**	**203**	**34**	**548**	**8**	**68.50**	
1978-79	West Indies	Tour of Sri Lanka	SL	1	2		33	22	16.50				3	1	8	1	8.00	
1979	Worcestershire	Counties	E	14	12	6	119	*24	19.83			5	405	75	1041	32	32.53	
1980	Worcestershire	Counties	E	6	8	1	78	34	11.14			4	161.2	26	439	15	29.26	
1985-86	Orange Free State	Currie Cup	SA	2	4		34	28	8.50			1	33	3	117	2	58.50	
		Barbados		43	57	11	742	122	16.13	1	1	16	1282.3	328	3140	134	23.43	
		West Indies		85	97	18	1186	89	15.01		2	23	2497.4	632	6402	225	28.45	
		Worcestershire		181	196	51	1553	52	10.71		1	56	5316.5	1146	13530	586	23.08	
		Rest of World XI		2	4	1	78	30	26.00			2	42.1	12	111	3	37.00	
		Orange Free State		2	4		34	38	8.50			1	33	3	117	2	58.50	
		TEST RECORD		**40**	**59**	**11**	**682**	**42**	**14.20**	**0**	**0**	**16**	**1460.3**	**361**	**3627**	**109**	**33.27**	**6-28**
		CAREER		**313**	**358**	**81**	**3593**	**122**	**12.97**	**1**	**4**	**99**	**9172.1**	**2121**	**23300**	**950**	**24.52**	**7-40**

HOLDING, Michael Anthony

SEASON	TEAM	OPPONENTS	V	M	I	NO	RUNS	H.S.	AVGE	100	50	CT	OV	MD	RUNS	W	AVGE	B.B.
				BATTING									BOWLING					
1972-73	Jamaica	Shell Shield	IIs	3	5		33	15	6.60				67	13	217	5	43.40	
1972-73	Jamaica	Australian Tourist	WI	1	2		9	9	4.50			1	23	6	69	2	34.50	
1972-73	WI President's XI	Australian Tourist	WI	1	2	1	1	1	1.00			1	18	1	59	1	59.00	
1973-74	Jamaica	Shell Shield	IIs	2	1		1	1	1.00			1	48	7	162	1	162.00	
1973-74	WI President's XI	M.C.C. Tourist	WI	1	2		6	5	3.00				7	2	14	0		
1974-75	Jamaica	Shell Shield	IIs	4	5	1	44	*32	11.00			1	93.3	19	297	7	42.42	
1975-76	West Indies	Tour of Australia	A	2	4	1	131	62	43.66		2	1	56	5	212	9	23.55	
1975-76	**WEST INDIES**	**AUSTRALIA TESTS**	**A**	**5**	**9**		**95**	**34**	**10.55**			**3**	**140.5**	**15**	**614**	**10**	**61.40**	
1975-76	**WEST INDIES**	**INDIA TESTS**	**WI**	**4**	**6**	**1**	**77**	**55**	**15.40**		**1**		**138**	**35**	**378**	**19**	**19.89**	
1976	West Indies	Tour of England	E	8	8	1	111	42	15.85			5	180.2	57	435	27	16.11	
1976	**WEST INDIES**	**ENGLAND TESTS**	**E**	**4**	**5**		**41**	**32**	**8.20**				**159.3**	**54**	**356**	**28**	**12.71**	
1976-77	Jamaica	Shell Shield	IIs	1	2	1	33	*33	33.00			1	10	3	18	1	18.00	
1977-78	Jamaica	Australian Tourist	WI	1	2		28	17	14.00			2	35.2	8	83	7	11.85	
1979-80	West Indies	Tour of Australia	A	1	1		2	2	2.00			1	29	8	88	4	22.00	
1979-80	**WEST INDIES**	**AUSTRALIA TESTS**	**A**	**3**	**4**	**1**	**22**	**11**	**7.33**			**2**	**111**	**24**	**319**	**14**	**22.78**	
1979-80	West Indies	Tour of New Zealand	NZ	1	2		5	5	2.50				26	6	61	1	61.00	
1979-80	**WEST INDIES**	**NEW ZEALAND TESTS**	**NZ**	**3**	**5**	**1**	**28**	***16**	**7.00**				**94**	**21**	**236**	**7**	**33.70**	
1979-80	Jamaica	Shell Shield	IIs	1	2	1	14	*10	14.00			2	43	9	134	5	26.80	
1980	West Indies	Tour of England	E	6	5	2	38	20	12.66			1	161.2	40	464	24	19.33	
1980	**WEST INDIES**	**ENGLAND TESTS**	**E**	**5**	**6**	**4**	**61**	**35**	**30.50**			**1**	**230.5**	**56**	**632**	**20**	**31.60**	
1980-81	West Indies	Tour of Pakistan	P	3	3		24	19	8.00				57	12	169	6	28.16	
1980-81	Jamaica	Shell Shield	IIs	4	5		51	33	10.20			1	99	13	332	13	25.53	
1980-81	**WEST INDIES**	**ENGLAND TESTS**	**WI**	**4**	**4**	**1**	**84**	***58**	**28.00**		**1**	**1**	**132.2**	**38**	**315**	**17**	**18.52**	
1981	Lancashire	Counties	E	7	8	2	66	32	11.00			2	271.1	75	715	40	17.87	
1981-82	International XI	Tour of Pakistan	P	2	4	1	131	67	43.66		1		46.1	11	144	8	18.00	
1981-82	West Indies	Tour of Australia	A	3	2		30	24	15.00			1	70	12	191	8	23.87	
1981-82	**WEST INDIES**	**AUSTRALIA TESTS**	**A**	**3**	**5**		**26**	**9**	**5.20**			**2**	**140.3**	**37**	**344**	**24**	**14.33**	
1982-83	West Indies XI	International XI	WI	1	1	1	3	*3					14	5	33	0		
1982-83	Tasmania	Sheffield Shield	A	9	11	2	187	*47	20.77			3	371.4	93	946	36	26.27	
1982-83	Jamaica	Shell Shield	IIs	1	2		22	16	11.00			1	34.2	7	139	3	46.33	
1982-83	**WEST INDIES**	**INDIA TESTS**	**WI**	**5**	**5**		**27**	**24**	**5.40**			**3**	**162**	**23**	**502**	**12**	**41.83**	
1983	Derbyshire	Counties	E	6	5	1	90	63	22.50		1	2	169	41	451	21	21.47	
1983-84	West Indies	Tour of India	I	2	2		30	25	15.00			2	33	10	63	4	15.75	
1983-84	**WEST INDIES**	**INDIA TESTS**	**I**	**6**	**7**		**141**	**58**	**20.14**		**1**		**223.4**	**43**	**663**	**30**	**22.10**	
1983-84	**WEST INDIES**	**AUSTRALIA TESTS**	**WI**	**3**	**3**	**2**	**3**	***3**	**3.00**			**1**	**101.5**	**20**	**245**	**13**	**18.84**	
1984	West Indies	Tour of England	E	3	2		31	31	15.50			1	56.3	18	143	6	23.83	

SEASON	TEAM	OPPONENTS	V	M	I	NO	RUNS	H.S.	AVGE	100	50	CT	OV	MD	RUNS	W	AVGE	B.B.
1984	**WEST INDIES**	**ENGLAND TESTS**	**E**	**4**	**5**		**158**	**69**	**31.60**		**2**	**2**	**122.2**	**24**	**343**	**15**	**22.86**	
1984-85	West Indies	Tour of Australia	A	3	3		47	21	15.66			4	80.2	20	161	5	32.20	
1984-85	**WEST INDIES**	**AUSTRALIA TESTS**	**A**	**3**	**4**		**2**	**1**	**0.50**			**2**	**81.1**	**20**	**249**	**15**	**16.60**	
1984-85	**WEST INDIES**	**NEW ZEALAND TESTS**	**WI**	**3**	**3**		**21**	**12**	**7.00**			**1**	**82**	**24**	**218**	**9**	**4.79**	
1985	Derbyshire	Counties	E	12	19	1	413	80	22.94		3	6	354.5	67	1124	50	22.48	
1985-86	Jamaica	Shell Shield	IIs	5	9		114	34	12.66			7	77	17	251	15	16.73	
1985-86	Jamaica	English Tourist	WI	1	D								13.3	1	44	2	22.00	
1985-86	**WEST INDIES**	**ENGLAND TESTS**	**WI**	**4**	**4**		**124**	**73**	**31.00**		**1**	**3**	**102.4**	**16**	**385**	**16**	**24.06**	
1986	Derbyshire	Counties	E	14	20	2	295	*36	16.38			6	388.1	110	1045	52	20.09	
1986-87	West Indies	Tour of Australia	A	1	1		2	2	2.00			1	11	3	18	3	6.00	
1986-87	West Indies	Tour of New Zealand	NZ	1	1	1	34	*34				2	34	6	104	4	26.00	
1986-87	**WEST INDIES**	**NEW ZEALAND TESTS**	**NZ**	**1**	**1**		**0**	**0**				**1**	**37**	**8**	**99**	**0**		
1986-87	Jamaica	Shell Shield	IIs	2	3		4	4	1.33			1	56	10	157	12	13.08	
1986-87	Jamaica	Lancashire Tourist XI	WI	1	D								7	2	12	0		
1987	Derbyshire	Counties	E	13	18	2	278	*63	17.37		1	10	391.2	72	1194	49	24.36	
1987-88	Canterbury	N.Z. Shell Shield	NZ	7	11	4	62	31	8.85			9	258.5	90	488	29	16.82	
1987-88	Jamaica	Red Stripe Cup	IIs	2	2	1	30	24	30.00				45	8	140	7	20.00	
1988	Derbyshire	Counties	E	11	12	2	129	*30	12.90			7	279.1	49	827	24	34.45	
1988-89	Jamaica	Red Stripe Cup	IIs	5	7	1	71	15	11.83			11	92	15	268	10	26.80	
1989	Derbyshire	Counties	E	10	13	4	90	34	10.00			8	258	46	863	28	30.82	
		Jamaica		34	47	5	454	34	10.80			29	743.4	138	2323	90	25.81	
		West Indies		97	115	17	1405	73	14.33		8	42	2893.1	663	8113	351	23.11	
		Derbyshire		66	87	12	1295	80	17.26		5	39	1840.3	385	5504	224	24.57	
		Lancashire		7	8	2	66	32	11.00			2	271.1	75	715	40	17.87	
		Tasmania		9	11	2	187	*47	20.77			3	371.4	93	946	36	26.27	
		Canterbury		7	11	4	62	31	8.85			9	258.5	90	488	29	16.82	
		International XI		2	4	1	131	67	43.66		1		46.1	11	144	8	18.00	
		TEST RECORD		**60**	**76**	**10**	**910**	**73**	**13.78**	**0**	**6**	**22**	**2058.4**	**458**	**5898**	**249**	**23.68**	**8-92**
		CAREER		**222**	**283**	**43**	**3600**	**80**	**15.00**	**0**	**14**	**125**	**6425.1**	**1455**	**18233**	**778**	**22.43**	**8-92**

HOLFORD, David Anthony Jerome

				BATTING									BOWLING					
SEASON	TEAM	OPPONENTS	V	M	I	NO	RUNS	H.S.	AVGE	100	50	CT	OV	MD	RUNS	W	AVGE	B.B.
1960-61	Barbados	Trinidad	IIs	2	4		37	22	9.25			2	19.5	1	66	1	66.00	
1962-63	Trinidad	Barbados	IIs	1	2		22	14	11.00			1	17	0	82	0		
1962-63	N. Trinidad	South Trinidad BC	T	1	1		9	9	9.00									

SEASON	TEAM	OPPONENTS	V	BATTING M	I	NO	RUNS	H.S.	AVGE	100	50	CT	BOWLING OV	MD	RUNS	W	AVGE	B.B.
1965-66	Barbados	Shell Shield	IIs	4	3		21	11	7.00			4	152.3	36	386	18	21.44	
1966	West Indies	Tour of England	E	14	18	4	532	*107	38.00	1	3	7	416.3	104	1158	46	25.17	
1966	**WEST INDIES**	**ENGLAND TESTS**	**E**	**5**	**8**	**2**	**227**	***105**	**37.83**	**1**		**5**	**90.5**	**13**	**302**	**5**	**60.40**	
1966-67	West Indies	Tour of India	I	2	2		77	46	38.50			1	50	11	141	7	20.14	
1966-67	**WEST INDIES**	**INDIA TESTS**	**I**	**1**	**1**		**80**	**80**	**80.00**		**1**	**1**	**58.4**	**9**	**162**	**5**	**32.40**	
1966-67	Barbados	Shell Shield	IIs	2	2	1	80	80	80.00		1		46	9	179	2	89.50	
1967-68	Barbados	M.C.C. Tourist	WI	1	2		8	5	4.00				20	5	58	0		
1967-68	**WEST INDIES**	**ENGLAND TESTS**	**WI**	**4**	**7**		**50**	**35**	**7.14**			**1**	**156**	**39**	**335**	**6**	**55.83**	
1968-69	West Indies	Tour of Australia	A	8	13	5	308	54	38.50		1	8	156.7	17	709	13	54.33	
1968-69	**WEST INDIES**	**AUSTRALIA TESTS**	**A**	**2**	**4**		**96**	**80**	**24.00**		**1**	**3**	**72.5**	**8**	**290**	**4**	**72.50**	
1968-69	West Indies	Tour of New Zealand	NZ	3	6		112	63	18.66		1	2	52	3	314	6	52.33	
1968-69	**WEST INDIES**	**NEW ZEALAND TESTS**	**NZ**	**3**	**5**	**1**	**35**	**18**	**8.75**			**3**	**65**	**12**	**242**	**9**	**26.88**	
1969	Barbados	Tour of English Counties	E	2	4		135	53	33.75		1	1	87.2	17	287	9	31.88	
1969-70	Barbados	Shell Shield	IIs	4	6	2	181	65	45.25		1	4	148.4	22	462	14	33.00	
1969-70	Barbados	Duke of Norfolk's Tourist	WI	1	2		108	67	54.00		1	1	47.2	11	96	3	32.00	
1970-71	Barbados	Shell Shield	IIs	3	4		137	66	34.25		1	5	91.2	12	277	15	18.46	
1970-71	Barbados	Indian Tourist	WI	1	1		111	111	111.00	1			25	6	87	0		
1970-71	**WEST INDIES**	**INDIA TESTS**	**WI**	**1**	**2**		**53**	**44**	**26.50**				**55.3**	**8**	**131**	**3**	**43.66**	
1971-72	Barbados	Shell Shield	IIs	4	6	3	188	93	62.66		2	6	139.4	40	342	13	26.30	
1971-72	Barbados	New Zealand Tourist	WI	1	2		50	35	25.00			3	47	10	101	2	50.50	
1971-72	**WEST INDIES**	**NEW ZEALAND TESTS**	**WI**	**5**	**7**	**2**	**175**	**50**	**35.00**		**1**	**4**	**179**	**62**	**312**	**8**	**39.00**	
1972-73	Barbados	Shell Shield	IIs	4	8	1	218	96	31.14		1	2	124	31	297	12	24.75	
1972-73	Barbados	Australian Tourist	WI	1	2		31	31	15.50				18	0	70	1	70.00	
1973-74	Barbados	Shell Shield	IIs	4	6	2	175	*47	43.75			2	57.4	15	141	10	14.10	
1973-74	Barbados	M.C.C. Tourist	WI	1	1	1	52	*52			1		33	10	79	2	39.50	
1975-76	Barbados	Shell Shield	IIs	3	5	2	207	*74	69.00		2	2	94	33	183	11	16.63	
1975-76	Barbados	Indian Tourist	WI	1	1		15	15	15.00			3	26	2	86	2	43.00	
1975-76	**WEST INDIES**	**INDIA TESTS**	**WI**	**2**	**3**		**13**	**9**	**4.33**				**45.1**	**7**	**126**	**6**	**21.00**	
1976-77	Barbados	Shell Shield	IIs	4	6		157	90	26.16		1	7	116	36	281	14	20.07	
1976-77	Barbados	Pakistan Tourist	WI	1	1		39	39	39.00			1	44	5	137	1	137.00	
1976-77	**WEST INDIES**	**PAKISTAN TESTS**	**WI**	**1**	**2**		**39**	**37**	**19.50**			**1**	**34**	**6**	**109**	**5**	**21.80**	
1978-79	Barbados	Shell Shield	IIs	2	2	1	43	*30	43.00			3	37	12	68	0		
		Barbados		46	68	13	1993	111	36.23	1	12	46	1374.2	313	3683	130	28.33	
		Trinidad		1	2		22	14	11.00			1	17	0	82	0		
		North Trinidad		1	1		9	9	9.00									
		West Indies		51	78	14	1797	*107	28.07	2	8	36	1432.2	299	4331	123	35.21	

				M	I	NO	RUNS	H.S.	AVGE	100	50	CT	OV	MD	RUNS	W	AVGE	B.B.
		TEST RECORD		**24**	**39**	**5**	**768**	***105**	**22.58**	**1**	**3**	**18**	**757**	**164**	**2009**	**51**	**39.39**	**5-23**
		CAREER		**99**	**149**	**27**	**3821**	**111**	**31.31**	**3**	**20**	**83**	**2823.4**	**612**	**8096**	**253**	**32.00**	**8-52**

HOLT (Jnr), John Kenneth

				BATTING									BOWLING					
SEASON	TEAM	OPPONENTS	V	M	I	NO	RUNS	H.S.	AVGE	100	50	CT	OV	MD	RUNS	W	AVGE	B.B.
1945-46	Jamaica	Trinidad	IIs	3	3		151	94	50.33		2	1	4	0	10	1	10.00	
1946-47	Jamaica	Barbados	IIs	1	2		39	32	19.50			1	1	0	10	0		
1947-48	Jamaica	British Guiana	IIs	2	3		173	172	57.66	1		1	1	0	3	0		
1947-48	Jamaica	M.C.C. Tourist	WI	2	4		133	87	33.25		1							
1949-50	Comm. XI	Tour of India	I	17	24	3	838	162	39.90	1	5	2						
1950-51	Jamaica	British Guiana	IIs	2	4	1	130	63	43.33		1	4						
1952-53	Jamaica	Indian Tourist	WI	1	2		34	22	17.00			1						
1953-54	Jamaica	M.C.C. Tourist	WI	2	4		230	152	57.50	1		1/1	12	3	29	1	29.00	
1953-54	**WEST INDIES**	**ENGLAND TESTS**	**WI**	**5**	**9**	**1**	**432**	**166**	**54.00**	**1**	**2**	**2**						
1954-55	Jamaica	Trinidad	IIs	2	4		111	55	27.75		1	1						
1954-55	Jamaica	Australian Tourist	WI	1	2	1	31	25	31.00				6	1	16	1	16.00	
1954-55	**WEST INDIES**	**AUSTRALIA TESTS**	**WI**	**5**	**10**		**251**	**60**	**25.10**		**1**	**2**	**4**	**1**	**20**	**1**	**20.00**	
1956-57	Jamaica	British Guiana	IIs	1	1		13	13	13.00			1						
1956-57	Jamaica	Duke of Norfolk's Tourist	WI	3	6	2	317	*93	79.25		3	1	14	1	57	1	57.00	
1957-58	Jamaica	Pakistan Tourist	WI	1	2		139	124	69.50	1		1						
1958-59	Jamaica	Leeward Islands	IIs	1	1		81	81	81.00		1	2	7	2	10	0		
1958-59	Jamaica	Barbados	IIs	2	4		143	104	35.75	1		3	8	2	18	0		
1958-59	West Indies	Tour of India	I	9	13	3	561	105	56.10	2	3	1	1	0	4	0		
1958-59	**WEST INDIES**	**INDIA TESTS**	**I**	**5**	**8**	**1**	**343**	**123**	**49.00**	**1**	**2**	**4**						
1958-59	West Indies	Tour of Pakistan	P	2	2		57	43	28.50									
1958-59	**WEST INDIES**	**PAKISTAN TESTS**	**P**	**2**	**4**		**40**	**29**	**10.00**				**1**	**1**	**0**	**0**		
1959-60	Jamaica	M.C.C. Tourist	WI	1	2		6	6	3.00									
1961-62	Jamaica	Barbados	IIs	1	1		5	5	5.00									
		Jamaica		26	45	4	1736	172	42.34	4	9	18/1	53	9	153	4	38.25	
		West Indies		28	46	5	1684	166	41.07	4	8	9	6	2	24	1	24.00	
		Comm. XI		17	24	3	838	162	39.90	1	5	2						
		TEST RECORD		**17**	**31**	**2**	**1066**	**166**	**36.75**	**2**	**5**	**8**	**5**	**2**	**20**	**1**	**20.00**	**1-20**
		CAREER		**71**	**115**	**12**	**4258**	**172**	**41.33**	**9**	**22**	**29/1**	**59**	**11**	**177**	**5**	**35.40**	**1-1**

HOOPER, Carl Llewellyn

				BATTING									BOWLING					
SEASON	TEAM	OPPONENTS	V	M	I	NO	RUNS	H.S.	AVGE	100	50	CT	OV	MD	RUNS	W	AVGE	B.B.
1983-84	Demerara	Berbice JC	G	1	2		16	15	8.00									
1984-85	Demerara	Berbice GT	G	1	2		37	32	18.50			1	47.4	6	142	9	15.77	
1984-85	Guyana	Shell Shield	IIs	5	7		267	126	38.14	1		6	91.4	11	327	12	27.25	
1984-85	WI Shell Awards XI	New Zealand Tourist	WI	1	1		36	36	36.00			1	4	0	24	0		
1984-85	WI Under 23 XI	New Zealand Tourist	WI	1	1		37	37	37.00			1	31	4	94	5	18.80	
1984-85	WI President's XI	New Zealand Tourist	WI	1	1		0	0					17.5	2	59	2	29.50	
1986-87	Demerara	Berbice GT	G	1	1	1	25	*25				1	13	5	21	4	5.25	
1986-87	West Indies 'B'	Tour of Zimbabwe	Z	5	6	1	262	88	32.40		2	7	57	10	181	5	36.20	
1986-87	West Indies	Tour of New Zealand	NZ	2	3		93	69	31.00		1	2	7	0	50	0		
1986-87	Guyana	Shell Shield	IIs	3	4	1	58	25	19.33			2	82	19	211	8	26.37	
1987-88	West Indies	Tour of India	I	2	2		42	41	21.00			6	20	3	73	1	73.00	
1987-88	**WEST INDIES**	**INDIA TESTS**	**I**	**3**	**4**	**1**	**147**	***100**	**49.00**	**1**			**38**	**9**	**102**	**2**	**51.00**	
1987-88	WI President's XI	Pakistan Tourist	WI	1	1		67	67	67.00		1	2	57.2	7	161	5	32.20	
1987-88	**WEST INDIES**	**PAKISTAN TESTS**	**WI**	**3**	**6**		**156**	**54**	**26.00**		**1**	**2**	**47.1**	**6**	**164**	**3**	**54.66**	
1988	West Indies	Tour of England	E	9	13	1	459	87	38.25		4	6	82.1	13	246	9	27.33	
1988	**WEST INDIES**	**ENGLAND TESTS**	**E**	**5**	**7**		**166**	**84**	**23.71**		**1**	**3**	**24**	**3**	**57**	**0**		
1988-89	West Indies	Tour of Australia	A	6	9		337	83	37.44		2	4	131.1	23	339	14	24.21	
1988-89	**WEST INDIES**	**AUSTRALIA TESTS**	**A**	**5**	**9**		**170**	**64**	**18.88**		**1**	**5**	**79.3**	**17**	**198**	**2**	**99.00**	
1988-89	WI Board XI	Indian Tourist	WI	1	1	1	54	*54			1	2						
1989-90	West Indies 'B'	Tour of Zimbabwe	Z	3	3		104	86	34.66		1	4	43	16	71	6	11.83	
1989-90	Guyana	Red Stripe Cup	IIs	3	5		201	102	40.20	1	1	2	100.4	21	240	9	26.67	
1989-90	**WEST INDIES**	**ENGLAND TESTS**	**WI**	**3**	**5**		**71**	**32**	**14.00**			**3**	**24**	**5**	**54**	**0**		
		Guyana		11	16	1	526	126	35.06	2	1	10	274.2	51	778	29	26.82	
		Demerara		3	5	1	78	32	19.50			2	60.4	11	163	13	12.53	
		West Indies		51	72	4	2201	*100	32.36	1	15	48	663.1	118	1873	54	34.68	
		TEST RECORD		**19**	**31**	**1**	**710**	***100**	**23.66**	**1**	**3**	**13**	**212.4**	**40**	**575**	**7**	**82.14**	**2-42**
		CAREER		**65**	**93**	**6**	**2805**	**126**	**32.24**	**3**	**16**	**60**	**998.1**	**180**	**2814**	**96**	**29.31**	**5-33**

HOWARD, Anthony Bourne

				BATTING									BOWLING					
SEASON	TEAM	OPPONENTS	V	M	I	NO	RUNS	H.S.	AVGE	100	50	CT	OV	MD	RUNS	W	AVGE	B.B.
1965-66	Barbados	Shell Shield	IIs	3	2	1	19	10	19.00				74.1	29	163	7	23.28	
1966-67	Barbados	Shell Shield	IIs	4	3	1	5	5	2.50			3	120.5	27	285	13	21.92	
1967-68	Barbados	M.C.C. Tourist	WI	1	1		17	17	17.00				36	7	106	3	35.33	

1968-69	Barbados	Shell Shield	IIs	3	4	1	57	*42	19.00			2	89.2	26	191	7	27.28	
1970-71	Barbados	Shell Shield	IIs	4	7	1	58	29	9.66			1	135.3	24	333	9	37.00	
1970-71	Barbados	Indian Tourist	WI	1	1		16	16	16.00			1	24.4	5	59	4	14.75	
1971-72	Barbados	Shell Shield	IIs	4	4		26	18	6.50			1	130	33	355	13	27.30	
1971-72	Barbados	New Zealand Tourist	WI	1	1	1	11	*11					65.2	13	133	8	16.62	
1971-72	**WEST INDIES**	**NEW ZEALAND TESTS**	**WI**	**1**	**D**								**62**	**16**	**140**	**2**	**70.00**	
1972-73	Barbados	Shell Shield	IIs	4	6	1	9	5	1.80				122	31	315	11	28.63	
1972-73	Barbados	Australian Tourist	WI	1	2		10	5	5.00				13.3	0	76	3	25.33	
1973-74	Barbados	Shell Shield	IIs	2	4	1	61	24	20.33				11	6	16	0		
1974-75	Barbados	Shell Shield	IIs	2	3		21	8	7.00			2	66.4	16	149	5	29.80	
		Barbados		30	38	7	310	*42	10.00			10	889	217	2181	83	26.27	
		West Indies		1	D								62	16	140	2	70.00	
		TEST RECORD		**1**	**0**	**0**	**0**	**0**		**0**	**0**	**0**	**62**	**16**	**140**	**2**	**70.00**	**2-140**
		CAREER		**31**	**38**	**7**	**310**	***42**	**10.00**	**0**	**0**	**10**	**951**	**233**	**2321**	**85**	**27.30**	**5-46**

HUNTE, Conrad Cleophas

				BATTING									BOWLING					
SEASON	TEAM	OPPONENTS	V	M	I	NO	RUNS	H.S.	AVGE	100	50	CT/St	OV	MD	RUNS	W	AVGE	B.B.
1950-51	Barbados	Trinidad	IIs	2	4		89	63	22.25		1							
1951-52	Barbados	British Guiana	IIs	2	3		83	66	27.66		1	0/1						
1951-52	Barbados	Jamaica	IIs	2	3		188	80	62.66		2							
1952-53	Barbados	Indian Tourist	WI	1	1		29	29	29.00									
1954-55	Barbados	British Guiana	IIs	2	3		160	70	53.33		2	3						
1954-55	Barbados	Australian Tourist	WI	1	2		3	3	1.50									
1955-56	Barbados	E.W. Swanton's Tourist	WI	2	3		266	151	88.66	1	1	1	2	0	6	0		
1955-56	West Indies XI	E.W. Swanton's Tourist	WI	1	2	1	86	*55	86.00		1	1						
1956	Comm. XI	England XI	E	1	1	1	28	*28										
1957-58	Barbados	Pakistan Tourist	WI	1	2		84	77	42.00		1		4	0	18	0		
1957-58	**WEST INDIES**	**PAKISTAN TESTS**	**WI**	**5**	**9**	**1**	**622**	**260**	**77.75**	**3**								
1958-59	West Indies	Tour of India	I	9	16	2	727	137	51.92	1	7	1	7	4	6	0		
1958-59	**WEST INDIES**	**INDIA TESTS**	**I**	**5**	**8**		**216**	**92**	**27.00**		**1**	**2**	**4**	**2**	**4**	**0**		
1958-59	West Indies	Tour of Pakistan	P	3	6	1	163	52	32.60		1							
1958-59	**WEST INDIES**	**PAKISTAN TESTS**	**P**	**1**	**2**		**21**	**21**	**10.50**									
1959-60	Barbados	M.C.C. Tourist	WI	1	2	1	83	69	83.00		1							
1959-60	**WEST INDIES**	**ENGLAND TESTS**	**WI**	**5**	**8**	**1**	**291**	***72**	**41.57**		**1**	**3**	**12**	**3**	**26**	**1**	**26.00**	
1960-61	West Indies	Tour of Australia	A	6	10		354	105	35.40	1	1	13	4	0	16	1	16.00	

SEASON	TEAM	OPPONENTS	V	BATTING M	I	NO	RUNS	H.S.	AVGE	100	50	CT/St	BOWLING OV	MD	RUNS	W	AVGE	B.B.
1960-61	**WEST INDIES**	**AUSTRALIA TESTS**	**A**	**5**	**10**		**377**	**110**	**37.70**	**1**	**2**	**4**						
1961	Comm. XI	England XI	E	1	2		55	43	27.50			2	16	2	63	1	63.00	
1961-62	Barbados	Jamaica	IIs	1	1		263	263	263.00	1								
1961-62	Barbados	British Guiana	IIs	1	2		79	58	39.50		1	1						
1961-62	Barbados	Indian Tourist	WI	1	1		23	23	23.00			2	3	0	15	0		
1961-62	**WEST INDIES**	**INDIA TESTS**	**WI**	**5**	**8**	**1**	**195**	**59**	**27.85**		**2**	**2**						
1963	West Indies	Tour of England	E	16	27	4	896	103	38.95	1	6	8	44.1	8	112	5	22.40	
1963	**WEST INDIES**	**ENGLAND TESTS**	**E**	**5**	**10**	**2**	**471**	**182**	**58.87**	**2**	**1**	**4**						
1963-64	West Indies XI	The Rest XI	WI	1	2		66	65	33.00		1	2	22	2	68	1	68.00	
1963-64	C. Hunte's XI	F. Worrell's XI	WI	1	2		38	33	19.00			1	7	0	33	1	33.00	
1963-64	Indian Prime Minister's XI	President's XI	I	1	2		51	30	25.50			3	5	1	20	1	20.00	
1963-64	Barbados	British Guiana	IIs	1	2		148	129	74.00	1								
1963-64	Barbados	Jamaica	IIs	1	2	1	128	*88	128.00		1	1						
1963-64	Barbados	Trinidad	IIs	1	2		35	25	17.50			2						
1964-65	Jamaica XI	Cavaliers Touring XI	WI	1	2		90	78	45.00		1							
1964-65	Barbados	Australian Tourist	WI	1	1		53	53	53.00		1		9	0	31	0		
1964-65	**WEST INDIES**	**AUSTRALIA TESTS**	**WI**	**5**	**10**	**1**	**550**	**89**	**61.11**		**6**		**5**	**2**	**9**	**0**		
1965	Rest of World XI	England XI	E	1	2		93	63	46.50		1							
1965-66	Barbados	Shell Shield	IIs	4	5	1	141	61	35.25		1	2						
1966	West Indies	Tour of England	E	14	19		727	206	38.26	1	5	8	19	6	52	1	52.00	
1966	**WEST INDIES**	**ENGLAND TESTS**	**E**	**5**	**8**		**243**	**135**	**30.57**	**1**		**1**	**13**	**2**	**41**	**0**		
1966-67	West Indies	Tour of India	I	4	7		282	132	40.28	1			29	6	75	4	18.75	
1966-67	**WEST INDIES**	**INDIA TESTS**	**I**	**3**	**5**		**259**	**101**	**51.80**	**1**			**11**	**2**	**30**	**1**	**30.00**	
1966-67	Barbados	Shell Shield	IIs	1	2	1	98	*80	98.00		1		5	1	16	0		
1966-67	Barbados	Rest of World XI	WI	1	2		51	36	25.50				3	0	3	0		
1967	Rest of World XI	Sussex	E	1	1		11	11	11.00			1						
		Barbados		27	43	4	2004	263	51.38	3	14	12/1	26	1	89	0		
		West Indies		98	167	14	6546	260	42.78	13	35	49	170.1	37	439	14	31.35	
		Jamaican XI		1	2		90	78	45.00		1							
		C. Hunte's XI		1	2		38	33	19.00			1	7	0	33	1	33.00	
		Comm. XI		2	3	1	83	43	41.50			2	16	2	63	1	63.00	
		Rest of World XI		2	3		104	63	34.66		1	1						
		Indian Prime Minister's XI		1	2		51	30	25.50			3	5	1	20	1	20.00	
		TEST RECORD		**44**	**78**	**6**	**3245**	**260**	**45.06**	**8**	**13**	**16**	**45**	**11**	**110**	**2**	**55.00**	**1-17**
		CAREER		**132**	**222**	**19**	**8916**	**263**	**43.92**	**16**	**51**	**68/1**	**224.1**	**41**	**644**	**17**	**37.88**	**3-5**

HUNTE, Errol Ashton Clairmore

SEASON	TEAM	OPPONENTS	V	BATTING M	I	NO	RUNS	H.S.	AVGE	100	50	CT/St	BOWLING OV	MD	RUNS	W	AVGE	B.B.
1928-29	Trinidad	British Guiana	IIs	1	2		38	26	19.00			1						
1928-29	Trinidad	Barbados	IIs	1	1		1	1	1.00			3						
1929-30	Trinidad	British Guiana	IIs	1	2		17	17	8.50			4						
1929-30	Trinidad	M.C.C. Tourist	WI	1	2	2	32	*20				5/2						
1929-30	**WEST INDIES**	**ENGLAND TESTS**	**WI**	**3**	**6**	**1**	**166**	**58**	**33.20**		**2**	**5**						
1930-31	West Indies	Tour of Australia	A	6	9	2	135	29	19.28			6/2						
1931-32	Trinidad	Barbados	IIs	1	2		65	56	32.50		1	0/1						
1931-32	Trinidad	British Guiana	IIs	1	2		14	10	7.00			2/1						
1933-34	Trinidad	Barbados	IIs	1	2		4	2	2.00			2/2						
		Trinidad		7	13	2	171	56	15.54		2	17/6						
		West Indies		9	15	3	301	58	25.08		1	11/2						
		TEST RECORD		**3**	**6**	**1**	**166**	**58**	**33.20**	**0**	**2**	**5**						
		CAREER		**16**	**28**	**5**	**472**	**58**	**20.52**	**0**	**3**	**28/8**						

HYLTON, Leslie George

SEASON	TEAM	OPPONENTS	V	BATTING M	I	NO	RUNS	H.S.	AVGE	100	50	CT	BOWLING OV	MD	RUNS	W	AVGE	B.B.
1926-27	Jamaica	L.H. Tennyson's Tourist	WI	3	4	3	69	*32	69.00			5	58.5	8	221	9	24.55	
1927-28	Combined J/B XI	Combined Trin/BG XI	IIs	2	3		21	10	7.00			1	20	1	77	3	25.66	
1927-28	Jamaica	L.H. Tennyson's Tourist	WI	3	5	1	173	60	43.25		2	3	86.1	15	242	9	26.88	
1928-29	Jamaica	Julien Cahn's Tourist	WI	2	3		58	39	19.33			3	57	16	157	8	19.62	
1929-30	Jamaica	M.C.C Tourist	WI	1	1		7	7	7.00				20.1	3	35	1	35.00	
1931-32	Jamaica	L.H. Tennyson's Tourist	WI	2	1		11	11	11.00			1	104	21	252	12	21.00	
1932-33	G.C. Grant's XI	C.A. Merry's XI	IIs	1	2		2	2	1.00				40.3	7	75	4	18.75	
1934-35	Jamaica	M.C.C. Tourist	WI	1	1		1	1	1.00			3	24.4	3	61	3	20.33	
1934-35	**WEST INDIES**	**ENGLAND TESTS**	**WI**	**4**	**5**	**1**	**53**	**19**	**13.25**			**1**	**96.5**	**22**	**251**	**13**	**19.30**	
1935-36	Jamaica	Yorkshire Tourist	WI	3	5		177	80	35.40		2	2	123.3	13	347	6	57.83	
1938-39	Jamaica	Combined University Tourist	WI	1	2		34	31	17.00			2	24	2	107	5	21.40	
1938-39	Jamaica	Trinidad	IIs	1	2		0	0					38	6	131	5	26.20	
1938-39	Jamaica	West Indies XI	IIs	1	1		22	22	22.00				15	2	38	3	12.66	
1939	West Indies	Tour of England	E	13	16	3	198	55	15.23		1	10	253	23	914	36	25.38	
1939	**WEST INDIES**	**ENGLAND TESTS**	**E**	**2**	**3**	**1**	**17**	**13**	**8.50**				**48**	**9**	**167**	**3**	**55.66**	

SEASON	TEAM		M	I	NO	RUNS	H.S.	AVGE	100	50	CT	OV	MD	RUNS	W	AVGE	B.B.
			BATTING									BOWLING					
		Jamaica	18	25	4	552	80	26.28		4	19	551.2	89	1591	61	26.08	
		West Indies	19	24	5	268	55	14.10		1	11	397.5	54	1332	52	25.61	
		Combined J/B XI	2	3		21	10	7.00			1	20	1	77	3	25.66	
		G.C. Grant's XI	1	2		2	2	1.00				40.3	7	75	4	18.75	
		TEST RECORD	**6**	**8**	**2**	**70**	**19**	**11.66**	**0**	**0**	**1**	**144.5**	**31**	**418**	**16**	**26.12**	**4-27**
		CAREER	**40**	**54**	**9**	**843**	**80**	**18.73**	**0**	**5**	**31**	**1009.4**	**151**	**3075**	**120**	**25.62**	**5-24**

JOHNSON, Hophnie Horace Hines

SEASON	TEAM	OPPONENTS	V	M	I	NO	RUNS	H.S.	AVGE	100	50	CT	OV	MD	RUNS	W	AVGE	B.B.
				BATTING									BOWLING					
1934-35	Jamaica	M.C.C. Tourist	WI	1	D								37	7	96	5	19.20	
1935-36	Jamaica	Yorkshire Tourist	WI	1	1		0	0				1	25	6	42	1	42.00	
1938-39	Jamaica	Combined University Tourist	WI	2	3	3	10	*9				2	35.3	3	103	6	17.16	
1938-39	Jamaica	Trinidad	IIs	1	1		0	0					27	3	85	2	42.50	
1938-39	Jamaica	West Indies XI	WI	1	1	1	0	*0				1	13	2	44	2	22.00	
1945-46	Jamaica	Trinidad	IIs	2	3	2	57	*39	57.00			2	31.3	5	100	6	16.66	
1947-48	Jamaica	M.C.C. Tourist	WI	1	2		1	1	0.50			2	27.1	6	42	2	21.00	
1947-48	**WEST INDIES**	**ENGLAND TESTS**	**WI**	**1**	**1**		**8**	**8**	**8.00**				**65.5**	**24**	**96**	**10**	**9.60**	
1950	West Indies	Tour of England	E	15	13	4	154	*39	17.11			5	370.1	89	812	31	26.19	
1950	**WEST INDIES**	**ENGLAND TESTS**	**E**	**2**	**3**		**30**	**22**	**10.00**				**65.4**	**13**	**142**	**3**	**47.33**	
1950-51	Jamaica	British Guiana	IIs	1	2	2	56	*34					13	2	27	0		
		Jamaica		10	13	8	124	*39	24.80			8	209.1	34	539	24	22.45	
		West Indies		18	17	4	192	*39	14.76			5	501.4	126	1050	44	23.86	
		TEST RECORD		**3**	**4**	**0**	**38**	**22**	**9.50**	**0**	**0**	**0**	**131.3**	**37**	**238**	**13**	**18.30**	**5-41**
		CAREER		**28**	**30**	**12**	**316**	***39**	**17.55**	**0**	**0**	**13**	**710.5**	**160**	**1589**	**68**	**23.36**	**5-33**

JOHNSON, Tyrell Francis

SEASON	TEAM	OPPONENTS	V	M	I	NO	RUNS	H.S.	AVGE	100	50	CT	OV	MD	RUNS	W	AVGE	B.B.
				BATTING									BOWLING					
1935-36	Trinidad	Barbados	IIs	1	2	2	7	*5					35	11	73	2	36.50	
1935-36	Trinidad	British Guiana	IIs	1	2	1	2	*2	2.00			1	17	4	34	2	17.00	
1936-37	Trinidad	Barbados	IIs	1	1		27	27	27.00				32	9	70	2	35.00	

SEASON	TEAM	OPPONENTS	V	M	I	NO	RUNS	H.S.	AVGE	100	50	CT	OV	MD	RUNS	W	AVGE	B.B.
1936-37	Trinidad	British Guiana	IIs	1	1	1	4	*4				1	33	13	53	4	13.25	
1937-38	Trinidad	British Guiana	IIs	1	2		8	8	4.00				45	11	114	2	57.00	
1938-39	Trinidad	Barbados	IIs	1	1	1	1	*1				1	17.6	3	44	3	14.66	
1938-39	Trinidad	British Guiana	IIs	1	1	1	2	*2				1	23.3	8	46	7	6.57	
1938-39	Trinidad	Jamaica	IIs	1	1	1	9	*9					21	5	55	5	11.00	
1938-39	West Indies XI	Jamaica	IIs	1	1		0	0					23	5	66	7	9.42	
1939	West Indies	Tour of England	E	8	8	3	21	12	4.20			3	127.1	23	391	13	30.07	
1939	**WEST INDIES**	**ENGLAND TESTS**	**E**	**1**	**1**	**1**	**9**	***9**				**1**	**30**	**3**	**129**	**3**	**43.00**	
		Trinidad		8	11	7	60	27	15.00			4	224.1	64	489	27	18.11	
		West Indies		10	10	4	30	12	5.00			4	180.1	31	586	23	25.47	
		TEST RECORD		**1**	**1**	**1**	**9**	***9**		**0**	**0**	**1**	**30**	**3**	**129**	**3**	**43.00**	**2-53**
		CAREER		**18**	**21**	**11**	**90**	**27**	**9.00**	**0**	**0**	**8**	**404.2**	**95**	**1075**	**50**	**21.50**	**6-41**

JONES, Charles Ernest Llewellyn

				BATTING									BOWLING					
SEASON	TEAM	OPPONENTS	V	M	I	NO	RUNS	H.S.	AVGE	100	50	CT	OV	MD	RUNS	W	AVGE	B.B.
1925-26	British Guiana	Barbados	IIs	1	1		14	14	14.00			1	20	4	62	1	62.00	
1925-26	British Guiana	Trinidad	IIs	1	2		1	1	0.50				10	0	33	0		
1926-27	British Guiana	Barbados	IIs	1	2		54	30	27.00				55	14	133	1	133.00	
1927-28	Combined T/BG XI	Combined Jam/Bar XI	IIs	2	2		39	34	19.50			2	37	11	91	5	18.20	
1927-28	Barbados XI	West Indies XI	IIs	1	1		0	0					21	0	93	0		
1928-29	British Guiana	Trinidad	IIs	1	2		13	12	6.50			1	27	7	72	2	36.00	
1929-30	British Guiana	Barbados	IIs	1	2	1	101	*89	101.00			1	29	7	69	2	34.50	
1929-30	British Guiana	Trinidad	IIs	1	1		27	27	27.00		1		19.1	4	58	3	19.33	
1929-30	British Guiana	M.C.C. Tourist	WI	2	4		31	15	7.75			2	55	7	157	1	157.00	
1929-30	**WEST INDIES**	**ENGLAND TESTS**	**WI**	**1**	**2**		**8**	**6**	**4.00**			**2**	**10**	**7**	**5**	**0**		
1931-32	British Guiana	Trinidad	IIs	1	2		52	43	26.00				17	1	51	1	51.00	
1933-34	British Guiana	Barbados	IIs	1	2		29	28	14.50			2	12	2	26	0		
1934-35	British Guiana	Barbados	IIs	1	2		130	85	65.00		1		4	1	7	0		
1934-35	British Guiana	Trinidad	IIs	1	2	1	77	69	77.00		1		12	2	19	0		
1934-35	British Guiana	M.C.C. Tourist	WI	2	4	1	95	*72	31.66		1	2	22	4	85	3	28.33	
1934-35	**WEST INDIES**	**ENGLAND TESTS**	**WI**	**3**	**5**		**55**	**19**	**11.00**			**1**	**7**	**4**	**6**	**0**		
1935-36	British Guiana	Trinidad	IIs	1	1		16	16	16.00			1	8	3	16	1	16.00	
1937-38	British Guiana	Barbados	IIs	1	1		13	13	13.00			2	10	3	12	2	6.00	
1937-38	British Guiana	Trinidad	IIs	1	2		75	48	37.50			1	16	2	29	1	29.00	
1938-39	British Guiana	R.S. Grant's XI	IIs	1	2		64	51	32.00		1	2	14	3	35	1	35.00	

SEASON	TEAM	OPPONENTS	V	M	I	NO	RUNS	H.S.	AVGE	100	50	CT	OV	MD	RUNS	W	AVGE	B.B.
				BATTING									**BOWLING**					
1938-39	R.S. Grant's XI	British Guiana	IIs	1	1		14	14	14.00									
1938-39	British Guiana	Trinidad	IIs	1	2		9	7	4.50			1						
		British Guiana		19	34	3	801	*89	25.83		5	16	330.1	64	864	19	45.47	
		West Indies		4	7		63	19	9.00			3	17	11	11	0		
		R.S. Grant's XI		1	1		14	14	14.00									
		Barbados XI		1	1		0	0					21	0	93	0		
		Combined T/BG XI		2	2		39	34	19.50			2	37	11	91	5	18.20	
		TEST RECORD		**4**	**7**	**0**	**63**	**19**	**9.00**	**0**	**0**	**3**	**17**	**11**	**11**	**0**		
		CAREER		**27**	**45**	**3**	**917**	***819**	**21.83**	**0**	**6**	**21**	**405.1**	**86**	**1059**	**24**	**44.12**	**3-19**

JONES, Prior Erskine

SEASON	TEAM	OPPONENTS	V	M	I	NO	RUNS	H.S.	AVGE	100	50	CT	OV	MD	RUNS	W	AVGE	B.B.
				BATTING									**BOWLING**					
1940-41	Trinidad	Barbados	IIs	1	1		43	43	43.00				25	0	96	2	48.00	
1941-42	Trinidad	Barbados	IIs	4	7		74	15	10.57				93.3	12	327	15	21.80	
1942-43	Trinidad	Barbados	IIs	2	2	1	95	*48	95.00			2	49.6	2	227	5	45.40	
1943-44	Trinidad	Barbados	IIs	2	3	1	71	*60	35.50		1	3	50.7	3	190	7	27.14	
1944-45	Trinidad	Barbados	IIs	2	2		54	41	27.00				49	6	185	5	37.00	
1945-46	Trinidad	British Guiana	IIs	2	4	1	64	34	21.33				53.2	11	116	9	12.88	
1945-46	Trinidad	Barbados	IIs	2	3		62	47	20.66				65.4	10	271	5	54.20	
1945-46	Trinidad	Jamaica	IIs	3	5		14	10	2.80				68.6	3	237	11	21.54	
1946-47	Trinidad	British Guiana	IIs	1	2	1	31	27	31.00				35	11	63	3	21.00	
1947-48	Trinidad	M.C.C. Tourist	WI	1	D								16	4	41	1	41.00	
1947-48	**WEST INDIES**	**ENGLAND TESTS**	**WI**	**1**	**2**	**1**	**17**	***10**	**17.00**				**34.2**	**7**	**83**	**4**	**20.75**	
1948-49	West Indies	Tour of India	I	5	5	2	18	8	6.00			2	146.2	41	356	20	17.80	
1948-49	**WEST INDIES**	**INDIA TESTS**	**I**	**5**	**5**	**1**	**21**	**10**	**5.25**			**2**	**191**	**44**	**479**	**17**	**28.17**	
1948-49	West Indies	Tour of Pakistan	P	1	1		31	31	31.00			1	26.1	9	49	4	12.25	
1948-49	West Indies	Tour of Ceylon	C	1	D								25.4	7	62	10	6.20	
1949-50	Trinidad	Jamaica	IIs	1	D							2	32	8	79	3	26.33	
1950	West Indies	Tour of England	E	15	14	4	82	20	8.20			12	349.5	75	875	32	27.34	
1950	**WEST INDIES**	**ENGLAND TESTS**	**E**	**2**	**2**		**1**	**1**	**0.50**			**2**	**38.4**	**7**	**105**	**1**	**105.00**	
1950-51	Trinidad	Barbados	IIs	1	2	1	9	5	9.00			1	28	9	86	3	28.66	
1951-52	West Indies	Tour of Australia	A	6	7	3	63	46	15.75			5	122	19	398	6	66.33	
1951-52	**WEST INDIES**	**AUSTRALIA TESTS**	**A**	**1**	**2**		**8**	**7**	**4.00**				**32**	**6**	**84**	**3**	**28.00**	

SEASON	TEAM	OPPONENTS	V	M	I	NO	RUNS	H.S.	AVGE	100	50	CT	OV	MD	RUNS	W	AVGE	B.B.
1951-52	West Indies	Tour of New Zealand	NZ	2	2		17	10	8.50			1	57	16	122	3	40.66	
		Trinidad		22	31	5	517	*60	19.88		1	8	566.4	79	1918	69	27.79	
		West Indies		39	40	11	258	46	8.89			25	1023	231	2613	100	26.13	
		TEST RECORD		**9**	**11**	**2**	**47**	***10**	**5.22**	**0**	**0**	**4**	**295.2**	**64**	**751**	**25**	**30.04**	**5-85**
		CAREER		**61**	**71**	**16**	**775**	***60**	**14.09**	**0**	**1**	**33**	**1589.4**	**310**	**4531**	**169**	**26.81**	**7-29**

JULIEN, Bernard Denis

SEASON	TEAM	OPPONENTS	V	BATTING M	I	NO	RUNS	H.S.	AVGE	100	50	CT	BOWLING OV	MD	RUNS	W	AVGE	B.B.
1967-68	N. Trinidad	South Trinidad BC	T	1	1		8	8	8.00			1	18	5	47	3	15.66	
1968-69	Trinidad	Shell Shield	IIs	1	2		10	9	5.00				34	6	111	2	55.50	
1968-69	N. Trinidad	South Trinidad BC	T	1	1		54	54	54.00		1	1	56	20	108	9	12.00	
1969-70	Trinidad	Shell Shield	IIs	4	4		107	49	26.75			3	90.5	13	275	10	27.50	
1969-70	Trinidad	Duke of Norfolk's Tourist	WI	1	1		24	24	24.00			2	51.2	11	113	4	28.25	
1969-70	Trinidad	Glamorgan Tourist	WI	1	1		1	1	1.00			1	14	6	30	1	30.00	
1970	Kent	Counties	E	1	1		5	5	5.00			1	24	10	58	2	29.00	
1970-71	Trinidad	Shell Shield	IIs	3	4	1	153	46	51.00			2	124.2	26	313	13	24.07	
1970-71	Trinidad	Indian Tourist	WI	1	1		0	0					33	8	94	2	47.00	
1970-71	WI President's XI	Indian Tourist	WI	1	1		3	3	3.00			1	38	11	61	3	20.33	
1970-71	N. Trinidad	Central Trinidad BC	T	1	1	1	68	*68			1		46.5	6	171	4	42.75	
1971	Kent	Counties	E	23	34	4	407	47	13.56			14	398.1	88	1244	44	28.27	
1971-72	Trinidad	Shell Shield	IIs	4	5		94	44	18.80			2	128.5	20	384	19	20.21	
1971-72	Trinidad	New Zealand Tourist	WI	1	2		34	26	17.00				20	0	46	0		
1971-72	WI President's XI	New Zealand Tourist	WI	1	1		2	2	2.00				35.4	10	102	1	102.00	
1971-72	N. Trinidad	South Trinidad BC	T	1	2		51	50	50.50		1	2	27	7	60	1	60.00	
1972	Kent	Counties	E	18	24	4	414	90	20.70		2	19	461.2	84	1517	49	30.95	
1972-73	Trinidad	Shell Shield	IIs	4	4	1	126	*82	42.00		1	3	122.2	21	355	12	29.58	
1972-73	WI President's XI	Australian Tourist	WI	1	2		88	59	44.00		1		18	5	50	1	50.00	
1973	West Indies	Tour of England	E	8	8		301	127	37.62	1	1	6	143	25	456	20	22.80	
1973	**WEST INDIES**	**ENGLAND TESTS**	**E**	**3**	**5**		**220**	**121**	**44.00**	**1**	**1**		**110**	**27**	**266**	**7**	**38.00**	
1973	Kent	Counties	E	5	4	2	251	98	125.50		2		140	40	388	14	27.71	
1973-74	Trinidad	Shell Shield	IIs	4	7	2	145	*43	29.00			3	56	5	207	5	41.40	
1973-74	Trinidad	M.C.C. Tourist	WI	1	1		6	6	6.00				29	5	76	2	38.00	
1973-74	**WEST INDIES**	**ENGLAND TESTS**	**WI**	**5**	**5**	**1**	**172**	***86**	**43.00**		**2**	**3**	**174**	**51**	**378**	**16**	**23.62**	
1974	Kent	Counties	E	4	8		78	28	9.75			1	93	21	266	12	22.16	
1974-75	West Indies	Tour of India	I	7	9	2	152	41	21.71			2	160	32	482	12	40.16	

SEASON	TEAM	OPPONENTS		V	M	I	NO	RUNS	H.S.	AVGE	100	50	CT	OV	MD	RUNS	W	AVGE	B.B.
					BATTING									BOWLING					
1974-75	**WEST INDIES**	**INDIA TESTS**		**I**	**4**	**6**	**2**	**93**	**45**	**23.25**			**3**	**99**	**30**	**250**	**9**	**27.77**	
1974-75	West Indies	Tour of Sri Lanka		SL	1	2		83	43	41.50				14	1	46	2	23.00	
1974-75	West Indies	Tour of Pakistan		P	1	2		28	21	14.00			1	11.3	1	66	1	66.00	
1974-75	**WEST INDIES**	**PAKISTAN TESTS**		**P**	**2**	**2**		**103**	**101**	**51.50**	**1**		**1**	**44**	**12**	**145**	**2**	**72.50**	
1974-75	Trinidad	Shell Shield		IIs	4	8		227	77	34.62		3	3	71	14	269	6	44.83	
1975	Kent	Counties		E	13	17	2	451	*73	30.06		3	8	270	76	707	40	17.67	
1975-76	West Indies	Tour of Australia		A	5	8	1	155	78	22.14		1	3	99	12	408	9	45.33	
1975-76	**WEST INDIES**	**AUSTRALIA TESTS**		**A**	**3**	**5**	**1**	**124**	***46**	**31.00**			**2**	**68.4**	**8**	**303**	**11**	**27.54**	
1975-76	Trinidad	Indian Tourist		WI	1	1		3	3	3.00			1	27	8	55	1	55.00	
1975-76	**WEST INDIES**	**INDIA TESTS**		**WI**	**4**	**6**	**2**	**111**	**47**	**27.75**			**4**	**101**	**30**	**270**	**2**	**135.00**	
1976	West Indies	Tour of England		E	16	22	3	511	89	26.89		3	8	382.4	98	1171	49	23.89	
1976	**WEST INDIES**	**ENGLAND TESTS**		**E**	**2**	**4**		**38**	**21**	**9.50**			**1**	**86**	**28**	**168**	**2**	**84.00**	
1976-77	Trinidad	Shell Shield		IIs	4	7	2	182	77	36.40		2	5	84.3	27	293	10	29.30	
1976-77	N. Trinidad	Central Trinidad	TC	T	1	2		13	9	6.50				23	10	44	4	11.00	
1976-77	**WEST INDIES**	**PAKISTAN TESTS**		**WI**	**1**	**1**		**5**	**5**	**5.00**				**37**	**5**	**88**	**1**	**88.00**	
1977	Kent	Counties		E	16	21	2	451	*55	25.05		2	4	421.4	119	1076	37	29.08	
1979-80	Trinidad	Shell Shield		IIs	3	5		50	30	10.00			4	56	12	170	3	56.60	
1979-80	N/E Trinidad	S/C Trinidad	BC	T	1	2		4	4	2.00			2	17	5	48	1	48.00	
1981-82	Trinidad	Shell Shield		IIs	4	7	1	67	37	11.16			7	128	18	422	21	20.09	
1983-84	WI Rebels XI	Tour of South Africa		SA	3	6	1	119	*33	23.80			3	59	11	215	4	53.75	
		Trinidad			41	60	7	1229	*82	23.18		6	36	1070.1	200	3212	111	28.93	
		North Trinidad			5	7	1	194	*68	32.33		3	4	170.5	48	430	21	20.47	
		N.E. Trinidad			1	2		4	4	2.00			2	17	5	48	1	48.00	
		West Indies			65	89	12	2189	127	28.42	3	9	35	1621.3	386	4710	148	31.82	
		Kent			80	109	15	2057	98	21.88		9	47	1808.1	438	5256	198	26.54	
		WI Rebels XI			3	6	1	119	*33	23.80			3	59	11	215	4	53.75	
		TEST RECORD			**24**	**34**	**6**	**866**	**121**	**30.92**	**2**	**3**	**14**	**719.4**	**191**	**1868**	**50**	**37.36**	**5-57**
		CAREER			**195**	**273**	**36**	**5792**	**127**	**24.43**	**3**	**27**	**127**	**4746.4**	**1088**	**13871**	**483**	**28.72**	**9-97**

JUMADEEN, Raphick Rasif

SEASON	TEAM	OPPONENTS		V	M	I	NO	RUNS	H.S.	AVGE	100	50	CT	OV	MD	RUNS	W	AVGE	B.B.
					BATTING									BOWLING					
1966-67	S. Trinidad	North Trinidad	BC	T	1	2	1	11	10	11.00				18	4	47	1	47.00	
1967-68	S. Trinidad	North Trinidad	BC	T	1	1	1	0	*0					20	4	53	3	17.66	

1969-70	S. Trinidad	North Trinidad	BC	T	1	2	1	12	*10	12.00			16	5	63	4	15.75
1970-71	S. Trinidad	East Trinidad	BC	T	1	2		12	12	6.00			62.4	17	148	9	16.44
1970-71	Trinidad	Shell Shield		IIs	1	1		0	0				26	2	104	1	104.00
1971-72	Trinidad	Shell Shield		IIs	3	3	1	30	*17	15.00		3	120.5	32	287	15	19.13
1971-72	Trinidad	New Zealand Tourist		WI	1	1		13	13	13.00			36.4	11	79	2	39.50
1971-72	WI President's XI	New Zealand Tourist		WI	1	1		0	0				40	9	116	1	116.00
1971-72	S. Trinidad	N & E Trinidad	TC	T	2	3		10	8	3.33			123	46	211	15	14.06
1971-72	**WEST INDIES**	**NEW ZEALAND TESTS**		**WI**	**1**	**2**	**2**	**5**	***3**				**64**	**31**	**64**	**1**	**64.00**
1972-73	Trinidad	Shell Shield		IIs	4	2		1	1	0.50		1	196	54	494	15	32.93
1972-73	Trinidad	Australian Tourist		WI	1	1	1	3	*3			1	74.4	20	183	4	45.75
1972-73	**WEST INDIES**	**AUSTRALIA TESTS**		**WI**	**1**	**1**	**1**	**11**	***11**				**58**	**14**	**121**	**2**	**60.50**
1972-73	S. Trinidad	E & N Trinidad	TC	T	2	2		4	4	2.00		1	90.5	30	190	12	15.83
1973-74	Trinidad	Shell Shield		IIs	4	5	3	13	7	6.50		1	121.1	38	254	9	28.22
1973-74	Trinidad	M.C.C. Tourist		WI	1	1		7	7	7.00		1	73.4	20	126	6	21.00
1973-74	S. Trinidad	North Trinidad	TC	T	1	1		11	11	11.00			45	11	117	3	39.00
1974-75	Trinidad	Shell Shield		IIs	4	7	4	50	23	16.66		2	145.4	29	422	9	46.88
1974-75	S. Trinidad	North Trinidad	TC	T	1	2		14	12	7.00			52	15	106	7	15.14
1975-76	Trinidad	Shell Shield		IIs	4	5	4	5	*3	5.00		1	196.1	78	296	13	22.76
1975-76	S. Trinidad	Central Trinidad	TC	T	1	2	1	3	*3	3.00			34.4	15	49	11	4.45
1975-76	**WEST INDIES**	**INDIA TESTS**		**WI**	**4**	**3**	**1**	**4**	**3**	**2.00**		**1**	**138**	**40**	**278**	**9**	**30.88**
1976	West Indies	Tour of England		E	16	11	3	49	21	6.12		12	556	132	1676	57	29.40
1976	**WEST INDIES**	**ENGLAND TESTS**		**E**	**1**	**1**	**1**	**0**	***0**			**2**	**28**	**8**	**64**	**1**	**64.00**
1976-77	Trinidad	Shell Shield		IIs	4	4	2	16	*8	5.33		2	231	82	389	24	16.20
1976-77	Trinidad	Pakistan Tourist		WI	1	2	1	16	*16	16.00		1	41	13	89	5	17.80
1976-77	**WEST INDIES**	**PAKISTAN TESTS**		**WI**	**1**	**1**		**0**	**0**				**51**	**16**	**127**	**2**	**63.50**
1976-77	S. Trinidad	East Trinidad	TC	T	1	2		5	4	2.50			52	12	136	5	27.20
1976-77	S/C Trinidad	N/E Trinidad	BC	T	1	2	2	16	*15				40.2	11	112	4	28.00
1977-78	Trinidad	Shell Shield		IIs	4	8	2	24	8	3.42		3	232	73	506	13	38.92
1977-78	S. Trinidad	C, E & N Trinidad	TC	T	3	4	1	20	10	6.66			139.4	43	280	16	17.50
1977-78	Trinidad	Australian Tourist		WI	1	2		1	1	1.00			42	9	115	5	23.80
1977-78	**WEST INDIES**	**AUSTRALIA TESTS**		**WI**	**2**	**4**	**4**	**6**	***4**			**1**	**100.4**	**15**	**279**	**11**	**25.36**
1978-79	West Indies	Tour of India		I	7	8	3	71	52	14.20	1	3	175	37	519	11	47.18
1978-79	**WEST INDIES**	**INDIA TESTS**		**I**	**2**	**2**	**1**	**58**	**56**	**58.00**	**1**		**83.4**	**13**	**208**	**3**	**69.33**
1978-79	West Indies	Tour of Sri Lanka		SL	2	3	3	15	*10			1	62	15	133	4	33.25
1978-79	Trinidad	Shell Shield		IIs	4	5	2	60	40	20.00		1	201.3	59	488	13	37.53
1979-80	Trinidad	Shell Shield		IIs	4	6	1	17	*10	3.40		1	164	51	376	11	34.14
1979-80	S/C Trinidad	N/E Trinidad	BC	T	1	1		2	2	2.00		3	24	6	57	3	19.00
1980-81	Trinidad	Shell Shield		IIs	3	3	1	9	*4	4.44		3	140.5	38	324	7	46.28

SEASON	TEAM	OPPONENTS	V	M	I	NO	BATTING RUNS	H.S.	AVGE	100	50	CT	BOWLING OV	MD	RUNS	W	AVGE	B.B.
		Trinidad		44	56	22	265	40	7.79			21	2043.1	609	4532	152	29.81	
		South Trinidad		15	23	5	102	12	5.66			1	653.5	202	1400	86	16.27	
		S/C Trinidad		2	3	2	18	10	18.00			3	64.2	17	169	7	24.14	
		West Indies		38	37	19	219	56	12.16		2	20	1356.2	330	3585	102	35.14	
		TEST RECORD		**12**	**14**	**10**	**84**	**56**	**21.00**	**0**	**1**	**4**	**523.2**	**136**	**1142**	**29**	**39.34**	**4-72**
		CAREER		**99**	**119**	**48**	**604**	**56**	**8.50**	**0**	**2**	**45**	**4117.4**	**1158**	**9686**	**347**	**27.91**	**6-30**

KALLICHARRAN, Alvin Isaac

SEASON	TEAM	OPPONENTS	V	M	I	NO	BATTING RUNS	H.S.	AVGE	100	50	CT	BOWLING OV	MD	RUNS	W	AVGE	B.B.
1966-67	Guyana	Shell Shield	IIs	1	2		16	14	8.00			1						
1968-69	Guyana	Shell Shield	IIs	3	6		206	99	34.33		2	3	2	0	17	0		
1969-70	Guyana	Shell Shield	IIs	4	7		397	137	56.71	1	4	1	3	0	17	0		
1970-71	Guyana	Shell Shield	IIs	4	5		183	96	36.60		2	2	14	2	45	0		
1970-71	Guyana	Indian Tourist	WI	1	2		63	55	31.50		1		3	0	20	0		
1970-71	WI President's XI	Indian Tourist	WI	1	2	1	63	*57	63.00		1		1	0	5	0		
1971	Warwickshire	Counties	E	2	2		39	27	19.50			2	7	0	32	0		
1971-72	Guyana	Shell Shield	IIs	4	7		307	83	43.85		3	3	14	2	53	0		
1971-72	Guyana	New Zealand Tourist	WI	1	2		205	154	102.50	1	1		4	0	14	0		
1971-72	WI President's XI	New Zealand Tourist	WI	1	1		51	51	51.00		1		9	3	20	0		
1971-72	**WEST INDIES**	**NEW ZEALAND TESTS**	**WI**	**2**	**3**	**1**	**219**	**101**	**109.50**	**2**			**7**	**2**	**17**	**0**		
1972	Warwickshire	Counties	E	22	33	6	1153	164	42.70	2	5	14	64.4	7	258	7	36.85	
1972-73	Berbice	Demerara JC	G	1	2		6	4	3.00				1	0	4	0		
1972-73	Guyana	Shell Shield	IIs	4	6	1	241	135	48.20	1	1	4	10.2	0	48	0		
1972-73	**WEST INDIES**	**AUSTRALIA TESTS**	**WI**	**5**	**9**	**1**	**294**	**91**	**36.75**		**3**	**7**						
1973	West Indies	Tour of England	E	10	15	1	677	135	48.35	3	1	8						
1973	**WEST INDIES**	**ENGLAND TESTS**	**E**	**3**	**5**		**212**	**80**	**42.40**		**2**	**5**						
1973	Warwickshire	Counties	E	9	12	2	418	154	41.80	1	2	5						
1973-74	Berbice	Demerara JC	G	1	1		0	0										
1973-74	Rest of World XI	Tour of Pakistan	P	2	4		177	103	44.25	1		1	2.4	0	20	0		
1973-74	Guyana	Shell Shield	IIs	4	6		325	197	54.16	1		5	6	0	30	1	30.00	
1973-74	Guyana	M.C.C. Tourist	WI	1	2		23	23	11.50									
1973-74	**WEST INDIES**	**ENGLAND TESTS**	**WI**	**5**	**7**		**397**	**158**	**56.71**	**2**	**1**	**1**	**4**	**0**	**17**	**0**		
1974	Warwickshire	Counties	E	24	39	2	1309	132	35.37	3	7	10	34	4	119	2	59.50	

1974-75	West Indies	Tour of India	I	6	9	1	496	151	62.00	1	3	5	3	1	12	0	
1974-75	**WEST INDIES**	**INDIA TESTS**	**I**	**5**	**9**	**1**	**454**	**124**	**56.75**	**1**	**3**	**7**					
1974-75	**West Indies**	**Tour of Sri Lanka**	**SL**	**1**	**2**		**23**	**12**	**11.50**								
1974-75	West Indies	Tour of Pakistan	P	1	2		25	24	12.50				2.7	0	15	1	15.00
1974-75	**WEST INDIES**	**PAKISTAN TESTS**	**P**	**2**	**3**	**1**	**251**	**115**	**125.50**	**1**	**1**	**1**					
1974-75	Guyana	Shell Shield	IIs	4	6	2	270	110	67.50	1	2	4	0.3	0	1	1	1.00
1975	Warwickshire	Counties	E	17	33	1	1247	137	38.96	2	9	19	11.3	0	59	2	29.50
1975-76	West Indies	Tour of Australia	A	6	10	1	309	78	34.33		4	3	8	1	60	2	30.00
1975-76	**WEST INDIES**	**AUSTRALIA TESTS**	**A**	**6**	**11**		**421**	**101**	**38.27**	**1**	**3**	**3**	**3.1**	**1**	**21**	**1**	**21.00**
1975-76	**WEST INDIES**	**INDIA TESTS**	**WI**	**4**	**6**	**1**	**237**	***103**	**47.00**	**1**	**1**	**1**					
1976	West Indies	Tour of England	E	9	15	1	498	104	35.57	1	3	4					
1976	**WEST INDIES**	**ENGLAND TESTS**	**E**	**3**	**6**	**1**	**180**	**97**	**36.00**		**1**	**1**	**10**	**3**	**18**	**0**	
1976-77	Guyana	Shell Shield	IIs	1	1		68	68	68.00		1	1					
1976-77	Guyana	Pakistan Tourist	WI	1	2		24	18	12.00			1					
1976-77	WI President's XI	Pakistan Tourist	WI	1	1		134	134	134.00	1							
1976-77	**WEST INDIES**	**PAKISTAN TESTS**	**WI**	**5**	**9**	**1**	**258**	**72**	**32.25**		**1**	**8**					
1977	Warwickshire	Counties	E	22	36	4	1343	*149	41.96	1	10	15	2	0	7	0	
1977-78	Queensland	Sheffield Shield	A	7	14	1	402	*129	30.92	1	2	9					
1977-78	Guyana	Australian Tourist	WI	1	1		32	32	32.00								
1977-78	**WEST INDIES**	**AUSTRALIA TESTS**	**WI**	**5**	**8**		**408**	**127**	**51.00**	**2**	**1**	**1**					
1978	Warwickshire	Counties	E	16	29	5	1041	129	43.37	3	5	10	19	5	48	4	12.00
1978-79	West Indies	Tour of India	I	5	8		363	99	40.33		3	2	15	1	50	1	50.00
1978-79	**WEST INDIES**	**INDIA TESTS**	**I**	**6**	**10**	**1**	**538**	**187**	**59.77**	**1**	**3**	**3**	**5.5**	**2**	**9**	**0**	
1978-79	West Indies	Tour of Sri Lanka	SL	1	1		49	49	49.00			1	14	1	37	0	
1979	Warwickshire	Counties	E	17	26	5	1098	*170	52.28	4	6	14	119.1	20	403	6	67.16
1979-80	West Indies	Tour of Australia	A	3	5	1	352	138	88.00	2		2	6.2	1	8	1	8.00
1979-80	**WEST INDIES**	**AUSTRALIA TESTS**	**A**	**3**	**5**	**1**	**202**	**106**	**50.50**	**1**		**5**	**18**	**0**	**32**	**0**	
1979-80	West Indies	Tour of New Zealand	NZ	2	4		73	29	18.25			1	6	0	25	0	
1979-80	**WEST INDIES**	**NEW ZEALAND TESTS**	**NZ**	**3**	**6**		**146**	**75**	**24.33**		**1**	**1**	**10.4**	**5**	**16**	**3**	**5.33**
1980	West Indies	Tour of England	E	10	13	1	551	90	45.91		5	8	8	2	31	2	15.50
1980	**WEST INDIES**	**ENGLAND TESTS**	**E**	**5**	**6**		**102**	**37**	**17.00**			**6**	**7**	**1**	**24**	**0**	
1980	Warwickshire	Counties	E	5	9		223	52	24.77		1	1	11	2	51	0	
1980-81	West Indies	Tour of Pakistan	P	5	8	2	183	*55	30.50		1	2					
1980-81	**WEST INDIES**	**PAKISTAN TESTS**	**P**	**4**	**6**	**1**	**80**	**27**	**16.00**			**1**	**1**	**0**	**4**	**0**	
1980-81	Guyana	Shell Shield	IIs	3	3	1	192	184	96.00	1		3	24	2	41	1	41.00
1981	Warwickshire	Counties	E	13	23	6	923	135	54.29	3	4	7	35.5	3	133	2	66.50
1981-82	Transvaal	Currie Cup	SA	6	10	1	484	129	53.77	2	1	3	6	1	51	1	51.00
1982	Warwickshire	Counties	E	23	37	5	2120	235	66.25	8	5	8	154.2	21	578	14	41.28
1982-83	WI Rebels XI	Tour of South Africa	SA	2	4		160	89	40.00		1	1					

SEASON	TEAM	OPPONENTS	V	BATTING M	I	NO	RUNS	H.S.	AVGE	100	50	CT	BOWLING OV	MD	RUNS	W	AVGE	B.B.
1982-83	Transvaal	Currie Cup	SA	9	13	1	662	151	55.16	2	2	4	62	9	206	7	29.42	
1983	Warwickshire	Counties	E	22	34	4	1637	*243	54.56	6	4	16	135	18	476	8	59.50	
1983-84	WI Rebels XI	Tour of South Africa	SA	8	15	1	465	103	33.21	1	3	5	14.3	3	62	4	15.50	
1983-84	Transvaal	Currie Cup	SA	2	4		90	73	22.50		1	1	13	4	54	3	18.00	
1984	Warwickshire	Counties	E	26	50	6	2301	*200	52.29	9	7	17	10	5	12	0		
1984-85	Orange Free State	Castle Bowl	SA	6	11	2	623	110	69.22	1	7	3	41	9	107	1	107.00	
1985	Warwickshire	Counties	E	21	35	2	1052	*152	31.87	2	6	6	11	4	56	0		
1986	Warwickshire	Counties	E	14	23	5	1005	*163	55.83	5	2	13	9	0	65	2	32.50	
1986-87	Orange Free State	Currie Cup	SA	7	13		555	110	42.69	1	5	5	134.2	25	398	4	99.50	
1987-88	Orange Free State	Currie Cup	SA	4	8		70	37	8.75			2	23	1	69	1	69.00	
1988	Warwickshire	Counties	E	9	15	1	418	*117	29.85	1	2	4						
1989	Warwickshire	Counties	E	16	26	2	610	119	25.41	2	1	8	28.5	8	55	2	27.50	
1990	Warwickshire	Counties	E	7	10	1	221	72	24.55		2	5						
		Guyana		37	58	4	2552	197	47.25	6	17	28	80.5	6	286	3	95.33	
		Berbice		2	3		6	4	2.00				1	0	4	0		
		West Indies		128	205	19	8246	187	44.33	20	43	87	140.1	24	421	11	38.27	
		Warwickshire		285	472	57	18158	*243	43.75	52	78	174	652.2	97	2352	49	48.00	
		Rest of World XI		2	4		177	103	44.25	1		1	2.4	0	20	0		
		Queensland		7	14	1	402	*129	30.92	1	2	9						
		WI Rebels XI		10	19	1	625	103	34.72	1	4	6	14.3	3	62	4	15.50	
		Transvaal		17	27	2	1236	151	49.44	4	4	8	81	14	311	11	28.27	
		Orange Free State		17	32	2	1248	110	41.60	2	12	10	198.2	35	574	6	95.66	
		TEST RECORD		**66**	**109**	**10**	**4399**	**187**	**44.43**	**12**	**21**	**51**	**66.4**	**14**	**158**	**4**	**39.00**	**2-16**
		CAREER		**505**	**834**	**86**	**32650**	***243**	**43.64**	**87**	**160**	**323**	**1170.5**	**179**	**4030**	**84**	**47.97**	**5-45**

KANHAI, Rohan Babulal

SEASON	TEAM	OPPONENTS	V	BATTING M	I	NO	RUNS	H.S.	AVGE	100	50	CT/St	BOWLING OV	MD	RUNS	W	AVGE	B.B.
1954-55	British Guiana	Barbados	IIs	1	2		15	14	7.50			1						
1954-55	British Guiana	Australian Tourist	WI	1	2		78	51	39.00		1	1						
1955-56	West Indies XI	E.W. Swanton's Tourist	WI	1	2		28	23	14.00			1						
1956-57	British Guiana	Jamaica	IIs	1	1		129	129	129.00	1								
1956-57	British Guiana	Barbados	IIs	1	1		195	195	195.00	1								

1957	West Indies	Tour of England	E	17	29	3	887	95	34.11		7	15/5					
1957	**WEST INDIES**	**ENGLAND TESTS**	**E**	**5**	**10**	**1**	**206**	**47**	**22.88**			**5**					
1957-58	British Guiana	Pakistan Tourist	WI	1	1		48	48	48.00				5	1	30	0	
1957-58	**WEST INDIES**	**PAKISTAN TESTS**	**WI**	**5**	**9**	**1**	**299**	**96**	**37.37**		**2**						
1958-59	West Indies	Tour of India	I	8	12	2	503	*100	55.88	1	4	3	1	0	6	0	
1958-59	**WEST INDIES**	**INDIA TESTS**	**I**	**5**	**8**		**538**	**256**	**67.25**	**1**	**2**	**3**					
1958-59	West Indies	Tour of Pakistan	P	2	3		203	114	67.66	1	1	2/2					
1958-59	**WEST INDIES**	**PAKISTAN TESTS**	**P**	**3**	**5**		**274**	**217**	**54.80**	**1**		**1**					
1959-60	Berbice	M.C.C. Tourist	WI	1	1		13	13	13.00								
1959-60	British Guiana	Jamaica	IIs	1	2	1	137	*75	137.00		2						
1959-60	British Guiana	M.C.C. Tourist	WI	1	1		14	14	14.00								
1959-60	**WEST INDIES**	**ENGLAND TESTS**	**WI**	**5**	**8**		**325**	**110**	**40.62**	**1**	**2**	**2**	**4**	**3**	**2**	**0**	
1960	Comm. XI	England XI	E	1	1		10	10	10.00			1					
1960	A.E.R. Gilligan's XI	South African Tourist	E	1	2		64	62	32.00		1	3	2	0	15	1	15.00
1960-61	West Indies	Tour of Australia	A	6	8	1	590	252	84.28	2	2	2					
1960-61	**WEST INDIES**	**AUSTRALIA TESTS**	**A**	**5**	**10**		**503**	**117**	**50.30**	**2**	**2**	**2**					
1961-62	Western Australia	Sheffield Shield	A	8	14	1	533	135	41.00	2	2	3	7	0	21	0	
1961-62	**WEST INDIES**	**INDIA TESTS**	**WI**	**5**	**7**		**495**	**139**	**70.71**	**2**	**1**	**3**	**2**	**1**	**5**	**0**	
1962-63	Comm. XI	Tour of Rhodesia	R	2	4		232	110	58.00	1	1	1					
1962-63	British Guiana	Barbados	IIs	1	2		36	36	18.00			1					
1963	West Indies	Tour of England	E	16	23	4	652	119	34.31	1	5	7					
1963	**WEST INDIES**	**ENGLAND TESTS**	**E**	**5**	**9**		**497**	**92**	**55.22**		**4**	**5**					
1963-64	West Indies XI	The Rest XI	WI	1	2		178	103	89.00	1	1	1	7	0	43	0	
1963-64	C. Hunte's XI	F. Worrell's XI	WI	1	2		37	28	18.50			1	5	1	21	0	
1963-64	Comm. XI	Tour of Pakistan	P	6	10	1	484	161	53.78	2	1	5	19	4	78	1	78.00
1963-64	Indian President's XI	Prime Minister's XI	I	1	2		83	43	41.50				6	0	39	1	39.00
1963-64	British Guiana	Barbados	IIs	1	1		108	108	108.00	1							
1963-64	British Guiana	Trinidad	IIs	1	2		131	79	65.50		2		4	0	21	0	
1964	West Indies XI	England XI	E	3	4		307	170	76.75	2		2					
1964-65	Trinidad	Australian Tourist	WI	1	2		86	52	43.00		1						
1964-65	**WEST INDIES**	**AUSTRALIA TESTS**	**WI**	**5**	**10**		**462**	**129**	**46.20**	**2**	**2**	**3**	**1**	**0**	**4**	**0**	
1965	Rest of World XI	England XI	E	1	2	1	32	17	32.00			1					
1965-66	Guyana	Shell Shield	IIs	4	7	1	260	69	43.33		2	7	3.5	0	4	1	4.00
1966	West Indies	Tour of England	E	14	20	1	704	*192	37.05	2	1	12	5.1	0	47	1	47.00
1966	**WEST INDIES**	**ENGLAND TESTS**	**E**	**5**	**8**		**324**	**104**	**40.50**	**1**	**1**	**1**					
1966-67	West Indies	Tour of India	I	4	7		236	138	33.71	1		2	16.4	2	93	2	46.50
1966-67	**WEST INDIES**	**INDIA TESTS**	**I**	**3**	**4**		**227**	**90**	**56.75**		**2**	**3**					
1966-67	Guyana	Shell Shield	IIs	4	6	1	459	164	91.80	2	1	3	3.2	2	1	1	1.00
1966-67	Rest of World XI	Barbados	WI	1	2		20	16	10.00			1					

				BATTING									BOWLING					
SEASON	**TEAM**	**OPPONENTS**	**V**	**M**	**I**	**NO**	**RUNS**	**H.S.**	**AVGE**	**100**	**50**	**CT/St**	**OV**	**MD**	**RUNS**	**W**	**AVGE**	**B.B.**
1967	Rest of World XI	Tour of England	E	2	3	1	203	107	101.50	1	1	2						
1967-68	Guyana	M.C.C. Tourist	WI	1	2		34	28	17.00			1	4	0	20	0		
1967-68	**WEST INDIES**	**ENGLAND TESTS**	**WI**	**5**	**10**	**1**	**535**	**153**	**59.44**	**2**	**1**	**2**						
1968	Warwickshire	Counties	E	29	42	3	1819	253	46.64	6	5	22	3	0	7	0		
1968-69	West Indies	Tour of Australia	A	6	11	1	476	*174	47.60	2		2						
1968-69	**WEST INDIES**	**AUSTRALIA TESTS**	**A**	**5**	**10**		**371**	**94**	**37.10**		**3**	**2**	**1**	**0**	**10**	**0**		
1968-69	West Indies	Tour of New Zealand	NZ	1	1		4	4	4.00			1						
1969	Warwickshire	Counties	E	17	29	4	1044	173	41.76	1	4	18						
1969-70	Tasmania	Victoria & NZ Tourist	A	2	2	2	308	*200		2		5	5.4	1	39	1	39.00	
1970	Rest of World XI	England	E	5	9		284	100	31.55	1	1	3	1	0	4	0		
1970	Rest of World XI	T.N. Pearce's XI	E	1	2	1	81	*81	81.00		1	2						
1970	Warwickshire	Counties	E	15	26	3	1529	*187	66.47	6	4	20	1.2	0	15	0		
1970-71	Rest of World XI	Tour of Pakistan	P	1	2		80	65	40.00		1	1	1	0	5	2	2.50	
1970-71	Guyana	Shell Shield	IIs	3	4	1	258	*186	86.00	1	1	1	20	4	69	2	34.50	
1970-71	Guyana	Indian Tourist	WI	1	2		126	92	63.00		1	1	3	2	2	0		
1970-71	**WEST INDIES**	**INDIA TESTS**	**WI**	**5**	**9**	**1**	**433**	***158**	**54.12**	**1**	**2**	**1**	**1**	**0**	**1**	**0**		
1971	Warwickshire	Counties	E	24	41	9	1529	*135	47.78	3	10	15	12	0	62	0		
1971-72	Rest of World XI	Australia	A	6	11	3	525	*121	65.62	3	1		3	0	14	0		
1972	Warwickshire	Counties	E	21	30	5	1607	199	64.28	8	3	28	8	1	23	0		
1972-73	Guyana	Shell Shield	IIs	4	5		273	117	54.60	1	2	9	5	2	7	0		
1972-73	**WEST INDIES**	**AUSTRALIA TESTS**	**WI**	**5**	**8**	**1**	**358**	**105**	**51.14**	**1**	**3**	**7**	**11.1**	**2**	**34**	**0**		
1973	West Indies	Tour of England	E	9	11	3	430	*119	53.75	1	3	3	6.3	0	37	1	37.00	
1973	**WEST INDIES**	**ENGLAND TESTS**	**E**	**3**	**5**		**223**	**157**	**44.60**	**1**	**1**	**3**	**7**	**1**	**21**	**0**		
1973	Warwickshire	Counties	E	5	6	1	476	*230	95.20	2	1	4						
1973-74	Rest of World XI	Tour of Pakistan	P	2	4		139	70	34.75		1		14	2	63	0		
1973-74	Guyana	Shell Shield	IIs	3	5		84	46	16.80			4	6	0	17	0		
1973-74	**WEST INDIES**	**ENGLAND TESTS**	**WI**	**5**	**7**	**1**	**157**	**44**	**26.16**			**7**	**3**	**1**	**8**	**0**		
1974	Warwickshire	Counties	E	14	22	4	936	*213	52.00	3	4	3	3	0	9	0		
1975	Warwickshire	Counties	E	13	22	9	1073	*178	82.53	3	6	11						
1976	Warwickshire	Counties	E	17	28	4	864	*111	36.00	1	4	15	1	0	5	1	5.00	
1977	Warwickshire	Counties	E	18	26	5	738	176	35.14	2	2	19	28	6	90	3	30.00	
1981-82	International XI	Tour of Pakistan	P	3	6		135	54	22.50		1	2	3	0	17	0		
		British Guiana/Guyana		30	46	4	2385	195	56.78	7	12	29	54.1	11	171	4	42.75	
		Berbice		1	1		13	13	13.00									
		West Indies		167	270	21	11425	256	45.88	29	52	103/7	66.3	10	311	4	77.75	
		Trinidad		1	2		86	52	43.00		1							

	M	I	NO	RUNS	H.S.	AVGE	100	50	CT	OV	MD	RUNS	W	AVGE	B.B.
Comm. XI	9	15	1	726	161	51.85	3	2	7	19	4	78	1	78.00	
A.E.R. Gilligan's XI	1	2		64	62	32.00		1	3	2	0	15	1	15.00	
C. Hunte's XI	1	2		37	28	18.50			1	5	1	21	0		
Western Australia	8	14	1	533	135	41.00	2	2	3	7	0	21	0		
Indian President's XI	1	2		83	43	41.50				6	0	39	1	39.00	
Rest of World XI	19	35	6	1364	*121	47.03	5	6	10	19	2	86	2	43.00	
Warwickshire	173	272	47	11615	253	51.62	35	43	155	56.2	7	211	4	52.75	
Tasmania	2	2	2	308	*200		2		5	5.4	1	39	1	39.00	
International XI	3	6		135	54	22.50		1	2	3	0	17	0		
TEST RECORD	**79**	**137**	**6**	**6227**	**256**	**47.53**	**15**	**28**	**50**	**30.1**	**8**	**85**	**0**		
CAREER	**416**	**669**	**82**	**28774**	**256**	**49.01**	**83**	**120**	**318/7**	**243.4**	**36**	**1009**	**18**	**56.05**	**2-5**

KENTISH, Esmond Seymour Maurice

				BATTING									BOWLING					
SEASON	**TEAM**	**OPPONENTS**	**V**	**M**	**I**	**NO**	**RUNS**	**H.S.**	**AVGE**	**100**	**50**	**CT**	**OV**	**MD**	**RUNS**	**W**	**AVGE**	**B.B.**
1947-48	Jamaica	British Guiana	IIs	2	2	2	17	*15					46	5	133	4	33.25	
1947-48	Jamaica	M.C.C. Tourist	WI	1	D								26	0	77	4	19.25	
1947-48	**WEST INDIES**	**ENGLAND TESTS**	**WI**	**1**	**1**	**1**	**1**	***1**					**47**	**15**	**106**	**3**	**35.33**	
1949-50	Jamaica	Trinidad	IIs	2	3	3	22	*13				1	36	3	144	1	144.00	
1952-53	Jamaica	Indian Tourist	WI	1	2	1	12	*10	12.00			1	19	4	48	1	48.00	
1953-54	Jamaica	M.C.C. Tourist	WI	2	3	2	18	*10	18.00				58	10	150	5	30.00	
1953-54	**WEST INDIES**	**ENGLAND TESTS**	**WI**	**1**	**1**		**0**	**0**				**1**	**43**	**16**	**72**	**5**	**14.40**	
1954-55	Jamaica	Trinidad	IIs	2	3	2	19	*10	19.00				46	13	115	5	23.00	
1956	Oxford University	Counties	E	14	13	10	18	*6	6.00			3	362.3	77	1134	44	25.77	
1956-57	Jamaica	Duke of Norfolk's Tourist	WI	1	1		2	2	2.00				30.2	3	105	6	17.50	
		Jamaica		11	14	10	90	*15	22.50			2	261.2	38	772	26	29.69	
		West Indies		2	2	1	1	*1	1.00			1	90	31	178	8	22.25	
		Oxford University		14	13	10	18	*6	6.00			3	362.3	77	1134	44	25.77	
		TEST RECORD		**2**	**2**	**1**	**1**	***1**	**1.00**	**0**	**0**	**1**	**90**	**31**	**178**	**8**	**22.25**	**5-49**
		CAREER		**27**	**29**	**21**	**109**	***15**	**13.62**	**0**	**0**	**6**	**713.5**	**146**	**2084**	**78**	**26.71**	**5-36**

KING, Collis Llewellyn

SEASON	TEAM	OPPONENTS	V	BATTING M	I	NO	RUNS	H.S.	AVGE	100	50	CT	BOWLING OV	MD	RUNS	W	AVGE	B.B.
1972-73	Barbados	Shell Shield	IIs	2	4	1	37	22	12.33			2	1	0	5	0		
1973-74	Barbados	Shell Shield	IIs	4	7		232	81	33.14		2	4	52	11	124	7	17.71	
1973-74	Barbados	M.C.C. Tourist	WI	1	1		60	60	60.00		1	2	8.2	0	37	2	18.50	
1974-75	Barbados	Shell Shield	IIs	4	8	2	431	*103	71.83	1	4	3	79	18	216	4	54.00	
1975-76	Barbados	Shell Shield	IIs	3	5		188	66	37.60		2	6	62.4	13	165	8	20.62	
1975-76	Barbados	Indian Tourist	WI	1	1		14	14	14.00				14	2	30	1	30.00	
1976	West Indies	Tour of England	E	18	29	9	1153	163	57.65	6	2	25	309.4	80	833	25	33.32	
1976	**WEST INDIES**	**ENGLAND TESTS**	**E**	**3**	**5**	**1**	**167**	**63**	**41.75**		**2**	**2**	**39**	**11**	**95**	**2**	**47.50**	
1976-77	Barbados	Shell Shield	IIs	4	7	1	254	130	42.33	1		3	63.4	13	205	11	18.63	
1976-77	Barbados	Pakistan Tourist	WI	1	2	1	59	39	59.00			3	37.3	7	98	4	24.50	
1976-77	WI President's XI	Pakistan Tourist	WI	1	1		2	2	2.00			1	1	0	1	0		
1976-77	**WEST INDIES**	**PAKISTAN TESTS**	**WI**	**1**	**2**		**44**	**41**	**22.00**			**1**	**7**	**2**	**18**	**0**		
1977	Glamorgan	Counties	E	16	27	1	811	78	31.19		6	13	259.1	58	730	20	36.50	
1977-78	Barbados	Australian Tourist	WI	1	2		43	37	21.50			1	21.5	2	57	2	28.50	
1978-79	Barbados	Shell Shield	IIs	1	1		156	156	156.00	1								
1979-80	West Indies	Tour of Australia	A	3	6	1	198	92	39.60		1		52	15	133	5	26.60	
1979-80	**WEST INDIES**	**AUSTRALIA TESTS**	**A**	**1**	**2**	**1**	**8**	***8**	**8.00**			**1**	**27**	**7**	**63**	**1**	**63.00**	
1979-80	West Indies	Tour of New Zealand	NZ	2	4		134	88	33.50		1		42	14	81	5	16.20	
1979-80	**WEST INDIES**	**NEW ZEALAND TESTS**	**NZ**	**3**	**6**	**1**	**187**	***100**	**37.40**	**1**		**1**	**12**	**1**	**74**	**0**		
1979-80	Barbados	Shell Shield	IIs	4	5		254	117	50.80	1	1	6	19	3	52	3	17.33	
1980	West Indies	Tour of England	E	8	10	2	74	26	9.55			4	86	21	269	7	38.42	
1980	**WEST INDIES**	**ENGLAND TESTS**	**E**	**1**	**1**		**12**	**12**	**12.00**				**12**	**3**	**32**	**0**		
1980-81	Barbados	Shell Shield	IIs	3	4		50	26	12.50			1	24	10	48	0		
1980-81	Barbados	English Tourist	WI	1	1		76	76	76.00		1	1	20	5	34	0		
1981-82	International XI	Tour of Pakistan	P	1	2		45	34	22.50				20	4	62	2	31.00	
1981-82	Barbados	Shell Shield	IIs	5	7	1	319	*88	53.16		3	2	25.4	9	59	4	14.75	
1982	D.B. Close's XI	Pakistan Tourist	E	1	1		22	22	22.00				4	1	11	0		
1982-83	WI Rebels XI	Tour of South Africa	SA	2	4		172	101	43.00	1		2	8	2	32	1	32.00	
1983	Worcestershire	Counties	E	2	3		158	123	52.66	1		1	15	2	39	1	39.00	
1983	D.B. Close's XI	New Zealand Tourist	E	1	2		26	26	13.00			2	3	0	18	0		
1983-84	WI Rebels XI	Tour of South Africa	SA	7	13	2	450	83	40.50		4	2	52	9	191	4	47.75	
1984-85	Natal	Currie Cup	SA	7	10		361	94	36.10		2	6	46	4	200	1	200.00	
1985-86	Natal	Currie Cup	SA	5	7		374	154	53.42	1	2	2	48	14	138	5	46.00	
1986	D.B. Close's XI	New Zealand Tourist	E	1	2		49	48	24.50				4	0	39	0		
1986-87	Natal	Currie Cup	SA	6	10	1	150	30	16.66			1	71	17	191	3	63.66	

OPPONENTS	M	I	NO	RUNS	H.S.	AVGE	100	50	CT	OV	MD	RUNS	W	AVGE	B.B.
Barbados	35	55	6	2173	156	44.34	4	14	34	428.4	93	1130	46	24.56	
West Indies	41	66	15	1979	163	38.80	7	6	35	587.4	154	1599	45	35.53	
WI Rebels XI	9	17	2	622	101	41.46	1	4	4	60	11	223	5	44.60	
Glamorgan	16	27	1	811	78	31.19		6	13	259.1	58	730	20	36.50	
Worcestershire	2	3		158	123	52.66	1		1	15	2	39	1	39.00	
International XI	1	2		45	34	22.50				20	4	62	2	31.00	
D.B. Close's XI	3	5		97	48	19.40			2	11	1	68	0		
Natal	18	27	1	885	154	34.03	1	4	9	165	35	529	9	58.77	
TEST RECORD	**9**	**16**	**3**	**418**	***100**	**32.15**	**1**	**2**	**5**	**97**	**24**	**282**	**3**	**94.00**	**1-30**
CAREER	**125**	**202**	**25**	**6770**	**163**	**38.24**	**14**	**34**	**98**	**1546.3**	**358**	**4380**	**128**	**34.21**	**5-91**

KING, Frank McDonald

				BATTING									BOWLING					
SEASON	TEAM	OPPONENTS	V	M	I	NO	RUNS	H.S.	AVGE	100	50	CT	OV	MD	RUNS	W	AVGE	B.B.
1947-48	Barbados	M.C.C. Tourist	WI	2	D								54	13	156	3	52.00	
1948-49	Barbados	Trinidad	IIs	2	2	1	8	*7	8.00			3	68.5	3	269	7	38.42	
1949-50	Barbados	British Guiana	IIs	2	2		4	4	2.00				67	13	194	7	27.71	
1950-51	Trinidad	Barbados	IIs	2	2	2	4	*4					47	4	202	3	67.33	
1951-52	Barbados	Jamaica	IIs	2	3		20	9	6.66			4	71.2	20	192	13	14.76	
1952-53	**WEST INDIES**	**INDIA TESTS**	**WI**	**5**	**6**		**33**	**19**	**5.50**				**238.1**	**78**	**480**	**17**	**28.23**	
1953-54	**WEST INDIES**	**ENGLAND TESTS**	**WI**	**3**	**3**	**1**	**24**	***10**	**12.00**			**2**	**110.2**	**41**	**247**	**8**	**30.87**	
1954-55	Barbados	British Guiana	IIs	2	2	1	6	4	6.00			2	63.5	21	150	15	10.00	
1954-55	**WEST INDIES**	**AUSTRALIA TESTS**	**WI**	**4**	**7**	**1**	**46**	**21**	**7.66**			**2**	**113**	**16**	**403**	**3**	**134.33**	
1955-56	West Indies	Tour of New Zealand	NZ	3	4		39	17	9.75			3	68	14	177	9	19.66	
1955-56	**WEST INDIES**	**NEW ZEALAND TESTS**	**NZ**	**2**	**1**	**1**	**13**	***13**				**1**	**17**	**5**	**29**	**1**	**29.00**	
1956-57	Barbados	Trinidad	IIs	1	1	1	30	*30					11.5	3	28	3	9.33	
1956-57	Barbados	British Guiana	IIs	1	1		10	10	10.00				16.5	3	61	1	61.00	
		Barbados		12	11	3	78	*30	9.75			9	353.4	76	1050	49	21.42	
		Trinidad		2	2	2	4	*4					47	4	202	3	67.33	
		West Indies		17	21	3	155	21	8.61			8	546.3	154	1336	38	35.15	
		TEST RECORD		**14**	**17**	**3**	**116**	**21**	**8.28**	**0**	**0**	**5**	**478.3**	**140**	**1159**	**29**	**39.96**	**5-74**
		CAREER		**31**	**34**	**8**	**237**	***30**	**9.11**	**0**	**0**	**17**	**947.1**	**234**	**2588**	**90**	**28.75**	**5-35**

KING, Lester Anthony

SEASON	TEAM	OPPONENTS	V	BATTING M	I	NO	RUNS	H.S.	AVGE	100	50	CT	BOWLING OV	MD	RUNS	W	AVGE	B.B.
1961-62	Jamaica	Barbados	IIs	1	2	1	6	5	6.00			2	44.5	8	129	4	32.25	
1961-62	Jamaica	Indian Tourist	WI	1	1		12	12	12.00			1	28	1	97	1	97.00	
1961-62	**WEST INDIES**	**INDIA TESTS**	**WI**	**1**	**2**		**13**	**13**	**6.50**				**32**	**7**	**64**	**7**	**9.14**	
1962-63	Bengal	Ranji Trophy	I	2	4		68	32	17.00				36	1	192	6	32.00	
1962-63	East Zone	Duleen Trophy	I	1	2		4	4	2.00				9	1	57	0		
1962-63	Chidambaram's XI	Gold Cup	I	1	2		52	35	26.00			1	36.6	6	114	7	16.28	
1962-63	Chief Minister's XI	Defence Fund	I	1	D								11	2	44	1	44.00	
1962-63	Bombay Governor's XI	Defence Fund	I	1	2		14	14	7.00				22	3	92	5	18.40	
1963	West Indies	Tour of England	E	18	22	7	202	*27	13.46			10	493.5	100	1284	47	27.31	
1963-64	The Rest XI	West Indies XI	WI	1	2		28	15	14.00			2	10	1	40	2	20.00	
1963-64	C. Hunte's XI	F. Worrell's XI	WI	1	2		18	10	9.00			1	12	3	25	0		
1963-64	Jamaica	Cavaliers Touring XI	WI	3	3	1	114	75	57.00		1	3	68	25	171	7	24.42	
1963-64	Jamaica	Barbados	IIs	1	2		26	23	13.00				28	3	106	0		
1963-64	Jamaica	Trinidad	IIs	1	2		91	89	45.50		1		27	4	76	2	38.00	
1963-64	Jamaica	British Guiana	IIs	1	2	1	13	11	13.00			1	27	1	77	2	38.50	
1964	West Indies XI	England XI	E	2	2	1	60	*46	60.00				32	4	99	4	24.75	
1964-65	Jamaica	Cavaliers Touring XI	WI	2	2		21	19	10.50			1	46	6	141	5	28.20	
1964-65	Jamaica	Australian Tourist	WI	1	2		79	77	39.50		1		30	6	120	1	120.00	
1966-67	West Indies	Tour of India	I	6	10	5	169	39	33.80			4	118	27	333	11	30.27	
1966-67	West Indies	Tour of Ceylon	C	1	D								18	4	31	2	15.50	
1966-67	Jamaica	Shell Shield	IIs	4	5		171	58	34.20		3	4	138.2	25	404	10	40.40	
1967-68	Jamaica	M.C.C. Tourist	WI	1	2		18	10	9.00			2	38	10	105	3	35.00	
1967-68	**WEST INDIES**	**ENGLAND TESTS**	**WI**	**1**	**2**		**28**	**20**	**14.00**			**2**	**47.2**	**12**	**90**	**2**	**45.00**	
1968-69	West Indies	Tour of Australia	A	6	7	2	100	39	20.00			2	117.4	16	417	8	52.12	
1968-69	West Indies	Tour of New Zealand	NZ	2	3	1	76	*33	38.00			1	41	6	120	3	40.00	
1968-69	NZ Governor's XI	West Indies	NZ	1	2		21	15	10.50			1	9	0	35	2	17.50	
		Jamaica		16	23	3	551	89	27.55		6	14	475.1	89	1426	35	40.74	
		West Indies		37	48	16	648	*46	20.25			19	899.5	176	2438	84	29.02	
		The Rest XI		1	2		28	15	14.00			2	10	1	40	2	20.00	
		C. Hunte's XI		1	2		18	10	9.00			1	12	3	25	0		
		Bengal		2	4		68	32	17.00				36	1	192	6	32.00	
		East Zone		1	2		4	4	2.00				9	1	57	0		
		Chidambaram's XI		1	2		52	35	26.00			1	36.6	6	114	7	16.28	
		Chief Minister's XI		1	D								11	2	44	1	44.00	
		Bombay Governor's XI		1	2		14	14	7.00				22	3	92	5	18.40	

		N.Z. Governor's XI		1	2		21	15	10.50			1	9	0	35	2	17.50	
		TEST RECORD		**2**	**4**	**0**	**41**	**20**	**10.25**	**0**	**0**	**2**	**79.2**	**19**	**154**	**9**	**17.11**	**5-46**
		CAREER		**62**	**87**	**19**	**1404**	**89**	**20.64**	**0**	**6**	**38**	**1521**	**282**	**4463**	**142**	**31.42**	**5-46**

LASHLEY, Patrick Douglas

				BATTING									BOWLING					
SEASON	TEAM	OPPONENTS	V	M	I	NO	RUNS	H.S.	AVGE	100	50	CT	OV	MD	RUNS	W	AVGE	B.B.
1957-58	Barbados	Pakistan Tourist	WI	1	2		10	9	5.00				2	0	6	0		
1958-59	Barbados	Jamaica	IIs	2	4		122	62	30.50		1		6.4	3	15	2	7.50	
1958-59	Barbados	British Guiana	IIs	2	2	1	218	*200	218.00	1		4	22	7	48	3	16.00	
1959-60	Barbados	M.C.C. Tourist	WI	1	1		45	45	45.00			1	13	2	44	1	44.00	
1960-61	West Indies	Tour of Australia	A	7	11		213	69	19.36		1	6						
1960-61	**WEST INDIES**	**AUSTRALIA TESTS**	**A**	**2**	**4**		**78**	**41**	**19.50**									
1961-62	Barbados	Jamaica	IIs	1	1		58	58	58.00		1		2	0	10	0		
1961-62	Barbados	British Guiana	IIs	1	2		83	61	41.50		1	1						
1961-62	Barbados	Indian Tourist	WI	1	1		9	9	9.00			1						
1962-63	Barbados	Trinidad	IIs	1	D													
1962-63	Barbados	British Guiana	IIs	1	2		50	48	25.00			1						
1963-64	Barbados	Trinidad	IIs	1	2		53	43	26.50				4	1	12	0		
1964-65	Barbados	Cavaliers Touring XI	WI	2	4	2	233	*113	116.50	1	1	2	3	0	15	0		
1964-65	Barbados	Australian Tourist	WI	1	1		28	28	28.00				13	2	52	0		
1965-66	Barbados	Shell Shield	IIs	4	4	1	387	121	129.00	2	2	5	3	2	3	0		
1966	West Indies	Tour of England	E	16	21	2	566	78	29.40		6	11	159.2	38	406	13	31.23	
1966	**WEST INDIES**	**ENGLAND TESTS**	**E**	**2**	**3**		**81**	**49**	**27.00**			**4**	**3**	**2**	**1**	**1**	**1.00**	
1966-67	Barbados	Shell Shield	IIs	4	5		510	204	102.00	2	2	3	33	5	132	4	33.00	
1966-67	Barbados	Rest of World XI	WI	1	2		16	10	8.00			2	3.4	0	11	1	11.00	
1967-68	Barbados	M.C.C. Tourist	WI	1	2		27	18	13.50				13	4	32	1	32.00	
1968-69	Barbados	Shell Shield	IIs	4	7		318	94	45.42		3	5	35	12	92	1	92.00	
1969	Barbados	Tour of England	E	2	4		140	56	35.00		1	3	3	1	7	0		
1969-70	Barbados	Shell Shield	IIs	4	8		454	118	56.75	1	3		22	8	56	0		
1970-71	Barbados	Shell Shield	IIs	4	8	1	205	98	29.28		2	2	4	2	2	0		
1970-71	Barbados	Indian Tourist	WI	1	2		8	8	4.00									
1971-72	Barbados	Shell Shield	IIs	4	6	2	228	78	57.00		3	5	2	0	14	0		
1971-72	Barbados	New Zealand Tourist	WI	1	2	1	37	*23	37.00									
1972-73	Barbados	Shell Shield	IIs	4	6	1	381	*144	76.20	1	2	2						
1972-73	Barbados	Australian Tourist	WI	1	2		110	76	55.00		1							
1973-74	Barbados	Shell Shield	IIs	4	7		197	62	28.14		2	6						

SEASON	TEAM	OPPONENTS	V	M	I	NO	BATTING RUNS	H.S.	AVGE	100	50	CT	BOWLING OV	MD	RUNS	W	AVGE	B.B.
1973-74	Barbados	M.C.C. Tourist	WI	1	2	1	11	*6	11.00			1						
1974-75	Barbados	Shell Shield	IIs	3	4	1	56	44	18.66			1						
		Barbados		58	93	11	3994	204	48.70	8	25	45	184.2	49	551	13	42.38	
		West Indies		27	39	2	938	78	25.35		7	21	162.2	40	407	14	29.07	
		TEST RECORD		**4**	**7**	**0**	**159**	**49**	**22.71**	**0**	**0**	**4**	**3**	**2**	**1**	**1**	**1.00**	**1-1**
		CAREER		**85**	**132**	**13**	**4932**	**204**	**41.44**	**8**	**32**	**66**	**345.4**	**89**	**958**	**27**	**35.48**	**3-15**

LEGALL, Ralph Archibald

SEASON	TEAM	OPPONENTS	V	M	I	NO	BATTING RUNS	H.S.	AVGE	100	50	CT/St	BOWLING OV	MD	RUNS	W	AVGE	B.B.
1946-47	Trinidad	British Guiana	IIs	2	1	1	2	*2	2.00			2/5						
1950-51	Trinidad	Barbados	IIs	2	4		67	48	16.75			2/1						
1951-52	Trinidad	British Guiana	IIs	2	4	1	107	59	35.66		1	11/1						
1952-53	Trinidad	Indian Tourist	WI	1	1		41	41	41.00			2						
1952-53	**WEST INDIES**	**INDIA TESTS**	**WI**	**4**	**5**		**50**	**23**	**10.00**			**8/1**						
1953-54	Trinidad	M.C.C. Tourist	WI	1	2		50	42	25.00			1						
1954-55	Trinidad	Jamaica	IIs	2	4		161	68	40.25		1	4						
1954-55	Trinidad	Australian Tourist	WI	1	2		3	3	1.50			0/1						
1957-58	Trinidad	Pakistan Tourist	WI	1	1		4	4	4.00			2/1						
		Trinidad		12	19	12	435	68	25.58		2	24/9						
		West Indies		4	5		50	23	10.00			8/1						
		TEST RECORD		**4**	**5**	**0**	**50**	**23**	**10.00**	**0**	**0**	**8/1**						
		CAREER		**16**	**24**	**2**	**485**	**68**	**22.04**	**0**	**2**	**32/10**						

LEWIS, Desmond Michael

SEASON	TEAM	OPPONENTS	V	M	I	NO	BATTING RUNS	H.S.	AVGE	100	50	CT/St	BOWLING OV	MD	RUNS	W	AVGE	B.B.
1970	Jamaica	Tour of England	E	4	5		64	24	12.80			9						
1970-71	Jamaica	Shell Shield	IIs	4	6		230	91	38.33		2	6/2						
1970-71	Jamaica	Indian Tourist	WI	1	2	1	163	96	163.00		2	5						
1970-71	**WEST INDIES**	**INDIA TESTS**	**WI**	**3**	**5**	**2**	**259**	**88**	**86.33**		**3**	**8**						

SEASON	TEAM	OPPONENTS	V	M	I	NO	RUNS	H.S.	AVGE	100	50	CT
1971-72	Jamaica	Shell Shield	IIs	4	7		152	43	21.71			10/1
1971-72	Jamaica	New Zealand Tourist	WI	1	1		24	24	24.00			2
1972-73	Jamaica	Shell Shield	IIs	4	8		75	15	9.37			4
1972-73	Jamaica	Australian Tourist	WI	1	2		70	61	35.00		1	2
1973-74	Jamaica	Shell Shield	IIs	4	5		131	49	26.20			8/3
1973-74	Jamaica	M.C.C. Tourist	WI	1	2	1	47	*24	47.00			2/1
1974-75	Jamaica	Shell Shield	IIs	4	7	1	266	65	44.33		2	6/3
1975-76	Jamaica	Shell Shield	IIs	4	4		74	56	18.50		1	3/1
1975-76	Jamaica	Indian Tourist	WI	1	2		68	53	34.00		1	2
		Jamaica		33	51	3	1364	96	28.41		9	59/11
		West Indies		3	5	2	259	88	86.33		3	8
		TEST RECORD		**3**	**5**	**2**	**259**	**88**	**86.33**	**0**	**3**	**8**
		CAREER		**36**	**56**	**5**	**1623**	**96**	**31.82**	**0**	**12**	**67/11**

LLOYD, Clive Hubert

				BATTING									BOWLING					
SEASON	**TEAM**	**OPPONENTS**	**V**	**M**	**I**	**NO**	**RUNS**	**H.S.**	**AVGE**	**100**	**50**	**CT**	**OV**	**MD**	**RUNS**	**W**	**AVGE**	**B.B.**
1963-64	British Guiana	Jamaica	IIs	1	1		11	11	11.00			1						
1964-65	British Guiana	Australian Tourist	WI	1	2		19	17	9.50			1						
1965-66	Guyana	Shell Shield	IIs	3	5	1	344	194	86.00	2		6	11	1	19	0		
1966-67	West Indies	Tour of India	I	5	8	1	395	118	56.42	1	2	5	65	7	256	10	25.60	
1966-67	**WEST INDIES**	**INDIA TESTS**	**I**	**3**	**5**	**1**	**227**	**82**	**56.75**		**2**	**2**	**43**	**12**	**90**	**2**	**45.00**	
1966-67	West Indies	Tour of Ceylon	C	1	1		138	138	138.00	1			22	5	95	1	95.00	
1966-67	Guyana	Shell Shield	IIs	2	3		188	79	62.66		3	1	19	4	61	0		
1967	Rest of World XI	England XI	E	1	2	1	27	*27	27.00			2	21	3	70	3	23.33	
1967-68	Guyana	M.C.C. Tourist	WI	1	2		63	63	31.50		1							
1967-68	**WEST INDIES**	**ENGLAND TESTS**	**WI**	**5**	**9**	**2**	**369**	**118**	**52.71**	**2**		**3**	**15**	**5**	**34**	**0**		
1968	Lancashire	Counties	E	1	1		1	1	1.00									
1968	Rest of World XI	England XI & Hampshire	E	2	4		74	37	18.50			2	36	8	117	4	29.25	
1968-69	West Indies	Tour of Australia	A	9	14	1	484	97	37.23		3	6	34	4	139	2	69.50	
1968-69	**WEST INDIES**	**AUSTRALIA TESTS**	**A**	**4**	**8**		**315**	**129**	**39.37**	**1**	**2**	**2**	**22**	**2**	**78**	**2**	**39.00**	
1968-69	West Indies	Tour of New Zealand	NZ	2	4	1	352	*205	117.33	1	2	1	6	1	11	0		
1968-69	**WEST INDIES**	**NEW ZEALAND TESTS**	**NZ**	**3**	**5**		**65**	**44**	**13.00**			**1**						
1968-69	N.Z. Governor's XI	West Indies	NZ	1	2		76	71	38.00		1							
1969	West Indies	Tour of England	E	13	15	5	721	*210	72.10	2	3	5	37.5	9	106	2	53.00	
1969	**WEST INDIES**	**ENGLAND TESTS**	**E**	**3**	**6**		**183**	**70**	**30.50**		**2**	**1**						

SEASON	TEAM	OPPONENTS	V	BATTING M	I	NO	RUNS	H.S.	AVGE	100	50	CT	BOWLING OV	MD	RUNS	W	AVGE	B.B.
1969	Lancashire	Counties	E	10	15	1	554	99	39.57		5	3	62	16	161	4	40.25	
1969-70	Guyana	Shell Shield	IIs	4	7	2	334	*100	66.80	1	2	3	36	12	86	3	28.66	
1970	Lancashire	Counties	E	18	28	2	1203	163	46.26	3	6	10	270	72	698	22	31.72	
1970	Rest of World XI	England	E	5	9	1	400	*114	50.00	2	1	3	53	13	120	6	20.00	
1970-71	Rest of World XI	Tour of Pakistan	P	1	2		45	29	22.50			3						
1970-71	Guyana	Shell Shield	IIs	3	4		176	77	44.00		2	2	50	9	87	3	29.00	
1970-71	Guyana	Indian Tourist	WI	1	2		74	57	37.00		1		8	0	33	0		
1970-71	**WEST INDIES**	**INDIA TESTS**	**WI**	**5**	**10**		**295**	**64**	**29.50**		**3**	**3**	**12**	**1**	**46**	**0**		
1971	Lancashire	Counties	E	22	33	4	1124	*217	38.75	2	7	20	201	52	506	15	33.73	
1971-72	Rest of World XI	Tour of Australia	A	6	10	1	370	69	41.11		3	2	3	0	11	0		
1971-72	Guyana	Shell Shield	IIs	2	3		67	60	22.33		1	1	1	0	8	0		
1971-72	Guyana	New Zealand Tourist	WI	1	2	1	237	133	237.00	2		1	11	5	12	0		
1971-72	**WEST INDIES**	**NEW ZEALAND TESTS**	**WI**	**2**	**3**		**66**	**43**	**22.00**			**1**	**39**	**11**	**84**	**1**	**84.00**	
1972	Lancashire	Counties	E	18	26	4	895	181	40.68	3	2	9	105.2	17	276	9	30.66	
1972-73	Guyana	Shell Shield	IIs	4	5	1	198	*100	49.50	1		2	52	15	88	3	29.33	
1972-73	Guyana	Australian Tourist	WI	1	2		143	124	71.50	1			4	0	14	0		
1972-73	WI President's XI	Australian Tourist	WI	1	2		85	59	42.50		1							
1972-73	**WEST INDIES**	**AUSTRALIA TESTS**	**WI**	**3**	**6**	**1**	**297**	**178**	**59.40**	**1**	**1**	**1**	**37**	**12**	**89**	**0**		
1973	West Indies	Tour of England	E	12	18	4	810	174	57.85	2	5	5	42	9	102	4	25.50	
1973	**WEST INDIES**	**ENGLAND TESTS**	**E**	**3**	**5**		**318**	**132**	**63.60**	**1**	**2**	**2**	**14**	**3**	**31**	**2**	**15.50**	
1973	Lancashire	Counties	E	6	10	1	271	*66	30.11		3	7	26	4	76	1	76.00	
1973-74	Rest of World XI	Tour of Pakistan	P	2	3		123	91	41.00		1		12	2	53	0		
1973-74	Guyana	Shell Shield	IIs	3	4	1	385	134	128.33	2	2		25.4	7	46	2	23.00	
1973-74	Guyana	M.C.C. Tourist	WI	1	2		89	65	44.50		1		2	0	3	0		
1973-74	**WEST INDIES**	**ENGLAND TESTS**	**WI**	**5**	**7**	**1**	**147**	**52**	**24.50**		**1**	**3**	**56**	**21**	**71**	**3**	**23.67**	
1974	Lancashire	Counties	E	20	31	8	1458	*178	63.39	4	7	15	23	9	47	2	23.50	
1974-75	West Indies	Tour of India	I	5	5	3	399	126	199.50	1	3	6	7	0	21	1	21.00	
1974-75	**WEST INDIES**	**INDIA TESTS**	**I**	**5**	**9**	**1**	**636**	***242**	**79.50**	**2**	**1**	**6**						
1974-75	West Indies	Tour of Sri Lanka	SL	2	3	1	63	50	31.50		1	4						
1974-75	West Indies	Tour of Pakistan	P	1	2	2	101	*59			1	1						
1974-75	**WEST INDIES**	**PAKISTAN TESTS**	**P**	**2**	**3**		**164**	**83**	**54.66**		**2**	**1**						
1974-75	Guyana	Shell Shield	IIs	3	3		191	68	63.66		3	1	4	0	10	0		
1975	Lancashire	Counties	E	18	27	4	1423	*167	61.86	6	6	18	22	6	45	2	22.50	
1975-76	West Indies	Tour of Australia	A	5	8		307	105	38.37	1	1	5	3	1	5	1	5.00	
1975-76	**WEST INDIES**	**AUSTRALIA TESTS**	**A**	**6**	**11**	**1**	**469**	**149**	**46.90**	**2**	**2**	**5**	**17**	**4**	**56**	**0**		
1975-76	**WEST INDIES**	**INDIA TESTS**	**WI**	**4**	**6**		**283**	**102**	**47.16**	**1**	**2**		**10**	**1**	**33**	**0**		
1976	West Indies	Tour of England	E	14	17	4	1067	*201	80.07	3	5	18	32	10	81	3	27.00	

1976	**WEST INDIES**	**ENGLAND TESTS**	**E**	**5**	**9**		**296**	**84**	**32.88**		**2**	**5**	**7**	**3**	**9**	**0**	
1976-77	Guyana	Shell Shield	IIs	1	1		36	36	36.00								
1976-77	Guyana	Pakistan Tourist	WI	1	2	1	126	*126	126.00	1		2	6	0	19	1	19.00
1976-77	**WEST INDIES**	**PAKISTAN TESTS**	**WI**	**5**	**9**	**1**	**336**	**157**	**42.00**	**1**		**5**					
1977	Lancashire	Counties	E	5	3	1	164	95	82.00		1	1					
1977-78	**WEST INDIES**	**AUSTRALIA TESTS**	**WI**	**2**	**2**		**128**	**86**	**64.00**		**1**	**2**					
1978	Lancashire	Counties	E	21	36	6	1116	120	37.20	4	6	21					
1979	Lancashire	Counties	E	17	22	4	880	*104	48.88	3	3	11					
1979-80	West Indies	Tour of Australia	A	4	6		114	77	19.00		1	2					
1979-80	**WEST INDIES**	**AUSTRALIA TESTS**	**A**	**2**	**3**		**201**	**121**	**67.00**	**1**		**4**					
1979-80	**WEST INDIES**	**NEW ZEALAND TESTS**	**NZ**	**3**	**6**		**103**	**42**	**17.16**			**1**					
1980	West Indies	Tour of England	E	8	8	2	318	116	53.00	2		4					
1980	**WEST INDIES**	**ENGLAND TESTS**	**E**	**4**	**4**		**169**	**101**	**42.25**	**1**	**1**	**2**	**1**	**0**	**1**	**0**	
1980	Lancashire	Counties	E	2	3		134	101	44.66	1		3					
1980-81	West Indies	Tour of Pakistan	P	4	4		169	97	42.25		2	7					
1980-81	**WEST INDIES**	**PAKISTAN TESTS**	**P**	**4**	**6**	**1**	**106**	**37**	**21.20**			**5**					
1980-81	Guyana	Shell Shield	IIs	3	4	2	345	144	172.50	2		5					
1980-81	**WEST INDIES**	**ENGLAND TESTS**	**WI**	**4**	**5**		**383**	**100**	**76.60**	**1**	**3**	**7**					
1981	Lancashire	Counties	E	18	31	2	1324	145	45.65	1	10	13					
1981-82	West Indies	Tour of Australia	A	2	2		119	68	59.50		2	2					
1981-82	**WEST INDIES**	**AUSTRALIA TESTS**	**A**	**3**	**6**	**1**	**275**	***77**	**55.00**		**3**	**1**					
1981-82	Guyana	Shell Shield	IIs	1	2		38	38	19.00			3					
1982	Lancashire	Counties	E	21	29	2	1135	100	42.03	1	9	19					
1982-83	West Indies XI	International XI	WI	1	1		60	60	60.00		1	1					
1982-83	Guyana	Shell Shield	IIs	5	8	1	412	136	58.85	2	1	3					
1982-83	**WEST INDIES**	**INDIA TESTS**	**WI**	**5**	**6**		**407**	**143**	**67.83**	**2**	**2**	**5**					
1983	Lancashire	Counties	E	11	16	1	447	86	29.80		3	11					
1983-84	West Indies	Tour of India	I	3	4	1	175	85	58.33		2	2					
1983-84	**WEST INDIES**	**INDIA TESTS**	**I**	**6**	**8**	**2**	**496**	***161**	**82.66**	**2**	**2**	**4**					
1983-84	**WEST INDIES**	**AUSTRALIA TESTS**	**WI**	**4**	**4**		**170**	**76**	**42.50**		**1**	**4**					
1984	West Indies	Tour of England	E	4	3	1	109	72	54.50		1	3					
1984	**WEST INDIES**	**ENGLAND TESTS**	**E**	**5**	**6**	**1**	**255**	**71**	**51.00**		**2**	**9**					
1984-85	West Indies	Tour of Australia	A	5	8	1	376	95	53.71		3	2					
1984-85	**WEST INDIES**	**AUSTRALIA TESTS**	**A**	**5**	**8**	**1**	**356**	**114**	**50.85**	**1**	**2**	**5**					
1985	Lancashire	Counties	E	4	7	1	288	131	48.00	1	1	3					
1986	Lancashire	Counties	E	7	8	1	347	128	49.57	1	2						
		British Guiana/Guyana		42	64	10	3476	194	64.37	14	17	32	229.4	53	486	12	40.50
		West Indies		211	308	41	13877	*242	51.97	33	78	169	521.5	121	1438	34	42.29

SEASON	TEAM		M	I	NO	RUNS	H.S.	AVGE	100	50	CT	OV	MD	RUNS	W	AVGE	B.B.
			BATTING									BOWLING					
		Lancashire	219	326	42	12764	*217	44.94	30	71	164	709.2	176	1809	55	32.89	
		Rest of World XI	17	30	3	1039	*114	38.48	2	5	12	125	26	371	13	28.53	
		N.Z. Governor's XI	1	2		76	71	38.00		1							
		TEST RECORD	**110**	**175**	**14**	**7515**	***242**	**46.67**	**19**	**39**	**90**	**273**	**75**	**622**	**10**	**62.20**	**2-13**
		CAREER	**490**	**730**	**96**	**31232**	***242**	**49.26**	**79**	**172**	**377**	**1585.5**	**376**	**4104**	**114**	**36.00**	**4-48**

LOGIE, Augustine Lawrence

SEASON	TEAM	OPPONENTS	V	M	I	NO	RUNS	H.S.	AVGE	100	50	CT/St	OV	MD	RUNS	W	AVGE	B.B.
				BATTING									BOWLING					
1977-78	S. Trinidad	C. N. & E. Trinidad TC	T	3	6	2	56	23	14.00			2	4	0	9	1	9.00	
1978-79	Trinidad	Shell Shield	IIs	1	2		19	11	9.50									
1978-79	S. Trinidad	C. N. & E Trinidad & TobagoTC	T	4	4		137	57	34.25		2	1	13	3	26	1	26.00	
1978-79	S/C Trinidad	N/E Trinidad BC	T	1	2		136	114	68.00	1		3	11	5	26	0		
1979-80	Trinidad	Shell Shield	IIs	4	7		79	18	11.28			2	2	0	11	0		
1979-80	S/C Trinidad	N/E Trinidad BC	T	1	2		46	42	23.00			1						
1980-81	Trinidad	Shell Shield	IIs	4	5	1	258	125	64.50	1	2	1	6	0	22	0		
1980-81	Trinidad	English Tourist	WI	1	1		30	30	30.00				1	0	1	0		
1981-82	West Indies Under 26 XI	Tour of Zimbabwe	Z	3	5	1	87	29	21.75			1						
1981-82	West Indies	Tour of Australia	A	3	4		81	43	20.25									
1981-82	Trinidad	Shell Shield	IIs	4	7		317	171	45.28	1								
1982-83	Trinidad	Shell Shield	IIs	5	10	2	540	138	67.50	2	2	1						
1982-83	Trinidad	Indian Tourist	WI	1	2		20	13	10.00									
1982-83	**WEST INDIES**	**INDIA TESTS**	**WI**	**5**	**6**		**167**	**130**	**27.83**	**1**		**1**						
1983-84	West Indies	Tour of India	I	5	8	1	151	56	21.57		1	1						
1983-84	**WEST INDIES**	**INDIA TESTS**	**I**	**3**	**4**		**63**	**63**	**15.75**		**1**	**1**						
1983-84	Trinidad	Australian Tourist	WI	1	2		25	13	12.50									
1983-84	**WEST INDIES**	**AUSTRALIA TESTS**	**WI**	**1**	**1**		**97**	**97**	**97.00**		**1**	**1**	**0.1**	**0**	**4**	**0**		
1984	West Indies	Tour of England	E	8	10	2	585	141	73.12	2	4	3						
1984-85	West Indies	Tour of Australia	A	5	7		250	134	35.71	1			10	1	29	1	29.00	
1984-85	**WEST INDIES**	**NEW ZEALAND TESTS**	**WI**	**4**	**6**	**1**	**166**	**52**	**33.20**		**1**	**4**	**1**	**1**	**0**	**0**		
1985-86	Trinidad	Shell Shield	IIs	5	9		206	79	22.88		1	2						
1986-87	West Indies	Tour of Pakistan	P	2	3		58	29	19.33			4						
1986-87	West Indies	Tour of Australia	A	1	2		61	36	30.50			1						
1986-87	West Indies	Tour of New Zealand	NZ	2	2		9	9	4.50			3						
1986-87	**WEST INDIES**	**NEW ZEALAND TESTS**	**NZ**	**3**	**4**		**62**	**34**	**15.50**			**8**						

SEASON	TEAM	OPPONENTS	V	M	I	NO	RUNS	H.S.	AVGE	100	50	CT	OV	MD	RUNS	W	AVGE	B.B.
1986-87	Trinidad	Shell Shield	IIs	1	2		30	28	15.00									
1987-88	West Indies	Tour of India	I	2	3		125	54	41.66		2	1						
1987-88	**WEST INDIES**	**INDIA TESTS**	**I**	**4**	**7**	**1**	**250**	**101**	**41.66**	**1**	**1**	**2**						
1987-88	Trinidad	Red Stripe Cup	IIs	2	4		113	46	28.25			3/1						
1987-88	**WEST INDIES**	**PAKISTAN TESTS**	**WI**	**3**	**6**		**126**	**80**	**21.00**		**1**	**5**						
1988	West Indies	Tour of England	E	8	11	2	222	53	24.66		1	3						
1988	**WEST INDIES**	**ENGLAND TESTS**	**E**	**5**	**7**	**2**	**364**	***95**	**72.80**		**2**	**6**						
1988-89	West Indies	Tour of Australia	A	5	7	1	403	134	67.16	2	1	2						
1988-89	**WEST INDIES**	**AUSTRALIA TESTS**	**A**	**5**	**9**	**1**	**198**	**93**	**24.75**		**1**	**8**						
1988-89	Trinidad	Red Stripe Cup	IIs	1	2	1	56	50	56.00		1							
1988-89	**WEST INDIES**	**INDIA TESTS**	**WI**	**4**	**6**	**1**	**214**	**87**	**42.80**		**1**	**5**						
1989-90	Trinidad	Red Stripe Cup	IIs	2	4		156	75	39.00		1	1						
1989-90	WI President's XI	English Tourist	WI	1	2		66	40	33.00									
1989-90	**WEST INDIES**	**ENGLAND TESTS**	**WI**	**3**	**5**		**212**	**98**	**42.40**		**1**	**1**						
		Trinidad		32	57	4	1849	171	34.88	4	7	10/1	9	0	34	0		
		South Trinidad		7	10	2	193	57	24.12	0	2	3	17	3	35	2	17.50	
		S/C Trinidad		2	4		182	114	45.50	1	0	4	11	5	26	0		
		West Indies		85	125	13	4017	141	35.86	7	19	61	11.1	2	33	1	33.00	
		TEST RECORD		**40**	**61**	**6**	**1919**	**130**	**34.89**	**2**	**10**	**42**	**1.1**	**1**	**4**	**0**		
		CAREER		**126**	**196**	**19**	**6241**	**171**	**35.26**	**12**	**28**	**78/1**	**48.1**	**10**	**128**	**3**	**42.66**	**1-2**

McMORRIS, Easton Dudley Ashton St. John

				BATTING									BOWLING					
SEASON	TEAM	OPPONENTS	V	M	I	NO	RUNS	H.S.	AVGE	100	50	CT	OV	MD	RUNS	W	AVGE	B.B.
1956-57	Jamaica	British Guiana	IIs	1	1		34	34	34.00									
1956-57	Jamaica	Duke of Norfolk's Tourist	WI	3	6		247	114	41.16	1	1	3						
1957-58	Jamaica	Pakistan Tourist	WI	1	2		51	27	25.50									
1957-58	**WEST INDIES**	**PAKISTAN TESTS**	**WI**	**1**	**2**		**29**	**16**	**14.50**									
1959-60	Jamaica	Trinidad	IIs	1	2		178	102	89.00	1	1							
1959-60	Jamaica	British Guiana	IIs	1	2	1	228	*136	228.00	1	1							
1959-60	Jamaica	M.C.C. Tourist	WI	1	2		178	104	89.00	1	1	1						
1959-60	**WEST INDIES**	**ENGLAND TESTS**	**WI**	**4**	**6**		**124**	**73**	**20.66**		**1**	**1**						
1961-62	Jamaica	Barbados	IIs	1	2		175	175	87.50	1								
1961-62	Jamaica	Indian Tourist	WI	1	2		154	154	77.00	1		1						
1961-62	**WEST INDIES**	**INDIA TESTS**	**WI**	**4**	**6**		**349**	**125**	**58.16**	**1**	**2**	**3**						

SEASON	TEAM	OPPONENTS	V	M	I	NO	RUNS	H.S.	AVGE	100	50	CT	OV	MD	RUNS	W	AVGE	B.B.
				BATTING									BOWLING					
1963	West Indies	Tour of England	E	15	25	5	842	*190	36.58	2	4	4	3	0	26	0		
1963	**WEST INDIES**	**ENGLAND TESTS**	**E**	**2**	**4**		**36**	**16**	**9.00**			**1**						
1963-64	The Rest XI	West Indies XI	WI	1	2		59	37	29.50			1	4	0	44	0		
1963-64	F. Worrell's XI	C. Hunte's XI	WI	1	2		33	22	16.50			3						
1963-64	Jamaica	Cavaliers Touring XI	WI	3	6	1	239	*103	47.80	1	1							
1963-64	Jamaica	Barbados	IIs	1	2		66	55	33.00		1	1						
1963-64	Jamaica	Trinidad	IIs	1	2		31	27	15.50									
1963-64	Jamaica	British Guiana	IIs	1	2		111	59	55.50		2	1						
1964-65	Jamaica	Cavaliers Touring XI	WI	2	4		166	61	41.50		1	1						
1964-65	Jamaica	Australian Tourist	WI	1	2		61	32	30.50									
1965-66	Jamaica	Shell Shield	IIs	4	8	2	553	190	92.16	3			3	3	0	0		
1965-66	Jamaica	Worcestershire Tourist	WI	1	2		4	4	2.00			1						
1966	West Indies	Tour of England	E	15	22	3	608	*157	32.00	2	1	2						
1966	**WEST INDIES**	**ENGLAND TESTS**	**E**	**2**	**3**		**26**	**14**	**8.66**									
1966-67	Jamaica	Shell Shield	IIs	3	5	1	343	218	82.75	1	1	2	1	0	8	0		
1967-68	Jamaica	M.C.C. Tourist	WI	1	2		26	26	13.00			1						
1968-69	Jamaica	Shell Shield	IIs	4	4	1	77	41	25.66			1						
1969-70	Jamaica	Shell Shield	IIs	4	7	1	299	*105	49.83	1	1	1						
1969-70	Jamaica	Cavaliers Touring XI	WI	1	2	1	142	*197	142.00	1								
1970	Jamaica	Tour of English Counties	E	3	4	1	36	25	12.00			2						
1970-71	Jamaica	Shell Shield	IIs	4	6	1	199	70	39.80		2	1	7	1	29	0		
1970-71	Jamaica	Indian Tourist	WI	1	1		4	4	4.00			3						
1971-72	Jamaica	Shell Shield	IIs	4	7		187	68	26.71		1		1	1	0	0		
1971-72	Jamaica	New Zealand Tourist	WI	1	1		11	11	11.00			1						
		Jamaica		50	86	10	3800	218	50.00	13	14	21	12	5	37	0		
		West Indies		43	68	8	2014	*190	33.56	5	8	11	3	0	26	0		
		The Rest XI		1	2		59	37	29.50			1	4	0	44	0		
		F. Worrell's XI		1	2		33	22	16.50			3						
		TEST RECORD		**13**	**21**	**0**	**564**	**125**	**26.85**	**1**	**3**	**5**						
		CAREER		**95**	**158**	**18**	**5906**	**218**	**42.18**	**18**	**22**	**36**	**19**	**5**	**107**	**0**		

McWATT, Clifford Aubrey

SEASON	TEAM	OPPONENTS	V	BATTING M	I	NO	RUNS	H.S.	AVGE	100	50	CT/St	BOWLING OV	MD	RUNS	W	AVGE	B.B.
1943-44	British Guiana	Trinidad	IIs	2	4		90	46	22.50			2/1						
1944-45	British Guiana	Barbados	IIs	2	4		132	64	33.00		1							
1946-47	British Guiana	Barbados	IIs	2	4		98	40	24.50				3	0	17	1	17.00	
1946-47	British Guiana	Trinidad	IIs	2	4	1	190	*123	63.33	1	1	3						
1947-48	British Guiana	Jamaica	IIs	2	4		62	34	15.50			3						
1948-49	West Indies	Tour of India	I	8	9		250	51	27.77		1	11/1						
1948-49	West Indies	Tour of Pakistan	P	2	2	1	24	20	24.00			2/1						
1948-49	West Indies	Tour of Ceylon	C	1	1		12	12	12.00									
1949-50	British Guiana	Barbados	IIs	2	4		95	47	23.75			1						
1950-51	British Guiana	Jamaica	IIs	1	2	1	19	17	19.00			1						
1951-52	British Guiana	Trinidad	IIs	2	4		93	44	23.25			4	9	1	41	0		
1952-53	British Guiana	Indian Tourist	WI	1	1		1	1	1.00									
1953-54	British Guiana	Trinidad	IIs	2	4	2	208	128	104.00	1	1	4/2						
1953-54	British Guiana	M.C.C. Tourist	WI	1	2		38	29	19.00									
1953-54	**WEST INDIES**	**ENGLAND TESTS**	**WI**	**5**	**8**	**2**	**198**	**54**	**33.00**		**2**	**7/1**	**4**	**2**	**16**	**1**	**16.00**	
1954-55	British Guiana	Barbados	IIs	2	4		76	58	19.00		1	3	4	0	21	0		
1954-55	British Guiana	Australian Tourist	WI	1	2		42	28	21.00			2						
1954-55	**WEST INDIES**	**AUSTRALIA TESTS**	**WI**	**1**	**1**		**4**	**4**	**4.00**			**2**						
1956-57	British Guiana	Jamaica	IIs	1	D													
1956-57	British Guiana	Barbados	IIs	1	1		41	41	41.00									
		British Guiana		24	44	4	1185	128	29.62	2	4	23/3	16	1	79	1	79.00	
		West Indies		17	21	3	488	54	27.11		3	22/3	4	2	16	1	16.00	
		TEST RECORD		**6**	**9**	**2**	**202**	**54**	**28.85**	**0**	**2**	**9/1**	**4**	**2**	**16**	**1**	**16.00**	**1-16**
		CAREER		**41**	**65**	**7**	**1673**	**128**	**28.84**	**2**	**7**	**45/6**	**20**	**3**	**95**	**2**	**47.50**	**1-17**

MADRAY, Ivan Samuel

SEASON	TEAM	OPPONENTS	V	BATTING M	I	NO	RUNS	H.S.	AVGE	100	50	CT	BOWLING OV	MD	RUNS	W	AVGE	B.B.
1954-55	British Guiana	Australian Tourist	WI	1	2		1	1	0.50				23	0	122	3	40.66	
1956-57	British Guiana	Jamaica	IIs	1	1		25	25	25.00				84	18	168	4	42.00	
1956-57	British Guiana	Barbados	IIs	1	1		16	16	16.00			2	24.2	4	79	5	15.80	
1957-58	British Guiana	Pakistan Tourist	WI	1	1		28	28	28.00			1	51	3	144	4	36.00	
1957-58	**WEST INDIES**	**PAKISTAN TESTS**	**WI**	**2**	**3**		**3**	**2**	**1.00**			**2**	**35**	**6**	**108**	**0**		

SEASON	TEAM	OPPONENTS	M	I	NO	RUNS	H.S.	AVGE	100	50	CT	OV	MD	RUNS	W	AVGE	B.B.
			BATTING									**BOWLING**					
		British Guiana	4	5		70	28	14.00			3	182.2	25	513	16	32.06	
		West Indies	2	3		3	2	1.00			2	35	6	108	0		
		TEST RECORD	**2**	**3**	**0**	**3**	**2**	**1.00**	**0**	**0**	**2**	**35**	**6**	**108**	**0**		
		CAREER	**6**	**8**	**0**	**73**	**28**	**9.12**	**0**	**0**	**5**	**217.2**	**31**	**621**	**16**	**38.81**	**4-61**

MARSHALL, Malcolm Denzil

SEASON	TEAM	OPPONENTS	V	M	I	NO	RUNS	H.S.	AVGE	100	50	CT	OV	MD	RUNS	W	AVGE	B.B.
				BATTING									**BOWLING**					
1977-78	Barbados	Shell Shield	IIs	1	1		0	0					33.4	7	97	7	13.85	
1978-79	West Indies	Tour of India	I	6	7	1	140	59	15.55		1	5	165.3	43	452	34	13.29	
1978-79	**WEST INDIES**	**INDIA TESTS**	**I**	**3**	**5**	**1**	**8**	**5**	**2.00**			**1**	**78**	**11**	**265**	**3**	**88.33**	
1978-79	West Indies	Tour of Sri Lanka	SL	2	3		12	9	4.00				42	16	93	5	18.60	
1978-79	Barbados	Shell Shield	IIs	4	5	1	38	17	9.50			2	142.2	22	401	25	16.04	
1979	Hampshire	Counties	E	19	25	2	197	38	8.56			12	476	146	1051	47	22.36	
1979-80	West Indies	Tour of Australia	A	2	3	1	39	*23	19.50				52	14	144	7	20.57	
1979-80	West Indies	Tour of New Zealand	NZ	2	3	1	20	13	10.00			2	55	10	149	7	21.28	
1979-80	Barbados	Shell Shield	IIs	4	4	1	142	55	47.33		1	1	105.1	29	273	18	15.16	
1980	West Indies	Tour of England	E	8	7	2	121	52	24.20		1		164	44	428	34	12.58	
1980	**WEST INDIES**	**ENGLAND TESTS**	**E**	**4**	**5**		**90**	**45**	**18.00**			**2**	**172.3**	**42**	**436**	**15**	**29.06**	
1980	Hampshire	Counties	E	5	10	1	251	*72	27.88		2	4	141	42	306	17	18.00	
1980-81	West Indies	Tour of Pakistan	P	3	3		57	24	19.00			1	52.5	8	146	12	12.16	
1980-81	**WEST INDIES**	**PAKISTAN TESTS**	**P**	**4**	**5**		**13**	**9**	**2.60**			**1**	**98.3**	**11**	**319**	**13**	**24.53**	
1980-81	Barbados	Shell Shield	IIs	4	5	1	137	*49	34.25			2	112	25	308	17	18.11	
1980-81	Barbados	English Tourist	WI	1	1	1	29	*29					37	13	67	4	16.75	
1980-81	WI President's XI	English Tourist	WI	1	2		58	31	29.00				43	14	102	4	25.50	
1980-81	**WEST INDIES**	**ENGLAND TESTS**	**WI**	**1**	**1**		**15**	**15**	**15.00**				**21**	**2**	**64**	**3**	**21.33**	
1981	Hampshire	Counties	E	17	23	3	425	*75	21.25		1	6	531.3	166	1321	68	19.42	
1981-82	West Indies Under 26 XI	Tour of Zimbabwe	Z	3	4		175	109	43.75	1			80.4	18	192	7	27.42	
1981-82	West Indies	Tour of Australia	A	2	2		66	66	33.00		1		46	14	105	11	9.54	
1982	Hampshire	Counties	E	22	31	3	633	*116	22.60	1	1	4	822	225	2108	134	15.73	
1982-83	West Indies XI	International XI	WI	1	1		40	40	40.00				15	3	25	1	25.00	
1982-83	Barbados	Shell Shield	IIs	5	8		209	71	26.12		1	4	196.2	46	525	20	26.25	
1982-83	**WEST INDIES**	**INDIA TESTS**	**WI**	**5**	**6**	**1**	**74**	**27**	**14.80**			**3**	**174.1**	**40**	**495**	**21**	**23.57**	
1983	Hampshire	Counties	E	16	16	4	563	112	46.91	2	2	6	532.5	143	1327	80	16.58	
1983-84	West Indies	Tour of India	I	1	1		61	61	61.00		1		13	5	20	1	20.00	

1983-84	**WEST INDIES**	**INDIA TESTS**	**I**	**6**	**7**		**244**	**92**	**34.85**		**2**	**1**	**221**	**59**	**621**	**33**	**18.61**	
1983-84	**WEST INDIES**	**AUSTRALIA TESTS**	**WI**	**4**	**4**		**45**	**19**	**11.25**			**2**	**158.5**	**24**	**480**	**21**	**22.85**	
1984	West Indies	Tour of England	E	4	4		56	34	14.00			1	93	25	209	16	13.06	
1984	**WEST INDIES**	**ENGLAND TESTS**	**E**	**4**	**5**		**47**	**29**	**9.40**			**2**	**167.4**	**50**	**437**	**24**	**18.20**	
1984-85	West Indies	Tour of Australia	A	2	3	1	38	35	19.00				52.1	14	145	8	18.12	
1984-85	**WEST INDIES**	**AUSTRALIA TESTS**	**A**	**5**	**6**	**1**	**174**	**57**	**34.80**		**2**	**4**	**215.2**	**45**	**554**	**28**	**19.78**	
1984-85	**WEST INDIES**	**NEW ZEALAND TESTS**	**WI**	**4**	**4**		**90**	**63**	**22.50**		**1**	**3**	**170.2**	**30**	**486**	**27**	**18.00**	
1985	Hampshire	Counties	E	22	33	2	768	*66	24.77		5	10	688.1	193	1680	95	17.68	
1985-86	Barbados	Shell Shield	IIs	4	6	1	51	17	10.20			4	127	22	353	23	15.34	
1985-86	**WEST INDIES**	**ENGLAND TESTS**	**WI**	**5**	**5**	**1**	**153**	**76**	**38.25**		**2**	**4**	**169.3**	**36**	**482**	**27**	**17.85**	
1986	Hampshire	Counties	E	23	23	2	263	*51	12.52		1	5	656.3	171	1508	100	15.08	
1986-87	West Indies	Tour of Pakistan	P	1	1	1	16	*16					17	3	61	1	61.00	
1986-87	**WEST INDIES**	**PAKISTAN TESTS**	**P**	**3**	**5**	**1**	**32**	***13**	**8.00**				**114**	**27**	**266**	**16**	**15.62**	
1986-87	**WEST INDIES**	**NEW ZEALAND TESTS**	**NZ**	**3**	**4**		**83**	**45**	**20.75**				**119**	**21**	**289**	**9**	**32.11**	
1986-87	Barbados	Shell Shield	IIs	1	D								26	9	54	7	7.71	
1987	Hampshire	Counties	E	21	22	5	610	99	35.88		3	6	571.4	149	1445	72	20.06	
1987	M.C.C.	Rest of World XI	E	1	D							1	22.3	3	63	4	15.75	
1987-88	Barbados	Red Stripe Cup	IIs	5	9	1	298	77	37.25		4	5	159.5	35	466	27	17.26	
1987-88	**WEST INDIES**	**PAKISTAN TESTS**	**WI**	**2**	**4**	**1**	**75**	**48**	**25.00**				**91.4**	**14**	**284**	**15**	**18.93**	
1988	West Indies	Tour of England	E	4	4		154	76	38.50		1	2	42.3	7	110	7	15.71	
1988	**WEST INDIES**	**ENGLAND TESTS**	**E**	**5**	**6**	**1**	**135**	**72**	**27.00**		**1**	**1**	**203.1**	**49**	**443**	**35**	**12.65**	
1988-89	West Indies	Tour of Australia	A	2	3	1	53	31	26.50				51	10	163	1	163.00	
1988-89	**WEST INDIES**	**AUSTRALIA TESTS**	**A**	**5**	**8**		**76**	**23**	**9.50**			**1**	**192**	**42**	**488**	**17**	**28.70**	
1988-89	Barbados	Red Stripe Cup	IIs	1	1		89	89	89.00		1		19	3	60	1	60.00	
1988-89	**WEST INDIES**	**INDIA TESTS**	**WI**	**3**	**4**	**1**	**84**	***40**	**28.00**				**111.2**	**18**	**290**	**19**	**15.26**	
1989	Hampshire	Counties	E	15	21	5	412	*68	25.75		2	2	428.3	115	1067	64	16.67	
1989-90	Barbados	Red Stripe Cup	IIs	2	2		62	59	31.00		1	1	53	16	134	6	22.33	
1989-90	Barbados	English Tourist	WI	1	2		55	31	27.50				21	3	73	3	24.33	
1989-90	**WEST INDIES**	**ENGLAND TESTS**	**WI**	**2**	**4**	**1**	**19**	***8**	**6.33**				**59**	**16**	**132**	**3**	**44.00**	
1990	Hampshire	Counties	E	18	24	3	962	117	45.80	2	6	7	554.2	141	1381	72	19.18	
		Barbados		33	44	6	1110	89	29.21		8	19	1032.2	230	2811	158	17.79	
		West Indies		112	139	17	2563	109	21.00	1	13	36	3521.4	785	9375	485	19.32	
		Hampshire		178	228	30	5084	117	25.67	5	23	62	5402.3	1491	13194	749	17.61	
		M.C.C.		1	D							1	22.3	3	63	4	15.75	
		TEST RECORD		**68**	**88**	**9**	**1457**	**92**	**18.44**	**0**	**8**	**25**	**2536.5**	**537**	**6831**	**329**	**20.76**	**7-22**
		CAREER		**324**	**411**	**53**	**8757**	**117**	**24.46**	**6**	**44**	**118**	**9979**	**2509**	**25443**	**1396**	**18.22**	**8-71**

MARSHALL, Norman Edgar

SEASON	TEAM	OPPONENTS	V	M	I	NO	RUNS	H.S.	AVGE	100	50	CT	OV	MD	RUNS	W	AVGE	B.B.
				BATTING									BOWLING					
1940-41	Barbados	Trinidad	IIs	1	2	1	0	*0					15	0	100	0		
1942-43	Barbados	Trinidad	IIs	1	2		14	14	7.00				12	1	50	0		
1943-44	Barbados	Trinidad	IIs	2	2	1	77	44	77.00				30	2	111	3	37.00	
1944-45	Barbados	British Guiana	IIs	2	3		134	80	44.66		1	1	58	11	157	4	39.25	
1944-45	Barbados	Trinidad	IIs	2	4		47	16	11.75				40	6	155	6	25.83	
1945-46	Barbados	Trinidad	IIs	2	3	1	148	84	74.00		1		63	13	180	2	90.00	
1946-47	Barbados	British Guiana	IIs	2	3		54	45	18.00				79.1	27	164	6	27.33	
1946-47	Barbados	Jamaica	IIs	2	3	1	45	23	22.50				120	37	339	10	33.90	
1947-48	Barbados	M.C.C. Tourist	WI	1	D								56	24	90	1	90.00	
1948-49	Barbados	Trinidad	IIs	2	3		65	43	21.66			2	78	32	149	3	49.66	
1949-50	Barbados	British Guiana	IIs	1	D								28	7	20	1	20.00	
1950-51	Barbados	Trinidad	IIs	2	4	1	88	49	29.33				85.4	31	199	7	28.42	
1951-52	Barbados	British Guiana	IIs	2	3		182	134	60.66	1			100.1	28	213	4	53.25	
1951-52	Barbados	Jamaica	IIs	2	3		84	59	28.00		1	2	69.5	46	179	6	29.83	
1953-54	Trinidad	British Guiana	IIs	2	2		50	35	25.00				117.2	58	202	10	20.20	
1954-55	Trinidad	Jamaica	IIs	2	4		88	66	22.00		1	1	106	56	133	8	16.62	
1954-55	**WEST INDIES**	**AUSTRALIA TESTS**	**WI**	**1**	**2**		**8**	**8**	**4.00**				**46.3**	**22**	**62**	**2**	**31.00**	
1954-55	Barbados	Australian Tourist	WI	1	2		26	19	13.00				52	22	109	5	21.80	
1955-56	Barbados	E.W. Swanton's Tourist	WI	2	3	1	161	100	80.50	1			113	46	211	12	17.58	
1958-59	N. Trinidad	South Trinidad BC	T	1	2		66	57	33.00		1		8	1	32	0		
		Barbados		27	40	6	1125	134	33.08	2	3	5	999.5	333	2426	70	34.65	
		Trinidad		4	6		138	66	23.00		1	1	223.2	114	335	18	18.61	
		North Trinidad		1	2		66	57	33.00		1		8	1	32	0		
		West Indies		1	2		8	8	4.00				46.3	22	62	2	31.00	
		TEST RECORD		**1**	**2**	**0**	**8**	**8**	**4.00**	**0**	**0**	**0**	**46.3**	**22**	**62**	**2**	**31.00**	**1-22**
		CAREER		**33**	**50**	**6**	**1337**	**134**	**30.38**	**2**	**5**	**6**	**1277.4**	**470**	**2855**	**90**	**31.72**	**6-117**

MARSHALL, Roy Edwin

SEASON	TEAM	OPPONENTS	V	M	I	NO	RUNS	H.S.	AVGE	100	50	CT	OV	MD	RUNS	W	AVGE	B.B.
				BATTING									BOWLING					
1945-46	Barbados	Trinidad	IIs	1	1		2	2	2.00									
1948-49	Barbados	Trinidad	IIs	2	3		316	149	105.33	2	1	1	33.2	10	74	5	14.80	
1949-50	Barbados	British Guiana	IIs	2	3		250	191	83.33	1		3	51	17	143	3	47.66	

1950	West Indies	Tour of England	E	20	28		1117	188	39.89	3	3	14	120.5	36	336	7	48.00
1950-51	Barbados	Trinidad	IIs	2	4		102	52	25.50		1	2	56	17	145	5	29.00
1951-52	West Indies	Tour of Australia	A	6	10		267	114	26.70	1		3	68.5	15	218	6	36.33
1951-52	**WEST INDIES**	**AUSTRALIA TESTS**	**A**	**2**	**4**		**101**	**30**	**25.25**			**1**	**5**	**1**	**12**	**0**	
1951-52	West Indies	Tour of New Zealand	NZ	2	4	2	213	*102	106.50	1	1	2	12	2	32	1	32.00
1951-52	**WEST INDIES**	**NEW ZEALAND TESTS**	**NZ**	**2**	**3**		**42**	**26**	**14.00**				**2**	**1**	**3**	**0**	
1952-53	Barbados	Indian Tourist	WI	1	1		25	25	25.00								
1953	Hampshire	Counties	E	3	6		170	71	28.33		1	6	55.4	14	139	3	46.33
1953	Comm. XI	Essex	E	1	2		8	7	4.00				41	6	143	6	23.83
1953-54	Comm. XI	Tour of India	I	17	25	4	761	90	36.23		5	8	14	5	15	2	7.50
1954	Hampshire	Counties	E	1	2		0	0					284	75	738	25	29.62
1954	The South XI	The North XI	E	1	2		74	42	37.00			1	16	9	14	1	14.00
1954	Comm. XI	England XI	E	2	3		92	59	30.66		1	4	7	0	45	0	
1955	Hampshire	Counties	E	30	56	4	1890	*110	36.34	3	10	29	22	4	76	2	38.00
1955	Comm. XI	England XI	E	1	2		119	72	59.50		1	1	168.4	68	370	26	14.27
1955	The South XI	The North XI	E	1	2		106	72	53.00		1	2					
1956	Hampshire	Counties	E	31	51	1	1310	133	26.20	2	6	26	20	1	69	2	34.50
1956-57	Duke of Norfolk's XI	Tour of Jamaica	WI	3	6		273	97	45.50		2	4	350.3	116	740	36	20.55
1957	Hampshire	Counties	E	29	53	1	1708	163	32.44	4	10	13	9	0	32	1	32.00
1957	Comm. XI	England XI	E	1	2		73	47	36.50			1	60	18	153	2	76.50
1957	The South XI	The North XI	E	1	2		52	43	26.00								
1957	Rest of League XI	Surrey	E	1	2		55	55	27.50		1	1					
1958	Hampshire	Counties	E	30	51	2	1876	193	38.28	5	9	20					
1958	The Players XI	The Gentlemen's XI	E	2	4	1	161	76	53.66		1	1	99.5	38	199	4	49.75
1958	T.N. Pearce's XI	New Zealand Tourist	E	1	2		81	78	40.50		1		9	2	36	2	18.00
1959	Hampshire	Counties	E	31	57		2279	150	39.38	4	17	19	20	7	44	2	22.00
1959	M.C.C.	Scotland	E	1	2		106	85	53.00		1	4	149.4	45	424	10	42.40
1959	T.N. Pearce's XI	Indian Tourist	E	1	2		99	61	49.50		1						
1959	The Players XI	The Gentlemen's XI	E	1	2	1	48	41	48.00								
1959-60	Comm. XI	Tour of South Africa	SA	3	6	1	100	25	20.00			2					
1960	Hampshire	Counties	E	33	58	5	2262	168	42.67	5	11	12	40	13	115	0	
1960	The Players XI	The Gentlemen's XI	E	1	2		34	32	17.00				58	25	102	5	20.40
1960	T.N. Pearce's XI	South African Tourist	E	1	2		84	67	42.00		1						
1961	Hampshire	Counties	E	32	62	2	2607	212	43.45	5	15	8					
1961-62	International XI	World Tour	R.I.NZ	6	10	1	302	76	33.55		2	3	5	1	13	0	
1962	Hampshire	Counties	E	27	50	3	2095	*228	44.57	6	8	16	40	11	117	5	23.40
1962	M.C.C.	Surrey	E	1	2		29	19	14.50				104	8	11	1	11.00
1962-63	Comm. XI	Tour of Rhodesia	R	1	2		40	32	20.00								
1963	Hampshire	Counties	E	29	54	3	1800	*161	35.29	5	7	7	2	0	3	0	
													7	0	67	0	

SEASON	TEAM	OPPONENTS	V	M	I	NO	RUNS	H.S.	AVGE	100	50	CT	OV	MD	RUNS	W	AVGE	B.B.
				BATTING									BOWLING					
1963	M.C.C.	Surrey	E	1	1		0	0										
1963-64	Cavaliers XI	Tour of Jamaica	WI	2	4		101	38	25.25				11	2	38	0		
1964	Hampshire	Counties	E	23	39	1	1341	163	35.28	4	4	9						
1964	West Indies XI	England XI	E	3	5		90	33	18.00			3	7	1	16	1	16.00	
1964-65	Cavaliers XI	Tour of West Indies	WI	3	6		70	23	11.66				62.2	7	243	5	48.60	
1965	Hampshire	Counties	E	29	54	2	1644	132	31.61	2	8	7	11	5	26	2	13.00	
1966	Hampshire	Counties	E	29	54	2	1882	133	36.19	3	13	11	47	14	116	5	23.20	
1967	Hampshire	Counties	E	29	50	3	1493	160	31.76	4	6	18	2	0	18	0		
1968	Hampshire	Counties	E	30	48	5	1179	*112	27.41	1	7	6						
1968	Rest of World XI	Kent	E	1	2		29	24	14.50									
1969	Hampshire	Counties	E	19	26		595	87	22.88		6	6						
1970	Hampshire	Counties	E	25	41	2	1590	*189	40.76	2	10	10	16	10	7	1	7.00	
1971	Hampshire	Counties	E	26	47	7	1543	*142	38.57	3	7	8						
1972	Hampshire	Counties	E	18	31	6	1039	203	41.56	2	5	2						
		Barbados		8	12		695	191	57.91	3	2	6	196	58	501	16	31.31	
		West Indies		35	54	2	1830	188	35.19	5	4	23	215.4	56	617	15	41.13	
		Hampshire		504	890	49	30303	*228	36.03	60	160	233	1135.4	363	2403	99	24.27	
		Comm. XI		26	42	5	1193	90	32.24		7	16	362	97	947	29	32.65	
		M.C.C.		3	5		135	85	27.00		1	4						
		The South XI		3	6		232	72	38.66		1	3	27	1	114	2	57.00	
		Duke of Norfolk's XI		3	6		273	97	45.50		2	4	9	0	32	1	32.00	
		The Players XI		4	8	2	243	76	40.50		1	1	9	2	36	2	18.00	
		T.N. Pearce's XI		3	6		264	78	44.00		3		20	7	44	2	22.00	
		Rest of League XI		1	2		55	55	27.50		1	1						
		International XI		6	10	1	302	76	33.55		2	3	40	11	117	5	23.40	
		Cavaliers XI		5	10		171	38	17.10				73.2	9	281	5	56.20	
		Rest of World XI		1	2		29	24	14.50									
		TEST RECORD		**4**	**7**	**0**	**143**	**30**	**20.42**	**0**	**0**	**1**	**7**	**2**	**15**	**0**		
		CAREER		**602**	**1053**	**59**	**35725**	***228**	**35.94**	**68**	**184**	**294**	**2087.4**	**604**	**5092**	**176**	**28.93**	**6-36**

MARTIN, Frank Reginald

SEASON	TEAM	OPPONENTS	V	M	I	NO	RUNS	H.S.	AVGE	100	50	CT	OV	MD	RUNS	W	AVGE	B.B.
				BATTING									BOWLING					
1924-25	Jamaica	Barbados	IIs	3	5		292	195	58.40	1		2	44	8	120	0		

1925-26	Jamaica	M.C.C. Tourist	WI	3	5		190	80	38.00		2	1	80	20	184	7	26.28	
1926-27	Jamaica	L.H. Tennyson's Tourist	WI	3	4	1	274	*204	91.33	1		2	112	20	234	6	39.00	
1927-28	Jamaica	L.H. Tennyson's Tourist	WI	3	5	3	272	*141	136.00	1	2	1	63	22	95	1	95.00	
1928	West Indies	Tour of England	E	26	40	4	1195	165	33.16	1	8	7	325.2	80	822	19	43.26	
1928	**WEST INDIES**	**ENGLAND TESTS**	**E**	**3**	**6**		**175**	**44**	**29.16**				**10**	**3**	**31**	**0**		
1928-29	Jamaica	Julien Cahn's Tourist	WI	2	4	2	103	64	51.50		1		44	13	88	1	88.00	
1928-29	West Indies XI	Julien Cahn's Tourist	WI	1	2		36	32	18.00				16	5	40	0		
1929-30	Jamaica	M.C.C. Tourist	WI	1	2		131	*106	65.50	1		1	49	11	124	2	62.00	
1929-30	**WEST INDIES**	**ENGLAND TESTS**	**WI**	**1**	**2**		**57**	**33**	**28.50**				**54**	**7**	**140**	**1**	**140.00**	
1930-31	West Indies	Tour of Australia	A	8	14	1	352	*79	27.07		2		172	29	502	14	35.85	
1930-31	**WEST INDIES**	**AUSTRALIA TESTS**	**A**	**5**	**10**	**1**	**254**	***123**	**28.22**	**1**		**2**	**160.2**	**17**	**448**	**7**	**64.00**	
1933	West Indies	Tour of England	E	6	9		258	67	28.66		1	3	135.2	31	321	16	20.06	
		Jamaica		15	25	6	1262	*204	66.42	4	5	7	392	94	845	17	49.70	
		West Indies		50	83	6	2327	165	30.22	2	11	12	873	172	2304	57	40.42	
		TEST RECORD		**9**	**18**	**1**	**486**	***123**	**28.58**	**1**	**0**	**2**	**224.2**	**27**	**619**	**8**	**77.37**	**3-91**
		CAREER		**65**	**108**	**12**	**3589**	***204**	**37.78**	**6**	**16**	**19**	**1265**	**266**	**3149**	**74**	**42.55**	**5-90**

MARTINDALE, Emmanuel Alfred

				BATTING									BOWLING					
SEASON	**TEAM**	**OPPONENTS**	**V**	**M**	**I**	**NO**	**RUNS**	**H.S.**	**AVGE**	**100**	**50**	**CT**	**OV**	**MD**	**RUNS**	**W**	**AVGE**	**B.B.**
1929-30	Barbados	British Guiana	IIs	1	2		17	10	8.50			1	58.4	12	180	4	45.00	
1929-30	Barbados	M.C.C. Tourist	WI	1	1		0	0					30	3	120	1	120.00	
1931-32	Barbados	Trinidad	IIs	1	2	1	30	*30	30.00				25	6	72	4	18.00	
1932-33	C.A. Merry's XI	G.C. Grant's XI	IIs	1	2		70	42	35.00				28	8	69	5	13.80	
1933	West Indies	Tour of England	E	22	27	8	231	*25	12.15			12	595.5	100	1910	89	21.46	
1933	**WEST INDIES**	**ENGLAND TESTS**	**E**	**3**	**6**	**2**	**21**	***9**	**5.25**			**1**	**72.3**	**9**	**251**	**14**	**17.92**	
1933-34	Barbados	British Guiana	IIs	1	2		25	16	12.50			2	45	8	128	7	18.28	
1933-34	Barbados	Trinidad	IIs	1	2	1	43	*35	43.00				52	7	197	9	21.88	
1934-35	Barbados	British Guiana	IIs	1	2		44	28	22.00			3	30	7	86	1	86.00	
1934-35	Barbados	M.C.C. Tourist	WI	2	2		55	45	27.50			1	53	6	170	0		
1934-35	**WEST INDIES**	**ENGLAND TESTS**	**WI**	**4**	**4**	**1**	**9**	**9**	**3.00**			**3**	**100.3**	**23**	**239**	**19**	**12.57**	
1935-36	Barbados	Trinidad	IIs	1	2		141	134	70.50	1		1	40	3	196	4	49.00	
1939	West Indies	Tour of England	E	17	26	7	258	39	13.57			4	324	33	1273	42	30.30	
1939	**WEST INDIES**	**ENGLAND TESTS**	**E**	**3**	**4**		**28**	**22**	**7.00**			**1**	**70.7**	**8**	**314**	**4**	**78.50**	
		Barbados		9	15	2	355	134	27.30	1		8	333.4	52	1149	30	38.30	

SEASON	TEAM	OPPONENTS	V	BATTING M	I	NO	RUNS	H.S.	AVGE	100	50	CT	BOWLING OV	MD	RUNS	W	AVGE	B.B.
		West Indies		49	67	18	547	39	11.66			21	1163.4	173	3987	168	23.73	
		C.A. Merry's XI		1	2		70	42	35.00				28	8	69	5	13.80	
		TEST RECORD		**10**	**14**	**3**	**58**	**22**	**5.27**	**0**	**0**	**5**	**243.7**	**40**	**804**	**37**	**21.72**	**5-22**
		CAREER		**59**	**84**	**20**	**972**	**134**	**15.18**	**1**	**0**	**29**	**1525.2**	**233**	**5205**	**203**	**25.64**	**8-32**

MATTIS, Everton Hugh

SEASON	TEAM	OPPONENTS	V	BATTING M	I	NO	RUNS	H.S.	AVGE	100	50	CT	BOWLING OV	MD	RUNS	W	AVGE	B.B.
1976-77	Jamaica	Shell Shield	IIs	2	3	1	49	*24	24.50			1						
1977-78	Jamaica	Shell Shield	IIs	3	5	1	186	95	46.50		1							
1977-78	Jamaica	Australian Tourist	WI	1	2		13	10	6.50									
1978-79	Jamaica	Shell Shield	IIs	4	5		210	125	42.00	1		3	20	7	32	2	16.00	
1979-80	Jamaica	Shell Shield	IIs	4	8		244	132	30.50	1		3	5.4	1	14	1	14.00	
1980-81	Jamaica	Shell Shield	IIs	3	6		332	92	55.33		4	2						
1980-81	Jamaica	English Tourist	WI	1	1		15	15	15.00			1	14	6	22	4	5.50	
1980-81	WI President's XI	English Tourist	WI	1	2		87	46	43.50			1						
1980-81	**WEST INDIES**	**ENGLAND TESTS**	**WI**	**4**	**5**		**145**	**71**	**29.00**		**1**	**3**	**6**	**1**	**14**	**0**		
1981-82	West Indies Under 26 XI	Tour of Zimbabwe	Z	3	4		118	106	29.50	1		4	2	0	5	0		
1981-82	Jamaica	Shell Shield	IIs	5	10	1	441	98	49.00		4	3	3	1	2	1	2.00	
1982-83	WI Rebels XI	Tour of South Africa	SA	2	4		43	21	10.75									
1983-84	WI Rebels XI	Tour of South Africa	SA	5	10		181	51	18.10		1	3	0.4	0	0	1		
		Jamaica		23	40	3	1490	132	40.27	2	9	13	42.4	14	70	8	8.75	
		West Indies		8	11		350	106	31.81	1	1	8	8	1	19	0		
		WI Rebels XI		7	14		224	51	16.00		1	3	0.4	0	0	1		
		TEST RECORD		**4**	**5**	**0**	**145**	**71**	**29.00**	**0**	**1**	**3**	**6**	**1**	**14**	**0**		
		CAREER		**38**	**65**	**3**	**2064**	**132**	**33.29**	**3**	**11**	**24**	**51.2**	**16**	**89**	**9**	**9.88**	**4-22**

MENDONCA, Ivor Leon

SEASON	TEAM	OPPONENTS	V	BATTING M	I	NO	RUNS	H.S.	AVGE	100	50	CT/St	BOWLING OV	MD	RUNS	W	AVGE	B.B.
1958-59	British Guiana	Barbados	IIs	2	4		175	74	43.75		2	6						
1959-60	British Guiana	Jamaica	IIs	1	2		7	5	3.50			1/1						

1959-60	British Guiana	M.C.C. Tourist	WI	1	2	2	38	*31				3/1						
1960-61	British Guiana	E.W. Swanton's Tourist	WI	1	2		31	26	15.50			3/1						
1961-62	British Guiana	Windward Islands	IIs	1	1		37	37	37.00			2						
1961-62	British Guiana	Trinidad	IIs	1	1		22	22	22.00			1						
1961-62	British Guiana	Barbados	IIs	1	2	1	16	9	16.00			1						
1961-62	**WEST INDIES**	**INDIA TESTS**	**WI**	**2**	**2**		**81**	**78**	**40.50**		**1**	**8/2**						
		British Guiana		8	14	3	326	74	29.63		2	17/3						
		West Indies		2	2		81	78	40.50		1	8/2						
		TEST RECORD		**2**	**2**	**0**	**81**	**78**	**40.50**	**0**	**1**	**8/2**						
		CAREER		**10**	**16**	**3**	**407**	**78**	**31.30**	**0**	**3**	**25/5**						

MERRY, Cyril Arthur

				BATTING									BOWLING					
SEASON	TEAM	OPPONENTS	V	M	I	NO	RUNS	H.S.	AVGE	100	50	CT	OV	MD	RUNS	W	AVGE	B.B.
1929-30	Trinidad	M.C.C. Tourist	WI	2	4		72	30	18.00			2	14.3	2	28	5	5.60	
1931-32	Trinidad	Barbados	IIs	1	2		13	12	6.50			3						
1931-32	Trinidad	British Guiana	IIs	1	2	1	79	*46	79.00									
1932-33	C.A. Merry's XI	G.C. Grant's XI	IIs	1	2		30	30	15.00			1	5.1	1	19	2	9.50	
1933	West Indies	Tour of England	E	19	30	4	822	146	31.61	1	3	14	150	25	420	13	32.30	
1933	**WEST INDIES**	**ENGLAND TESTS**	**E**	**2**	**4**		**34**	**13**	**8.50**			**1**						
1933-34	Trinidad	Barbados	IIs	1	2		48	27	24.00			1	2	1	4	0		
1934-35	Trinidad	M.C.C. Tourist	WI	2	4		81	49	20.25			2	30	6	73	4	18.25	
1935-36	Trinidad	Barbados	IIs	1	2		24	20	12.00			3	27	6	59	3	19.66	
1935-36	Trinidad	British Guiana	IIs	1	2		18	10	9.00			1	2.3	1	4	1	4.00	
1936-37	Trinidad	Barbados	IIs	1	2	1	64	*37	64.00				9	3	20	2	10.00	
1936-37	Trinidad	British Guiana	IIs	1	1		6	6	6.00			2	7	4	13	0		
1937-38	Trinidad	British Guiana	IIs	1	2		113	88	56.50		1		23	4	68	0		
1938-39	Trinidad	British Guiana	IIs	1	2	1	63	*43	63.00			2	4	1	6	1	6.00	
1938-39	Trinidad	Jamaica	IIs	1	2		57	32	28.50			1	9	3	25	0		
1938-39	Trinidad	Barbados	IIs	1	1		23	23	23.00				6	1	7	2	3.50	
		Trinidad		15	28	3	661	88	26.44		1	17	134	32	307	18	17.05	
		West Indies		21	34	4	856	146	28.53	1	3	15	150	25	420	13	32.30	
		C.A. Merry's XI		1	2		30	30	15.00			1	5.1	1	19	2	9.50	
		TEST RECORD		**2**	**4**	**0**	**34**	**13**	**8.50**	**0**	**0**	**1**						
		CAREER		**37**	**64**	**7**	**1547**	**146**	**27.14**	**1**	**4**	**33**	**289.1**	**58**	**746**	**33**	**22.60**	**3-13**

MILLER, Roy

SEASON	TEAM	OPPONENTS	V	M	I	NO	RUNS	H.S.	AVGE	100	50	CT	OV	MD	RUNS	W	AVGE	B.B.
				BATTING									BOWLING					
1950-51	Jamaica	British Guiana	IIs	1	1		17	17	17.00				42	11	117	3	39.00	
1951-52	Jamaica	Barbados	IIs	2	4	1	54	*22	18.00			2	86	16	277	7	39.57	
1952-53	Jamaica	British Guiana	IIs	2	2	1	98	86	98.00		1		59	10	159	3	53.00	
1952-53	**WEST INDIES**	**INDIA TESTS**	**WI**	**1**	**1**		**23**	**23**	**23.00**				**16**	**8**	**28**	**0**		
1953-54	Jamaica	M.C.C. Tourist	WI	2	3		39	12	13.00				23	1	54	1	54.00	
		Jamaica		7	10	2	208	86	26.00		1	2	213	38	607	14	43.35	
		West Indies		1	1		23	23	23.00				16	8	28	0		
		TEST RECORD		**1**	**1**	**0**	**23**	**23**	**23.00**	**0**	**0**	**0**	**16**	**8**	**28**	**0**		
		CAREER		**8**	**11**	**2**	**231**	**86**	**25.66**	**0**	**1**	**2**	**229**	**46**	**635**	**14**	**45.35**	

MOSELEY, Ezra Alphonsa

SEASON	TEAM	OPPONENTS	V	M	I	NO	RUNS	H.S.	AVGE	100	50	CT	OV	MD	RUNS	W	AVGE	B.B.
				BATTING									BOWLING					
1980	Glamorgan	Counties	E	14	16	6	294	*70	29.40		2	2	430	94	1340	51	26.27	
1981	Glamorgan	Counties	E	15	19	3	306	57	19.12		2	5	355.4	87	942	52	18.11	
1981-82	Barbados	Shell Shield	IIs	5	5	1	81	30	20.25			4	161.2	28	476	18	26.44	
1982-83	WI Rebels XI	Tour of South Africa	SA	1	2		33	25	16.50				33	4	112	4	28.00	
1983-84	WI Rebels XI	Tour of South Africa	SA	6	9	1	164	35	20.50			2	174.5	34	597	24	24.87	
1984-85	Eastern Province	Currie Cup & SA Defence XI	SA	9	12	2	115	40	11.50			2	291.3	90	665	34	19.55	
1986	Glamorgan	Counties	E	6	8	1	55	19	7.85				124.3	14	447	11	40.63	
1989-90	Barbados	Red Stripe Cup	IIs	5	8	1	176	48	25.14			1	159.1	28	542	22	24.63	
1989-90	**WEST INDIES**	**ENGLAND TESTS**	**WI**	**2**	**4**		**35**	**26**	**8.75**			**1**	**87**	**13**	**261**	**6**	**43.50**	
1990	Rest of World XI	Indian Tourist	E	1	D								21	3	58	1	58.00	
		Barbados		10	13	2	257	48	23.36			5	320.3	56	1018	40	25.45	
		West Indies		2	4		35	26	8.75			1	87	13	261	6	43.50	
		WI Rebels XI		7	11	1	197	35	19.70			2	207.5	38	709	28	25.32	
		Glamorgan		35	43	10	655	*70	19.84		4	7	910.1	195	2729	114	23.93	
		Eastern Province		9	12	2	115	40	11.50			2	291.3	90	665	34	19.55	
		Rest of World XI		1	D								21	3	58	1	58.00	
		TEST RECORD		**2**	**4**	**0**	**35**	**26**	**8.75**	**0**	**0**	**1**	**87**	**13**	**261**	**6**	**43.50**	**2-70**
		CAREER		**64**	**83**	**15**	**1259**	***70**	**18.51**	**0**	**4**	**17**	**1838**	**395**	**5440**	**223**	**24.39**	**6-23**

MUDIE, George H.

SEASON	TEAM	OPPONENTS	V	BATTING M	I	NO	RUNS	H.S.	AVGE	100	50	CT	BOWLING OV	MD	RUNS	W	AVGE	B.B.
1931-32	Jamaica	L.H. Tennyson's Tourist	WI	1	1		6	6	6.00				18	5	37	0		
1932-33	G.C. Grant's XI	C.A. Merry's XI	WI	1	2		8	7	4.00				36	11	83	3	27.66	
1934-35	Jamaica	M.C.C. Tourist	WI	2	2	1	154	94	154.00		2		38	9	85	0		
1934-35	**WEST INDIES**	**ENGLAND TESTS**	**WI**	**1**	**1**		**5**	**5**	**5.00**				**29**	**12**	**40**	**3**	**13.33**	
1935-36	Jamaica	Yorkshire Touring XI	WI	1	2		8	6	4.00				6	1	16	0		
1938-39	Jamaica	Combined Universities Tourist	WI	2	3		47	26	15.66			3	43.3	8	166	12	13.83	
1938-39	Jamaica	Trinidad	IIs	1	2	1	11	6	11.00				23.7	1	81	2	40.50	
1938-39	Jamaica	West Indies XI	IIs	1	1		53	53	53.00		1		8.2	0	29	1	29.00	
1945-46	Jamaica	Trinidad	IIs	2	4		12	9	3.00			1	87	10	216	7	30.85	
1946-47	Jamaica	Barbados	IIs	2	3	1	62	26	31.00			3	69	14	159	3	53.00	
1949-50	Jamaica	Trinidad	IIs	2	4	1	38	22	12.66				75.1	6	216	3	72.00	
1950-51	Jamaica	British Guiana	IIs	1	2		52	52	26.00		1	1	43	8	117	4	29.25	
1951-52	Jamaica	Barbados	IIs	2	4	1	122	45	40.66			3	87.4	9	244	4	61.00	
		Jamaica		17	28	4	565	94	23.54		4	11	499.3	71	1366	36	37.94	
		West Indies		1	1		5	5	5.00				29	12	40	3	13.33	
		G.C. Grant's XI		1	2		8	7	4.00				36	11	83	3	27.66	
		TEST RECORD		**1**	**1**	**0**	**5**	**5**	**5.00**	**0**	**0**	**0**	**29**	**12**	**40**	**3**	**13.33**	**2-23**
		CAREER		**19**	**31**	**5**	**578**	**94**	**22.23**	**0**	**4**	**11**	**564.3**	**94**	**1489**	**42**	**35.45**	**5-32**

MURRAY, David Anthony

SEASON	TEAM	OPPONENTS	V	BATTING M	I	NO	RUNS	H.S.	AVGE	100	50	CT/St	BOWLING OV	MD	RUNS	W	AVGE	B.B.
1970-71	Barbados	Shell Shield	IIs	3	4		27	20	6.75			6/2						
1971-72	Barbados	Shell Shield	IIs	2	2		15	13	7.50			5						
1971-72	Barbados	New Zealand Tourist	WI	1	2	1	10	*7	10.00			2						
1972-73	Barbados	Shell Shield	IIs	4	8	4	283	*86	70.75		3	9/1						
1972-73	Barbados	Australian Tourist	WI	1	2		49	33	24.50			2/1						
1972-73	WI President's XI	Australian Tourist	WI	1	2		45	24	22.50			1						
1973	West Indies	Tour of England	E	10	13	5	285	*107	35.62	1	1	28/8	1	0	10	0		
1973-74	Barbados	Shell Shield	IIs	4	7	1	205	68	34.16		1	5/1						
1973-74	Barbados	M.C.C. Tourist	WI	1	1		57	57	57.00		1	2						
1973-74	WI President's XI	M.C.C. Tourist	WI	1	2		36	28	18.00			1/1						
1974-75	West Indies	Tour of India	I	5	5	1	237	*103	59.25	1	1	9/3						

SEASON	TEAM	OPPONENTS	V	M	I	NO	RUNS	H.S.	AVGE	100	50	CT/St	OV	MD	RUNS	W	AVGE	B.B.
				BATTING									BOWLING					
1974-75	West Indies	Tour of Sri Lanka	SL	2	3		11	10	3.66			2						
1974-75	West Indies	Tour of Pakistan	P	1	2		100	91	50.00		1	2						
1974-75	Barbados	Shell Shield	IIs	4	8	1	179	*106	25.57	1		13						
1975-76	West Indies	Tour of Australia	A	3	4	1	67	*23	22.23			10/2						
1975-76	Barbados	Indian Tourist	WI	1	2	1	42	37	42.00			3/2						
1976-77	Barbados	Shell Shield	IIs	4	7		309	113	41.14	1	2	10/1						
1976-77	Barbados	Pakistan Tourist	WI	1	2	1	59	57	59.00		1							
1977-78	Barbados	Shell Shield	IIs	4	6		301	143	50.16	1	1	8						
1977-78	Barbados	Australian Tourist	WI	1	2		117	108	58.50	1		1/1						
1977-78	**WEST INDIES**	**AUSTRALIA TESTS**	**WI**	**3**	**6**		**67**	**21**	**11.16**			**6/3**						
1978-79	West Indies	Tour of India	I	4	7	2	293	*206	58.60	1		5/1						
1978-79	**WEST INDIES**	**INDIA TESTS**	**I**	**6**	**10**	**1**	**261**	**84**	**29.00**		**2**	**17/1**						
1978-79	West Indies	Tour of Sri Lanka	SL	1	1		9	9	9.00									
1978-79	Barbados	Shell Shield	IIs	2	3		80	42	26.66			8						
1979-80	West Indies	Tour of Australia	A	2	3		51	23	17.00			5						
1979-80	West Indies	Tour of New Zealand	NZ	1	2		12	11	6.00			2						
1979-80	Barbados	Shell Shield	IIs	2	2		63	38	31.50			5/1						
1980	West Indies	Tour of England	E	6	8	2	161	49	26.83			16/1	1	0	1	0		
1980-81	West Indies	Tour of Pakistan	P	3	4		31	12	7.75			5						
1980-81	**WEST INDIES**	**PAKISTAN TESTS**	**P**	**4**	**6**		**142**	**50**	**23.66**		**1**	**9/1**						
1980-81	Barbados	Shell Shield	IIs	3	4	1	142	92	47.33		1	8						
1980-81	Barbados	English Tourist	WI	1	1		19	19	19.00			5						
1980-81	**WEST INDIES**	**ENGLAND TESTS**	**WI**	**4**	**5**	**1**	**75**	**46**	**18.75**			**13**						
1981-82	West Indies	Tour of Australia	A	2	2	1	83	72	83.00		1	7						
1981-82	**WEST INDIES**	**AUSTRALIA TESTS**	**A**	**2**	**4**	**1**	**56**	***32**	**18.66**			**12**						
1981-82	Barbados	Shell Shield	IIs	3	5	2	179	*55	59.67		1	12						
1982-83	WI Rebels XI	Tour of South Africa	SA	2	4		42	27	10.50			4						
1983-84	WI Rebels XI	Tour of South Africa	SA	9	15	3	303	43	25.25			34						
		Barbados		42	68	12	2136	143	38.14	4	11	104/10						
		West Indies		61	89	15	2022	*206	27.32	3	7	150/21	2	0	11	0		
		WI Rebels XI		11	19	3	345	43	21.56			38						
		TEST RECORD		**19**	**31**	**3**	**601**	**84**	**21.46**	**0**	**3**	**57/5**						
		CAREER		**114**	**176**	**30**	**4503**	***206**	**30.84**	**7**	**18**	**292/31**	**2**	**0**	**11**	**0**		

MURRAY, Deryck Lance

SEASON	TEAM	OPPONENTS	V	BATTING M	I	NO	RUNS	H.S.	AVGE	100	50	CT/St	BOWLING OV	MD	RUNS	W	AVGE	B.B.
1960-61	Trinidad	E.W. Swanton's Tourist	WI	1	2		36	32	18.00			2						
1960-61	N. Trinidad	South Trinidad BC	T	1	1		7	7	7.00									
1961-62	Trinidad	British Guiana	IIs	1	2	1	35	*35	35.00			1						
1961-62	Trinidad	Indian Tourist	WI	1	1		6	6	6.00			1						
1961-62	N. Trinidad	South Trinidad BC	T	1	2	1	29	22	29.00			2						
1962-63	Trinidad	Barbados	IIs	1	2		27	15	13.50									
1963	West Indies	Tour of England	E	10	12	2	176	67	17.60		1	20/5						
1963	**WEST INDIES**	**ENGLAND TESTS**	**E**	**5**	**8**	**2**	**93**	**34**	**15.50**			**22/2**						
1963-64	West Indies XI	The Rest XI	WI	1	2		38	24	19.00			2/2						
1963-64	F. Worrell's XI	C. Hunte's XI	WI	1	2	2	108	*102		1		4						
1964	West Indies XI	England XI	E	3	4	1	17	*8	5.66			6/2						
1964	M.C.C.	Lancashire & Cambridge Univ.	E	2	2	1	57	52	57.00		1	6/2						
1965	Cambridge Univ.	Counties	E	10	19		622	108	32.73	1	5	12/2						
1966	Cambridge Univ.	Counties	E	14	26	2	626	133	26.08	1	3	21/3	12	3	66	1	66.00	
1966	Nottinghamshire	Counties	E	12	23	3	672	*166	33.60	1	2	9	1	0	8	0		
1966	Rest of World XI	England XI	E	1	2	1	60	*50	60.00		1	3/2						
1966	A.E.R. Gilligan's XI	West Indies	E	1	D							0/2						
1966-67	West Indies	Tour of India	I	6	11		183	52	16.63		1	6/7	10.4	1	50	2	25.00	
1966-67	West Indies	Tour of Ceylon	C	1	1		20	20	20.00			2/1	6	0	23	0		
1966-67	Trinidad	Shell Shield	IIs	4	6		225	82	37.50		3	5/3						
1967	Nottinghamshire	Counties	E	29	45	5	1284	139	32.10	1	10	20/2	10	2	39	1	39.00	
1967-68	WI President's XI	M.C.C. Tourist	WI	1	1		63	63	63.00		1	2						
1967-68	Trinidad	M.C.C. Tourist	WI	1	2		67	42	33.50			3						
1967-68	**WEST INDIES**	**ENGLAND TESTS**	**WI**	**5**	**9**	**1**	**104**	**27**	**13.00**			**13/1**						
1968	Nottinghamshire	Counties	E	29	42	6	1044	*102	29.00	1	4	68/8						
1968-69	Trinidad	Shell Shield	IIs	4	6		139	58	23.16		1	4/2						
1969	Nottinghamshire	Counties	E	27	38	10	873	101	31.17	1	6	61/5	3	0	18	0		
1970	Rest of World XI	England XI	E	3	4		172	95	43.00		1	15						
1970	Rest of World XI	T.N. Pearce's XI	E	1	2		51	37	25.50			2						
1972	Warwickshire	Counties	E	14	21	6	412	54	27.46		1	40/4						
1972-73	Trinidad	Shell Shield	IIs	4	5	2	241	*105	80.33	1	1	9/3						
1972-73	N. Trinidad	South Trinidad BC	T	1	1		2	2	2.00			2						
1972-73	Trinidad	Australian Tourist	WI	1	1		45	45	45.00			2						
1972-73	**WEST INDIES**	**AUSTRALIAN TESTS**	**WI**	**4**	**7**		**182**	**90**	**26.00**		**1**	**5**						
1973	West Indies	Tour of England	E	9	10	3	184	*53	26.28		1	18/5						
1973	**WEST INDIES**	**ENGLAND TESTS**	**E**	**3**	**5**		**76**	**28**	**15.20**			**8**						

SEASON	TEAM	OPPONENTS	V	BATTING M	I	NO	RUNS	H.S.	AVGE	100	50	CT/St	BOWLING OV	MD	RUNS	W	AVGE	B.B.
1973	Warwickshire	Counties	E	7	8		249	76	31.12		1	12/4	1	1	0	0		
1973-74	Trinidad	Shell Shield	IIs	4	7	1	139	44	23.16			6/6	0.5	0	8	0		
1973-74	Trinidad	M.C.C. Tourist	WI	1	1		148	148	148.00	1								
1973-74	**WEST INDIES**	**ENGLAND TESTS**	**WI**	**5**	**5**	**2**	**113**	***53**	**37.66**		**1**	**14/1**						
1974	Warwickshire	Counties	E	22	34	2	707	78	22.09		2	47/3	7	3	23	0		
1974-75	West Indies	Tour of India	I	7	9	6	317	81	105.66		4	10/1	1	1	0	0		
1974-75	**WEST INDIES**	**INDIA TESTS**	**I**	**5**	**8**		**154**	**91**	**19.25**		**1**	**14/1**						
1974-75	West Indies	Tour of Sri Lanka	SL	1	1		65	65	65.00		1	1						
1974-75	West Indies	Tour of Pakistan	P	1	2		32	28	16.00				3	0	29	0		
1974-75	**WEST INDIES**	**PAKISTAN TESTS**	**P**	**2**	**3**	**1**	**30**	**19**	**15.00**			**6**						
1974-75	Trinidad	Shell Shield	IIs	4	8		184	67	23.00		1	9/5	1.5	0	18	0		
1975	Warwickshire	Counties	E	15	24	4	405	59	20.25		1	37/4	17	4	60	0		
1975-76	West Indies	Tour of Australia	A	4	7		213	47	30.42			11/1						
1975-76	**WEST INDIES**	**AUSTRALIA TESTS**	**A**	**6**	**11**		**342**	**66**	**31.09**		**4**	**17**						
1975-76	Trinidad	Indian Tourist	WI	1	1		6	6	6.00									
1975-76	**WEST INDIES**	**INDIA TESTS**	**WI**	**4**	**6**		**189**	**71**	**31.50**		**1**	**10/2**						
1976	West Indies	Tour of England	E	13	17	7	274	55	27.40		1	18/1	5	2	12	0		
1976	**WEST INDIES**	**ENGLAND TESTS**	**E**	**5**	**8**	**2**	**123**	**36**	**20.50**			**19**						
1976-77	Trinidad	Shell Shield	IIs	3	6	3	149	46	49.66			4/3						
1976-77	Trinidad	Pakistan Tourist	WI	1	2		24	23	12.00			0/1						
1976-77	**WEST INDIES**	**PAKISTAN TESTS**	**WI**	**5**	**8**		**218**	**52**	**27.25**		**1**	**14/1**						
1976-77	N. Trinidad	Central Trinidad TC	T	1	2	1	60	*43	60.00			5						
1976-77	N/E Trinidad	S/C Trinidad BC	T	1	1		8	8	8.00			3						
1977-78	Trinidad	Shell Shield	IIs	1	2		30	26	15.00			1/1						
1977-78	Trinidad	Australian Tourist	WI	1	2		87	63	43.50		1	1	3	0	13	1	13.00	
1977-78	**WEST INDIES**	**AUSTRALIA TESTS**	**WI**	**2**	**2**		**81**	**60**	**40.50**		**1**	**8**						
1978-79	Trinidad	Shell Shield	IIs	1	2	1	57	*50	57.00		1	4/1						
1979-80	West Indies	Tour of Australia	A	3	3	1	147	103	73.50	1		12/1						
1979-80	**WEST INDIES**	**AUSTRALIA TESTS**	**A**	**3**	**4**		**77**	**28**	**19.25**			**10**						
1979-80	West Indies	Tour of New Zealand	NZ	1	2	2	33	*19										
1979-80	**WEST INDIES**	**NEW ZEALAND TESTS**	**NZ**	**3**	**6**	**1**	**66**	**30**	**13.20**			**7**						
1979-80	Trinidad	Shell Shield	IIs	3	4		60	50	15.00		1	6/1						
1979-80	N/E Trinidad	S/C Trinidad BC	T	1	2		16	13	8.00			0/1						
1980	West Indies	Tour of England	E	7	8	2	170	64	28.33		1	19/2						
1980	**WEST INDIES**	**ENGLAND TESTS**	**E**	**5**	**6**		**145**	**64**	**24.16**		**1**	**14**						
1980-81	Trinidad	Shell Shield	IIs	4	4		122	82	30.50		1	4/4						
1980-81	Trinidad	English Tourist	WI	1	1		75	75	75.00		1	2						

	M	I	NO	RUNS	H.S.	AVGE	100	50	CT	OV	MD	RUNS	W	AVGE	B.B.
Trinidad	43	67	8	1902	148	32.33	3	11	64/30	5.4	0	39	1	39.00	
North Trinidad	4	6	2	98	*43	24.50			9						
N/E Trinidad	2	3		24	13	8.00			3/1						
West Indies	130	186	33	3925	103	25.65	1	22	308/36	25.4	4	114	2	57.00	2-50
Cambridge University	24	45	2	1248	133	29.02	2	8	33/5	12	3	66	1	66.00	
Nottinghamshire	97	148	24	3873	*166	31.23	3	22	158/15	14	2	65	1	65.00	
Warwickshire	58	87	12	1773	78	23.64		5	136/15	25	8	83	0		
Rest of World XI	5	8	1	283	95	40.42		2	20/2						
M.C.C.	2	2	1	57	52	57.00		1	6/2						
A.E.R. Gilligan's XI	1	D							0/2						
F. Worrell's XI	1	2	2	108	*102		1		4						
TEST RECORD	**62**	**96**	**9**	**1993**	**91**	**22.90**	**0**	**11**	**181/8**						
CAREER	**367**	**554**	**85**	**13291**	***166**	**28.33**	**10**	**71**	**741/108**	**82.2**	**17**	**367**	**5**	**73.40**	**2-50**

NANAN, Ranjie

					BATTING									BOWLING					
SEASON	**TEAM**	**OPPONENTS**		**V**	**M**	**I**	**NO**	**RUNS**	**H.S.**	**AVGE**	**100**	**50**	**CT**	**OV**	**MD**	**RUNS**	**W**	**AVGE**	**B.B.**
1972-73	C. Trinidad	East Trinidad	TC	T	1	2		58	49	29.00			2	17.4	2	47	6	7.83	
1972-73	Trinidad	Shell Shield		IIs	1	D								14	0	64	0		
1973-74	C. Trinidad	East Trinidad	TC	T	1	1		11	11	11.00				38.4	9	82	3	27.33	
1973-74	Trinidad	M.C.C. Tourist		WI	1	1		21	21	21.00				56	12	149	0		
1974-75	Trinidad	Shell Shield		IIs	1	2		8	8	4.00				19	0	66	1	66.00	
1974-75	C. Trinidad	East Trinidad	TC	T	1	1		19	19	19.00			1	30	11	66	2	33.00	
1975-76	Trinidad	Shell Shield		IIs	1	1		51	51	51.00		1	1	24	7	53	0		
1975-76	C. Trinidad	N.S. & E. Trinidad	TC	T	3	5		60	28	12.00			2	81.1	27	167	14	11.92	
1975-76	S/C Trinidad	N/E Trinidad	BC	T	1	1		57	57	57.00		1	3	13	2	20	1	20.00	
1976-77	Trinidad	Shell Shield		IIs	1	1		0	0				1	22	4	47	1	47.00	
1976-77	Trinidad	Pakistan Tourist		WI	1	2	1	35	*23	35.00			1	22	13	31	3	10.33	
1976-77	C. Trinidad	N. & E. Trinidad	TC	T	2	3		6	4	2.00			3	59.3	13	115	11	10.45	
1976-77	S/C Trinidad	N/E Trinidad	BC	T	1	2		4	3	2.00				22	7	65	2	32.50	
1977-78	Trinidad	Shell Shield		IIs	3	6	1	145	*78	29.00		1	1	144.3	42	323	14	23.07	
1977-78	Trinidad	Australian Tourist		WI	1	2	1	20	*13	20.00			1	48.4	14	106	3	35.33	
1977-78	C. Trinidad	E.S. & N. Trinidad	TC	T	3	3		71	35	23.66			7	130.4	42	246	13	18.92	
1978-79	Trinidad	Shell Shield		IIs	4	5		96	48	19.20			2	202	63	479	18	26.61	
1978-79	C. Trinidad	N. & E. Trinidad	TC	T	2	2		12	11	6.00			1	34.4	8	71	8	8.87	
1979-80	Trinidad	Shell Shield		IIs	4	6	1	115	41	23.00			2	201.1	71	465	24	19.37	
1979-80	S/C Trinidad	N/E Trinidad	BC	T	1	1		0	0				2	40.1	7	113	6	18.83	

1980-81	West Indies	Tour of Pakistan		P	3	4		55	32	13.75			1	74	18	200	14	14.28	
1980-81	**WEST INDIES**	**PAKISTAN TESTS**		**P**	**1**	**2**		**16**	**8**	**8.00**			**2**	**36**	**7**	**91**	**4**	**22.75**	
1980-81	Trinidad	Shell Shield		IIs	3	3		63	36	21.00				173	68	341	11	31.00	
1980-81	Trinidad	English Tourist		WI	1	1	1	66	*66	66.00		1	1	49	9	116	2	58.00	
1981-82	Trinidad	Shell Shield		IIs	5	9	3	122	40	20.33			1	310.3	105	677	32	21.15	
1982-83	Trinidad	Shell Shield		IIs	5	8		234	125	29.25	1		6	337.3	69	791	24	32.95	
1982-83	Trinidad	Indian Tourist		WI	1	2		23	18	11.50				41	13	78	2	39.00	
1983-84	Trinidad	Shell Shield		IIs	5	8	1	234	*98	33.42		1	2	261.1	68	507	15	33.80	
1983-84	Trinidad	Australian Tourist		WI	1	2	1	78	40	78.00			1	23.2	3	75	3	25.00	
1983-84	S/C Trinidad	N/E Trinidad	BC	T	1	2	1	91	*75	91.00		1	2	56	13	113	6	18.83	
1984-85	Trinidad	Shell Shield		IIs	5	8		115	46	14.37			2	161.5	40	302	15	20.13	
1984-85	S/C Trinidad	N/E Trinidad	BC	T	1	2		45	42	22.50			1	24	5	67	4	16.75	
1985-86	Trinidad	Shell Shield		IIs	5	9	2	133	61	19.00		1	4	202.4	47	442	30	14.73	
1985-86	Trinidad	English Tourist		WI	1	1		26	26	26.00				32	9	66	3	22.00	
1986-87	Trinidad	Shell Shield		IIs	2	4		60	29	15.00			1	98	14	286	5	57.20	
1987-88	Trinidad	Red Stripe Cup		IIs	5	7	2	101	48	20.20			2	196	72	305	20	15.25	
1988-89	Trinidad	Red Stripe Cup		IIs	5	8	1	187	59	26.71		2	5	244.1	69	512	23	22.26	
1989-90	Trinidad	Red Stripe Cup		IIs	4	8	1	95	*36	13.57				116.4	25	265	8	33.12	
		Trinidad			66	104	16	2028	125	23.04	1	7	34	3000.1	837	6546	257	25.47	
		Central Trinidad			13	17		237	49	13.94			16	392.2	112	794	57	13.92	
		S/C Trinidad			5	8	1	197	*75	28.14		2	8	155.1	34	378	19	19.89	
		West Indies			4	6		71	32	11.83			3	110	25	291	18	16.16	
		TEST RECORD			**1**	**2**	**0**	**16**	**8**	**8.00**	**0**	**0**	**2**	**36**	**7**	**91**	**4**	**22.75**	**2-37**
		CAREER			**88**	**135**	**17**	**2533**	**125**	**21.46**	**1**	**9**	**61**	**3657.4**	**1008**	**8009**	**351**	**22.81**	**7-109**

NEBLETT, James M.

						BATTING							BOWLING			
SEASON	TEAM	OPPONENTS	V	M	I	NO	RUNS	H.S.	AVGE	100	50	CT	OV	MD	RUNS	W	AVGE	B.B.
1925-26	British Guiana	M.C.C. Tourist	WI	2	2		13	9	6.50			1	46.4	11	112	6	18.66	
1925-26	West Indies XI	M.C.C. Tourist	WI	1	1		0	0					45	12	104	3	34.66	
1927-28	Combined J/B XI	Combined BG/Trin XI	IIs	2	4	1	98	59	32.66		1	1	37	6	115	3	38.33	
1927-28	Barbados XI	West Indies XI	IIs	1	2	1	30	*23	30.00				33	7	114	4	28.50	
1928	West Indies	Tour of England	E	8	13	1	181	61	15.08		1	9	86	12	325	6	54.16	
1929-30	British Guiana	M.C.C. Tourist	WI	2	4		89	32	22.25			3	36	3	134	0		
1934-35	British Guiana	M.C.C. Tourist	WI	2	3	1	54	33	27.00				44.1	11	122	3	40.66	
1934-35	**WEST INDIES**	**ENGLAND TESTS**	**WI**	**1**	**2**	**1**	**16**	***11**	**16.00**				**36**	**11**	**75**	**1**	**75.00**	

SEASON	TEAM	OPPONENTS		V	M	I	NO	RUNS	H.S.	AVGE	100	50	CT	OV	MD	RUNS	W	AVGE	B.B.
1938-39	British Guiana	R.S. Grant's XI		WI	1	2		45	36	22.50			1	44	9	104	3	34.66	
		British Guiana			7	11	1	201	36	20.10			6	170.5	34	472	12	39.33	
		Barbados XI			1	2	1	30	*23	30.00				33	7	114	4	28.50	
		Combined J/B XI			2	4	1	98	59	32.66		1	1	37	6	115	3	38.33	
		West Indies			10	16	2	197	61	14.07		1	9	167	35	504	10	51.40	
		TEST RECORD			**1**	**2**	**1**	**16**	***11**	**16.00**	**0**	**0**	**0**	**36**	**11**	**75**	**1**	**75.00**	**1-44**
		CAREER			**20**	**33**	**5**	**526**	**61**	**18.78**	**0**	**2**	**16**	**407.5**	**82**	**1205**	**29**	**41.55**	**4-82**

NOREIGA, Jack Mollison

								BATTING								BOWLING			
SEASON	**TEAM**	**OPPONENTS**		**V**	**M**	**I**	**NO**	**RUNS**	**H.S.**	**AVGE**	**100**	**50**	**CT**	**OV**	**MD**	**RUNS**	**W**	**AVGE**	**B.B.**
1961-62	Trinidad	Indian Tourist		WI	1	1		13	13	13.00				44	6	146	1	146.00	
1961-62	N. Trinidad	South Trinidad	BC	T	1	2		15	9	7.50				34	14	83	4	20.75	
1968-69	N. Trinidad	South Trinidad	BC	T	1	1		0	0				1	56	26	81	5	16.20	
1970-71	Trinidad	Shell Shield		IIs	3	3	1	0	*0					143	41	313	19	16.47	
1970-71	Trinidad	Indian Tourist		WI	1	1		6	6	6.00				48	19	106	0		
1970-71	**WEST INDIES**	**INDIA TESTS**		**WI**	**4**	**5**	**2**	**11**	**9**	**3.66**			**2**	**220.2**	**47**	**493**	**17**	**28.00**	
1970-71	E. Trinidad	North Trinidad	BC	T	1	2	2	13	*7				1	26	6	81	1	81.00	
1971-72	Trinidad	Shell Shield		IIs	3	4	1	22	*12	7.33				106.5	24	247	5	49.40	
1971-72	Trinidad	New Zealand Tourist		WI	1	1	1	1	*1					40	8	110	0		
1971-72	E. Trinidad	C. & S. Trinidad	TC	T	2	3		44	25	14.66				77.4	23	168	8	21.00	
1972-73	E. Trinidad	C. & S. Trinidad	TC	T	2	4	1	50	20	16.66				42	10	98	3	33.66	
1974-75	E. Trinidad	North Trinidad	TC	T	1	1		6	6	6.00				40	10	92	5	18.40	
		Trinidad			9	10	3	42	13	6.00				381.5	98	922	25	36.88	
		North Trinidad			2	3		15	9	5.00			1	90	40	164	9	18.22	
		East Trinidad			6	10	3	113	25	16.14			1	185.4	49	439	17	25.82	
		West Indies			4	5	2	11	9	3.66			2	220.2	47	493	17	29.00	
		TEST RECORD			**4**	**5**	**2**	**11**	**9**	**3.66**	**0**	**0**	**2**	**220.2**	**47**	**493**	**17**	**29.00**	**9-95**
		CAREER			**21**	**28**	**8**	**181**	**25**	**9.05**	**0**	**0**	**4**	**877.5**	**234**	**2018**	**68**	**29.67**	**9-95**

NUNES, Robert Karl

SEASON	TEAM	OPPONENTS	V	BATTING M	I	NO	RUNS	H.S.	AVGE	100	50	CT/St	BOWLING OV	MD	RUNS	W	AVGE	B.B.
1923	West Indies	Tour of England	E	15	24	1	455	89	19.73		3							
1924-25	Jamaica	Barbados	IIs	3	5		127	43	25.40			1	26	2	83	3	27.66	
1925-26	Jamaica	M.C.C. Tourist	WI	3	5	1	305	*140	76.25	1	1	6/1						
1926-27	Jamaica	L.H. Tennyson's Tourist	WI	3	3	1	313	*200	156.50	2		2/4						
1927-28	Jamaica	L.H. Tennyson's Tourist	WI	3	5	1	134	53	33.50		2	5/3						
1928	West Indies	Tour of England	E	23	32	4	711	*127	23.47	1	3	13						
1928	**WEST INDIES**	**ENGLAND TESTS**	**E**	**3**	**6**		**87**	**37**	**14.50**			**1**						
1928-29	Jamaica	Julien Cahn's Tourist	WI	2	4		162	112	40.50	1								
1928-29	West Indies XI	Julien Cahn's Tourist	WI	1	2		21	21	10.50			1						
1929-30	Jamaica	M.C.C. Tourist	WI	2	3		68	31	22.66									
1929-30	**WEST INDIES**	**ENGLAND TESTS**	**WI**	**1**	**2**		**158**	**92**	**79.00**		**2**	**1**						
1931-32	Jamaica	L.H. Tennyson's Tourist	WI	2	3		154	125	51.33	1		1						
		Jamaica		18	28	3	1263	*200	50.52	5	3	15/8	26	2	83	3	27.66	
		West Indies		43	66	5	1432	*127	23.47	1	8	16						
		TEST RECORD		**4**	**8**	**0**	**245**	**92**	**30.62**	**0**	**2**	**2**						
		CAREER		**61**	**94**	**8**	**2695**	***200**	**31.33**	**6**	**11**	**31/8**	**26**	**2**	**83**	**3**	**27.66**	**2-49**

NURSE, Seymour MacDonald

SEASON	TEAM	OPPONENTS	V	BATTING M	I	NO	RUNS	H.S.	AVGE	100	50	CT	BOWLING OV	MD	RUNS	W	AVGE	B.B.
1958-59	Barbados	Jamaica	IIs	2	4	1	192	*128	64.00	1		2						
1958-59	Barbados	British Guiana	IIs	2	4	1	178	131	59.33	1		1						
1959-60	Barbados	M.C.C. Tourist	WI	1	1		213	213	213.00	1		1						
1959-60	**WEST INDIES**	**ENGLAND TESTS**	**WI**	**1**	**2**		**81**	**70**	**40.50**		**1**							
1960-61	West Indies	Tour of Australia	A	7	12		317	97	26.41		2	5						
1960-61	**WEST INDIES**	**AUSTRALIA TESTS**	**A**	**3**	**6**		**181**	**70**	**30.16**		**1**	**3**						
1961-62	Barbados	Jamaica	IIs	1	1		64	64	64.00		1							
1961-62	Barbados	British Guiana	IIs	1	2		9	9	4.50									
1961-62	Barbados	Indian Tourist	WI	1	1		19	19	19.00			1						
1961-62	**WEST INDIES**	**INDIA TESTS**	**WI**	**1**	**2**	**1**	**47**	***46**	**47.00**			**3**						
1962-63	Barbados	Trinidad	IIs	1	1		210	210	210.00	1								
1962-63	Barbados	British Guiana	IIs	1	2		2	1	1.00			2						
1963	West Indies	Tour of England	E	17	29	2	911	*116	33.74	3	3	15	13	1	53	3	17.66	

1963-64	The Rest XI	West Indian XI	WI	1	2		27	20	13.50			1	10	0	85	2	42.50	
1963-64	C. Hunte's XI	F. Worrell's XI	WI	1	1	1	65	*65			1	1	4	0	44	0		
1963-64	Comm. XI	Tour of Pakistan	P	6	11	2	369	*126	41.00	1	2	4	23	3	91	2	45.50	
1963-64	Indian Prime Minister's XI	President's XI	I	1	2		90	78	45.00		1							
1963-64	Barbados	British Guiana	IIs	1	2		23	21	11.00									
1963-64	Barbados	Jamaica	IIs	1	1		20	20	20.00									
1963-64	Barbados	Trinidad	IIs	1	2		206	163	103.00	1								
1963-64	E.W. Swanton's XI	Tour of India	I	1	2	1	241	*135	241.00	2								
1964	West Indies XI	Tour of England	E	3	5	1	266	116	66.50	1	1	2						
1964-65	Barbados	Cavaliers Touring XI	WI	1	1		100	100	100.00	1		1	2	2	0	1		
1964-65	Barbados	Australian Tourist	WI	1	1		29	29	29.00			2	6	0	27	0		
1964-65	**WEST INDIES**	**AUSTRALIA TESTS**	**WI**	**4**	**8**		**291**	**201**	**36.37**	**1**		**4**						
1965-66	Barbados	Shell Shield	IIs	4	4		364	153	91.00	2	1	4	3	0	11	0		
1966	West Indies	Tour of England	E	14	18	1	604	155	35.52	1	4	12	2	0	3	0		
1966	**WEST INDIES**	**ENGLAND TESTS**	**E**	**5**	**8**		**501**	**137**	**62.62**	**1**	**4**	**5**						
1966-67	West Indies	Tour of India	I	4	6	1	116	*32	23.20			1						
1966-67	**WEST INDIES**	**INDIA TESTS**	**I**	**2**	**3**		**82**	**56**	**27.33**		**1**	**1**	**4**	**1**	**7**	**0**		
1966-67	West Indies	Tour of Ceylon	C	1	1		22	22	22.00			1	8.1	4	36	3	12.00	
1966-67	Barbados	Shell Shield	IIs	4	6		166	92	27.66		2	2						
1966-67	Barbados	Rest of World XI	WI	1	2		48	48	24.00			2						
1967	Rest of World XI	Tour of England	E	2	3		160	121	53.33	1			3	2	2	0		
1967-68	Barbados	M.C.C. Tourist	WI	1	2	1	151	144	151.00	1		1						
1967-68	**WEST INDIES**	**ENGLAND TESTS**	**WI**	**5**	**10**		**434**	**136**	**43.40**	**1**	**1**	**2**	**3**	**3**	**0**	**0**		
1968	Rest of World XI	Tour of England	E	4	8	1	115	51	16.42		1	2						
1968-69	West Indies	Tour of Australia	A	7	11	1	346	94	34.60		2	7	1.4	0	12	0		
1968-69	**WEST INDIES**	**AUSTRALIA TESTS**	**A**	**5**	**10**		**348**	**137**	**34.80**	**1**	**1**	**3**						
1968-69	West Indies	Tour of New Zealand	NZ	2	4		268	124	67.00	1	1	2	1	0	5	0		
1968-69	**WEST INDIES**	**NEW ZEALAND TESTS**	**NZ**	**3**	**5**		**558**	**258**	**111.60**	**2**	**1**							
1969	Barbados	Tour of England	E	2	4	1	123	52	41.00		1	1						
1969-70	Barbados	Shell Shield	IIs	4	7		275	102	39.28	1	1	3						
1970-71	Barbados	Shell Shield	IIs	4	7	1	269	68	44.83		3	7						
1970-71	Barbados	Indian Tourist	WI	1	2	1	26	*26	26.00			4						
1971-72	Barbados	Shell Shield	IIs	4	7	1	286	*93	47.66		2	5	4	0	13	1	13.00	
1971-72	Barbados	New Zealand Tourist	WI	1	2		76	76	38.00		1	3						
		Barbados		41	66	7	3049	213	51.67	10	12	42	15	2	51	2	25.50	
		West Indies		84	140	7	5373	258	40.39	12	23	66	32.5	9	116	6	19.33	3-36
		Rest of World XI		6	11	1	275	121	27.50	1	1	2	3	2	2	0		
		The Rest XI		1	2		27	20	13.50			1	10	0	85	2	42.50	

SEASON	TEAM			BATTING M	I	NO	RUNS	H.S.	AVGE	100	50	CT	BOWLING OV	MD	RUNS	W	AVGE	B.B.
		C. Hunte's XI		1	1	1	65	*65			1	1	4	0	44	0		
		Comm. XI		6	11	2	369	*126	41.00	1	2	4	23	3	91	2	45.50	
		Indian Prime Minister's XI		1	2		90	78	45.00		1							
		E.W. Swanton's XI		1	2	1	241	*135	241.00	2								
		TEST RECORD		**29**	**54**	**1**	**2523**	**258**	**47.60**	**6**	**10**	**21**	**7**	**4**	**7**	**0**		
		CAREER		**141**	**235**	**19**	**9489**	**258**	**43.93**	**26**	**40**	**116**	**87.5**	**16**	**389**	**12**	**32.41**	**3-36**

PADMORE, Albert Leroy

SEASON	TEAM	OPPONENTS	V	BATTING M	I	NO	RUNS	H.S.	AVGE	100	50	CT	BOWLING OV	MD	RUNS	W	AVGE	B.B.
1972-73	Barbados	Shell Shield	IIs	2	3		8	8	2.66			2	70.5	21	144	6	24.00	
1972-73	Barbados	Australian Tourist	WI	1	1	1	0	0					36	2	138	2	69.00	
1973-74	Barbados	Shell Shield	IIs	4	5	3	20	7	10.00				93.2	23	180	7	25.71	
1973-74	Barbados	M.C.C. Tourist	WI	1	1	1	1	*1				2	34	8	102	3	34.00	
1973-74	WI President's XI	M.C.C. Tourist	WI	1	2		7	7	3.50			1	61.3	10	186	3	62.00	
1974-75	West Indies	Tour of India	I	6	1		30	30	30.00			3	125.2	52	563	26	21.65	
1974-75	West Indies	Tour of Sri Lanka	SL	2	2		5	4	2.50			1	80	29	159	3	53.00	
1974-75	West Indies	Tour of Pakistan	P	1	D								31	5	130	2	65.00	
1974-75	Barbados	Shell Shield	IIs	3	4	1	12	*5	4.00				116.2	42	206	3	68.66	
1975-76	West Indies	Tour of Australia	A	4	5	3	34	20	17.00			2	146.5	31	509	12	42.41	
1975-76	Barbados	Shell Shield	IIs	1	D								13	4	24	0		
1975-76	Barbados	Indian Tourist	WI	1	1		3	3	3.00			2	35.4	13	63	7	9.00	
1975-76	**WEST INDIES**	**INDIA TESTS**	**WI**	**1**	**1**		**0**	**0**					**76**	**21**	**134**	**1**	**134.00**	
1976	West Indies	Tour of England	E	15	15	5	91	*26	9.10			4	494.3	126	1380	59	23.38	
1976	**WEST INDIES**	**ENGLAND TESTS**	**E**	**1**	**1**	**1**	**8**	***8**					**3**	**2**	**1**	**0**		
1976-77	Barbados	Shell Shield	IIs	4	5	3	33	15	16.50			1	124.3	38	287	12	23.91	
1976-77	Barbados	Pakistan Tourist	WI	1	D							2	58	15	155	4	38.75	
1977-78	Barbados	Australian Tourist	WI	1	2	1	126	79	126.00		1		45	10	92	2	46.00	
1978-79	Barbados	Shell Shield	IIs	1	D								2	0	3	0		
1979-80	Barbados	Shell Shield	IIs	4	4		60	50	15.00		1	2	96.4	19	245	7	35.00	
1980-81	Barbados	Shell Shield	IIs	4	4	1	63	39	21.00			4	128.2	22	320	10	32.00	
1980-81	Barbados	English Tourist	WI	1	1		0	0					9	1	122	5	24.40	
1981-82	Barbados	Shell Shield	IIs	5	5	1	43	25	10.75			1	168	45	360	14	25.71	
1983-84	WI Rebels XI	Tour of South Africa	SA	3	3	2	18	*9	18.00			2	108	20	277	5	55.40	

SEASON	TEAM	OPPONENTS	V	M	I	NO	RUNS	H.S.	AVGE	100	50	CT	OV	MD	RUNS	W	AVGE	B.B.
		Barbados		34	36	12	369	79	15.37		2	16	1030.4	263	2441	82	29.76	
		West Indies		31	27	9	175	30	9.72			11	1018.1	276	3062	106	28.88	
		WI Rebels XI	3	3	2	18	*9	18.00			2	108	20	277	5	55.40		
		TEST RECORD		**2**	**2**	**1**	**8**	***8**	**8.00**	**0**	**0**	**0**	**79**	**23**	**135**	**1**	**135.00**	**1-36**
		CAREER		**68**	**66**	**23**	**562**	**79**	**13.06**	**0**	**2**	**29**	**2156.5**	**559**	**5780**	**193**	**29.94**	**6-69**

PAIRAUDEAU, Bruce Hamilton

				BATTING									BOWLING					
SEASON	TEAM	OPPONENTS	V	M	I	NO	RUNS	H.S.	AVGE	100	50	CT	OV	MD	RUNS	W	AVGE	B.B.
1946-47	British Guiana	Trinidad	IIs	2	4		32	19	8.00			1	1	0	13	0		
1947-48	British Guiana	Jamaica	IIs	2	4		219	130	54.75	1		3	2	0	19	0		
1947-48	British Guiana	M.C.C. Tourist	WI	1	1		6	6	6.00									
1949-50	British Guiana	Barbados	IIs	2	4		257	161	64.25	1		1						
1950	Comm. XI	England XI	E	1	1		20	20	20.00									
1952-53	British Guiana	Jamaica	IIs	2	3		304	126	101.33	2	1	2						
1952-53	British Guiana	Indian Tourist	WI	1	2	1	75	*54	75.00		1	1	1	0	12	0		
1952-53	**WEST INDIES**	**INDIA TESTS**	**WI**	**5**	**8**		**257**	**115**	**32.12**	**1**	**1**	**2**						
1953-43	British Guiana	Trinidad	IIs	2	4	1	143	105	47.66	1		1						
1953-54	**WEST INDIES**	**ENGLAND TESTS**	**WI**	**2**	**3**		**76**	**71**	**25.33**		**1**	**1**	**1**	**0**	**3**	**0**		
1954-55	British Guiana	Barbados	IIs	2	4		139	85	34.75		1	3						
1954-55	British Guiana	Australian Tourists	WI	1	2		21	17	10.50			1						
1955-56	West Indies	Tour of New Zealand	NZ	2	3		186	104	62.00	1	1	3						
1955-56	**WEST INDIES**	**NEW ZEALAND TESTS**	**NZ**	**4**	**6**		**101**	**68**	**16.83**		**1**	**2**						
1956-57	British Guiana	Jamaica	II	1	2		149	111	74.50	1		1						
1956-57	British Guiana	Barbados	IIs	1	1		41	41	41.00			2						
1957	West Indies	Tour of England	E	16	29		761	163	26.24	2	2	6						
1957	**WEST INDIES**	**ENGLAND TESTS**	**E**	**2**	**4**		**20**	**7**	**5.00**			**1**						
1957-58	British Guiana	Pakistan Tourist	WI	1	1		17	17	17.00				1	0	3	0		
1958-59	Northern Districts	Plunket Shield	NZ	6	11	1	456	80	45.60		6	4	0.4	0	2	0		
1959-60	Northern Districts	Plunket Shield	NZ	5	9		365	80	40.55		4	2						
1960-61	Northern Districts	Plunket Shield	NZ	4	8		188	88	23.50		1	1						
1961-62	Northern Districts	Plunket Shield (& Pres. XI)	NZ	6	12		420	102	35.00	1	2	4						
1962-63	Northern Districts	Plunket Shield (& Inv. XI)	NZ	6	11	1	243	*68	24.30		1	7	1.2	0	9	0		
1963-64	Northern Districts	Plunket Shield	NZ	5	9		204	87	22.66		1	6						
1964-65	Northern Districts	Plunket Shield	NZ	5	9	1	183	93	22.87		1	6	1	0	12	0		
1966-67	Northern Districts	Plunket Shield	NZ	2	4		47	32	11.75			3	2.4	0	9	0		

SEASON	TEAM	OPPONENTS	V	M	I	NO	RUNS	H.S.	AVGE	100	50	CT	OV	MD	RUNS	W	AVGE	B.B.
				BATTING									BOWLING					
		British Guiana		18	32	2	1403	161	46.76	6	3	16	5	0	47	0		
		West Indies		31	53		1401	163	26.43	4	6	15	1	0	3	0		
		Northern Districts		39	73	3	2106	102	30.08	1	16	33	5.4	0	32	0		
		Comm. XI		1	1		20	20	20.00									
		TEST RECORD		**13**	**21**	**0**	**454**	**115**	**21.61**	**1**	**3**	**6**	**1**	**0**	**3**	**0**		
		CAREER		**89**	**159**	**5**	**4930**	**163**	**32.01**	**11**	**25**	**64**	**11.4**	**0**	**82**	**0**		

PARRY, Derick Ricaldo

SEASON	TEAM	OPPONENTS	V	M	I	NO	RUNS	H.S.	AVGE	100	50	CT	OV	MD	RUNS	W	AVGE	B.B.
				BATTING									BOWLING					
1975-76	Leeward Islands	Windward Islands	IIs	1	2		46	29	23.00				21	4	69	3	23.00	
1976-77	Leeward Islands	Windward Islands	IIs	2	2		88	85	44.00		1	3	64	12	171	5	34.20	
1976-77	Combined Islands	Shell Shield	IIs	4	6		154	57	25.66		1	8	172	43	412	12	34.33	
1976-77	Leeward Islands	Pakistan Tourist	WI	1	2		30	19	15.00			2	30	5	105	4	26.25	
1977-78	Leeward Islands	Windward Islands	IIs	2	4	1	72	*44	24.00			1	51	8	196	8	24.50	
1977-78	Combined Islands	Shell Shield	IIs	4	5		147	96	29.40		1	3	174.2	42	455	19	23.94	
1977-78	Leewards Islands	Australian Tourist	WI	1	2		9	9	4.50				48.5	8	142	5	28.40	
1977-78	**WEST INDIES**	**AUSTRALIA TESTS**	**WI**	**5**	**9**	**2**	**193**	**65**	**27.57**		**2**	**2**	**124.4**	**19**	**360**	**12**	**30.00**	
1978-79	West Indies	Tour of India	I	4	7	3	278	72	69.50		2	1	71	10	203	3	67.66	
1978-79	**WEST INDIES**	**INDIA TESTS**	**I**	**6**	**9**	**1**	**170**	**55**	**21.25**		**1**	**2**	**171.3**	**41**	**513**	**9**	**57.00**	
1978-79	West Indies	Tour of Sri Lanka	SL	2	3		61	31	20.33			1	47	8	161	4	40.25	
1978-79	Combined Islands	Shell Shield	IIs	4	6	1	170	59	28.33		1	6	215	57	500	23	21.73	
1979-80	West Indies	Tour of Australia	A	3	3		104	41	34.66				126.4	23	399	11	36.27	
1979-80	West Indies	Tour of New Zealand	NZ	2	3	1	30	16	12.00				62	11	198	7	43.50	
1979-80	**WEST INDIES**	**NEW ZEALAND TESTS**	**NZ**	**1**	**2**		**18**	**17**	**9.00**				**22**	**6**	**63**	**2**	**31.50**	
1979-80	Combined Islands	Shell Shield	IIs	4	6		140	55	23.33		1	3	232	68	537	25	21.48	
1980	West Indies	Tour of England	E	11	13	8	103	*26	20.60			1	303.1	93	800	40	20.00	
1980-81	West Indies	Tour of Pakistan	P	4	6	1	101	42	20.20			3	111.4	21	367	12	30.58	
1980-81	Combined Islands	Shell Shield	IIs	4	6	1	201	92	40.20		2	3	155.1	39	368	13	28.30	
1980-81	Leeward Islands	English Tourist	WI	1	2		22	21	11.00			1	36	9	101	1	101.00	
1981-82	Leeward Islands	Shell Shield	IIs	4	8	2	126	*27	21.00			5	192	46	525	13	40.38	
1982-83	WI Rebels XI	Tour of South Africa	SA	2	4		82	29	20.50			2	87	19	233	9	25.88	
1983-84	WI Rebels XI	Tour of South Africa	SA	5	9	3	207	63	34.50		2	3	146	31	390	11	35.45	
		Leeward Islands		12	22	3	393	85	20.68		1	12	442.5	92	1309	39	33.56	

				M	I	NO	RUNS	H.S.	AVGE	100	50	CT	OV	MD	RUNS	W	AVGE	B.B.
		Combined Islands		20	29	2	812	96	30.07		6	23	948.3	249	2272	92	24.69	
		West Indies		38	55	16	1058	72	27.12		5	10	1039.4	232	3064	100	30.64	
		WI Rebels XI		7	13	3	289	63	28.90		2	5	233	50	623	20	31.15	
		TEST RECORD		**12**	**20**	**3**	**381**	**65**	**22.41**	**0**	**3**	**4**	**318.1**	**66**	**936**	**23**	**40.69**	**5-15**
		CAREER		**77**	**119**	**24**	**2552**	**96**	**26.86**	**0**	**14**	**50**	**2664**	**623**	**7268**	**251**	**28.95**	**9-76**

PASSAILAIGUE, Clarence Charles

				BATTING									BOWLING					
SEASON	TEAM	OPPONENTS	V	M	I	NO	RUNS	H.S.	AVGE	100	50	CT	OV	MD	RUNS	W	AVGE	B.B.
1929-30	Jamaica	M.C.C. Tourist	WI	1	1		183	183	183.00	1		1						
1929-30	**WEST INDIES**	**ENGLAND TESTS**	**WI**	**1**	**2**	**1**	**46**	**44**	**46.00**			**3**	**2**	**0**	**15**	**0**		
1931-32	Jamaica	L.H. Tennyson's Tourist	WI	3	5	1	307	*261	76.75	1		5						
1932-33	G.C. Grant's XI	C.A. Merry's XI	IIs	1	2		9	9	4.50									
1934-35	Jamaica	M.C.C. Tourist	WI	2	2		29	19	14.50				3	1	7	0		
1935-36	Jamaica	Yorkshire Touring XI	WI	2	3		142	82	47.33		1		3	0	12	0		
1938-39	Jamaica	Trinidad	IIs	1	2	1	71	65	71.00		1							
1938-39	Jamaica	West Indies XI	IIs	1	1		1	1	1.00			2	2	0	22	1	22.00	
		Jamaica		10	14	2	733	*261	61.08	2	2	8						
		West Indies		1	2	1	46	44	46.00			3	2	0	15	0		
		G.C. Grant's XI		1	2		9	9	4.50				8	1	41	1	41.00	
		TEST RECORD		**1**	**2**	**1**	**46**	**44**	**46.00**	**0**	**0**	**3**	**2**	**0**	**15**	**0**		
		CAREER		**12**	**18**	**3**	**788**	***261**	**52.53**	**2**	**2**	**11**	**10**	**1**	**56**	**1**	**56.00**	**1-22**

PATTERSON, Balfour Patrick

				BATTING									BOWLING					
SEASON	TEAM	OPPONENTS	V	M	I	NO	RUNS	H.S.	AVGE	100	50	CT	OV	MD	RUNS	W	AVGE	B.B.
1982-83	Jamaica	Shell Shield	IIs	1	2		3	3	1.50			1	22	4	78	3	26.00	
1982-83	Jamaica	Indian Tourist	WI	1	1		3	3	3.00				16	1	50	1	50.00	
1984	Lancashire	Counties	E	1	2		10	10	5.00				21	3	51	0		
1984-85	Tasmania	Sheffield Shield	A	10	9	2	27	12	3.85			1	376	51	1359	37	36.72	
1985	Lancashire	Counties	E	16	15	5	38	22	3.80			4	364.3	59	1144	41	27.90	
1985-86	Jamaica	Shell Shield	IIs	5	8	4	8	*3	2.00			3	128.4	26	387	22	17.59	
1985-86	**WEST INDIES**	**ENGLAND TESTS**	**WI**	**5**	**5**	**3**	**12**	**9**	**6.00**			**1**	**118.1**	**18**	**426**	**19**	**22.42**	
1986	Lancashire	Counties	E	18	15	5	54	*12	5.40			4	391.4	69	1309	48	27.27	

				BATTING									BOWLING					
SEASON	TEAM	OPPONENTS	V	M	I	NO	RUNS	H.S.	AVGE	100	50	CT	OV	MD	RUNS	W	AVGE	B.B.
1986-87	West Indies	Tour of Pakistan	P	2	2		12	9	6.00				23	6	72	5	14.40	
1986-87	**WEST INDIES**	**PAKISTAN TESTS**	**P**	**1**	**2**	**1**	**6**	***6**	**6.00**			**1**	**31**	**4**	**101**	**3**	**33.66**	
1986-87	West Indies	Tour of New Zealand	NZ	1	D							2	21	2	102	1	102.00	
1986-87	Jamaica	Shell Shield	IIs	1	1		0	0					4	0	19	0		
1987	Lancashire	Counties	E	17	16	8	65	29	8.12			1	419.1	61	1359	52	26.13	
1987-88	West Indies	Tour of India	I	1	1	1	11	*11					18	7	49	2	24.50	
1987-88	**WEST INDIES**	**INDIA TESTS**	**I**	**4**	**4**	**4**	**26**	***21**					**117.1**	**14**	**456**	**17**	**26.82**	
1987-88	Jamaica	Red Stripe Cup	IIs	3	3	2	18	*15	18.00				80.3	16	282	10	28.20	
1987-88	**WEST INDIES**	**PAKISTAN TESTS**	**WI**	**1**	**2**		**10**	**10**	**5.00**				**26**	**1**	**101**	**4**	**25.25**	
1988	West Indies	Tour of England	E	7	5	2	58	*23	19.33			1	122	20	362	21	17.23	
1988	**WEST INDIES**	**ENGLAND TESTS**	**E**	**2**	**2**		**2**	**2**	**1.00**				**74.5**	**13**	**270**	**4**	**67.50**	
1988-89	West Indies	Tour of Australia	A	5	7	1	41	*18	6.83			1	122	23	381	10	38.10	
1988-89	**WEST INDIES**	**AUSTRALIA TESTS**	**A**	**4**	**6**	**3**	**32**	**13**	**10.66**				**107.1**	**11**	**405**	**12**	**33.75**	
1988-89	Jamaica	Red Stripe Cup	IIs	2	3		12	7	4.00				34	2	131	4	32.75	
1988-89	WI Board XI	Indian Tourist	WI	1	D								19	3	47	5	9.40	
1989	Lancashire	Counties	E	8	9	5	15	*4	3.75			1	210.3	43	618	32	19.31	
1989-90	Jamaica	Red Stripe Cup	IIs	3	4	1	24	19	8.00				88.3	13	277	17	16.29	
1989-90	WI President's XI	English Tourist	WI	1	2	1	11	11	11.00				32.5	8	104	3	34.66	
1989-90	**WEST INDIES**	**ENGLAND TESTS**	**WI**	**1**	**2**		**2**	**2**	**1.00**			**1**	**21**	**3**	**85**	**1**	**85.00**	
1990	Lancashire	Counties	E	10	4	1	5	*4	1.66			2	282.4	45	1015	29	35.00	
		Jamaica		16	22	7	68	19	4.53			4	373.4	62	1224	57	21.47	
		West Indies		36	40	16	223	*23	9.29			7	853.1	133	2961	107	27.67	
		Lancashire		70	61	24	187	29	5.05			12	1689.3	280	5496	202	27.20	
		Tasmania		10	9	2	27	12	3.85			1	376	51	1359	37	36.72	
		TEST RECORD		**18**	**23**	**11**	**90**	***21**	**7.50**	**0**	**0**	**3**	**495.2**	**64**	**1844**	**60**	**30.73**	**5-24**
		CAREER		**132**	**132**	**49**	**505**	**29**	**6.08**	**0**	**0**	**24**	**3292.2**	**526**	**11040**	**403**	**27.39**	**7-24**

PAYNE, Thelston Rodney O'Neal

				BATTING									BOWLING					
SEASON	TEAM	OPPONENTS	V	M	I	NO	RUNS	H.S.	AVGE	100	50	CT/St	OV	MD	RUNS	W	AVGE	B.B.
1978-79	Barbados	Shell Shield	IIs	4	5		222	97	44.40		2	6						
1979-80	Barbados	Shell Shield	IIs	4	6	2	290	140	72.50	1	2	8/1						
1980-81	Barbados	Shell Shield	IIs	4	6		93	53	15.50		1	5						
1980-81	WI President's XI	English Tourist	WI	1	2		2	1	1.00			2						

1981-82	Barbados	Shell Shield	IIs	1	2		5	3	2.50			2						
1982-83	Barbados	Shell Shield	IIs	5	9	2	517	123	78.85	3	2	4						
1982-83	Barbados	Indian Tourist	WI	1	1		26	26	26.00			1						
1983-84	West Indies 'B'	Tour of Zimbabwe	Z	1	2		44	28	22.00			1						
1983-84	Barbados	Shell Shield	IIs	5	10		372	76	37.20		4	10						
1983-84	Barbados	Australian Tourist	WI	1	2	1	67	*51	67.00		1							
1984	West Indies	Tour of England	E	7	8	3	191	44	38.20			4/1						
1984-85	West Indies	Tour of Australia	A	3	5		93	55	18.60		1	9						
1984-85	WI President's XI	New Zealand Tourist	WI	1	2		65	56	32.50		1	3						
1985-86	Barbados	Shell Shield	IIs	5	9	2	257	62	36.71		2	6/3						
1985-86	Barbados	English Tourist	WI	1	2		8	7	4.00			5/1						
1985-86	**WEST INDIES**	**ENGLAND TESTS**	**WI**	**1**	**1**		**5**	**5**	**5.00**			**5**						
1986-87	West Indies	Tour of Pakistan	P	2	2		14	14	7.00			4						
1986-87	Barbados	Shell Shield	IIs	2	2	1	75	*65	75.00		1	6						
1986-87	West Indies	Tour of Australia	A	1	1	1	60	*60			1							
1986-87	West Indies	Tour of New Zealand	NZ	1	2		51	51	25.50		1	1						
1987-88	Barbados	Red Stripe Cup	IIs	5	9		461	127	51.22	1	3	14/1						
1987-88	WI President's XI	Pakistan Tourist	WI	1	2		4	4	2.00									
1988-89	Barbados	Red Stripe Cup	IIs	5	6	1	186	70	37.20		2	6/1						
1989-90	Barbados	Red Stripe Cup	IIs	5	8	1	270	*101	38.57	1	1	1						
1989-90	Barbados	English Tourist	WI	1	2		13	13	6.50									
		Barbados		49	79	10	2862	140	41.47	6	21	74/7						
		West Indies		19	27	4	529	*60	23.00		4	29/1						
		TEST RECORD		**1**	**1**	**0**	**5**	**5**	**5.00**	**0**	**0**	**5**						
		CAREER		**68**	**106**	**14**	**3391**	**140**	**36.85**	**6**	**25**	**103/8**						

PHILLIP, Norbert

				BATTING									BOWLING					
SEASON	TEAM	OPPONENTS	V	M	I	NO	RUNS	H.S.	AVGE	100	50	CT	OV	MD	RUNS	W	AVGE	B.B.
1969-70	Windward Islands	Glamorgan Touring XI	WI	1	2	1	129	96	129.00		1	1	20	4	54	2	28.00	
1970-71	Windward Islands	Leeward Islands	IIs	1	2		3	3	1.50				26	3	77	3	25.66	
1970-71	Combined Islands	Shell Shield	IIs	3	6	1	32	20	6.40			1	87.5	23	182	13	14.00	
1970-71	Windward Islands	Indian Tourist	WI	1	2		54	38	27.00			1	23	10	39	1	39.00	
1971-72	Windward Islands	Leeward Islands	IIs	1	2	1	71	*60	71.00		1		24	5	52	0		
1971-72	Combined Islands	Shell Shield	IIs	4	8	1	211	99	30.14		2	2	91	17	294	8	36.75	
1971-72	Windward Islands	New Zealand Tourist	WI	1	D								8	3	16	0		

SEASON	TEAM	OPPONENTS	V	BATTING M	I	NO	RUNS	H.S.	AVGE	100	50	CT	BOWLING OV	MD	RUNS	W	AVGE	B.B.
1972-73	Windward Islands	Leeward Islands	IIs	2	4		185	58	46.25		2		46	10	128	2	64.00	
1972-73	Combined Islands	Shell Shield	IIs	4	8		255	70	31.87		3	2	119.3	23	336	13	25.84	
1972-73	WI President's XI	Australian Tourist	WI	1	2		56	35	28.00				15	2	43	1	43.00	
1972-73	Windward Islands	Australian Tourist	WI	1	2		86	70	43.00		1		34.5	2	125	8	15.62	
1973-74	Windward Islands	Leeward Islands	IIs	1	2	1	97	*77	97.00		1		22	5	37	3	12.33	
1973-74	Combined Islands	Shell Shield	IIs	4	8	1	138	60	19.71		2	3	80.3	15	253	13	19.46	
1974-75	Windward Islands	Leeward Islands	IIs	2	3		53	25	17.66				54	28	104	5	20.80	
1975-76	Windward Islands	Leeward Islands	IIs	1	1		1	1	1.00			1	27	12	42	3	14.00	
1975-76	Combined Islands	Shell Shield	IIs	4	3		15	8	5.00				92	21	220	8	27.25	
1975-76	Windward Islands	Indian Tourist	WI	1	2		49	31	24.50			1	17	4	36	1	36.00	
1976-77	Windward Islands	Leeward Islands	IIs	2	3		84	49	28.00				35	11	105	3	35.00	
1976-77	Combined Islands	Shell Shield	IIs	4	6	1	126	51	25.20		1		130.2	30	310	20	15.50	
1976-77	WI President's XI	Pakistan Tourist	WI	1	1		17	17	17.00			1	14.1	1	63	2	31.50	
1976-77	Windward Islands	Pakistan Tourist	WI	1	2		25	25	12.50				26.3	2	49	4	12.25	
1977-78	Windward Islands	Leeward Islands	IIs	2	3		18	7	6.00			1	61.3	11	182	8	22.75	
1977-78	Combined Islands	Shell Shield	IIs	4	5	2	240	*90	80.00		2	2	135.3	39	372	21	17.71	
1977-78	**WEST INDIES**	**AUSTRALIA TESTS**	**WI**	**3**	**6**	**1**	**120**	**46**	**24.00**			**2**	**110**	**8**	**391**	**9**	**43.44**	
1978	Essex	Counties	E	20	28	4	645	134	26.87	1	3	4	583.1	113	1591	71	22.40	
1978-79	West Indies	Tour of India	I	4	4		61	47	15.25				94.3	25	253	14	18.07	
1978-79	**WEST INDIES**	**INDIA TESTS**	**I**	**6**	**9**	**4**	**177**	**47**	**35.40**			**3**	**193.2**	**38**	**650**	**19**	**34.21**	
1978-79	West Indies	Tour of Sri Lanka	SL	1	1		29	29	29.00				5	2	20	0		
1978-79	Combined Islands	Shell Shield	IIs	1	2		38	36	19.00				6	1	16	0		
1979	Essex	Counties	E	22	30	5	425	66	17.00		2	6	548.1	128	1506	70	21.51	
1979-80	Windward Islands	Leeward Islands	IIs	1	2		79	63	39.50		1		12	1	50	1	50.00	
1979-80	Combined Islands	Shell Shield	IIs	3	4		88	44	22.00			2	84	22	254	10	25.40	
1980	Essex	Counties	E	20	24	4	376	*77	18.80		2	5	412.2	59	1412	40	35.30	
1981	Essex	Counties	E	22	37	4	720	*80	21.81		3	10	521.1	87	1725	51	33.82	
1981-82	Windward Islands	Shell Shield	IIs	4	7	1	186	62	31.00		1	2	121	24	342	21	16.28	
1982	Essex	Counties	E	24	32	3	783	79	27.00		2	6	584.1	107	1842	82	22.46	
1982-83	Windward Islands	Shell Shield	IIs	4	8		183	49	22.87			1	116	12	370	14	26.42	
1982-83	Windward Islands	Indian Tourist	WI	1	2		10	9	5.00			1	36	6	108	6	18.00	
1983	Essex	Counties	E	19	26		413	80	15.88		1	8	477.2	88	1409	69	20.42	
1983-84	Windward Islands	Shell Shield	IIs	5	4		110	63	27.50		1		93	9	315	14	22.50	
1983-84	Windward Islands	Australian Tourist	WI	1	1		13	13	13.00				21	0	112	1	112.00	
1984	Essex	Counties	E	13	17	2	293	71	19.53		1	3	275.2	48	911	34	26.79	
1984-85	Windward Islands	Shell Shield	IIs	5	6		190	81	31.66		2	3	124.2	16	394	14	28.14	
1985	Essex	Counties	E	4	7		129	50	18.42		1	3	75.3	14	242	6	40.33	

SEASON	TEAM	OPPONENTS	V	M	I	NO	RUNS	H.S.	AVGE	100	50	CT	OV	MD	RUNS	W	AVGE	B.B.
		Windward Islands		39	60	4	1626	96	29.03		11	12	948.1	178	2737	114	24.00	
		Combined Islands		31	50	6	1143	99	25.97		10	12	825.4	191	2237	106	21.10	
		West Indies		16	23	5	460	47	25.55			6	432	76	1420	45	31.55	
		Essex		144	201	22	3784	134	21.13	1	15	45	3477.1	644	10638	423	25.14	
		TEST RECORD		**9**	**15**	**5**	**297**	**47**	**29.70**	**0**	**0**	**5**	**303.2**	**46**	**1041**	**28**	**37.17**	**4-48**
		CAREER		**230**	**334**	**37**	**7013**	**134**	**23.61**	**1**	**36**	**75**	**5683**	**1089**	**17032**	**688**	**24.75**	**7-33**

PIERRE, Lancelot Richard

				BATTING									BOWLING					
SEASON	**TEAM**	**OPPONENTS**	**V**	**M**	**I**	**NO**	**RUNS**	**H.S.**	**AVGE**	**100**	**50**	**CT**	**OV**	**MD**	**RUNS**	**W**	**AVGE**	**B.B.**
1940-41	Trinidad	Barbados	IIs	2	3	2	7	*6	7.00			1	44	4	212	9	23.55	
1941-42	Trinidad	Barbados	IIs	4	6	2	10	6	2.50			1	104	8	383	22	17.40	
1942-43	Trinidad	Barbados	IIs	2	1		0	0					66.1	3	300	11	27.27	
1943-44	Trinidad	Barbados	IIs	2	2		6	3	3.00			1	30	2	147	2	73.50	
1943-44	Trinidad	British Guiana	IIs	2	2	1	12	*11	12.00			1	32	2	138	5	27.60	
1944-45	Trinidad	Barbados	IIs	2	2	2	13	*13				1	37.7	1	191	9	21.22	
1945-46	Trinidad	British Guiana	IIs	2	3	2	11	*6	11.00			1	41	10	121	5	24.20	
1945-46	Trinidad	Barbados	IIs	2	3	3	34	*13				1	36	5	141	3	47.00	
1945-46	Trinidad	Jamaica	IIs	1	2	1	1	1	1.00				23.7	1	95	3	31.66	
1947-48	Trinidad	M.C.C. Tourist	WI	1	1		6	6	6.00			1	30	8	85	4	21.25	
1947-48	**WEST INDIES**	**ENGLAND TESTS**	**WI**	**1**	**D**								**7**	**0**	**28**	**0**		
1948-49	Trinidad	Barbados	IIs	1	2		27	23	13.50			1	19	2	63	1	63.00	
1949-50	Trinidad	Jamaica	IIs	1	1		2	2	2.00				28.2	8	61	4	15.25	
1950	West Indies	Tour of England	E	12	7	1	2	1	0.33			5	204	39	557	24	23.20	
		Trinidad		22	28	13	129	23	8.60			9	492.1	54	1937	78	24.83	
		West Indies		13	7	1	2	1	0.33			5	211	39	585	24	24.37	
		TEST RECORD		**1**	**D**								**7**	**0**	**28**	**0**		
		CAREER		**35**	**35**	**14**	**131**	**23**	**6.23**	**0**	**0**	**14**	**703.1**	**93**	**2522**	**102**	**24.72**	**8-51**

RAE, Allan Fitzroy

				BATTING									BOWLING					
SEASON	**TEAM**	**OPPONENTS**	**V**	**M**	**I**	**NO**	**RUNS**	**H.S.**	**AVGE**	**100**	**50**	**CT**	**OV**	**MD**	**RUNS**	**W**	**AVGE**	**B.B.**
1946-47	Jamaica	Barbados	IIs	2	3		240	128	80.00	2		1	1	0	4	0		
1948-49	West Indies	Tour of India	I	9	14		522	160	37.28	2	1	2						

SEASON	TEAM	OPPONENTS	V	M	I	NO	RUNS	H.S.	AVGE	100	50	CT	OV	MD	RUNS	W	AVGE	B.B.
				BATTING									BOWLING					
1948-49	**WEST INDIES**	**INDIA TESTS**	**I**	**5**	**7**		**374**	**109**	**53.42**	**2**	**1**	**4**						
1948-49	West Indies	Tour of Pakistan	P	1	2		1	1	0.50									
1948-49	West Indies	Tour of Ceylon	C	2	2		253	137	126.50	2			2	0	18	0		
1950	West Indies	Tour of England	E	22	31	3	953	179	34.03	2	3	13						
1950	**WEST INDIES**	**ENGLAND TESTS**	**E**	**4**	**7**	**1**	**377**	**109**	**62.83**	**2**	**1**	**2**						
1951-52	West Indies	Tour of Australia	A	7	11		454	171	41.27	2	1	1						
1951-52	**WEST INDIES**	**AUSTRALIA TESTS**	**A**	**3**	**6**		**87**	**25**	**14.50**			**2**						
1951-52	West Indies	Tour of New Zealand	NZ	2	4		92	46	23.00			2						
1951-52	**WEST INDIES**	**NEW ZEALAND TESTS**	**NZ**	**1**	**1**		**99**	**99**	**99.00**		**1**							
1952-53	Jamaica	British Guiana	IIs	2	3	1	144	103	72.00	1		1						
1952-53	Jamaica	Indian Tourist	WI	1	2		53	44	26.50			4	0.4	0	4	0		
1952-53	**WEST INDIES**	**INDIA TESTS**	**WI**	**2**	**3**	**1**	**79**	***63**	**39.50**		**1**	**2**						
1953-54	Jamaica	M.C.C. Tourist	WI	2	4		100	53	25.00		1							
1954-55	Jamaica	Trinidad	IIs	2	4		62	44	15.50			2						
1954-55	Jamaica	Australian Tourist	WI	1	2	1	22	*21	22.00			2						
1955-56	West Indies XI	E.W. Swanton's Tourist	WI	1	2		43	36	21.50									
1956-57	Jamaica	British Guiana	IIs	1	1		80	80	80.00		1	1						
1956-57	Jamaica	Duke of Norfolk's Tourist	WI	3	6		174	74	29.00		1	1						
1957-58	Jamaica	Pakistan Tourist	WI	1	2		138	110	69.00	1		1						
1958-59	Jamaica	Leeward Islands	IIs	1	1		6	6	6.00			1						
1958-59	Jamaica	Barbados	IIs	2	4		141	52	35.25		2							
1959-60	Jamaica	Trinidad	IIs	1	2		180	142	90.00	1								
1959-60	Jamaica	British Guiana	IIs	1	2		106	65	53.00		1							
1959-60	Jamaica	M.C.C. Tourist	WI	1	2		18	12	9.00									
		Jamaica		21	38	2	1464	142	40.66	5	6	14	1.4	0	8	0		
		West Indies		59	90	5	3334	179	39.22	12	9	28	2	0	18	0		
		TEST RECORD		**15**	**24**	**2**	**1016**	**109**	**46.18**	**4**	**4**	**10**						
		CAREER		**80**	**128**	**7**	**4798**	**179**	**39.65**	**17**	**15**	**42**	**3.4**	**0**	**26**	**0**		

RAMADHIN, Sonny

SEASON	TEAM	OPPONENTS	V	M	I	NO	RUNS	H.S.	AVGE	100	50	CT	OV	MD	RUNS	W	AVGE	B.B.
				BATTING									BOWLING					
1949-50	Trinidad	Jamaica	IIs	2	1	1	12	*12				1	98.5	26	231	12	19.25	
1950	West Indies	Tour of England	E	17	10	6	26	*7	6.50			3	666	228	1405	109	12.88	

1950	**WEST INDIES**	**ENGLAND TESTS**	**E**	**4**	**5**	**2**	**10**	**4**	**3.33**		**377.5**	**170**	**604**	**26**	**23.33**
1950-51	Comm. XI	Tour of India	I	20	16	6	74	19	7.40	5	774.5	261	1553	79	19.65
1951	Comm. XI	England XI	E	2	1		0	0		1	62	20	90	14	6.42
1951-52	West Indies	Tour of Australia	A	3	3	1	3	*3	1.50	1	92	23	233	8	29.12
1951-52	**WEST INDIES**	**AUSTRALIA TESTS**	**A**	**5**	**9**	**4**	**30**	***16**	**6.00**	**2**	**232.3**	**53**	**695**	**14**	**49.64**
1951-52	West Indies	Tour of New Zealand	NZ	2	2	1	4	*4	4.00	1	100	41	180	12	15.00
1951-52	**WEST INDIES**	**NEW ZEALAND TESTS**	**NZ**	**2**	**1**		**10**	**10**	**10.00**		**100**	**44**	**166**	**12**	**13.83**
1952	Comm. XI	England XI	E	1	D						45	10	140	8	17.50
1952-53	Trinidad	Indian Tourist	WI	1	1		0	0			44	15	84	2	42.00
1952-53	**WEST INDIES**	**INDIA TESTS**	**WI**	**4**	**5**	**3**	**40**	***16**	**20.00**		**232.4**	**96**	**471**	**13**	**36.23**
1953	Comm. XI	England XI	E	1	2	1	33	24	33.00	2	17.3	3	52	6	8.66
1953-54	Comm. XI	Tour of India	I	11	10	3	74	*27	10.57	4	361.2	118	801	29	37.62
1953-54	**WEST INDIES**	**ENGLAND TESTS**	**WI**	**5**	**6**		**23**	**10**	**3.83**	**3**	**304.3**	**133**	**559**	**23**	**24.30**
1954	Comm. XI	England XI	E	1	1	1	0	*0			32	8	77	6	12.83
1954-55	**WEST INDIES**	**AUSTRALIA TESTS**	**WI**	**4**	**6**	**1**	**27**	***12**	**5.40**	**1**	**139**	**33**	**380**	**5**	**76.00**
1955	Comm. XI	England XI	E	2	4	1	48	16	16.00		59	8	194	6	32.33
1955-56	West Indies	Tour of New Zealand	NZ	4	4	1	40	14	13.33		190.4	84	340	20	17.00
1955-56	**WEST INDIES**	**NEW ZEALAND TESTS**	**NZ**	**4**	**5**		**95**	**44**	**19.00**	**1**	**184.4**	**76**	**316**	**20**	**15.80**
1955-56	West Indies XI	E.W. Swanton's Tourist	WI	1	1	1	0	*0		1	85	35	140	7	20.00
1956	Comm. XI	England XI	E	1	D										
1957	West Indies	Tour of England	E	15	13	3	58	28	5.80	1	675.4	283	1117	105	10.63
1957	**WEST INDIES**	**ENGLAND TESTS**	**E**	**5**	**9**	**1**	**47**	**19**	**5.87**	**1**	**261.3**	**78**	**547**	**14**	**39.07**
1958-59	West Indies	Tour of India	I	8	4	1	16	8	5.33	2	136	48	254	19	13.26
1958-59	**WEST INDIES**	**INDIA TESTS**	**I**	**2**	**1**		**9**	**9**	**9.00**		**44.5**	**15**	**91**	**2**	**45.50**
1958-59	West Indies	Tour of Pakistan	P	3	2	1	41	*22	41.00		89.4	28	171	11	15.54
1958-59	**WEST INDIES**	**PAKISTAN TESTS**	**P**	**2**	**3**	**3**	**8**	***4**		**1**	**70.3**	**28**	**121**	**9**	**13.44**
1959-60	**WEST INDIES**	**ENGLAND TESTS**	**WI**	**4**	**4**		**41**	**23**	**10.25**		**248.3**	**83**	**491**	**17**	**28.88**
1960-61	West Indies	Tour of Australia	A	5	8	1	72	*16	10.28		133.3	13	493	21	23.47
1960-61	**WEST INDIES**	**AUSTRALIA TESTS**	**A**	**2**	**4**		**21**	**12**	**5.25**		**37**	**4**	**138**	**3**	**46.00**
1961	M.C.C.	Oxford University	E	1	2		47	41	23.50		76	25	169	8	21.12
1961-62	International XI	World Tour	R/P/NZ	6	7	2	24	8	4.80	2	256.1	73	715	21	34.04
1963-64	E.W. Swanton's XI	Tour of India	I	1	1	1	8	*8			25	8	60	0	
1964	Lancashire	Counties	E	28	33	18	126	13	8.40	5	952.1	305	2046	92	22.33
1965	Lancashire	Counties	E	5	7	1	25	10	4.16		97	29	221	5	44.20
		Trinidad		3	2	1	12	*12	12.00	1	142.5	41	315	14	22.50
		West Indies		101	105	30	621	44	8.28	18	4402	1596	8912	470	18.96
		Comm. XI		39	34	12	229	*27	10.40	12	1351.4	428	2907	148	19.64
		Lancashire		33	40	19	151	13	7.19	5	1049.1	334	2267	97	23.37

			BATTING									BOWLING					
SEASON	TEAM		M	I	NO	RUNS	H.S.	AVGE	100	50	CT	OV	MD	RUNS	W	AVGE	B.B.
		International XI	6	7	2	24	8	4.80			2	256.1	73	715	21	34.04	
		E.W. Swanton's XI	1	1	1	8	*8					25	8	60	0		
		M.C.C.	1	2		47	41	23.50				76	25	169	8	21.12	
		TEST RECORD	**43**	**58**	**14**	**361**	**44**	**8.20**	**0**	**0**	**9**	**2233.3**	**813**	**4579**	**158**	**28.98**	**7-49**
		CAREER	**184**	**191**	**65**	**1092**	**44**	**8.66**	**0**	**0**	**38**	**7302.5**	**2505**	**15345**	**758**	**20.24**	**8-15**

RICHARDS, Isaac Vivian Alexander

				BATTING									BOWLING					
SEASON	TEAM	OPPONENTS	V	M	I	NO	RUNS	H.S.	AVGE	100	50	CT/St	OV	MD	RUNS	W	AVGE	B.B.
1971-72	Leewards Islands	Windward Islands	IIs	1	2		46	26	23.00				1	0	9	0		
1971-72	Combined Islands	Shell Shield	IIs	4	8		217	58	27.12		2							
1971-72	Leeward Islands	New Zealand Tourist	WI	1	2		82	82	41.00		1							
1972-73	Leewards Islands	Windward Islands	IIs	2	2		84	56	42.00		1	4	32	12	68	2	34.00	
1972-73	Combined Islands	Shell Shield	IIs	4	8		102	52	12.75		1	2	64	18	160	6	26.66	
1972-73	WI President's XI	Australian Tourist	WI	1	2		23	18	11.50				10	1	30	0		
1972-73	Leeward Islands	Australian Tourist	WI	1	1		5	5	5.00			1	35	4	85	3	28.33	
1973-74	Combined Islands	Shell Shield	IIs	4	8	1	270	78	38.57		2	1	38	7	85	1	85.00	
1973-74	Leewards Islands	M.C.C. Tourist	WI	1	2	1	94	*52	94.00		1		16	3	40	1	40.00	
1974	Somerset	Counties	E	23	38	1	1223	107	33.05	2	6	18	95	31	273	6	45.50	
1974-75	West Indies	Tour of India	I	7	11	5	544	*103	90.66	2	3	6	28	8	88	3	29.33	
1974-75	**WEST INDIES**	**INDIA TESTS**	**I**	**5**	**9**	**2**	**353**	***192**	**50.42**	**1**	**1**	**5**	**7**	**2**	**10**	**0**		
1974-75	West Indies	Tour of Sri Lanka	SL	2	3		231	151	77.00	1	1	1						
1974-75	West Indies	Tour of Pakistan	P	1	2		122	79	61.00		1	1						
1974-75	**WEST INDIES**	**PAKISTAN TESTS**	**P**	**2**	**3**		**17**	**10**	**5.66**			**3**	**9**	**2**	**17**	**1**	**17.00**	
1974-75	Combined Islands	Shell Shield	IIs	4	7		363	112	51.85	2	2	5	59	20	102	1	102.00	
1975	Somerset	Counties	E	18	32	1	1151	*217	37.12	3	3	27	130	33	358	10	35.86	
1975	International XI	Yorkshire	E	1	2		23	20	11.50			2	2	1	6	1	6.00	
1975-76	West Indies	Tour of Australia	A	6	10	2	681	175	85.12	3	2	5	22.4	2	99	2	49.50	
1975-76	**WEST INDIES**	**AUSTRALIA TESTS**	**A**	**6**	**11**		**426**	**101**	**38.76**	**1**	**2**	**6**	**8.1**	**0**	**44**	**0**		
1975-76	Leeward Islands	Indian Tourist	WI	1	1	1	27	*27				2	11	5	10	0		
1975-76	**WEST INDIES**	**INDIA TESTS**	**WI**	**4**	**6**		**556**	**177**	**92.66**	**3**	**1**	**3**	**6**	**0**	**17**	**0**		
1976	West Indies	Tour of England	E	12	18	1	895	176	52.64	3	5	15/1						
1976	**WEST INDIES**	**ENGLAND TESTS**	**E**	**4**	**7**		**829**	**291**	**118.42**	**3**	**2**	**2**	**31**	**12**	**56**	**1**	**56.00**	
1976-77	Queensland	Sheffield Shield	A	5	8		349	143	43.62	1	2	4	4	0	41	0		
1976-77	Combined Islands	Shell Shield	IIs	1	2		169	124	84.50	1			9	2	30	0		

1976-77	Leeward Islands	Pakistan Tourist	WI	1	2		94	60	47.00		1		29	7	62	2	31.00
1976-77	**WEST INDIES**	**PAKISTAN TESTS**	**WI**	**5**	**9**		**257**	**92**	**28.55**		**2**	**4**	**40.3**	**11**	**91**	**2**	**45.50**
1977	Somerset	Counties	E	20	35	2	2161	*241	65.48	7	9	16	89.5	24	248	7	35.42
1977-78	Combined Islands	Shell Shield	IIs	1	2		51	51	25.50		1	4	27	11	60	2	30.00
1977-78	**WEST INDIES**	**AUSTRALIA TESTS**	**WI**	**2**	**2**		**62**	**39**	**31.00**			**3**					
1978	Somerset	Counties	E	21	38	4	1558	118	45.82	2	10	21					
1979	Somerset	Counties	E	16	26		1043	156	40.11	3	4	13	89.5	16	268	8	33.50
1979-80	West Indies	Tour of Australia	A	2	2		206	127	103.00	1	1	4	77.3	11	270	5	54.00
1979-80	**WEST INDIES**	**AUSTRALIA TESTS**	**A**	**3**	**4**		**386**	**140**	**96.50**	**1**	**3**	**3**	3	1	2	0	
1979-80	Combined Islands	Shell Shield	IIs	4	7		165	78	23.57		1	4	**2**	**0**	**7**	**0**	
1980	West Indies	Tour of England	E	8	11	1	532	131	53.20	3	2	7	84	23	210	8	26.25
1980	**WEST INDIES**	**ENGLAND TESTS**	**E**	**5**	**6**		**379**	**145**	**63.16**	**1**	**2**	**6**	62	9	92	1	92.00
1980	Somerset	Counties	E	4	8		306	170	38.25	1	1	6	**36**	**12**	**85**	**0**	
1980-81	West Indies	Tour of Pakistan	P	4	5		79	32	15.80			3	30	2	110	3	36.66
1980-81	**WEST INDIES**	**PAKISTAN TESTS**	**P**	**4**	**6**	**1**	**364**	***120**	**72.80**	**1**	**3**	**9**	**26.2**	**5**	**61**	**4**	**15.25**
1980-81	Combined Islands	Shell Shield	IIs	4	7	1	323	*168	53.83	2		2	50.1	16	116	2	58.00
1980-81	**WEST INDIES**	**ENGLAND TESTS**	**WI**	**4**	**5**	**1**	**340**	***182**	**85.00**	**2**		**3**	**100**	**35**	**206**	**5**	**41.20**
1981	Somerset	Counties	E	20	33	3	1718	196	57.26	7	5	18	185.5	38	585	13	45.00
1981-82	West Indies	Tour of Australia	A	4	5	1	276	121	69.00	1	2	3	71.5	15	195	6	32.50
1981-82	**WEST INDIES**	**AUSTRALIA TESTS**	**A**	**3**	**6**		**160**	**50**	**26.66**		**1**	**1**	**49**	**13**	**109**	**0**	
1981-82	Leeward Islands	Shell Shield	IIs	4	7		433	167	61.85	1	3	12	42	8	103	1	103.00
1982	Somerset	Counties	E	20	31	2	1324	*181	45.65	4	5	11	265.3	75	671	16	41.93
1982-83	Leeward Islands	Shell Shield	IIs	1	2		45	45	22.50			2					
1982-83	**WEST INDIES**	**INDIA TESTS**	**WI**	**5**	**6**		**282**	**109**	**47.00**	**1**	**2**	**8**	**36**	**9**	**87**	**1**	**87.00**
1982-83	Somerset	Counties	E	12	20	4	1204	216	75.25	5	3	6	188	61	462	12	38.50
1983-84	West Indies	Tour of India	I	4	5		221	109	44.20	1	1	2	18.3	4	80	3	26.66
1983-84	**WEST INDIES**	**INDIA TESTS**	**I**	**6**	**9**		**306**	**120**	**34.00**	**1**	**1**	**8**	**3**	**1**	**8**	**0**	
1983-84	Leeward Islands	Shell Shield	IIs	1	1		37	37	37.00			2	24	7	58	1	58.00
1983-84	**WEST INDIES**	**AUSTRALIA TESTS**	**WI**	**5**	**5**		**270**	**178**	**54.00**	**1**	**1**	**3**	**53**	**13**	**102**	**3**	**34.00**
1984	West Indies	Tour of England	E	7	8		375	170	48.87	1	2	7	73	20	183	3	61.00
1984	**WEST INDIES**	**ENGLAND TESTS**	**E**	**5**	**7**	**1**	**250**	**117**	**41.66**	**1**	**1**	**5**	**1**	**0**	**2**	**0**	
1984-85	West Indies	Tour of Australia	A	5	8		264	102	33.00	1	1	6	78	22	143	6	23.83
1984-85	**WEST INDIES**	**AUSTRALIA TESTS**	**A**	**5**	**9**	**1**	**342**	**208**	**42.71**	**1**	**1**	**3**	**16**	**4**	**32**	**1**	**32.00**
1984-85	**WEST INDIES**	**NEW ZEALAND TESTS**	**WI**	**4**	**6**	**1**	**310**	**105**	**62.00**	**1**	**2**	**2**	**39**	**7**	**89**	**1**	**89.00**
1985	Somerset	Counties	E	19	24		1836	322	76.50	9	6	9	183	48	494	7	70.57
1985-86	Leeward Islands	Shell Shield	IIs	4	5		187	132	37.40	1		4	121	28	236	7	33.71
1985-86	**WEST INDIES**	**ENGLAND TESTS**	**WI**	**5**	**6**	**1**	**331**	**110**	**66.20**	**1**	**2**	**2**	**20**	**7**	**29**	**0**	
1986	Somerset	Counties	E	18	28	1	1174	136	43.48	4	5	19	161	32	500	9	55.55
1986-87	West Indies	Tour of Pakistan	P	3	3		101	54	33.66		1	3	9	1	26	0	

SEASON	TEAM	OPPONENTS	V	M	I	NO	RUNS	H.S.	AVGE	100	50	CT/St	OV	MD	RUNS	W	AVGE	B.B.
				BATTING									BOWLING					
1986-87	**WEST INDIES**	**PAKISTAN TESTS**	**P**	**3**	**5**		**175**	**70**	**35.00**		**1**	**1**	**5**	**2**	**9**	**1**	**9.00**	
1986-87	West Indies	Tour of New Zealand	NZ	1	1	1	117	*117		1								
1986-87	**WEST INDIES**	**NEW ZEALAND TESTS**	**NZ**	**3**	**4**		**77**	**38**	**19.25**			**5**	**67**	**19**	**147**	**2**	**73.50**	
1986-87	Leeward Islands	Shell Shield	IIs	1	2		58	42	29.00				9	0	35	1	35.00	
1987-88	West Indies	Tour of India	I	2	2		144	138	72.00	1			9	5	28	2	14.00	
1987-88	**WEST INDIES**	**INDIA TESTS**	**I**	**4**	**6**	**1**	**295**	***109**	**59.00**	**1**	**2**	**5**	**50**	**11**	**103**	**3**	**34.33**	
1987-88	Leeward Islands	Red Stripe Cup	IIs	2	2		189	119	94.50	1	1	2	15	4	20	1	20.00	
1987-88	**WEST INDIES**	**PAKISTAN TESTS**	**WI**	**2**	**4**		**278**	**123**	**69.50**	**1**	**1**	**6**	**17**	**4**	**44**	**3**	**14.66**	
1988	West Indies	Tour of England	E	8	10	1	401	128	44.55	1	3	6	35.4	9	94	3	31.33	
1988	**WEST INDIES**	**ENGLAND TESTS**	**E**	**5**	**6**		**223**	**80**	**37.16**		**2**	**3**	**10**	**1**	**28**	**0**		
1988-89	West Indies	Tour of Australia	A	2	2		237	136	118.50	2		2	51.1	8	141	5	28.20	
1988-89	**WEST INDIES**	**AUSTRALIA TESTS**	**A**	**5**	**9**	**1**	**446**	**146**	**55.75**	**1**	**4**	**3**	**117**	**12**	**299**	**3**	**99.67**	
1988-89	**WEST INDIES**	**INDIA TESTS**	**WI**	**4**	**5**		**135**	**110**	**27.00**	**1**		**10**	**51**	**8**	**128**	**1**	**128.00**	
1989-90	Leeward Islands	Red Stripe Cup	IIs	2	3	1	58	*25	29.00			1	41	12	91	3	30.33	
1989-90	**WEST INDIES**	**ENGLAND TESTS**	**WI**	**3**	**5**		**141**	**70**	**28.20**		**1**	**4**	**28**	**10**	**47**	**0**		
1990	Glamorgan	Counties	E	18	28	5	1425	*164	61.95	7	3	8	137	26	426	5	85.20	
		Leeward Islands		23	34	3	1439	167	46.41	3	8	30	376	90	817	22	37.13	
		Combined Islands		26	49	2	1660	*168	35.31	5	9	18	331.1	97	763	20	38.15	
		West Indies		190	274	22	13439	291	53.32	46	63	187/1	1299.5	305	3058	66	46.33	
		Somerset		191	313	18	14698	322	49.82	47	57	164	1495.3	371	4239	96	44.15	
		Glamorgan		18	28	5	1425	*164	61.95	7	3	8	137	26	426	5	85.20	
		Queensland		5	8		349	143	43.62	1	2	4	4	0	41	0		
		International XI		1	2		23	20	11.50			2	2	1	6	1	6.00	
		TEST RECORD		**111**	**166**	**10**	**7990**	**291**	**51.21**	**24**	**38**	**116**	**828**	**200**	**1857**	**32**	**58.03**	**2-17**
		CAREER		**454**	**708**	**50**	**33033**	**322**	**50.20**	**109**	**142**	**413/1**	**3645.3**	**890**	**9350**	**210**	**44.52**	**5-88**

RICHARDSON, Richard Benjamin

SEASON	TEAM	OPPONENTS	V	M	I	NO	RUNS	H.S.	AVGE	100	50	CT	OV	MD	RUNS	W	AVGE	B.B.
				BATTING									BOWLING					
1981-82	Leeward Islands	Shell Shield	IIs	2	4		111	76	27.75		1	1						
1982-83	Leeward Islands	Shell Shield	IIs	5	10		396	156	39.60	2		7	3	1	2	0		
1982-83	Leeward Islands	Indian Tourist	WI	1	2		21	17	21.00			2						
1983-84	West Indies	Tour of India	I	6	10		354	77	35.40		2	5						
1983-84	**WEST INDIES**	**INDIA TESTS**	**I**	**1**	**2**		**26**	**26**	**13.00**									

1983-84	Leeward Islands	Shell Shield	IIs	1	1		162	162	162.00	1								
1983-84	Leeward Islands	Australian Tourist	WI	1	2		7	7	3.50									
1983-84	**WEST INDIES**	**AUSTRALIA TESTS**	**WI**	**5**	**5**	**1**	**327**	**154**	**81.75**	**2**		**5**						
1984	West Indies	Tour of England	E	8	10		335	111	33.50	1	1	3						
1984-85	West Indies	Tour of Australia	A	5	8	1	321	145	45.85	1	2	7	10	1	40	0		
1984-85	**WEST INDIES**	**AUSTRALIA TESTS**	**A**	**5**	**9**		**236**	**138**	**26.22**	**1**	**1**	**9**						
1984-85	West Indies Under 23 XI	New Zealand Tourist	WI	1	1		1	1	1.00			1						
1984-85	**WEST INDIES**	**NEW ZEALAND TESTS**	**WI**	**4**	**6**		**378**	**185**	**63.00**	**1**	**2**	**5**						
1985-86	Leeward Islands	Shell Shield	IIs	4	6		142	55	23.66		2	1	5	0	19	0		
1985-86	Leeward Islands	English Tourist	WI	1	2		46	27	23.00			1	20	2	44	5	8.80	
1985-86	**WEST INDIES**	**ENGLAND TESTS**	**WI**	**5**	**9**	**2**	**387**	**160**	**55.28**	**2**		**6**	**1**	**0**	**5**	**0**		
1986-87	West Indies	Tour of Pakistan	P	3	5	1	116	67	29.00		1	3						
1986-87	**WEST INDIES**	**PAKISTAN TESTS**	**P**	**3**	**5**		**148**	**54**	**29.60**		**1**	**5**						
1986-87	West Indies	Tour of Australia	A	1	2		10	7	5.00									
1986-87	West Indies	Tour of New Zealand	NZ	2	4	1	193	121	64.33	1	1	1						
1986-87	**WEST INDIES**	**NEW ZEALAND TESTS**	**NZ**	**3**	**5**	**1**	**134**	**41**	**33.50**			**5**	**4**	**1**	**4**	**0**		
1986-87	Leeward Islands	Shell Shield	IIs	3	5		83	44	16.60									
1987-88	West Indies	Tour of India	I	3	4		230	147	57.50	1		1						
1987-88	**WEST INDIES**	**INDIA TESTS**	**I**	**4**	**8**	**2**	**226**	**89**	**37.66**		**2**	**9**						
1987-88	Leeward Islands	Red Stripe Cup	IIs	2	3	1	193	176	96.50	1		3						
1987-88	**WEST INDIES**	**PAKISTAN TESTS**	**WI**	**3**	**6**		**240**	**75**	**40.00**		**2**	**2**						
1988	West Indies	Tour of England	E	7	10		208	82	20.80		1	4	4	0	22	0		
1988	**WEST INDIES**	**ENGLAND TESTS**	**E**	**3**	**4**		**71**	**26**	**17.75**			**4**						
1988-89	West Indies	Tour of Australia	A	5	7		238	121	34.00	1		8						
1988-89	**WEST INDIES**	**AUSTRALIA TESTS**	**A**	**5**	**10**	**1**	**528**	**122**	**58.66**	**2**	**2**	**4**						
1988-89	Leeward Islands	Red Stripe Cup	IIs	1	2		14	14	7.00			1						
1988-89	**WEST INDIES**	**INDIA TESTS**	**WI**	**4**	**7**		**619**	**194**	**88.42**	**2**	**3**	**2**						
1989-90	Leeward Islands	Red Stripe Cup	IIs	5	9	3	421	*125	70.16	2		4						
1989-90	Leeward Islands	English Tourist	WI	1	2		88	83	44.00		1		8	3	21	0		
1989-90	**WEST INDIES**	**ENGLAND TESTS**	**WI**	**4**	**7**		**195**	**45**	**27.85**			**4**	**2**	**1**	**3**	**0**		
1990	Rest of World XI	Indian Tourist	E	1	2		107	65	53.50		1	1						
		Leeward Islands		27	48	4	1684	176	38.27	6	4	20	36	6	86	5	17.20	
		West Indies		90	144	10	5521	194	41.20	15	21	93	21	3	74	0		
		Rest of World XI		1	2		107	65	53.50		1	1						
		TEST RECORD		**49**	**83**	**7**	**3515**	**194**	**46.25**	**10**	**13**	**60**	**7**	**2**	**12**	**0**		
		CAREER		**118**	**194**	**14**	**7312**	**194**	**40.62**	**21**	**26**	**114**	**57**	**9**	**160**	**5**	**32.00**	**5-40**

RICKARDS, Kenneth Roy

SEASON	TEAM	OPPONENTS	V	BATTING M	I	NO	RUNS	H.S.	AVGE	100	50	CT	BOWLING OV	MD	RUNS	W	AVGE	B.B.
1945-46	Jamaica	Trinidad	IIs	3	6	1	170	67	34.00		2		3	0	17	0		
1946-47	Jamaica	Barbados	IIs	2	4	1	78	44	26.00				17	0	76	1	76.00	
1947-48	Jamaica	British Guiana	IIs	2	3		151	77	50.33		2		2	0	5	0		
1947-48	Jamaica	M.C.C. Tourist	WI	2	4	3	179	*112	179.00	1		1	3	0	15	0		
1947-48	**WEST INDIES**	**ENGLAND TESTS**	**WI**	**1**	**1**		**67**	**67**	**67.00**		**1**							
1948-49	West Indies	Tour of India	I	6	7		247	99	35.28		2	2						
1948-49	West Indies	Tour of Pakistan	P	1	1		72	72	72.00		1	2	2	0	15	0		
1948-49	West Indies	Tour of Ceylon	C	2	1		11	11	11.00			2						
1949-50	Jamaica	Trinidad	IIs	2	4		251	83	62.75		3							
1950-51	Jamaica	British Guiana	IIs	2	3		220	195	73.33	1								
1951-52	West Indies	Tour of Australia	A	4	7		189	59	27.00		1	1						
1951-52	**WEST INDIES**	**AUSTRALIA TESTS**	**A**	**1**	**2**		**37**	**22**	**18.50**									
1951-52	West Indies	Tour of New Zealand	NZ	2	4	1	19	10	6.33			1						
1952	Comm. XI	England XI & Indian Tourist	E	2	4	1	133	69	44.33		1							
1953	Essex	Comm. XI	E	1	2		25	13	12.50									
1953-54	Jamaica	M.C.C. Tourist	WI	2	4		111	75	27.75		1							
1958-59	Jamaica	Leeward Islands	IIs	1	1		56	56	56.00		1		1	1	0	0		
1958-59	Jamaica	Barbados	IIs	1	2		49	28	24.50			1						
		Jamaica		17	31	5	1265	195	48.65	2	9	2	26	1	113	1	113.00	
		West Indies		17	23	1	642	99	29.18		5	8	2	0	15	0		
		Comm. XI		2	4	1	133	69	44.33		1							
		Essex		1	2		25	13	12.50									
		TEST RECORD		**2**	**3**	**0**	**104**	**67**	**34.66**	**0**	**1**	**0**						
		CAREER		**37**	**60**	**7**	**2065**	**195**	**38.96**	**2**	**15**	**10**	**28**	**1**	**128**	**1**	**128.00**	**1-66**

ROACH, Clifford Archibald

SEASON	TEAM	OPPONENTS	V	M	I	NO	RUNS	H.S.	AVGE	100	50	CT	OV	MD	RUNS	W	AVGE	B.B.
				BATTING									BOWLING					
1923-24	Trinidad	British Guiana	IIs	1	2		66	44	33.00				6	2	20	0		
1925-26	Trinidad	M.C.C. Tourist	WI	2	3		65	32	21.66			1						
1926-27	Trinidad	Barbados	IIs	1	2		40	32	20.00			1	15	7	27	0		
1927-28	Combined T/BG XI	Combined Bar/Jam XI	IIs	2	2		98	84	49.00		1	2	4	0	14	0		
1927-28	West Indies XI	Barbados XI	IIs	1	2		34	27	17.00			1	8	0	27	0		
1928	West Indies	Tour of England	E	25	41	1	1091	92	27.27		7	11	48	4	194	2	97.00	
1928	**WEST INDIES**	**ENGLAND TESTS**	**E**	**3**	**6**		**131**	**53**	**21.83**		**2**	**2**						
1928-29	Trinidad	British Guiana	IIs	1	2		52	48	26.00									
1928-29	Trinidad	Barbados	IIs	1	1		86	86	86.00		1	1						
1929-30	Trinidad	British Guiana	IIs	1	2		98	72	49.00		1							
1929-30	Trinidad	M.C.C. Tourist	WI	2	4		24	13	6.00			2	3	1	11	0		
1929-30	**WEST INDIES**	**ENGLAND TESTS**	**WI**	**4**	**8**		**467**	**209**	**58.37**	**2**	**1**		**37**	**5**	**103**	**2**	**51.50**	
1930-31	West Indies	Tour of Australia	A	9	16		443	104	27.68	1	2	7	14	4	63	0		
1930-31	**WEST INDIES**	**AUSTRALIA TESTS**	**A**	**5**	**10**		**194**	**56**	**19.40**		**1**	**3**						
1931-32	Trinidad	Barbados	IIs	1	2		31	25	15.50									
1931-32	Trinidad	British Guiana	IIs	1	2		23	14	11.50									
1932-33	C.A. Merry's XI	G.C. Grant's XI	IIs	1	2		53	33	26.50									
1933	West Indies	Tour of England	E	25	46	2	1145	180	26.02	1	5	9	15	2	42	1	42.00	
1933	**WEST INDIES**	**ENGLAND TESTS**	**E**	**3**	**6**		**141**	**64**	**23.50**		**2**							
1933-34	Trinidad	Barbados	IIs	1	2		39	32	19.50									
1934-35	Trinidad	British Guiana	IIs	1	2		166	128	83.00	1								
1934-35	Trinidad	M.C.C. Tourist	WI	1	2		28	28	14.00				2	0	4	0		
1934-35	**WEST INDIES**	**ENGLAND TESTS**	**WI**	**1**	**2**	**1**	**19**	***10**	**19.00**									
1935-36	Trinidad	Barbados	IIs	1	2		60	46	30.00									
1935-36	Trinidad	British Guiana	IIs	1	2		78	64	39.00		1		4	0	10	0		
1936-37	Trinidad	Barbados	IIs	1	2		96	89	48.00		1	1	3	0	11	0		
1936-37	Trinidad	British Guiana	IIs	1	2		35	28	17.50			1						
1937-38	Trinidad	British Guiana	IIs	1	2		48	31	24.00			1						
		Trinidad		19	36		1035	128	28.75	1	4	8	33	10	83	0		
		West Indies		76	137	4	3665	209	27.55	4	20	33	122	15	429	5	85.80	
		Combined T/BG XI		2	2		98	84	49.00		1	2	4	0	14	0		
		C.A. Merry's XI		1	2		53	33	26.50									
		TEST RECORD		**16**	**32**	**1**	**952**	**209**	**30.70**	**2**	**6**	**5**	**37**	**5**	**103**	**2**	**51.50**	**1-18**
		CAREER		**98**	**177**	**4**	**4851**	**209**	**28.04**	**5**	**25**	**43**	**159**	**25**	**526**	**5**	**105.20**	**1-18**

ROBERTS, *Alphonso Theodore*

SEASON	TEAM	OPPONENTS	V	BATTING M	I	NO	RUNS	H.S.	AVGE	100	50	CT	BOWLING OV	MD	RUNS	W	AVGE	B.B.
1955-56	West Indies	Tour of New Zealand	NZ	4	6	1	109	45	21.80			2						
1955-56	**WEST INDIES**	**NEW ZEALAND TESTS**	**NZ**	**1**	**2**		**28**	**28**	**14.00**									
1956-57	Trinidad	Barbados	IIs	1	2		15	15	7.50									
1959-60	Windward Is.	M.C.C. Tourist	WI	1	2		1	1	0.50			1						
		Trinidad		1	2		15	15	7.50									
		Windward Islands		1	2		1	1	0.50			1						
		West Indies		5	8	1	137	45	19.57			2						
		TEST RECORD		**1**	**2**	**0**	**28**	**28**	**14.00**	**0**	**0**	**0**						
		CAREER		**7**	**12**	**1**	**153**	**45**	**13.90**	**0**	**0**	**3**						

ROBERTS, *Anderson Montgomery Everton*

SEASON	TEAM	OPPONENTS	V	BATTING M	I	NO	RUNS	H.S.	AVGE	100	50	CT	BOWLING OV	MD	RUNS	W	AVGE	B.B.
1969-70	Leeward Islands	Windward Islands	IIs	1	2		17	9	8.50				37	9	64	4	16.00	
1970-71	Leeward Islands	Windward Islands	IIs	1	1		17	17	17.00			1	30	10	74	5	14.80	
1970-71	Combined Islands	Shell Shield	IIs	3	6		64	17	10.66			1	70.4	11	260	9	28.88	
1970-71	Leeward Islands	Indian Tourist	WI	1	2	1	33	27	33.00				16	4	51	0		
1971-72	Leeward Islands	Windward Islands	IIs	1	2	1	12	*6	12.00				19	9	25	1	25.00	
1971-72	Combined Islands	Shell Shield	IIs	2	4	1	37	*26	12.33				48.5	11	119	4	29.75	
1971-72	Leeward Islands	New Zealand Tourist	WI	1	2		10	6	5.00				25.4	7	50	1	50.00	
1972-73	Leeward Islands	Windward Islands	IIs	2	1	1	3	*3					76	30	146	11	13.27	
1972-73	Combined Islands	Shell Shield	IIs	1	1		1	1	1.00				11	0	38	0		
1973	Hampshire	Counties	E	1	2	1	10	10	10.00				34.3	4	144	1	144.00	
1973-74	Combined Islands	Shell Shield	IIs	4	7	4	23	*10	7.66				108.1	18	310	16	19.37	
1973-74	WI President's XI	M.C.C. Tourist	WI	1	2	2	48	*48					34	8	91	2	45.40	
1973-74	Leeward Islands	M.C.C. Tourist	WI	1	1		2	2	2.00				43.3	6	140	5	28.00	
1973-74	**WEST INDIES**	**ENGLAND TESTS**	**WI**	**1**	**1**	**1**	**9**	***9**				**1**	**50**	**12**	**124**	**3**	**41.33**	
1974	Hampshire	Counties	E	21	20	10	67	15	6.70			2	727.4	198	1621	119	13.62	
1974-75	West Indies	Tour of India	I	4	1	1	2	*2					89	11	279	13	21.46	
1974-75	**WEST INDIES**	**INDIA TESTS**	**I**	**5**	**6**	**1**	**26**	**17**	**5.20**			**1**	**208.3**	**51**	**585**	**32**	**18.28**	
1974-75	West Indies	Tour of Sri Lanka	SL	1	1	1	13	*13				1	32	4	71	6	11.83	
1974-75	**WEST INDIES**	**PAKISTAN TESTS**	**P**	**2**	**2**		**6**	**6**	**3.00**				**190**	**12**	**322**	**12**	**26.83**	
1974-75	Combined Islands	Shell Shield	IIs	4	7	1	58	*16	9.66				131.5	39	318	25	12.72	

1975	Hampshire	Counties	E	13	16	5	195	39	17.72		5	418.3	141	901	57	15.80
1975-76	West Indies	Tour of Australia	A	4	5		104	32	20.80		1	94.1	11	313	13	24.07
1975-76	**WEST INDIES**	**AUSTRALIA TESTS**	**A**	**5**	**9**		**40**	**17**	**4.44**			**141.6**	**15**	**580**	**22**	**26.36**
1975-76	Leeward Islands	Indian Tourist	WI	1	D						1	13	2	27	2	13.50
1975-76	**WEST INDIES**	**INDIA TESTS**	**WI**	**2**	**3**	**1**	**5**	***4**	**2.50**			**53**	**12**	**176**	**6**	**29.33**
1976	West Indies	Tour of England	E	7	5	2	90	*56	30.00	1	2	189.5	40	552	16	34.50
1976	**WEST INDIES**	**ENGLAND TESTS**	**E**	**5**	**5**		**45**	**19**	**9.00**		**3**	**221.4**	**69**	**537**	**28**	**19.17**
1976-77	New South Wales	Sheffield Shield	A	2	2	1	12	8	12.00			32.3	5	87	3	29.00
1976-77	Combined Islands	Shell Shield	IIs	3	5		38	14	7.60		2	99.5	19	300	16	18.75
1976-77	Leeward Islands	Pakistan Tourist	WI	1	2		13	13	6.50			23	4	56	0	
1976-77	**WEST INDIES**	**PAKISTAN TESTS**	**WI**	**5**	**8**	**2**	**87**	**35**	**10.87**			**236.3**	**37**	**763**	**19**	**40.15**
1977	Hampshire	Counties	E	14	13	2	102	19	9.27		4	349.2	109	793	40	19.82
1977-78	**WEST INDIES**	**AUSTRALIA TESTS**	**WI**	**2**	**2**		**11**	**7**	**5.50**			**64.3**	**14**	**211**	**12**	**17.58**
1978	Hampshire	Counties	E	9	14	5	209	*37	23.22			254.1	74	617	27	22.85
1978-79	Combined Islands	Shell Shield	IIs	1	2		62	62	31.00	1		36.1	11	94	3	31.33
1979-80	West Indies	Tour of Australia	A	2	1		11	11	11.00		1	56.3	11	157	7	22.42
1979-80	**WEST INDIES**	**AUSTRALIA TESTS**	**A**	**3**	**4**		**78**	**54**	**19.50**	**1**	**2**	**112**	**20**	**296**	**11**	**26.90**
1979-80	West Indies	Tour of New Zealand	NZ	1	1		0	0				10	1	39	0	
1979-80	**WEST INDIES**	**NEW ZEALAND TESTS**	**NZ**	**2**	**3**	**2**	**78**	***35**	**78.00**			**72**	**14**	**196**	**3**	**65.33**
1979-80	Combined Islands	Shell Shield	IIs	4	6	2	104	*29	26.00		3	127	29	330	9	36.67
1980	West Indies	Tour of England	E	6	6		36	31	6.00			129	33	395	16	24.68
1980	**WEST INDIES**	**ENGLAND TESTS**	**E**	**3**	**4**	**1**	**78**	**24**	**26.00**			**105.2**	**24**	**262**	**11**	**23.81**
1980-81	Leeward Islands	Windward Islands	IIs	1	1		20	20	20.00		1	22	5	51	2	25.50
1980-81	Combined Islands	Shell Shield	IIs	4	6		96	63	16.00	1	4	104.1	28	248	25	9.92
1980-81	**WEST INDIES**	**ENGLAND TESTS**	**WI**	**3**	**4**	**1**	**77**	***50**	**25.66**	**1**	**1**	**104**	**28**	**251**	**8**	**31.37**
1981	Leicestershire	Counties	E	11	17	2	347	57	23.13	2	2	310.1	80	923	37	24.94
1981-82	West Indies	Tour of Australia	A	2	2	1	33	33	33.00		1	71	20	140	7	20.00
1981-82	**WEST INDIES**	**AUSTRALIA TESTS**	**A**	**2**	**3**		**70**	**42**	**23.33**			**76**	**24**	**178**	**6**	**29.66**
1981-82	Leeward Islands	Shell Shield	IIs	4	7	1	35	22	5.87		2	142.4	37	398	24	16.58
1982	Leicestershire	Counties	E	13	20	3	338	47	19.88		4	427.2	114	1081	55	19.65
1982-83	West Indies XI	International XI	WI	1	1		34	34	34.00			17	3	44	2	22.00
1982-83	Leeward Is.lands	Shell Shield	IIs	5	9	2	62	16	8.85		2	162.1	29	514	28	18.35
1982-83	**WEST INDIES**	**INDIA TESTS**	**WI**	**5**	**6**	**1**	**84**	**36**	**16.80**		**1**	**187.5**	**36**	**545**	**24**	**22.70**
1983	Leicestershire	Counties	E	4	3		22	15	7.33			101.2	19	294	16	18.37
1983-84	West Indies	Tour of India	I	5	5	2	63	29	21.00			92	29	207	6	34.50
1983-84	**WEST INDIES**	**INDIA TESTS**	**I**	**2**	**2**	**1**	**68**	**68**	**68.00**	**1**		**55.4**	**14**	**148**	**5**	**29.60**
1983-84	Leeward Islands	Shell Shield	IIs	5	6	1	123	54	24.60	1	1	142.5	34	374	21	17.80
		Leeward Islands		25	36	7	347	54	11.96	1	8	752.5	186	1970	104	18.94

SEASON	TEAM			M	I	NO	RUNS	H.S.	AVGE	100	50	CT	OV	MD	RUNS	W	AVGE	B.B.
				BATTING									BOWLING					
		Combined Islands		26	44	8	483	63	13.41		2	10	737.4	166	2017	107	18.85	
		West Indies		81	92	20	1196	68	16.61		4	15	2693.3	553	7462	290	25.73	
		Hampshire		58	65	23	583	39	13.88			11	1784.1	526	4076	244	16.70	
		Leicestershire		28	40	5	707	57	20.20		2	6	838.5	213	2298	108	21.27	
		New South Wales		2	2	1	12	8	12.00				32.3	5	87	3	29.00	
		TEST RECORD		**47**	**62**	**11**	**762**	**68**	**14.94**	**0**	**3**	**9**	**1878.4**	**382**	**5174**	**202**	**25.61**	**7-54**
		CAREER		**220**	**279**	**64**	**3328**	**68**	**15.47**	**0**	**9**	**50**	**6839.3**	**1649**	**17910**	**856**	**20.92**	**8-47**

RODRIGUEZ, William Vincente

SEASON	TEAM	OPPONENTS		V	M	I	NO	RUNS	H.S.	AVGE	100	50	CT	OV	MD	RUNS	W	AVGE	B.B.
					BATTING									BOWLING					
1953-54	Trinidad	British Guiana		IIs	1	2		64	38	32.00									
1954-55	Trinidad	Australian Tourist		WI	1	2		33	26	16.50				4	0	22	1	22.00	
1957-58	Trinidad	Pakistan Tourist		WI	1	1		105	105	105.00	1			14	0	56	0		
1958-59	West Indies	Tour of India		I	8	10	2	114	30	14.25			6	88	10	382	16	23.87	
1958-59	West Indies	Tour of Pakistan		P	2	3		96	58	32.00		1	4	19.4	3	74	2	37.00	
1959-60	Trinidad	M.C.C. Tourist		WI	2	4		30	25	7.50				7.2	2	35	0		
1960-61	Trinidad	Barbados		IIs	1	2		45	40	22.50			1						
1960-61	Trinidad	E.W. Swanton's Tourist		WI	1	2		65	40	32.50			1	10	0	34	0		
1960-61	N. Trinidad	South Trinidad	BC	T	1	1		33	33	33.00			1	11	4	30	2	15.00	
1961-62	Trinidad	British Guiana		IIs	1	2		101	80	50.50		1		53	14	180	4	45.00	
1961-62	Trinidad	Indian Tourist		WI	1	2	1	80	77	80.00		1	1	37	12	99	4	24.75	
1961-62	**WEST INDIES**	**INDIA TESTS**		**WI**	**2**	**2**		**53**	**50**	**26.50**		**1**	**3**	**36.3**	**3**	**143**	**3**	**47.66**	
1961-62	N. Trinidad	South Trinidad	BC	T	1	2		62	42	31.00				26	5	97	4	24.25	
1963	West Indies	Tour of England		E	11	15	4	380	93	34.54		3	8	59	6	240	4	60.00	
1963	**WEST INDIES**	**ENGLAND TESTS**		**E**	**1**	**2**		**33**	**28**	**16.50**									
1963-64	West Indies XI	The Rest XI		WI	1	2		23	16	11.50			1	2	0	4	1	4.00	
1963-64	C. Hunte's XI	F. Worrell's XI		WI	1	2		80	43	40.00				16	0	86	1	86.00	
1963-64	Trinidad	Jamaica		IIs	1	2		99	79	49.50		1		23.4	6	81	3	27.00	
1963-64	Trinidad	British Guiana		IIs	1	2	1	9	9	9.00				16	2	86	0		
1963-64	N. Trinidad	South Trinidad	BC	T	1	2		3	3	1.50			2	6	0	21	2	10.50	
1964-65	Trinidad	Australian Tourist		WI	1	2	1	36	28	36.00				22	1	87	2	43.50	
1964-65	**WEST INDIES**	**AUSTRALIA TESTS**		**WI**	**1**	**2**		**10**	**9**	**5.00**				**14**	**2**	**52**	**0**		
1965-66	Trinidad	Shell Shield		IIs	4	7		149	55	21.28		1	1	104.3	18	327	12	27.25	
1965-66	N. Trinidad	South Trinidad	BC	T	1	2		40	25	20.00			1	7	1	111	8	13.87	

SEASON	TEAM	OPPONENTS	V	M	I	NO	RUNS	H.S.	AVGE	100	50	CT	OV	MD	RUNS	W	AVGE	B.B.
1966-67	Trinidad	Shell Shield	IIs	4	7	2	102	29	20.40			1	51.3	7	159	1	159.00	
1966-67	N. Trinidad	South Trinidad BC	T	1	1		1	1	1.00			2	32	6	93	3	31.00	
1967-68	Trinidad	M.C.C. Tourist	WI	1	1		22	22	22.00				25.2	9	63	6	10.50	
1967-68	**WEST INDIES**	**ENGLAND TESTS**	**WI**	**1**	**1**		**0**	**0**					**45**	**5**	**179**	**4**	**44.75**	
1967-68	N. Trinidad	South Trinidad BC	T	1	1		6	6	6.00				10	3	27	1	27.00	
1968-69	Trinidad	Shell Shield	IIs	4	6	1	101	*40	20.20			1	87.3	22	241	17	14.17	
1969-70	Trinidad	Shell Shield	IIs	4	4	2	60	*39	30.00			2	98	20	263	17	15.47	
1969-70	Trinidad	Glamorgan Tourist	WI	1	2	1	26	*25	26.00				25	5	70	1	70.00	
		Trinidad		30	50	9	1127	105	27.48	1	4	8	578.5	118	1803	68	26.51	
		North Trinidad		6	9		145	42	16.11			6	92	19	379	20	18.95	
		West Indies		27	37	6	709	93	22.87		5	22	264.1	29	1074	30	35.80	
		C. Hunte's XI		1	2		80	43	40.00				16	0	86	1	86.00	
		TEST RECORD		**5**	**7**	**0**	**96**	**50**	**13.71**	**0**	**1**	**3**	**95.3**	**10**	**374**	**7**	**53.42**	**3-51**
		CAREER		**64**	**98**	**15**	**2061**	**105**	**24.83**	**1**	**9**	**36**	**951**	**166**	**3342**	**119**	**28.08**	**7-90**

ROWE, Lawrence George

				BATTING									BOWLING					
SEASON	TEAM	OPPONENTS	V	M	I	NO	RUNS	H.S.	AVGE	100	50	CT	OV	MD	RUNS	W	AVGE	B.B.
1968-69	Jamaica	Shell Shield	IIs	4	6		84	54	14.00		1	1						
1969	Cavaliers XI	Barbados Touring XI	E	1	2		9	8	4.50			1						
1969-70	Jamaica	Cavaliers Touring XI	WI	1	2		152	109	76.00	1		3						
1969-70	Jamaica	Shell Shield	IIs	4	8	1	285	88	40.71		2	4						
1970	Jamaica	Tour of England	E	4	5		125	52	25.00		1	5	10	4	23	0		
1970-71	Jamaica	Shell Shield	IIs	4	6		312	114	52.00	1	1	4						
1970-71	WI President's XI	Indian Tourist	WI	1	2		50	27	25.00									
1970-71	Jamaica	Indian Tourist	WI	1	2	1	38	*19	38.00									
1971-72	Jamaica	Shell Shield	IIs	4	7		249	147	35.57	1		6						
1971-72	Jamaica	New Zealand Tourist	WI	1	1		227	227	227.00	1			1	0	2	0		
1971-72	**WEST INDIES**	**NEW ZEALAND TESTS**	**WI**	**4**	**7**	**1**	**419**	**214**	**69.83**	**2**	**1**	**1**	**5**	**0**	**28**	**0**		
1972-73	Jamaica	Shell Shield	IIs	4	8	1	238	69	34.00		2	3						
1972-73	Jamaica	Australian Tourist	WI	1	2		173	149	86.50	1		1						
1972-73	**WEST INDIES**	**AUSTRALIA TESTS**	**WI**	**3**	**3**		**96**	**76**	**32.00**		**1**	**2**						
1973	West Indies	Tour of England	E	8	13	1	344	84	28.66		2	6						
1973-74	Jamaica	Shell Shield	IIs	4	6	1	342	204	68.40	1	1	8	4	1	17	0		
1973-74	Jamaica	M.C.C. Tourist	WI	1	2		159	118	79.50	1								
1973-74	**WEST INDIES**	**ENGLAND TESTS**	**WI**	**5**	**7**		**616**	**302**	**88.00**	**3**		**5**	**3**	**1**	**6**	**0**		

				BATTING									BOWLING					
SEASON	TEAM	OPPONENTS	V	M	I	NO	RUNS	H.S.	AVGE	100	50	CT	OV	MD	RUNS	W	AVGE	B.B.
1974	Derbyshire	Counties	E	17	30	1	1059	94	36.51		7	15	27.4	7	84	1	84.00	
1974-75	West Indies	Tour of India	I	2	3	1	16	*15	8.00									
1974-75	Jamaica	Shell Shield	IIs	4	7		269	92	38.42		3	3						
1975-76	West Indies	Tour of Australia	A	4	6		164	74	27.32		1	3	2	0	13	0		
1975-76	**WEST INDIES**	**AUSTRALIA TESTS**	**A**	**6**	**11**		**270**	**107**	**24.54**	**1**	**1**	**2**	**1**	**0**	**6**	**0**		
1975-76	Jamaica	Indian Tourist	WI	1	2	1	92	76	92.00		1		1	0	2	0		
1975-76	**WEST INDIES**	**INDIA TESTS**	**WI**	**4**	**7**	**1**	**179**	**47**	**29.83**			**3**						
1976	West Indies	Tour of England	E	15	24	1	845	152	36.73	2	2	11						
1976	**WEST INDIES**	**ENGLAND TESTS**	**E**	**2**	**3**		**126**	**70**	**42.00**		**2**							
1976-77	Jamaica	Shell Shield	IIs	2	2		20	18	10.00			1						
1977-78	Jamaica	Australian Tourist	WI	1	2		57	31	28.50									
1979-80	West Indies	Tour of Australia	A	3	4		127	82	31.75		1							
1979-80	**WEST INDIES**	**AUSTRALIA TESTS**	**A**	**3**	**5**		**162**	**50**	**32.40**		**1**	**3**						
1979-80	West Indies	Tour of New Zealand	NZ	2	4		129	74	32.25		1							
1979-80	**WEST INDIES**	**NEW ZEALAND TESTS**	**NZ**	**3**	**6**		**179**	**100**	**29.83**	**1**	**1**	**1**	**5**	**2**	**4**	**0**		
1979-80	Jamaica	Shell Shield	IIs	2	4		141	94	35.25		1	4	10	0	30	1	30.00	
1980	West Indies	Tour of England	E	3	2		13	13	6.50			2						
1980-81	Jamaica	Shell Shield	IIs	4	7	1	230	76	38.33		5	4						
1980-81	Jamaica	English Tourist	WI	1	1		116	116	116.00	1								
1981-82	Jamaica	Shell Shield	IIs	5	9		178	73	19.77		1	10						
1982-83	West Indies XI	International XI	WI	1	1		47	47	47.00				1	0	9	0		
1982-83	WI Rebels XI	Tour of South Africa	SA	2	4		35	26	8.75			3						
1983-84	WI Rebels XI	Tour of South Africa	SA	7	12		383	157	31.91	1		3						
		Jamaica		53	89	6	3487	227	42.01	8	19	57	26	5	74	1	74.00	
		West Indies		69	108	5	3782	302	36.71	9	14	39	17	3	66	0		
		Derbyshire		17	30	1	1059	94	36.51		7	15	27.4	7	84	1	84.00	
		WI Rebels XI		9	16		418	157	26.12	1		6						
		Cavaliers XI		1	2		9	8	4.50			1						
		TEST RECORD		**30**	**49**	**2**	**2047**	**302**	**43.55**	**7**	**7**	**17**	**14**	**3**	**44**	**0**		
		CAREER		**149**	**245**	**12**	**8755**	**302**	**37.58**	**18**	**40**	**118**	**70.4**	**15**	**224**	**2**	**112.00**	**1-19**

ST. HILL, Edwin Lloyd

SEASON	TEAM	OPPONENTS	V	BATTING M	I	NO	RUNS	H.S.	AVGE	100	50	CT	BOWLING OV	MD	RUNS	W	AVGE	B.B.
1923-24	Trinidad	British Guiana	IIs	1	2	1	0	*0				2	40	18	56	6	9.33	
1923-24	Trinidad	Barbados	IIs	1	2		41	35	20.50			1	40.1	10	101	5	20.20	
1924-25	Trinidad	Barbados	IIs	1	2	1	23	17	23.00				54	13	101	2	50.50	
1925-26	Trinidad	British Guiana	IIs	1	1		0	0				2	77	11	155	5	31.00	
1925-26	Trinidad	M.C.C. Tourist	WI	2	3	2	29	*19	29.00				51.4	10	137	4	34.25	
1926-27	Trinidad	Barbados	IIs	1	2		31	27	15.50				76	23	171	3	57.00	
1928-29	Trinidad	British Guiana	IIs	1	2		13	8	6.50			1	39	20	48	2	24.00	
1928-29	Trinidad	Barbados	IIs	1	1	1	20	*20	20.00			1	20	4	58	4	14.50	
1929-30	Trinidad	British Guiana	IIs	1	2		77	67	38.50		1		83.4	25	204	10	20.40	
1929-30	Trinidad	M.C.C. Tourist	WI	1	2		6	3	3.00				42.4	9	103	4	25.75	
1929-30	**WEST INDIES**	**ENGLAND TESTS**	**WI**	**2**	**4**		**18**	**12**	**4.50**				**93**	**29**	**221**	**3**	**73.66**	
1930-31	West Indies	Tour of Australia	A	4	6	1	16	9	3.20			2	151.1	10	477	16	29.81	
		Trinidad		11	19	5	240	67	17.14		1	7	524.1	143	1134	45	25.20	
		West Indies		6	10	1	34	12	3.77			2	244.1	39	698	19	36.73	
		TEST RECORD		**2**	**4**	**0**	**18**	**12**	**4.50**	**0**	**0**	**0**	**93**	**29**	**221**	**3**	**73.66**	**2-110**
		CAREER		**17**	**29**	**6**	**274**	**67**	**11.91**	**0**	**1**	**9**	**768.2**	**182**	**1832**	**64**	**28.62**	**6-117**

ST. HILL, Wilton H.

SEASON	TEAM	OPPONENTS	V	BATTING M	I	NO	RUNS	H.S.	AVGE	100	50	CT	BOWLING OV	MD	RUNS	W	AVGE	B.B.
1911-12	Trinidad	British Guiana	IIs	1	1		4	4	4.00									
1911-12	Trinidad	Barbados	IIs	1	2	1	62	*59	62.00		1	1						
1912-13	Trinidad	M.C.C. Tourist	WI	2	3		76	33	25.33			1						
1919-20	Trinidad	Barbados	IIs	2	4		157	96	39.25		1	1	6.4	0	50	0		
1921-22	Trinidad	British Guiana	IIs	1	1		104	104	104.00	1			16.5	6	31	3	10.33	
1921-22	Trinidad	Barbados	IIs	1	2		54	48	27.00				3	1	7	0		
1922-23	Trinidad	British Guiana	IIs	1	2		13	13	6.50				2	1	1	0		
1922-23	Trinidad	Barbados	IIs	1	2		36	36	18.00			1	3	0	17	0		
1923-24	Trinidad	British Guiana	IIs	1	2		23	17	11.50									
1923-24	Trinidad	Barbados	IIs	1	2	1	8	6	8.00			1						
1924-25	Trinidad	British Guiana	IIs	1	2		42	29	21.00			2						
1924-25	Trinidad	Barbados	IIs	1	2		130	66	65.00		2		2	0	6	0		
1925-26	Trinidad	British Guiana	IIs	1	2		100	100	50.00	1								

				BATTING									BOWLING					
SEASON	TEAM	OPPONENTS	V	M	I	NO	RUNS	H.S.	AVGE	100	50	CT	OV	MD	RUNS	W	AVGE	B.B.
1925-26	Trinidad	M.C.C. Tourist	WI	2	3		170	105	56.66	1			2	0	17	0		
1925-26	West Indies XI	M.C.C. Tourist	WI	3	4		141	72	35.25		1	1						
1926-27	Trinidad	Barbados	IIs	1	2		18	18	9.00			1	4	0	6	0		
1927-28	Combined T/BG XI	Combined Bar/Jam XI	IIs	2	2		189	144	94.50	1		1						
1927-28	West Indies XI	Barbados XI	IIs	1	2		115	71	57.50		1	1	10	0	33	2	16.50	
1928	West Indies	Tour of England	E	12	21	1	208	58	10.40		1	2						
1928	**WEST INDIES**	**ENGLAND TESTS**	**E**	**2**	**4**		**54**	**38**	**13.50**			**1**						
1928-29	Trinidad	British Guiana	IIs	1	2		27	23	13.50									
1928-29	Trinidad	Barbados	IIs	1	1		5	5	5.00									
1929-30	Trinidad	British Guiana	IIs	1	2		11	6	10.50				7	0	32	0		
1929-30	Trinidad	M.C.C. Tourist	WI	1	2		118	102	59.00	1								
1929-30	**WEST INDIES**	**ENGLAND TESTS**	**WI**	**1**	**2**		**63**	**33**	**31.50**				**2**	**0**	**9**	**0**		
		Trinidad		22	39	2	1158	105	31.29	4	4	8	46.3	8	167	3	55.66	
		West Indies		19	33	1	581	72	18.15		3	5	12	0	42	2	21.00	
		Combined T/BG XI		2	2		189	144	94.50	1		1						
		TEST RECORD		**3**	**6**	**0**	**117**	**38**	**19.50**	**0**	**0**	**1**	**2**	**0**	**9**	**0**		
		CAREER		**43**	**74**	**3**	**1928**	**144**	**27.15**	**5**	**7**	**14**	**58.3**	**8**	**209**	**5**	**41.80**	**2-14**

SCARLETT, Reginald Osmond

				BATTING									BOWLING					
SEASON	TEAM	OPPONENTS	V	M	I	NO	RUNS	H.S.	AVGE	100	50	CT	OV	MD	RUNS	W	AVGE	B.B.
1951-52	Jamaica	Barbados	IIs	1	2		7	7	3.50				30	5	108	3	36.00	
1952-53	Jamaica	British Guiana	IIs	2	3	1	40	28	20.00			1	23	4	58	0		
1953-54	Jamaica	M.C.C. Tourist	WI	2	3		6	3	2.00			1	87	17	234	8	29.25	
1954-55	Jamaica	Trinidad	IIs	1	2		38	21	19.00				11	1	34	1	34.00	
1954-55	Jamaica	Australian Tourist	WI	1	1		25	25	25.00			1	46	6	137	3	45.66	
1957-58	Jamaica	Pakistan Tourist	WI	1	1		34	34	34.00				41	7	114	5	22.80	
1958-59	Jamaica	Leeward Islands	IIs	1	1	1	11	*11					48	13	101	1	101.00	
1958-59	Jamaica	Barbados	IIs	2	4		58	34	14.50			1	88.5	19	277	14	19.78	
1959-60	Jamaica	Trinidad	IIs	1	2	2	54	*49					45.3	14	128	5	25.60	
1959-60	Jamaica	British Guiana	IIs	1	2	1	19	*11	19.00				62	23	125	3	41.66	
1959-60	Jamaica	M.C.C. Tourist	WI	1	2	1	131	*72	131.00		2		33.3	9	113	3	37.66	
1959-60	**WEST INDIES**	**ENGLAND TESTS**	**WI**	**3**	**4**	**1**	**54**	***29**	**18.00**			**2**	**134**	**53**	**209**	**2**	**104.50**	

SEASON	TEAM	OPPONENTS	V	M	I	NO	RUNS	H.S.	AVGE	100	50	CT	OV	MD	RUNS	W	AVGE	B.B.
		Jamaica		14	23	6	423	*72	24.88		2	4	515.5	118	1429	46	31.06	
		West Indies		3	4	1	54	*29	18.00			2	134	53	209	2	104.50	
		TEST RECORD		**3**	**4**	**1**	**54**	***29**	**18.00**	**0**	**0**	**2**	**134**	**53**	**209**	**2**	**104.50**	**1-46**
		CAREER		**17**	**27**	**7**	**477**	***72**	**23.85**	**0**	**2**	**6**	**649.5**	**171**	**1638**	**48**	**34.12**	**5-69**

SCOTT, Alfred P. H.

				BATTING									BOWLING					
SEASON	**TEAM**	**OPPONENTS**	**V**	**M**	**I**	**NO**	**RUNS**	**H.S.**	**AVGE**	**100**	**50**	**CT**	**OV**	**MD**	**RUNS**	**W**	**AVGE**	**B.B.**
1952-53	Jamaica	British Guiana	IIs	2	1	1	17	*17				2	87.1	13	270	9	30.00	
1952-53	Jamaica	Indian Tourist	WI	1	2		13	13	6.50			1	38	9	96	7	13.71	
1952-53	**WEST INDIES**	**INDIA TESTS**	**WI**	**1**	**1**		**5**	**5**	**5.00**				**44**	**9**	**140**	**0**		
1953-54	Jamaica	M.C.C. Tourist	WI	1	1	1	3	*3					30	4	88	2	44.00	
		Jamaica		4	4	2	33	*17	11.00			3	155.1	26	454	18	25.22	
		West Indies		1	1		5	5	5.00				44	9	140	0		
		TEST RECORD		**1**	**1**	**0**	**5**	**5**	**5.00**	**0**	**0**	**0**	**44**	**9**	**140**	**0**		
		CAREER		**5**	**5**	**2**	**38**	***17**	**12.66**	**0**	**0**	**3**	**199.1**	**35**	**594**	**18**	**33.00**	**4-46**

SCOTT, Oscar Charles

				BATTING									BOWLING					
SEASON	**TEAM**	**OPPONENTS**	**V**	**M**	**I**	**NO**	**RUNS**	**H.S.**	**AVGE**	**100**	**50**	**CT**	**OV**	**MD**	**RUNS**	**W**	**AVGE**	**B.B.**
1910-11	Jamaica	M.C.C. Tourist	WI	1	2		3	2	1.50			1	43	7	138	11	12.54	
1924-25	Jamaica	Barbados	IIs	3	5		197	94	39.40		2	1	37	1	123	2	61.50	
1925-26	Jamaica	M.C.C. Tourist	WI	3	5		260	72	52.00		4	1	100	9	353	8	44.12	
1926-27	Jamaica	L.H. Tennyson's Tourist	WI	3	3		28	15	9.33			3	166.4	29	506	15	33.73	
1927-28	Jamaica	L.H. Tennyson's Tourist	WI	3	4		78	24	19.50			1	191	42	479	24	19.95	
1928	West Indies	Tour of England	E	10	15	2	248	75	19.07		2	4	210.4	19	803	23	34.91	
1928	**WEST INDIES**	**ENGLAND TESTS**	**E**	**2**	**4**	**1**	**74**	**35**	**24.66**				**23.2**	**1**	**103**	**2**	**51.50**	
1928-29	Jamaica	Julien Cahn's Tourist	WI	2	3	1	106	44	53.00				120	17	396	14	28.28	
1928-29	West Indies XI	Julien Cahn's Tourist	WI	1	2	1	21	*20	21.00				35	5	170	3	56.66	
1929-30	Jamaica	M.C.C. Tourist	WI	1	1	1	24	*24					75	9	256	10	25.60	
1929-30	**WEST INDIES**	**ENGLAND TESTS**	**WI**	**1**	**1**		**8**	**8**	**8.00**				**105.2**	**13**	**374**	**9**	**41.55**	
1930-31	West Indies	Tour of Australia	A	7	11	3	162	*67	20.25		1		187.5	7	877	29	30.24	
1930-31	**WEST INDIES**	**AUSTRALIA TESTS**	**A**	**5**	**8**	**2**	**89**	***20**	**14.83**				**104.5**	**3**	**448**	**11**	**40.72**	
1931-32	Jamaica	L.H. Tennyson's Tourist	WI	2	1		4	4	4.00			3	124	14	448	19	23.57	

SEASON	TEAM	OPPONENTS	V	M	I	NO	RUNS (Batting)	H.S.	AVGE (Batting)	100	50	CT	OV	MD	RUNS (Bowling)	W	AVGE (Bowling)	B.B.
1934-35	Jamaica	M.C.C. Tourist	WI	1	1	1	15	*15					22	0	82	2	41.00	
		Jamaica		19	25	3	715	94	32.50		6	10	878.4	128	2781	105	26.48	
		West Indies		26	41	9	602	75	18.81		3	4	667	48	2775	77	36.03	
		TEST RECORD		**8**	**13**	**3**	**171**	**35**	**17.10**	**0**	**0**	**0**	**233.3**	**17**	**925**	**22**	**42.04**	**5-266**
		CAREER		**45**	**66**	**12**	**1317**	**94**	**24.38**	**0**	**9**	**14**	**1545.4**	**176**	**5556**	**182**	**30.52**	**8-67**

SEALEY, Benjamin James

SEASON	TEAM	OPPONENTS	V	M	I	NO	RUNS (Batting)	H.S.	AVGE (Batting)	100	50	CT	OV	MD	RUNS (Bowling)	W	AVGE (Bowling)	B.B.
1923-24	Trinidad	British Guiana	IIs	1	2		15	9	7.50			1	9.1	1	26	4	6.50	
1923-24	Trinidad	Barbados	IIs	1	2		15	15	7.50			1	3	1	5	0		
1925-26	Trinidad	British Guiana	IIs	1	2	2	10	*8					8	1	27	0		
1926-27	Trinidad	Barbados	IIs	1	2	1	99	*98	99.00		1		9	0	29	0		
1927-28	Combined T/BG XI	Combined Bar/Jam XI	IIs	2	2		54	47	27.00									
1927-28	Barbados XI	West Indies XI	IIs	1	1		5	5	5.00			2	29	2	147	3	49.00	
1928-29	Trinidad	British Guiana	IIs	1	2		24	19	12.00			2	5	2	4	0		
1928-29	Trinidad	Barbados	IIs	1	1		37	37	37.00			1	10	1	25	5	5.00	
1929-30	Trinidad	British Guiana	IIs	1	2		11	11	5.50				17	7	29	0		
1929-30	Trinidad	M.C.C. Tourist	WI	2	4		60	48	15.00			2	42	22	77	8	9.62	
1931-32	Trinidad	Barbados	IIs	1	2	1	24	*15	24.00				28	10	50	5	10.00	
1931-32	Trinidad	British Guiana	IIs	1	2		99	90	49.50		1		56	20	89	3	29.66	
1932-33	C.A. Merry's XI	G.C. Grant's XI	IIs	1	2		37	37	18.50				16	1	66	4	16.50	
1933	West Indies	Tour of England	E	21	32	7	1031	*106	41.24	3	5	8	261	45	715	18	39.72	
1933	**WEST INDIES**	**ENGLAND TESTS**	**E**	**1**	**2**		**41**	**29**	**20.50**				**5**	**1**	**10**	**1**	**10.00**	
1933-34	Trinidad	Barbados	IIs	1	2		11	9	5.50			1	17	9	22	1	22.00	
1934-35	Trinidad	British Guiana	IIs	1	2		41	23	20.50				6	3	6	0		
1934-35	Trinidad	M.C.C. Tourist	WI	1	2		9	8	4.50				23	8	42	5	8.40	
1935-36	Trinidad	Barbados	IIs	1	2		65	49	32.50				40	12	74	0		
1935-36	Trinidad	British Guiana	IIs	1	2		16	16	8.00				16	3	28	1	28.00	
1936-37	Trinidad	Barbados	IIs	1	2		56	38	28.00				27	5	66	1	66.00	
1936-37	Trinidad	British Guiana	IIs	1	2	1	69	*58	69.00		1		34	9	66	4	16.50	
1937-38	Trinidad	British Guiana	IIs	1	2		87	83	43.50		1	1	57	19	103	5	20.60	
1938-39	R.S. Grant's XI	British Guiana	IIs	2	3		39	24	19.50				90	16	237	4	59.25	
1938-39	Trinidad	Barbados	IIs	1	1		116	116	116.00	1			6	1	10	0		

SEASON	TEAM	OPPONENTS	V	M	I	NO	RUNS	H.S.	AVGE	100	50	CT/St	OV	MD	RUNS	W	AVGE	B.B.
1938-39	Trinidad	British Guiana	IIs	1	1		2	2	2.00			2	5	2	11	2	5.50	
1938-39	Trinidad	Jamaica	IIs	1	2		10	8	5.00				16.1	5	32	4	8.00	
1940-41	Trinidad	Barbados	IIs	1	1		32	32	32.00			1	5	0	30	0		
		Trinidad		23	42	5	908	116	24.54	1	4	12	439.2	141	851	48	17.72	
		West Indies		22	34	7	1072	*106	39.70	3	5	8	266	46	725	19	38.15	
		C.A. Merry's XI		1	2		37	37	18.50				16	1	66	4	16.50	
		Combined T/BG XI		2	2		54	47	27.00									
		R.S. Grant's XI		2	3		39	24					90	16	237	4	59.25	
		Barbados XI		1	1		5	5	5.00			2	29	2	147	3	49.00	
		TEST RECORD		**1**	**2**	**0**	**41**	**29**	**20.50**	**0**	**0**	**0**	**5**	**1**	**10**	**1**	**10.00**	**1-10**
		CAREER		**51**	**84**	**12**	**2115**	**116**	**29.37**	**4**	**9**	**22**	**840.2**	**206**	**2026**	**78**	**25.97**	**5-22**

SEALY, James Edward Derek

				BATTING									BOWLING					
SEASON	TEAM	OPPONENTS	V	M	I	NO	RUNS	H.S.	AVGE	100	50	CT/St	OV	MD	RUNS	W	AVGE	B.B.
1928-29	Barbados	Trinidad	IIs	1	2		16	9	8.00									
1929-30	Barbados	British Guiana	IIs	1	2		6	6	3.00			1	3	0	15	0		
1929-30	Barbados	M.C.C. Tourist	WI	2	3		202	100	67.33	1	1	3	10	1	31	0		
1929-30	**WEST INDIES**	**ENGLAND TESTS**	**WI**	**2**	**4**		**83**	**58**	**20.75**		**1**							
1930-31	West Indies	Tour of Australia	A	6	9	3	304	92	50.66		2	9	22.2	2	95	2	47.50	
1930-31	**WEST INDIES**	**AUSTRALIA TESTS**	**A**	**2**	**4**	**1**	**30**	***16**	**10.00**			**2**	**3**	**0**	**32**	**0**		
1931-32	Barbados	Trinidad	IIs	1	2		4	4	2.00				3	1	20	0		
1932-33	C.A. Merry's XI	G.C. Grant's XI	IIs	1	2		16	15	8.00			2/2						
1933-34	Barbados	British Guiana	IIs	1	2		46	36	23.00				26	6	55	3	18.33	
1933-34	Barbados	Trinidad	IIs	1	2		133	107	66.50	1		4	30	10	51	3	17.00	
1934-35	Barbados	British Guiana	IIs	1	2		9	8	4.50				33	6	76	2	38.00	
1934-35	Barbados	M.C.C. Tourist	WI	2	3		107	87	35.66		1	1						
1934-35	**WEST INDIES**	**ENGLAND TESTS**	**WI**	**4**	**6**		**270**	**92**	**45.00**		**2**		**19**	**4**	**41**	**3**	**13.66**	
1935-36	Trinidad	Barbados	IIs	1	2		148	123	74.00	1			23	1	82	4	20.50	
1935-36	Trinidad	British Guiana	IIs	1	2		57	38	28.50				5	0	15	0		
1936-37	Barbados	Trinidad	IIs	1	2		42	40	21.00				12	0	36	0		
1937-38	Barbados	British Guiana	IIs	1	2		45	44	22.50			2	30.1	6	71	3	23.66	
1938-39	R.S. Grant's XI	British Guiana	IIs	2	3		281	141	93.66	2		3	11	1	40	1	40.00	
1938-39	Barbados	Trinidad	IIs	1	2		28	19	14.00				12	1	25	0		
1938-39	Barbados	British Guiana	IIs	1	2		84	71	42.00		1	2	8	1	20	0		
1938-39	West Indies XI	Jamaica	IIs	1	2	1	11	*9	11.00			2	4	0	24	0		

SEASON	TEAM	OPPONENTS	V	BATTING M	I	NO	RUNS	H.S.	AVGE	100	50	CT/St	BOWLING OV	MD	RUNS	W	AVGE	B.B.
1939	West Indies	Tour of England	E	20	30		853	181	28.43	2	4	12/2	44	4	153	5	30.60	
1939	**WEST INDIES**	**ENGLAND TESTS**	**E**	**3**	**5**	**1**	**95**	**29**	**23.75**			**4/1**	**3**	**0**	**21**	**0**		
1940-41	Barbados	Trinidad	IIs	2	4		97	71	24.25		1		21	2	81	4	20.25	
1941-42	Barbados	Trinidad	IIs	4	7		263	87	37.57		1	1	61.1	7	184	14	13.14	
1942-43	Barbados	Trinidad	IIs	2	4		53	42	13.25			1	29.1	4	106	4	26.50	
1943-44	Trinidad	Barbados	IIs	2	3		55	46	18.33			2	38	3	159	3	53.00	
1943-44	Trinidad	British Guiana	IIs	1	2		43	40	21.50			1	17.5	1	73	5	14.60	
1944-45	Trinidad	Barbados	IIs	2	3		24	16	8.00			6/4						
1945-46	Trinidad	British Guiana	IIs	2	4	1	43	*27	14.33			4/2						
1945-46	Trinidad	Barbados	IIs	2	3		54	26	18.00			4/2						
1945-46	Trinidad	Jamaica	IIs	2	4	1	70	*44	23.33			1	16.3	0	54	6	9.00	
1946-47	Trinidad	British Guiana	IIs	1	1		7	7	7.00				16	3	59	1	59.00	
1947-48	Trinidad	M.C.C. Tourist	WI	1	D								24	6	61	0		
1947-48	Trinidad	Barbados	IIs	2	4		252	112	63.00	1	2		28	4	122	0		
		Barbados		22	41		1135	107	27.68	2	5	15	278.3	45	771	33	23.36	
		Trinidad		17	28	2	753	123	28.96	2	2	18/8	168.2	18	625	19	32.89	
		West Indies		38	60	6	1646	181	30.48	2	9	29/3	95.2	10	366	10	36.60	
		C.A. Merry's XI		1	2		16	15	8.00			2/2						
		R.S. Grant's XI		2	3		281	141	93.66	2		3	1	1	40	1	40.00	
		TEST RECORD		**11**	**19**	**2**	**478**	**92**	**28.11**	**0**	**3**	**6/1**	**25**	**4**	**94**	**3**	**31.33**	**2-7**
		CAREER		**80**	**134**	**8**	**3831**	**181**	**30.40**	**8**	**16**	**67/13**	**553.1**	**74**	**1802**	**63**	**28.60**	**8-8**

SHEPHERD, John Neil

SEASON	TEAM	OPPONENTS	V	BATTING M	I	NO	RUNS	H.S.	AVGE	100	50	CT	BOWLING OV	MD	RUNS	W	AVGE	B.B.
1964-65	Barbados	Cavaliers Touring XI	WI	1	2		55	33	27.00				33	3	111	2	55.50	
1966	Kent	Oxford University	E	1	1		17	17	17.00				37	11	85	5	17.00	
1967	Kent	Counties	E	29	41	6	951	*73	27.17		7	37	568.3	182	1113	54	20.61	
1967-68	Barbados	M.C.C. Tourist	WI	1	2		10	6	5.00				27	9	87	0		
1968	Kent	Counties	E	28	42	3	1157	170	29.66	3	7	27	752.3	238	1798	96	18.72	
1968-69	Barbados	Shell Shield	IIs	4	7		186	73	23.07		1	6	90.2	28	202	7	28.85	
1969	West Indies	Tour of England	E	10	11	2	121	22	11.00			5	191.4	56	537	17	31.58	
1969	**WEST INDIES**	**ENGLAND TESTS**	**E**	**3**	**5**		**65**	**32**	**13.00**			**1**	**137.5**	**44**	**266**	**12**	**22.16**	
1969	Kent	Counties	E	4	6	2	69	*30	11.06			2	55	13	127	2	63.50	

1970	Kent	Counties	E	25	36	4	734	105	22.93	1	2	23	894.5	231	2320	86	26.97	
1970-71	Barbados	Shell Shield	IIs	3	5	1	104	*68	26.00		1	6	49	14	124	6	20.66	
1970-71	Barbados	Indian Tourist	WI	1	1		2	2	2.00				26	5	68	4	17.00	
1970-71	**WEST INDIES**	**INDIA TESTS**	**WI**	**2**	**3**		**12**	**9**	**4.00**			**3**	**103**	**26**	**213**	**7**	**30.42**	
1971	Kent	Counties	E	26	40	5	792	81	22.62		5	26	768.5	199	1946	59	32.98	
1972	Kent	Counties	E	20	27	7	333	51	16.65		1	9	591.2	165	1469	48	30.60	
1973	Kent	Counties	E	24	35	4	804	87	25.93		5	11	800.3	229	2054	92	22.32	
1973-74	D.H. Robins XI	Tour of South Africa	SA	7	7		169	53	24.14		1	4	199	45	566	15	37.73	
1974	D.H. Robins XI	Indian Tourist	E	1	2	1	33	*25	16.05				28	9	47	2	23.50	
1974	Kent	Counties	E	20	28	5	576	79	25.04		2	6	613	145	1644	53	31.01	
1974-75	International XI	Tour of South Africa	SA	2	4	2	164	*71	82.00		2	1	76.4	14	181	9	20.11	
1974-75	D. H. Robins XI	Tour of South Africa	SA	5	8	3	233	*50	29.01		1	4	141.5	27	467	14	33.35	
1975	Kent	Counties	E	19	30	7	734	116	31.91	1	3	9	579.2	146	1465	52	28.17	
1975-76	International XI	Tour of Rhodesia	R	2	3		7	6	2.33			5	84	20	199	7	28.42	
1975-76	Rhodesia	Currie Cup	SA	3	5		189	65	37.80		2	1	85	22	191	6	31.83	
1975-76	International XI	Tour of South Africa	SA	4	8	1	102	42	14.57				97.5	20	272	13	20.92	
1976	Kent	Counties	E	16	29	6	895	87	38.91		8	11	496.2	106	1347	48	28.06	
1977	Kent	Counties	E	20	25	4	446	77	21.23		2	18	738.4	216	1734	87	19.93	
1978	Kent	Counties	E	20	28	6	785	101	35.68	2	3	12	601.2	166	1573	44	35.75	
1979	Kent	Counties	E	16	20	1	370	86	19.47		1	9	418.3	114	1075	34	31.61	
1980	Kent	Counties	E	20	23	8	428	100	28.53	1	1	8	473.1	118	1220	44	27.72	
1981	Kent	Counties	E	15	20	6	310	59	22.14		2	4	424.3	111	1136	28	40.57	
1982	Gloucestershire	Counties	E	22	34	9	590	*67	23.60		3	13	742.1	177	2026	63	32.15	
1983	Gloucestershire	Counties	E	23	34	6	1025	168	36.60	2	6	16	776.1	209	2047	67	30.55	
1984	Gloucestershire	Counties	E	24	39	7	885	87	22.65		6	13	800.3	209	2225	72	30.90	
1985	Gloucestershire	Counties	E	1	D								14	3	41	0		
1987	Gloucestershire	Counties	E	1	2		6	5	3.00			2	28	9	92	2	46.00	
		Barbados		10	17	1	357	73	22.31		2	12	255.2	59	592	19	31.15	
		West Indies		15	19	2	198	32	11.64			9	432.3	126	1016	36	28.22	
		Kent		303	431	74	9401	170	26.33	8	49	212	8813.2	2390	22106	832	26.56	
		Gloucestershire		71	109	22	2506	168	28.80	2	15	44	2360.5	607	6431	204	31.52	
		D.H. Robins XI		13	17	4	435	53	33.46		2	8	368.5	81	1080	31	34.83	
		International XI		8	15	3	273	*71	22.75		2	6	258.3	54	652	29	22.48	
		Rhodesia		3	5		189	65	37.80		2	1	85	22	191	6	31.83	
		TEST RECORD		**5**	**8**	**0**	**77**	**32**	**9.62**	**0**	**0**	**4**	**240.5**	**70**	**479**	**19**	**25.21**	**5-104**
		CAREER		**423**	**613**	**106**	**13359**	**170**	**26.34**	**10**	**72**	**292**	**12544.2**	**3339**	**32068**	**1157**	**27.71**	**8-40**

SHILLINGFORD, Grayson Cleophas

SEASON	TEAM	OPPONENTS	V	BATTING M	I	NO	RUNS	H.S.	AVGE	100	50	CT	BOWLING OV	MD	RUNS	W	AVGE	B.B.
1967-68	Windward Islands	M.C.C. Tourist	WI	1	1	1	1	*1					16	2	40	0		
1968-69	Windward Islands	Shell Shield	IIs	2	3	1	11	*10	5.50				36	4	89	3	29.66	
1969	West Indies	Tour of England	E	9	5		21	10	4.20			1	161.4	29	509	30	16.96	
1969	**WEST INDIES**	**ENGLAND TESTS**	**E**	**2**	**3**	**1**	**11**	***5**	**5.50**				**59.4**	**12**	**160**	**6**	**26.66**	
1969-70	Windward Islands	Leeward Islands	IIs	1	2	1	10	*10	10.00				20	3	38	4	9.50	
1969-70	Combined Islands	Shell Shield	IIs	4	8	3	51	*15	10.20			1	124	13	383	13	29.46	
1969-70	Windward Islands	Duke of Norfolk's Tourist	WI	1	1		13	13	13.00				18	2	51	1	51.00	
1969-70	Windward Islands	Glamorgan Tourist	WI	1	1		11	11	11.00				23	2	64	2	32.00	
1970-71	Windward Islands	Leeward Islands	IIs	1	2	1	11	*9	11.00			1	21	9	59	1	59.00	
1970-71	Combined Islands	Shell Shield	IIs	4	8	1	67	37	9.57			2	94	17	291	14	20.78	
1970-71	WI President's XI	Indian Tourist	WI	1	1		1	1	1.00				30	5	86	3	28.66	
1970-71	Windward Islands	Indian Tourist	WI	1	2		15	12	7.50				16.5	1	79	2	39.50	
1970-71	**WEST INDIES**	**INDIA TESTS**	**WI**	**3**	**4**		**31**	**25**	**7.75**			**2**	**75**	**9**	**217**	**4**	**54.25**	
1971-72	Windward Islands	Leeward Islands	IIs	1	2		16	16	8.00				31.1	10	69	2	34.50	
1971-72	Combined Islands	Shell Shield	IIs	4	8	3	52	42	10.40			1	106.3	19	351	17	20.64	
1971-72	Windward Islands	New Zealand Tourist	WI	1	D							1	6	1	18	0		
1971-72	**WEST INDIES**	**NEW ZEALAND TESTS**	**WI**	**2**	**1**		**15**	**15**	**15.00**				**62.1**	**17**	**160**	**5**	**32.00**	
1972-73	Windward Islands	Leeward Islands	IIs	2	4	2	46	35	23.00			1	46	4	151	7	21.57	
1972-73	Combined Islands	Shell Shield	IIs	4	7	3	52	17	13.00			2	112	22	360	9	40.00	
1972-73	Windward Islands	Australian Tourist	WI	1	2		17	9	8.50				33	0	136	3	45.33	
1973	West Indies	Tour of England	E	11	8	5	65	*35	21.66			1	224.5	46	720	22	32.72	
1973-74	Combined Islands	Shell Shield	IIs	4	7	2	68	29	13.60				76.2	10	245	5	49.00	
1974-75	Windward Islands	Leeward Islands	IIs	2	3	1	32	13	16.00			1	64.1	16	167	5	33.40	
1974-75	Combined Islands	Shell Shield	IIs	1	1		13	13	13.00			1	8	2	25	0		
1975-76	Windward Islands	Leeward Islands	IIs	1	1		12	12	12.00				19	3	58	3	19.33	
1975-76	Combined Islands	Shell Shield	IIs	4	3	1	41	*23	20.50			1	84	15	252	11	22.90	
1975-76	Windward Islands	Indian Tourist	WI	1	2		22	20	11.00				16	3	51	2	25.50	
1976-77	Windward Islands	Leeward Islands	IIs	2	3		34	25	11.33				45	8	149	4	37.25	
1976-77	Combined Islands	Shell Shield	IIs	2	3	1	16	15	5.33				70.2	14	196	5	39.20	
1976-77	Windward Islands	Pakistan Tourist	WI	1	2		6	6	3.00			2	17	6	44	4	11.00	
1978-79	Windward Islands	Leeward Islands	IIs	2	2		13	13	6.50				59	11	170	9	18.88	
1978-79	Combined Islands	Shell Shield	IIs	4	6	1	17	*9	3.66			4	132.2	26	372	21	17.71	
		Windward Islands		22	33	7	270	35	10.38			6	487.1	85	1433	52	27.55	
		Combined Islands		31	51	15	377	42	10.47			12	807.3	138	2475	95	26.05	

		West Indies		28	22	6	144	*35	9.00			4	613.2	118	1852	70	26.45	
		TEST RECORD		**7**	**8**	**1**	**57**	**25**	**8.14**	**0**	**0**	**2**	**196.5**	**38**	**537**	**15**	**35.80**	**3-63**
		CAREER		**81**	**106**	**28**	**791**	**42**	**10.14**	**0**	**0**	**22**	**1908**	**341**	**5760**	**217**	**26.54**	**6-49**

SHILLINGFORD, Irvine Theodore

				BATTING									BOWLING					
SEASON	**TEAM**	**OPPONENTS**	**V**	**M**	**I**	**NO**	**RUNS**	**H.S.**	**AVGE**	**100**	**50**	**CT**	**OV**	**MD**	**RUNS**	**W**	**AVGE**	**B.B.**
1961-62	Combined Islands	British Guiana	IIs	1	1		12	12	12.00									
1964-65	Windward Islands	Australian Tourist	WI	1	2		72	46	36.00									
1965-66	Windward Islands	Leeward Islands	IIs	1	2		29	18	14.50			2						
1965-66	Combined Islands	Shell Shield	IIs	4	7	1	308	*113	51.33	1	2	7	4	0	14	0		
1966-67	Windward Islands	Shell Shield	IIs	3	6		142	37	23.66			3						
1967-68	Windward Islands	M.C.C. Tourist	WI	1	1		69	69	69.00		1	1						
1968-69	Windward Islands	Shell Shield	IIs	2	3		75	41	25.00				1	0	6	0		
1969-70	Windward Islands	Leeward Islands	IIs	1	2		14	14	7.00									
1969-70	Combined Islands	Shell Shield	IIs	4	8		207	51	25.87		1	2						
1969-70	Windward Islands	Duke of Norfolk's Tourist	WI	1	1		26	26	26.00			1						
1969-70	Windward Islands	Glamorgan Tourist	WI	1	2		70	37	35.00			1	2	0	7	0		
1970-71	Windward Islands	Leeward Islands	IIs	1	2		62	58	31.00		1							
1970-71	Combined Islands	Shell Shield	IIs	4	8	1	253	105	36.14	1	1	4						
1970-71	Windward Islands	Indian Tourist	WI	1	2		38	32	19.00			2	1	0	7	0		
1971-72	Windward Islands	Leeward Islands	IIs	1	2		67	47	33.50			2						
1971-72	Combined Islands	Shell Shield	IIs	4	8		258	116	32.25	1	1	7						
1971-72	WI President's XI	New Zealand Tourist	WI	1	1		124	124	124.00	1			2	0	9	0		
1971-72	Windward Islands	New Zealand Tourist	WI	1	D													
1972-73	Windward Islands	Leeward Islands	IIs	2	4		107	78	26.75		1	4						
1972-73	Combined Islands	Shell Shield	IIs	4	8		243	111	30.37	1	1	7						
1972-73	Windward Islands	Australian Tourist	WI	1	2		72	69	36.00		1	1						
1973-74	Windward Islands	Leeward Islands	IIs	1	2		21	21	10.50			3						
1973-74	Combined Islands	Shell Shield	IIs	1	2		54	31	27.00									
1974-75	Windward Islands	Leeward Islands	IIs	2	4	1	196	97	65.33		2	3	3	2	4	0		
1974-75	Combined Islands	Shell Shield	IIs	4	7		159	82	22.71		1	5	3	1	3	0		
1975-76	Windward Islands	Leeward Islands	IIs	1	1		75	75	75.00		1							
1975-76	Combined Islands	Shell Shield	IIs	4	3		257	111	85.66	1	2	2						
1975-76	Windward Islands	Indian Tourist	WI	1	2		143	127	71.50	1			3	0	7	0		
1976-77	Windward Islands	Leeward Islands	IIs	2	4	1	190	77	63.33		2		10	4	15	1	15.00	
1976-77	Combined Islands	Shell Shield	IIs	4	7	1	210	120	35.00	1		2	2	1	1	0		
1976-77	WI President's XI	Pakistan Tourist	WI	1	1		69	69	69.00		1							

SEASON	TEAM	OPPONENTS	V	M	I	NO	RUNS	H.S.	AVGE	100	50	CT	OV	MD	RUNS	W	AVGE	B.B.
				BATTING									BOWLING					
1976-77	**WEST INDIES**	**PAKISTAN TESTS**	**WI**	**3**	**5**		**199**	**120**	**39.80**	**1**		**1**						
1977-78	Windward Islands	Leeward Islands	IIs	2	3		284	238	94.66	1		2						
1977-78	Combined Islands	Shell Shield	IIs	4	6	1	287	87	57.40		3	8	3	0	12	0		
1977-78	Windward Islands	Australian Tourist	WI	1	2		24	16	12.00									
1977-78	**WEST INDIES**	**AUSTRALIA TESTS**	**WI**	**1**	**2**		**19**	**16**	**9.50**									
1978-79	Windward Islands	Leeward Islands	IIs	2	3		195	104	65.00	1	1	3						
1978-79	Combined Islands	Shell Shield	IIs	4	6		152	65	25.33		1	3						
1979-80	Windward Islands	Leeward Islands	IIs	1	2		59	41	29.50			4						
1979-80	Combined Islands	Shell Shield	IIs	4	7	1	241	67	40.16		2	3						
1980-81	Windward Islands	Leeward Islands	IIs	1	2		97	66	48.50		1	1						
1980-81	Combined Islands	Shell Shield	IIs	3	5		147	63	29.40		1	4						
1981-82	Windward Islands	Shell Shield	IIs	4	7	1	112	48	18.66			3						
		Windward Islands		37	65	3	2250	238	36.29	3	11	39	20	6	46	1	46.00	
		Combined Islands		49	83	5	2788	120	35.74	6	16	54	12	2	30	0		
		West Indies		6	9		411	124	45.66	2	1	1	2	0	9	0		
		TEST RECORD		**4**	**7**	**0**	**218**	**120**	**31.14**	**1**	**0**	**1**						
		CAREER		**92**	**157**	**8**	**5449**	**238**	**36.57**	**11**	**28**	**94**	**34**	**8**	**85**	**1**	**85.00**	**1-15**

SHIVNARINE, Sewdatt

SEASON	TEAM	OPPONENTS	V	M	I	NO	RUNS	H.S.	AVGE	100	50	CT	OV	MD	RUNS	W	AVGE	B.B.
				BATTING									BOWLING					
1970-71	Guyana	Shell Shield	IIs	2	2		1	1	0.50				58.1	16	131	4	32.75	
1970-71	Guyana	Indian Tourist	WI	1	1		9	9	9.00			2	48.4	14	89	5	17.80	
1971-72	Berbice	Demerara	JC G	1	1	1	6	*6				2	27	4	86	3	28.66	
1971-72	Guyana	Shell Shield	IIs	2	3		68	36	22.66			2	70	16	204	4	51.00	
1972-73	Guyana	Australian Tourist	WI	1	2		28	14	14.00				49	8	178	4	44.50	
1973-74	Berbice	Demerara	JC G	1	2	1	63	*32	63.00				6	2	17	0		
1974-75	Berbice	Demerara	JC G	1	2	2	105	*73			1	2	29	13	49	1	49.00	
1975-76	Berbice	Demerara	JC G	1	1		22	22	22.00			1	26	2	75	4	18.75	
1975-76	Guyana	Shell Shield	IIs	2	3		16	6	5.33			2	10	4	21	0		
1976-77	Berbice	Demerara	JC G	1	2		105	82	52.50		1	1	27	5	71	0		
1976-77	Guyana	Shell Shield	IIs	4	7		254	101	36.28	1	1	1	72	20	152	5	30.00	
1976-77	Guyana	Pakistan Tourist	WI	1	2		33	30	16.50			2	29.3	10	88	3	29.33	
1977-78	Berbice	Demerara	JC G	1	2		28	21	14.00			1	43	10	64	2	32.00	

SEASON	TEAM	OPPONENTS		V	M	I	NO	RUNS	H.S.	AVGE	100	50	CT	OV	MD	RUNS	W	AVGE	B.B.
1977-78	Guyana	Shell Shield		IIs	4	5		76	49	15.20			4	102.5	35	241	11	21.90	
1977-78	Guyana	Australian Tourist		WI	1	2	1	64	*56	64.00		1		54	7	176	4	44.00	
1977-78	**WEST INDIES**	**AUSTRALIA TESTS**		**WI**	**3**	**6**		**217**	**63**	**36.16**		**3**	**1**	**44**	**6**	**139**	**1**	**139.00**	
1978-79	West Indies	Tour of India		I	6	11	4	455	*131	65.00	2	1	6	55	9	177	5	35.40	
1978-79	**WEST INDIES**	**INDIA TESTS**		**I**	**5**	**8**	**1**	**162**	**62**	**23.14**		**1**	**5**	**12**	**4**	**28**	**0**		
1978-79	West Indies	Tour of Sri Lanka		SL	1	1		6	6	6.00			1	8	1	14	0		
1978-79	Guyana	Shell Shield		IIs	4	5		202	98	40.40		2		66.4	23	140	4	35.00	
1979-80	Berbice	Demerara	JC	G	1	1	1	9	*9										
1979-80	Guyana	Shell Shield		IIs	4	7		243	87	34.71		3	3	85	21	239	6	39.83	
1980-81	Guyana	Shell Shield		IIs	1	2		10	7	5.00			2	26	2	68	1	68.00	
		Guyana			27	41	1	1004	101	25.10	1	7	18	671.5	176	1727	51	33.86	
		Berbice			7	11	5	338	82	56.33		2	7	158	36	362	10	36.20	
		West Indies			15	26	5	840	*131	40.00	2	5	13	119	20	358	6	59.66	
		TEST RECORD			**8**	**14**	**1**	**379**	**63**	**29.15**	**0**	**4**	**6**	**56**	**10**	**167**	**1**	**167.00**	**1-13**
		CAREER			**49**	**78**	**11**	**2182**	***131**	**32.56**	**3**	**14**	**38**	**948.5**	**232**	**2447**	**67**	**36.52**	**4-29**

SIMMONS, Philip Verant

					BATTING									BOWLING					
SEASON	TEAM	OPPONENTS		V	M	I	NO	RUNS	H.S.	AVGE	100	50	CT	OV	MD	RUNS	W	AVGE	B.B.
1982-83	N/E Trinidad	S/C Trinidad	BC	T	1	2		44	24	22.00				1	0	9	0		
1982-83	Trinidad	Shell Shield		IIs	5	10		325	106	32.50	1	1	1	52.1	7	168	3	56.00	
1982-83	Trinidad	Indian Tourist		WI	1	2		103	81	51.50		1	2	4	0	11	0		
1983-84	West Indies 'B'	Tour of Zimbabwe		Z	1	2		10	9	5.00			1	1	0	1	0		
1983-84	N/E Trinidad	S/C Trinidad	BC	T	1	2		69	68	34.50		1	3						
1983-84	Trinidad	Shell Shield		IIs	5	10		289	72	28.90		2	6	19	3	53	0		
1983-84	Trinidad	Australian Tourist		WI	1	2		46	42	23.00			2	2	1	7	0		
1984-85	N/E Trinidad	S/C Trinidad	BC	T	1	1		71	71	71.00		1							
1984-85	Trinidad	Shell Shield		IIs	5	8		390	118	48.75	1	3	9	3	0	19	0		
1984-85	West Indies Under 23 XI	New Zealand Tourist		WI	1	1		1	1	1.00			2						
1984-85	WI President's XI	New Zealand Tourist		WI	1	2		12	7	6.00									
1985-86	Trinidad	Shell Shield		IIs	4	8		203	65	25.37		2	6	16	0	78	0		
1985-86	Trinidad	English Tourist		WI	1	2		30	24	15.00			1	6	2	18	0		
1986-87	West Indies 'B'	Tour of Zimbabwe		Z	5	8	1	190	107	27.14	1		7	23	5	69	3	23.00	
1986-87	Trinidad	Shell Shield		IIs	2	4		138	82	34.50		1		19	1	91	1	91.00	
1987-88	West Indies	Tour of India		I	3	4		129	72	32.25		1	4						
1987-88	**WEST INDIES**	**INDIA TESTS**		**I**	**1**	**2**		**22**	**14**	**11.00**									

				BATTING									BOWLING					
SEASON	TEAM	OPPONENTS	V	M	I	NO	RUNS	H.S.	AVGE	100	50	CT	OV	MD	RUNS	W	AVGE	B.B.
1987-88	Trinidad	Red Stripe Cup	IIs	3	4		141	64	35.25		1		11	0	34	1	34.00	
1987-88	WI President's XI	Pakistan Tourist	WI	1	1		39	39	39.00			1						
1987-88	WI Board XI	Pakistan Tourist	WI	1	2	1	61	*41	61.00			1						
1987-88	**WEST INDIES**	**PAKISTAN TESTS**	**WI**	**1**	**2**		**27**	**16**	**13.50**			**1**						
1988	West Indies	Tour of England	E	1	1	1	53	*53			1							
1988-89	Trinidad	Red Stripe Cup	IIs	5	10	1	189	*46	21.00			10	15	6	38	1	38.00	
1988-89	WI President's XI	Indian Tourist	WI	1	2	1	122	*116	122.00	1								
1988-89	WI Board XI	Indian Tourist	WI	1	1		35	35	35.00			1						
1989-90	Trinidad	Red Stripe Cup	IIs	4	8		141	65	17.62		1	4	12	0	61	2	30.50	
		Trinidad		36	68	1	1995	118	29.77	2	12	41	159.1	20	578	8	72.25	
		N/E Trinidad		3	5		184	71	36.80		2	3	1	0	9	0		
		West Indies		18	28	4	701	*116	29.20	2	2	18	24	5	70	3	23.33	
		TEST RECORD		**2**	**4**		**49**	**16**	**12.25**			**1**						
		CAREER		**57**	**101**	**5**	**2880**	**118**	**30.00**	**4**	**16**	**62**	**184.1**	**25**	**657**	**11**	**59.72**	**2-50**

SINGH, Charran Kamkaran

				BATTING									BOWLING					
SEASON	TEAM	OPPONENTS	V	M	I	NO	RUNS	H.S.	AVGE	100	50	CT	OV	MD	RUNS	W	AVGE	B.B.
1959-60	Trinidad	Jamaica	IIs	1	1		0	0				1	54	18	127	5	25.40	
1959-60	Trinidad	M.C.C. Tourist	WI	1	1		0	0					48	11	127	6	21.16	
1959-60	**WEST INDIES**	**ENGLAND TESTS**	**WI**	**2**	**3**		**11**	**11**	**3.66**			**2**	**84.2**	**35**	**166**	**5**	**33.20**	
1959-60	N. Trinidad	South Trinidad BC	T	1	1		0	0					45	17	71	5	14.20	
1960-61	Trinidad	Barbados	IIs	2	3	2	52	*29	52.00			2	142.2	62	228	13	17.53	
1960-61	Trinidad	E.W. Swanton's Tourist	WI	1	2		15	15	7.50			3	69.1	17	182	7	26.00	
1960-61	N. Trinidad	South Trinidad BC	T	1	1		9	9	9.00				35	15	54	1	54.00	
1961-62	Trinidad	British Guiana	IIs	1	2	1	12	8	12.00				40	16	87	1	87.00	
1961-62	Trinidad	Indian Tourist	WI	1	1		3	3	3.00				39.3	12	107	5	21.40	
		Trinidad		7	10	3	82	*29	11.71			6	393	136	858	37	23.18	
		North Trinidad		2	2		9	9	9.00				80	32	125	6	20.83	
		West Indies		2	3		11	11	3.66			2	84.2	35	166	5	33.20	
		TEST RECORD		**2**	**3**	**0**	**11**	**11**	**3.66**	**0**	**0**	**2**	**84.2**	**35**	**166**	**5**	**33.20**	**2-28**
		CAREER		**11**	**15**	**3**	**102**	***29**	**8.50**	**0**	**0**	**8**	**557.2**	**203**	**1149**	**48**	**23.93**	**7-38**

SMALL, Joseph A.

SEASON	TEAM	OPPONENTS	V	BATTING M	I	NO	RUNS	H.S.	AVGE	100	50	CT	BOWLING OV	MD	RUNS	W	AVGE	B.B.
1909-10	Trinidad	W.C. Shepherd's Tourist	WI	1	2		13	13	6.50			1	2	0	8	0		
1909-10	Trinidad	British Guiana	IIs	1	1		7	7	7.00			1	19	5	32	4	8.00	
1909-10	Trinidad	Barbados	IIs	1	2		25	17	12.50			1	27	6	52	1	52.00	
1910-11	Trinidad	Barbados	IIs	1	2	1	4	4	4.00				9	2	31	1	31.00	
1911-12	Trinidad	British Guiana	IIs	1	1	1	4	*4				2	19	3	54	3	18.00	
1911-12	Trinidad	Barbados	IIs	1	2		23	15	11.50				18	3	43	0		
1912-13	Trinidad	M.C.C. Tourist	WI	2	3		79	28	26.33			2	66	27	122	9	13.55	
1912-13	West Indies XI	M.C.C. Tourist	WI	1	1		6	6	6.00				10	3	14	0		
1919-20	Trinidad	Barbados	IIs	2	4	1	200	*102	66.66	1	1	1	41.1	3	181	3	60.33	
1921-22	Trinidad	British Guiana	IIs	1	1		3	3	3.00			1	11	4	19	2	9.50	
1921-22	Trinidad	Barbados	IIs	1	2		22	12	11.00				2	0	7	0		
1922-23	Trinidad	British Guiana	IIs	1	2		115	82	57.50		1	1	29	5	75	3	25.00	
1922-23	Trinidad	Barbados	IIs	1	2		41	36	20.50				35	5	111	2	55.50	
1923	West Indies	Tour of England	E	18	27	2	776	94	31.04		7	20	196	28	636	19	33.47	
1923-24	Trinidad	British Guiana	IIs	1	2		76	62	38.00		1	3	13	5	26	0		
1923-24	Trinidad	Barbados	IIs	1	2		3	3	1.50			2	24	7	49	2	24.50	
1924-25	Trinidad	British Guiana	IIs	1	2		81	72	40.50		1	1	36	12	54	6	9.00	
1924-25	Trinidad	Barbados	IIs	1	2		38	36	19.00			1	61.1	21	96	9	10.66	
1925-26	Trinidad	British Guiana	IIs	1	2		155	133	77.50	1			31	11	58	3	19.33	
1925-26	Trinidad	M.C.C. Tourist	WI	2	3		69	57	23.00		1	3	55	10	132	4	33.00	
1925-26	West Indies XI	M.C.C. Tourist	WI	3	5		37	19	7.40			2	101	16	309	7	44.14	
1926-27	Trinidad	Barbados	IIs	1	2		142	100	71.00	1		2	73.3	15	191	5	38.20	
1927-28	Combined T/BG XI	Combined Jam/Bar XI	IIs	2	3	1	108	*45	54.00			1	52	15	114	5	22.80	
1927-28	West Indies XI	Barbados XI	IIs	1	2	1	109	*81	109.00		1	1	30	4	80	0		
1928	West Indies	Tour of England	E	20	32	4	541	*106	19.32	1	1	16	510.4	103	1338	48	27.87	
1928	**WEST INDIES**	**ENGLAND TESTS**	**E**	**2**	**4**		**54**	**52**	**13.50**		**1**	**2**	**30**	**3**	**106**	**2**	**53.00**	
1928-29	Trinidad	British Guiana	IIs	1	2		80	43	40.00				36	12	54	6	9.00	
1928-29	Trinidad	Barbados	IIs	1	1		6	6	6.00				15	5	49	3	16.33	
1928-29	West Indies XI	Julien Cahn's Tourist	WI	1	2		41	27	20.50			1	43	7	124	9	13.77	
1929-30	Trinidad	British Guiana	IIs	1	2		40	22	20.00				68	17	159	2	79.50	
1929-30	Trinidad	M.C.C. Tourist	WI	1	2		34	26	17.00			3	31	15	48	2	24.00	
1929-30	**WEST INDIES**	**ENGLAND TESTS**	**WI**	**1**	**2**		**25**	**20**	**12.50**			**1**	**31**	**8**	**78**	**1**	**78.00**	
1931-32	Trinidad	Barbados	IIs	1	2		15	14	7.50			1	37	11	59	3	19.66	
1931-32	Trinidad	British Guiana	IIs	1	2		91	66	45.50		1	2	48.2	16	80	1	80.00	
		Trinidad		28	50	3	1366	133	29.06	3	6	28	807.1	220	1790	74	24.18	

SEASON	TEAM	OPPONENTS	V	M	I	NO	RUNS	H.S.	AVGE	100	50	CT	OV	MD	RUNS	W	AVGE	B.B.
				BATTING									BOWLING					
		West Indies		47	75	7	1589	*106	23.36	1	10	43	951.4	172	2685	86	31.22	
		Combined T/BG XI		2	3	1	108	*45	54.00			1	52	15	114	5	22.80	
		TEST RECORD		**3**	**6**	**0**	**79**	**52**	**13.16**	**0**	**1**	**3**	**61**	**11**	**184**	**3**	**61.33**	**2-67**
		CAREER		**77**	**128**	**11**	**3063**	**133**	**26.17**	**4**	**16**	**72**	**1810.5**	**407**	**4589**	**165**	**27.81**	**7-49**

SMALL, Milton Aster

SEASON	TEAM	OPPONENTS	V	M	I	NO	RUNS	H.S.	AVGE	100	50	CT	OV	MD	RUNS	W	AVGE	B.B.
				BATTING									BOWLING					
1983-84	Barbados	Shell Shield	IIs	4	6	3	5	*2	1.66			1	110.1	15	332	18	18.44	
1983-84	Barbados	Australian Tourist	WI	1	1		8	8	8.00				39	7	138	1	138.00	
1983-84	**WEST INDIES**	**AUSTRALIA TESTS**	**WI**	**1**	**D**								**24**	**5**	**75**	**1**	**75.00**	
1984	West Indies	Tour of England	E	4	2	1	3	*2	3.00			1	79	15	243	10	24.30	
1984	**WEST INDIES**	**ENGLAND TESTS**	**E**	**1**	**1**	**1**	**3**	***3**					**21**	**2**	**78**	**3**	**26.00**	
1984-85	Barbados	Shell Shield	IIs	1	2		0	0					33	3	147	3	49.00	
1988-89	Barbados	Red Stripe Cup	IIs	5	4		31	15	7.75			3	160.4	25	441	20	22.05	
		Barbados		11	13	3	44	15	4.40			4	342.5	50	1058	42	25.19	
		West Indies		6	3	2	6	*3	6.00			1	124	22	396	14	28.28	
		TEST RECORD		**2**	**1**	**1**	**3**	***3**		**0**	**0**	**0**	**45**	**7**	**153**	**4**	**38.25**	**3-40**
		CAREER		**17**	**16**	**5**	**50**	**15**	**4.54**	**0**	**0**	**5**	**466.5**	**72**	**1454**	**56**	**25.96**	**6-55**

SMITH, Cameron Wilberforce

SEASON	TEAM	OPPONENTS	V	M	I	NO	RUNS	H.S.	AVGE	100	50	CT	OV	MD	RUNS	W	AVGE	B.B.
				BATTING									BOWLING					
1951-52	Barbados	British Guiana	IIs	1	1		80	80	80.00		1		10	0	35	0		
1951-52	Barbados	Jamaica	IIs	2	3		241	140	80.33	1	1	1						
1953-54	Barbados	M.C.C. Tourist	WI	1	2		47	25	23.50			1						
1954-55	Barbados	British Guiana	IIs	2	3		115	55	38.33		1	3						
1954-55	Barbados	Australian Tourist	WI	1	2		28	24	14.00			1						
1955-56	Barbados	E.W. Swanton's Tourist	WI	1	1		41	41	41.00			2						
1956-57	Barbados	Trinidad	IIs	1	1		43	43	43.00									
1956-57	Barbados	British Guiana	IIs	1	2		0	0										
1958-59	Barbados	Jamaica	IIs	2	4		256	116	64.00	2		7						

1958-59	Barbados	British Guiana	IIs	2	4		188	80	47.00		2	4						
1959-60	Barbados	M.C.C. Tourist	WI	1	2	2	44	*40					3	0	13	0		
1960-61	West Indies	Tour of Australia	A	7	13		354	59	27.23		1	2/2						
1960-61	**WEST INDIES**	**AUSTRALIA TESTS**	**A**	**4**	**8**		**206**	**55**	**25.75**		**1**	**3**						
1960-61	N.Z. Gov/Gen's XI	M.C.C. Tourist	NZ	1	2		53	35	26.50			2	7	0	24	2	12.00	
1961-62	Barbados	Jamaica	IIs	1	1		127	127	127.00	1								
1961-62	Barbados	British Guiana	IIs	1	2		2	1	1.00			1						
1961-62	Barbados	Indian Tourist	WI	1	1		61	61	61.00		1							
1961-62	**WEST INDIES**	**INDIA TESTS**	**WI**	**1**	**2**	**1**	**16**	**12**	**16.00**			**1/1**						
1962-63	Barbados	Trinidad	IIs	1	1		140	140	140.00	1		2	7	2	12	1	12.00	
1962-63	Barbados	British Guiana	IIs	1	2		21	11	10.50				5	0	13	0		
1964	West Indies XI	England XI	E	3	5		140	68	28.00		1	2						
1964-65	Comm. XI	Tour of India	I	1	2		74	68	37.00		1							
		Barbados		20	32	2	1434	140	47.80	5	6	22	25	2	73	1	73.00	
		West Indies		15	28	1	716	68	26.51		3	8/3						
		Comm. XI		1	2		74	68	37.00		1							
		N.Z. Governor General's XI		1	2		53	35	26.50			2	7	0	24	2	12.00	
		TEST RECORD		**5**	**10**	**1**	**222**	**55**	**24.66**	**0**	**1**	**4/1**						
		CAREER		**37**	**64**	**3**	**2277**	**140**	**37.32**	**5**	**10**	**32/3**	**32**	**2**	**97**	**3**	**32.33**	**2-24**

SMITH, O'Neil Gordon

				BATTING									BOWLING					
SEASON	**TEAM**	**OPPONENTS**	**V**	**M**	**I**	**NO**	**RUNS**	**H.S.**	**AVGE**	**100**	**50**	**CT**	**OV**	**MD**	**RUNS**	**W**	**AVGE**	**B.B.**
1954-55	Jamaica	Trinidad	IIs	2	4	1	117	*58*	39.00		1	3	66.1	15	166	8	20.75	
1954-55	Jamaica	Australian Tourist	WI	1	1		169	169	169.00	1		1	50.4	10	128	4	32.00	
1954-55	**WEST INDIES**	**AUSTRALIA TESTS**	**WI**	**4**	**8**		**206**	**104**	**25.75**	**1**			**134.4**	**38**	**340**	**5**	**68.00**	
1955-56	West Indies	Tour of New Zealand	NZ	3	3		145	80	48.33		1	1	43	28	95	2	47.50	
1955-56	**WEST INDIES**	**NEW ZEALAND TESTS**	**NZ**	**4**	**5**		**78**	**64**	**15.60**		**1**	**3**	**115.5**	**43**	**241**	**13**	**18.53**	
1955-56	West Indies XI	E.W. Swanton's Tourist	WI	1	1		33	33	33.00			1	46	15	77	2	38.50	
1956-57	Jamaica	British Guiana	IIs	1	1		109	109	109.00	1			69	20	140	0		
1956-57	Jamaica	Duke of Norfolk's Tourist	WI	3	6		370	118	61.66	2	1	2	126	18	385	11	35.00	
1957	West Indies	Tour of England	E	21	35	9	1087	133	41.80	1	8	13	316.3	121	697	29	24.03	
1957	**WEST INDIES**	**ENGLAND TESTS**	**E**	**5**	**10**		**396**	**168**	**39.60**	**2**			**89**	**14**	**223**	**5**	**44.60**	
1957-58	Jamaica	Pakistan Tourist	WI	1	2		108	93	54.00		1		24	10	40	3	13.33	
1957-58	**WEST INDIES**	**PAKISTAN TESTS**	**WI**	**5**	**6**		**283**	**86**	**47.16**		**3**	**2**	**236**	**71**	**494**	**13**	**38.00**	
1958	Comm. XI	England XI	E	1	2		29	17	14.50			1	21	5	67	1	67.00	

SEASON	TEAM	OPPONENTS	V	M	I	NO	BATTING RUNS	H.S.	AVGE	100	50	CT	BOWLING OV	MD	RUNS	W	AVGE	B.B.
1958-59	West Indies	Tour of India	I	9	14	2	529	*140	44.08	1	2	8	89	18	288	11	26.18	
1958-59	**WEST INDIES**	**INDIA TESTS**	**I**	**5**	**8**		**287**	**100**	**35.87**	**1**	**2**	**2**	**124**	**33**	**267**	**9**	**29.66**	
1958-59	West Indies	Tour of Pakistan	P	1	1		4	4	4.00				21	5	46	2	23.00	
1958-59	**WEST INDIES**	**PAKISTAN TESTS**	**P**	**3**	**5**		**81**	**39**	**16.20**			**2**	**39**	**20**	**60**	**3**	**20.00**	
		Jamaica		8	14	1	873	169	67.15	4	3	6	335.5	73	859	26	33.03	
		West Indies		61	96	11	3129	168	36.81	6	17	32	1254	406	2828	94	30.08	
		Comm. XI		1	2		29	17	14.50			1	21	5	67	1	67.00	
		TEST RECORD		**26**	**42**	**0**	**1331**	**168**	**31.69**	**4**	**6**	**9**	**738.3**	**219**	**1625**	**48**	**33.85**	**5-90**
		CAREER		**70**	**112**	**12**	**4031**	**169**	**40.31**	**10**	**20**	**39**	**1610.5**	**484**	**3754**	**121**	**31.02**	**5-63**

SOBERS, Garfield St. Aubrun

SEASON	TEAM	OPPONENTS	V	M	I	NO	BATTING RUNS	H.S.	AVGE	100	50	CT	BOWLING OV	MD	RUNS	W	AVGE	B.B.
1952-53	Barbados	Indian Tourist	WI	1	1	1	7	*7					89	40	142	7	20.28	
1953-54	Barbados	M.C.C. Tourist	WI	1	2		73	46	36.50				53	15	139	2	69.50	
1953-54	**WEST INDIES**	**ENGLAND TESTS**	**WI**	**1**	**2**	**1**	**40**	**26**	**40.00**				**29.5**	**9**	**81**	**4**	**20.25**	
1954-55	Barbados	British Guiana	IIs	2	3	1	142	*104	71.00	1		3	57.1	16	121	5	24.20	
1954-55	Barbados	Australian Tourist	WI	1	2		62	62	31.00		1		20	10	42	0		
1954-55	**WEST INDIES**	**AUSTRALIA TESTS**	**WI**	**4**	**8**	**2**	**231**	**64**	**38.50**		**1**	**1**	**93.5**	**36**	**213**	**6**	**35.50**	
1955-56	West Indies	Tour of New Zealand	NZ	3	4	1	131	53	43.66		1	2	57	24	120	2	60.00	
1955-56	**WEST INDIES**	**NEW ZEALAND TESTS**	**NZ**	**4**	**5**		**81**	**27**	**16.20**			**4**	**46.5**	**26**	**49**	**2**	**24.50**	
1955-56	West Indies XI	E.W. Swanton's Tourist	WI	1	1		71	71	71.00		1		67.1	22	134	6	22.33	
1956-57	Barbados	Trinidad	IIs	1	1		10	10	10.00				35	21	38	4	9.50	
1956-57	Barbados	British Guiana	IIs	1	2	1	109	77	109.00		1		56	20	108	1	108.00	
1957	West Indies	Tour of England	E	20	34	6	1324	*219	47.28	3	6	25	343.3	120	817	32	25.53	
1957	**WEST INDIES**	**ENGLAND TESTS**	**E**	**5**	**10**		**320**	**66**	**32.00**		**2**	**1**	**134**	**25**	**355**	**5**	**71.00**	
1957-58	Barbados	Pakistan Tourist	WI	1	2	1	183	*183	183.00	1			42	22	48	2	24.00	
1957-58	**WEST INDIES**	**PAKISTAN TESTS**	**WI**	**5**	**8**	**2**	**824**	***365**	**137.33**	**3**	**3**	**2**	**171.3**	**53**	**377**	**4**	**94.25**	
1958	A.E.R. Gilligan's XI	New Zealand Tourist	E	1	1		75	75	75.00		1		8	2	27	0		
1958	Comm. XI	England XI	E	2	4		177	74	44.25		2	4	20	6	33	1	33.00	
1958-59	West Indies	Tour of India	I	7	10	2	605	*161	75.62	2	3	6	75.1	13	222	8	27.75	
1958-59	**WEST INDIES**	**INDIA TESTS**	**I**	**5**	**8**	**2**	**557**	**198**	**92.83**	**3**		**5**	**119.1**	**33**	**292**	**10**	**29.20**	
1958-59	West Indies	Tour of Pakistan	P	2	3	1	97	75	48.50		1	3	13	4	49	2	24.50	
1958-59	**WEST INDIES**	**PAKISTAN TESTS**	**P**	**3**	**5**		**160**	**72**	**32.00**		**1**	**2**	**66**	**36**	**77**	**0**		

1959	A.E.R. Gilligan's XI	Indian Tourist	E	1	2		119	74	59.50		1	1	5	0	36	0	
1959-60	Barbados	M.C.C. Tourist	WI	1	1		154	154	154.00	1		1	41	9	116	0	
1959-60	**WEST INDIES**	**ENGLAND TESTS**	**WI**	**5**	**8**	**1**	**709**	**226**	**101.28**	**3**	**1**	**7**	**114**	**14**	**355**	**9**	**39.55**
1960-61	West Indies	Tour of Australia	A	7	12		375	119	31.25	1	2	11	165	18	621	19	32.68
1960-61	**WEST INDIES**	**AUSTRALIA TESTS**	**A**	**5**	**10**		**430**	**168**	**43.00**	**2**	**1**	**12**	**191**	**27**	**588**	**15**	**39.20**
1961	M.C.C.	Counties	E	2	3	1	116	103	58.00	1			50	17	119	6	19.83
1961	Comm. XI	England XI	E	1	2		94	54	47.00		1	1	28	2	95	7	13.57
1961-62	South Australia	Sheffield Shield	A	7	13		573	251	44.07	1	2	9	210.7	19	769	35	21.97
1961-62	Barbados	Indian Tourist	WI	1	1		27	27	27.00				23.2	9	48	4	12.00
1961-62	**WEST INDIES**	**INDIA TESTS**	**WI**	**5**	**7**	**1**	**424**	**153**	**70.66**	**2**	**1**	**11**	**223.3**	**61**	**473**	**23**	**20.56**
1962	M.C.C.	Surrey	E	1	2		38	28	19.00			1	50	10	164	2	82.00
1962-63	South Australia	Sheffield Shield	A	10	18	2	1006	196	62.87	3	6	2	384.3	48	1355	51	26.56
1963	West Indies	Tour of England	E	19	26	6	1011	112	50.55	3	4	21	527.3	132	1273	62	20.53
1963	**WEST INDIES**	**ENGLAND TESTS**	**E**	**5**	**8**		**322**	**102**	**40.25**	**1**	**2**	**8**	**231**	**50**	**571**	**20**	**28.55**
1963-64	West Indies XI	The Rest XI	WI	1	2	1	143	89	143.00		2	1	38	4	135	5	27.00
1963-64	C. Hunte's XI	F. Worrell's XI	WI	1	2		118	107	59.00	1			27	1	135	5	27.00
1963-64	South Australia	Sheffield Shield	A	9	14		1128	195	80.57	6	2	15	411.4	50	1441	51	28.25
1963-64	E.W. Swanton's XI	Tour of India	I	1	2	1	130	123	130.00	1			46	9	141	9	15.66
1964	West Indies XI	England XI	E	3	4	2	104	44	52.00			3	93	14	336	10	33.60
1964-65	Comm. XI	Tour of India	I	1	2		185	102	92.50	1	1	1	39	4	167	4	41.75
1964-65	Jamaican XI	Cavaliers Touring XI	WI	1	2		147	129	73.50	1		2	31.4	8	79	5	15.80
1964-65	Barbados	Cavaliers Touring XI	WI	1	1		52	52	52.00		1		32	4	100	3	33.33
1964-65	Barbados	Australian Tourist	WI	1	1	1	183	*183		1			26	6	88	2	44.00
1964-65	**WEST INDIES**	**AUSTRALIA TESTS**	**WI**	**5**	**10**	**1**	**352**	**69**	**39.11**		**2**	**8**	**192.3**	**53**	**490**	**12**	**41.00**
1965	Rest of World XI	England XI	E	1	2		5	5	2.50				17	4	45	1	45.00
1965-66	Jamaican XI	Worcestershire Touring XI	WI	1	1		120	120	120.00	1			47	11	126	2	63.00
1965-66	Barbados	Shell Shield	IIs	4	3	1	290	204	145.00	1	1	6	94.3	20	288	14	20.57
1966	West Indies	Tour of England	E	13	17	2	627	153	41.80	1	1	13	287.4	90	690	40	17.25
1966	**WEST INDIES**	**ENGLAND TESTS**	**E**	**5**	**8**	**1**	**722**	**174**	**103.14**	**3**	**2**	**10**	**269.4**	**78**	**545**	**20**	**27.25**
1966-67	West Indies	Tour of India	I	2	2		84	49	42.00			5	62.3	17	196	9	21.77
1966-67	**WEST INDIES**	**INDIA TESTS**	**I**	**3**	**5**	**2**	**342**	**95**	**114.00**		**5**	**7**	**155.1**	**51**	**350**	**14**	**25.00**
1966-67	West Indies	Tour of Ceylon	C	1	1		115	115	115.00	1		1	18	4	56	0	
1966-67	Barbados	Shell Shield	IIs	4	6	1	389	165	77.80	1	1	6	116	31	292	9	32.44
1966-67	Barbados	Rest of World XI	WI	1	2		35	32	17.50			1	30	9	54	2	27.00
1967	Rest of World XI	England XI & Sussex	E	2	2		50	26	25.00			3	75.5	16	195	11	17.72
1967-68	Barbados	M.C.C. Tourist	WI	1	2		93	56	46.50		1	1	20	8	54	0	
1967-68	**WEST INDIES**	**ENGLAND TESTS**	**WI**	**5**	**9**	**3**	**545**	**152**	**90.83**	**2**	**2**	**4**	**232.5**	**72**	**508**	**13**	**39.07**
1968	Northamptonshire	Counties	E	26	42	7	1570	*105	44.85	2	13	25	773.4	226	1882	83	22.67
1968	Rest of World XI	England XI	E	1	2		20	20	10.00				25	3	82	1	82.00

SEASON	TEAM	OPPONENTS	V	BATTING									BOWLING					
				M	I	NO	RUNS	H.S.	AVGE	100	50	CT	OV	MD	RUNS	W	AVGE	B.B.
1968-69	West Indies	Tour of Australia	A	5	7	2	514	132	102.80	3	1	7	104	12	387	18	21.50	
1968-69	**WEST INDIES**	**AUSTRALIA TESTS**	**A**	**5**	**10**		**497**	**113**	**49.70**	**2**	**2**	**6**	**206.1**	**37**	**733**	**18**	**40.72**	
1968-69	West Indies	Tour of New Zealand	NZ	1	2		85	54	42.50		1		15	1	89	2	44.50	
1968-69	**WEST INDIES**	**NEW ZEALAND TESTS**	**NZ**	**3**	**5**		**70**	**39**	**14.00**			**5**	**105**	**23**	**301**	**7**	**45.00**	
1969	West Indies	Tour of England	E	9	9	1	282	81	35.25		2	10	122.1	31	305	11	27.72	
1969	**WEST INDIES**	**ENGLAND TESTS**	**E**	**3**	**6**	**1**	**150**	***50**	**30.00**		**1**	**2**	**145**	**47**	**318**	**11**	**28.90**	
1969	Nottinghamshire	Counties	E	8	11		591	104	53.72	2	3	7	263.1	77	696	32	21.75	
1969-70	Cavaliers XI	Jamaica	WI	1	2		43	35	21.50			2	49	16	126	2	63.00	
1969-70	Barbados	Shell Shield	IIs	1	1	1	116	*116		1		2	42	6	143	2	71.50	
1970	Nottinghamshire	Counties	E	14	23	8	1154	160	76.93	5	4	13	403.3	87	1088	43	25.30	
1970	Rest of World XI	England	E	5	9	1	588	183	23.50	2		7	272.4	106	452	21	21.52	
1970-71	Rest of World XI	Tour of Pakistan	P	1	2		25	25	12.50			3	20.3	4	62	2	31.00	
1970-71	Barbados	Shell Shield	IIs	3	4	1	157	76	52.33		1	1	84.3	31	172	10	17.20	
1970-71	Barbados	Indian Tourist	WI	1	1		135	135	135.00	1			28	6	52	3	17.33	
1970-71	**WEST INDIES**	**INDIA TESTS**	**WI**	**5**	**10**	**2**	**597**	***178**	**74.62**	**3**	**1**	**4**	**220**	**70**	**401**	**12**	**33.50**	
1971	Nottinghamshire	Counties	E	23	38	6	1485	*151	46.40	3	8	29	660.4	189	1641	53	30.96	
1971-72	Rest of World XI	Tour of Australia	A	9	14	4	562	254	56.20	2		7	129.6	8	528	14	37.71	
1971-72	**WEST INDIES**	**NEW ZEALAND TESTS**	**WI**	**5**	**8**	**1**	**253**	**142**	**36.14**	**1**		**2**	**181**	**56**	**332**	**10**	**33.20**	
1972	Nottinghamshire	Counties	E	6	9	1	222	71	27.75		1	4	157	45	351	15	23.40	
1972-73	Barbados	Shell Shield	IIs	1	2		43	23	21.50				16	4	40	0		
1973	**WEST INDIES**	**ENGLAND TESTS**	**E**	**3**	**5**	**1**	**306**	***150**	**76.50**	**1**	**2**	**7**	**82.1**	**24**	**169**	**6**	**28.16**	
1973	Nottinghamshire	Counties	E	15	24	4	909	128	45.45	2	4	15	244	74	619	26	23.80	
1973-74	Barbados	Shell Shield	IIs	2	2		95	60	47.50		1	1	20	6	48	1	48.00	
1973-74	**WEST INDIES**	**ENGLAND TESTS**	**WI**	**4**	**5**		**100**	**57**	**20.00**		**1**	**1**	**223.2**	**92**	**421**	**14**	**30.07**	
1974	Nottinghamshire	Counties	E	15	27	4	1110	*132	48.26	4	6	17	350.4	79	925	29	31.89	
		Barbados		30	40	9	2355	204	75.96	8	8	22	925.3	293	2133	71	30.04	
		West Indies		187	294	45	13600	*365	54.61	40	55	217	5422.1	1479	13429	461	29.13	
		Nottinghamshire		107	174	30	7041	160	48.99	18	39	110	2852.4	777	7202	281	25.62	
		South Australia		26	45	2	2707	251	62.95	10	10	26	1006.6	117	3565	137	26.02	
		Rest of World XI		19	31	5	1250	254	48.07	4		20	540.6	141	1364	50	17.28	
		Comm. XI		4	8		456	102	57.00	1	4	6	87	12	295	12	24.58	
		M.C.C.		3	5	1	154	103	38.50	1		1	100	27	283	8	35.37	
		Jamaican XI		2	3		267	129	89.00	2		2	78.4	19	205	7	29.28	
		Cavaliers XI		1	2		43	35	21.50			2	49	16	126	2	63.00	
		A.E.R. Gilligan's XI		2	3		194	75	64.66		2	1	13	2	63	0		
		C. Hunte's XI		1	2		118	107	59.00	1			27	1	135	5	27.00	

		OPPONENTS	V	M	I	NO	RUNS	H.S.	AVGE	100	50	CT	OV	MD	RUNS	W	AVGE	B.B.
		E.W. Swanton's XI		1	2	1	130	123	130.00	1			46	9	141	9	15.66	
		TEST RECORD		**93**	**160**	**21**	**8032**	***365**	**57.78**	**26**	**30**	**109**	**3433.3**	**973**	**7999**	**235**	**34.03**	**6-73**
		CAREER		**383**	**609**	**93**	**28315**	***365**	**54.87**	**86**	**118**	**407**	**11148.6**	**2893**	**28941**	**1043**	**27.74**	**9-49**

SOLOMON, Joseph Stanislaus

				BATTING									BOWLING					
SEASON	TEAM	OPPONENTS	V	M	I	NO	RUNS	H.S.	AVGE	100	50	CT	OV	MD	RUNS	W	AVGE	B.B.
1956-57	British Guiana	Jamaica	IIs	1	1	1	114	*114		1								
1956-57	British Guiana	Barbados	IIs	1	1		108	108	108.00	1		1						
1957-58	British Guiana	Pakistan Tourist	WI	1	1		121	121	121.00	1			9	1	23	0		
1958-59	West Indies	Tour of India	I	8	9	2	231	*55	33.00		3	2	23	3	66	1	66.00	
1958-59	**WEST INDIES**	**INDIA TESTS**	**I**	**4**	**6**	**3**	**351**	***100**	**117.00**	**1**	**2**	**3**	**33**	**14**	**76**	**0**		
1958-59	West Indies	Tour of Pakistan	P	1	1		30	30	30.00			1						
1958-59	**WEST INDIES**	**PAKISTAN TESTS**	**P**	**3**	**5**		**144**	**66**	**28.80**		**2**		**4**	**1**	**8**	**0**		
1959-60	British Guiana	Jamaica	IIs	1	1		53	53	53.00		1		5	1	17	0		
1959-60	British Guiana	M.C.C. Tourist	WI	1	2	1	65	37	65.00				4	0	28	0		
1959-60	Berbice	M.C.C. Tourist	WI	1	1	1	201	*201		1		2	20	0	83	1	83.00	
1959-60	**WEST INDIES**	**ENGLAND TESTS**	**WI**	**2**	**4**	**1**	**50**	**23**	**16.66**			**1**	**17**	**2**	**51**	**1**	**51.00**	
1960-61	West Indies	Tour of Australia	A	6	11	2	226	55	25.11		1	2	12	1	66	1	66.00	
1960-61	**WEST INDIES**	**AUSTRALIA TESTS**	**A**	**5**	**10**	**1**	**250**	**65**	**27.77**		**1**	**5**	**3**	**2**	**1**	**0**		
1960-61	Berbice	E.W. Swanton's Tourist	WI	1	2		133	79	66.50		2		7	0	48	0		
1960-61	British Guiana	E.W. Swanton's Tourist	WI	1	2		39	35	19.50									
1961-62	British Guiana	Combined Islands	IIs	1	D													
1961-62	British Guiana	Trinidad	IIs	1	2		176	166	88.00	1		1	6	0	22	0		
1961-62	British Guiana	Barbados	IIs	1	2		179	146	89.50	1								
1961-62	**WEST INDIES**	**INDIA TESTS**	**WI**	**4**	**5**		**148**	**96**	**29.60**		**1**	**2**	**31**	**17**	**36**	**0**		
1962-63	British Guiana	Barbados	IIs	1	2		45	33	22.50			1						
1963	West Indies	Tour of England	E	18	27	6	570	61	27.14		4	7	152.5	25	540	26	20.76	
1963	**WEST INDIES**	**ENGLAND TESTS**	**E**	**5**	**8**		**204**	**62**	**25.50**		**2**	**2**						
1963-64	West Indies XI	The Rest XI	WI	1	2		6	5	3.00				18	2	67	2	33.50	
1963-64	C. Hunte's XI	F. Worrell's XI	WI	1	2		105	74	52.50		1		21	0	136	1	136.00	
1963-64	British Guiana	Barbados	IIs	1	2	1	111	63	111.00		1	2	3	0	7	0		
1963-64	British Guiana	Jamaica	IIs	1	1		39	39	39.00			1	15	2	45	2	22.50	
1963-64	British Guiana	Trinidad	IIs	1	2	1	207	107	207.00	2		1	5	1	13	0		
1964-65	**WEST INDIES**	**AUSTRALIA TESTS**	**WI**	**4**	**8**	**2**	**179**	**76**	**29.83**		**1**		**28**	**3**	**96**	**3**	**32.00**	
1965-66	British Guiana	Shell Shield	IIs	4	6	1	264	110	52.80	1	1	1	90	25	203	10	20.30	
1966	West Indies	Tour of England	E	17	21	4	585	*104	34.41	1	3	6	54	10	204	1	204.00	

SEASON	TEAM	OPPONENTS	V	M	I	NO	RUNS	H.S.	AVGE	100	50	CT	OV	MD	RUNS	W	AVGE	B.B.
				BATTING									BOWLING					
1966-67	Guyana	Shell Shield	IIs	3	4	1	103	68	34.33		1		30	5	84	0		
1968-69	Guyana	Shell Shield	IIs	3	5		281	169	56.20	1		5	14	3	30	2	15.00	
		British Guiana/Guyana		23	34	6	1905	179	68.03	9	4	13	181	38	472	14	33.71	
		Berbice		2	3	1	334	*201	167.00	1	2	2	27	0	131	1	131.00	
		West Indies	78	117	21		2974	*104	30.97	2	20	31	375.5	80	1211	35	34.60	
		C. Hunte's XI		1	2		105	74	52.50		1		21	0	136	1	136.00	
		TEST RECORD		**27**	**46**	**7**	**1326**	***100**	**34.00**	**1**	**9**	**13**	**116**	**39**	**268**	**4**	**67.00**	**1-20**
		CAREER		**104**	**156**	**28**	**5318**	***201**	**41.54**	**12**	**27**	**46**	**604.5**	**118**	**1950**	**51**	**38.23**	**4-28**

STAYERS, Sven Conrad

SEASON	TEAM	OPPONENTS	V	M	I	NO	RUNS	H.S.	AVGE	100	50	CT	OV	MD	RUNS	W	AVGE	B.B.
				BATTING									BOWLING					
1957-58	British Guiana	Pakistan Tourist	WI	1	1		1	1	1.00			1	48.4	9	158	5	31.60	
1958-59	British Guiana	Barbados	IIs	2	4		184	120	46.00	1			59	7	210	6	35.00	
1959-60	British Guiana	Jamaica	IIs	1	1		14	14	14.00			1	40.1	8	111	6	18.50	
1959-60	British Guiana	M.C.C. Tourist	WI	1	1	1	19	*19					29	4	114	1	114.00	
1960-61	British Guiana	E.W. Swanton's Tourist	WI	1	2		1	1	0.50				28.2	3	96	5	19.20	
1961-62	British Guiana	Combined Islands	IIs	1	1		22	22	22.00			1	24	5	83	7	11.85	
1961-62	British Guiana	Trinidad	IIs	1	1		2	2	2.00				47	4	184	6	30.66	
1961-62	British Guiana	Barbados	IIs	1	2	1	93	83	93.00		1		32	1	134	9	14.88	
1961-62	**WEST INDIES**	**INDIA TESTS**	**WI**	**4**	**4**	**1**	**58**	***35**	**19.33**				**106**	**20**	**364**	**9**	**40.44**	
1962-63	Bombay	Ranji Trophy	I	2	1		53	53	53.00		1		53	8	215	11	19.54	
1962-63	West Zone	South Zone	I	1	1		22	22	22.00				12	8	66	3	22.00	
1962-63	Chief Minister's XI	Indian Governor's XI	I	1	2	1	16	12	16.00				7	0	40	0		
		British Guiana		9	13	2	336	120	30.54	1	1	3	308.1	41	1090	45	24.22	
		West Indies		4	4	1	58	*35	19.33				106	20	364	9	40.44	
		Bombay		2	1		53	53	53.00		1		53	8	215	11	19.54	
		West Zone		1	1		22	22	22.00				12	8	66	3	22.00	
		Chief Minister's XI		1	2	1	16	12	16.00				7	0	40	0		
		TEST RECORD		**4**	**4**	**1**	**58**	***35**	**19.33**	**0**	**0**	**0**	**106**	**20**	**364**	**9**	**40.44**	**3-65**
		CAREER		**17**	**21**	**4**	**485**	**120**	**28.52**	**1**	**2**	**3**	**486.1**	**77**	**1775**	**68**	**26.10**	**6-36**

STOLLMEYER, Jeffrey Baxter

				BATTING									BOWLING					
SEASON	TEAM	OPPONENTS	V	M	I	NO	RUNS	H.S.	AVGE	100	50	CT	OV	MD	RUNS	W	AVGE	B.B.
1938-39	R.S. Grant's XI	British Guiana	IIs	1	1		118	118	118.00	1			20	2	69	1	69.00	
1938-39	Trinidad	Barbados	IIs	1	1		11	11	11.00			2	7	0	32	3	10.66	
1938-39	Trinidad	Jamaica	IIs	1	2		40	28	20.00				15	0	48	0		
1939	West Indies	Tour of England	E	15	26	1	783	117	31.32	1	5	5	34	2	182	3	60.66	
1939	WEST INDIES	ENGLAND TESTS	E	3	5		133	59	26.60		2	1						
1940-41	Trinidad	Barbados	IIs	1	2		176	92	88.00		2		20	2	81	3	27.00	
1941-42	Trinidad	Barbados	IIs	4	8	1	256	106	36.57	1		6	46.5	4	215	4	53.75	
1942-43	Trinidad	Barbados	IIs	2	4	2	209	107	104.50	1	1	3	22	1	100	2	50.00	
1943-44	Trinidad	Barbados	IIs	2	4		296	210	74.00	1		1	29	0	162	3	54.00	
1943-44	Trinidad	British Guiana	IIs	2	3		101	88	33.66		1	1	30	4	122	4	30.50	
1944-45	Trinidad	Barbados	IIs	2	4	1	143	45	47.66				10	0	54	1	54.00	
1945-46	Trinidad	Jamaica	IIs	3	5	1	122	74	30.50		1							
1946-47	Trinidad	British Guiana	IIs	2	3		450	324	150.00	1	2	2	17	1	77	2	38.50	
1947-48	Trinidad	M.C.C.Tourist	WI	2	1		16	16	16.00			3	19	4	65	1	65.00	
1947-48	WEST INDIES	ENGLAND TESTS	WI	2	4	1	164	78	54.66		1		24	8	47	3	15.66	
1948-49	West Indies	Tour of India	I	7	12	3	569	*244	63.22	1	3	7	59	6	191	3	63.66	
1948-49	WEST INDIES	INDIA TESTS	I	4	5		342	160	68.40	1	2	3	33	2	133	2	66.50	
1948-49	West Indies	Tour of Pakistan	P	2	4	2	87	*36	43.50			3	43	7	136	4	34.00	
1948-49	West Indies	Tour of Ceylon	C	1	1		93	93	93.00		1	3	22	0	101	0		
1949-50	Trinidad	Jamaica	IIs	2	2		273	261	136.50	1		3	10	3	19	0		
1950	West Indies	Tour of England	E	21	30		1029	198	34.30	1	5	18	27	3	117	2	58.50	
1950	WEST INDIES	ENGLAND TESTS	E	4	7	1	305	78	50.83		2	5						
1950-51	Trinidad	Barbados	IIs	2	4		358	208	89.50	1	1	2	1	0	5	0		
1951-52	West Indies	Tour of Australia	A	6	10		201	94	20.10		1	6	31	3	138	6	23.00	
1951-52	WEST INDIES	AUSTRALIA TESTS	A	5	10		328	104	32.80	1	1	3						
1951-52	WEST INDIES	NEW ZEALAND TESTS	NZ	2	3		188	152	62.66	1		3	6	1	12	2	6.00	
1952-53	Trinidad	Indian Tourist	WI	1	1		64	64	64.00		1	2	7	1	21	0		
1952-53	WEST INDIES	INDIA TESTS	WI	5	9	3	354	*104	59.00	1	2	2	71	13	231	3	77.00	
1953-54	Trinidad	M.C.C. Tourist	WI	1	2		137	89	68.50		1	1	6	0	19	0		
1953-54	WEST INDIES	ENGLAND TESTS	WI	5	9		256	64	28.44		2	2	23	4	72	3	24.00	
1954-55	Trinidad	Jamaica	IIs	2	4		117	55	29.25		1	3	3	0	21	0		
1954-55	Trinidad	Australian Tourist	WI	1	2		104	95	52.00		1	1						
1954-55	WEST INDIES	AUSTRALIA TESTS	WI	2	4		89	42	22.25			1	6	0	12	0		
1956-57	Trinidad	Barbados	IIs	1	2		30	28	15.00			1						
		Trinidad		32	54	5	2903	324	59.24	6	12	62	242.5	20	1041	23	45.26	

SEASON	TEAM			BATTING M	I	NO	RUNS	H.S.	AVGE	100	50	CT	BOWLING OV	MD	RUNS	W	AVGE	B.B.
		West Indies		84	139	11	4921	*244	38.44	7	27	31	379	49	1318	31	42.51	
		R.S. Grant's XI		1	1		118	118	118.00	1			20	2	69	1	69.00	
		TEST RECORD		**32**	**56**	**5**	**2159**	**160**	**42.33**	**4**	**12**	**20**	**163**	**28**	**507**	**13**	**39.00**	**3-32**
		CAREER		**117**	**194**	**16**	**7942**	**324**	**44.61**	**14**	**39**	**93**	**641.5**	**71**	**2482**	**55**	**45.12**	**3-32**

STOLLMEYER, Victor Humphrey

SEASON	TEAM	OPPONENTS	V	BATTING M	I	NO	RUNS	H.S.	AVGE	100	50	CT	BOWLING OV	MD	RUNS	W	AVGE	B.B.
1935-36	Trinidad	British Guiana	IIs	1	2		1	1	0.50									
1936-37	Trinidad	British Guiana	IIs	1	2		144	139	72.00	1		1	25	2	77	3	25.66	
1937-38	Trinidad	British Guiana	IIs	1	2		122	121	61.00	1			14	1	60	1	60.00	
1938-39	Trinidad	Barbados	IIs	1	1		86	86	86.00		1		2	0	17	0		
1938-39	Trinidad	British Guiana	IIs	1	2	1	107	83	107.00		1	1						
1938-39	Trinidad	Jamaica	IIs	1	1		66	66	66.00		1		6	0	22	1	22.00	
1939	West Indies	Tour of England	E	12	21	4	446	*73	26.23		2	3	6	1	33	1	33.00	
1939	**WEST INDIES**	**ENGLAND TESTS**	**E**	**1**	**1**		**96**	**96**	**96.00**		**1**							
1940-41	Trinidad	Barbados	IIs	2	4	1	173	*86	57.66		1	5	15.3	0	96	3	32.00	
1941-42	Trinidad	Barbados	IIs	4	8	1	414	121	59.14	2	2	2	9.4	0	53	1	53.00	
1942-43	Trinidad	Barbados	IIs	2	4	1	127	83	42.33		1	2	5	0	25	1	25.00	
1943-44	Trinidad	British Guiana	IIs	2	3		150	92	50.00		2	1	9	0	49	1	49.00	
1944-45	Trinidad	Barbados	IIs	2	4	1	66	38	22.00			1	9	1	31	0		
1945-46	Trinidad	Barbados	IIs	2	3		98	67	32.66		1		29	0	149	3	49.66	
		Trinidad		20	36	5	1554	139	50.12	4	10	13	124.1	4	579	14	41.35	
		West Indies		13	22	4	542	96	30.11		3	3	6	1	33	1	33.00	
		TEST RECORD		**1**	**1**	**0**	**96**	**96**	**96.00**	**0**	**1**	**0**						
		CAREER		**33**	**58**	**9**	**2096**	**139**	**42.77**	**4**	**13**	**16**	**130.1**	**5**	**612**	**15**	**40.80**	**3.38**

TAYLOR, Jaswick Ossie

SEASON	TEAM	OPPONENTS	V	BATTING M	I	NO	RUNS	H.S.	AVGE	100	50	CT	BOWLING OV	MD	RUNS	W	AVGE	B.B.
1953-54	Trinidad	British Guiana	IIs	2	2	1	0	*0				1	47.1	8	143	3	47.66	
1953-54	Trinidad	M.C.C. Tourist	WI	1	2	1	0	*0				1	32	9	67	2	33.50	

SEASON	TEAM	OPPONENTS	V	M	I	NO	RUNS	H.S.	AVGE	100	50	CT	OV	MD	RUNS	W	AVGE	B.B.
1954-55	Trinidad	Jamaica	IIs	1	2	1	2	2	2.00				7	2	23	1	23.00	
1957-58	Trinidad	Pakistan Tourist	WI	1	1		12	12	12.00				33	2	129	2	64.50	
1957-58	**WEST INDIES**	**PAKISTAN TESTS**	**WI**	**1**	**2**	**1**	**4**	***4**	**4.00**				**36.5**	**6**	**109**	**5**	**21.80**	
1958-59	West Indies	Tour of India	I	6	4	2	35	18	17.50			2	142	51	342	24	14.25	
1958-59	**WEST INDIES**	**INDIA TESTS**	**I**	**1**	**1**	**1**	**0**	***0**					**48.1**	**18**	**106**	**5**	**21.20**	
1958-59	West Indies	Tour of Pakistan	P	2	2		1	1	0.50				43	8	135	6	22.50	
1958-59	**WEST INDIES**	**PAKISTAN TESTS**	**P**	**1**	**2**	**1**	**0**	***0**					**27**	**9**	**58**	**0**		
1959-60	Trinidad	Jamaica	IIs	1	2	2	7	*6					30.5	3	114	1	114.00	
1959-60	Trinidad	M.C.C. Tourist	WI	1	1		1	1	1.00				32.5	6	85	1	85.00	
		Trinidad		7	10	5	22	12	4.40			2	182.5	30	561	10	56.10	
		West Indies		11	11	5	40	18	6.66			2	297	92	750	40	18.75	
		TEST RECORD		**3**	**5**	**3**	**4**	***4**	**2.00**	**0**	**0**	**0**	**112**	**33**	**273**	**10**	**27.30**	**5-109**
		CAREER		**18**	**21**	**10**	**62**	**18**	**5.63**	**0**	**0**	**4**	**479.5**	**122**	**1311**	**50**	**26.22**	**5-36**

TRIM, John

SEASON	TEAM	OPPONENTS	V	BATTING									BOWLING					
				M	I	NO	RUNS	H.S.	AVGE	100	50	CT	OV	MD	RUNS	W	AVGE	B.B.
1943-44	British Guiana	Trinidad	IIs	2	4		17	17	4.25			1	46.5	6	228	5	45.60	
1944-45	British Guiana	Barbados	IIs	2	4	1	36	16	12.00			1	55	3	288	5	57.60	
1945-46	British Guiana	Trinidad	IIs	2	4	1	9	6	3.00			2	40	5	135	6	22.50	
1946-47	British Guiana	Barbados	IIs	1	1		17	17	17.00				18	0	98	1	98.00	
1946-47	British Guiana	Trinidad	IIs	2	4	2	24	*10	12.00				40	4	180	2	90.00	
1947-48	British Guiana	M.C.C. Tourist	WI	1	1		3	3	3.00			1	47.1	10	104	9	11.55	
1947-48	**WEST INDIES**	**ENGLAND TESTS**	**WI**	**1**	**D**								**23**	**8**	**44**	**3**	**14.66**	
1948-49	West Indies	Tour of India	I	6	3	1	22	12	11.00			4	149	25	386	14	27.57	
1948-49	**WEST INDIES**	**INDIA TESTS**	**I**	**2**	**3**	**1**	**21**	**12**	**10.50**			**2**	**80**	**15**	**188**	**10**	**18.80**	
1948-49	West Indies	Tour of Pakistan	P	2	1		16	16	16.00			1	54	23	110	3	36.66	
1948-49	West Indies	Tour of Ceylon	C	2	D								59	12	134	10	13.40	
1949-50	British Guiana	Barbados	IIs	2	4	2	22	22	11.00			1	63	11	269	5	53.80	
1950-51	British Guiana	Jamaica	IIs	2	4		71	26	17.75			3	53	2	245	5	49.00	
1951-52	West Indies	Tour of Australia	A	3	5	1	27	8	6.75				50	2	191	10	19.10	
1951-52	**WEST INDIES**	**AUSTRALIA TESTS**	**A**	**1**	**2**		**0**	**0**					**22**	**5**	**59**	**5**	**11.80**	
1951-52	West Indies	Tour of New Zealand	NZ	2	2		23	15	11.50			1	49.4	9	155	3	51.66	
1952-53	British Guiana	Indian Tourist	WI	1	1	1	78	*78			1		25	4	67	0		
		British Guiana		15	27	7	277	*78	13.85		1	9	388	45	1614	38	42.47	

SEASON	TEAM		M	I	NO	RUNS	H.S.	AVGE	100	50	CT	OV	MD	RUNS	W	AVGE	B.B.
			BATTING									BOWLING					
		West Indies	19	16	3	109	16	8.38			8	486.4	99	1267	58	21.84	
		TEST RECORD	**4**	**5**	**1**	**21**	**12**	**5.25**	**0**	**0**	**2**	**125**	**28**	**291**	**18**	**16.16**	**5-34**
		CAREER	**34**	**43**	**10**	**386**	***78**	**11.69**	**0**	**1**	**17**	**874.4**	**144**	**2881**	**96**	**30.01**	**5-34**

VALENTINE, Alfred Lewis

SEASON	TEAM	OPPONENTS	V	M	I	NO	RUNS	H.S.	AVGE	100	50	CT	OV	MD	RUNS	W	AVGE	B.B.
				BATTING									BOWLING					
1949-50	Jamaica	Trinidad	IIs	2	3		23	12	7.66			1	78.2	16	190	2	95.00	
1950	West Indies	Tour of England	E	17	14	3	34	*9	3.09			5	763	278	1533	90	17.03	
1950	**WEST INDIES**	**ENGLAND TESTS**	**E**	**4**	**5**		**15**	**9**	**3.00**			**2**	**422.3**	**197**	**674**	**33**	**20.42**	
1950-51	Jamaica	British Guiana	IIs	2	3	1	12	7	6.00			2	119.5	22	367	22	16.68	
1951-52	West Indies	Tour of Australia	A	5	8	3	11	6	2.20			3	199.6	40	610	29	21.03	
1951-52	**WEST INDIES**	**AUSTRALIA TESTS**	**A**	**5**	**9**	**2**	**37**	**14**	**5.28**			**1**	**218.1**	**39**	**691**	**24**	**28.79**	
1951-52	**WEST INDIES**	**NEW ZEALAND TESTS**	**NZ**	**2**	**1**	**1**	**0**	***0**					**113.4**	**55**	**153**	**8**	**19.12**	
1952	Comm. XI	Indian Tourist	E	1	1	1	0	*0					53	8	171	3	57.00	
1952-53	Jamaica	British Guiana	IIs	2	1		18	18	18.00			2	133.5	37	346	10	34.60	
1952-53	Jamaica	Indian Tourist	WI	1	2		8	8	4.00				17	4	28	0		
1952-53	**WEST INDIES**	**INDIA TESTS**	**WI**	**5**	**6**	**2**	**23**	**13**	**5.75**			**3**	**430**	**178**	**828**	**28**	**29.57**	
1953	Comm. XI	Essex	E	1	2	1	1	1					47.1	25	54	2	27.00	
1953-54	Jamaica	M.C.C. Tourist	WI	1	2		5	5	2.50				18	1	99	0		
1953-54	**WEST INDIES**	**ENGLAND TESTS**	**WI**	**3**	**4**	**1**	**0**	***0**					**190.5**	**82**	**378**	**7**	**54.00**	
1954-55	Jamaica	Trinidad	IIs	2	3		28	23	9.33			1	119.5	40	232	13	17.84	
1954-55	**WEST INDIES**	**AUSTRALIA TESTS**	**WI**	**3**	**4**	**3**	**8**	***4**	**8.00**			**2**	**140**	**42**	**349**	**5**	**69.80**	
1955-56	West Indies	Tour of New Zealand	NZ	2	3	1	4	2	2.00				123	61	164	8	20.50	
1955-56	**WEST INDIES**	**NEW ZEALAND TESTS**	**NZ**	**4**	**5**		**10**	**5**	**2.00**			**1**	**201.4**	**99**	**283**	**15**	**18.86**	
1956-57	Jamaica	British Guiana	IIs	1	1		5	5	5.00				91.5	32	166	2	83.00	
1956-57	Jamaica	Duke of Norfolk's Tourist	WI	2	4	1	9	5	3.00			1	68	10	209	3	69.66	
1957	West Indies	Tour of England	E	14	7	4	15	7	5.00			4	486	156	1092	60	18.20	
1957	**WEST INDIES**	**ENGLAND TESTS**	**E**	**2**	**4**	**2**	**4**	***2**	**2.00**				**26**	**4**	**88**	**0**		
1957-58	**WEST INDIES**	**PAKISTAN TESTS**	**WI**	**1**	**1**	**1**	**5**	***5**					**45.2**	**9**	**124**	**3**	**41.33**	
1959-60	Jamaica	Trinidad	IIs	1	1		17	17	17.00			2	63	18	159	6	26.50	
1959-60	Jamaica	British Guiana	IIs	1	1		7	7	7.00				31	10	91	1	91.00	
1959-60	Jamaica	M.C.C. Tourist	WI	1	1		0	0					44	10	108	2	54.00	
1960-61	West Indies	Tour of Australia	A	6	7	1	6	2	1.00			3	206.3	32	593	25	23.72	
1960-61	**WEST INDIES**	**AUSTRALIA TESTS**	**A**	**5**	**9**	**8**	**21**	***10**	**21.00**			**3**	**170.4**	**42**	**533**	**14**	**38.07**	

SEASON	TEAM	OPPONENTS	V	M	I	NO	RUNS	H.S.	AVGE	100	50	CT	OV	MD	RUNS	W	AVGE	B.B.
1961-62	Jamaica	Barbados	IIs	1	2	1	4	*4	4.00				44	5	140	0		
1961-62	Jamaica	Indian Tourist	WI	1	1		4	4	4.00				55	14	157	4	39.25	
1961-62	**WEST INDIES**	**INDIA TESTS**	**WI**	**2**	**3**	**1**	**18**	***7**	**9.00**			**1**	**72**	**39**	**114**	**2**	**57.00**	
1963	West Indies	Tour of England	E	15	11	5	10	*6	1.66			5	306.3	98	822	24	34.25	
1963-64	The Rest XI	West Indies XI	IIs	1	2	2	25	*24					21.2	6	119	6	19.83	
1963-64	F. Worrell's XI	C. Hunte's XI	IIs	1	D							1						
1963-64	Jamaica	Cavaliers Touring XI	WI	2	2		25	24	12.50			2	53	5	268	9	29.77	
1963-64	Jamaica	Barbados	IIs	1	1		10	10	10.00				42.3	10	101	2	50.50	
1963-64	Jamaica	Trinidad	IIs	1	2	1	12	11	12.00				64.1	11	150	4	37.50	
1963-64	Jamaica	British Guiana	IIs	1	2		20	16	10.00				28.5	7	69	5	13.80	
1964-65	Jamaica	Cavaliers Touring XI	WI	1	1		0	0					16	4	56	2	28.00	
1964-65	Jamaican XI	Cavaliers Touring XI	WI	1	1	1	1	*1					25.3	12	61	2	30.50	
1964-65	Jamaica	Australian Tourist	WI	1	2	1	15	11	15.00				16	1	81	0		
		Jamaica		26	36	6	223	24	7.43			11	1129.4	269	3078	89	34.58	
		West Indies		95	101	38	221	14	3.50			33	4115.5	1451	9029	375	24.07	
		Comm. XI		2	3	2	1	1	1.00				100.1	33	225	5	45.00	
		The Rest XI		1	2	2	25	*24					21.2	6	119	6	19.83	
		F. Worrell's XI		1	D							1						
		TEST RECORD		**36**	**51**	**21**	**141**	**14**	**4.70**	**0**	**0**	**13**	**2030.5**	**786**	**4215**	**139**	**30.32**	**8-104**
		CAREER		**125**	**142**	**48**	**470**	***24**	**5.00**	**0**	**0**	**45**	**5367**	**1759**	**12451**	**475**	**26.21**	**8-26**

VALENTINE, Vincent A.

				BATTING									BOWLING					
SEASON	TEAM	OPPONENTS	V	M	I	NO	RUNS	H.S.	AVGE	100	50	CT	OV	MD	RUNS	W	AVGE	B.B.
1931-32	Jamaica	L.H. Tennyson's Tourist	WI	1	D								50.2	13	128	4	32.00	
1932-33	G.C. Grant's XI	C.A. Merry's XI	IIs	1	2	1	5	3	5.00				25	5	67	1	67.00	
1933	West Indies	Tour of England	E	17	23	3	356	*59	17.80		1	11	539	112	1437	35	41.05	
1933	**WEST INDIES**	**ENGLAND TESTS**	**E**	**2**	**4**	**1**	**35**	***19**	**11.66**				**48**	**14**	**104**	**1**	**104.00**	
1935-36	Jamaica	Yorkshire Touring XI	WI	2	3		93	36	31.00				92	16	227	7	32.42	
1938-39	Jamaica	Universities Touring XI	WI	1	1		11	11	11.00				12	7	17	1	17.00	
		Jamaica		4	4		104	36	26.00				154.2	36	372	12	31.00	
		West Indies		19	27	4	391	*59	17.00		1	11	587	126	1541	36	42.80	
		G.C. Grant's XI		1	2	1	5	3	5.00				25	5	67	1	67.00	
		TEST RECORD		**2**	**4**	**1**	**35**	***19**	**11.66**	**0**	**0**	**0**	**48**	**14**	**104**	**1**	**104.00**	**1-55**
		CAREER		**24**	**33**	**5**	**500**	***59**	**17.85**	**0**	**1**	**11**	**766.2**	**167**	**1980**	**49**	**40.40**	**4-83**

WALCOTT, Clyde Leopold

SEASON	TEAM	OPPONENTS	V	BATTING M	I	NO	RUNS	H.S.	AVGE	100	50	CT/St	BOWLING OV	MD	RUNS	W	AVGE	B.B.
1941-42	Barbados	Trinidad	IIs	3	5		195	70	39.00		3	1	5	0	20	0		
1942-43	Barbados	Trinidad	IIs	2	4		148	58	37.00		2		4	0	24	1	24.00	
1943-44	Barbados	Trinidad	IIs	2	3		100	55	33.33		1	0/1	4.7	0	12	1	12.00	
1944-45	Barbados	British Guiana	IIs	2	3		175	125	58.33	1		3/1						
1944-45	Barbados	Trinidad	IIs	2	4		173	103	43.25	1	1	1						
1945-46	Barbados	Trinidad	IIs	2	4	1	397	*314	132.33	1		5/2						
1946-47	Barbados	Jamaica	IIs	2	4		88	42	22.00			1	6	2	7	0		
1947-48	Barbados	M.C.C. Tourist	WI	2	3	1	142	120	71.00	1		3	3	2	2	0		
1947-48	**WEST INDIES**	**ENGLAND TESTS**	**WI**	**4**	**7**	**1**	**133**	**45**	**22.16**			**11/5**						
1948-49	West Indies	Tour of India	I	7	11	2	692	128	76.88	2	4	8/1	22	7	68	0		
1948-49	**WEST INDIES**	**INDIA TESTS**	**I**	**5**	**7**		**452**	**152**	**64.57**	**2**	**2**	**9/2**	**3**	**0**	**12**	**0**		
1948-49	West Indies	Tour of Pakistan	P	1	2	1	43	41	43.00				18	9	24	0		
1948-49	West Indies	Tour of Ceylon	C	2	2	1	179	*125	179.00	1	1	7	20	2	26	1	26.00	
1949-50	Barbados	British Guiana	IIs	2	3	1	293	*211	146.50	1	1	3	50.3	11	124	8	15.50	
1950	West Indies	Tour of England	E	21	30	4	1445	149	55.57	6	5	26/15	8	5	10	0		
1950	**WEST INDIES**	**ENGLAND TESTS**	**E**	**4**	**6**	**1**	**229**	***168**	**45.80**	**1**		**4/3**	**4**	**1**	**12**	**0**		
1950-51	Barbados	Trinidad	IIs	2	4		409	209	102.25	1	2	1	13	5	29	0		
1951-52	West Indies	Tour of Australia	A	7	13	1	664	186	55.33	2	4	6/2						
1951-52	**WEST INDIES**	**AUSTRALIA TESTS**	**A**	**3**	**6**		**87**	**60**	**14.50**		**1**	**4/1**						
1951-52	West Indies	Tour of New Zealand	NZ	1	1		148	148	148.00	1			8	3	8	1	8.00	
1951-52	**WEST INDIES**	**NEW ZEALAND TESTS**	**NZ**	**2**	**3**		**199**	**115**	**66.33**	**1**	**1**	**2**						
1951-52	Barbados	Indian Tourist	WI	1	1		51	51	51.00		1	2	26	12	40	0		
1952-53	**WEST INDIES**	**INDIA TESTS**	**WI**	**5**	**7**	**1**	**457**	**125**	**76.16**	**2**	**1**	**6**	**35**	**14**	**48**	**2**	**24.00**	
1953	Comm. XI	England XI & Essex	E	2	4		141	115	35.25	1		4	4	0	13	0		
1953-54	Barbados	M.C.C. Tourist	WI	1	2		25	25	12.50			1	30.3	14	65	4	16.25	
1953-54	**WEST INDIES**	**ENGLAND TESTS**	**WI**	**5**	**10**	**2**	**698**	**220**	**87.25**	**3**	**3**	**3**	**53**	**24**	**94**	**4**	**27.50**	
1954	Comm. XI	England XI	E	1	2	1	42	*39	42.00									
1954-55	British Guiana	Barbados	IIs	1	2		67	50	33.50		1							
1954-55	British Guiana	Australian Tourist	WI	1	1	1	51	*51			1		1	0	4	0		
1954-55	**WEST INDIES**	**AUSTRALIA TESTS**	**WI**	**5**	**10**		**827**	**155**	**82.70**	**5**	**2**	**5**	**71**	**24**	**152**	**4**	**38.00**	
1955-56	Barbados	E.W. Swanton's Tourist	WI	2	3		132	130	44.00	1		1	34	12	86	2	43.00	
1955-56	West Indies XI	E.W. Swanton's Tourist	WI	1	1		17	17	17.00			1	16	2	30	1	30.00	
1956-57	British Guiana	Jamaica	IIs	1	1		26	26	26.00			2	4	2	2	0		
1956-57	British Guiana	Barbados	IIs	1	1		64	64	64.00		1	2						
1957	West Indies	Tour of England	E	16	26	4	1167	131	53.04	3	6	24	7	2	24	0		
1957	**WEST INDIES**	**ENGLAND TESTS**	**E**	**5**	**10**	**1**	**247**	**90**	**27.44**		**1**	**4**	**1**	**0**	**4**	**0**		

SEASON	TEAM	OPPONENTS	V	M	I	NO	RUNS	H.S.	AVGE	100	50	CT/St	OV	MD	RUNS	W	AVGE	B.B.
1957-58	British Guiana	Pakistan Tourist	WI	1	1		29	29	29.00			1	11	5	13	0		
1957-58	**WEST INDIES**	**PAKISTAN TESTS**	**WI**	**4**	**5**	**1**	**385**	**145**	**96.25**	**1**	**2**	**3**	**12**	**5**	**16**	**0**		
1958-59	British Guiana	Barbados	IIs	2	4	1	195	*70	65.00		2	2	19.3	2	68	0		
1959-60	British Guiana	Jamaica	IIs	1	2	1	110	*61	110.00		1	3	13	3	32	0		
1959-60	British Guiana	M.C.C. Tourist	WI	1	1		83	83	83.00		1		5	1	12	0		
1959-60	**WEST INDIES**	**ENGLAND TESTS**	**WI**	**2**	**3**		**84**	**53**	**28.00**		**1**	**2**	**20**	**4**	**70**	**1**	**70.00**	
1960-61	British Guiana	E.W. Swanton's Tourist	WI	1	2	1	154	108	154.00	1		1						
1961-62	British Guiana	Combined Islands	IIs	1	1		59	59	59.00		1	1						
1961-62	British Guiana	Trinidad	IIs	1	2	1	13	8	13.00				6	3	8	0		
1961-62	British Guiana	Barbados	IIs	1	2		17	12	8.50			5	1	0	4	0		
1962-63	British Guiana	Barbados	IIs	1	2		17	13	8.50			3						
1963-64	The Rest XI	West Indies XI	IIs	1	2		99	82	49.50		1	1	8	2	29	0		
1963-64	F. Worrell's XI	C. Hunte's XI	IIs	1	2		146	105	73.00	1			20.1	4	61	5	12.20	
1963-64	British Guiana	Jamaica	IIs	1	1		2	2	2.00			1						
1963-64	British Guiana	Trinidad	IIs	1	2		24	23	12.00			1	7	2	16	0		
		Barbados		25	43	3	2328	*314	58.20	7	11	22/4	176.5	58	409	16	25.56	
		British Guiana		16	25	5	911	108	45.55	1	8	22	67.3	18	159	0		
		West Indies		100	160	20	8153	220	58.23	30	34	125/29	298	102	598	14	42.71	
		Comm. XI		3	6	1	183	115	36.60	1		4	4	0	13	0		
		The Rest XI		1	2		99	82	49.50		1	1	8	2	29	0		
		F. Worrell's XI		1	2		146	105	73.00	1			20.1	4	61	5	12.20	
		TEST RECORD		**44**	**74**	**7**	**3798**	**220**	**56.68**	**15**	**14**	**53/11**	**199**	**72**	**408**	**11**	**37.09**	**3-50**
		CAREER		**146**	**238**	**29**	**11820**	***314**	**56.55**	**40**	**54**	**174/33**	**574.3**	**184**	**1269**	**35**	**36.25**	**5-41**

WALCOTT, Leslie Arthur

				BATTING									BOWLING					
SEASON	**TEAM**	**OPPONENTS**	**V**	**M**	**I**	**NO**	**RUNS**	**H.S.**	**AVGE**	**100**	**50**	**CT/St**	**OV**	**MD**	**RUNS**	**W**	**AVGE**	**B.B.**
1925-26	Barbados	British Guiana	IIs	1	2		45	40	22.50									
1926-27	Barbados	British Guiana	IIs	1	1		62	62	62.00		1		4	0	18	0		
1928-29	Barbados	Trinidad	IIs	1	2		9	9	4.50			1	6.1	1	30	3	10.00	
1929-30	Barbados	M.C.C. Tourist	WI	2	3	1	113	*73	56.50		1	1	44.5	3	145	4	36.25	
1929-30	**WEST INDIES**	**ENGLAND TESTS**	**WI**	**1**	**2**	**1**	**40**	**24**	**40.00**				**8**	**1**	**32**	**1**	**32.00**	
1931-32	Barbados	Trinidad	IIs	1	2		26	18	13.00			1	9	2	31	1	31.00	
1933-34	Barbados	British Guiana	IIs	1	2	1	95	*59	95.00		1	1	12	4	32	2	16.00	
1933-34	Barbados	Trinidad	IIs	1	2		58	51	29.00		1	4	19	1	59	1	59.00	
1934-35	Barbados	M.C.C. Tourist	WI	2	3		39	33	13.00			0/1	6	0	30	1	30.00	

SEASON	TEAM	OPPONENTS	V	M	I	NO	RUNS	H.S.	AVGE	100	50	CT/St	OV	MD	RUNS	W	AVGE	B.B.
				BATTING									BOWLING					
1935-36	Barbados	Trinidad	IIs	1	2		68	53	34.00		1		21	3	95	3	31.66	
		Barbados		11	19	2	515	*73	30.29		5	8/1	122	14	440	15	29.33	
		West Indies		1	2	1	40	24	40.00				8	1	32	1	32.00	
		TEST RECORD		**1**	**2**	**1**	**40**	**24**	**40.00**	**0**	**0**	**0**	**8**	**1**	**32**	**1**	**32.00**	**1-17**
		CAREER		**12**	**21**	**3**	**555**	***73**	**30.83**	**0**	**5**	**8/1**	**130**	**15**	**472**	**16**	**29.50**	**3-30**

WALSH, Courtney Andrew

SEASON	TEAM	OPPONENTS	V	M	I	NO	RUNS	H.S.	AVGE	100	50	CT	OV	MD	RUNS	W	AVGE	B.B.
				BATTING									BOWLING					
1981-82	Jamaica	Shell Shield	IIs	4	6		38	21	6.33			1	114.1	21	378	15	25.20	
1982-83	Jamaica	Shell Shield	IIs	4	7	1	43	18	7.16			3	117	22	351	8	43.87	
1982-83	Jamaica	Indian Tourist	WI	1	1		6	6	6.00				34	8	94	4	23.50	
1983-84	West Indies 'B'	Tour of Zimbabwe	Z	2	4		26	12	6.50				80	22	222	11	20.18	
1983-84	Jamaica	Shell Shield	IIs	5	8	3	49	19	9.80			4	154	20	602	30	20.06	
1984	West Indies	Tour of England	E	8	5	2	2	*2	0.66			1	156.1	32	557	14	39.78	
1984	Gloucestershire	Counties	E	6	10	1	96	30	10.66				185.2	48	622	18	34.55	
1984-85	West Indies	Tour of Australia	A	4	4	3	23	16	23.00			1	164.5	29	514	24	21.41	
1984-85	**WEST INDIES**	**AUSTRALIA TESTS**	**A**	**5**	**6**	**3**	**32**	**18**	**10.66**			**1**	**146.2**	**29**	**432**	**13**	**33.23**	
1984-85	West Indies Under 23 XI	New Zealand Tourist	WI	1	1	1	10	*10					27	7	94	0		
1984-85	WI President's XI	New Zealand Tourist	WI	1	1		13	13	13.00				33	1	141	6	23.50	
1984-85	**WEST INDIES**	**NEW ZEALAND TESTS**	**WI**	**1**	**1**	**1**	**12**	***12**				**1**	**25**	**6**	**75**	**3**	**25.00**	
1985	Gloucestershire	Counties	E	21	18	6	189	37	15.75			4	560.3	124	1706	85	20.07	
1985-86	Jamaica	Shell Shield	IIs	5	8	1	51	19	7.28			4	138	19	461	29	15.89	
1985-86	Jamaica	English Tourist	WI	1	2	2	0	*0				1	45	12	116	5	23.20	
1985-86	**WEST INDIES**	**ENGLAND TESTS**	**WI**	**1**	**1**		**3**	**3**	**3.00**				**33**	**5**	**103**	**5**	**20.60**	
1986	Gloucestershire	Counties	E	23	24	6	221	52	12.27		1	7	789.5	193	2145	118	18.17	
1986-87	West Indies	Tour of Pakistan	P	1	1		0	0					20	2	70	3	23.33	
1986-87	**WEST INDIES**	**PAKISTAN TESTS**	**P**	**3**	**5**	**1**	**12**	**8**	**3.00**			**1**	**97.3**	**27**	**195**	**11**	**17.72**	
1986-87	West Indies	Tour of Australia	A	1	1	1	0	*0					17	1	57	1	57.00	
1986-87	West Indies	Tour of New Zealand	NZ	1	D							1	36	9	91	2	45.50	
1986-87	**WEST INDIES**	**NEW ZEALAND TESTS**	**NZ**	**3**	**3**	**2**	**23**	**14**	**23.00**				**120.2**	**28**	**306**	**13**	**23.53**	
1986-87	Jamaica	Shell Shield	IIs	2	3	2	20	*12	20.00			1	60.2	5	212	13	16.30	
1987	Gloucestershire	Counties	E	17	21	2	166	27	8.73			10	471.3	95	1433	59	24.28	
1987	Rest of World XI	M.C.C. & Gloucester	E	2	2		23	21	11.50				53.1	13	176	4	44.00	

SEASON	TEAM	OPPONENTS	V	M	I	NO	RUNS	H.S.	AVGE	100	50	CT	OV	MD	RUNS	W	AVGE	B.B.
1987-88	West Indies	Tour of India	I	1	1		50	50	50.00		1		10	1	35	3	11.66	
1987-88	**WEST INDIES**	**INDIA TESTS**	**I**	**4**	**4**		**29**	**16**	**7.25**				**137.1**	**24**	**437**	**26**	**16.80**	
1987-88	Jamaica	Red Stripe Cup	IIs	3	3		61	29	20.33			1	93	19	286	14	20.42	
1987-88	**WEST INDIES**	**PAKISTAN TESTS**	**WI**	**3**	**5**	**1**	**52**	**14**	**13.00**			**1**	**86**	**15**	**230**	**4**	**57.50**	
1988	West Indies	Tour of England	E	4	2		5	4	2.50				175	15	210	6	35.00	
1988	**WEST INDIES**	**ENGLAND TESTS**	**E**	**5**	**5**	**3**	**26**	***9**	**13.00**				**157.2**	**40**	**412**	**12**	**34.33**	
1988-89	West Indies	Tour of Australia	A	2	2		12	12	6.00			2	42	7	121	6	20.16	
1988-89	**WEST INDIES**	**AUSTRALIA TESTS**	**A**	**5**	**8**	**5**	**68**	***30**	**20.66**				**176.5**	**32**	**500**	**17**	**29.41**	
1988-89	Jamaica	Red Stripe Cup	IIs	2	4	3	57	*21	57.00				43	9	129	4	32.25	
1988-89	**WEST INDIES**	**INDIA TESTS**	**WI**	**4**	**5**		**20**	**6**	**4.00**				**123.2**	**35**	**268**	**18**	**14.88**	
1989	Gloucestershire	Counties	E	18	25	5	360	47	18.00			2	627.4	134	1675	81	20.67	
1989-90	Jamaica	Red Stripe Cup	IIs	3	4	2	56	*34	28.00			1	87.2	11	308	7	44.00	
1989-90	**WEST INDIES**	**ENGLAND TESTS**	**WI**	**3**	**5**	**1**	**25**	***8**	**6.25**				**93.2**	**14**	**243**	**12**	**20.25**	
1990	Gloucestershire	Counties	E	20	20	3	464	*63	27.29		3	6	611.1	107	2022	72	28.08	
		Jamaica		30	46	14	381	*34	11.90			16	885.5	146	2937	129	22.76	
		West Indies		63	70	24	443	50	9.63		1	9	1957.1	381	5313	210	25.30	
		Gloucestershire		105	118	23	1496	*63	15.74		4	29	3246	701	9603	433	22.17	
		Rest of World XI		2	2		23	21	11.50				53.1	13	176	4	44.00	
		TEST RECORD		**37**	**48**	**17**	**302**	***30**	**9.74**	**0**	**0**	**4**	**1196.1**	**255**	**3201**	**134**	**23.88**	**6-62**
		CAREER		**200**	**236**	**61**	**2343**	***63**	**13.38**	**0**	**5**	**54**	**6142.1**	**1241**	**18029**	**776**	**23.23**	**9-72**

WATSON, Chester Donald

				BATTING									BOWLING					
SEASON	TEAM	OPPONENTS	V	M	I	NO	RUNS	H.S.	AVGE	100	50	CT	OV	MD	RUNS	W	AVGE	B.B.
1958-59	Jamaica	Leeward Islands	IIs	1	D							1	32	12	48	3	16.00	
1958-59	Jamaica	Barbados	IIs	2	3	1	4	4	2.00			1	68.3	12	209	8	26.12	
1959-60	Jamaica	Trinidad	IIs	1	1		0	0				1	45.5	13	140	7	20.00	
1959-60	Jamaica	British Guiana	IIs	1	1		4	4	4.00				34.5	9	89	4	22.25	
1959-60	Jamaica	M.C.C. Tourist	WI	1	1		8	8	8.00			1	27	3	94	0		
1959-60	**WEST INDIES**	**ENGLAND TESTS**	**WI**	**5**	**3**	**1**	**3**	**3**	**1.50**				**199**	**39**	**593**	**16**	**37.06**	
1960-61	West Indies	Tour of Australia	A	6	7	4	47	16	15.66			4	105	9	364	11	33.09	
1960-61	**WEST INDIES**	**AUSTRALIA TESTS**	**A**	**1**	**2**		**9**	**5**	**4.50**			**1**	**21**	**2**	**105**	**2**	**52.50**	
1961-62	Jamaica	Indian Tourist	WI	1	1		9	9	9.00				22	2	87	0		
1961-62	**WEST INDIES**	**INDIA TESTS**	**WI**	**1**	**1**		**0**	**0**					**16**	**6**	**26**	**1**	**26.00**	
1962-63	Comm. XI	Tour of Rhodesia	R	2	2		0	0					70.3	16	160	5	32.00	
1962-63	New Delhi	Rajasthan	I	1	2		57	50	28.50		1	1	24	1	97	4	24.25	

SEASON	TEAM	OPPONENTS	V	M	I	NO	RUNS	H.S.	AVGE	100	50	CT/St	OV	MD	RUNS	W	AVGE	B.B.
1962-63	West Zone	East Zone & North Zone	I	2	2		23	12	11.50			2	42	5	154	7	22.00	
1962-63	Indian Governor's XI	Chief Minister's XI	I	2	4	1	27	12	9.00				35	6	175	3	58.33	
1962-63	Cavaliers XI	Indian XI	I	1	1		0	0					22.5	5	55	7	7.85	
1963-64	Comm. XI	Tour of Pakistan	P	4	3	1	6	*3	3.00			3	93.4	22	330	7	47.14	
		Jamaica		7	7	1	25	9	4.16			4	230.1	51	667	22	30.31	
		West Indies		13	13	5	59	16	7.37			5	341	56	1088	30	26.26	
		Comm. XI		6	5	1	6	*3	1.50			3	164.1	38	490	12	40.83	
		New Delhi		1	2		57	50	28.50			1	24	1	97	4	24.25	
		West Zone		2	2		23	12	11.50			2	42	5	154	7	22.00	
		Indian Governor's XI		2	4	1	27	12	9.00				35	6	175	3	58.33	
		Cavaliers XI		1	1		0	0					22.5	5	55	7	7.85	
		TEST RECORD		**7**	**6**	**1**	**12**	**5**	**2.40**	**0**	**0**	**1**	**235**	**47**	**724**	**19**	**38.10**	**4-62**
		CAREER		**32**	**34**	**8**	**197**	**50**	**7.57**	**0**	**1**	**15**	**859.1**	**162**	**2726**	**85**	**32.07**	**6-33**

WEEKES, Everton de Courcey

				BATTING									BOWLING					
SEASON	TEAM	OPPONENTS	V	M	I	NO	RUNS	H.S.	AVGE	100	50	CT/St	OV	MD	RUNS	W	AVGE	B.B.
1944-45	Barbados	Trinidad	IIs	2	4		76	53	19.00		1		4	1	15	0		
1945-46	Barbados	Trinidad	IIs	2	4		57	29	14.25			1	5	0	16	0		
1946-47	Barbados	British Guiana	IIs	2	4	1	250	129	83.33	1	1	2						
1946-47	Barbados	Jamaica	IIs	2	4		223	123	55.75	1	1	2						
1947-48	Barbados	M.C.C. Tourist	WI	2	3	2	145	*118	145.00	1								
1947-48	**WEST INDIES**	**ENGLAND TESTS**	**WI**	**4**	**6**		**293**	**141**	**48.83**	**1**		**1**						
1948-49	West Indies	Tour of India	I	6	8	3	317	*172	63.40	1	1	4	18	1	68	1	68.00	
1948-49	**WEST INDIES**	**INDIA TESTS**	**I**	**5**	**7**		**779**	**194**	**111.28**	**4**	**2**	**1**	**2**	**0**	**5**	**0**		
1948-49	West Indies	Tour of Pakistan	P	2	2		111	56	55.50		2	1						
1948-49	West Indies	Tour of Ceylon	C	2	2	1	143	*133	143.00	1		2	3	0	14	0		
1949-50	Barbados	British Guiana	IIs	2	3	1	439	*236	219.50	2	1	2	8	2	12	0		
1950	West Indies	Tour of England	E	19	27	4	1972	*304	85.73	6	6	20	9	0	41	2	20.50	
1950	**WEST INDIES**	**ENGLAND TESTS**	**E**	**4**	**6**		**338**	**129**	**56.33**	**1**	**3**	**11**						
1950-51	Barbados	Trinidad	IIs	2	4		155	75	38.75		2	1	20	3	75	3	25.00	
1951	Comm. XI	England XI	E	1	1		117	117	117.00	1		1						
1951-52	West Indies	Tour of Australia	A	4	6		177	66	29.50		1	3	1	0	3	0		
1951-52	**WEST INDIES**	**AUSTRALIA TESTS**	**A**	**5**	**10**		**245**	**70**	**24.50**		**2**	**5**						
1951-52	West Indies	Tour of New Zealand	NZ	1	1		75	75	75.00		1	1/1	2	0	5	0		
1951-52	**WEST INDIES**	**NEW ZEALAND TESTS**	**NZ**	**2**	**3**		**60**	**51**	**20.00**		**1**	**2**						
1952-53	Barbados	Indian Tourist	WI	1	1		253	253	253.00	1			9	3	13	0		

1952-53	**WEST INDIES**	**INDIA TESTS**	**WI**	**5**	**8**	**1**	**716**	**207**	**102.28**	**3**	**2**	**9**	**3**	**0**	**11**	**0**		
1953	Comm. XI	Essex	E	1	2		44	40	22.00			2						
1953-54	Barbados	M.C.C. Tourist	WI	1	2		64	47	32.00									
1953-54	**WEST INDIES**	**ENGLAND TESTS**	**WI**	**4**	**8**	**1**	**487**	**206**	**69.57**	**1**	**3**	**3**	**7**	**1**	**39**	**0**		
1954-55	Barbados	Australian Tourist	WI	1	2		142	132	71.00	1		1						
1954-55	**WEST INDIES**	**AUSTRALIA TESTS**	**WI**	**5**	**10**	**2**	**469**	**139**	**58.62**	**1**	**3**	**3**	**2.2**	**0**	**8**	**1**	**8.00**	
1955-56	West Indies	Tour of New Zealand	NZ	4	5	1	522	156	130.50	3	1							
1955-56	**WEST INDIES**	**NEW ZEALAND TESTS**	**NZ**	**4**	**5**		**418**	**156**	**83.60**	**3**		**5**						
1955-56	West Indies XI	E.W. Swanton's Tourist	WI	1	2	1	125	89	125.00		1							
1956-57	Barbados	Trinidad	IIs	1	1		54	54	54.00		1	1						
1956-57	Barbados	British Guiana	IIs	1	2		67	63	33.50		1		3	0	15	0		
1957	West Indies	Tour of England	E	18	30	1	901	105	31.06	1	9	13	6	0	32	1	32.00	
1957	**WEST INDIES**	**ENGLAND TESTS**	**E**	**5**	**10**		**195**	**90**	**19.50**		**1**	**4**						
1957-58	Barbados	Pakistan Tourist	WI	1	2		69	45	34.50			1	8	0	23	0		
1957-58	**WEST INDIES**	**PAKISTAN TESTS**	**WI**	**5**	**8**	**1**	**455**	**197**	**65.00**	**1**	**2**	**5**	**6**	**2**	**14**	**0**		
1958-59	Barbados	British Guiana	IIs	2	3	1	81	52	40.50		1	2	2	0	8	0		
1959-60	Barbados	M.C.C. Tourist	WI	1	D								14.3	2	38	4	9.50	
1960-61	Barbados	Trinidad	IIs	2	4	1	105	*68	35.00		1	1	10	0	43	0		
1960-61	E.W. Swanton's XI	Tour of West Indies	WI	4	6		211	63	35.16		1	3	16	2	60	3	20.00	
1961-62	Barbados	Jamaica	IIs	1	1		49	49	49.00			1	4	0	18	0		
1961-62	Barbados	British Guiana	IIs	1	2		73	73	36.50		1		3	0	21	0		
1961-62	International XI	World Tour	R/D/NZ	7	11	1	231	55	23.10		1	8						
1962-63	Barbados	Trinidad	IIs	1	1		41	41	41.00									
1962-63	Barbados	British Guiana	IIs	1	2		22	16	11.00			1						
1963-64	The Rest XI	West Indies XI	IIs	1	2		60	41	30.00			1	5	0	38	0		
1963-64	F. Worrell's XI	C. Hunte's XI	IIs	1	2	1	31	*27	31.00			1	14	0	96	2	48.00	
1963-64	Barbados	British Guiana	IIs	1	1		14	14	14.00									
1963-64	Barbados	Jamaica	IIs	1	1		107	107	107.00	1								
1963-64	Barbados	Trinidad	IIs	1	2		32	19	16.00									
		Barbados		32	53	6	2518	253	53.37	8	11	16	90.3	11	297	7	42.42	
		West Indies		105	164	16	8798	*304	59.44	27	41	93/1	59.2	4	240	5	48.00	
		Comm. XI		2	3		161	117	53.66	1		3						
		E.W. Swanton's XI		4	6		211	63	35.16		1	3	16	2	60	3	20.00	
		International XI		7	11	1	231	55	23.10		1	8						
		The Rest XI		1	2		60	41	30.00			1	5	0	38	0		
		F. Worrell's XI		1	2	1	31	*27	31.00			1	14	0	96	2	48.00	
		TEST RECORD		**48**	**81**	**5**	**4455**	**207**	**58.61**	**15**	**19**	**49**	**20.2**	**3**	**77**	**1**	**77.00**	**1-8**
		CAREER		**152**	**241**	**24**	**12010**	***304**	**55.34**	**36**	**54**	**125/1**	**184.5**	**17**	**731**	**17**	**43.00**	**4-38**

WEEKES, Kenneth Hunnell

SEASON	TEAM	OPPONENTS	V	BATTING M	I	NO	RUNS	H.S.	AVGE	100	50	CT/St	BOWLING OV	MD	RUNS	W	AVGE	B.B.
1938-39	Jamaica	Combined Universities	WI	2	3		176	106	58.66	1	1	1	12	2	53	3	17.66	
1938-39	Jamaica	Trinidad	IIs	1	2	1	90	88	90.00		1	1						
1938-39	Jamaica	West Indies XI	IIs	1	2	1	118	*100	118.00	1		4/1						
1939	West Indies	Tour of England	E	17	25	1	630	146	26.25	1	5	6						
1939	**WEST INDIES**	**ENGLAND TESTS**	**E**	**2**	**3**		**173**	**137**	**57.66**	**1**								
1945-46	Jamaica	Trinidad	IIs	3	5	1	249	72	62.25		3	2	42.4	7	107	5	21.40	
1946-47	Jamaica	Barbados	IIs	2	4		222	84	55.50		2		44	4	134	1	134.00	
1947-48	Jamaica	British Guiana	IIs	2	3		73	41	24.33			7	47	1	170	3	56.66	
		Jamaica		11	19	3	928	106	58.00	2	7	15/1	145.4	14	464	12	38.66	
		West Indies		19	28	1	803	146	29.74	2	5	6						
		TEST RECORD		**2**	**3**	**0**	**173**	**137**	**57.66**	**1**	**0**	**0**						
		CAREER		**30**	**47**	**4**	**1731**	**146**	**40.25**	**4**	**12**	**21/1**	**145.4**	**14**	**464**	**12**	**38.66**	**3-84**

WHITE, Anthony Wilbur

SEASON	TEAM	OPPONENTS	V	BATTING M	I	NO	RUNS	H.S.	AVGE	100	50	CT	BOWLING OV	MD	RUNS	W	AVGE	B.B.
1958-59	Barbados	Jamaica	IIs	2	4		110	53	27.50		2	4	92	36	167	9	18.55	
1959-60	Barbados	British Guiana	IIs	2	3		84	53	28.00		1	4	112	42	245	9	27.22	
1959-60	Barbados	M.C.C. Tourist	WI	1	1	1	6	*6				2	59	16	156	5	31.20	
1960-61	Barbados	Trinidad	IIs	2	3		30	19	10.00			5	99.5	41	195	7	27.85	
1961-62	Barbados	Jamaica	IIs	1	1		18	18	18.00			1	48	17	114	3	38.00	
1961-62	Barbados	British Guiana	IIs	1	2	1	129	75	129.00		2	2	48.4	6	155	4	38.75	
1961-62	Barbados	Indian Tourist	WI	1	1		35	35	35.00				18	4	61	1	61.00	
1962-63	Barbados	Trinidad	IIs	1	1		12	12	12.00				41.1	15	55	7	7.85	
1962-63	Barbados	British Guiana	IIs	1	2		43	38	21.50			1	39	18	72	2	36.00	
1963	West Indies	Tour of England	E	9	14	3	228	*68	20.72		1	8	286	83	647	28	23.10	
1963-64	The Rest XI	West Indies XI	WI	1	2		71	71	35.50		1	1	22	4	77	2	38.50	
1963-64	F. Worrell's XI	C. Hunte's XI	WI	1	1		42	42	42.00				37	1	133	2	66.50	
1963-64	Barbados	British Guiana	IIs	1	1		16	16	16.00			3	28	4	86	1	86.00	
1963-64	Barbados	Jamaica	IIs	1	2	1	74	57	74.00		1		39.1	15	96	4	24.00	
1963-64	Barbados	Trinidad	IIs	1	2		7	5	3.50				52	21	96	5	19.20	
1964-65	Barbados	Cavaliers Touring XI	WI	1	D								33	5	84	1	84.00	

1964-65	Barbados	Australian Tourist	WI	1	1		17	17	17.00				21.3	5	58	2	29.00	
1964-65	**WEST INDIES**	**AUSTRALIA TESTS**	**WI**	**2**	**4**	**1**	**71**	***57**	**23.66**		**1**	**1**	**81.5**	**27**	**152**	**3**	**50.66**	
1965-66	Barbados	Shell Shield	IIs	1	1		3	3	3.00				7	2	16	0		
		Barbados		18	25	3	584	75	26.54		6	22	738.2	247	1656	60	27.60	
		West Indies		11	18	4	299	*68	21.35		2	9	367.5	110	799	31	25.77	
		The Rest XI		1	2		71	71	35.50		1	1	22	4	77	2	38.50	
		F. Worrell's XI		1	1		42	42	42.00				37	1	133	2	66.50	
		TEST RECORD		**2**	**4**	**1**	**71**	***57**	**23.66**	**0**	**1**	**1**	**81.5**	**27**	**152**	**3**	**50.66**	**2-34**
		CAREER		**31**	**46**	**7**	**996**	**75**	**25.53**	**0**	**9**	**32**	**1165.1**	**362**	**2665**	**95**	**28.05**	**6-80**

WIGHT, Claude Vibart

				BATTING									BOWLING					
SEASON	TEAM	OPPONENTS	V	M	I	NO	RUNS	H.S.	AVGE	100	50	CT	OV	MD	RUNS	W	AVGE	B.B.
1925-26	British Guiana	Barbados	IIs	1	2		8	4	4.00			1						
1925-26	British Guiana	Trinidad	IIs	1	2		71	37	35.50									
1925-26	British Guiana	M.C.C. Tourist	WI	2	2		65	46	32.50									
1925-26	West Indies XI	M.C.C. Tourist	WI	1	1		90	90	90.00		1	2						
1926-27	British Guiana	Barbados	IIs	1	2		64	47	32.00				5	0	16	0		
1927-28	Combined T/BG XI	Combined Jam/Bar XI	IIs	2	2		21	11	10.50			2						
1927-28	West Indies XI	Barbados XI	IIs	1	1	1	119	*119		1		2						
1928	West Indies	Tour of England	E	16	24	8	308	40	19.25			9						
1928	**WEST INDIES**	**ENGLAND TESTS**	**E**	**1**	**2**	**1**	**35**	**23**	**35.00**									
1929-30	British Guiana	Barbados	IIs	1	2		22	13	11.00				1	0	1	0		
1929-30	British Guiana	Trinidad	IIs	1	2		51	43	25.50				2	0	11	0		
1929-30	British Guiana	M.C.C. Tourist	WI	2	4		126	51	31.50		1		24	4	104	2	52.00	
1929-30	**WEST INDIES**	**ENGLAND TESTS**	**WI**	**1**	**2**		**32**	**22**	**16.00**				**5**	**1**	**6**	**0**		
1931-32	British Guiana	Trinidad	IIs	1	2		61	39	30.50			1	6	2	19	0		
1934-35	British Guiana	Barbados	IIs	1	2		206	130	103.00	1	1	1						
1934-35	British Guiana	Trinidad	IIs	1	1		2	2	2.00			1						
1934-35	British Guiana	M.C.C. Tourist	WI	2	3	1	49	*30	24.50				4	0	22	1	22.00	
1937-38	British Guiana	Barbados	IIs	1	1		12	12	12.00			1						
1937-38	British Guiana	Trinidad	IIs	1	1		127	127	127.00	1			2	0	15	0		
1938-39	British Guiana	R.S. Grant's XI	IIs	2	3		78	40	26.00				6	1	15	0		
		British Guiana		18	29	1	942	130	33.64	2	3	5	50	7	203	3	67.66	
		West Indies		20	30	10	584	*119	29.20	1		13	5	1	6	0		

SEASON	TEAM	OPPONENTS	V	M	I	NO	RUNS	H.S.	AVGE	100	50	CT	OV	MD	RUNS	W	AVGE	B.B.
				BATTING									BOWLING					
		Combined T/BG XI		2	2		21	11	10.50			2						
		TEST RECORD		**2**	**4**	**1**	**67**	**23**	**22.33**	**0**	**0**	**0**	**5**	**1**	**6**	**0**		
		CAREER		**40**	**61**	**11**	**1547**	**130**	**30.94**	**3**	**3**	**20**	**55**	**8**	**209**	**3**	**69.66**	**1-18**

WIGHT, George Leslie

SEASON	TEAM	OPPONENTS	V	M	I	NO	RUNS	H.S.	AVGE	100	50	CT	OV	MD	RUNS	W	AVGE	B.B.
				BATTING									BOWLING					
1949-50	British Guiana	Barbados	IIs	2	4		177	58	44.25		2	3						
1950-51	British Guiana	Jamaica	IIs	2	4		161	64	40.25		2	1						
1951-52	British Guiana	Barbados	IIs	2	3	2	412	*262	412.00	2		3						
1951-52	British Guiana	Trinidad	IIs	2	4		213	114	106.50	1	1	3						
1952-53	British Guiana	Jamaica	IIs	2	3		192	138	64.00	1		2						
1952-53	British Guiana	Indian Tourist	WI	1	2		84	79	42.00		1							
1952-53	**WEST INDIES**	**INDIA TESTS**	**WI**	**1**	**1**		**21**	**21**	**21.00**									
		British Guiana		11	20	2	1239	*262	68.83	4	6	12						
		West Indies		1	1		21	21	21.00									
		TEST RECORD		**1**	**1**	**0**	**21**	**21**	**21.00**	**0**	**0**	**0**						
		CAREER		**12**	**21**	**2**	**1260**	***262**	**66.31**	**4**	**6**	**12**						

WILES, Charles Archibald

SEASON	TEAM	OPPONENTS	V	M	I	NO	RUNS	H.S.	AVGE	100	50	CT	OV	MD	RUNS	W	AVGE	B.B.
				BATTING									BOWLING					
1919-20	Trinidad	Barbados	IIs	2	4		52	22	13.00									
1921-22	Trinidad	British Guiana	IIs	1	1		76	76	76.00		1	1						
1921-22	Trinidad	Barbados	IIs	1	2	1	118	88	118.00		1							
1922-23	Trinidad	British Guiana	IIs	1	2		0	0										
1922-23	Trinidad	Barbados	IIs	1	2		29	16	14.50									
1924-25	Trinidad	British Guiana	IIs	1	2		156	110	78.00	1		1						
1924-25	Trinidad	Barbados	IIs	1	2		32	32	16.00									
1925-26	Trinidad	British Guiana	IIs	1	2		14	12	7.00									
1925-26	Trinidad	M.C.C. Tourist	WI	2	3	1	60	30	30.00			2						
1925-26	West Indies XI	M.C.C. Tourist	WI	1	2		92	75	46.00		1							

SEASON	TEAM	OPPONENTS	V	M	I	NO	RUNS	H.S.	AVGE	100	50	CT	OV	MD	RUNS	W	AVGE	B.B.
1926-27	Trinidad	Barbados	IIs	1	2		205	192	102.50	1								
1927-28	Combined T/BG XI	Combined Jam/Bar XI	IIs	2	2		16	13	8.00			1						
1927-28	Barbados XI	West Indies XI	IIs	1	2	1	57	*34	57.00									
1928-29	Trinidad	British Guiana	IIs	1	2		7	7	3.50									
1928-29	Trinidad	Barbados	IIs	1	1		46	46	46.00			1						
1929-30	Trinidad	British Guiana	IIs	1	2		21	19	10.50									
1929-30	Trinidad	M.C.C. Tourist	WI	2	4		83	31	20.75									
1931-32	Trinidad	Barbados	IIs	1	2	1	66	43	66.00									
1931-32	Trinidad	British Guiana	IIs	1	2		76	76	38.00		1							
1932-33	C.A. Merry's XI	G.C. Grant's XI	IIs	1	2		78	43	39.00									
1933	West Indies	Tour of England	E	12	22	1	429	71	20.42		2	1						
1933	**WEST INDIES**	**ENGLAND TESTS**	**E**	**1**	**2**		**2**	**2**	**1.00**									
1935-36	Trinidad	Barbados	IIs	1	2		51	44	25.50									
		Trinidad		20	37	3	1092	192	32.11	2	3	5						
		West Indies		14	26	1	523	75	20.92		3	1						
		Barbados XI		1	2	1	57	34	57.00									
		C.A. Merry's XI		1	2		78	43	39.00									
		Combined T/BG XI		2	2		16	13	8.00			1						
		TEST RECORD		**1**	**2**	**0**	**2**	**2**	**1.00**	**0**	**0**	**0**						
		CAREER		**38**	**69**	**5**	**1766**	**192**	**27.59**	**2**	**6**	**7**						

WILLETT, Elquemedo Tonito

				BATTING									BOWLING					
SEASON	**TEAM**	**OPPONENTS**	**V**	**M**	**I**	**NO**	**RUNS**	**H.S.**	**AVGE**	**100**	**50**	**CT**	**OV**	**MD**	**RUNS**	**W**	**AVGE**	**B.B.**
1970-71	Leeward Islands	Windward Islands	IIs	1	1		0	0					28	6	44	4	11.00	
1970-71	Combined Islands	Shell Shield	IIs	4	8	3	52	21	10.40			3	86	22	250	10	25.00	
1970-71	Leeward Islands	Indian Tourist	WI	1	2		2	2	1.00			1	44	3	135	3	45.00	
1971-72	Leeward Islands	Windward Islands	IIs	1	1		12	12	12.00				74.1	20	178	10	17.80	
1971-72	Combined Islands	Shell Shield	IIs	4	8	3	37	*16	7.40			3	141	24	363	5	72.60	
1971-72	Leeward Islands	New Zealand Tourist	WI	1	1		5	5	5.00				44	16	66	5	13.20	
1972-73	Leeward Islands	Windward islands	IIs	2	1	1	23	*23	23.00			1	86.1	31	191	13	14.69	
1972-73	Combined Islands	Shell Shield	IIs	4	8	2	162	47	27.00			5	188.2	56	428	18	23.77	
1972-73	WI President's XI	Australian Tourist	WI	1	2	1	20	*17	20.00			1	49	15	132	7	18.85	
1972-73	Leeward Islands	Australian Tourist	WI	1	1	1	16	*16				1	48.2	23	84	8	10.50	
1972-73	**WEST INDIES**	**AUSTRALIA TESTS**	**WI**	**3**	**5**	**2**	**19**	**12**	**6.33**				**145**	**49**	**327**	**7**	**46.71**	
1973	West Indies	Tour of England	E	11	9	5	115	56	28.75		1	8	251.4	77	694	30	23.13	

							BATTING								BOWLING			
SEASON	TEAM	OPPONENTS	V	M	I	NO	RUNS	H.S.	AVGE	100	50	CT	OV	MD	RUNS	W	AVGE	B.B.
1973-74	Combined Islands	Shell Shield	IIs	4	7		30	9	4.28			2	155.3	41	305	13	23.46	
1973-74	Leeward Islands	M.C.C. Tourist	WI	1	1	1	0	*0					51	15	88	4	22.00	
1974-75	West Indies	Tour of India	I	4	2	1	63	47	63.00				100	30	259	5	51.80	
1974-75	**WEST INDIES**	**INDIA TESTS**	**I**	**2**	**3**	**1**	**55**	**26**	**27.50**				**76**	**29**	**155**	**4**	**38.75**	
1974-75	West Indies	Tour of Sri Lanka	SL	2	3		9	5	3.00			1	37	9	96	5	19.20	
1974-75	West Indies	Tour of Pakistan	P	1	D								51	9	173	4	43.25	
1974-75	Combined Islands	Shell Shield	IIs	4	7	1	56	15	9.33			3	190.5	51	390	11	35.45	
1975-76	Leeward Islands	Windward Islands	IIs	1	2		14	14	7.00			1	37	15	62	5	12.40	
1975-76	Combined Islands	Shell Shield	IIs	4	3	1	17	12	8.50			1	116	27	265	4	65.75	
1975-76	Leeward Islands	Indian Tourist	WI	1	D								24	3	49	2	24.50	
1976-77	Leeward Islands	Windward Islands	IIs	2	2	1	30	*24	30.00			3	65.4	19	151	10	15.10	
1976-77	Combined Islands	Shell Shield	IIs	1	1		0	0					40	13	74	0		
1977-78	Leeward Islands	Windward Islands	IIs	2	4		26	13	6.50			2	88.4	25	179	8	22.37	
1977-78	Combined Islands	Shell Shield	IIs	4	5		40	22	8.00			7	144	33	285	6	47.50	
1977-78	Leeward Islands	Australian Tourist	WI	1	2	2	10	*10				1	71	14	205	10	20.50	
1978-79	Leeward Islands	Windward Islands	IIs	2	2		2	2	1.00				100	19	253	6	42.16	
1978-79	Combined Islands	Shell Shield	IIs	3	4	3	13	*5	13.00			4	115.1	30	242	4	60.50	
1979-80	Leeward Islands	Windward Islands	IIs	1	2	1	32	*23	32.00			1	68.4	15	138	5	27.60	
1979-80	Combined Islands	Shell Shield	IIs	1	2		14	13	7.00			1	29	5	85	2	42.50	
1982-83	Leeward Islands	Shell Shield	IIs	4	6	3	34	12	11.33			2	166.3	48	372	13	28.61	
1982-83	Leeward Islands	Indian Tourist	WI	1	2	1	6	*6	6.00				41	14	87	1	87.00	
1983-84	Leeward Islands	Shell Shield	IIs	4	5	3	18	12	9.00			4	138.4	33	343	10	34.30	
1984-85	Leeward Islands	Shell Shield	IIs	5	7	4	71	40	23.66			1	157.2	44	306	13	23.53	
1985-86	Leeward Islands	Shell Shield	IIs	1	1		0	0				1	66	25	139	3	46.33	
1986-87	Leeward Islands	Shell Shield	IIs	3	4	4	47	*20					111	19	262	5	52.40	
1987-88	Leeward Islands	Red Stripe Cup	IIs	4	5	1	28	*14	7.00			8	102	26	249	12	20.75	
1988-89	Leeward Islands	Red Stripe Cup	IIs	1	2		22	17	11.00				13	1	28	1	28.00	
		Leeward Islands		41	54	23	398	40	12.83			27	1626.1	434	3609	151	23.90	
		Combined Islands		33	53	13	421	47	10.52			29	1205.5	302	2687	73	36.80	
		West Indies		24	24	10	281	56	6.85		1	10	709.4	218	1836	62	29.61	
		TEST RECORD		**5**	**8**	**3**	**74**	**26**	**14.80**	**0**	**0**	**0**	**221**	**78**	**482**	**11**	**43.81**	**3-33**
		CAREER		**98**	**131**	**46**	**1100**	**56**	**12.94**	**0**	**1**	**66**	**3541.4**	**954**	**8132**	**286**	**28.43**	**8-73**

WILLIAMS, Alvadon Basil

							BATTING								BOWLING			
SEASON	TEAM	OPPONENTS	V	M	I	NO	RUNS	H.S.	AVGE	100	50	CT	OV	MD	RUNS	W	AVGE	B.B.
1969-70	Jamaica	Shell Shield	IIs	1	2		21	20	10.50									
1970-71	Jamaica	Shell Shield	IIs	1	2		15	15	7.50			1	1	0	7	0		
1976-77	Jamaica	Shell Shield	IIs	4	6		301	123	50.16	1	1	1	5	1	8	0		
1976-77	Jamaica	Pakistan Tourist	WI	1	2		13	8	6.50									
1977-78	Jamaica	Shell Shield	IIs	4	6	1	399	96	79.80		5	1	2	0	7	0		
1977-78	**WEST INDIES**	**AUSTRALIA TESTS**	**WI**	**3**	**6**		**257**	**100**	**42.83**	**1**	**1**	**4**						
1978-79	West Indies	Tour of India	I	5	8	1	339	*126	48.42	1	3	2						
1978-79	**WEST INDIES**	**INDIA TESTS**	**I**	**4**	**6**		**212**	**111**	**35.33**	**1**		**1**						
1978-79	Jamaica	Shell Shield	IIs	4	6		180	82	30.00		1		4	1	18	0		
1979-80	Jamaica	Shell Shield	IIs	4	8		206	72	25.75		1	1	1	0	4	0		
1980-81	Jamaica	Shell Shield	IIs	3	6		46	24	7.66			2						
1980-81	Jamaica	English Tourist	WI	1	1		10	10	10.00			1	2	0	5	0		
1983-84	Jamaica	Shell Shield	IIs	5	9		220	41	24.44			2						
1984-85	Jamaica	Shell Shield	IIs	5	8		380	102	47.50	1	3							
1984-85	WI Shield Awards XI	New Zealand Tourist	WI	1	1		4	4	4.00			2						
		Jamaica		33	56	1	1791	123	32.56	2	11	9	15	2	49	0		
		West Indies		13	21	1	812	*126	40.60	3	4	9						
		TEST RECORD		**7**	**12**	**0**	**469**	**111**	**39.08**	**2**	**1**	**5**						
		CAREER		**46**	**77**	**2**	**2603**	***126**	**34.70**	**5**	**15**	**18**	**15**	**2**	**49**	**0**		

WILLIAMS, Ernest Albert Vivian

							BATTING								BOWLING			
SEASON	TEAM	OPPONENTS	V	M	I	NO	RUNS	H.S.	AVGE	100	50	CT	OV	MD	RUNS	W	AVGE	B.B.
1934-35	Barbados	British Guiana	IIs	1	2		13	10	6.50			1	48.2	12	110	4	27.50	
1934-35	Barbados	M.C.C. Tourist	WI	2	3	1	24	*13	12.00				33	4	147	3	49.00	
1935-36	Barbados	Trinidad	IIs	1	2	2	142	*131		1			35	4	110	6	18.33	
1936-37	Barbados	Trinidad	IIs	1	2		95	80	47.50		1	1	40.5	4	163	5	32.60	
1937-38	Barbados	British Guiana	IIs	1	2		15	15	7.50				24	6	94	1	94.00	
1938-39	Barbados	Trinidad	IIs	1	2		27	23	13.50				23	1	92	4	23.00	
1938-39	Barbados	British Guiana	IIs	1	2		60	34	30.00			1	27	2	108	3	36.00	
1938-39	West Indies XI	Jamaica	IIs	1	1		28	28	28.00				27	1	106	4	26.50	
1939	West Indies	Tour of England	E	10	14	3	369	*126	33.54	1	1	5	110.4	13	438	14	31.28	
1939	**WEST INDIES**	**ENGLAND TESTS**	**E**	**1**	**1**		**1**	**1**	**1.00**			**1**	**9**	**1**	**23**	**0**		

SEASON	TEAM	OPPONENTS	V	M	I	NO	RUNS	H.S.	AVGE	100	50	CT	OV	MD	RUNS	W	AVGE	B.B.
				BATTING									BOWLING					
1940-41	Barbados	Trinidad	IIs	2	4	1	109	67	36.33		1	1	36.1	4	141	5	28.20	
1941-42	Barbados	Trinidad	IIs	4	6		92	39	15.33			3	93.5	7	323	15	21.53	
1942-43	Barbados	Trinidad	IIs	1	1		7	7	7.00				21	3	78	1	78.00	
1943-44	Barbados	Trinidad	IIs	1	2		21	11	10.50			1	16	1	61	2	30.50	
1944-45	Barbados	British Guiana	IIs	1	2		77	48	38.50				34	2	115	7	16.42	
1944-45	Barbados	Trinidad	IIs	2	4		84	39	21.00			2	49	6	182	6	30.33	
1945-46	Barbados	Trinidad	IIs	2	1		0	0				1	56.5	9	203	6	33.83	
1946-47	Barbados	British Guiana	IIs	2	3	1	141	58	70.50		2		67	17	212	5	43.00	
1947-48	Barbados	M.C.C. Tourist	WI	2	1		33	33	33.00				90.4	18	218	10	21.80	
1947-48	**WEST INDIES**	**ENGLAND TESTS**	**WI**	**3**	**5**		**112**	**72**	**22.40**		**1**	**1**	**120.4**	**45**	**218**	**9**	**24.22**	
1948-49	Barbados	Trinidad	IIs	2	3		29	26	9.66			1	74	12	245	6	40.83	
		Barbados		27	42	5	969	*131	26.18	1	4	12	769.2	112	2602	89	29.23	
		West Indies		15	21	3	510	*126	28.33	1	2	7	267.2	60	785	27	29.07	
		TEST RECORD		**4**	**6**	**0**	**113**	**72**	**18.83**	**0**	**1**	**2**	**129.4**	**46**	**241**	**9**	**26.77**	**3-51**
		CAREER		**42**	**63**	**8**	**1479**	***131**	**26.89**	**2**	**6**	**19**	**1036.4**	**172**	**3387**	**116**	**29.19**	**5-73**

WISHART, Kenneth Leslie

SEASON	TEAM	OPPONENTS	V	M	I	NO	RUNS	H.S.	AVGE	100	50	CT	OV	MD	RUNS	W	AVGE	B.B.
				BATTING									BOWLING					
1928-29	British Guiana	Trinidad	IIs	1	2		31	24	15.50			1						
1929-30	British Guiana	M.C.C. Tourist	WI	2	4		235	88	58.75		2							
1931-32	British Guiana	Trinidad	IIs	1	2		30	15	15.00			1						
1934-35	British Guiana	Barbados	IIs	1	2		83	54	41.50		1							
1934-35	British Guiana	Trinidad	IIs	1	2		9	7	4.50									
1934-35	British Guiana	M.C.C. Tourist	WI	2	4	1	97	56	32.33		1	1						
1934-35	**WEST INDIES**	**ENGLAND TESTS**	**WI**	**1**	**2**		**52**	**52**	**26.00**		**1**							
1935-36	British Guiana	Trinidad	IIs	1	2		16	15	8.00			1						
1936-37	British Guiana	Trinidad	IIs	1	2		18	16	9.00			1						
1938-39	British Guiana	Trinidad	IIs	1	2		41	35	20.50			1						
1938-39	British Guiana	Barbados	IIs	1	2	1	38	38	38.00			1						
1946-47	British Guiana	Barbados	IIs	1	2		16	12	8.00									
1946-47	British Guiana	Trinidad	IIs	2	4		40	17	10.00									
		British Guiana		15	30	2	654	88	23.35		4	7						

	M	I	NO	RUNS	H.S.	AVGE	100	50	CT						
West Indies	1	2		52	52	26.00		1							
TEST RECORD	**1**	**2**	**0**	**52**	**52**	**26.00**	**0**	**1**	**0**						
CAREER	**16**	**32**	**2**	**706**	**88**	**23.53**	**0**	**5**	**7**						

WORRELL, Frank Mortimore Maglinne

				BATTING									BOWLING					
SEASON	TEAM	OPPONENTS	V	M	I	NO	RUNS	H.S.	AVGE	100	50	CT	OV	MD	RUNS	W	AVGE	B.B.
1941-42	Barbados	Trinidad	IIs	4	7	2	134	48	26.80			3	78	9	300	15	20.00	
1942-43	Barbados	Trinidad	IIs	2	4	1	322	188	107.33	1	2	1	32	6	110	1	110.00	
1943-44	Barbados	Trinidad	IIs	2	3	1	347	*308	173.50	1		3	46	3	145	10	14.50	
1944-45	Barbados	British Guiana	IIs	2	3		77	41	25.66			2	59.3	11	203	8	25.37	
1944-45	Barbados	Trinidad	IIs	2	4		248	113	62.00	1	2	2	19	0	90	0		
1945-46	Barbados	Trinidad	IIs	1	2	1	271	*255	271.00	1			25	6	77	2	38.50	
1946-47	Barbados	Jamaica	IIs	2	4	1	148	*67	49.33		1	4	74.1	15	223	7	31.85	
1947-48	Jamaica	British Guiana	IIs	2	2		96	65	48.00		1		65.3	12	189	7	27.00	
1947-48	Jamaica	M.C.C. Tourist	WI	2	4	2	178	*106	89.00	1	1	2	50	17	121	3	40.33	
1947-48	**WEST INDIES**	**ENGLAND TESTS**	**WI**	**3**	**4**	**2**	**294**	***131**	**147.00**	**1**	**1**	**2**	**70**	**10**	**156**	**1**	**156.00**	
1949-50	Comm. XI	Tour of India	I	17	26	4	1640	*223	74.54	5	8	7	341.4	123	611	26	23.50	
1950	West Indies	Tour of England	E	18	25	5	1236	*241	61.80	4	4	7	381.3	134	788	33	23.87	
1950	**WEST INDIES**	**ENGLAND TESTS**	**E**	**4**	**6**		**539**	**261**	**89.83**	**2**	**1**	**4**	**98.2**	**36**	**182**	**6**	**30.33**	
1950-51	Comm. XI	Tour of India	I	22	33	3	1900	285	63.33	5	12	16	578.8	195	1176	39	30.15	
1951	Comm. XI	England XI	E	2	3		88	52	29.33		1		4	2	2	0		
1951-52	West Indies	Tour of Australia	A	4	7	2	282	*160	56.40	1	1	5	53.4	9	155	8	19.37	
1951-52	**WEST INDIES**	**AUSTRALIA TESTS**	**A**	**5**	**10**		**337**	**108**	**33.70**	**1**	**1**	**4**	**89.1**	**10**	**329**	**17**	**17.35**	
1951-52	West Indies	Tour of New Zealand	NZ	1	2	1	20	*16	20.00			1	8	3	18	1	18.00	
1951-52	**WEST INDIES**	**NEW ZEALAND TESTS**	**NZ**	**2**	**3**	**1**	**233**	**100**	**116.50**	**1**	**2**	**2**	**47**	**15**	**81**	**2**	**40.50**	
1952	Comm. XI	England XI	E	1	2		97	62	48.50		1							
1952-53	Jamaica	Indian Tourist	WI	1	2	1	48	*47	48.00				8	1	21	0		
1952-53	**WEST INDIES**	**INDIA TESTS**	**WI**	**5**	**8**		**398**	**237**	**49.75**	**1**	**1**	**8**	**135**	**35**	**262**	**7**	**37.42**	
1953	Comm. XI	Essex & England XI	E	2	4		83	37	20.75				38	13	52	5	10.40	
1953-54	Comm. XI	Tour of India	I	11	16		833	165	52.06	4	2	14	329.5	103	658	24	27.41	
1953-54	**WEST INDIES**	**ENGLAND TESTS**	**WI**	**4**	**8**	**1**	**334**	**167**	**47.71**	**1**	**2**	**4**	**69**	**9**	**193**	**2**	**96.50**	
1954	Comm. XI	England XI	E	2	3	1	116	74	58.00		1	2	27	6	52	1	52.00	
1954-55	Jamaica	Trinidad	IIs	2	4		148	100	37.00	1		1	14	4	25	0		
1954-55	Jamaica	Australian Tourist	WI	1	1		24	24	24.00			1	27.5	5	107	5	21.40	
1954-55	**WEST INDIES**	**AUSTRALIA TESTS**	**WI**	**4**	**8**		**206**	**61**	**25.75**		**2**	**2**	**115**	**23**	**311**	**3**	**103.66**	
1955	Comm. XI	England XI	E	2	4		178	100	44.50	1		2	52	7	185	6	30.83	

SEASON	TEAM	OPPONENTS	V	M	I	NO	RUNS	H.S.	AVGE	100	50	CT	OV	MD	RUNS	W	AVGE	B.B.
				BATTING									BOWLING					
1957	West Indies	Tour of England	E	15	24	8	1120	135	70.00	3	8	9	278.3	69	606	29	20.89	
1957	**WEST INDIES**	**ENGLAND TESTS**	**E**	**5**	**10**	**1**	**350**	***191**	**38.88**	**1**	**1**	**1**	**128.2**	**25**	**343**	**10**	**34.30**	
1958	Comm. XI	England XI	E	1	2		72	68	36.00		1	1	10	2	21	0		
1958	A.E.R. Gilligan's XI	New Zealand Tourist	E	1	1		101	101	101.00	1		1	10	3	45	1	45.00	
1959	A.E.R. Gilligan's XI	Indian Tourist	E	1	2		79	54	39.50		1		20	4	63	3	21.00	
1959-60	Jamaica	M.C.C. Tourist	WI	1	1		75	75	75.00		1		4	0	19	0		
1959-60	**WEST INDIES**	**ENGLAND TESTS**	**WI**	**4**	**6**	**1**	**320**	***197**	**64.00**	**1**	**1**	**4**	**115.5**	**37**	**233**	**6**	**38.83**	
1960-61	West Indies	Tour of Australia	A	7	12	3	443	82	49.22		5	2	108	8	391	12	32.58	
1960-61	**WEST INDIES**	**AUSTRALIA TESTS**	**A**	**5**	**10**		**375**	**82**	**37.50**		**5**	**2**	**134**	**34**	**357**	**10**	**35.70**	
1961	M.C.C.	Cambridge & Oxford Univ.	E	2	3		46	29	15.33			2	62.3	14	141	6	23.50	
1961-62	Jamaica	Indian Tourist	WI	1	2	1	71	*57	71.00		1		57	2	57	2	28.50	
1961-62	**WEST INDIES**	**INDIA TESTS**	**WI**	**5**	**6**	**2**	**332**	***98**	**83.00**		**4**	**7**	**69.1**	**25**	**121**	**2**	**60.50**	
1963	West Indies	Tour of England	E	13	15	1	380	71	27.14		1	3	159	40	376	10	37.60	
1963	**WEST INDIES**	**ENGLAND TESTS**	**E**	**5**	**8**	**1**	**142**	***74**	**20.28**		**1**	**3**	**45**	**16**	**104**	**3**	**34.66**	
1963-64	West Indies XI	The Rest XI	WI	1	2	1	76	73	76.00		1		8	1	60	2	30.00	
1963-64	F. Worrell's XI	C. Hunte's XI	WI	1	1		24	24	24.00			1	30.1	5	81	4	20.25	
1963-64	Jamaica	Cavaliers Touring XI	WI	3	3		58	38	19.33			2	31	6	111	3	37.00	
1964	M.C.C.	Lancashire	E	1	2	1	38	*37	38.00				5	1	20	0		
1964	Free Foresters XI	Oxford University	E	1	2		42	42	21.00			1	27	6	72	3	24.00	
1964	West Indies XI	England XI	E	3	2		26	25	13.00				23	4	72	4	18.00	
		Barbados		15	27	6	1547	*308	73.66	4	5	15	333.4	50	1148	43	26.69	
		Jamaica		13	19	4	698	*106	46.53	2	4	6	257.2	47	650	20	32.50	
		West Indies		113	176	30	7443	261	53.16	17	42	71	2135.3	543	5138	168	30.58	
		Comm. XI		60	93	8	5007	285	58.90	15	26	42	1381	451	2757	101	27.29	
		M.C.C.		3	5	1	84	*37	21.00			2	67.3	15	161	6	26.83	
		A.E.R. Gilligan's XI		2	3		180	101	60.00	1	1	1	30	7	108	4	27.00	
		F. Worrell's XI		1	1		24	24	24.00			1	30.1	5	81	4	20.25	
		Free Foresters XI		1	2		42	42	21.00			1	27	6	72	3	24.00	
		TEST RECORD		**51**	**87**	**9**	**3860**	**261**	**49.48**	**9**	**22**	**43**	**1114.5**	**275**	**2672**	**69**	**38.72**	**7-70**
		CAREER		**208**	**326**	**49**	**15025**	***308**	**54.24**	**39**	**78**	**139**	**4262.1**	**1124**	**10115**	**349**	**28.98**	**7-70**

APPENDIX C

Career Statistics for West Indian-born Cricketers who have played Test Cricket for England

BUTCHER, Roland Orlando

SEASON	TEAM	OPPONENTS	V	BATTING M	I	NO	RUNS	H.S.	AVGE	100	50	CT/St	BOWLING OV	MD	RUNS	W	AVGE	B.B.
1974	Middlesex	Counties	E	5	8	1	150	*53	21.42		1	3						
1974-75	Barbados	Shell Shield	IIs	1	2		67	38	34.50									
1975	Middlesex	Counties	E	5	10		201	53	20.10		1	7						
1976	Middlesex	Counties	E	11	18	1	465	74	27.35		4	10	2	0	30	0		
1976	T.N. Pearce's XI	West Indies	E	1	2	1	54	*54	54.00		1	2						
1977	Middlesex	Counties	E	8	15		298	42	19.86			6						
1978	Middlesex	Counties	E	10	14		464	142	33.14	1	3	18						
1979	Middlesex	Counties	E	14	22		513	106	23.31	1	2	13	1	0	4	0		
1980	Middlesex	Counties	E	16	22	2	792	179	39.60	2	3	16						
1980-81	Middlesex	Tour of Zimbabwe	Z	3	6		162	52	27.00		2							
1980-81	England	Tour of West Indies	WI	4	8	2	314	*77	52.33		2	4						
1980-81	**ENGLAND**	**WEST INDIES TESTS**	**WI**	**3**	**5**		**71**	**32**	**14.20**			**3**						
1981	Middlesex	Counties	E	20	33	3	695	*106	23.16	1	5	32						
1981-82	International XI	Tour of Pakistan	P	3	6		92	35	15.33			4/1	3	1	12	0		
1982	Middlesex	Counties	E	21	28	3	1058	197	42.32	3	2	22	1	10	0			
1982-83	International XI	West Indies XI	WI	1	1		15	15	15.00									
1982-83	Tasmania	Sheffield Shield	A	12	19	2	423	53	24.88		3	12	4	1	9	0		
1983	Middlesex	Counties	E	15	19	3	657	179	41.06	2	3	36	3	1	11	0		
1984	Middlesex	Counties	E	23	40	7	1326	116	40.18	2	10	17						
1985	Middlesex	Counties	E	26	38	6	1210	120	37.81	1	9	24	19	5	46	2	23.00	
1986	Middlesex	Counties	E	26	37	4	1016	171	30.78	1	7	15	13.4	2	49	2	24.50	
1987	Middlesex	Counties	E	16	20	1	530	118	27.61	1	2	15	2.3	1	9	0		
1987	M.C.C.	Yorkshire	E	1	2		50	25	25.00									
1988	Middlesex	Counties	E	19	29	3	796	134	30.61	1	4	15						
1989	Middlesex	Counties	E	11	20	2	519	126	28.83	1	1	13						
1990	Middlesex	Counties	E	2	4	2	83	32	41.50			3	2	0	2	0		
		Barbados		1	2		67	38	34.50									
		Middlesex		251	383	38	10935	197	31.69	17	59	265	44.1	9	161	4	40.25	
		England		7	13	2	385	*77	35.00			7						
		International XI		4	7		107	35	15.28			4/1	3	1	12	0		
		Tasmania		12	19	2	423	53	24.88		3	12	4	1	9	0		
		T.N. Pearce's XI		1	2	1	54	*54	54.00		1	2						
		M.C.C.		1	2		50	25	25.00									
		TEST RECORD		**3**	**5**	**0**	**71**	**32**	**14.20**	**0**	**0**	**3**						
		CAREER		**277**	**428**	**43**	**12021**	**197**	**31.22**	**17**	**65**	**290/1**	**51.1**	**11**	**182**	**4**	**45.50**	**2-37**

COWANS, Norman George

SEASON	TEAM	OPPONENTS	V	M	I	NO	RUNS	H.S.	AVGE	100	50	CT	OV	MD	RUNS	W	AVGE	B.B.
				BATTING									BOWLING					
1980	Middlesex	Counties	E	1	1		1	1	1.00				16	4	42	1	42.00	
1980-81	Middlesex	Tour of Zimbabwe	Z	1	1		1	1	1.00				12	0	44	1	44.00	
1981	Middlesex	Counties	E	3	1		10	10	10.00			2	54	9	155	8	19.37	
1982	Middlesex	Counties	E	11	10	1	63	16	7.00			8	222.3	50	721	33	21.84	
1982-83	England	Tour of Australia	A	4	6	1	2	1	0.40			2	106.4	24	349	15	23.26	
1982-83	**ENGLAND**	**AUSTRALIA TESTS**	**A**	**4**	**7**	**1**	**68**	**36**	**11.33**			**3**	**107**	**14**	**396**	**11**	**36.00**	
1983	Middlesex	Counties	E	11	8	3	34	10	6.80			2	161	35	465	18	25.83	
1983	**ENGLAND**	**NEW ZEALAND TESTS**	**E**	**4**	**7**	**1**	**22**	**10**	**3.66**				**125**	**25**	**447**	**12**	**37.25**	
1983-84	England	Tour of New Zealand	NZ	3	D							2	61	20	174	6	29.00	
1983-84	**ENGLAND**	**NEW ZEALAND TESTS**	**NZ**	**2**	**3**		**32**	**21**	**10.66**			**1**	**52**	**13**	**154**	**5**	**30.80**	
1983-84	**ENGLAND**	**PAKISTAN TESTS**	**P**	**2**	**4**	**3**	**7**	***3**	**7.00**			**2**	**57.3**	**11**	**175**	**7**	**25.00**	
1984	Middlesex	Counties	E	19	23	1	255	66	11.59		1	8	445.1	73	1386	71	19.52	
1984	M.C.C.	Essex	E	1	D								29	1	131	2	65.50	
1984	**ENGLAND**	**WEST INDIES TESTS**	**E**	**1**	**2**		**14**	**14**	**7.00**			**1**	**19**	**2**	**76**	**0**		
1984-85	England	Tour of India	I	5	3		11	10	3.66			1	86	19	289	11	26.27	
1984-85	**ENGLAND**	**INDIA TESTS**	**I**	**5**	**5**	**1**	**10**	**9**	**2.50**			**2**	**181.5**	**41**	**627**	**14**	**44.78**	
1985	Middlesex	Counties	E	21	15	2	105	*15	8.07			5	385.2	67	1377	65	21.18	
1985	**ENGLAND**	**AUSTRALIA TESTS**	**E**	**1**	**1**	**1**	**22**	***22**					**33**	**6**	**128**	**2**	**64.00**	
1985	M.C.C.	Essex	E	1	1	1	3	*3					46	9	153	6	25.50	
1985	D.B. Close's XI	Rest of World XI	E	1	D								10	3	18	0		
1985-86	England 'B'	Tour of Sri Lanka	SL	3	2	2	2	*2					83	22	229	7	32.71	
1986	Middlesex	Counties	E	21	21	7	223	*44	15.92			3	435.2	94	1380	58	23.79	
1987	Middlesex	Counties	E	13	15	3	79	24	6.58			3	308.3	70	877	46	19.06	
1987	M.C.C.	Yorkshire	E	1	1	1	8	*8					33	8	81	5	16.20	
1988	Middlesex	Counties	E	20	21	7	119	*27	8.50			4	491.5	123	1290	71	18.16	
1989	Middlesex	Counties	E	20	24	7	127	*21	7.47			2	492.3	117	1321	62	21.30	
1990	Middlesex	Counties	E	17	16	6	81	31	8.10			3	442	119	1208	38	31.78	
1990	M.C.C.	Worcester	E	1	1	1	46	*46					18	5	39	1	39.00	
		Middlesex		158	156	37	1098	66	9.22		1	40	3466.1	761	10266	472	21.75	
		England		34	40	10	190	36	6.33			14	912	197	3044	90	33.82	
		M.C.C.		4	3	3	57	*46					126	23	404	14	28.85	
		D.B. Close's XI		1	D								10	3	18	0		
		TEST RECORD		**19**	**29**	**7**	**175**	**36**	**7.95**	**0**	**0**	**9**	**575.2**	**112**	**2003**	**51**	**39.27**	**6-77**
		CAREER		**197**	**199**	**50**	**1345**	**66**	**9.02**	**0**	**1**	**54**	**4514.1**	**984**	**13732**	**576**	**23.84**	**6-31**

DeFREITAS, Phillip Anthony Jason

SEASON	TEAM	OPPONENTS	V	BATTING M	I	NO	RUNS	H.S.	AVGE	100	50	CT	BOWLING OV	MD	RUNS	W	AVGE	B.B.
1985	Leicestershire	Counties	E	9	12	3	117	*30	13.00			2	234.2	43	703	27	26.03	
1986	Leicestershire	Counties	E	26	30	2	645	106	23.03	1	3	6	704.3	129	2073	91	22.78	
1986	T.C.C.B. XI	New Zealand Tourist	E	1	D							1	39	10	98	3	32.66	
1986-87	England	Tour of Australia	A	3	5	1	53	22	13.25				97.2	19	308	13	23.69	
1986-87	**ENGLAND**	**AUSTRALIA TESTS**	**A**	**4**	**5**	**1**	**77**	**40**	**19.25**			**1**	**141.4**	**24**	**446**	**9**	**49.55**	
1987	Leicestershire	Counties	E	16	21	2	398	74	20.94		2	9	443.2	99	1284	46	27.91	
1987	**ENGLAND**	**PAKISTAN TESTS**	**E**	**1**	**1**		**11**	**11**	**11.00**				**12**	**4**	**36**	**1**	**36.00**	
1987	M.C.C.	Essex	E	1	1		3	3	3.00				32	4	130	9	14.44	
1987-88	England	Tour of Pakistan	P	1	2		41	25	20.50				11.2	4	25	3	8.33	
1987-88	**ENGLAND**	**PAKISTAN TESTS**	**P**	**2**	**4**		**38**	**15**	**9.50**				**52.5**	**10**	**170**	**6**	**28.33**	
1987-88	England	Tour of New Zealand	NZ	2	3		44	41	14.66			1	59	7	208	4	52.00	
1987-88	**ENGLAND**	**NEW ZEALAND TESTS**	**NZ**	**2**	**2**		**20**	**16**	**10.00**			**1**	**91.1**	**33**	**175**	**4**	**43.75**	
1988	Leicestershire	Counties	E	14	20	1	481	113	25.31	1	3	6	465.3	111	1302	61	21.34	
1988	**ENGLAND**	**WEST INDIES TESTS**	**E**	**3**	**5**		**36**	**18**	**7.20**			**2**	**92**	**16**	**253**	**3**	**84.33**	
1989	Lancashire	Counties	E	16	26	2	558	78	23.25		5	2	551.2	115	1602	65	24.64	
1989	Lancashire	Tour of Zimbabwe	Z	1	2		9	6	4.50				38	10	85	4	21.25	
1989	**ENGLAND**	**AUSTRALIA TESTS**	**E**	**1**	**2**		**22**	**21**	**11.00**				**63.3**	**10**	**216**	**3**	**72.00**	
1989-90	England	Tour of West Indies	WI	4	7	4	63	*17	21.00			1	117.5	17	455	15	30.33	
1989-90	**ENGLAND**	**WEST INDIES TESTS**	**WI**	**2**	**4**		**45**	**24**	**11.25**			**1**	**78.5**	**11**	**242**	**6**	**40.33**	
1990	Lancashire	Counties	E	16	18	3	608	102	40.53	2	2	7	429.5	100	1265	34	37.20	
1990	**ENGLAND**	**NEW ZEALAND TESTS**	**E**	**2**	**2**		**52**	**38**	**26.00**				**59.4**	**9**	**175**	**6**	**29.16**	
		Leicestershire		65	83	8	1641	113	21.88	2	8	23	1847.4	382	5362	225	23.83	
		Lancashire		33	46	5	1175	102	28.65	2	7	9	1019.1	225	2952	103	28.66	
		England		27	42	6	502	41	13.94			7	877.1	164	2709	73	37.10	
		M.C.C.		1	1		3	3	3.00				32	4	130	9	14.44	
		T.C.C.B. XI		1	D							1	39	10	98	3	32.66	
		TEST RECORD		**17**	**25**	**1**	**505**	**40**	**21.04**	**0**	**0**	**5**	**591.4**	**117**	**1713**	**38**	**45.07**	**5-86**
		CAREER		**127**	**172**	**19**	**3321**	**113**	**21.70**	**4**	**15**	**40**	**3815**	**785**	**11251**	**413**	**27.24**	**7-21**

LEWIS, Christopher Clairmonte

				BATTING									BOWLING					
SEASON	TEAM	OPPONENTS	V	M	I	NO	RUNS	H.S.	AVGE	100	50	CT	OV	MD	RUNS	W	AVGE	B.B.
1987	Leicestershire	Counties	E	4	4		53	42	13.25			1	63	9	167	5	33.40	
1988	Leicestershire	Counties	E	16	23	4	400	40	21.05			10	391.4	83	1210	42	28.80	
1989	Leicestershire	Counties	E	12	19	1	277	69	15.38		2	12	300.3	59	986	45	21.91	
1989-90	England	Tour of West Indies	WI	2	3		33	21	11.00			1	35	6	128	2	64.00	
1990	Leicestershire	Counties	E	14	23	5	661	*189	36.72	1	2	11	430.2	87	1289	47	27.42	
1990	**ENGLAND**	**NEW ZEALAND TESTS**	**E**	**1**	**2**		**33**	**32**	**16.50**				**41**	**8**	**127**	**4**	**31.75**	
1990	**ENGLAND**	**INDIA TESTS**	**E**	**2**	**1**		**3**	**3**	**3.00**			**4**	**65**	**8**	**281**	**5**	**56.20**	
		Leicestershire		46	69	10	1391	*189	23.57	1	4	34	1185.3	238	3652	139	26.27	
		England		5	6		69	32	11.50			5	141	22	536	11	48.72	
		TEST RECORD		**3**	**3**	**0**	**36**	**32**	**12.00**	**0**	**0**	**4**	**106**	**16**	**408**	**9**	**45.33**	**3-76**
		CAREER		**51**	**75**	**10**	**1460**	***189**	**22.46**	**1**	**4**	**39**	**1326.3**	**260**	**4188**	**150**	**27.92**	**6-22**

MALCOLM, Devon Eugene

				BATTING									BOWLING					
SEASON	TEAM	OPPONENTS	V	M	I	NO	RUNS	H.S.	AVGE	100	50	CT	OV	MD	RUNS	W	AVGE	B.B.
1984	Derbyshire	Counties	E	7	8	1	40	23	5.71			4	156.2	24	674	16	42.12	
1985	Derbyshire	Counties	E	1	1		0	0					17	2	82	3	27.33	
1986	Derbyshire	Counties	E	9	7	4	37	*29	12.33			2	216.2	38	765	28	27.32	
1987	Derbyshire	Counties	E	13	16	4	43	*9	3.58			4	255	45	898	26	34.53	
1988	Derbyshire	Counties	E	20	21	5	119	22	7.43			1	488.1	93	1676	56	29.92	
1989	Derbyshire	Counties	E	11	14	7	172	51	24.57		1	1	253.5	38	956	46	20.78	
1989	**ENGLAND**	**AUSTRALIA TESTS**	**E**	**1**	**2**		**14**	**9**	**7.00**				**44**	**2**	**166**	**1**	**166.00**	
1989-90	England	Tour of West Indies	WI	3	3		12	8	4.00			2	97	17	371	13	28.53	
1989-90	**ENGLAND**	**WEST INDIES TESTS**	**WI**	**4**	**6**	**3**	**17**	**12**	**5.66**			**1**	**161.2**	**21**	**577**	**19**	**30.86**	
1990	Derbyshire	Counties	E	10	7	2	44	*20	8.80				289.4	47	983	30	32.76	
1990	**ENGLAND**	**NEW ZEALAND TESTS**	**E**	**3**	**4**	**2**	**4**	***4**	**2.00**				**118.4**	**38**	**269**	**15**	**17.93**	
1990	**ENGLAND**	**INDIA TESTS**	**E**	**3**	**2**	**1**	**28**	***15**	**28.00**				**110**	**16**	**436**	**7**	**62.68**	
		Derbyshire		71	74	23	455	51	8.92		1	12	1676.2	287	6034	205	29.43	
		England		14	17	6	75	*15	6.81			3	531	94	1819	55	33.07	
		TEST RECORD		**11**	**14**	**6**	**63**	***15**	**7.87**	**0**	**0**	**1**	**434**	**77**	**1448**	**42**	**34.47**	**6-77**
		CAREER		**85**	**91**	**29**	**530**	**51**	**8.54**	**0**	**1**	**15**	**2207.2**	**381**	**7853**	**260**	**30.20**	**6-68**

SLACK, Wilfred Norris

				BATTING									BOWLING					
SEASON	TEAM	OPPONENTS	V	M	I	NO	RUNS	H.S.	AVGE	100	50	CT	OV	MD	RUNS	W	AVGE	B.B.
1977	Middlesex	Counties	E	3	5		65	30	13.00									
1978	Middlesex	Counties	E	10	16	1	268	52	17.86		1	7						
1979	Middlesex	Counties	E	6	12		236	66	19.66		1	2	6	3	3	0		
1980	Middlesex	Counties	E	10	13		276	47	21.23			1						
1980-81	Middlesex	Tour of Zimbabwe	Z	3	6		215	94	35.83		2	3						
1981	Middlesex	Counties	E	18	32	3	1372	*248	47.31	3	9	6	10	1	33	0		
1981-82	International XI	Tour of Pakistan	P	2	4		32	17	8.00			4						
1981-82	Windward Islands	Shell Shield	IIs	4	8	1	290	*68	41.42		1	6	7.1	1	20	2	10.00	
1982	Middlesex	Counties	E	25	40	6	1499	*203	44.08	2	10	20	81	18	225	10	22.50	
1982-83	Windward Islands	Shell Shield	IIs	4	7		166	66	23.71		1	5	6	2	18	0		
1982-83	Windward Islands	Indian Tourist	WI	1	2		129	97	64.50		1	2	2	1	3	0		
1983	Middlesex	Counties	E	18	28	4	1034	140	43.08	3	6	17	44	20	84	6	14.00	
1984	Middlesex	Counties	E	25	46	8	1631	145	42.92	4	6	23	28	3	76	0		
1985	Middlesex	Counties	E	26	43	8	1900	*201	54.28	4	11	27	9	1	29	0		
1985-86	England 'B'	Tour of Sri Lanka	SL	6	10		431	96	43.10		4		8	1	15	0		
1985-86	England	Tour of West Indies	WI	2	4	1	72	37	18.00			1						
1985-86	**ENGLAND**	**WEST INDIES TESTS**	**WI**	**2**	**4**		**62**	**52**	**15.50**		**1**	**1**						
1986	Middlesex	Counties	E	22	33	3	1205	106	38.05	3	7	17	17	3	75	1	75.00	
1986	**ENGLAND**	**INDIA TESTS**	**E**	**1**	**2**		**19**	**19**	**9.50**			**2**						
1986-87	England	Tour of Australia	A	5	9		184	89	20.44		1	5						
1987	Middlesex	Counties	E	25	42		1636	173	38.95	3	7	14	33	9	93	2	46.50	
1988	Middlesex	Counties	E	19	32	5	1228	*163	45.08	3	6	11	2	1	14	0		
		Middlesex		210	348	38	12565	*248	40.53	25	66	148	230	59	632	19	33.26	
		Windward Islands		9	17	1	585	97	36.56		3	13	15.1	4	41	2	20.50	
		England		16	29	1	768	96	27.42		6	9	8	1	15	0		
		International XI		2	4		32	17	8.00			4						
		TEST RECORD		**3**	**6**	**0**	**81**	**52**	**13.50**	**0**	**1**	**3**						
		CAREER		**237**	**398**	**40**	**13950**	***248**	**38.96**	**25**	**75**	**174**	**253.1**	**64**	**688**	**21**	**32.76**	**3-17**

SMALL, Gladstone Cleophas

SEASON	TEAM	OPPONENTS	V	BATTING M	I	NO	RUNS	H.S.	AVGE	100	50	CT	BOWLING OV	MD	RUNS	W	AVGE	B.B.
1979-70	D.H. Robins XI	Tour of New Zealand	NZ	1	D								16	5	50	0		
1980	Warwickshire	Counties	E	15	15	4	64	16	5.81			3	240	52	864	24	36.00	
1981	Warwickshire	Counties	E	19	26	4	198	*21	9.00			8	395.3	52	1590	42	37.85	
1981-82	International XI	Tour of Pakistan	P	2	4	2	54	*21	27.00				47	8	161	4	40.25	
1982	Warwickshire	Counties	E	25	29	5	309	*57	12.87		1	6	589.1	107	1925	63	30.55	
1983	Warwickshire	Counties	E	6	8	3	62	31	12.40			2	110.5	19	349	10	34.90	
1984	Warwickshire	Counties	E	24	30	8	400	41	18.18			6	643.4	127	2027	71	28.54	
1985	Warwickshire	Counties	E	21	27	8	285	*31	15.00			7	592.3	114	1850	69	26.81	
1985-86	South Australia	Sheffield Shield	A	10	15	2	144	33	11.07			2	415.4	74	1244	39	31.89	
1986	Warwickshire	Counties	E	23	24	6	290	*45	16.11			4	575.3	138	1647	73	22.56	
1986	**ENGLAND**	**NEW ZEALAND TESTS**	**E**	**2**	**2**	**1**	**14**	**12**	**14.00**				**64**	**20**	**134**	**4**	**33.50**	
1986-87	England	Tour of Australia	A	6	8	2	65	26	10.83			3	180	49	446	21	21.23	
1986-87	**ENGLAND**	**AUSTRALIA TESTS**	**A**	**2**	**3**	**1**	**35**	***21**	**17.50**			**1**	**78.4**	**23**	**180**	**12**	**15.00**	
1987	Warwickshire	Counties	E	12	20	4	257	42	16.06			4	350	71	1067	34	31.38	
1988	Warwickshire	Counties	E	18	26	5	521	70	24.80		3	7	564.2	159	1387	76	18.25	
1988	**ENGLAND**	**WEST INDIES TESTS**	**E**	**1**	**2**	**1**	**12**	**7**	**12.00**				**37.5**	**6**	**140**	**4**	**35.00**	
1988	M.C.C.	Nottinghamshire	E	1	1	1	21	*21					26	5	78	0		
1989	Warwickshire	Counties	E	17	22	4	232	34	12.88			4	477	122	1202	51	23.56	
1989	**ENGLAND**	**AUSTRALIA TESTS**	**E**	**1**	**1**		**59**	**59**	**59.00**		**1**		**60**	**12**	**198**	**4**	**49.50**	
1989-90	England	Tour of West Indies	WI	1	D							1	40	8	139	6	23.16	
1989-90	**ENGLAND**	**WEST INDIES**	**WI**	**4**	**6**	**1**	**17**	**8**	**3.40**			**3**	**161**	**33**	**505**	**17**	**29.70**	
1990	Warwickshire	Counties	E	12	18	2	212	55	13.25		1	3	325.4	78	900	27	33.33	
1990	**ENGLAND**	**NEW ZEALAND TESTS**	**E**	**3**	**4**	**2**	**84**	***44**	**42.00**			**1**	**104**	**27**	**290**	**5**	**58.00**	
		Warwickshire		192	245	53	2830	70	14.73		5	54	4864.1	1039	14808	540	27.42	
		England		20	26	8	286	59	15.88		1	9	725.3	178	2032	73	27.83	
		D.H. Robins XI		1	D								16	5	50	0		
		International XI		2	4	2	54	*21	27.00				47	8	161	4	40.25	
		M.C.C.		1	1	1	21	*21					26	5	78	0		
		South Australia		10	15	2	144	33	11.07			2	415.4	74	1244	39	31.89	
		TEST RECORD		**13**	**18**	**6**	**221**	**59**	**18.41**	**0**	**1**	**5**	**505.3**	**121**	**1447**	**46**	**31.45**	**5-48**
		CAREER		**226**	**291**	**66**	**3335**	**70**	**14.82**	**0**	**6**	**65**	**6094.2**	**1309**	**18373**	**656**	**28.00**	**7-15**

WILLIAMS, Neil Fitzgerald

				BATTING									BOWLING					
SEASON	TEAM	OPPONENTS	V	M	I	NO	RUNS	H.S.	AVGE	100	50	CT	OV	MD	RUNS	W	AVGE	B.B.
1982	Middlesex	Counties	E	12	11	5	112	*27	18.66			2	236.4	34	819	23	35.60	
1982-83	Windward Islands	Shell Shield	IIs	3	5	1	120	*51	30.00		1	2	81	16	239	12	19.91	
1982-83	Windward Islands	Indian Tourist	WI	1	2		14	13	7.00				33.2	6	128	5	25.60	
1983	Middlesex	Counties	E	25	25	7	407	63	22.61		2	6	532.2	114	1659	63	26.33	
1983-84	Tasmania	Sheffield Shield	A	7	11	1	131	34	13.10			4	221.5	47	841	22	38.22	
1984	Middlesex	Counties	E	18	21	3	285	44	15.83			6	447.5	90	1568	42	37.33	
1984	M.C.C.	Essex	E	1	D								26.2	5	85	7	12.14	
1984-85	English Counties XI	Tour of Zimbabwe	Z	2	2	2	75	*62			1	1	60	13	201	13	15.46	
1985	Middlesex	Counties	E	21	21	4	378	67	22.23		1	3	462.2	67	1649	55	29.98	
1985	M.C.C.	Australian Tourist	E	1	D								28	2	135	3	45.00	
1986	Middlesex	Counties	E	5	4	1	51	*23	17.00				79.3	9	264	10	26.40	
1987	Middlesex	Counties	E	10	9	4	64	*18	12.80			1	189.4	32	575	13	44.23	
1988	Middlesex	Counties	E	8	11	2	186	*63	20.66		1	1	178.3	33	511	30	17.03	
1989	Middlesex	Counties	E	15	19	5	317	*69	22.64		1	4	327.2	58	970	31	31.29	
1989-90	Windward Islands	Red Stripe Cup	WI	3	6	2	189	*66	47.25		1	1	62.5	7	217	11	19.72	
1990	Middlesex	Counties	E	20	23	3	410	*55	20.50		2	4	488.1	93	1470	52	28.26	
1990	**ENGLAND**	**INDIA TESTS**	**E**	**1**	**1**		**38**	**38**	**38.00**				**41**	**5**	**148**	**2**	**74.00**	
		Windward Islands		7	13	3	323	*66	32.30		2	3	177.1	29	584	28	20.85	
		Middlesex		134	144	34	2210	*69	20.09		7	27	2942.2	530	9485	319	29.73	
		Tasmania		7	11	1	131	34	13.10			4	221.5	47	841	22	38.22	
		M.C.C.		2	D								54.2	7	220	10	22.00	
		English Counties XI		2	2	2	75	*62			1	1	60	13	201	13	15.46	
		England		1	1		38	38	38.00				41	5	148	2	74.00	
		TEST RECORD		**1**	**1**	**0**	**38**	**38**	**38.00**	**0**	**0**	**0**	**41**	**5**	**148**	**2**	**74.00**	**2-148**
		CAREER		**153**	**171**	**40**	**2777**	***69**	**21.19**	**0**	**10**	**35**	**3496.4**	**631**	**11479**	**394**	**29.13**	**7-55**

APPENDIX D

West Indian Test Players - Island by Island & Players who have represented the West Indies in First-Class matches other than Test matches

Player	*Island Born*	*Island Played For*	*Tours*	*Tests*
Allan D.W.	Barbados	Barbados	E(2)	5
Atkinson D.S.	Barbados	Barbados, Trinidad	I, P, C, A, NZ(2), E	22
Atkinson E.S.	Barbados	Barbados	I, P	8
Bartlett E.L.	Barbados	Barbados	E, A	5
Best C.A.	Barbados	Barbados	Z	6
Birkett L.S.	Barbados	Barbados, Trinidad, B. Guiana	A	4
Boyce K.D.	Barbados	Barbados	E, A, I, P, SL	21
Browne C.R.	Barbados	Barbados, British Guiana	E(2)	4
Bynoe M.R.	Barbados	Barbados	I, P, C	4
Carew G.M.	Barbados	Barbados	I, C	4
Challenor G.	Barbados	Barbados	E(3)	3
Clarke C.B.	Barbados	Barbados	E	3
Clarke S.T.	Barbados	Barbados	I, SL, P, A	11
Daniel W.W.	Barbados	Barbados	E, Z, I	10
Depeiza C.C.	Barbados	Barbados	NZ	5
Edwards R.M.	Barbados	Barbados	A, NZ	5
Francis G.N.	Barbados	Barbados	E(3), A	10
Frederick M.C.	Barbados	Barbados, Jamaica	None	1
Garner J.	Barbados	Barbados	E(2), A(4), NZ(2), P	58
Goddard J.D.C.	Barbados	Barbados	I, P, C, E(2), A, NZ(2)	27
Greenidge A.E.	Barbados	Barbados	I, SL	6
Greenidge C.G.	Barbados	Barbados	E(4), A(6), NZ(2), P(3), I(3)	
Greenidge G.A.	Barbados	Barbados	None	5
Griffith C.C.	Barbados	Barbados	E(2), I, A, NZ	28
Hall W.W.	Barbados	Barbados, Trinidad	E(3), I(2), P, A(2), C, NZ	48
Haynes D.L.	Barbados	Barbados	E(3), A(5), NZ(2), P(2), I(2), Z	
Hoad E.L.G.	Barbados	Barbados	E(2)	4
Holder V.A.	Barbados	Barbados	E(3), I(2), SL(2), P, A	40
Holford D.A.J.	Barbados	Barbados, Trinidad	E, I, A, NZ	24
Howard A.B.	Barbados	Barbados	None	1
Hunte C.C.	Barbados	Barbados	I(2), P, A, E(2)	44
King C.L.	Barbados	Barbados	E(2), A, NZ	9
King F.M.	Barbados	Barbados, Trinidad	NZ	14
Lashley P.D.	Barbados	Barbados	A, E	4
Legall R.A.	Barbados	Trinidad	None	4
Marshall M.D.	Barbados	Barbados	E(3), A(4), NZ(2), P(2), I(2), Z, SL	
Marshall N.E.	Barbados	Barbados, Trinidad	None	1
Marshall R.E.	Barbados	Barbados	E, A, NZ	4
Martindale E.A.	Barbados	Barbados	E(2)	10
Moseley E.A.	Barbados	Barbados	None	2
Murray D.A.	Barbados	Barbados	E(2), I(2), SL(2), P(2), A(3), NZ	19
Neblett J.M.	Barbados	British Guiana, Barbados XI	E	1
Nurse S.M.	Barbados	Barbados	A(2), E(2), I, C, NZ	29
Padmore A.L.	Barbados	Barbados	I, SL, P, A, E	2
Payne T.R.O.	Barbados	Barbados	Z, E, A(2), P, NZ	1
Sealy J.E.D.	Barbados	Barbados, Trinidad	A, E	11
Shepherd J.N.	Barbados	Barbados	E	5
Small M.A.	Barbados	Barbados	E	2
Smith C.W.	Barbados	Barbados	A	5
Sobers G.S.	Barbados	Barbados, Jamaica XI	E(5), A(2), NZ(2), I(2), P, C	93
Walcott C.L.	Barbados	Barbados, British Guiana	E(2), I, P, C, A, NZ	44
Walcott L.A.	Barbados	Barbados	None	1
Weekes E.D.	Barbados	Barbados	E(2), I, P, C, A, NZ(2)	48
White A.W.	Barbados	Barbados	E	2
Wiles C.A.	Barbados	Trinidad, Barbados XI	E	1
Williams E.A.V.	Barbados	Barbados	E	4
Worrell F.M.M.	Barbados	Barbados, Jamaica	E(3), A(2), NZ	51

BARBADOS 57

Player	Island Born	Island Played For	Tours	Tests
Achong E.E.	Trinidad	Trinidad	E	6
Imtiaz Ali	Trinidad	Trinidad	None	1
Inshan Ali	Trinidad	Trinidad	E, A	12
Asgarali N.S.	Trinidad	Trinidad	E	2
Betancourt N.	Trinidad	Trinidad	None	1
Bishop I.R.	Trinidad	Trinidad	E, A	
Butler L.S.	Trinidad	Trinidad	None	1
Carew M.C.	Trinidad	Trinidad	E(3), A, NZ	19
Constantine L. N.	Trinidad	Trinidad, Barbados	E(4), A	18
Davis B.A.	Trinidad	Trinidad	I, C	4
Davis C.A.	Trinidad	Trinidad	A, NZ, E	15
Ferguson W.F.	Trinidad	Trinidad	I, C, A, NZ	8
Furlonge H.A.	Trinidad	Trinidad	NZ	3
Ganteaume A.G.	Trinidad	Trinidad	E	1
Gomes H.A.	Trinidad	Trinidad	E(2), I(2), SL, A(4), NZ(2), P(2)	60
Gomez G.E.	Trinidad	Trinidad	E(2), I, P, C, A, NZ	29
Grant G.C.	Trinidad	Trinidad	A, E	12
Grant R.S.	Trinidad	Trinidad	E	7
Gray A.H.	Trinidad	Trinidad	P, NZ, Z	5
Grell M.G.	Trinidad	Trinidad	None	1
Griffith H.C.	Trinidad	Barbados	E(2), A	13
Guillen S.C.	Trinidad	Trinidad	A, NZ	5
Hunte E.A.C.	Trinidad	Trinidad	A	3
Johnson T.F.	Trinidad	Trinidad	E	1
Jones P.E.	Trinidad	Trinidad	I, P, C, E, A, NZ	9
Julien B.D.	Trinidad	Trinidad	E(2), I, SL, P, A	24
Jumadeen R.R.	Trinidad	Trinidad	E, I, SL	12
Logie A.L.	Trinidad	Trinidad	Z, A(4), E(2), I(2), P, NZ	
Merry C.A.	(Tobago)	Trinidad	E	2
Murray D.L.	Trinidad	Trinidad	E(4), I(2), C(2), P, A(3), NZ	62
Nanan R.	Trinidad	Trinidad	P	1
Noreiga J.M.	Trinidad	Trinidad	None	4
Pierre L.R.	Trinidad	Trinidad	E	1
Ramadhin S.	Trinidad	Trinidad	E(2), A(2), NZ(2), I, P	43
Roach C.A.	Trinidad	Trinidad	E(2), A	16
Rodriguez W.V.	Trinidad	Trinidad	I, P, E	5
St. Hill E.L.	Trinidad	Trinidad	A	2
St. Hill W.H.	Trinidad	Trinidad	E	3
Sealey B.J.	Trinidad	Trinidad, Barbados XI	E	1
Simmons P.V.	Trinidad	Trinidad	Z(2), I, E	
Singh C.K.	Trinidad	Trinidad	None	2
Small J.A.	Trinidad	Trinidad	E(2)	3
Stollmeyer J.B.	Trinidad	Trinidad	E(2), I, P, C, A, NZ	32
Stollmeyer V.H.	Trinidad	Trinidad	E	1
Taylor J.O.	Trinidad	Trinidad	I, P	3

TRINIDAD 45

Player	Island Born	Island Played For	Tours	Tests
Alexander F.C.M.	Jamaica	Jamaica	E, I, P, A, NZ	25
Austin R.A.	Jamaica	Jamaica	None	2
Barrett A.G.	Jamaica	Jamaica	I, P	6
Barrow I.	Jamaica	Jamaica	A, E(2)	11
Binns A.P.	Jamaica	Jamaica	NZ	5
Cameron F.J.	Jamaica	Jamaica	I, P, C	5
Cameron J.H.	Jamaica	Jamaica	E	2
Chang H.S.	Jamaica	Jamaica	I, SL	1
Da Costa O.C.	Jamaica	Jamaica	E	5
Dewdney D.T.	Jamaica	Jamaica	NZ, E, A	9
Dowe U.G.	Jamaica	Jamaica	None	4

Player	Island Born	Island Played For	Tours	Tests
Dujon P.J.L	Jamaica	Jamaica	Z, A(3), I(2), E(2), P, NZ	
Foster M.L.C.	Jamaica	Jamaica	E(2)	14
Fuller R.L.	Jamaica	Jamaica	None	1
Gilchrist R.	Jamaica	Jamaica	E, I	13
Gladstone G.	Jamaica	Jamaica	None	1
Headley G.A.	Panama	Jamaica	A, E(2), I, P	22
Headley R.G.A	Jamaica	Jamaica	E	2
Hendriks J.L.	Jamaica	Jamaica	I(2), P, A(2), E(2), NZ	20
Holding M.A.	Jamaica	Jamaica	E(3), A(5), NZ(2), P, I	60
Holt (Jnr.) J.K.	Jamaica	Jamaica	I, P	17
Hylton L.G.	Jamaica	Jamaica	E	6
Johnson H.H.H.	Jamaica	Jamaica	E	3
Kentish E.S.M.	Jamaica	Jamaica	None	2
King L.A.	Jamaica	Jamaica	E, I, C, A, NZ	2
Lewis D.M.	Jamaica	Jamaica	None	3
McMorris E.D.A.S.	Jamaica	Jamaica	E(2)	13
Martin F.R.	Jamaica	Jamaica	E(2), A	9
Mattis E.H.	Jamaica	Jamaica	Z	4
Miller R.	Jamaica	Jamaica	None	1
Mudie G.H.	Jamaica	Jamaica	None	1
Nunes R.K.	Jamaica	Jamaica	E(2)	4
Passailaigue C.C.	Jamaica	Jamaica	None	1
Patterson B.P.	Jamaica	Jamaica	P, NZ, I, E, A	
Rae A.F.	Jamaica	Jamaica	I, P, C, E, A, NZ	15
Rickards K.R.	Jamaica	Jamaica	I, P, C, A, NZ	2
Rowe L.G.	Jamaica	Jamaica	E(3), I, A(2), NZ	30
Scarlett R.O.	Jamaica	Jamaica	None	3
Scott A.P.H.	Jamaica	Jamaica	None	1
Scott O.C.	Jamaica	Jamaica	E, A	8
Smith O.G.	Jamaica	Jamaica	NZ, E, I, P	26
Valentine A.L.	Jamaica	Jamaica	E(3), A(2), NZ(2)	36
Valentine V.A.	Jamaica	Jamaica	E	2
Walsh C.A.	Jamaica	Jamaica	Z, E(2), A(3), P, NZ, I	
Watson C.D.	Jamaica	Jamaica	A	7
Weekes K.H.	USA	Jamaica	E	2
Williams A.B.	Jamaica	Jamaica	I	7

JAMAICA 47

Player	Island Born	Island Played For	Tours	Tests
Bacchus S.F.A.F	British Guiana	Guyana	I, SL, E, P, Z, A	19
Baichan L.	British Guiana	Guyana	I, SL, P, A	3
Butcher B.F.	British Guiana	British Guiana	I(2), P, E(3), C,A, NZ	44
Butts C.G.	British Guiana	Guyana	Z, P, NZ, I	
Camacho G.S.	British Guiana	Guyana	A, NZ, E(2)	11
Christiani C.M.	British Guiana	British Guiana	E	4
Christiani R.J.	British Guiana	British Guiana	I(2), P, C, E, A, NZ	22
Croft C.E.H.	British Guiana	Guyana	A(2), NZ, E, P	27
De Caires F. I.	British Guiana	British Guiana	A	3
Fernandes M.P.	British Guiana	British Guiana	E(2)	2
Fredericks R.C.	British Guiana	Guyana	A(2), NZ, E(3), I, SL, P	59
Gaskin B.B.M.	British Guiana	British Guiana	None	2
Gibbs G.L.	British Guiana	British Guiana	None	1
Gibbs L.R.	British Guiana	British Guiana	I(3), P(2), A(3), E(4), C, NZ	79
Harper R.A.	British Guiana	Guyana	I(2), E(2), A(2), P	
Hooper C.L.	Guyana	Guyana	Z(2), NZ, I, E, A	
Jones C.E.L.	British Guiana	British Guiana	None	4
Kallicharran A.I.	British Guiana	Guyana	E(3), I(2), SL(2), P(2), A(2), NZ	66
Kanhai R.B.	British Guiana	British Guiana	E(4), I(2), P, A(2), NZ	79
Lloyd C.H.	British Guiana	Guyana	E(5), A(5), NZ(2), P(2), I(3), SL(2)	110

Player	*Island Born*	*Island Played For*	*Tours*	*Tests*
McWatt C.A.	British Guiana	British Guiana	I, P, C	6
Madray I.S.	British Guiana	British Guiana	None	2
Mendonca I.V.	British Guiana	British Guiana	None	2
Pairaudeau B.H.	British Guiana	British Guiana	NZ, E	13
Shivnarine S.	Guyana	Guyana	I, SL	8
Solomon J.S.	British Guiana	British Guiana	I, P, A, E(2)	27
Stayers S.C.	British Guiana	British Guiana	None	4
Trim J.	British Guiana	British Guiana	I, P, C, A, NZ	4
Wight C.V.	British Guiana	British Guiana	E	2
Wight G.L.	British Guiana	British Guiana	None	1
Wishart K.L.	British Guiana	British Guiana	None	1

GUYANA 31

Player	*Island Born*	*Island Played For*	*Tours*	*Tests*
Ambrose C.E.L.	Leeward Islands	Leeward Islands	E, A	
Arthurton K.L.T.	Leeward Islands	Leeward Islands	E, A	
Baptiste E.A.L.	Leeward Islands	Leeward Islands	I(2), E, A, Z	
Benjamin W.K.M.	Leeward Islands	Leeward Islands	P, A(2), I, E	
Parry D.R.	Leeward Islands	Leeward Islands	I, SL, A, NZ, E, P	12
Richards I.V.A.	Leeward Islands	Leeward Islands	E(4), A(5), NZ, I(3), P(3), SL	
Richardson R.B.	Leeward Islands	Leeward Islands	E(2), A(3), NZ, I(2), P	
Roberts A.M.E.	Leeward Islands	Leeward Islands	E(2), A(3), NZ, I(2), P, SL	47
Willett E.T.	Leeward Islands	Leeward Islands	E, I, SL, P	5

LEEWARD ISLANDS 9

Player	*Island Born*	*Island Played For*	*Tours*	*Tests*
Davis W.W.	Windward Islands	Windward Islands	Z, I(2), E, A	
Findlay T.M.	Windward Islands	Windward Islands	A, NZ, E(2)	10
Phillip N.	Windward Islands	Windward Islands	I, SL	9
Roberts A.T.	Windward Islands	Windward Islands, Trinidad	NZ	1
Shillingford G.C.	Windward Islands	Windward Islands	E(2)	7
Shillingford I.T.	Windward Islands	Windward Islands	None	4

WINDWARD ISLANDS 6

Player	*Island Born*	*Island Played For*	
Butcher R.O.	Barbados	Barbados	English West Indian born Test Players
Cowans N.G.	Jamaica		
DeFreitas P.A.J.	Windward Islands		
Lewis C.C.	Guyana		
Malcolm D.E.	Jamaica		
Slack W.N.	Windwards Islands	Windward Islands	
Small G.C.	Barbados		
Williams N.F.	Windward Islands	Windward Islands	

PLAYERS WHO HAVE REPRESENTED THE WEST INDIES IN FIRST-CLASS MATCHES OTHER THAN TEST MATCHES

(West Indies, W.I. XI, President's XI, 'B'XI, Under 26XI etc.)

M. Smith	T
L.S. D'Ade	T
S.W. Sproston	BG
H.B.G. Austin	B
A.B. Clarke	NG
O. Weber	BG
R.S.A. Warner	T
L.S. Constantine	T
D.M. McAuley	B
C.E. Goodman	B
A. Cumberbatch	T
G.C. Learmond	T
P.I. Cox	B
V.C. Challenor	B
A.E. Harragin	T
C.H. King	BG
F. Hinds	B
O.H. Layne	B
T.J. Burton	BG
W.C. Shepherd	B
J. Woods	BG
W.P. Weber	BG
S.G. Smith	T
H.C. Bayley	BG
G.B.Y. Cox	B
P.A. Goodman	B
R.C. Ollivierre	T
W. Bowring	B
W. Hoad	B
C.K. Bancroft	B
W.G.M. Sarel	T
W.J. Cumberbatch	T
C.S. Morrison	J
C.P. Cumberbatch	T
J.E. Parker	BG
J.J. Cameron	J
P.H. Tarilton	B
C.A. Browne	B
W.O. Gibbs	B
C. Simpson	BG
L.F. Archer	B
S.M. Worme	B
F.E.W.G Austin	B
E.R.D. Moulder	BG
J.C.S. Rogers	T

H.A. Croal	BG
G. John	T
S. Hinds	BG
C.V. Hunter	BG
W.V. Sherlock	BG
C.A. Reid	BG
E.A. Fraser	BG
R.L. Challenor	B
C.D. Phillips	B
V.S. Pascall	T
H.W. Ince	B
A. Cipriani	T
J.M. Kidney	B
M.B.G Austin	BG
J.E. Blackman	BG
J.K. Holt (Sen.)	J
G.A. Dewhurst	T
O.S. Wight	BG
C.A. Nascimonto	BG
E.A. Rae	J
W.S. Beckford	J
C. de L. Inniss	B
H.P. Bayley	BG
K.B. Trestrail	T
C.B. Williams	B
R. Griffith	B
J.L. Parris	B
R. Cohen	J
R.C. Branker	B
R.C. Collymore	BG
R.M. de Souza	T
W. English	G
K. Laurent	WI
P.D. Blair	G
P. Roberts	T
V.A. Amory	LI
A.J. Lewis	T
S.A. Morgan	J
S. Matthews	G
C. Campbell	J
C.E. Lawson	J
R.S. Gabriel	T
L.C. Sebastian	WI
M.A. Tucker	J
R.R. Wynter	J
V.A. Eddy	LI
A.A. Lyght	G
D.I. Kallicharran	G
S.W. Julien	WI

O.W. Peters	J
R.O. Estwick	B
G.D. Armstrong	B
A. Persand	G
E.E. Brown	J
J.R. Lyon	T
T. Mohamed	G
M.R. Pydanna	G
H.L. Alleyne	B
S.I. Williams	LI
A.E. Daniel	T
H. Joseph	T
G. Powell	J
R.C. Haynes	J
A.L Kelly	LI
E.E. Lewis	LI
A.G. Daley	J
M.C. Worrell	B
D. Williams	T
G. Mahabir	T
A.F.D. Jackman	G
R.M. Otto	LI
V.S. Greene	B
L.L. Lawrence	LI
T.A. Merrick	LI
J.D. Charles	WI
J.T. Etienne	WI
F.D.C. Stephenson	B
E.N. Trotman	B
M.A. Lynch	G
R. Seeram	G
W.W. Lewis	J
C.B. Lambert	G
R. Dhanraj	T
G.J.F. Ferris	LI
D.A. Joseph	WI
S. Dhaniram	G
D.J. Collymore	WI
D.S. Morgan	J
R.I.C. Holder	B
J.C. Adams	J
J.R. Murray	WI
N.O. Perry	J
B. St. A. Brown	G
I.B.A. Allen	WI
K.C.G. Benjamin	LI
L.A. Joseph	G
C.A. Davidson	J
L.L. Harris	LI